NT Network Plumbing: Routers, Proxies, and Web Services

NT Network Plumbing: Routers, Proxies, and Web Services

Anthony Northrup

IDG Books Worldwide, Inc.
An International Data Group Company
Foster City, CA ◆ Chicago, IL ◆ Indianapolis, IN ◆ New York, NY

NT Network Plumbing: Routers, Proxies, and Web Services

Published by
IDG Books Worldwide, Inc.
An International Data Group Company
919 E. Hillsdale Blvd., Suite 400
Foster City, CA 94404
www.idgbooks.com (IDG Books Worldwide Web site)

Library of Congress Catalog Card No.: 98-71151

ISBN: 0-7645-3209-X

Printed in the United States of America

10 9 8 7 6 5 4 3

1B/SZ/QW/ZY/FC

Distributed in the United States by IDG Books Worldwide, Inc.

Distributed by Macmillan Canada for Canada; by Transworld Publishers Limited in the United Kingdom; by IDG Norge Books for Norway; by IDG Sweden Books for Sweden; by Woodslane Pty. Ltd. for Australia; by Woodslane (NZ) Ltd. for New Zealand; by Addison Wesley Longman Singapore Pte Ltd. for Singapore, Malaysia, Thailand, Indonesia, and Korea; by Norma Comunicaciones S.A. for Colombia; by Intersoft for South Africa; by International Thomson Publishing for Germany, Austria, and Switzerland; by Toppan Company Ltd. for Japan; by Distribuidora Cuspide for Argentina; by Livraria Cultura for Brazil; by Ediciencia S.A. for Ecuador; by Ediciones ZETA S.C.R. Ltda. for Peru; by WS Computer Publishing Corporation, Inc., for the Philippines; by Unalis Corporation for Taiwan; by Contemporanea de Ediciones for Venezuela; by Computer Book & Magazine Store for Puerto Rico; by Express Computer Distributors for the Caribbean and West Indies. Authorized Sales Agent: Anthony Rudkin Associates for the Middle East and North Africa.

For general information on IDG Books Worldwide's books in the U.S., please call our Consumer Customer Service department at 800-762-2974. For reseller information, including discounts and premium sales, please call our Reseller Customer Service department at 800-434-3422.

For information on where to purchase IDG Books Worldwide's books outside the U.S., please contact our International Sales department at 650-655-3200 or fax 650-655-3297.

For information on foreign language translations, please contact our Foreign & Subsidiary Rights department at 650-655-3021 or fax 650-655-3281.

For sales inquiries and special prices for bulk quantities, please contact our Sales department at 650-655-3200 or write to the address above.

For information on using IDG Books Worldwide's books in the classroom or for ordering examination copies, please contact our Educational Sales department at 800-434-2086 or fax 317-595-5499.

For press review copies, author interviews, or other publicity information, please contact our Public Relations department at 650-655-3000 or fax 650-655-3299.

For authorization to photocopy items for corporate, personal, or educational use, please contact Copyright Clearance Center, 222 Rosewood Drive, Danvers, MA 01923, or fax 978-750-4470.

ABOUT IDG BOOKS WORLDWIDE

Welcome to the world of IDG Books Worldwide.

IDG Books Worldwide, Inc., is a subsidiary of International Data Group, the world's largest publisher of computer-related information and the leading global provider of information services on information technology. IDG was founded more than 25 years ago and now employs more than 8,500 people worldwide. IDG publishes more than 275 computer publications in over 75 countries (see listing below). More than 90 million people read one or more IDG publications each month.

Launched in 1990, IDG Books Worldwide is today the #1 publisher of best-selling computer books in the United States. We are proud to have received eight awards from the Computer Press Association in recognition of editorial excellence and three from *Computer Currents'* First Annual Readers' Choice Awards. Our best-selling ...*For Dummies*® series has more than 50 million copies in print with translations in 38 languages. IDG Books Worldwide, through a joint venture with IDG's Hi-Tech Beijing, became the first U.S. publisher to publish a computer book in the People's Republic of China. In record time, IDG Books Worldwide has become the first choice for millions of readers around the world who want to learn how to better manage their businesses.

Our mission is simple: Every one of our books is designed to bring extra value and skill-building instructions to the reader. Our books are written by experts who understand and care about our readers. The knowledge base of our editorial staff comes from years of experience in publishing, education, and journalism — experience we use to produce books for the '90s. In short, we care about books, so we attract the best people. We devote special attention to details such as audience, interior design, use of icons, and illustrations. And because we use an efficient process of authoring, editing, and desktop publishing our books electronically, we can spend more time ensuring superior content and spend less time on the technicalities of making books.

You can count on our commitment to deliver high-quality books at competitive prices on topics you want to read about. At IDG Books Worldwide, we continue in the IDG tradition of delivering quality for more than 25 years. You'll find no better book on a subject than one from IDG Books Worldwide.

John Kilcullen
John Kilcullen
CEO
IDG Books Worldwide, Inc.

Steven Berkowitz
Steven Berkowitz
President and Publisher
IDG Books Worldwide, Inc.

Eighth Annual Computer Press Awards ≥1992

Ninth Annual Computer Press Awards ≥1993

Tenth Annual Computer Press Awards ≥1994

XI WINNER
Eleventh Annual Computer Press Awards ≥1995

Credits

ACQUISITIONS EDITORS
Anne Hamilton
Tracy Thomsic

DEVELOPMENT EDITORS
Janet Andrews
Ellen Dendy
Kenyon Brown

TECHNICAL EDITOR
Teri Northrup

COPY EDITORS
Robert Campbell
Larisa North

PROJECT COORDINATOR
Susan Parini

BOOK DESIGNERS
Catalin Dulfu
Kurt Krames

COVER DESIGN
© mark parsons design

GRAPHICS AND PRODUCTION SPECIALISTS
Stephanie Hollier
Chris Pimentel

QUALITY CONTROL SPECIALISTS
Mick Arellano
Mark Schumann

GRAPHICS TECHNICIANS
Linda J. Marousek
Hector Mendosa

ILLUSTRATOR
Joan Carol

PROOFREADER
David Wise

INDEXER
Sherry Massey

About the Author

Anthony Northrup, Microsoft Certified Systems Engineer and Compaq Accredited Systems Engineer, is the chief engineer in charge of NT Web hosting at an international communications company. He is ultimately responsible for many of the largest NT-based Web sites on the Internet. He is also the coauthor of *Network Essentials Unleashed*.

This book is dedicated to my most talented colleague, my best friend, my technical editor, my career consultant, my accountant, and my wife. I love you, Teri, for playing so many roles so perfectly.

Preface

The key to understanding complex systems lies in the details. This understanding of details is what separates senior personnel from junior personnel, regardless of the discipline. Generally, this understanding comes from experience. Experience is a terrible teacher; it teaches with pain and expense and is rarely, if ever, forgiving. Worse yet, experience teaches a lesson only after the student needs the knowledge.

With *NT Network Plumbing: Routers, Proxies, and Web Services*, I teach details that lead you to an understanding of the big picture and allow you to perform your job better. I hope to be a swifter and kinder teacher than experience.

Technical disciplines – in particular, systems and network engineering – require an incredible understanding of details. These details are intimidating, and most people do not learn the details until after they need them. *NT Network Plumbing* is filled with details that enable you to anticipate and plan around complex systems problems without ever experiencing those problems.

Who Should Read This Book

I have not written *NT Network Plumbing* with the beginner in mind; I've written it for experienced professionals who wish to deepen their understanding of Windows NT and internetworking. The ambitious beginner would certainly benefit from reading this book; it will not be an easy read, but I do provide background information where I think it is needed. You will *not* find a step-by-step description of how to use the Windows NT user interface. Throughout the book, I assume you are familiar with the basics of Windows NT and networking, or that you have online help files handy. *NT Network Plumbing* is unique because it is *not* geared for the beginner.

Windows NT evolved from Microsoft's desktop operating systems. Perhaps this is why networking aspects of Windows NT have been underemphasized until now. Documentation for the networking aspects of Windows NT has been superficial, as if only the developers within Microsoft really needed to understand how everything actually worked. Indeed, research was the most difficult part of creating this work, and much of it had to be done manually using tools like a protocol analyzer.

I hope to increase the knowledge of each person reading this book to the point where he or she has a real and deep understanding of each topic I cover. I want readers to truly understand how networking in Windows NT works. The person who completes this book will have the knowledge he or she needs to do high-level systems and network engineering based on Windows NT *and* perform low-level troubleshooting. Indeed, high-level work must rely on the low-level understanding; the best network architectures break down because of simple oversights.

Versions of Windows NT

The most common version of Windows NT, at the time of writing, is 4.0 (with service pack 3). Therefore, NT 4 is the focus of *NT Network Plumbing.* This book will remain useful long after these software versions are considered "legacy" because I have focused on both the protocols, as implemented by Microsoft and other software vendors, and the underlying standards. Standards typically have a lifetime of several years, and while Microsoft may make minor adjustments to the protocol implementations between versions, they remain largely consistent. To further extend the lifetime of this book, I included explanations of new software, including a great deal of information about the next release of NT.

How This Book Is Organized

This book is divided into four parts and five appendixes.

Part I, **Internetworking Fundamentals,** provides baseline information. While most readers will already know most of this material, this part fills in any gaps that may exist in their knowledge.

Part II, **Connectivity,** covers network design and optimization issues.

Part III, **Implementation,** provides the information you need to make specific products work correctly and efficiently.

Part IV, **Noteworthy Products,** examines several specific products that build upon the Windows NT foundation.

Finally, the five appendixes provide important reference information. Appendix A describes well-known TCP/UDP port numbers. Appendix B lists *request for commands* terms. Appendix C presents important header information. Appendix D defines common acronyms. Appendix E lists CIDR (classless interdomain routing) names.

You may choose to read the book from cover to cover. If you do, you will fill your head with an incredible amount of useful information. However, the book is also intended to be used during the troubleshooting and researching processes. So, if you are having a problem with Routing and Remote Access Services, you may turn directly to Chapter 13 and read through it. If your company is in the process of implementing the Common Internet File System (CIFS), read Chapter 14. If understanding the information in one chapter depends on reading another chapter, the book refers you to that chapter.

Reader Feedback

I am very interested in hearing from every reader. Your comments will help me improve the content of this book in future editions. The easiest way to contact me is via e-mail at northrup@ultranet.com. I'm interested in getting to know my readers, and I will make a sincere effort to respond to each e-mail message I receive.

Acknowledgments

This book could not have been written without the help of many different people, many of whom worked "behind the scenes." I'd like to thank everyone who helped, especially Tracy Thomsic, Kenyon Brown, Ellen Dendy, Michael Lohrey, and Teri Northrup for their amazing patience, kindness, and leadership, and always at just the right time. Without their experience and guidance, this book would not have been possible. The whole group at IDG Books Worldwide has demonstrated an unparalleled professionalism that is key to producing quality books.

My friends and family have my sincerest gratitude, though they may not even realize how they contributed. Thanks to Rick and Angie for listening to me whine and making me laugh. Thanks to the gang at work — Scott, Chris, Eric, Kurt, and Ari — for tolerating my elevated stress level. Thank you Jimmy and Stephanie, for making me leave my office once in a while. Thanks to Bonnie and Allen for making me gamble (literally). My mom and dad deserve credit for chasing me down from a distance of 2,000 miles and making me stay in touch.

Finally, thanks to my wife, Teri Northrup, for sacrificing so much and always supporting me. I can't wait to return the favor.

Contents at a Glance

Contents

Part I

Internetworking Fundamentals

Chapter 1

Networking Fundamentals

IN THIS CHAPTER

- ◆ Using the OSI model to organize a network
- ◆ Examining the various network protocols supported by Windows NT
- ◆ Understanding routing and routing protocols

THIS CHAPTER INTRODUCES several key networking concepts and is intended to provide an overview of the technology. It is meant to fill in gaps in your technical experience and to introduce concepts that are key to this book but may not be common in the networking industry. Those with extensive experience in network and systems engineering may be tempted to skip this chapter. I have always believed in reading material that I am already familiar with. First, it gives me the opportunity to brush up on topics I may have let become stale in my own memory. Second, each author brings his or her own viewpoints and opinions to a topic. Finally, I have proved to myself, time and time again, that there is still a great deal I do not know about networking. I am often surprised to learn something new from an article in a book that I thought would be strictly review.

The OSI Model

The Open Systems Interconnection (OSI) model was developed by the International Standards Organization (ISO) in 1983 to provide a conceptual model on which networks could be based. In the process of developing this framework, the ISO established a vocabulary that assisted engineers worldwide by giving them a common set of words to use to describe concepts they already understood and took for granted. The OSI model divides communications functions into seven layers. These layers aid in envisioning the structure of communications between applications and users on a network. They allow vendors and software engineers to work on one piece of the communication model at a time, following clear-cut guidelines.

Each layer of the OSI model has a simple task to perform – to provide services for the layer directly above it. Each layer is aware that the layer below is at its disposal, eagerly awaiting a command. Each layer receives data from the layer above, in a standardized way, and must provide all the services assigned to it. According to this model, each layer behaves as if it could communicate directly with the corresponding layer on the remote computer.

The OSI model uses several important terms that are not commonly used in the networking industry. When layers communicate across a network with their opposing peer, for instance, the data they transfer is called a *protocol data unit* (PDU). When a layer passes data to the layer below, that data is referred to as a *service data unit* (SDU). Figure 1-1 illustrates this concept.

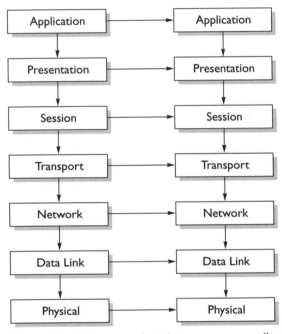

Figure 1–1: PDUs communicate between corresponding layers on different hosts. SDUs communicate from layer to layer within a single host.

It is critical for any network or systems engineer to have a strong understanding of the OSI model. It is not intuitive for most, and it does not make sense to many until they have spent years in the industry. Nonetheless, the vocabulary is extremely common in the real world and is used extensively throughout this book. The layers of the OSI model are outlined in Table 1-1.

TABLE 1-1 LAYERS OF THE OSI MODEL

Layer	Function	Application
Application	Provides an interface for applications to use to access the network	Telnet, FTP, HTTP
Presentation	Provides the final layer of abstraction before the application layer, hiding the specifics of the application from the session layer	Workstation service, network redirectors
Session	Provides complex conversation controls. Rarely referenced	NetBIOS over TCP/IP
Transport	Provides connections, error-checking, and guaranteed delivery	TCP, UDP, SPX
Network	Provides for addressing, navigation, and routing of an internetwork	IP, IPX
Data Link	Provides for addressing within a network segment, collision avoidance, and some error-checking	Ethernet, Token Ring, FDDI
Physical	Specifies how signals are transmitted, received, and carried between hosts on a network segment	Cat 5 copper, fiber optics, hubs

The OSI model should not be confused with a protocol — it is simply a theoretical model. Indeed, very few protocols actually conform to any of the OSI specifications. TCP/IP, for example, was designed many years before OSI and is based on an unrelated, four-layer model. A suite of protocols have been designed to conform closely to the OSI model, including a protocol called Connectionless Network Protocol (CLNP), roughly equivalent to IP in function, and a routing protocol called Intermediate System to Intermediate System (IS-IS). You will find few references to these protocols in this book; they are rarely encountered in the industry and are not implemented in Windows NT.

The next sections describe each of these layers in detail. You will find that I have included more detail on some layers, such as the network and transport layers, than on others. This is a reflection of the importance of each layer in the real world, and it reflects what I thought was most critical to understanding the model as a whole. I have also made an effort to teach "conversational OSI," an important skill for communicating with other engineers.

Layer 1 — the Physical Layer

The physical layer consists of all cabling, electrical properties, pinouts, and connectors on a network. It is commonly referred to as layer 1. If you can touch it or feel it (and that includes electrical shocks!), then it belongs in this layer. This is the layer I will touch on the very least. Physical topologies vary from network to network; the beauty of the OSI model is that I can discuss higher-layer networking without concern for the specific physical implementation of the network.

Layer 2 — the Data-Link Layer

Layer 2, the data-link layer, defines the topology of network connections (for example, star, ring, or bus) and identification of machines on a single network segment. The most common layer-2 protocol in a LAN is Ethernet, but Token Ring and FDDI are also popular. Frame relay is a commonly used data-link-layer WAN protocol and hints at another key vocabulary term.

 Data, when transmitted across a network with a data-link-layer header and footer, is referred to as a *frame*. When you are using a protocol analyzer to investigate network traffic, you can refer to the data being analyzed as a frame if the data-link-layer header or footer is of significance. For example, if you are troubleshooting the resolution of media access control (MAC) addresses, you are analyzing the *frames*.

Though each layer-2 protocol is different, most include a MAC address. The Ethernet MAC address is a flat, 48-bit number assigned to a specific network interface. The assignment of numbers is globally administered by the Internet Assigned Numbers Authority, a practice that ensures that this number is always unique to a network card. Other popular layer-2 fields include a field that indicates the size of the frame and a CRC (cyclical redundancy check) field that is used to verify that no data in the frame header was altered.

The data-link layer includes the capability to address multiple systems. This is accomplished by including a special broadcast address in place of the destination MAC address.

Two common network devices exist at the second layer of the OSI model: bridges and switches. The popularity of bridges has begun to fade in recent years, as routed protocols become more popular than bridged protocols and the cost of layer-3 switching decreases. A bridge connects two physically separate networks, listening for frames transmitted onto one segment that must be forwarded onto another segment. Bridges exist at layer 2 of the OSI model and by definition do not contain the intelligence to analyze traffic at layer 3. This is a limitation, but this simplicity gives bridges the advantage of speed. By decreasing the amount of analysis that must be performed on each frame, the bridge can forward more traffic between networks. Internally, a bridge builds a map of its directly connected networks and the MAC addresses of the hosts attached to each, as Figure 1-2 and Table 1-2 illustrate.

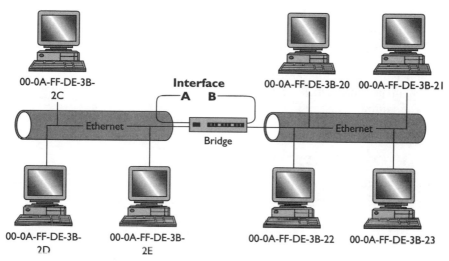

Figure 1–2: A bridge forwards traffic between network segments based on the destination MAC address of the frame.

A bridge listens to each frame on a segment and compares the destination MAC address to a table it stores in memory. By consulting the table in RAM, the bridge is able to determine if the destination MAC address is on the correct network segment or not. If it is a broadcast frame or belongs on another segment, the frame is copied.

TABLE 1-2 SAMPLE BRIDGE ROUTING TABLE

MAC Address	Interface
00-0A-FF-DE-3B-2C	A
00-0A-FF-DE-3B-2D	A
00-0A-FF-DE-3B-2E	A
00-0A-FF-DE-3B-20	B
00-0A-FF-DE-3B-21	B
00-0A-FF-DE-3B-22	B
00-0A-FF-DE-3B-23	B

Switches perform many of the same functions as bridges and have replaced them in many networks. Bridges also forward frames based on the MAC address, but they are characterized by having eight or more network interfaces. Each of these interfaces may connect directly to a host, or it may connect to another switch or hub. The cost per port on switches has decreased in recent years to such a degree that switches are actually replacing hubs, which operate strictly at the physical layer. Windows NT includes only weak bridging capabilities within RAS, the Remote Access Service. Because bridging is not a critical component of NT, it will not be a topic of much discussion in this book.

Remember that the entire purpose of stratifying network communications is to make each layer independent of the other layers. Because of this, bridges and switches forwarding frames make no distinction between frames that carry TCP/IP and frames that carry IPX/SPX.

Layer 3 – the Network Layer

Layer 3 of the OSI model, the network layer, defines how traffic gets across networks. It defines an addressing scheme that includes both network and host addresses, mechanisms for traffic control, and, often, a checksum. Later in the book, several key concepts of the network layer will be discussed in detail: addressing (Chapter 2), routing (Chapters 2 and 13), and flow control (Chapters 2 and 9).

The most well-known examples of layer-3 protocols are Internet Protocol (IP), Internet Control Message Protocol (ICMP), Internetwork Packet Exchange, X.25 (IPX), and Asynchronous Transfer Mode (ATM).

The network layer includes an addressing scheme that allows for greater robustness than is provided by the data-link layer. The network layer allows any two systems to address each other, regardless of whether or not they are directly connected. In order to accomplish this, the network layer includes routing protocols such as IS-IS, RIP, and OSPF. It also includes packet fragmentation and reassembly, which allows packets to traverse networks with different maximum packet sizes, also called MTUs, or maximum transfer units.

Network components that connect different networks and switch packets are called *routers*. The OSI model refers to them as *Intermediate Systems* (ISs), hence the routing protocol name IS-IS. You will also hear the term *gateway*. The two words, "router" and "gateway," are usually synonymous. Routers, by definition, exist at the network layer. As network technology evolves, the distinct capabilities of bridges, routers, and switches merge into single devices. Modern routers commonly include bridging functions (occasionally called *brouters*). Modern switches often include layer-3 routing capabilities.

Network-layer addresses are different from data-link-layer addresses in that they are hierarchical. They include an address for the network, which aids routers in finding the destination. They include a distinctly different address for the host, which allows a computer to identify itself within a specific network. IP has 32 bits to be shared between both the network and host addresses, with a variable number of bits dedicated to each. In contrast, IPX has a 32-bit network address and uses the MAC address as the host portion of the address.

Layer 4 – the Transport Layer

The fourth layer of the OSI model, the transport layer, is responsible for maintaining a conversation between two nodes on a network. It provides for error correction and for data fragmentation and reassembly.

Transport layer protocols for the IP protocol suite include TCP (Transmission Control Protocol) and UDP (User Datagram Protocol). SPX (Sequenced Packet Exchange) is a common layer-4 protocol for the IPX layer-3 protocol.

Layer-4 protocols come in two distinct flavors: connection-oriented and connectionless. *Connection-oriented* protocols allow two-way conversations to take place between hosts. They provide for guaranteed delivery and order. TCP is the connection-oriented transport protocol in the TCP/IP stack. Common uses of TCP are World Wide Web requests, Windows NT file transfers, and Telnet traffic.

Connectionless layer-4 protocols have the advantage of requiring less overhead. They allow for "fire and forget" communications, where a message must be sent but the sender does not need to be notified if the packet is not transmitted correctly. Connectionless protocols are more efficient because they do not need to maintain header fields for order and the sender has no need to wait for an acknowledgment from the destination. However, they are only suited to traffic for which delivery is not critical. UDP is the connectionless transport protocol in the TCP/IP stack. Common uses of UDP are DNS queries, Windows NT browser notifications, and network broadcasts.

Layer 5 – the Session Layer

Layer 5, the session layer, provides for complex conversation controls. It allows for the management and synchronization of communications between hosts. The session layer is also responsible for user authentication.

In reality, the session layer is one of the least practical of the OSI layers and is rarely referred to. Indeed, there is no corresponding layer in the Department of Defense model on which TCP/IP is based. I will spend very little time on the session and presentation layers simply because this book is centered around TCP/IP and these two layers have no direct correlation. One of the few examples of a session-layer protocol implemented over TCP/IP is NetBIOS over TCP/IP, which is covered in detail in Chapter 10.

Layer 6 – the Presentation Layer

The presentation layer, layer 6 of the OSI model, provides a layer of abstraction to the application layer of the OSI model. This allows applications to agree on standardized representations for data. Network redirectors such as the Workstation service typically work with the presentation layer.

The ISO intended this layer to provide conversion between different formats, such as converting carriage returns to carriage return/line feed combinations when necessary. Tasks such as compression and encryption should be implemented here, though they are often implemented in protocols at other layers. Like the session layer, the presentation layer is not a common topic of conversation at dinner parties.

Layer 7 – the Application Layer

The top of the OSI food chain is the seventh layer, the application layer. The application layer does not describe applications; instead, it provides an interface to the network *for* applications. In this way, applications have a simple way to communicate across a network, without prior knowledge of the physical topology, the network architecture, or the network protocol. Based on input from applications, the application layer makes use of the layers beneath it to communicate across a network and exchange useful data between hosts.

Protocols that are commonly used and exist at layer 7 of the OSI model are HTTP (Web requests), FTP (Internet file transfers), and Telnet (remote consoles).

How the OSI Model Works

To tie things together, let's go through an example of network communications and consider how each layer of the OSI model is used. If you launch a Web browser and visit a Web site, the Web browser makes requests with an application-layer protocol, HTTP. In theory, HTTP communicates directly with the Web server's HTTP service, also at the application layer. Think back to Figure 1-1, which showed protocol data units being passed horizontally from the application layer of the client directly to the application layer of the server – the HTTP protocol is an example of how this theory works in practice.

When sending a request to retrieve a Web page, the protocol is not concerned about the network topology in any way – it relies on the lower layers to take care of those details. HTTP creates a request that it wants the HTTP server to receive, something like, "GET /." It passes this data to the transport-layer protocol. In this case, the transport-layer protocol is TCP. (TCP/IP does not include the session and presentation layers, so they are not present in this example.)

As shown in Figure 1-3, TCP adds a header and passes its SDU to the network-layer protocol, IP. IP, in turn, pads the data it received from TCP with a header and passes it to the layer-2 protocol, which may be Ethernet, Token Ring, FDDI, or something else. The data-link-layer protocol passes it to the layer-1 protocol (which is generally dependent on the layer-2 protocol), and the layer-1 protocol converts it into actual electrical signals that can be received by the destination host's network interface card.

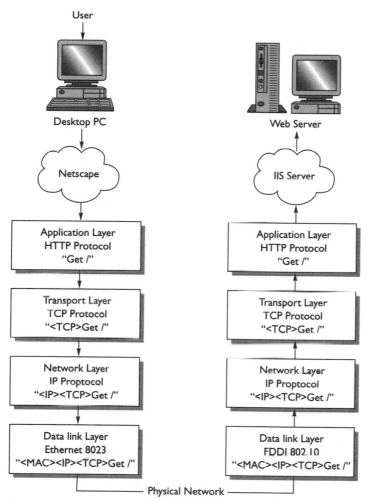

Figure 1-3: A request from a user traverses the OSI model until it is converted into network traffic. Once it reaches the host, it moves back up the OSI model so that a server application may interpret the request.

In summary, the OSI model's greatest value to most network engineers comes from providing a convenient method of describing protocols in conversation. For example, as a network engineer armed with a strong knowledge of the OSI model, you can use catch phrases in conversation such as, "Of course TCP isn't responsible for getting the traffic through the routers! It's a layer-4 protocol!" Rest assured you will soon be the life of any party.

The purpose of the OSI model is to provide entirely separated layers so that protocols residing at a particular layer may be "mixed and matched" with protocols at other layers. In reality, however, layer-3 protocols are used only with specific layer-4, -5, -6, and -7 protocols. For example, you cannot use the transport-layer TCP protocol with the network-layer IPX protocol. TCP is only used with the network-layer IP protocol. This grouping of protocols at multiple layers has led to the development of *protocol suites*. The next section describes the protocol suites supported by Windows NT.

Sorting Out the Most Common Network Protocols

As networks evolved over the years, different vendors developed different ways of communicating. For communication to occur successfully and reliably, all hosts on a network must be speaking the same language, with no dialects. Though people from England and people from the United States use the English language differently, we are still able to exchange ideas. Computers are never that flexible, so strict standards have been developed to define every bit of every byte of every packet sent between hosts. These standards arose from the efforts of groups of organizations, all putting their heads together for the common cause of communication.

Many protocols were developed, but few remain. Those that did not make the cut failed for different reasons — poor design, poor implementation, or lack of support. Those that remain today have withstood the test of time and have proved an effective method of communicating. The three most common protocols in today's local area networks are Microsoft's NetBEUI, Novell's IPX/SPX, and the cross-platform TCP/IP.

NetBEUI

NetBEUI was developed for IBM as a nonroutable protocol to carry NetBIOS traffic. NetBEUI's lack of support for routing and network-layer addresses is the reason for its greatest advantage and disadvantage. Because it does not require the additional overhead of network addresses and a network-layer header and footer, it is fast and efficient. This makes it well suited to small workgroup environments where there is a single network or the entire environment is bridged.

NetBEUI will never be the primary protocol in enterprise networking because it does not support routing. The only address included in a NetBEUI frame is the data-link-layer media access control (MAC) address, which identifies an interface card but does not identify a network. Routers depend on network addresses to forward packets to their final destination, and NetBEUI frames lack that information entirely.

Bridges are capable of forwarding traffic between networks based on the data-link-layer address, but bridges have many drawbacks. Bridges do not scale well, because all broadcast traffic must be forwarded to every network. NetBEUI in particular includes a significant amount of broadcast traffic and depends on it for name resolution. Your mileage may vary, but bridged NetBEUI networks rarely scale above 100 hosts.

In recent years, networks based on a hierarchy of layer-2 switches have become popular. Entirely switched environments reduce network utilization, although broadcasts must still be forwarded to each host on the network. This fact, combined with the adoption of 100-base-T Ethernet, allows switched NetBIOS networks to scale as high as 350 nodes before broadcast traffic becomes overwhelming.

IPX/SPX

Adopted by Novell for their NetWare client/server software, the IPX protocol suite does not suffer from the weaknesses of NetBEUI. Instead, it introduces new, different weaknesses.

IPX is fully routable, allowing it to be used in large enterprise networks. It includes a 32-bit network address, permitting an incredible number of routed networks in a single environment.

The scalability of IPX is hampered by its high level of broadcast traffic and extremely high overhead. The Service Advertising Protocol (SAP), in particular, limits the number of hosts on a routed network to several thousand. While the limitations of SAP have been overcome in part by intelligent routers and conservative server configurations, management of large-scale IPX networks has proved to be an extremely difficult task.

TCP/IP

Every network protocol has its advantages, but only TCP/IP allows full connectivity to the Internet. TCP/IP was developed by persons at the Massachusetts Institute of Technology and several commercial organizations for the Department of Defense in the late 1960s, as a network protocol resilient enough to continue communications in the event a nuclear attack were to destroy large sections of the network. Gradually, the ARPANET, which developed around this protocol, evolved into the Internet, a medium of communication for scientists and engineers.

TCP/IP was designed for scalability and reliability, and it meets both of these requirements extremely well. Unfortunately, speed and efficiency were sacrificed. (Remember: development was funded by the government!)

After the Internet became public, people began to discover the power of worldwide networking. The resulting popularity of the Internet is the primary reason TCP/IP is still used today. Often without realizing it, users have installed TCP/IP stacks onto their home PCs, making this network protocol the most widely used in the world.

TCP/IP's 32-bit addressing scheme is not sufficient to support the number of hosts and networks that will soon participate in the Internet. The most likely standard to replace the current implementation is IPv6, also referred to as IPng (IP, the Next Generation, a reference anyone reading this book probably understands). You will find more information on IPv6 in Chapter 2, which covers TCP/IP-specific topics in detail.

Exploring Basic Routing Concepts

When traveling through unfamiliar territory, people must rely on directions to guide them to their final destination. These directions come in several forms. People may refer to a map containing streets and landmarks, or they may remember verbal directions, describing the path as a series of left and right turns. Or they may simply follow the road signs.

Despite the fact that I have a map, directions, and signs to follow, I still get lost. In fact, I get lost *all the time*! So how do packets, mere electrical signals, make it through the many turns in a network? When a router receives a packet, how does it know which interface to forward the packet to? When a section of a network fails, how do the other routers know to reroute traffic?

The answers to the first and second questions are *routing tables*. Routing tables each contain a database of information about each of the networks a particular router knows the path to. So when a router receives a packet that it must forward, it compares the network number of the packet to the network numbers listed in its routing table and forwards the packet toward the destination.

The example routing table shown in Table 1-3 includes a basic set of information. Each row in a routing table contains, at a minimum, a network address, a distance, and the address of the next router to receive a packet. By comparing the network address of an incoming packet to this table, the router is able to determine where it should forward the packet.

TABLE 1-3 EXAMPLE ROUTING TABLE

Network	Distance	Next Hop
A	2	Router C
D	3	Router A
F	5	Router A

The answer to the third question (When a section of a network fails, how do the other routers know to reroute traffic?) is *routing protocols*. Routing protocols are network-layer protocols that routers use to communicate with each other. Routers rely on these protocols to exchange the information contained in their routing tables: *where* a specific network is, how fast the connection is, and whether or not it is working at all. By exchanging this information, a router can add a new network and all other routers will know the best route to that destination. Similarly, if a router or network segment fails, the routing protocol will propagate news of the failure throughout the rest of the network.

When all routers on a network have exchanged the information they have in their routing tables and no changes are being made, the routers are said to have *converged*. The time it takes for a network to converge after a change is made is called the *convergence delay*. This is an important consideration when choosing a routing protocol because it allows changes to be made more quickly. It also makes troubleshooting easier by decreasing the time it takes for problems to manifest themselves and for the corrected information to be propagated. In large networks such as the Internet, routers have a great deal of information to exchange to keep their routing tables up to date, and they may never reach a state of convergence.

This section provides a general background in routing protocols. Chapter 13 provides information about specific routing protocols commonly used with the TCP/IP protocol suite and details on Microsoft's implementation of the Routing and Remote Access Service.

Routing and Windows NT

Systems administrators and systems engineers typically focus on the individual hosts and think of networks as a transparent way of connecting those hosts. With the introduction of static and RIP routing in Windows NT 3.51, NT systems could be more than just nodes on a network – they could *be* the network. An NT server could now forward traffic between network segments using either IPX/SPX or TCP/IP. It could share a network with traditional dedicated network hardware and communicate with it. These new forms of routing now offered an inexpensive way for small networks with an NT server to segment their traffic without sacrificing connectivity.

Shortly after Windows NT 4.0 was released, Microsoft released an add-on package called the Routing and Remote Access Service (RRAS). With this package, routing in Windows NT becomes more robust and flexible. Windows NT now includes support for RIP v2 and can interoperate with another modern routing protocol, OSPF. More important, Microsoft has provided an open application programming interface to allow third-party vendors to develop routing protocols that plug into the RRAS.

As Microsoft continues scaling its operating systems both up and down, it will introduce systems that are dedicated routers running a simplified version of the Windows NT or Windows CE operating system, and it will take traditional vendors such as Cisco and 3-Com head on.

Adding routing for NT provides an excellent opportunity for you as a systems engineer to expand your career and build your skills as a network engineer. For this reason, routing concepts are a focus within this book — they will be required knowledge for NT systems engineers in the future.

Classes of Routing Protocols

Just as every network is different, different routing protocols are better suited to one network configuration or another. There are many different types of routing protocols, but they all fall into one of two categories: interior gateway protocols (IGPs) and exterior gateway protocols (EGPs).

Exterior gateway protocols describe the flow of traffic between *autonomous systems* (ASs). An AS, covered in more detail in Chapter 13, is a group of routers that are administered and owned by a single organization. The most widespread use of EGPs is on the Internet — it allows ISPs and other organizations with an Internet connection to describe the location of their network to everyone else on the Internet. EGPs are not currently supported in Windows NT and so will not receive much attention in this book.

Interior gateway protocols provide information to neighboring routers about the flow of traffic within an autonomous system. For example, if a network administrator adds an IP network to a router located on the fourth floor of a building, routers on the first, second, and third floors must learn about it before they can forward traffic. Several IGPs are supported by Windows NT and RRAS and are described in detail in Chapter 13, on the Routing and Remote Access Service.

Interior gateway protocols are further subdivided by the method they use to exchange information. *Distance-vector routing protocols* are the simpler of the two kinds, exchanging information only with routers on directly connected networks. Each router, in turn, passes this information on to other directly connected routers. In this way, information is propagated through a network step by step, router by router, as Figure 1-4 illustrates. The name "distance-vector" comes from the two components that are typically exchanged: the distance (number of hops) and the vector (direction, or next hop). Routers typically exchange information on a regular, timed basis using broadcast frames on each active network interface.

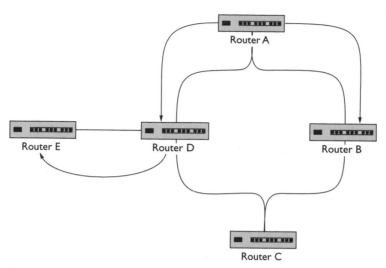

Figure 1–4: Distance–vector routing protocols exchange routing information only with their directly attached neighboring routers.

The primary advantage of this method is simplicity: routers only communicate through broadcasts to directly connected neighbors. The drawbacks are many: convergence time is very slow, problems such as routing loops are common, and traffic overhead is high because the entire routing table is typically exchanged.

The other, more modern, method of exchanging routing information is the *link-state routing protocol*. Link-state routing protocols are protocols in which a router exchanges its routing table with every individual router on a network. Additional advantages over distance-vector protocols include the ability to exchange information immediately as a change takes place, reducing convergence time. To further reduce convergence time, information is sent directly to every affected gateway, rather than to one router at a time, as with distance-vector routing protocols. This concept is illustrated in Figure 1-5.

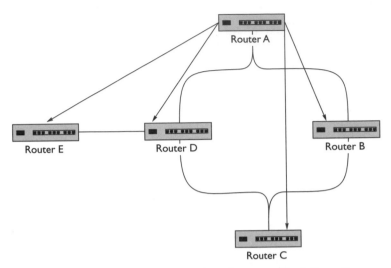

Figure 1-5: Link-state routing protocols exchange routing information directly with all routers within their autonomous system.

Common Routing Problems

Routing protocols do not get the credit they deserve. The fact of the matter is that everything that happens on the Internet is entirely dependent on the functions of these routing protocols, which very few people really understand well. If you have ever noticed that large sections of the Internet disappear from time to time, chances are good it was because a routing table had been misconfigured.

These problems are not confined to the public Internet, however. Even experienced network administrators have brought down an entire company network because of a mistake configuring a routing protocol or a routing table. Worse yet, these problems often take several hours to fully manifest themselves. Because routers exchange information among themselves, misinformation in a routing table spreads like a computer virus, making this kind of bug a very difficult process to troubleshoot. Once a problem is isolated and corrected, the correction must be passed from router to router, and the problem may not disappear completely for several hours.

Probably the most common source of routing problems stems from *human error*. If someone mistakenly adds a network to a router's routing table, and that network exists somewhere else already, traffic may not get to the correct location. Routers will forward traffic to whichever occurrence of the network is closer to them. The root cause of a problem such as this may be as simple as a typographical error, but finding and resolving the problem can take hours. The most effective way to reduce human error is through education; make sure that everyone who has access to routing tables has the knowledge necessary to really understand the effects a change may have. Another method is to have an approval system such that two people must always verify that a change is accurate before it is implemented.

Routing loops commonly occur with distance-vector routing protocols. The router connected to the failed network notifies its neighbor routers of the failed network and asks them to remove it from their routing tables. Ideally, each router would remove the entry in its routing table for the failed network and no longer attempt to forward traffic to it. A routing loop occurs when a router that has not yet been notified of the failed network broadcasts its own routing table, which includes a path to the failed network through the router that originally advertised its failure. At this point, the router attached directly to the failed network will add the network back into its routing table and attempt to forward traffic through the router that advertised it.

This is a difficult concept to describe and is best appreciated through an example. For example, suppose a simple network uses the RIP routing protocol, a distance-vector protocol. This network has five routers (A, B, C, D, and E) and five networks, and it is in a completely converged state. Figure 1-6 shows the network, and Tables 1-4, 1-5, 1-6, 1-7, and 1 8 show the routing tables of each of the five routers.

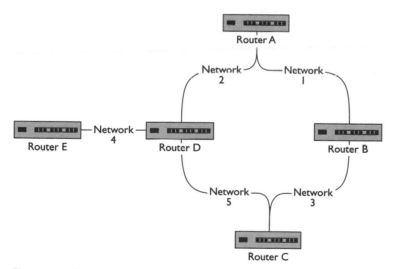

Figure 1-6: An example network with five routers and five network segments. Currently, the network is stable and converged.

TABLE 1-4 ROUTER A'S ROUTING TABLE (STEP A — PRIOR TO THE CHANGE)

Network	Distance	Next Hop
1	1	Local
2	1	Local
3	2	Router B
4	2	Router D
5	2	Router D

TABLE 1-5 ROUTER B'S ROUTING TABLE (STEP A — PRIOR TO THE CHANGE)

Network	Distance	Next Hop
1	1	Local
2	2	Router A
3	1	Local
4	3	Router C
5	2	Router C

TABLE 1-6 ROUTER C'S ROUTING TABLE (STEP A — PRIOR TO THE CHANGE)

Network	Distance	Next Hop
1	2	Router B
2	2	Router D
3	1	Local
4	2	Router D
5	1	Local

TABLE 1-7 ROUTER D'S ROUTING TABLE (STEP A – PRIOR TO THE CHANGE)

Network	Distance	Next Hop
1	2	Router A
2	1	Local
3	2	Router C
4	1	Local
5	1	Local

TABLE 1-8 ROUTER E'S ROUTING TABLE (STEP A – PRIOR TO THE CHANGE)

Network	Distance	Next Hop
1	3	Router D
2	2	Router D
3	3	Router D
4	1	Local
5	2	Router D

Suddenly, disaster strikes. While looking for paper for the fax machine, the receptionist accidentally unplugs the hub for Network 1. Now, in a perfect world, traffic going through Network 1 (for example, traffic from Router A bound for Network 3) would simply be rerouted and only connectivity to Network 1 would be lost. In that same perfect world, all the routers would instantly know that Network 1 was temporarily down and would drop packets bound for that network.

Routers A and B have a direct connection to the network, so they will recognize that it can no longer receive traffic. The problem begins because of a serious weakness in some distance-vector routing protocols (like RIP): they send updates on a timed interval, not immediately when something fails. In this example, Router A's timed interval occurs immediately after the change, and it notifies Router D that Network 1 is down. Unfortunately, Router B sent an update just before the network failed, so it will have to wait until its next scheduled update to notify Router C. At this point, only Routers A, B, and D have updated routing tables, as illustrated in Tables 1-9, 1-10, and 1-11.

TABLE 1-9 ROUTER A'S ROUTING TABLE (STEP B — IMMEDIATELY AFTER THE
          NETWORK FAILURE)

Network	Distance	Next Hop
1	**	**
2	1	Local
3	2	Router B
4	2	Router D
5	2	Router D

TABLE 1-10 ROUTER B'S ROUTING TABLE (STEP B — IMMEDIATELY AFTER THE
           NETWORK FAILURE)

Network	Distance	Next Hop
1	3	Router C
2	2	Router A
3	1	Local
4	3	Router C
5	2	Router C

TABLE 1-11 ROUTER D'S ROUTING TABLE (STEP B — IMMEDIATELY AFTER THE
           NETWORK FAILURE)

Network	Distance	Next Hop
1	3	Router C
2	1	Local
3	2	Router C
4	1	Local
5	1	Local

Now, if Router C really did have another connection to Network 1, everything would begin to work. Traffic would be neatly rerouted, and the network administrator would have no reason to panic. Unfortunately for the network administrator, Router C has just told the adjoining routers that it has a path to a failed network, and now those routers will begin to propagate false information.

Everything is going well until Router C transmits its timed update. Router C still has an entry in its routing table for Network 1, and it includes that network in its scheduled update, which it broadcasts to Router D and Router B. Both routers receive this update and are happy to add the entry to their own routing tables under the assumption that Router C has some way to get to the network. Unfortunately, Router C's path to the network is through Router B. So it still thinks it has a clean path to Network 1 only because it hasn't heard the news of the failure from Router B.

After Router C's update, Routers D and B have updated routing tables, as illustrated in Tables 1-12 and 1-13. This update removes Network 1 from the routing table.

 Remember that the distance between a router and the destination network is always equal to the distance from the next-hop router *plus one* to count the extra link.

TABLE 1-12 ROUTER B'S ROUTING TABLE (STEP C — NETWORK FAILURE BEGINS TO PROPAGATE)

Network	Distance	Next Hop
1	**	**
2	2	Router A
3	1	Local
4	3	Router C
5	2	Router C

TABLE 1-13 ROUTER D'S ROUTING TABLE (STEP C — NETWORK FAILURE BEGINS TO PROPAGATE)

Network	Distance	Next Hop
1	**	**
2	1	Local
3	2	Router C
4	1	Local
5	1	Local

The time finally comes for Router B to perform its scheduled update. It broadcasts an update to the only neighbor it can currently reach, Router C. This update includes the connection to Network 1 with a distance of 3. Router C will receive this and, because Router B is listed as the next hop in its routing table to Network 1, will update its own routing table with the new distance information. Remember that Router C automatically adds one to the distance to account for the link between Routers B and C. After this update, Router C's routing table has removed the path to Network 1. This change is reflected in Table 1-14.

TABLE 1-14 ROUTER C'S ROUTING TABLE (STEP D — NETWORK FAILURE PROPAGATES COMPLETELY, NETWORK CONVERGES)

Network	Distance	Next Hop
1	4	Router B
2	2	Router D
3	1	Local
4	2	Router D
5	1	Local

By now the trend of the routing loop should be becoming clear to you: *the routers will continue to propagate misinformation.* As Routers C and B transmit their scheduled updates, the distance they *think* it is to Network 1 will increment by one. Eventually, the distance will increase to 16, which in RIP means the network is unreachable. At this point, the route will be dropped from the routing tables and the network will be able to converge. The time to convergence is painfully slow, however, with updates occurring only every thirty seconds.

Until the network is converged, the network's ability to forward traffic will be reduced. When Router B receives a packet from a host on Network 3 that is bound for Network 1, it will forward it to the next hop listed in its routing table for Network 1 – Router C. Router C will receive the packet and forward it to the listed next hop in its routing table – Router B. In turn, Router B will forward the packet to Router C, and so on until the time to live (TTL) listed in the packet decrements to zero. (See the sidebar that accompanies this section for more information on TLLs.)

Several methods exist to reduce the chances for routing loops to occur. These include *hold-down times, triggered updates,* and *split horizons.*

A hold-down time specifies an amount of time that must pass before a route that was removed will be readded. This reduces the chance that a routing loop will occur because a router will not accept an alternate path to a failed network until after the hold-down time, which should be long enough to ensure that the network converges completely after any change. In the example, Router D would not have accepted the misinformation from Router C because it had been recently updated by Router A. Further, Router B would have ignored Router C because Router B had just updated its routing table.

TTLs and Looping Traffic

Time to Live (TTL) is a field in the IP header of a packet that keeps track of how many routers a packet has passed through. This field is filled in by the host sending the packet with a value that is configurable. In the Windows NT operating system, the value is 32 by default. Each router in a network decrements the value in the TTL field by one before retransmitting it, and when it reaches 0, the packet is dropped.

This method ensures that no packet will ever loop forever between two routers that are involved in a routing loop. However, with a high TTL of 32, that packet could bounce between two routers 32 times! This means that a single packet would generate 32 times the amount of traffic it normally would. This can cripple a network.

On the plus side, a routing loop that cripples the network means that the network administrator discovers it more quickly than he or she would otherwise. On the down side, network downtime is highly visible and extremely expensive.

The TTL in Windows NT can be adjusted — simply add the registry value HKEY_LOCAL_MACHINE\SYSTEM\CurrentControlSet\Services\Tcpip\Parameters\Default TTL and set the value to the desired default TTL.

Triggered updates reduce the chances of a routing loop and improve the time to convergence. Instead of being withheld until the next timed update, changes to the routing table are broadcast immediately. This translates to additional traffic when a network fails, but the quicker response time is generally worth the trouble.

A split horizon prevents two-node routing loops from occurring by disallowing a route to be advertised over the same interface it was learned from. In this way, a router that learns it has a failed route will not immediately learn from a neighboring router that an active route exists. I have covered the split-horizon concept in great detail in Chapter 13, covering the Routing and Remote Access Service.

Summary

This chapter discussed the OSI model, which was developed to organize work being done in the networking industry. It became a critical aspect of all networking and continues to be an important concept today. This chapter also covered one of the most important topics in networking – routing. Among systems engineers, routing is generally misunderstood, and yet routing is a critical concept because all network communications depend on it. Windows NT now has significant routing capabilities, and you should become proficient in routing concepts before moving on in this text.

In this chapter you learned that:

◆ The OSI model breaks network communications into seven distinct layers: the application layer, the presentation layer, the session layer, the transport layer, the network layer, the data-link layer, and the physical layer.

◆ Each layer of the OSI model has a separate, distinct set of responsibilities and provides services to the layer directly above it.

◆ Routers forward packets between physically separate network segments, allowing hosts on different segments to communicate.

◆ Routers communicate with each other using *routing protocols*. There are many different kinds of routing protocols, including link-state protocols, distance-vector protocols, IGPs, and EGPs.

I remember a basketball coach I had in grade school who felt I could never be a successful basketball player until I mastered the fundamentals of the game. So I practiced dribbling, passing, and shooting hour after hour after hour. If I never became a good basketball player, it was not because I did not focus on the fundamentals — it was because I had no talent. Nonetheless, it is important to build a strong foundation of knowledge before attempting to master more complex concepts. If you have read and understood this first chapter, then you have the basic knowledge you need to make this book a useful tool.

The next chapter continues building a foundation of basic networking knowledge. The scope, however, is narrowed to the TCP/IP protocol suite. You will learn the history, the present status, and the future of the most common network protocol in the world.

Chapter 2

Everything You Need to Know About TCP/IP and the Internet

IN THIS CHAPTER

◆ A description of the Department of Defense layered protocol model

◆ An introduction to the various organizations you'll interoperate with on the Internet

◆ Windows NT standards (the way things should work)

◆ Microsoft's implementation of Windows NT (the way things are)

◆ Factors specific to the Windows NT TCP/IP stack

◆ The basics you need to implement Windows NT on a TCP/IP-based network

◆ Pointers on how to secure an NT system on a TCP/IP network

THIS CHAPTER WILL provide a detailed look at the Windows NT standards (the way things should work) and the Microsoft implementation of Windows NT (the way things are). I will also provide you with the basics you need to implement Windows NT on a TCP/IP-based network. This chapter starts with a description of the Department of Defense layered protocol model, moves into an introduction to the various organizations you will need to know to interoperate on the Internet, discusses factors specific to the Windows NT TCP/IP stack, and gives you pointers to secure an NT system on a TCP/IP network.

Understanding the DOD Model

At this point, you should feel comfortable enough with the OSI model to use terms like *layer-2 protocol* and *transport-layer filtering* in casual conversation. This is a good thing, because the OSI model is commonly used to describe protocols and their various roles. Unfortunately, TCP/IP was not designed to fit into the OSI model. In fact, there is an entirely *new* model to learn: the Department of Defense (DOD) model.

Why two models? Why didn't the Department of Defense simply comply with the OSI specifications? Why duplicate the effort of designing a model and require everyone to learn two ways of thinking? The short answer is that the DOD designed the model that TCP/IP would be based on more than a decade before the OSI model was designed. Now that TCP/IP is the standard protocol for internetworking, everyone still refers to the OSI model. Go figure.

The DOD model is based on four distinct layers: *application, transport, internetwork,* and *network access.* These layers and the services they provide are outlined in Table 2-1.

TABLE 2-1 THE DOD MODEL

Protocol Layer	Services Provided
Application	FTP, Telnet, SNMP, and DNS
Transport	TCP and UDP
Internet	IP, ARP, ICMP, and IGMP
Network Interface	NDIS, Adapter Card Driver

The Application Layer

The application layer provides for high-level network communications between computers. It takes on the roles of the first two layers from the OSI model, which are the application and presentation layers. Application-layer protocols specify commands to be sent between clients and servers, providing a standardized method of access. For example, the File Transfer Protocol (FTP) allows files to be exchanged between systems on an internetwork. Any standard FTP server understands the same set of commands, such as USER and PASS, that identify a user. Other examples of application-layer protocols include HTTP, SMTP, POP, Telnet, NNTP, and IRC. The messages these protocols exchange are very understandable, especially compared to such alternatives as NetBIOS traffic.

To continue the FTP example, launch a Telnet client and connect to any FTP server on port 21. To TELNET into a server-side application, Windows users can choose Run from the Start menu and enter **telnet ftp.microsoft.com 21.** If you connect properly, the remote FTP server introduces itself with the numeric message "220."

At this point, you are expected to identify yourself using the USER and PASS commands. Type **USER anonymous** and press Enter (you may not see your characters echoed to the screen). The FTP server returns the message "330," which has been defined by the FTP standard to mean that the username was accepted. To complete identification, provide a password (in this case an e-mail address) by entering **PASS anony@mous.co'**. If the server allows anonymous connections, it will return a "230" code and perhaps a text message. The commands and responses you just exchanged with the FTP server are a demonstration of an application-layer protocol. Because of the layered nature of the DOD model, you were able to execute these commands and receive the responses without concern for the transport, internetwork, or network-access layers. Remember to close your FTP session before continuing!

The exact language clients and servers use to communicate is spelled out very clearly in Requests for Comments (RFCs). The commands described here are not the commands a user would enter into his client application; rather, they describe the actual characters transmitted over the network from the client to the server. Indeed, these commands are rarely seen by users. Commonly used protocols such as FTP are often defined in multiple RFCs, with newer documents adding features or fixing problems. FTP is primarily defined by RFC 959, but several other documents define commonly used extensions to the original RFCs.

Just as a good understanding of IP addressing is important to troubleshoot internetwork-layer problems, a strong knowledge of the workings of different protocols is necessary to solve problems occurring at this layer. The most common Internet protocols have chapters dedicated to them in this book; please refer to Appendix B for a listing of RFCs that define these protocols.

TIP

For the curious and/or masochistic, the InterNIC maintains the official database of RFCs. More information on finding RFCs can be found at `http://ds.internic.net/ds/dspg1intdoc.html` and `http://info.internet.isi.edu/1/in-notes/rfc`. You have been warned.

Besides the traditional Internet applications, two application programming interfaces are provided by Microsoft with Windows NT. One is Windows Sockets (Winsock), which gives you a standard communication mechanism and is utilized by common applications such as FTP and Telnet. The other is NetBIOS over TCP/IP (NBT), which allows support of NetBIOS messaging and naming services. For more on NBT, see Chapter 10, which is dedicated to this subject.

The Transport Layer

The transport layer of the DOD model is extremely similar to the transport layer of the OSI model. This layer provides for both connection-oriented and connectionless traffic between hosts on a network. Because it must provide services to the application layer, the transport-layer header contains a field that identifies a specific application, known as a port number. The specific port number used for any given application can vary depending on the configuration of a system, but the standards are provided in RFC 1700 (http://ds2.internic.net/rfc/rfc1700.txt).

The most common transport-layer protocols in the DOD model are the connectionless UDP (User Datagram Protocol) and the connection-oriented TCP (Transmission Control Protocol). UDP is used for multisystem broadcast messaging and network traffic for which efficiency is more important than reliability, such as DNS queries and browsing updates. UDP is useful when you do not need acknowledgment of receipt, or if you are transferring small amounts of data. TCP is used for most traffic, providing full connection capabilities, including flow control and acknowledgments.

This layer also handles taking a data stream from Winsock and arranging it into packets that can be transmitted over the network. TCP and UDP each add a *header* to the data segments that are transmitted from Winsock. The header, in general, is information added to the beginning of a datagram that is useful to that specific layer. Headers carry information in fields, including information that identifies which process on the server should handle the data, information on how the data was broken into packets, and a checksum that verifies that the information is intact. A TCP header follows the internetwork header, supplying information specific to the TCP protocol. Table 2-2 describes the TCP header fields, and Figure 2-1 shows the TCP header format.

TABLE 2–2 TCP HEADER FORMAT

Field Name	Field Description
Source Port (16 bits)	Identifies the port (corresponding to a process or application) sending the data.
Destination Port (16 bits)	Identifies the destination port (or process) on the receiving host that should handle this packet.
Sequence Number (32 bits)	Provides a unique identifier for the packet. Since TCP is a connection-oriented protocol, this number also helps to guarantee the delivery by assigning an acknowledgment number to each data segment.

Continued

Field Name	Field Description
Acknowledgment Number (32 bits)	Identifies what the next Sequence Number transmitted by the remote host should be. Used to confirm receipt of all packets with a lower Acknowledgment Number.
Data Offset (4 bits)	Gives the length of the TCP header. This field is used by the receiving computer to determine the beginning of the data portion of the packet. This field is only four bits and represents the four most significant bits of a byte. Therefore, multiply the number in this field by 32 to determine the total bytes in the TCP header (Network Monitor does this automatically).
Reserved (6 bits)	Since this field is reserved for future use, it must be set to zero.
URG (1 Bit)	Urgent Pointer field. This field is rarely used.
ACK (1 Bit)	Acknowledgment field. Set to zero only for the initial connection and disconnection requests.
PSH (1 Bit)	Push Function. Forces the receiving computer to process the data immediately rather than buffering it.
RST (1 Bit)	Forces a connection reset. Set to one when closing a TCP connection.
SYN (1 Bit)	Synchronizes sequence numbers between client and server. This field is set to one only when establishing a connection.
FIN (1 Bit)	Indicates there is no more data from the sender. Closes the connection.
Window (16 bits)	Indicates the size of the TCP sliding window buffer. This is the number of bytes that may be transmitted before an acknowledgment is required.
Checksum (16 bits)	A value the sender calculates from the TCP header and data. The sender recalculates this value to verify that none of the data has changed during the transfer. If an error is detected, the data may be retransmitted.
Urgent Pointer (16 bits)	Indicates where the urgent data is within the packet. Rarely used.

Continued

TABLE 2-2 TCP HEADER FORMAT *(Continued)*

Options (variable)	Used to convey information not allowed within other fields. Options may be in one of two formats. The first format is a single byte indicating the option type. The second format uses the first byte to indicate the option type, the second byte to indicate the length of the option data, and all bytes thereafter to hold the actual option data.
Padding (variable)	This field is filled with zeros to ensure that the TCP header ends and data begins on an even 32-bit boundary.

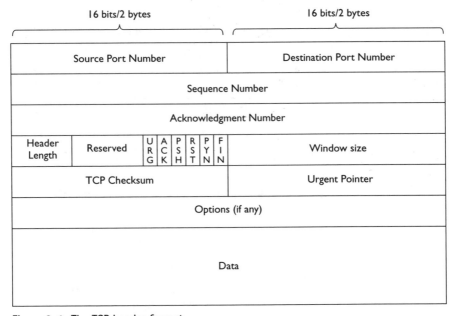

Figure 2-1: The TCP header format

Just as TCP carries certain information in its header, so does UDP. Since UDP does not have guaranteed delivery and does not provide error correction, the header is much simpler. The UDP header fields are described in Table 2-3; Figure 2-2 shows the UDP header format.

TABLE 2-3 UDP HEADER FORMAT

Field Name	Field Description
Source Port (16 bits)	Identifies the port (corresponding to a process or application) sending the data
	It is an optional field, and the default source port value is 0. It is only used when the two hosts are using UDP for two-way communications
Destination Port (16 bits)	Identifies the destination port (or process) on the receiving host that should handle this packet
Length (16 bits)	Indicates the length of the UDP header and data
Checksum (16 bits)	A value the sender calculates from the UDP header and data. The sender recalculates this value to verify that none of the data has changed during the transfer. If an error is detected, the data may be discarded.

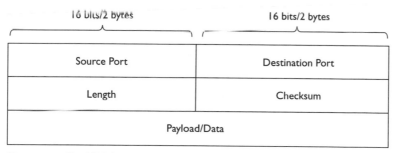

Figure 2-2: The UDP header format

When a client wishes to connect to a server using TCP, it must establish a session. To begin a TCP session, a "three-way handshake" establishes the source and destination port numbers and synchronizes the sending and receiving of data using the SYN and ACK fields. The synchronization process is as follows:

1. A client begins the three-way handshake process by transmitting a packet with the SYN flag set to 1. All other flags are set to 0.

2. Once the server receives the SYN packet, it returns an acknowledgment. The acknowledgment packet has both the SYN and ACK flags set to 1. The value of the Sequence Number field is set to indicate the first byte it is ready to receive.

3. The client responds with an acknowledgment that has the Acknowledgment Number field incremented to one greater than the Sequence Number field from the packet sent in step 2. The connection is established!

The Internetwork Layer

Similar to the network layer of the OSI model, the DOD internetwork layer allows for identifying other hosts on an internetwork, controlling the flow of traffic between machines, and identifying routes through the use of routing protocols.

Two common internetwork-layer protocols are included in the TCP/IP suite: IP (Internet Protocol) and ICMP (Internet Control and Messaging Protocol). Almost all of the traffic on any internetwork is IP. IP provides IP addresses, among other things, allowing any host to be uniquely identified on an internetwork. ICMP provides for flow control and error notification. For example, if a router must request that a host slow the flow of traffic, the router sends an ICMP packet. The IP header is complicated and confusing; Table 2-4 defines the header fields.

TABLE 2-4 IP HEADER FORMAT

Field Name	Field Description
Version (4 bits)	These four bits denote the version of IP in use. The current version is four, so the first four bits are always 0100.
Header Length (4 bits)	Multiply this value by four to determine the number of bytes in the IP header. Because the maximum value is fifteen, there can be only sixty bytes total in an IP header. This value is used to determine the start of the data that IP carries.
Type of Service (8 bits)	This field is intended to change the way a packet traverses a network. However, it is rarely supported in the real world and so is not covered in detail here.
Total Length (16 bits)	This field indicates the total length in bytes of the IP datagram, including the header length. Because this field is 16 bits, IP datagrams are limited to 65,535 bytes.
Identification (16 bits)	This field is used as a unique identifier for the packet. Its use will be covered in more detail in Chapter 9.

Continued

Field Name	Field Description
Flags/Fragmentation Offset (16 bits)	These flags are used in the fragmentation process, which gets pretty detailed. For more information, please refer to Chapter 9.
Time to Live (8 bits)	The TTL field is initially set by Windows NT 4.0 to 128. Each router that forwards the packet then decrements the TTL by one. When it reaches zero, the packet should be dropped. TTLs prevent a packet from looping infinitely in the event of a routing loop.
Protocol (8 bits)	This field indicates which protocol handed down the data to IP to be sent. TCP uses 6, UDP uses 17, ICMP uses 1.
Header Checksum (16 bits)	The header checksum allows the receiving computer to verify that the IP header is intact. It does not validate data within the header – that task is left to the transport layer. Each router that forwards the packet must recalculate the header checksum because fields such as TTL change.
Source IP Address (32 bits)	This is the IP address of the sending machine.
Destination IP Address (32 bits)	This is the IP address to which the packet is destined.
Options (variable length)	Options are rarely used in production and so are not covered in this text.

The most important protocols in this layer are Address Resolution Protocol (ARP), defined in RFC 826, and Reverse Address Resolution Protocol (RARP), defined in RFC 903. These protocols allow hosts on an internetwork to match IP addresses (a construct of TCP/IP) with media access control (MAC) addresses (MAC is an international addressing standard, independent of the network protocol).

The MAC addressing model is flat, meaning it does not contain a mechanism to identify the specific network a host is on. Using the MAC address to identify a packet is similar to addressing a letter with just the first and last name of the intended recipient – it works if you are in the same building, but the post office will not know how to deliver it. Similarly, MAC addresses alone are enough to deliver a packet if the destination is on the same subnet, but IP addresses are required to navigate routers.

The Network–Access Layer

The network-access layer corresponds to the bottom two layers of the OSI model: the data-link control layer and the physical layer. Even though MAC addresses are supported here, it is important to remember that the ARP process takes place in the internetwork layer. The main function of this layer is to send and receive data frames to and from other network interface cards. Some of the standards that work at this layer include Ethernet, Token Ring, and FDDI (Fiber Distributed Data Interface). When you have WAN networks, the network-access layer also supports serial lines, frame relay, and ATM.

The Internet's Humble Roots

TCP/IP is bloated, slow, and overly complicated. Who would guess that it was designed for the Department of Defense? Toward the end of the 1960s, ARPA (the Advanced Research Projects Agency) began experimenting with connecting computer networks. The first participants in this experiment were universities and private companies involved in research. ARPANet became a reality in December 1969. Four sites were connected via 56Kbps circuits, forming the first Internet backbone.

This is a very brief history, but it has a point. Those of us who work with TCP/IP and especially those of us who work with the Internet are haunted daily by issues that are a direct result of how the Internet evolved. Many aspects of the design of TCP/IP and the Internet do not make sense in its current context because the Internet has far outgrown its original design specifications. The fact that the Internet works at all is a tribute to the original designers — and to the scalability of their design. Nonetheless, it would be very different today if it had been designed to be a worldwide communication tool.

For example, 32 bits were used to define the IP address field in the IP header. This gives us over four billion addresses to play with — quite a few, even when considering that many of the bits must be used to describe the network number. However, the reality of the situation is that these addresses were given out in *huge* blocks, and the majority of these addresses today are wasted, completely unused.

Rest assured that the Internet is constantly improving. Groups like the Internet Engineering Task Force (IETF) continue to publish Requests for Comments (RFCs) that change the way the most basic components of the Internet work. These changes ensure that the Internet keeps up with the times (or at least follows closely behind!). This flexibility is accommodated by the layered nature of TCP/IP, otherwise known as the "DOD model."

The DOD (Department of Defense) invented this four-layer model. It is often compared to a similar, seven-layer model designed by ISO, the International Standards Organization. While these organizations developed the framework for network protocols, still more organizations are responsible for developing the actual protocols, including the Institute of Electrical and Electronics Engineers (IEEE) and the Internet Engineering Task Force (IETF). Keeping track of these individual organizations can be difficult in its own right, but the next section will help to sort them out.

Getting a Handle on the Various Internet Organizations

The Internet, since its inception, has constantly grown and changed. This growth has been slow at times and wild at other times, but it has never been out of control. Thousands of people forming several different organizations oversee what the Internet is today and what it will be in years to come, guiding its direction and providing standards for communication.

Anyone working on the Internet needs to understand which groups perform what services and how to reach them. Those interested in gaining a deep understanding of the Internet should consider joining one of the groups listed in Table 2-5; many are composed almost entirely of volunteers. Joining a group such as the IETF is an excellent opportunity to take part in the growth and development of the communication medium of the future: the Internet.

TABLE 2-5 SUMMARY OF INTERNET ORGANIZATIONS

Organization	Task
IANA	Assigns numbers
IAB	Organizes resources between Internet organizations
IETF	Creates Internet standards
InterNIC	Assigns IP addresses
ISOC	Provides high-level Internet direction

Internet Architecture Board (IAB)

The IAB was founded in 1983 and currently manages the engineering of standards and protocols on the Internet. The IAB works closely with the ISOC and other Internet organizations, acting as a binding force to coordinate the various efforts. Among other responsibilities, the IAB appoints people to important positions within the IETF. This organization is responsible for managing and publishing RFCs and for overseeing aspects of the IANA.

The home page for the IAB is `http://www.iab.org/iab`. This home page and RFC 1160 are good sources of information on this group.

Internet Engineering Task Force (IETF)

The Internet Engineering Task Force (IETF) is a division of the Internet Architecture Board (IAB). It is an international organization formed to resolve problems and create standards on the Internet. The people that make up the IETF are all volunteers, most of whom have very little free time to give but recognize the importance of the group and wish to contribute their part.

The most famous and most used products of the IETF are the Requests for Comments (RFCs). RFCs define standards on the Internet, including such core components as the number of bits in an IP address and the port number the HTTP protocol uses.

Working groups are another important part of the IETF. Working groups are composed of engineers interested in performing research on a specific topic. Standards and RFCs are often the product of IETF working groups.

For more information on the IETF, visit `http://www.ietf.cnri.reston.va.us/home.html`.

The IETF is divided into many technical areas:

- Applications

- IP: Next Generation

- Operational requirements

- Security

- User services

- Internet

- Network management

- Routing

- Transport

- General

The IETF is managed by the Internet Engineering Steering Group (IESG).

Internet Society (ISOC)

The Internet Society (ISOC) is an international organization founded in 1992, with the objective of helping the Internet grow and become more usable. Among other tasks, it helps developing countries with the infrastructure necessary to connect to the Internet, now a global communications standard. It works closely with the other Internet organizations to steer the direction and growth of the Internet.

The ISOC's home page is http://www.isoc.org.

Internet Assigned Numbers Authority (IANA)

As IP addresses become more scarce, the Internet Assigned Numbers Authority becomes more important. The IANA hands out IP addresses, domain names, port numbers, and protocol numbers. This organization makes sure that no two computers on the Internet ever have the same IP address, that no two domains have the same domain name, that no two protocols use the same protocol number, and that no two applications are assigned the same port number.

The IANA is located at the University of Southern California's Information Sciences Institute. Its home page on the Web is http://www.iana.org/iana. It was chartered by the Internet Society (ISOC) and the Federal Network Council (FNC).

Typically, ISPs and network application developers are the only ones who need to contact the IANA. Organizations generally receive IP addresses from a pool their ISP maintains. In this way, the IANA is capable of assigning a classless interdomain routing (CIDR) block of addresses consisting of multiple class C networks to a single group, rather than handling the assignment of each individual class C. More information on CIDR blocks can be found in this chapter in the section "Considering Addressing Issues."

This organization has delegated many of its responsibilities to other groups. The InterNIC, for example, now handles assignment of domain names for the United States.

Internet Network Information Center (InterNIC)

The Internet Network Information Center (InterNIC) is best known for providing and maintaining the master database of domain names. It was formed and funded in 1993 by the National Science Foundation, which still oversees the InterNIC.

Two groups make up the InterNIC. Network Solutions, Inc. manages the registration services and provides educational services to increase understanding of the Internet. The IANA has delegated to this group the task of managing all second-level domain names under the most popular of the first-level domains: EDU, COM, GOV, ORG, and NET. The IANA also delegates the task of allocating IP addresses to ISPs to the InterNIC.

The Directory and Database Services division is managed by AT&T, which provides white papers and directories for the Internet. Visit the InterNIC online at http://rs.internic.net.

The IANA is facing a very difficult challenge – to stretch the IP address range to fit the constantly expanding Internet. There are many things all of us can do to help with this challenge. The next section outlines some of the things we can do.

Considering Addressing Issues

When the IP addressing scheme was originally developed, the idea never occurred to anyone that more than four billion addresses would become completely consumed. However, the IANA is rapidly running out of available IP addresses. It is now much more difficult to get even a small block of addresses assigned to a particular organization, and practically impossible to get a block as large as an entire class B network.

IP addresses are composed of 32 bits and have two parts: a network ID and a host ID. Combined, these 32 bits give more than four billion possible addresses. Class D (multicast) and class E (reserved and unused) networks use about half a billion IP addresses, or one quarter of this total address space. Two billion of these addresses are allocated to class A networks, which were assigned to large organizations. In several cases, a single organization was assigned several class A addresses, which may never have been used. While efforts are underway to reclaim and reassign these IP addresses, little progress has been made to date. Setting aside class A, D, and E addresses, fewer than two billion IP addresses remain to be assigned.

The IP: Next Generation working group of the IETF is working to expand the address space to an astronomical 128 bits. The results of their work, though still in progress, will provide more than 300,000,000,000,000,000,000,000,000,000,000, 000,000 theoretically possible addresses. Once this is completed, the possible addressing space will be considerably expanded. Until then, the Internet community must make do with existing addresses while continuing to grow. For it to do this, several mechanisms have been developed to conserve the quantity of addresses consumed.

VLSMs (Variable-Length Subnet Masks)

Many of the wasted IP addresses on the Internet go unused because the original method of assigned networks was to assign addresses in large groups. Assigning a single class A address would immediately allocate $^1/_{256}$ of the total address space, or about sixteen million addresses. If the original addressing standards are followed, each of those sixteen million addresses would identify a separate host on a *single network segment*. This is far, far too large to ever be manageable.

Even the 256 addresses of a class C network provide for more hosts than most network segments can support. Modern layer-2 switched networks increase the maximum number of hosts on a single subnet, but fifty hosts is a more realistic maximum number on a modern network. With only fifty hosts on a network segment, more than 75 percent of the total address space will be wasted when assigning an entire class C network number to a single subnet! To reduce this waste, the concept of variable-length subnet masks was introduced. Instead of using a standard class C subnet mask (255.255.255.0) composed of 24 network bits and 8 host bits, the two or more bits from the host portion of the address are used as network bits. For example, the subnet may be divided into four more networks. Using this method, two of the eight bits from the host portion of the address are used as the subnet mask, providing a total of twenty-six bits to be used in the network mask. These two bits give the network administrator a total of four subnets that can be defined. The remaining eight bits of the host address allow a possible 64 hosts on each subnet — more than enough for a typical Ethernet network segment.

The downside of this technique is that the overhead associated with an IP network is multiplied. Normally, a class C network has an immediate overhead of three host addresses: the network number (host address all zeros), the broadcast address (host address all ones), and the default gateway IP address.

In the same way that host addresses that are all zeros or all ones must be set aside as overhead, subnet addresses that are all zeros or all ones are wasted. Therefore, as soon as you subnet a network, two of the subnets are wasted as overhead.

Wasting three addresses out of the 256 addresses in a full class C network results in a waste of 1.5 percent of the host addresses. This is the least amount of address waste possible; once you subnet a network, the percentage wasted increases. A one-bit subnet mask creates two subnets, but both subnets must be wasted because they are all zeros or all ones. Because of this overhead, one-bit subnet masks are illegal. (Address waste would be 100 percent!)

A two-bit subnet mask allows for four individual networks with 64 hosts each, but the waste increases to about 52 percent (61 usable host addresses * 2 usable networks / 256 possible addresses). Three out of sixteen available host addresses and two out of sixteen available network addresses are wasted when a four-bit subnet mask is used. This means about 29 percent of the total address space in each subnet is unusable. These calculations are carried out for all possible subnet masks of a class C address, as shown in Table 2-6. As you can see, the most efficient use of address space occurs with a three- or four-bit subnet mask.

Table 2-6 HOST ADDRESS SPACE LOST DUE TO VLSM

Subnet Mask Bits	Usable Networks	Usable Host Addresses	Percent Wasted
0	1	253	1%
1	0	0	100%
2	2	61	52%
3	6	29	32%
4	14	13	29%
5	30	5	41%
6	62	1	76%
7	126	0	100%

VLSM cannot be used on networks that use the RIP v1.0 routing protocol or IGRP. These protocols do not carry subnet masks as part of the information they transfer between routers – each router simply assumes a *classful* network architecture, meaning a network in which class A addresses use an 8-bit network mask, class B addresses use a 16-bit network mask, and class C addresses use a 24-bit network mask. RIP v2.0 and Enhanced IGRP both allow variable-length subnet masks. RIP v2.0 can be used with NT when the optional Routing and Remote Access Service is installed.

Windows NT has full support for variable-length subnet masks. In fact, Windows NT will let you put just about anything in as a subnet mask. Even illegal, noncontiguous subnet masks, such as 201.1.52.99, are allowed. Remember that all subnet masks must be contiguous to work with modern IP networks. So no matter what NT allows you to do, stick with the Internet standards to guarantee connectivity in the future.

CIDR

Classless interdomain routing (CIDR) is a general term applied to several different methods of combining multiple IP subnets. Other terms that are used interchangeably with CIDR are *supernetting* and *route aggregation*. In this section, I will explain all of these concepts as they relate to the term CIDR.

CIDR is used in several different circumstances. When an Internet service provider is assigned public networks from the InterNIC, the InterNIC generally assigns the ISP *a CIDR block* of networks. Assigning multiple, contiguous networks to the same ISP greatly simplifies routing on the Internet.

Earlier, we discussed class A, B, and C IP networks. While there are three different types, the only IP addresses that the InterNIC has left to be assigned are for class C addresses. Now there are more than 16 million class C networks total to be assigned to organizations and Internet service providers. Imagine if each of these networks were assigned to a different organization without consideration for their geographic location – the core routers on the Internet would need to keep track of the paths for all 16 million networks individually.

Even the most powerful routers have limitations. For each packet that comes in, the network portion of its IP address must be compared against this list of routes that resides within a router. While router manufacturers have made this an extremely efficient process, the number of routes stored within the router can significantly impact the overall performance of the router by increasing the time it takes to locate a particular network within the router's routing table.

Instead of distributing 16 million individual routes, the InterNIC has been assigning networks in CIDR blocks. In the following example, I'll use the 192.168.0.0 network; this is a private, reserved network address intended as an example only. Instead of assigning a class C network with a standard 24-bit subnet mask (for example, 192.168.10.0 255.255.255.0), they will assign an organization a class C network with a 21-bit subnet mask (for example, 192.168.17.0 255.255.224.0). This gives the organization a total of more than 2,000 IP addresses, or eight class C networks.

CIDR works with VLSM. Once the InterNIC assigns a CIDR block of public IP addresses, it expects the organization to conserve these addresses through the use of subnetting. In other words, a single CIDR block of addresses with a 21-bit subnet mask could be divided into 64 networks with 32 hosts on each network, rather than being used as eight traditional class C networks on eight separate subnets.

Another step the InterNIC is taking to reduce the size of the routing tables on the Internet is to assign class C networks only to ISPs (with very few exceptions). The ISPs, in turn, assign networks to their customers from the pool of addresses assigned to them. For example, an ISP is assigned a block of eight contiguous class C networks. When a customer requests Internet access and requires a single class C network (256 theoretical IP addresses), the ISP assigns one of the eight available to them. The backbone routers on the Internet still only need to have a single line within their routing table – all eight class C networks take the same route to the ISP's network. Once the traffic reaches the ISP, its routers will forward the traffic to the appropriate customer.

Private versus Public Addressing

There are two types of IP addresses, only one of which can be used on the Internet. These two types are *private* and *public* addresses. If you have ever worked at an organization that has internal telephone extensions and external telephone numbers, you are already familiar with the concept.

Public IP addresses are globally recognized and assigned by the InterNIC. The information for the IP address is entered into the Internet's global routing tables and can be accessed from any other valid IP address on the Internet. Thus, 99.5 percent of class A, B, and C IP addresses are public addresses. Public IPs should be used for all servers and network hardware that will be used from or by the Internet. For example, a Web server must have a public IP address.

Private IP addresses are part of the IP addressing scheme but are globally recognized. If a host has an Internet connection and is using a private IP address, it *cannot* use Internet-based services because routes to private IP networks are not entered into the global routing tables. Private IP networks are 10.0.0.0 255.0.0.0, 172.16.0.0 255.255.0.0, and 192.168.00 255.255.0.0. Half of one percent of class A, B, and C IP addresses are private addresses.

Private addresses are used for very different tasks than public addresses. Private addresses are often used for isolated, IP-based networks that will not be connected to the public Internet. The InterNIC encourages the use of private addresses for these situations because it reduces the waste of public IP addresses.

Private IPs can be used within organizations that have outgoing Internet connectivity, as well. There are two common methods for connecting networks with private numbering schemes to the public Internet. The first is to use an application-layer proxy.

Application-layer proxies, such as Microsoft Proxy Server, accept client connections from the internal, privately numbered IP network and create an outgoing client connection to the public Internet. More information on application-layer proxies can be found in Chapter 13, "Microsoft Proxy Server." The other common method of allowing public Internet access from privately numbered networks is called NAT, or network address translation. NAT gateways, also called transparent proxies, perform a similar function to routers on an IP network. However, they are intelligent enough to automatically translate between private and public IP addresses.

NAT has an advantage over application-layer proxy servers: it does not require the client to be reconfigured in any way. NAT gateways act exactly like any other router on the network, while clients must be configured with the IP address of an application-layer proxy server to make use of its services.

NAT gateways must be programmed with a table of private IP addresses and public IP addresses. When a packet is sent through the NAT gateway, it checks the NAT table to determine if the source address of the packet requires translation. If it does (that is, if it is a private IP address), the gateway replaces the private source IP address and the source port number. It notes these two items in its memory, and incoming communications from the public Internet to that IP address and port number are recognized as part of an established connection. When it receives a response from the Internet server, it translates the destination IP address (which was one of the addresses from its pool of public IP addresses) into the private address of the client before forwarding the packet. In this way, two-way connections from a privately numbered network may reach the public Internet. For more information on proxy servers, please turn to Chapter 18.

No software is currently available for Windows NT that allows it to act as a NAT gateway. Windows NT is often used with NAT gateways such as Cisco's Local Directory and PIX (Private Internet Exchange).

Private and public IP addresses complement each other in practice. To use address space efficiently, configure networks with private IP addresses and use an application-level proxy server such as Microsoft Proxy Server or a NAT gateway such as Cisco Local Director to reach the public Internet. Only Web servers should have permanent, public IP addresses.

RFC 1918 describes how to use private Internet addresses in great detail. RFC 1918 can be found at `http://ds.internic.net/rfc/rfc1918.txt`.

IP addressing on the Internet is a major problem. When IPv6 becomes a common standard, there will be more than enough IP addresses for the next several decades. Until then, we have to learn to make do. Understanding the different ways of conserving the IP address space, such as CIDR, VLSM, and private addressing, is critical for anyone who is responsible for addressing systems on TCP/IP networks.

The next section covers the Microsoft implementation of the Windows NT TCP/IP stack. This section moves away from general internetworking information and provides details specific to Windows NT.

Understanding the Windows NT TCP/IP Stack

Microsoft's network protocol structure is designed around the idea of layering. By defining the functions for individual layers and specifying the interfaces between them, you can replace any one layer without affecting the others. For example, you can update or change a network interface card driver without affecting the TCP/IP driver. The idea of layering was also used to design the OSI model, though Microsoft's layers do not correspond well with OSI.

The layering approach helps speed development by allowing a development group to focus on one specific area at a time. If the developers comply with the specifications for the interface into and out of their layer, they are assured it will function correctly. This also reduces the amount of time that must be spent in testing because it eliminates dependencies between separate layers. Finally, it allows anyone to replace one of these layers at will. The most common example is that manufacturers of network cards generally create a Windows NT driver for their product — yet they are not required to create a separate driver for each network-layer protocol. Because each protocol must use the same interface to speak to the network card, compatibility is guaranteed.

Getting Better with Age

Microsoft's implementation of the TCP/IP stack on Windows NT is still very young compared to those in various UNIX implementations, which have existed since the original specifications were created. This is not a factor many consider important; after all, Microsoft has a reputation for building reliable software. However, all complex software improves over time as flaws and weaknesses are discovered. Any piece of code that has not withstood the test of time is a potential risk.

No risk is greater to a networked system than the network protocol — it affects every system running that operating system and all applications that may be executing. Windows NT is a poor choice for a firewall for precisely this reason — the network protocol has a history of failure, and without a doubt, more weaknesses will be discovered.

Microsoft has divided the TCP/IP stack into five separate layers, which are shown in Table 2-7.

TABLE 2-7 WINDOWS NT NETWORK LAYERS

Layer	Function
Network Card Drivers	Closest to the physical network. Watches the network traffic for any traffic destined for the system by listening for the MAC address.
NDIS	Is a common language that protocols speak
Network Protocol	Controls formatting and flow of the incoming and outgoing data
TDI	Defines how application- and presentation-layer protocols will speak to network-layer protocols
Application	Includes high-level APIs such as Winsock and NetBEUI

Network Card Drivers

The layer closest to the physical network itself is the network card driver. This driver is specific to a manufacturer's network card and the physical network type — falling neatly into OSI's physical layer and the machine access control sublayer of the data-link layer. Ever notice that you do not have to load a specific network card driver for Ethernet or Token Ring? This is because the network card driver must have this functionality built in. For example, vendors may provide a network driver for a network card with both 10-base-T and 10-base-2 interfaces. Little is lost by combining these functions into the same layer; generally the physical interface card is different for different data-link layer topologies. The network driver must be written to speak to a specific interface type.

Network cards watch the network for traffic destined for them by listening for their MAC address in the data-link-layer header of a frame. If this MAC address matches their own or is a special broadcast address, the frame header and footer are stripped off, the computer is interrupted, and the remaining packet is passed through the NDIS layer to the network protocol. In this way, the network card passes only interesting traffic to the network layer.

Microsoft provides drivers for most common network cards as part of the Windows NT operating system. This work is often duplicated by the network card vendor. As a rule of thumb, make a point of finding the driver produced by the vendor; it is almost always more efficient and may substantially increase the performance of Web servers and file servers. Additionally, vendors may provide added functionality such as performance monitor objects and performance tuning tools. These drivers are normally available on the vendor's public Web site.

NDIS (Network Driver Interface Specification)

NDIS is a standard developed to replace ODI, the data-link layer interface made popular by Novell networking clients. The interface has been evolving for several years and is implemented in Windows NT 4.0 as NDIS version 4.0. NDIS acts as an interface between the network card and the network protocol. This added layer of abstraction is what allows a single network card driver to be used with NetBEUI, IPX/SPX, and TCP/IP. NDIS is the common language all protocols speak, and it is intelligent enough to translate that language into something network cards understand.

NDIS does more than simply act as an interface — it hides the physical configuration of network cards from the network protocols. For instance, TCP/IP and NetBEUI can be used with exactly the same network card within a computer. NDIS acts as an arbitrator, determining the order in which packets from different protocols are sent and passing responses back to the proper protocol. This layer helps to conserve memory and improve network performance on systems with multiple protocols and multiple network cards by allowing any protocol or network driver to be loaded only once, rather than requiring each protocol to be loaded individually for each network card. Figure 2-3 illustrates the TCP/IP network protocol and the IPX/SPX network protocol simultaneously accessing two individual network interface cards.

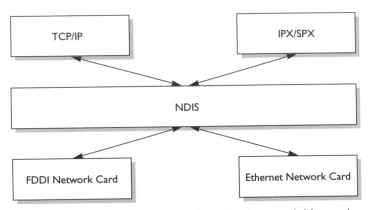

Figure 2–3: NDIS arbitrates between the network protocol driver and the network card driver.

By default, the NDIS layer binds all installed protocols to all active network cards. These bindings can be disabled in the Bindings section of the Network Control Panel. In fact, disabling any unnecessary bindings is encouraged because it can significantly reduce the amount of time it takes to find a destination computer. If all protocols are enabled, the system must try one after another until it locates the correct protocol, waiting for each to time out in turn. This Control Panel applet also allows a "pecking order" to be set, defining which protocols are attempted before others. The Bindings tab of the Network dialog box is shown in Figure 2-4.

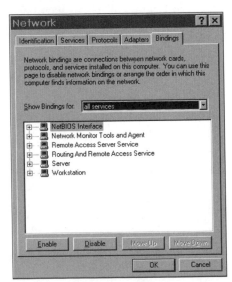

Figure 2–4: Network bindings may be disabled from the Network Control Panel applet.

Network Protocol

The network protocol, existing at the network and transport layers of the OSI model, controls the formatting and flow of data. Three full-featured protocols are available with Windows NT out of the box: TCP/IP, NetBEUI, and IPX/SPX. DLC is available with limited functionality for connecting to HP printers. Point-to-Point Tunneling Protocol (PPTP) is based on the PPP standard and provides for network-layer encapsulation of packets. Each network protocol has its own behavior. The distinctions between the different protocols can affect the overall behavior of a network tremendously. Though Microsoft provides the NetBIOS interface for network-protocol-transparent communications, most network applications are developed to work with a specific network protocol.

Microsoft has an open programming standard for creating network protocols. This allows third-party vendors to create protocols that can be installed in NT and offer full functionality. Firewall vendors tend to provide their own TCP/IP stack to overcome security and performance weaknesses in Microsoft's stock offering.

The network protocol receives packets from the network card driver and analyzes its network-layer header and footer. For example, the network protocol will examine the IP address of an incoming packet and discard the packet if it does not match its own IP address and is not a broadcast. If the IP address does match, the transport-layer header is examined to determine which application-layer protocol should receive it. For example, if an IP packet is received with the TCP port number 80, the data portion within the transport-layer header is passed to the Web service.

TDI (Transport Driver Interface)

The TDI layer is simply a standard that specifies how application- and presentation-layer protocols will speak to network-layer protocols. As with the NDIS standard, it does not translate between two languages; it simply provides a common language for both layers to speak. It most closely maps to the session layer of the OSI model.

It is important to understand that the TDI layer is only a theoretical layer — no DLL performs any action. This is advantageous because it avoids the additional overhead associated with additional processing. In this way, TDI offers the best of layering — compatibility and abstraction — without the performance hit.

Application

When you connect to another machine with Windows Explorer, the request is actually passed to an application-layer protocol. This protocol provides for finding the destination host, authenticating the user if necessary, and determining when a session is started or stopped. Widely used application-layer protocols in the Windows NT network stack are Winsock and NetBIOS. Winsock is commonly used for Internet-based applications, such as HTTP and Telnet. NetBIOS is used for Microsoft network services such as file sharing and remote applications such as User Manager.

In summary, applications that make use of the network are not part of this layer. These applications, such as mail clients and Web browsers, communicate directly to the application-layer protocols.

The Windows NT networking components are broken into five layers: network card drivers, NDIS, the network protocol, TDI, and application. Each of these layers performs an integral yet independent function from that of the other layers. The application layer makes calls to the network protocol via TDI. The network protocol communicates via NDIS to the network card driver, which knows how to talk to the physical network card itself.

Understanding *how* something works is never enough. Too many administrators install a Windows NT system onto a network without considering security. Windows NT is commonly attacked, perhaps *because* of this tendency. This risk of attack is greatly magnified when the Windows NT system is connected to the Internet. Always evaluate the security risks you take when placing an NT system on a network; security should always be your first concern.

Evaluating Your Security Requirements

This section covers the basics of security. You'll learn what your options are, and what type of security is best for your network.

What Is Security?

Securing systems and networks is a science that must be respected and studied but *never* underestimated. Perhaps the most common source of security problems on networks is a confident administrator — an administrator who feels he has made his network environment "secure." Security is not something that can be turned on or off like a light — it is an all-gray area. The best we network and systems engineers can hope for is to make our networks "more secure."

This may seem like a pessimistic introduction, but I am not trying to set you up for failure. Most networks can be configured such that they will never be the victim of a malicious attack, but this depends as much on how badly the wily hacker wants to compromise your network as it does on the level of security. If a network never attracts attention or has no information anyone would be interested in, it will probably never be attacked. Very few of us belong in this category, however. This section is for the rest of us, who need to guard our network as carefully as possible.

Effective security lets the good guys in while keeping the bad guys out. Reliable security grants as much functionality to the intended users as possible, while giving the least amount of information to the uninvited guests. Adding security is always a tradeoff between convenience and safety — even adding simple password protection inconveniences users by requiring them to remember passwords and type them in every so often.

Throughout this section, I will discuss compromises between functionality and safety. Before you read on, decide how important security is to you, what level of security you require, and what level of inconvenience you may impose on your legitimate users.

Network-Level Security

Network-level security covers all aspects of security that are implemented on routers and firewalls. For routers, network-level security includes packet filtering based on IP addresses and TCP or UDP port numbers.

When creating a network security scheme, keep several goals in mind:

1. Filter all incoming packets that are not useful to the systems. For example, packets with a destination port number of TCP 23 (from the Telnet application) but destined for a server that provides only HTTP services should always be filtered. This is advantageous for two reasons: it reduces the total network traffic, and it eliminates the possibility that an extraneous service such as Telnet will be used to compromise a system.

2. Filter all outgoing packets that have not been explicitly permitted beforehand. This may require you to implement a large access list on your router or firewall, but it significantly improves the overall security of a network. By filtering outgoing packets, you assure that systems on your network are less likely to be used to launch an attack on other hosts. For example, consider a scenario where a public Web server is compromised by a malicious "hacker." Once the hacker has access to your server, he can attack another host on the Internet without leaving any tracks. However, if you have implemented network security to filter outgoing packets that are not explicitly permitted, the router will drop a specific application's packets, such as Telnet packets, which may be used to attack outside hosts. Web servers are rarely used to initiate client-side connections, so most packets sent from a Web server can be dropped at the router if they are not already part of an established connection.

3. Never rely on system-level security (described in the next section). It may be tempting to allow all packets through for specific hosts, but system-level security should never be trusted. Even if you are creating the security policies for both the network and the systems, do not trust the operating system to be secure. The vast majority of the recent security problems with Windows NT could have been prevented entirely with adequate network-level security.

System-Level Security

Network-level security is simple compared to the complexity of system-level security. This complexity stems from the fact that operating systems are constantly evolving. Further, Windows NT is under close scrutiny by the security community and flaws are constantly being discovered and published. Each time a security flaw is published, systems engineers around the world must carefully consider whether it affects their systems. If it affects them, they must take steps to reduce the chance that the potential security problem becomes a realized security problem.

Systems, not network hardware, are the most common point of attack. Systems are more visible than network hardware because systems provide the actual services that people use, whether in the form of a public Web server, a corporate e-mail server, or a central Internet DNS server. In fact, it may not occur to many would-be malicious attackers to launch an attack directly against a router.

To reduce the likelihood that an attack will be successful, detailed system security policies are required. Most large organizations will have high-level security policies in place. In this case, a security policy should be written for each server operating system.

The next section details how to implement security on NT servers, from the top-level plan all the way down to the nitty-gritty details.

Creating a System Security Policy

This section will give you an understanding of what is required to secure a network (a Windows NT system in particular) on either a corporate intranet or the global Internet.

System security policies allow an organization to have a consistent level of system security. Security policies do not guarantee that systems will not suffer from security weaknesses, but they do help to ensure that a single server does not become a "weak link."

High-level policies define security methods used on all systems, regardless of the operating system. Low-level policies define operating system–specific security measures to be taken to allow hosts implemented on that platform to operate in a manner consistent with the goals outlined under the high-level policies.

High-Level Policies

How an organization implements security is very dependent on the organization itself. These decisions are impacted by factors such as Internet connectivity, remote access by users, and the types of users who will be using the systems. Policies need to be set separately for systems that are internal to the organization, such as corporate e-mail and file servers, and systems that are used externally, such as public Web and FTP servers.

CONSIDER YOUR USERS

First and foremost, consider your users when drafting security policies. All security is, at best, a slight inconvenience to users. At worst, security stops users from doing tasks that are critical to their jobs.

How much security your users can tolerate depends on the type of user. If your users consist of highly nontechnical people and contract employees, they will have a difficult time with complex security techniques such as one-time passwords. On the other hand, if your user base consists of systems and network engineers, they are more likely to understand *why* the policies are in place and to follow them carefully. Before mandating any security policy, make sure that everyone in your organization will be able to follow it.

For example, if you draft a policy that states all passwords must be changed every week, expect to see employees complaining they were not able to work for a full day because they forgot their newest password. You can also expect to see passwords written on those little sticky pads, sticking to the top of someone's monitor. This human element is a critical component and one of the most commonly overlooked in high-level policies. Do not make the mistake that others make and burden users with difficult security policies simply to ensure that your policy is airtight.

CONSIDER YOUR NETWORK CONNECTION

Many of your high-level security policies will relate to network-level security, such as policies in place to ensure that a password is not sniffed. These policies can become quite expensive and inconvenient, and in many cases they may not be entirely necessary. For example, if your network is totally isolated and all network connections are switched, the opportunity for sniffing other's passwords is extremely small. Therefore, it would be wasteful to implement expensive card-key access requirements simply to thwart sniffed passwords. If your users are connecting to computers over the public Internet and transmitting usernames and passwords, additional measures will have to be taken.

Also consider the impact of policies on bandwidth. The majority of networks in use today are bandwidth-constrained, meaning there simply is not enough room for all the traffic that needs to be sent. Many security methods actually increase the amount of traffic that needs to be transmitted. For example, Microsoft's Point-to-Point Tunneling Protocol can provide encryption for traffic traveling over public networks. It also adds an additional header and footer, however, which increase the bandwidth requirements of all encapsulated traffic. Once again, implementing security is a compromise between safety and cost. Decide what safety is worth in monetary terms and base your decisions on that information.

CONSIDER THE SERVICES PROVIDED

Naturally, you must decide which services your users require and ensure that they have access to them within the constraints of your security policy. Do your users require remote access? Do your users telecommute? Is everyone using the latest and greatest version of Windows NT, or do you need to support UNIX-based users who may require Telnet access?

Chances are good that a conservative security policy will break some functionality required by users. Work closely with your users to find out exactly what access they need before implementing a policy. If you don't, the best case scenario is that your users will not be able to do their job. The worst case scenario is that they will find a way to do their job by bypassing your security. Anytime users are required to break your rules to get their job done, it reduces the respect they have for security and adds another weak link to your security chain.

Low-Level Policies

The security policies an organization drafts have no value unless they are implemented on the systems themselves. Arguably, the more difficult task is determining how to carry out the mandates of the high-level security policy within the limitations of an operating system. While Windows NT was designed from the ground up to be a secure operating system, it is still very difficult to secure from the network.

This section will give useful suggestions for securing any Windows NT system. I have made specific suggestions for securing NT-based Web servers and servers that will be operating in a shared security environment.

PRACTICAL SECURITY VERSUS THEORETICAL SECURITY

Throughout this section, I will refer to practical and theoretical security concerns. These are terms I have made up for my own benefit, so don't feel that you've been left out if you haven't heard these terms before. Practical security concerns combat known weaknesses in the NT operating system and commonly accepted security standards. An example of a practical security measure is modifying the default Everyone/Full Control NTFS permissions of Windows NT. Theoretical security measures are more abstract and are used to combat problems that have not yet been discovered. For example, creating separate NTFS partitions for separate users reduces the risk that an as-yet-unknown bug with NTFS permissions will allow users to view each other's files.

DIRECTORY STRUCTURE AND FILE PERMISSIONS

The default NTFS permissions are completely without security. With the default permissions, anyone who can gain access to the computer can erase or replace system files. This section will cover a better way to handle these permissions. Additionally, I will point you toward the tools you need to set the permissions on existing NT systems on your network and new implementations of NT. Once you have set file permissions, I will show you what to do when applications stop working because you have been too restrictive.

CREATING A PARTITION STRUCTURE   It has always been common practice on UNIX systems to create separate partitions for the system to use and for various applications. This same structure can, and should, be used on NT-based systems. It has not been commonly used up to this point because NT evolved from desktop systems, which typically have a single hard drive and a single partition. Until recently, hard drive space was expensive enough that it was important to use it conservatively. Splitting a hard drive into multiple partitions wastes disk space by making less efficient use of it. Fortunately, hard drive space has become inexpensive enough in recent years to allow partitioning structures to adapt a more sensible methodology.

The desktop environment, commonly implemented with Windows NT Workstation, tends to be used by a single user who should not have administrative access to the system. It will benefit from creating a partition for the system, a partition for application files, and a partition for user documents. Consider an NT Workstation with a single 2GB hard drive. At least 500MB should be dedicated to the NT Workstation system directory and the swap file. The remaining 1.5GB should be divided between the application partition and the user partition. For most environments, 500MB is sufficient for applications files, leaving a full gigabyte for user files. Keep this partition structure in mind – I will be referring to the system, application, and user partitions in examples later on in this section. Figure 2-5 shows the user partitioning scheme.

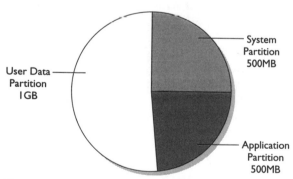

Figure 2-5: A sample workstation partitioning scheme designed with applications and users in mind

Server environments have different priorities and so will be partitioned differently. First and foremost, servers tend to have multiple physical hard drives. Depending on the budget of the organization's IT department, these may be accessed separately without RAID, they may be used in software-based RAID provided by Windows NT, or they may participate in hardware-based RAID provided by a RAID controller. In my humble opinion, software-based RAID should never be used; if redundancy and uptime are a priority, invest in a RAID controller and use hardware-based RAID. For those organizations using hardware-based

RAID, I suggest mirroring (RAID 1) if reliability and up time are the most important considerations.

I suggest striping with parity (RAID 5) if performance is a major factor. If you are using RAID 5, place as many hard drives into the array as possible to derive the greatest performance benefit and to provide the most flexible logical partitioning possible.

The typical server is accessed by many over the network, but only a handful of administrators have the permissions required to log on to the server actively. Further, those who do log on to the server will be doing so to perform administrative tasks and will have administrator access to the server. With these uses in mind, the top priority becomes to secure the server from users on the network rather than from users who will access the console directly.

As with the desktop environment, a partition should be dedicated to the system, the pagefile, and any application files. Servers tend to have many additional components installed, so 750MB may be dedicated. Another partition should be used for user and application data. This user partition will be used for user files if the server is a file server, SQL server databases if the server is a database server, or customer content files if the server is a Web server.

A third partition should be configured with a minimal 300MB space to be used as a *backup system* partition. This is a fairly rare concept for NT servers, but it is particularly important given the unreliability of the operating system and its tendency to fail and not boot successfully. This backup system partition should contain a minimal installation of Windows NT that can be used in the event the primary partition fails. Consider this example: an administrator installs the latest and greatest service pack on an NT server and reboots it. Each time the server reboots, the operating system blue-screens. If a backup system partition has been created, the administrator can boot to that partition and restore the files on the primary system partition that were replaced in the previous service pack without having to reinstall Windows NT or perform a time-consuming emergency repair. Figure 2-6 shows the server partitioning scheme.

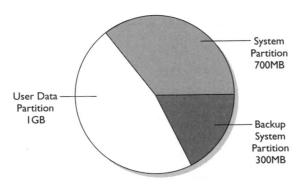

Figure 2-6: A sample server partitioning scheme designed with security in mind

SETTING FILE PERMISSIONS   The default file permissions on an NTFS partition are useful for allowing everyone to do whatever they need to do, an ideal situation for reducing the number of complaints that Microsoft receives. However, it is entirely inappropriate for the typical network environment. System files need to be restricted to allow only administrators to update them, user file permissions need to be configured so that users cannot touch each other's files, and users without explicit permissions to files should have no access at all.

The system partition on either a desktop PC or a server should allow Read Only access to all users who will be executing applications on the machine. On a desktop environment, these users are typically the people who sit at the desk where the desktop is placed. Avoid using built-in groups that include additional users, such as the Domain Users group or the Everyone group. While using these to assign permissions will accomplish the goal of allowing your users to run applications, they increase the opportunity for a network user to leverage an as-yet-unknown security weakness. Remember my description of theoretical security earlier? Over-restricting file and directory permissions is an excellent example of using theoretical security techniques to limit the potential damage to a system.

The system partition should have Full Control permissions for the systems administrators and for the built-in "SYSTEM" user account. Spend some time considering exactly what group you consider to be the system administrators — is this the local Administrators group on the local machine or the Domain Admins group in the domain? In a desktop environment, users logging onto the console have theoretical access to the local user database, so assigning permissions directly to the Domain Admins group may make more sense. Remember the GetAdmin utility that allowed a user to seize local administrator privileges? By following the guidelines of theoretical security and restricting the permissions granted to the local Administrators group, damage could have been controlled should the GetAdmin utility be used to compromise the integrity of the system. Some basic security suggestions are given in Table 2-8.

TABLE 2-8 SUGGESTED PERMISSIONS FOR THE SYSTEM PARTITION

User	Permissions
SYSTEM	Full Control
Domain Admins	Full Control
Users	Read Only

The GetAdmin Hack

For those who do not remember, a developer stumbled across a backdoor in Windows NT. This backdoor allowed any user on the system to execute a process in the context of SYSTEM, which has full rights over everything within Windows NT. The process the user launched, in turn, could do whatever it wanted — including adding users to the Administrators group. So a developer created a program that would use SYSTEM privileges to add the current user to the Administrators group. Convenient, eh?

The user partition is separated from the system and application partitions specifically so that Full Control can be granted to users without risking the integrity of the system overall. In server and shared desktop environments, different users will require separate directories on the partition so that they can secure their files from other users. The SYSTEM user may be granted minimal permissions to the content partition, in case a service requires access to files that are installed there. Access by the SYSTEM user is considered a security risk by many, so this can be handled on a case-by-case basis. If users are accessing the content partition strictly through file sharing, no service will ever need access to the files and there is no need to grant the SYSTEM user any explicit permissions. Similarly, the administrative user accounts do not require any explicit privileges to the user files. If they need access to the files, the option to "Take Ownership" is always available.

The application partition should be created on desktop environments where security and integrity of the system are a concern. In many environments, systems engineers choose to place the application program files in the system or content partitions. Even in these situations, the following file and directory permission guidelines should be followed.

Applications are difficult to secure in a desktop environment because they tend to place files in multiple directories. A typical Windows application places the majority of its files in a subdirectory beneath the \Program Files\ directory, places several DLLs into the \WINNT or \WINNT\SYSTEM directories, and creates and/or modifies several keys and values within the registry. In an ideal environment, the user would be able to use all the features of an application without being able to break it; granting the user accounts change permissions to application files is *asking* for support calls. So what file permissions do you grant to users that will allow them to change their application settings but *not* let them remove critical DLLs? Unfortunately, the answer is different for every single application. As a general rule, the application DLLs will be placed into the system directory and will inherit the Read Only permissions; this is sufficient for most applications. The application executable files will be placed into the \Program Files directory but will be accompanied by files that contain user settings and files that need to be updated (such as custom spelling dictionaries). On very rare occasions, the application developers include documentation describing the minimal file and directory permissions required by the application; this is the best-case scenario.

Implementing the majority of applications requires some trial and error. The following steps will refine the process of determining the minimal file and registry permissions required by an application:

1. Install the application with Read Only user permission to all files and directories.

2. Enable "File and Object Access" auditing within User Manager.

3. Enable failure auditing on all files and directories on the system.

4. Enable failure auditing on all registry keys and values.

5. Launch the application and use each of the features of the application.

6. If the application fails at some point during the test, check the Security Event Log to see what failure audits were reported. Modify the permissions on that file, directory, or registry value. Most important, document this change so that you can automate it later. Go back to step 5, and start your testing again.

7. Once all features of the application work without reporting a failure audit error, you have completely documented the minimal file and registry permissions required by the application. Turn off all the auditing you enabled in steps 2, 3, and 4.

Call to Arms

The way applications install themselves onto a system has a long-lasting effect on both the users and the support personnel. If you have ever had a problem using NTFS permissions to secure an application from the user or had a problem automating the installation of an application, do us all a favor and lobby Microsoft to build more robust restrictions into the Windows NT Logo requirements. Let's force all application developers to build setup routines that include an option for total automation, to include documentation describing minimal file and directory permissions, and to write a program in such a way that the user does not require administrative privileges to execute it and use all of its features. If you have ever tried to roll out a poorly behaved application to a thousand desktops, you'll sympathize with me!

AUTOMATING FILE PERMISSION ASSIGNMENT   Very few utilities exist to automate the assignment of file and directory permissions within Windows NT. The only utility that is included with the operating system out of the box is CACLS. The Windows NT Server 4.0 Resource Kit includes an improved utility called XCACLS, which allows a finer granularity of control over the permissions. A more robust and flexible utility is Perl for Win32, available from ActiveState software. Perl allows for flexible conditional statements and error checking, but the libraries included for file and directory permissions are poorly documented and difficult to use.

TIP ActiveState's build of Perl 5 can be found at www.activestate.com.

There are currently no publicly available utilities to automate the setting of registry permissions. Microsoft's default configuration of registry permissions is so poor, however, that they must *always* be reconfigured.

REGISTRY PERMISSIONS   Often overlooked and always overestimated, registry permissions are one of the greatest security weaknesses in most NT installations. The default permissions are more secure than the file permissions, but they still allow room for users to seriously damage the system.

Exactly how these permissions are configured is very dependent on what the system will be used for and what permissions are required. Keep in mind that troubleshooting registry permissions is similar to troubleshooting file and directory permissions. The security auditing tools built into Windows NT should be used liberally.

TROUBLESHOOTING FILE PERMISSIONS   Earlier, I described a method of trial and error to determine the required permissions on various files and directories when installing an application in a secure environment. These same techniques can be used to troubleshoot file and registry permissions. Consider a sample support call: a user calls the help desk and complains that he or she cannot run a utility that is included with the organization's standard application suite. As it turns out, nobody had ever tried to use that application before and it will not run on any system that was built from the organization's standard Windows NT environment. You suspect that the application is trying to access a file or registry key that the user does not have access to. To troubleshoot this situation, follow these steps:

1. Enable "File and Object Access" auditing within User Manager.

2. Enable failure auditing on all files and directories on the system.

3. Enable failure auditing on all registry keys and values.

4. Perform whatever action was failing previously.

5. When the action fails, check the Security Event Log to see what failure audits were reported. Modify the permissions on that file, directory, or registry value. Most important, document this change so that you may automate it later. Go back to step 4.

6. Once the activity succeeds without reporting a failure audit error, you know what changes are required to allow it to run in the future. Turn off all the auditing you enabled in steps 1, 2, and 3.

It is critical that auditing be turned off before you step away from the machine: enabling security auditing on all files and directories can *significantly* reduce performance of the system overall. Every time a process touches a file, directory, or registry entry that has auditing enabled, it has to check to see if it needs to add an event to the event log. The more auditing you have enabled, the greater the performance hit.

DOMAIN STRUCTURE

The domain architecture an organization uses has significant security implications. Microsoft suggests several different domain models: the single domain model, the master domain model, the multiple master domain model, and the complete trust model. Unfortunately, these domain models seem to have been created with the goal of increasing availability and functionality, with security assuming a lower priority.

Granted, most of the security weaknesses are theoretical. Keep in mind that trusted domains can view the entire domain user database. For example, in the typical master domain model, the resource domain can view the users and global groups in the user domain! This functionality is provided to allow administrators of the resources to assign permissions to users in the trusted domain, but it provides too much information to a domain that should have no privileges. It provides an insight into the structure of the trusted domain and lists usernames, valuable information for someone armed with a password-cracking utility.

RUNNING SERVICES

Earlier I discussed the default configuration of file and registry permissions, and I mentioned that they were entirely inappropriate for a secure configuration of Windows NT. The same holds true for the default configuration of running services.

In order to bring a Windows NT network system into a "more secure" state, several changes need to be made to the services.

When deciding how to configure services on a networked Windows NT installation, stay with the philosophy of minimizing possible points of entry by disabling everything you do not absolutely need. In this section, I will discuss what each of the various services does and how enabling it or disabling it will affect your Windows NT system. To start with, examine Table 2-9, which summarizes the suggested startup settings for each service.

TABLE 2-9 SERVICE STARTUP SECURITY SUGGESTIONS

Service	Startup Type	User Context
Alerter	Disabled	System
Clipbook Server	Disabled	System
Computer Browser	Disabled	System
DHCP Client	Disabled	System
Directory Replicator	Disabled	System
Event Log	Automatic	System
License Logging service	Automatic	System
Messenger	Automatic	System
MS SQL Server	Automatic	A user created specifically for this service
Net Logon	Automatic	System
Network DDE	Automatic	System
Network DDE DSDM	Automatic	System
Network Monitor Agent	Disabled	System
NT LM Security Support Provider	Automatic	System
Plug and Play	Automatic	System
Remote Procedure Call (RPC) Locator	Automatic	System
Remote Procedure Call (RPC) service	Automatic	System
Routing and Remote Access Service	Automatic	System

Continued

Service	Startup Type	User Context
Schedule	Disabled	A user created specifically for this service
Server	Disabled	System
Simple TCP/IP services	Disabled	System
Spooler	Disabled	System
SQL Executive	Enabled	A user created specifically for this service
TCP/IP NetBIOS Helper	Automatic	System
Telephony service	Disabled	System
UPS	Disabled	System
Workstation	Disabled	System

ALERTER, CLIPBOOK SERVER, MESSENGER   These services have been grouped together because they all rely strictly on NetBIOS over TCP/IP for all network communications.

The Alerter service allows a user to receive messages from other machines via the network. When a message is sent over the network to the Alerter service, a dialog box will appear on the user's screen showing the message that was sent.

The Clipbook Server allows clipboard contents to be shared over the network. It is not an efficient way of sharing information, in my humble opinion, and few rely on it.

The Messenger service, similar to the Alerter service in both function and operation, allows messages to be received and displayed on the user's screen.

Starting any of these services starts a NetBIOS listener with NetBIOS names based on the username and/or computer name. There are a couple of things to be concerned about because of security weaknesses in NetBIOS. These will be covered in great detail in Chapter 10. From a TCP/IP perspective, however, no new listeners are created because Windows NT is already listening to the NetBIOS ports.

Few people use these services on their network. To secure them, block the NetBIOS ports at the router or at the system, using port-based filtering such as that provided by the Routing and Remote Access Service. (This service is described in greater detail in Chapter 13.) A simpler way of securing them is to disable the services from the Services Control Panel applet.

COMPUTER BROWSER   The Computer Browser service, when run on all servers on a network, allows clients to open their "Network Neighborhood" on their desktop and view the available resources on the network. When the service is running on a server, the server will register its NetBIOS name either through NetBIOS broadcasts or to a WINS server. In an isolated network, the Computer Browser can be helpful to users, if it runs reliably. In most cases, I recommend disabling the Computer Browser service on all machines to reduce the amount of network traffic.

DHCP CLIENT   If the Windows NT server or workstation acquires its IP address through DHCP, this service should be set to automatic. If not, it should be disabled. This decision is not based on security, merely the method of address assignment.

DIRECTORY REPLICATOR   The Directory Replicator service allows NT servers to import and export entire directories of information. It may seem fairly obvious, but if you are not using directory replication on a particular host, disable this service.

EVENT LOG   Critical information is often placed into the Event Log – including security auditing information. This service should always be set to automatic on all hosts. Though the event log can be accessed over the network using NetBIOS over TCP/IP, this is not dependent on the event log service itself. This service has no impact on the network.

LICENSE LOGGING SERVICE   The License Logging service is used to track use of licenses by different server-side applications. It does not have an impact on the network and should be allowed to start automatically, as is the default.

NET LOGON   The Net Logon service is used by both servers and workstations to provide user authentication. On Windows NT workstations and Windows NT servers configured to be member servers in a domain, the Net Logon service submits requests to a domain controller for authentication on behalf of the user. On a domain controller, the Net Logon service accepts requests from the network from members of the domain and approves or denies authentication requests.

This service is required and should always start automatically. It must run as the built-in SYSTEM user.

NETWORK DDE AND NETWORK DDE DSDM   Two services provide for dynamic data exchange (DDE) in Windows NT: the Network DDE service and the Network DDE DSDM (DDE Share Database Manager) service. DDE is used for critical applications such as Chat and Hearts to be used on your network. Other applications may be created that use these interfaces, but for most situations these services are not necessary. They are configured to start manually by default; change this to disabled to make it more difficult to launch them.

These services should be considered a moderate risk because they accept TCP connections and run in the context of the built-in SYSTEM user. Anytime a service is listening and accepting traffic of any kind, it creates a risk.

NETWORK MONITOR AGENT   The Network Monitor Agent is used to monitor the traffic passing through a network interface card. When this service is running, the Network Monitor application that is included in Windows NT can be used to monitor traffic that is addressed to or from the host and broadcast traffic. The Network Monitor Agent can be used remotely by a computer that has the Network Monitor utility included with Microsoft's Systems Management Server. By using this utility, an administrator on a remote machine can monitor traffic on another segment.

It should be obvious that the Network Monitor Agent is a serious security weakness. It is also a useful diagnostic tool. Because it is a useful tool, you may want to install it ahead of time on machines that may need to be monitored. However, it is best to disable the service. By disabling the service, you minimize the chances that it will be used maliciously. If an administrator needs to make use of the utility, the startup type can be changed to manual and it can be started as needed. Please note that changing the startup type and remotely starting the service depend on the availability of the Server service.

NT LM SECURITY SUPPORT PROVIDER   NT LM Security Support Provider helps with backward compatibility and authentication with older Microsoft clients.

PLUG AND PLAY   This service is used to configure plug-and-play-compatible devices. There is no impact on the network, so the decision on whether or not to disable this service should be based on whether or not the hardware platform requires it.

REMOTE PROCEDURE CALL (RPC) LOCATOR AND REMOTE PROCEDURE CALL (RPC) SERVICES   RPC is a protocol used to start processes on local or remote hosts. In Windows NT, it is used by many critical applications and should be left to start automatically – this is the default configuration. RPC is a substantial security concern, and it is difficult, if not impossible, to restrict the service in any way and still guarantee full functionality of the system being secured.

The RPC services built into Windows NT highlight the importance of network-level security. Because RPC is a security weakness on the host that is difficult to restrict, undesired traffic destined for RPC should be filtered before it reaches the host.

ROUTING AND REMOTE ACCESS SERVICE   The Routing and Remote Access Service is an add-on service that supplements functionality built into NT. If you are using the RAS dial-out component only, leave this service startup type set to manual – it will start automatically when it is needed. If you are using the routing features of the service in a production environment, set the startup type to automatic so that the Windows NT server will begin to route as soon as the system boots.

SCHEDULE   The Schedule service is a common point of attack. Essentially, it allows an application to be executed at a prespecified time and date. However, the standard installation of Windows NT has this service run in the context of the built-in account SYSTEM. SYSTEM has security privileges that even administrators lack, such as the ability to view the security database. Fortunately, it's simple to set the service to run in the context of a user with more restrictive permissions, either a domain user account or a user account created in the local user database of the system. On any system that requires the use of this service, create a user account with minimal privileges and set the service to start automatically. On systems that do not immediately require the Schedule service, disable it.

Unless the Schedule service runs in the context of a domain user account, there is no potential impact on network security. If the Schedule service does run in the context of a domain user account, the service may be used by an administrator to assume the security profile of the domain user account in whose context the Schedule service runs.

SERVER   The Server service is key to many of the most serious security risks built into Windows NT. The Server service is used for all NetBIOS server-side applications. Without it, remote NetBIOS-based applications like registry editor, event viewer, and server manager cannot be used to administer a server from a remote machine. Without it, security is substantially improved.

This service should be disabled whenever possible, but disabling the service seriously impacts the functionality of a Windows NT system. As I stated earlier, remote applications that use NetBIOS will not be able to connect to a system if the Server service is not running. More is lost, however. File sharing is disabled. Print sharing is disabled. The ability to add users is lost. The facts are these: the server service is a serious security weakness, but you probably need it. One exception to this is the Windows NT–based Internet server: always disable the Server service and find another way to administer it; the risks are too great.

Using the SYSTEM Account to View the SAM

To exercise SYSTEM-level privileges, try scheduling the service account to launch the registry editor from the context of the SYSTEM user. To do this, first open the Services Control Panel applet and select the Schedule service. Enable the Allow Service to Interact with Desktop option and start the service.

The next step is to schedule the registry editor to start. The easiest way to do this is to schedule a command to execute in the next minute. So check the current time on the machine and execute the following command at a command prompt:

```
at 3:17pm regedt32
```

In this example, 3:17pm should be replaced with a time in the near future. Once the clock in the system hits the time specified by the at command, the registry editor will launch in the context of the built-in SYSTEM user account and you will have access to the SAM and SECURITY keys beneath the HKEY_LOCAL_MACHINE hive.

In order to allow the Server service to run while maintaining the most secure environment possible, implement router-based filtering. Configure your routers to filter all traffic destined for the NetBIOS ports except from authorized, internal hosts.

SPOOLER   The Spooler service is used to accept printing requests from clients and to allow the local system to spool jobs to network printers. Set this service to start automatically on any host that will be submitting print jobs and any printer server that will be accepting print jobs. Otherwise, leave it disabled.

TCP/IP NETBIOS HELPER   This service must remain running anytime the Net Logon service is running. Because I recommended that the Net Logon service be set to automatic, I will recommend that this service be set to automatic as well — this is the default configuration. It needs to run as the built-in SYSTEM user to avoid complications.

TELEPHONY SERVICE   The Telephony service is used to manage telephony drivers and dialing properties. This service is not needed in most server environments. Workstation environments that will be acting as RAS clients should have this service set to start manually or automatically, depending on user preference. The Telephony service has no impact on network security.

UPS   This service is used to facilitate serial communications with an Uninterruptible Power Supply (UPS). It has no impact on network security and should only be enabled if a serial connection to a UPS is being used.

WORKSTATION   The Workstation service allows outbound NetBIOS connections. Because the Workstation service is used for outgoing connections only, it does not create a security weakness on the host on which it is running. Therefore, it should be set to automatic in all circumstances.

ACCESS TO THE SERVER

A network is useless if users cannot gain access to the resources they need. Granting this access is a critical requirement. The real question is how this access will be granted, and to whom.

Out of the box, Windows NT provides many different ways to access systems over an internetwork. These include NetBIOS over TCP/IP, the Point-to-Point Tunneling Protocol, and Web services such as HTTP and FTP. Other utilities are available from third-party vendors that grant graphical access to the console and practically unlimited access.

NETBIOS   NetBIOS over TCP/IP is extremely useful for accessing a Windows NT computer. Using these services, users can access remote utilities such as Event Viewer and Server Manager, perform file management tasks and access all files on a system, reboot the computer, and more.

Though the functionality provided by NetBIOS over TCP/IP (NBT) is powerful, it is not secure. If at all possible, require these services to be disabled in your low-level security policies. If they are required, rely on network security to filter NBT traffic from external networks. For access from remote networks (for example, a user who telecommutes), use an encapsulation protocol such as the Point-to-Point Tunneling Protocol.

PPTP   PPTP allows private traffic to traverse a public network on its way to the destination. For example, if an organization has a persistent Internet connection, the network could be configured in such a way that a user could dial a local Internet service provider, launch the PPTP client, and connect to the PPTP server at the remote organization. Once this connection is made, all traffic will be encapsulated, encrypted, and tunneled over to the Internet.

PPTP brings remote networks together. It is an excellent protocol to enable in low-level security policies, and it should be required when using nonsecure protocols such as NetBIOS, FTP, and HTTP.

HTTP   As organizations develop intranets, secure access to HTTP becomes a priority. HTTP is a popular protocol, and accordingly several methods of secure authentication and data transfer have been created.

HTTP has two methods of authentication: Base64 encoding and the Microsoft Challenge-Response method.

Base64 encoding is universally supported by Web browsers and servers alike. It encodes the username and password with a method called Base64. Do not confuse encoding with encryption: if the encoded username and password are sniffed on a network, they can be decoded into clear text without sophisticated tools.

The second method, Microsoft Challenge-Response, is only supported by Microsoft's Internet Information Server Web service and the Microsoft Internet Explorer client. While Microsoft would like everyone to use these products, most people do not. Therefore, other alternatives should be explored.

A more secure protocol than HTTP is SSL. SSL uses TCP port 443 for all communications and provides functionality identical to HTTP. SSL is essentially a two-way encapsulation protocol, encrypting traffic before transmitting it between the client and the server. SSL is considered to be very secure and is supported by all popular Web browsers and servers. The downside to SSL is that it requires that a certificate from an authorized signing authority be installed. The only signing authority currently popular is Versign.

If your intranet servers include information that should not be publicly accessible, I suggest requiring that the SSL protocol be used and forbidding the HTTP protocol over remote connections.

FTP   With the success of HTTP-centric Web browsers over the last few years, the use of FTP has decreased. Today, FTP is considered nonsecure and inflexible. Nonetheless, it is still commonly used. Further, you may be surprised to find out that FTP can be a reasonably secure protocol.

FTP becomes a security concern for two major reasons:

◆ Passwords are sent between the client and server using clear-text, which is vulnerable to sniffers.

◆ Anonymous (not authenticated) access is commonly permitted.

These are both valid concerns. However, steps can be taken to make FTP more secure. Instead of creating a high-level policy forbidding the use of FTP, create a more complicated policy requiring the use of the measures I will now describe.

In Chapter 2, I walked the reader through logging into an FTP server using a simple Telnet client. If you carried out this exercise, you noticed that you typed the password in, and Telnet sent it, in clear text. Therefore, anyone with the capability to sniff traffic on the source network, the destination network, or any of the routers in between could have grabbed the password and stored it for later use. To make matters worse, people often use the same password for FTP as they do for other services. For example, a Windows NT server running the IIS Web services allows (often requires!) people to log on with their domain username and password. If someone were to sniff these packets, they could then access any domain resources available to that user. Figure 2-7 shows Network Monitor viewing the PASS command from an FTP client, complete with password. For more information on PASS and other FTP commands, please read Chapter 17.

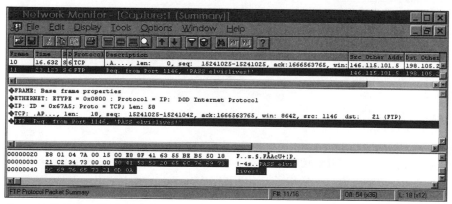

Figure 2-7: Network Monitor is useful for sniffing other users' passwords.

The solution to this problem is simple: don't give an FTP server your password! One option is to allow only anonymous access into your FTP server. This does not mean that security is completely discarded; it just means that the standard user authentication will not be used. Source-IP filtering at the router or FTP server can allow only people with an IP address internal to an organization to access an FTP server. This is not perfect: you may not want just anyone in the organization to have access, and you are still vulnerable to IP spoofing.

Another option is to use a one-time password (OTP). One OTP method, available on Windows NT from Security Dynamics, is called SecurID. It involves the user's carrying a card that displays passwords that change on a regular, timed basis. The card has been synchronized with an authentication server. When the user logs into the FTP server, he or she enters in the password displayed by the electronic card rather than the user's domain password. The FTP server verifies the password with the authentication server, and if the user provided a valid OTP, the user is allowed access.

REMOTE GUI ACCESS   Often, the access methods just described are not enough. For example, if a systems engineer needs to modify a setting within an application on a server at a remote site, he needs to log onto the console of the machine. Several third-party utilities provide this type of access: Avalan's Remotely Possible and PC/Anywhere are two of the most popular.

Any application that provides direct access to the graphical user interface is a security wildcard. Use such applications only when absolutely necessary.

I will say that the primary source of security for each of these methods is *security by obscurity*. This term means that the applications are only secure because nobody has taken the time to determine exactly how they work. Anyone implementing a low-level security policy should stay away from relying on security by obscurity to protect important information: it is a method of security that tends to break in major ways. For example, someone on the Internet may release code that bypasses the built-in authentication methods of these applications, invalidating any security you may have mandated in the low-level security policy.

Summary

TCP/IP was created almost thirty years ago for a government organization, the Department of Defense. It was created to be reliable and scalable, and it has accomplished those goals. Today, TCP/IP is the foundation of the Internet and the most commonly used network protocol in the world.

Windows NT is late out of the gate with TCP/IP, other operating systems such as UNIX having supported TCP/IP for many years. For this reason, there are many "quirks" to Microsoft's implementation of the protocol, and many ways that it can be fine-tuned over the default configuration.

Largely because of the immaturity of the IP stack in Windows NT, security is a primary concern. All organizations should outline detailed high-level and low-level security policies and implement them carefully. Understanding the issues at hand when drafting these documents is critical to creating a secure environment.

TCP/IP and internetworking are complicated topics, and this chapter has attempted to show that depth. Later chapters cover specific topics in greater detail but rely on the foundation provided by this chapter.

After reading this chapter, you should have a complete understanding of the following information:

- ◆ The DOD model is composed of four layers: the network-access layer, the internetwork layer, the transport layer, and the application layer.

- ◆ Many different organizations control how the Internet works. These include the IANA, IAB, IETF, InterNIC, and ISOC.

- ◆ There are simply not enough public IP addresses to go around. Most organizations do not use IP addresses efficiently, but many things can be done to improve that.

- ◆ The Windows NT TCP/IP stack is made up of five layers: network card drivers, NDIS, the network protocol, TDI, and the application.

- ◆ Default network security on Windows NT is nonexistent. Securing a networked system should always be your first consideration.

The next chapter will discuss how to physically configure your network to communicate with the outside world.

Part II

Connectivity

Chapter 3

Getting from Here to There

IN THIS CHAPTER

- ◆ Connecting Windows NT

- ◆ Understanding dial-up lines

- ◆ Understanding ISDN

- ◆ Connecting to your Internet service provider

- ◆ Using packet-switched networks within your wide area network

- ◆ Designing a network with leased lines

PROVIDING AN OVERVIEW of WAN technologies and how Windows NT fits into the picture is the primary goal of this chapter. I have also made an effort to tell you any specific considerations to keep in mind when using Windows-based networks with these links. This chapter will give you an overview of the various technologies that may be used to connect Windows NT for distances greater than a single building – whether you are connecting remote offices to a central office or your entire enterprise to the Internet.

Connecting Windows NT

Windows NT was originally designed to be a workgroup server – a server for a group of people who work on a local area network. This is very similar to the role that Novell's NetWare played for many organizations, and it seemed like a good marketplace for Microsoft to progress to from the desktop operating systems that it had been focusing on. However, the notion of the workgroup is changing, and modern networks have very little purpose unless connected to other larger networks such as corporate enterprise networks or the Internet.

Part of being a systems engineer in the modern network environment is understanding the various ways to get from here to there. Luckily, Microsoft has recognized this fact, providing several wide area network connectivity options with

Windows NT. Of these, Remote Access Service has been around the longest. RAS has always allowed remote users to use analog telephone lines to connect to Windows NT servers and perform any Windows NT networking task from a remote site. However, RAS is hardly sufficient for most modern wide area networking needs.

Enterprise networks usually need to connect their offices with higher bandwidth than analog lines can support. T1 circuits supporting up to 1.544Mbps have become common. Organizations implementing new networks often use ISDN, 56K leased lines, frame relay, or ATM networks to bridge the distance between remote offices.

Understanding Dial-up Lines

The most common form of remote connectivity is the dial-up link. Most people who connect to the Internet do so using an analog dial-up link. Additionally, many organizations provide dial-up access to employees, allowing network connectivity to the intranet. Dial-up networking is an important technology to understand simply because it is so common.

Windows NT, since version 3.1, has supported Remote Access Service (RAS). Remote Access Service allows a remote user to use a modem and an analog phone line to create a wide area network link to his or her Windows NT server. Figure 3-1 shows a RAS connection between a remote user and a remote network. These services have evolved a great deal since the original RAS. RAS is still included with Windows NT 4.0 and, among other advancements, now has the ability to support MPPP (Multilink Point-to-Point Protocol). This allows users to combine multiple analog phone lines into one single wide area network circuit, increasing the available bandwidth.

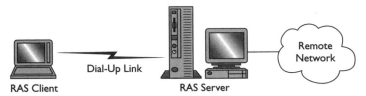

Figure 3–1: RAS allows NT systems to connect to a remote network via a standard analog telephone line.

While Windows NT supports MPPP, the majority of ISP dial-in modem banks do not support it. Because they rely on a phone system to rotate calls among many modems, there is no guarantee that the same dial-in server will receive both of the dual lines. Currently, Windows NT does not have the ability to demultiplex MPPP calls that are received by different servers.

Recently, Microsoft released Routing and Remote Access Service (RRAS), originally code named "Steelhead." RRAS adds a more robust feature set to the original RAS, allowing NT to use multiple analog phone lines, ISDN lines, or leased lines to create wide area network circuits that link not only a single user to a network, but entire networks to each other.

Although dial-up lines have become more flexible and powerful in recent years with modem technology improvements, the bandwidth available on a dial-up line is still insufficient for most enterprise networking purposes. Nonetheless, this sort of connection remains extremely common because of the low costs associated with it. Indeed, most organizations have a plethora of analog phone lines available to them. Modems are cheap as well. Both server- and client-side software is built into Windows NT, so the software is completely free.

Chapter 14, which covers Routing and Remote Access Service, provides more detail on how to use Windows NT with standard dial-up lines to create wide area network circuits. I will not go into a lot of detail here about RAS, outside of the context of RRAS, because RRAS has added such a great feature set that no one would want to be without it.

For more information on PPP, see RFC 1661. For more information on MPPP, see RFC 1990. Throughout this chapter, I have avoided providing detailed descriptions of the underlying protocols involved (trust me, I'm sparing you a lot of grief).

Making the Connection with ISDN

I have already discussed some of the weaknesses of standard dial-up lines. To make matters worse, analog lines, in general, are not well suited to carry digital data. Before digital data can be transmitted over an analog phone line, it has to be converted by a modem. Therefore, digital communications associated with analog lines tend to be inaccurate and low-bandwidth.

Does it seem odd to you, then, that more people connect to the Internet using analog lines than any other method? If so, you are not alone. In the 1970s, a group of telephone companies banded together to create the first Integrated Services Digital Network (ISDN). The goal of this network was to provide an alternative to the analog telephone lines that most of the world already used. This digital network would be more powerful than the analog network and would provide backward compatibility and connectivity.

ISDN is a dream for those of us who need remote access to a network but do not get enough bandwidth from a standard analog circuit. American dual-channel ISDN circuits provide 128Kbps of bandwidth, several times more than any conventional phone line can support. To make the transition even simpler, these circuits can be used for standard voice and fax calls if they are not in use for network communications.

2 + 2 = 5

Recently, many analog modems have been marketed as "56K" modems. But what does the 56K really mean? Don't be tricked into thinking that 56K modems mean you will achieve 56Kbps of throughput.

The fact is, 56K used in modern modem marketing is a theoretical bandwidth that can only be achieved through a great deal of compression. The 128Kbps that an ISDN circuit is capable of producing relies on no compression whatsoever. Instead of only being twice as fast as the figures might imply, ISDN circuits are capable of carrying five to ten times more traffic than a 56K modem used with an analog phone line.

So if someone tells you that you can achieve ISDN-level bandwidth by combining two analog phone lines using MPPP, don't believe them.

ISDN Billing

ISDN is now common enough that the majority of telephone companies support it and many ISPs allow users to connect to the Internet using an ISDN circuit. Unfortunately, there are many reasons ISDN has not become more popular. For one thing, it is still very expensive compared to analog lines. Additionally, many users still have a problem with the billing structure of ISDN. ISDN is billed on a per use basis, unlike analog lines, which provide unlimited local calling with a flat monthly rate. For users in most areas, every ISDN call is similar to a long-distance call, in that they are charged by the minute.

For those users who wish to use ISDN as a nailed-up Internet link and leave it connected at all times, this billing structure can lead to extremely high fees that may rival leased lines. For those users, leased lines are generally a better alternative. For the home user, both alternatives are too expensive.

NT Support

Windows NT supports ISDN NT1s from several different vendors. An NT1, in ISDN terminology, is very similar in function to an analog modem. It receives the signals from the computer and converts them into a format that can be sent across the ISDN circuit to the receiving ISDN switch. NT1s are also intelligent enough to send the proper control signals to route the call to the proper destination. NT1 cards for Windows NT systems are always more expensive than standard analog modems, costing more than $300.

Every component of Windows NT that works with a modem will also work with an ISDN NT1. This means that you can configure an NT server with an ISDN card as a RAS server and allow users to connect to it from their homes. Likewise, when using the Routing and Remote Access Service, you can configure both sides of a wide area network circuit with ISDN modems and use this ISDN connection as either a primary or a backup WAN link. Windows NT is smart enough to route traffic between the two points intelligently. To save the use-based costs, RRAS can even be configured to drop the call if traffic is only being transmitted intermittently.

ISDN connections are also commonly implemented in hardware-based routers. If this is the case, Windows NT systems are simply plugged into the network like any other node. The router is intelligent enough to recognize the IP address in packets as being destined for a network that lies on the far side of the ISDN circuit. When the router receives these packets, it routes them appropriately. Figure 3-2 shows four NT systems connected to an ISDN router via an Ethernet LAN. The ISDN router, in turn, connects the systems to the public Internet. In this way, Windows NT systems can make use of ISDN circuits without any special configuration on the systems themselves.

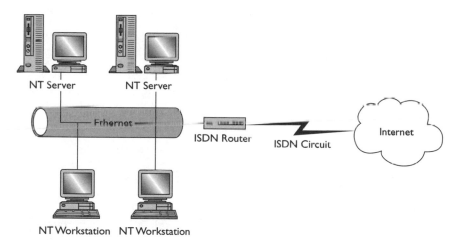

Figure 3-2: Entire networks can be connected to a remote network through an ISDN router.

An ISDN circuit supports 128Kbps throughput. If you plan to implement domain controllers on either side of an ISDN link, you will be glad to know that this is plenty of bandwidth for all of the background functions that occur within Windows NT. These include:

- ◆ Synchronizations between backup and primary domain controllers
- ◆ Intertrust communications
- ◆ Directory replication
- ◆ Domain authentications

Above and beyond these background communications, ISDN circuits can carry a substantial amount of traffic. While performance will be significantly less than it is on a local area network, it is still acceptable for many purposes. Table 3-1 compares common tasks on a LAN network and an ISDN dedicated circuit.

TABLE 3-1 TRANSFER TIMES COMPARED: ISDN VERSUS LAN

Activity	ISDN Completion Time	10-Base-T LAN Completion Time
Download a 100K Web page	approx. 8 seconds	approx. $1/_{10}$ second
Transfer a 1MB file	approx. 72 seconds	approx. 2 seconds
Transfer a 10MB file	approx. 10 minutes	approx. 20 seconds

ISDN circuits are becoming popular largely due to the high demand for bandwidth between homes and the Internet. Yet getting a fast digital circuit to an ISP is only one aspect to consider – an Internet connection is a complex entity and there are many factors to consider, as the next section will show you.

Considering ISP Connections

The majority of organizations today need to have some form of connectivity to the Internet. The way to do this is to lease some type of a wide area network circuit, as described in this section, to the ISP's offices. The ISP already has a connection to a higher-level Internet service provider, or, if it is a top-level ISP, a *peering relationship*.

ISP Hierarchy

In many Internet diagrams, the Internet is drawn as one big cloud. This seems to imply that there is no particular structure, that any connection to the cloud is the same as any other connection. Most of the world has the luxury of maintaining this level of understanding; we do not!

While this lack of structure would make everyone's life a little easier, the reality is that the Internet is extremely structured. This section will take you into that cloud and show you the different components and how they are connected. I will even give you some insight into how you are connected to the Internet.

Peering Relationships: Competing Yet Working Together

In a peering relationship, two same-tier ISPs establish network connections between their offices and agree to exchange traffic over that connection. For example, two competing tier-2 ISPs in the same town may commission a T1 line between their offices and configure the routers at each site to forward traffic between them. What is the advantage of establishing a peering relationship if you manage an ISP? First, this type of peering relationship does not charge according to the amount of traffic exchanged. Therefore, if people were connected to ISP A and visiting Web sites hosted at ISP B, ISP A would not have to pay a tier-1 ISP to carry its network traffic. It is also an inexpensive form of redundancy — if either of the two ISPs looses its primary Internet backbone connection, it can reroute traffic through the peering ISP until the connection is restored.

In the past, these types of friendly peering relationships were the foundation of the Internet. As bandwidth becomes more valuable, peering relationships have become less friendly. ISPs are now very wary of peers who misuse the connection, and they may begin to charge for the bandwidth usage if one peer is using more than the other. Soon, the friendly peering relationship may devolve into the type of relationship maintained between long-distance companies!

TIER 1

At the top of Internet provider hierarchy, tier-1 providers connect to each other. Tier-1 providers own the networks that make up what is called the Internet backbone. The backbone of the Internet provides functions similar to interstate highways. While very few people live directly off an interstate highway, many of us use the highway when traveling great distances. Similarly, very few Internet service providers are connected directly to the backbone, but most traffic must traverse it.

It takes a lot of money to be a tier-1 Internet provider. It takes so much money, in fact, that you'll probably recognize most of the names as some of the largest companies in the world. These are organizations such as Sprint, GTE Internetworking, and MCI. Not coincidentally, many of these companies also provide conventional long-distance and local phone services.

Tier-1 providers connect to each other to exchange Internet data. They connect at several specific points throughout the United States called NAPs, or network access points. ISPs connect their routers together at a NAP, allowing data to be exchanged between providers. There are many different NAPs in the United States, the largest being MAE-EAST in Washington, DC, MAE-WEST in Palo Alto, California, and the Sprint NAP in New York.

TIER 2, 3, AND SO ON

If tier-1 ISPs are so big and wonderful, why don't most of us dial into them? Probably because they're not all that interested in the home dial-up market. Most people in the United States get their Internet access from smaller ISPs. These ISPs, in turn, get their Internet access from the tier-1 ISPs.

You can think of tier-2 ISPs as being the smaller roads off a highway. While not as large or as fast as the interstate highways, the smaller roads do more than take you to a particular town or city. They take you to your workplace, a store, or your home.

Does this structure seem pretty simple so far? It's not. Unfortunately, the matter doesn't end with tier-2 ISPs. Tier-3 ISPs lease bandwidth from tier-2 ISPs. Tier-3 ISPs tend to be small, local, "mom and pop" type shops. Many people use tier-3 ISPs for dial-up access and for hosting personal home pages on the Web. Additionally, ISPs set up peering relationships with each other.

Evaluating Individual ISPs

All ISPs are not created equal. ISPs vary greatly in services offered, quality of service, reliability, and speed of Internet connectivity. To determine the quality of service of a particular ISP, talk to other people who use the same ISP. Things you want to know are:

◆ **Mean time to response:** The mean time to response is the average time that it takes an ISP representative to contact the customer when a customer reports a problem. This varies greatly from ISP to ISP. At best, the mean time to response is only a matter of a few minutes. At worst, it could take several days to respond to even the most critical customer problems.

◆ **Mean time to resolution (MTTR):** The MTTR is the time it takes for the ISP to solve a problem after the customer has reported it. As you can imagine, if the problem involves downtime, MTTR becomes extremely important. Most ISPs will track their mean time to resolution and have that information available for prospective customers. Many will also break that down by the severity of the issue. For instance, mean time to resolution for issues that involve downtime may be tracked separately from mean time to resolution for issues that are merely customer requests.

◆ **Flexibility:** How much is the ISP willing to work with you and meet your needs? Many ISPs are rigid on what they can and cannot do. Others will bend over backward to give the customers exactly what they want. The best way to find this out is to talk to current customers of the ISP and get their impressions. Another way is to discuss with the salesperson beforehand any request that you may have. The salesperson should be able to tell you whether or not it is feasible to meet your request.

Bandwidth

Another important consideration is *exit capacity*. Exit capacity is a term used to describe the amount of bandwidth from the ISP to the Internet backbone or to other ISPs. This exit capacity determines, to a great extent, how fast your Internet connection will be. Ideally, the exit capacity of the ISP would be greater than the total inbound traffic that they have from customers.

All ISPs, except the very new ones, overextend their exit capacity to some extent. For example, a tier-3 ISP may have a T3 connection to a tier-2 ISP. This T3 could theoretically support 32 full-capacity T1s. They may very well lease 50 to 60 T1s to customers and use that single T3 for all of that traffic. This has become common practice. In fact, it would be impossible for the ISP to make profits if they purchased bandwidth from their tier-2 provider on a one-to-one basis for customer bandwidth.

The tier level of an ISP is a good indicator of the overall bandwidth of the provider. However, most ISPs are not tier-1 providers. As you already know, tier-2 providers get their Internet connectivity from a tier-1 provider. Therefore, if you are using a tier-2 provider, their bandwidth may very well be bottlenecked by the bandwidth available to the tier-1 provider.

In summary, consider the exit capacity of your Internet service provider and any ISPs above them. Tier-3 providers are much more likely to have problems than tier-1 or tier-2 providers. For a tier-3 provider, bandwidth problems may occur at their offices, at the tier-2 ISP, or at the tier-1 ISP.

Windows NT Considerations

There are very few Windows NT–specific ISP considerations. However, network administrators responsible for the security of an ISP should consider compensating for Windows NT's weak internetworking security features. Further, choices for virtual private networking with Windows NT are still very limited – implementing VPNs using network hardware may be more effective.

SECURITY

The most important consideration is security. In my humble opinion, Windows NT provides very poor security from the dangers of the public Internet. It lacks the native ability to adequately filter incoming traffic according to source IP or TCP port number. Therefore, if you would like to make use of NetBIOS services, such as the Server service, from the public Internet, you will have to open it to all inbound traffic. You will end up allowing anyone in the world to attempt to connect to a shared drive on your server.

As a rule of thumb, it is a bad idea to have any TCP or UDP ports open to the world besides those ports that offer public services. For example, if the system is a public Web server, the only port that should be open is TCP port 80. All other ports should be blocked. Internet service providers should seriously consider offering port filtering as a service to customers who lease rack space at the ISP's offices.

If you plan to host Windows NT systems on the Internet, it is a very good idea to purchase some sort of firewalling service from your Internet service provider. Because Windows NT does not provide adequate filtering at the system level, the ISP may be able to provide filtering at the network level, either by configuring a router that provides source IP and TCP port number filtering or by inserting a firewall at their premises or yours.

If you must implement network security at the system level, Microsoft's Routing and Remote Access Service is your best bet. While not intended as a security tool for the NT system itself, the source IP and TCP port filtering may be used for all inbound traffic. Indeed, you do not have to use either the routing or remote access services to make use of the filtering capabilities. For more information on the Routing and Remote Access Service, see Chapter 13.

VIRTUAL PRIVATE NETWORKING

If you plan to use the Internet as a wide area network connection, consider purchasing virtual private networking services from your ISP. The VPN service will ensure that your data is transmitted to the remote site reliably and securely. Because VPN services are so new, inquire about your ISP's experience. You'll expect your VPN to be reliable and consistent, and your ISP needs to know how to provide that.

Many people will be tempted by the VPN capabilities built into Windows NT. These are right for you if you are on a tight budget and reliability is not the primary concern. Unfortunately, they are the opposite of reliable and consistent. Further, the built-in security has not withstood the test of time. History has shown us that new security features built into Windows NT tend to get broken sooner or later.

Other ISP Services

Another service commonly provided by ISPs that many customers are interested in is the option of colocating Web servers at the ISP's premises. When a customer colocates a Web server at the ISP, that customer benefits from being that much closer to the Internet backbone. This is opposed to locating the system on the customer's premises, where the bandwidth may very well be bottlenecked by the customer's Internet connection.

For example, the ISP may have dual T3s exiting their offices and connecting to multiple tier-1 providers. If the customer is connecting to that ISP through a T1 and placing a Web server on the customer side of the link, the most bandwidth the server will ever produce is 1.544Mbps. The concept of bottlenecking Web server bandwidth with a leased line is illustrated in Figure 3-3. Additionally, that bandwidth would be shared with other traffic that may be coming to or from the organization, such as employee e-mail and Web traffic. Most ISPs provide some sort of colocation service because it is an easy service for them to provide. They merely provide you with rack space, power, and a network connection.

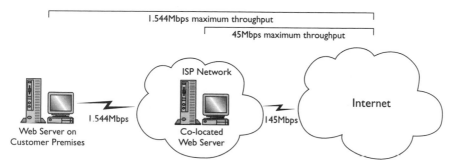

Figure 3-3: Colocating a Web server at an ISP's site yields much higher bandwidth.

Billing is usually based on the amount of rack space you consume and the amount of bandwidth that you use. Most colocation customers receive a monthly bill that describes how much bandwidth they use, and how much they will have to pay for it. This bill is useful for more than just understanding what is owed the ISP; it also provides an indicator of how busy the site has been.

Some ISPs provide additional services to colocation customers. These services may include backups, systems administration, database administration, monitoring, hardware maintenance, and content staging.

Redundancy and Reliability

Reliability is another extremely important consideration. Many people take for granted that their ISP will be as reliable as their telephone company has been. For most people, they merely pick up the phone, and it works. It always works. If it stopped working, it would be such a big deal that you would probably see it on the news!

This is not the case with ISPs. The Internet is not as refined as telephone networks are. Part of the problem is due to the hierarchical nature of the Internet. Tier-1 ISPs connect to each other, tier-2 ISPs connect to tier-1 ISPs, and tier-3 ISPs connect to tier-2 ISPs. If the tier-1 ISP has a problem, tier-2 and tier-3 ISPs underneath tier 1 will also have problems. You-know-what rolls downhill.

Smaller ISPs such as tier-3 ISPs tend to have more reliability problems than larger ISPs. This is caused by several factors:

- ◆ Smaller ISPs tend to be run by less experienced personnel.

- ◆ Smaller ISPs have smaller budgets.

- ◆ Smaller ISPs cater to the home customer rather than the business customer.

You can do several things to determine the reliability of your ISP. First and fore-most, try to contact some existing customers of the ISP and find out what their feelings are. You may also ask the ISP for their reliability statistics. Ideally, the ISP would provide you with detailed statistics about reliability and uptime, but these may not always be entirely honest. Customers always give a more accurate impres-sion than the ISP can possibly provide.

Always ask to see a network diagram of the ISP's Internet connections. It is important to determine that all connections are entirely redundant. There are many factors in making a redundant Internet connection. First, if the ISP has T1 connec-tivity, make sure that they have multiple T1s going to entirely different ISPs. If they do have redundant upstream connections, make sure that they really are redundant. The two connections need to go to entirely separate ISPs to avoid the problems that occur with the hierarchical nature of ISPs that I described earlier. In this way, if an upstream provider has a problem with the network, your ISP will be able to route traffic through the redundant ISP connection.

On a smaller scale, check that the ISP hardware internally is redundant. Each router between your connection and the Internet backbone should have redun-dancy built into it. All popular router manufacturers build their middle- to high-range routers with redundancy capabilities, albeit at an additional cost. Most routers have the ability to fail-over to another router that acts independently and acts as a hot spare should one of the routers fail.

Your ISP needs to use these techniques to provide entirely redundant connec-tions internally as well as externally. Their redundancy has a direct impact on your reliability.

ISP Billing Strategies

Finally, cost is always a consideration. Carefully consider the way your ISP bills you. Generally, they will have a fee for the installation and hookup for any con-nections that you lease. They will also have some sort of ongoing fee, perhaps a flat monthly fee and a fee that is based on the bandwidth used. Depending on the ISP, additional service charges may be tacked on as well. Just make sure that you have a good understanding of what your monthly fees are going to be before you sign a contract.

Use-based billing varies significantly between different ISPs. As a general strat-egy, ISPs want to bill you for the services that cost them money. Rack space in the data center will cost the ISP, so they will charge by the inch. Network traffic costs them in the form of switching hardware and support, so they will charge you by bandwidth used. Server hard drive space costs them money in the form of hardware and administration, so they may charge you by the megabyte. Exact policies vary widely between different ISPs, so consider several carefully.

Depending on the services that you provide internal to your own network, you may wish to purchase still more services from your ISP. ISPs generally have the ability to provide you Internet mail accounts, news accounts, and shell accounts, as well as some hard disk storage space. They will charge for these in most cases, so consider whether it is cheaper for them to provide the services or for you to configure your own servers. You will probably find that it is cheaper to have the ISP provide this.

The Internet is not the only packet-switched network around. Other packet-switched networks, such as X.25 and frame relay, knew commercial success long before the Internet became popular. These networks continue to improve and integrate with the public Internet, especially with recent advancements in ATM technology. The following section describes these packet-switched networks in more detail.

Exploring Packet–Switched Connections

A packet-switched network is one way for companies to create a wide area network link without the per-mile cost of a dedicated leased line such as a T1 or a T3. To the end user, packet-switched networks operate identically to a leased line because they provide exactly the same functionality. To the administrator, packet switched networks require a great deal more configuration than a typical leased line. However, the additional time required for administration is generally made up by reduced costs and greater flexibility.

Packet-switched networks break data into smaller packets. These packets are not to be confused with TCP/IP packets; the TCP/IP packet header is actually encapsulated as data and carried across the packet-switched network. These packets are then carried from one switch to another, from the beginning point to the final destination. At the destination, the packets are reassembled, and the data is returned to the final end node in a useable format. This really describes any type of modern network with the exception of circuit-switched networks. However, we are interested in a certain type of packet-switched network—the type of packet-switched network that is available from a network provider and can be used for wide area network connectivity. In general, these fall into one of three categories: X.25, frame relay, and ATM.

X.25

The oldest and most compatible are X.25 packet-switched networks. X.25 networks allow a maximum of 56Kbps bandwidth. For this reason, they are becoming less and less common. However, they are still commonly used for small provider network needs and for backward compatibility with equipment that may not have been modified to work with newer network architectures. The most common uses of the X.25 networks are for devices such as automated teller machines, credit card verification systems, and cash register systems that implement an inventory tracking mechanism. Additionally, X.25 is available to almost every corner of the earth. For this reason, some areas that may not have more modern packet-switched networks available still rely on X.25-based networking.

X.25 networks are used by customers who lease the use of a provider's network. Customers are charged according to the amount of traffic they generate. The network provider takes responsibility for carrying the traffic to the final destination, which must also be connected to the network. The X.25 protocol itself does not define the way in which the network carries the traffic from one node to another. The protocol only defines the interface between the DCE (data communications equipment) and DTE (data terminal equipment).

Windows NT actually supports the X.25 suite of standards through the RAS services. Because of this, a developer may write an application that connects to a server across an X.25 network. The specific implementation in Windows NT treats an X.25 PAD (packet assembler/disassembler) much as it treats a modem. I am not going to say much about the way X.25 networks work with Windows NT, because they are not commonly used.

Frame Relay

Frame relay is a much more modern packet-switched network than X.25 and is better suited to connecting remote offices than to automated teller machines. It uses permanent virtual circuits (PVCs) to create persistent paths through the packet-switched network. Some providers now offer switched virtual circuits (SVCs) to allow customers to communicate without defining the circuits beforehand.

In order to get access to a frame relay network, the customer must provision a leased line to the frame relay provider. Depending on the bandwidth desired, this leased line may be a 56K or T1 circuit. When you are provisioning a leased line for frame relay connectivity, it is important to remember that your bandwidth may never exceeded the bandwidth of the leased line connecting you to your frame relay provider. In other words, if you are paying for a maximum of 1Mbps bandwidth from the frame relay provider, a 56K link will not do. You will require a T1.

Frame relay networks have many advantages over leased lines. First, when you are connecting remote offices that are separated by great distances, it is much cheaper. This is because the organization only needs to lease circuits to the frame relay provider's closest point of presence (POP). If the organization were to connect remote offices on the east and west coasts, leased lines would be prohibitively expensive. Instead, the organization would use frame relay PVCs, essentially paying to share the cross-country circuits the frame relay provider already owns.

Another advantage of frame relay networks is increased flexibility. When purchasing leased lines, the lessee may use the entire bandwidth available to the circuits, no more, no less. However, when a customer allocates a PVC from a frame relay provider, that customer must specify several things about the bandwidth they will be using. The customer will specify a minimal amount of bandwidth that the frame relay provider will be required to provide at all times. This baseline is called the committed information rate (CIR).

If the customer ever wishes to exceed this bandwidth, that customer may specify a higher burst rate. The burst rate is the amount of bandwidth that the frame relay provider will allow the customer to transfer. However, the frame relay provider makes no guarantees that it will be able to support the increased traffic. This is good for the customer because it allows them to transfer more traffic at times of higher demand, and yet they will not have to foot the bill for the traffic if they do not need to use it. It is also good for the frame relay provider, because it allows them to take advantage of statistical multiplexing, making better use of the quiet times on their network.

Finally, frame relay networks provide for more redundancy than would otherwise be possible. The frame relay provider owns entirely redundant links between any two points on its network. The customer is able to benefit from this redundancy without the cost of owning multiple circuits.

Windows NT has no native support for frame relay; however, Windows NT may communicate across a frame relay packet-switched network just as it does across any other network.

ATM

Asynchronous Transfer Mode (ATM) is an emerging technology for high-speed switched networking. Though ATM has been in development for many years, it is still very much a young technology. Already, it has become known as the preferred method for transferring multimedia network traffic. However, it has earned a bad reputation for being highly expensive and extremely problematic.

ATM is similar to X.25 and frame relay networks in many ways. However, instead of switching packets, it switches cells. A cell is very similar to a packet except, by definition, a cell has a fixed length. ATM cells are always 53 bytes in length. Of those 53 bytes, five are used for the ATM cell header. The remaining 48 bytes are used to carry the data.

Unlike X.25 and frame relay, ATM is useful in both the local area network and the wide area network. It is ATM's support for local area networking, called LANE (local area network emulation), that allows high-speed, multimedia networking across the enterprise network.

The secret to ATM's ability to support high-speed, multimedia networking is the fixed-length cell. Because the cell is of fixed length, switches may forward many more cells than would otherwise be possible. The use of cells also allows for much more predictable data transfer. This structure reduces both latency and jitter that can kill real-time multimedia applications.

Windows NT supports ATM in LAN environments; however, I do not know of any mechanism for Windows NT to support ATM in the WAN circuits that are being discussed here. Honestly, I am not even sure how well the PC architecture would scale to the bandwidths that ATM would require. The minimum speeds for a wide area network ATM circuit are 155Mb, and the PCI architecture would probably have a difficult time keeping up with that bandwidth. Also becoming common are 622Mbps ATM-based lengths that far surpass the bandwidth available on a PCI network. For these reasons, I have serious doubts that we will see Windows NT based on the PC architecture supporting native WAN ATM circuits.

Hooking Up via Leased Lines

Organizations make use of three common leased lines for wide area network circuits. The first and cheapest of these is the 56K circuit. Adding 31 times the bandwidth of a 56K circuit, a T1 leased line is capable of carrying 1.544Mbps. The most powerful and expensive of the commonly available leased lines is the T3. T3 is used for large organizations that carry a great deal of traffic across a distance. They can carry a great deal of traffic from several miles to across the country, providing up to 45Mbps of sustained traffic.

These leased lines do not have properties, other than bandwidth, that make them unique.

Summary

Wide area networking is a complex topic. In this chapter, I've made an effort to provide you the basic information required to work with networks that use wide area network links. I have also shown you how Windows NT fits into this picture, and what special accommodations need to be made.

After reading this chapter, you should have a complete understanding of the following information:

◆ How to connect networks via analog dial-up links, ISDN, and packet-switched networks

◆ How ISPs connect to each other and how traffic flows between ISPs

◆ How to determine if a specific ISP suites your needs

The next chapter builds on the networking knowledge covered up to this point in the introductory material of this book. It will show you what types of traffic typically use the most bandwidth on Windows NT networks and how to estimate bandwidth requirements on your own network. Chapter 4 marks a transition from broad, conceptual lessons to detailed, Windows NT–specific knowledge.

Chapter 4

Bandwidth

IN THIS CHAPTER

- ◆ Estimating bandwidth based on actual statistics
- ◆ Estimating bandwidth based on speculation
- ◆ Reducing utilization by lowering traffic

AT ONE TIME, a computer's processing power was the most precious commodity. Later, with the introduction of Windows, hard drive space became the most sought-after, and consequently expensive, resource. As the end of the twentieth century approaches, bandwidth has taken the role of bottleneck in most computing systems.

The shift from standalone computers to small networks and from small networks to large networks has been a rapid one. It has been caused by the growth of the worldwide Internet. As the Internet grows, more and more people become Internet users and more and more organizations have an Internet presence. Unfortunately, the bandwidth required for this presence is scarce and expensive.

Internet connections are not the only ones that have become flooded with traffic. As the networking industry expands, private networks within organizations have grown. Existing networks have become overutilized. While new local area networking technologies such as layer-2 switching have effectively reduced total utilization, upgrades are expensive.

For these reasons, managing bandwidth has become an important skill for network engineers and systems engineers alike. The bulk of this chapter is dedicated to various ways of estimating bandwidth, using both actual statistics and speculation. For example, if your organization currently has enough bandwidth, you will learn to anticipate network trends and ensure that your organization continues to have enough bandwidth. In addition, if your organization is already overusing its existing network, you will learn what steps you can take to reduce existing network traffic without reducing functionality. You will also learn to determine exactly how much more bandwidth you need now, and how much you will need in the future. You will learn how to design a network with capacity in mind and how to ensure that future upgrades will be as painless as possible.

Estimating Bandwidth Based on Actual Statistics

As companies grow, so do network demands. Network administrators and network engineers who work for growing companies need to have a constant understanding of the condition of their network. When planning for upgrades, it is particularly important to understand what the bandwidth requirements will be as your organization continues to grow.

If you are concerned that their current network is reaching its full capacity, it is time to perform a usage analysis. A usage analysis, when done correctly, will tell you what types of network communications are generating all that traffic that's filling up your network. This information is also helpful for tuning the network — by giving you the information you need to optimize usage by modifying the network architecture, changing the configuration of the hosts on the network, or altering the settings on the network servers.

A usage analysis provides the most useful information you can have for optimizing how a network is used. While the network engineers have a great deal of control over what services are provided to users, it is these users who ultimately decide how much and what kind of traffic is generated on a network. By examining the network architecture, you may decide that a WINS server should be placed on every subnet of the network to ensure that WINS queries never cross a route. However, a network analysis may reveal that users make very few WINS queries and rely more heavily on DNS queries from applications such as Internet Explorer. A usage analysis can determine how much you will benefit from a change before you make that change.

This section guides you through performing a usage analysis and analyzing each specific type of information. From the data you gather you will be able to determine present and future bandwidth needs and steps you can take to reduce network utilization through network optimization. Architecture decisions will be made from solid information, rather than from educated guesses.

You will be guided through the requirements of performing a network analysis based on your current usage. This section also describes the most useful tools involved, as well as discussing specific types of traffic and what aspects of each protocol generate the most traffic.

You will also get help in estimating growth based on the number of users on your network. This section discusses the different types of users and helps you categorize people. Once you have this information, you can make more accurate estimates of future network requirements.

A third section shows you how to estimate network traffic based on changes in your business. Depending on your business, traffic can vary substantially and, as you will soon learn, predictably. Understanding how your organization's business and "busyness" affect network traffic allows you to know ahead of time how a marketing campaign may result in substantial network utilization changes. After reading this section, you will be able to correlate business activities with network activities.

Estimating by Typical Usage

The most accurate way to estimate future bandwidth requirements is to analyze your existing network usage. By analyzing how things really are, you build an understanding of how users make use of the network, rather than speculating on what "should" be happening. Windows NT provides several different tools to allow you to do this. Many third-party tools designed for this type of network analysis are also available.

TOOLS

There are many different ways to analyze your network traffic. The simplest of these is to use a utility built into both Windows NT Workstation and Windows NT Server. Also included with Windows NT Server and Workstation is the Network Monitor utility, which gives a more detailed insight into traffic on a network segment and can detail broadcast traffic and specific packets transmitted to or from a machine. This version of Network Monitor is a stripped-down version of the Network Monitor included with Systems Management Server (SMS). By upgrading to SMS's Network Monitor, you will find that a great deal of additional functionality is available. Finally, third-party products such as LANalyzer and hardware-based protocol analyzers also suit many situations.

PERFORMANCE MONITOR   Performance Monitor is a great utility to use because it has a lot of pretty charts. Fortunately, it also has robust features such as logging and remote monitoring.

Most systems engineers use Performance Monitor regularly to analyze and optimize the performance of systems. In fact, this book refers to Performance Monitor quite often when discussing the optimization of systems. However, it is underused as a network analysis tool, and it can provide useful information to guide you in focusing on more detailed analysis.

Because the Performance Monitor utility can be used to monitor remote servers by connecting to them with NetBIOS connections, it can be used to monitor network traffic on multiple network segments simultaneously. This is hardly a nonintrusive observation, however; the default update time of one second will generate a measurable amount of network traffic just in transmitting the performance data from the remote nodes to the management node!

For each update interval, three packets are transmitted. The first is an RPC query from the host, requesting the data from the system being monitored. The second packet is a response, which includes the performance data requested. The third packet is a TCP confirmation sent from the monitoring workstation to the monitored system. Table 4-1 shows the number of counters and the traffic generated when the update interval is set to one second. To determine the amount of traffic generated when the update interval is lengthened, simply divide the bandwidth given in this table by the number of seconds the update has been configured to.

TABLE 4-1 TRAFFIC GENERATED BY PERFORMANCE MONITOR WITH A ONE-SECOND UPDATE FREQUENCY

Objects Monitored	Traffic Generated
1	0.011Mbps
5	0.015Mbps
18	0.035Mbps
64	0.1Mbps

For monitoring network usage over long periods of time, be sure to reduce the update frequency to at least 300 seconds (five minutes). This will reduce the amount of traffic generated on any particular network segment to an insignificant amount. Network utilization data is better charted over periods of days and weeks, so reducing the granularity of the data loses nothing.

Performance Monitor is particularly useful because it can be used to correlate network traffic with a particular time of day. For example, people generally check their e-mail and launch several network applications first thing in the morning when they arrive for work. For many networks, this usage pattern results in a period of peak utilization occurring between 8 A.M. and 9 A.M. Knowing what time of day your peak utilization occurs is a critical piece of information because it allows you to focus your efforts on improving network performance when the users need it the most.

Performance Monitor's ability to chart and log over a long period of time allows you to determine which times of day peak utilization occurs. This is not obvious, since the charting mode of Performance Monitor does not include any counter for the current time. Nonetheless, you can tell what time of day spikes occur in a chart because you know the time interval between updates and the width of the chart. Therefore, you can configure the update interval so that the width of a chart is exactly one day, or any other period of time. Let me clarify this.

There are exactly one hundred columns in the chart mode of Performance Monitor. So if you have a goal of charting data over a specific time period, calculating the optimum Periodic Update Interval is easy. Simply convert the desired total chart time into seconds and divide by one hundred.

For example, to chart the objects over a period of an entire day and not have any data scroll off the screen, set the Periodic Update Interval in Performance Monitor to 864 (see Figure 4-1). This number was calculated by converting the time period of one day into 86,400 seconds (24 hours × 60 minutes × 60 seconds) and dividing that result by 100 (the number of columns in the Performance Monitor chart).

Figure 4-1: Performance Monitor's Chart Options dialog box

Table 4-2 provides a quick reference for the mathematically lazy.

TABLE 4-2 PERFORMANCE MONITOR UPDATE INTERVAL SETTINGS

Desired Chart Period	Periodic Update Interval
1 Hour	36
1 Day	864
1 Week	6,048
30 Days	25,920

If you are attempting to determine the busiest times of the day for network traffic, start by charting an entire day. At the end of the day, you will have a chart showing the ebb and the tide of network utilization. Take notes on what times of the day showed the highest utilization, and gather this information daily over a period of two weeks. After two weeks, examine your notes and see if there are consistent, daily traffic trends. In networks with more than 30 users, there will always be clear trends.

These trends are greatly affected by policies within the organization, such as having flexible or inflexible schedules. If everyone must be in before 8 A.M. and take a lunch hour at a specific time, you will see more distinct traffic spikes than if people tend to come in anywhere between 7 A.M. and 10 A.M. Also take into consideration times of high utilization when response time is not important, such as network backups. These are not a problem because backups are done during non-working hours, so the performance data may simply be discarded.

If you want to find the busiest days of the week, set Performance Monitor to chart over a period of five business days. At the end of this week, you will have a handy chart showing you the peak network utilization on different days. This will act as a starting point for alleviating weekly bursts of network traffic. To illustrate how this information may be put to use, consider this example: Performance Monitor may show you that Friday is by far the busiest day on the network. After further analysis, you may discover that accounting runs a huge weekly report on Friday, which generates a great deal of traffic between the accountant's desktop, the accounting server, and the accounting printer. This may lead you to suggest that the accountants run the report Thursday or Friday night, rather than in the middle of the day.

Trends similar to the weekly trend just described also tend to happen monthly as different parts of the organization produce monthly reports. The steps you need to take to analyze such use patterns are the same as the ones for analyzing over a period of a week. Analyzing cycles longer than a month is a lost cause with Performance Monitor in charting mode, but it can be done using the logging features described later in this section.

There are some specific counters to watch. For instance, Performance Monitor can chart and log:

◆ Network segment utilization

◆ Utilization by broadcasts

◆ Utilization by multicasts

The most interesting object in Performance Monitor for analyzing the utilization of a network segment is called Network Segment, ironically enough. Network Segment contains the following counters:

% **Network Utilization:** The Network Utilization object is the best starting point for network analysis. It gives you a quick view of the total traffic on a shared media network segment and should be used to determine whether or not a network segment requires further analysis. A critical step in the network analysis problem-solving process is to narrow down the location of your problem so that you can better focus your attention. This is an excellent time to make use of this counter!

To use Performance Monitor successfully on an enterprise network, connect to a single NT machine on each network segment within your network and add this counter. With a simple chart, you can get a summary of the enterprise network traffic and quickly determine which networks have the highest utilization. With this information, you are ready to focus your analysis to individual networks.

Please keep in mind that this particular counter has the most significant meaning on networks that use a shared medium of some kind. It works well when each Ethernet network segment uses a hub, because each host on that segment has the opportunity to measure all of the traffic being transmitted onto the shared medium. However, many modern networks are based on switched media. With switched media, each host has the opportunity to measure only broadcast traffic and frames destined for that switch port.

Does it really create a problem that hosts on a switched network cannot monitor network utilization for the entire segment? After all, if the ports the hosts are on are not receiving the traffic, bandwidth is not being utilized, right? This statement is true, but reducing the bandwidth utilized on individual ports may simply be shifting the bottleneck to the switch itself. Many switches support literally hundreds of Ethernet ports but cannot support switching the number of frames that would be necessary if each port was being fully utilized.

It would be nice if NT's Performance Monitor could tell you exactly how many frames the switch is processing and how it is performing, but switches cannot communicate in this way. Fortunately, most switches provide the functionality within the switch's operating system for monitoring and tuning the performance of the switch and some network statistics. Many switches, particularly those from Cisco, have the option of configuring a port to receive all frames that are being transmitted on the same virtual LAN. This is useful for network utilization analysis and for protocol analysis.

Total Bytes Received/Second: The Total Bytes Received/Second counter is perhaps the most useful counter for getting a snapshot of a subnet's usage. This counter provides the number of bytes being transmitted on the subnet that a particular host can see, including layer-2 headers, broadcasts, and multicasts of any protocol. As an indicator of overall network utilization, it is very similar to the % Network Utilization counter. Indeed, these two counters will rise and fall in direct proportion to one another. The % Network Utilization counter does not provide as much detail as this counter, but you may find that it is enough.

Please keep in mind that this is not a good indicator of utilization on a switched network. Because the network interface card on the machine can see only the number of frames sent to its particular port, you will only be able to measure the traffic addressed to a particular machine or to the broadcast MAC address. To measure the total traffic on a switched network, investigate the switch's methods of performance monitoring. Most switches have SNMP-based management built in, which allows them to be queried for performance statistics.

One possible use is to configure a counter to be monitored on many computers throughout the network. Consider using your desktop as a network monitoring workstation by running Performance Monitor and adding the Total Bytes Received/Second counter from one remote server on each remote network. By monitoring this counter from multiple subnets, you can get an idea of the overall traffic in the enterprise. Another possible usage is using this counter in conjunction with the Total Frames Received/Second counter to determine the average number of bytes in a frame.

% **Broadcast Frames:** Broadcast frames are a special type of frame that must be processed by every node on a network. Because these frames require processing time from every host on the same network segment, broadcast frames are worse than directed or multicast frames. This will not shock anyone who has gotten this far into the book; it is pretty common knowledge that broadcasts are bad. However, it may be worse than you think.

Back in the old days, networks were connected together by bridges. Bridges did their job better than most people would give them credit, and spanning tree algorithms gave them much of the functionality of modern routers. Nonetheless, layer-2 switching became more popular as networks grew because bridges, in their default configuration, forwarded all broadcasts packets to all network segments. The problem of broadcasts, which did not make up a substantial part of the bandwidth on any single segment, began to multiply as network segments grew in size. Networks with great amounts of broadcast traffic could easily consume thirty to forty percent of the CPU time of each connected host with just the overhead of processing and discarding network broadcast traffic. Granted, these CPUs were just 386s and could not do much anyway, but it was still a problem.

In networks with a small number of hosts on a single segment, broadcast traffic will never be a problem. However, many network administrators are increasing the bandwidth on Ethernet networks by replacing hubs with layer-2 switches (hereafter, I will simply refer to them as "switches"). Instead of a hub providing 10Mbps to all the hosts on a network segment, each host can receive a dedicated 10Mbps Ethernet port. This is a really great idea, but takes us back to the problems that bridges had: They must propagate broadcast frames to every known port.

Therefore, because broadcast frames defeat the advantages of switches, they are of particular concern to anyone implementing switched networks. For those organizations that are implementing hierarchical switched networks, broadcast traffic should be carefully monitored and analyzed. By connecting switches into switches, many organizations are implementing extremely large network segments, often hosting up to one thousand hosts on a single switched subnet. As you can imagine, the combined broadcast traffic of a thousand hosts can consume a substantial part of any network's total bandwidth.

The % Broadcast Frames Performance Monitor object allows you to watch what percentage of the total network bandwidth is consumed by broadcast frames. If during peak network usage times this counter averages more than five percent, you have a problem with broadcast traffic.

% **Multicast Frames:** I can't say this definitively, but I am pretty sure that very few people in the world have a problem with multicast traffic hogging all the bandwidth on a local area network. Multicast frames look just like broadcast frames at the data-link layer of the OSI model – they use the Ethernet address FF-FF-FF-FF-FF-FF and are received by every host on the same subnet. Therefore, the previously described properties for broadcast frames apply to multicast frames as well.

Multicast frames do not cause nearly as much trouble, however. The reason for this is that nobody actually uses multicast frames. Naturally, I don't mean this literally — applications such as OSPF and RIP v2 make extensive use of multicasting to identify similar hosts on a network. However, they do not produce enough traffic to affect the overall network performance.

These statements will not hold true much longer. The fact is, network applications such as teleconferencing and videoconferencing are beginning to make use of multicasting for distributing streaming data (such as audio or video) to a large number of hosts simultaneously. As this data is flooded through a network, the impact multicast frames have on network performance will increase. Nonetheless, very few applications currently use multicasting on a large scale, so keep this performance monitor counter in mind for the future.

Broadcast Frames Received/Second and Multicast Frames Received/Second: Providing similar information to the corresponding counters % Broadcast Frames and % Multicast Frames, the Broadcast/Multicast Frames Received/Second counter should only be used once you have determined that broadcast or multicast frames are worthy of further research. When you know the average number of each type of frame transmitted per second, it is possible to calculate the average number of bytes in each broadcast packet and determine if you are receiving many small broadcast packets or fewer, larger broadcast packets.

You could go through the trouble of logging both the Broadcast Frames/Second counter and the % Broadcast Frames counters, finding the average of both and performing the math to compute the average frame size, or you can just take my word for it: Your broadcast packets are really small. The most common source of broadcast packets in TCP/IP networks is the ARP request, a 42-byte frame. Other common sources such as the Browser service and the NetBIOS Name service create larger packets.

Total Frames Received/Second: Though not as useful as the other counters detailed in this section, this counter provides the number of frames that are sent onto the local network segment of a Windows NT system. The number of frames on a network is not immediately useful because it does not give an indicator of utilization, but you should keep this counter in mind should you ever need to calculate the average frame size on a network segment.

Frame size can be an important indicator of network usage. After determining the average frame size on a network, think about what types of traffic generate frames of that size. Some examples are shown in Table 4-3. Large frames of greater than 1,000 bytes tend to be the result of file transfers, indicating that the frame was filled to capacity and the data stream needed to be broken into multiple frames. Smaller frames are attributable to ARP broadcasts, name resolutions, and browser traffic. Typically, a great deal of optimization can be performed on traffic created by small frames. Large-frame traffic, such as file transfers, is not as flexible.

TABLE 4–3 AVERAGE FRAME SIZE INDICATORS

Average Frame Size	Possible High–Traffic Protocols
< 200	Browser traffic, WINS queries, DNS queries, domain authentications, ARP queries/responses
> 200	Large HTTP transfers, FTP transfers, NetBIOS/SMB file transfers

---

WINDOWS NT'S FREE NETWORK MONITOR   Network Monitor is a *really good* protocol analyzer. It is not for amateurs, but it's not so bad to use. It provides descriptions of each header field in each packet it can see, and it recognizes protocols at all layers of the OSI model. It can dissect the layer-2 headers in an Ethernet packet and identify packets bound for Web servers. As you read through this book, you'll find I'm a big fan of this product.

Unfortunately, this free version has some major weaknesses when it comes to using it as a tool for usage analysis. It lacks the capability to use the network interface card in promiscuous mode, meaning Network Monitor can analyze only traffic that is bound for or sent from one specific host. The capabilities it has to analyze the traffic on a network segment are limited to information also available from Performance Monitor. All else being equal, Performance Monitor is a more powerful tool for gathering network utilization statistics.

Though Network Monitor cannot view traffic bound for other hosts on the network, it can analyze broadcast traffic. For this reason, Network Monitor is useful after you have used Performance Monitor to determine that broadcast traffic is a problem. Simply start Network Monitor on any station on the network, allow it to collect data, and use the packet analysis capabilities to view the different types of broadcast traffic sent during the capture period. In this way, you can determine if the broadcast traffic is caused by ARP queries, NetBIOS name resolution, the Browser service, or some other protocol.

Broadcast traffic can be one of the most significant contributors to network congestion. Performance Monitor provides counters for measuring the amount of traffic on a network segment, but it cannot tell you what is generating the traffic. Network Monitor goes a step beyond: You can determine which hosts are transmitting the traffic, what type of traffic it is, and, depending on your familiarity with the protocol, whether or not it is even necessary.

By default, the freebie version of Network Monitor captures all traffic bound for the host it is executing on: directed, broadcast, and multicast frames. If you are attempting to analyze only broadcast traffic, there is no need to capture the directed frames. Capturing only the broadcast traffic reduces the processor overhead on the monitored host and allows you to capture traffic for a longer period of time, so it is very advisable to configure a filter before attempting to analyze broadcast traffic.

To configure Network Monitor to filter everything but broadcast traffic, follow these steps:

1. Launch Network Monitor on a host with an interface to the network segment you wish to analyze.

2. From the Capture menu, choose Filter (shortcut: press the F8 key).

3. Skip past the blatant-advertisement-for-SMS dialog box by pressing OK. You will see the Capture Filter dialog box, as illustrated in Figure 4-2, allowing you to filter traffic before it is captured. Do not confuse this with the filtering that can be performed on traffic after it has been captured. Capture filtering is much less flexible.

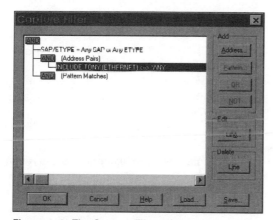

Figure 4-2: The Capture Filter dialog box

4. Beneath the (Address Pairs) branch, double-click the default filter (which is labeled "INCLUDE COMPUTERNAME (ETHERNET) <--> *ANY"). This will bring up a dialog box labeled Address Expression, as illustrated in Figure 4-3, allowing you to narrow down the frames that will be captured.

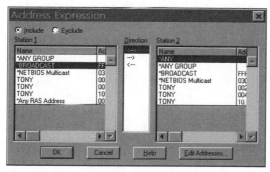

Figure 4-3: The Address Expression dialog box

5. The left list box gives several options for filtering. From these, choose "*BROADCAST." Make sure "<--> " is selected in the center list box and "*ANY" is selected in the right list box. Click OK to save your settings and return to the Capture Filter dialog box.

6. The (Address Pairs) field should now read "INCLUDE *BROADCAST (ETHERNET) <--> *ANY." At this point, only broadcast traffic will be captured. Broadcast traffic includes traffic generated by the host machine or any other machine on the same subnet. Because of the nature of broadcast traffic, even systems on a switched network can see others' traffic.

After configuring the filter to capture only broadcast traffic, I suggest increasing the buffer size to 10MB to reduce the chance that the buffer will overflow and begin to drop data. Press the F10 key to begin capturing. Feel free to let this run for a full day – the extra buffer allocation should be sufficient.

When you are ready to analyze the traffic, press F11 to stop capturing and begin analysis. From the capture window, quite a bit of useful information is readily available. The first place to look is in the Captured Statistics box. Examine the field labeled # Bytes. This is the total number of bytes that were not filtered by the Network Monitor filter – in this case, it should be all broadcast traffic on the network during the capture period. Next, convert the number shown for Time Elapsed at the top of the window into seconds.

Given these two pieces of information, you can calculate the average Mbps broadcast traffic generated on the network. To calculate this, multiply the number of bytes by eight to find the total number of broadcast bits transferred. Then divide this number by the number of seconds listed beside Time Elapsed. This yields the total bits per second of broadcast traffic on the network segment. Because bandwidth information is normally expressed as megabits per second, divide this number by one million. In a healthy network, you should achieve a result well below .25Mbps. Any number greater than .5Mbps requires further analysis.

If you determine that the bandwidth consumed by broadcast traffic deserves more attention, examine the pane at the bottom of the window. This window details the traffic collected by the station that transmitted and received it. To find out who the greatest consumers of bandwidth are, click on the Bytes Rcvd column heading. This sorts the column and brings the culprits to the top. After you have examined this summary information, take a look at the frame-by-frame capture by pressing F12.

This will take you to a screen displaying, frame by frame, every byte of broadcast traffic received by the host during the capture period. There's a lot of information here, but only a small fraction of it is useful for determining bandwidth usage. The most critical information that can be found in the frame analysis is which higher-level protocols are generating the greatest amount of broadcast traffic. Unfortunately, there is no simple way to determine this using the free version of Network Monitor; the summarizing features have been disabled. The quickest way is to scroll through the list of frames and "eyeball" it to determine which protocols are most commonly listed under the Protocol column header. Take note of the top three, and filter out just those protocols for further analysis. Filtering protocols in Network Monitor is a fundamental skill, so I will give a step-by-step description for filtering browser traffic.

To display only browser frames within Network Monitor:

1. From the Display menu, choose Filter. This will display the Display Filter dialog box, as shown in Figure 4-4.

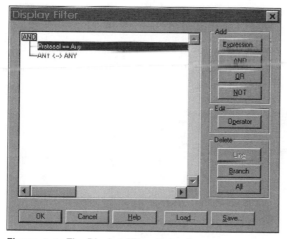

Figure 4-4: The Display Filter dialog box

2. The Display Filter dialog shows any active filters. The first line in the dialog box should read "Protocol == Any," which indicates that all protocols are being displayed. To edit this line, simply double-click on it. The expression editor, as illustrated in Figure 4-5, will greet you.

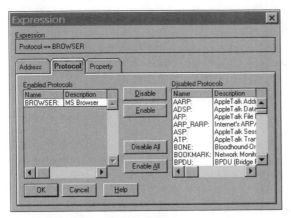

Figure 4-5: The expression editor

3. The expression editor allows you to specify which protocols you want to
   see, and which you want hidden. Because you want to filter everything
   except one specific protocol, start by pressing the Disable All button. All
   protocols listed in the left list box will be moved to the right list box. Next,
   select "BROWSER" from the right list box and choose the Enable button to
   move the MS Browser protocol to the list of enabled protocols. Click the OK
   button to return to the Display Filter, which should now look like Figure 4-6.

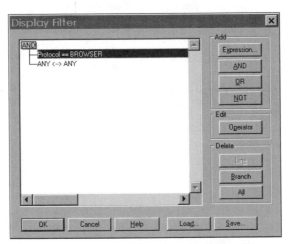

Figure 4-6: The result of changing the display filter

4. Click OK again to finalize your changes and view the filtered traffic.

If you followed the steps correctly, Network Monitor should show you only those frames generated by the Browser service. This greatly simplifies the task of examining the frames for that particular protocol, because you no longer have to squint at the display and scroll past all the protocols you are not interested in. The version of Network Monitor that is included with SMS allows you to total the number of bytes in the number of filtered frames. Unfortunately, the free version does not. When all else fails, use brute force: Scroll through the frames and total the number of bytes in each frame. With this number, it is simple to find the percentage of broadcast traffic that was generated by this particular protocol. You can also calculate the bandwidth used by this particular protocol in Mbps, as previously described. If you go through these laborious steps for each protocol, you will know which specific protocols are causing the most trouble.

Knowing what is causing the problem doesn't get you anywhere on its own; you still need to take steps to reduce the traffic. This is very protocol specific, though, so I will not attempt to cover it in this section. However, this book includes information about most common TCP/IP-related protocols, so it is only a matter of finding the right page to learn how to optimize a particular protocol.

After isolating traffic problems to a specific host, Network Monitor allows you to analyze that host's network traffic to determine which specific protocols are generating the traffic. To do this, you must run the free version of Network Monitor on that host and create a capture filter to avoid capturing broadcast frames. Alternatively, you may use the SMS version of Network Monitor to monitor the traffic from a remote workstation. This option is described in greater detail in the next section.

To configure Network Monitor to capture only traffic transmitted by a particular host or incoming traffic directed to that host, follow these steps:

1. Launch Network Monitor on the host to be monitored.

2. From the Capture menu, choose Filter (shortcut: press the F8 key).

3. Skip past the warning dialog box by pressing OK. You will see the Capture Filter dialog box, as illustrated in Figure 4-2, allowing you to filter traffic before it is captured. Do not confuse this with the filtering that can be performed on traffic after it has been captured. Capture filtering is much less flexible.

4. Beneath the (Address Pairs) branch, double-click the default filter (which is labeled "INCLUDE COMPUTERNAME (ETHERNET) <--> *ANY"). This will bring up a dialog box labeled Address Expression, as illustrated in Figure 4-7, allowing you to narrow down which frames will be captured.

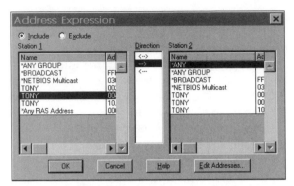

Figure 4-7: The Address Expression dialog box

5. The left list box gives several options for filtering. From these, choose the row that has the computer's name and the MAC address of the network interface card attached to the correct network. Make sure " → " is selected in the center list box and "*ANY" is selected in the right list box. Click OK to save your settings and return to the Capture Filter dialog.

6. The (Address Pairs) field should now read "INCLUDE *BROADCAST (ETHERNET) → *ANY." At this point, only traffic sent by or addressed to the host will be captured. Broadcast traffic will be captured only if it is transmitted by the host in question.

Assuming you have the disk space available, increase the buffer size to 20MB to reduce the chance that the buffer will overflow and begin to drop data. You may begin to collect data once the filter has been configured. Allow Network Monitor to capture for at least half an hour to get a reasonable sampling of data. If you have previously determined a specific time of day when this host generates the most traffic, capture data during that period for best results.

When half an hour has passed, press F11 to stop the capture. Take the time to note specific items in the summary information displayed in the capture windows before you examine the frames. The sampling period was too small to yield meaningful results, so it will not do you any good to calculate the bandwidth usage at this time. Instead, take a minute to find exactly which hosts are communicating most with the system being analyzed. To do this, click on the Bytes Rcvd column header in the lowest pane. This will sort the table by the traffic generated per host and tell you immediately if the high traffic is due to many users or a few isolated high-traffic systems. If there are specific hosts creating the bulk of the traffic, take note of those systems before pressing F12 to continue to the frame analysis screen.

At this point, you will see each frame as it was transmitted to or from the host you are analyzing. Earlier, I described a method to determine if the bulk of the traffic was coming to or from a few specific hosts. If you found this to be the case, take a few minutes to analyze the traffic on a host-by-host basis.

To filter frames within Network Monitor to show only those frames addressed to or from a particular host:

1. From the Display menu, choose Filter. This will display the Display Filter dialog box, as shown in Figure 4-4.

2. The Display Filter dialog box shows any active filters. The second line should read "ANY <--> ANY," indicating that all frames addressed to or from any address will be displayed. You want to filter all frames except those from specific hosts, so double-click on this line to edit it. The Expression Editor will open with the Address tab selected, as illustrated in Figure 4-8.

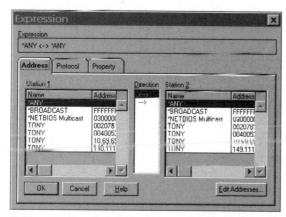

Figure 4-8: The Expression Editor with the Address tab selected

3. By default, no frames are filtered. However, you want to view only frames that are part of one specific conversation between two distinct hosts, so select the proper address of the system you are analyzing in the left column and the station it is conversing with in the right column. If the remote address already appears in the list, skip to step 5. Otherwise, step 4 will describe how to add that address to the list.

4. Click the Edit Addresses... button in the lower-right corner of the expression builder. Network Monitor will display a list of addresses that have already been registered. If the address of the remote system is not listed there, click the Add button. The Address Information dialog box appears as illustrated in Figure 4-9. You may enter the address as either the MAC address or the IP address. If the two hosts are on the same subnet, use the MAC address because it will filter traffic for all valid IP addresses on that network interface. If the two hosts are on different subnets, you are required to use the IP address. Click OK to add the address, and then click OK again to return to the expression builder.

Figure 4-9: The Address Information dialog box displays the address of the remote host.

5. Click OK twice to finalize your changes and view the filtered traffic.

Now that you have eliminated the distraction of all that extra traffic, you can better concentrate your efforts on finding the source of the traffic being exchanged between the two hosts. A great place to start is by examining the Protocol column. This column indicates the protocol based on several factors – but most often the TCP port number being used determines it. Eyeball this traffic and decide which protocols are the most significant, and then attempt to analyze the traffic deeper by looking into the frames and deciding what the application is attempting to do. For example, if the Protocol column shows a great deal of HTTP traffic, examine the GET requests to see what files the client is downloading. This may lead you to discover that the same files were being downloaded repeatedly by the same user, a good indicator that the user has disabled caching on the browser. This would require his system to redownload repeated images on the intranet server, wasting bandwidth. Or if the protocol shows SMB, you may discover that the client has been storing all of his files on a file server using a network drive, thereby wasting valuable network space.

These are just examples of what you may find when you analyze network traffic in this manner – your results may vary. Nonetheless, I hope this section has provided the foundation for performing network analysis using Network Monitor.

SMS'S NETWORK MONITOR   Until NT 4.0, Network Monitor was only a utility included with Microsoft's Systems Management Server (SMS), a component of BackOffice. With the release of NT 4.0, Microsoft began including a stripped-down version of this utility. In my humble opinion, Network Monitor was the most useful utility within SMS, and I was excited to see that they were now giving it away free.

The stripped-down version of SMS lacked many of the most powerful features of the full version. This was probably a good thing, overall. The most notable feature it lacked was the ability to place the network interface card into promiscuous mode and monitor all traffic on the network. I am glad it lacked that, because it would have turned any NT desktop into a serious security weakness, allowing anyone with an administrator account to snoop others' passwords.

Microsoft also eliminated Network Monitor's powerful ability to monitor network interface cards on remote systems, another potential security risk, because it extended the snooper's scope to remote networks. They also dropped the ability to summarize data; a useful feature for those of us who perform network analysis. There was no security risk associated with this feature; Microsoft just wanted to leave you something to pay for.

So if you have SMS, make a point of using it because it will make your life easier. In the previous sections, I have made a point of not assuming you are using it, giving directions only for the built-in Network Monitor, a poor man's protocol analyzer. This section provides details of using the extended features of SMS, supplementing the instructions provided in the previous section.

SMS's ability to monitor remote interfaces is a real advantage because it means you no longer have to walk over to the server and launch Network Monitor to analyze the traffic on the system. Essentially, you select the network interface card and you are able to monitor the traffic from your own desktop. To do this, follow these steps:

1. From the Capture menu, choose Network. You will see the Select Capture Network dialog box, allowing you to choose a network interface card. This dialog box is displayed in Figure 4-10.

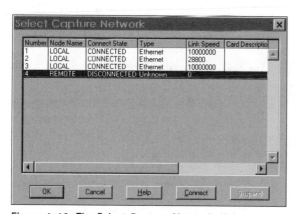

Figure 4-10: The Select Capture Network dialog box

2. Select the interface with a Node Name listed as REMOTE and click OK.

3. Enter in the name of the destination computer in the Agent Name field.

4. Click OK to connect to the server.

SMS adds other nifty things, too. Among them is the ability to sum up the total number of frames and bytes involved in any particular protocol in a capture. Let's say you've just captured all of the broadcast traffic on a subnet for an entire day, and you want to determine which protocols are generating the most traffic. Earlier in this chapter, I described a method of totaling the network traffic generated that required a great deal of patience and probably a calculator. Here is an easier method:

1. From the Tools menu, choose Protocol Distribution. The Protocol Distribution dialog box is pictured in Figure 4-11.

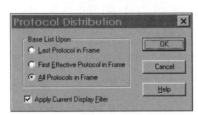

Figure 4-11: The Protocol Distribution dialog box

2. For a quick analysis, press the OK button. Network Monitor will display a Protocol Distribution Report, as pictured in Figure 4-12.

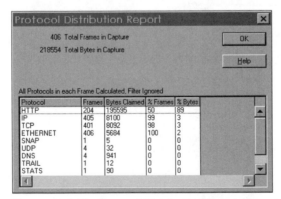

Figure 4-12: The Protocol Distribution Report dialog box

> **Caveat!**
>
> Please keep in mind that Network Monitor's remote agent abilities generate network traffic of their own. So if you are using Network Monitor in conjunction with Performance Monitor, Performance Monitor will reflect the additional network traffic and throw off your analysis.

3. The Protocol Distribution Report displays each of the protocols that were part of a captured frame, the total number of frames and bytes, and how that total compares to the rest of the traffic. You have the ability to sort a column quickly by clicking on the column headings. So to determine which protocols caused the most traffic, click on the "% Bytes" column heading. The most used protocols will float to the top.

As you can see, this is substantially easier than totaling the number of bytes in each frame one-by-one.

THIRD-PARTY PRODUCTS Microsoft does not have a monopoly on protocol analyzers. Many other vendors have produced products; a few of those products are described here.

A popular Protocol Analyzer is LANDecoder32 from Triticom. An evaluation version of this product can be downloaded from http://www.triticom.com/. It provides sniffing and analysis of network data.

The same vendor also produces EtherVision. Not as much a protocol analyzer as an Ethernet traffic monitor, EtherVision can also be downloaded from http://www.triticom.com/.

PrismLite is a hardware-based protocol analyzer that attaches to your laptop computer. It is capable of analyzing WAN, LAN, and ATM traffic. You can add and remove modules for various types of networks, so you are not bound to any particular topology. The real advantage to hardware-based protocol analyzers such as this one is the ability to carry it around and plug it into any port on just about any kind of network. When plugged into an Ethernet network, it will provide information similar to that provided with the SMS version of Network Monitor. However, Network Monitor is bound to a Windows NT system and is completely incapable of sniffing traffic on WAN circuits. You get what you pay for; prices start at $30,000 for an ATM-only configuration. For more information on PrismLite, visit http://www.radcom-inc.com.

PUTTING THAT DATA TO WORK

Now that you are familiar with the different tools and how they work, I want to go into more detail about how to use them together. In this section, I will focus primarily on the free, built-in tools that Windows NT provides: Performance Monitor and Network Monitor. This section goes past the technical aspects of traffic analysis and addresses the project management issues to make sure you use your time effectively. Because network analysis is such an expensive and time-consuming process, it is extremely important to make sure that you do not waste time optimizing underutilized subnets or rearranging the network architecture to make something more efficient – only to realize that the problem never had that substantial an impact.

PRIORITIZING SUBNETS   One of the best ways to start a network analysis is by analyzing the utilization on each subnet on your network. This will give you the information you need to find the real trouble spots in your organization and focus your attention there. As you read in the "Tools" section of this chapter, Performance Monitor is a handy way to determine the network utilization on remote subnets, but what do you do with that information once you have gathered it?

Unless you have a small network (less than five subnets), you will want to organize the information into something a little easier to look at than Performance Monitor charts. I suggest making a spreadsheet with a row for each subnet. Include a subnet identifier, the average utilization during prime time, and the peak utilization of the subnet. You should also include any other data that you have gathered that is useful in determining which networks are most in need of some help. An example of this type of spreadsheet is illustrated in Table 4-4.

TABLE 4-4 AN EXAMPLE SUBNET PRIORITIZATION

Description	Subnet	Prime Time Utilization	Peak Utilization
End-User Network 1	192.168.100.0	5%	11%
End-User Network 2	192.168.101.0	15%	15%
End-User Network 3	192.168.102.0	11%	12%
End-User Network 4	192.168.103.0	35%	35%
End-User Network 5	192.168.104.0	7%	7%
End-User Network 6	192.168.105.0	12%	12%
Backup Network	192.168.110.0	2%	56%
Server Network	192.168.115.0	48%	48%

Once you have created this table, you can tell at a glance which networks need help the most. Looking at the sample table, you see that two networks appear to be the most highly used: the backup network and the server network. This is not to say that the user networks are perfect – End-User Network 4 is definitely in the danger zone – but these two networks are the busiest.

Now consider the relative importance of each subnet. The server network, currently experiencing peak utilization of 48 percent, is extremely important because most traffic transmitted on the network will converge at this one point. Therefore, if this network is experiencing high utilization, all communications within the organization will suffer. In contrast, the backup network is unimportant. The type of traffic, high-speed file transfers, tends to saturate a network. The utilization becomes very high for a sustained period of time because several machines are backed up in sequence.

PRIORITIZING USAGE OPTIMIZATION   Usage optimization runs parallel to subnet optimization. Once you have performed a subnet optimization, isolating particular protocols that are causing a large portion of the traffic problem on the network, the next step is to attempt to reduce that traffic. Usage optimization is the process of identifying protocols that create a substantial amount of traffic on a crowded network and then attempting to reduce the amount of traffic that those protocols generate.

Earlier in this chapter, I outlined steps to use the free Network Monitor or the SMS version of Network Monitor to identify particular protocols that are creating a large portion of the traffic on a single subnet. Once you have used these methods to identify a protocol as being problematic, there are several things you can do to alleviate the amount of traffic being generated. Look for one or more of the following problems:

1. Packets that need to traverse several networks before reaching their final destination

2. Protocols that create a great deal of broadcast traffic. As I discussed earlier, broadcast frames are more costly than directed frames because each host on the subnet must process each frame. On switched networks, broadcast traffic is the only type of traffic that must be transmitted on each and every port. This means that the utilization created by broadcast traffic is significantly higher than for directed traffic.

3. Traffic that is not usage-based, that is, traffic that occurs in the background whether or not someone is using the network. An example of this is the traffic generated by the Browser service; browser broadcasts will happen regardless of whether someone is using it or not. Other types of background noise common on NT-based networks are WINS traffic, domain replication traffic, and intertrust communications.

Consider the example of WINS traffic, crossing several subnets between the client and the server. If you identified that a certain percentage of traffic, either on the server network or on a particular client network, was generated by WINS name resolutions, one of the best ways to alleviate this is to attempt to reduce the number of subnets the WINS packets must traverse before reaching their destination. One way to do this would be to add multiple network cards to the WINS server, connecting it to multiple networks simultaneously. Once the server is multihomed, simply change the WINS server address as configured on each of the clients so that they query the nearest interface card on the WINS server.

Estimating by Number of Users

When you are trying to scale the network to a growing organization, one of the different methods you can use is to estimate the traffic growth by estimating the growth in the number of users. Unfortunately, this is not as simple as it may seem! The simplest possibility would be to take the increase in the number of users and multiply it by the existing bandwidth needs. Following this logic, if the total number of users on a network is increasing by fifty percent, the network utilization will also increase by fifty percent. That is never the case, because users do not initiate much of the traffic on the network.

The first step you need to take when estimating future bandwidth needs based on the number of new users in your network is to isolate and measure the traffic that is generated by users. Consider the amount of traffic that is generated by various application-layer protocols. SMTP, POP, HTTP, and FTP are all entirely dependent on user actions. HTTP generates no traffic until a user launches a Web browser and visits a Web page. Similarly, POP and SMTP traffic is generated by the user's mail clients uploading and downloading mail messages. Other types of traffic that you will see increase in proportion to the number of users are domain authentications, Browser service broadcasts, and name resolution traffic.

Types of traffic that you will not see increase as the number of users increases are replication between the primary and backup domain controllers (PDCs and BDCs), synchronization between primary domain controllers on either side of a trust, and server monitoring using the SNMP protocol.

Estimating traffic by the number of users being added to a network is useful because network engineers and network administrators are commonly notified of growth plans this way. In most organizations, managers must plan months in advance to hire someone and usually provide estimates of staffing requirements as much as a year in advance. These estimates can be used by a skilled network engineer to ensure that the corporate network is never overutilized. Use the methods described in this chapter to identify traffic that is created per-user, ignoring traffic that is merely "background noise." Once you have determined this, the rest is just a simple calculation.

Estimating Growth

Rarely do people think to estimate bandwidth requirements based on the growth in the business of a company. To clarify, estimating by growth allows a network engineer to take something as abstract as a marketing plan and use it as part of a network needs analysis. If you know that marketing is planning on launching a campaign that will increase business by fifty percent, you should make sure the network is ready for the increased network utilization.

The first step in determining how traffic will increase is isolating the traffic that is generated on a per-customer basis. This is much more complicated than any method discussed previously, because you must analyze the packets deeper than the OSI application layer. You must actually look deeper into the individual packets and determine whether or not they are used as part of directly servicing the customer.

Some of the types of traffic you will see increase on a per-customer basis are e-mail traffic bound for the Internet. Because these communications are often directed to customers, they will increase as more customers are added. For organizations that connect to their customers through networks other than the Internet, such as leased lines or EDI connections, take growth in the customer base into account.

You should estimate growth by business at the same time you are considering traffic on a per-user basis. Optimistic companies plan on expanding both the number of employees and the number of customers. It is the job of the network engineer to associate traffic with users, customers, or other processes that may increase as the organization expands.

Estimating Bandwidth Based on Speculation

Estimating bandwidth requirements is a complex task, and the most useful information available to a network engineer is the current bandwidth usage. However, this information is not always available. If you are designing a new network for an organization, your estimates must be based purely on speculation. Likewise, if you are upgrading an existing network but will be adding new services and functionality, you must know the network requirements for each service. You will need to take the knowledge you have of the organization's plans for the network and extrapolate the bandwidth requirements.

Throughout this section I will use a sample company, Widgits, Inc., as an example. Consider the task of designing a network for Widgets, Inc. They have 500 employees in three separate locations. You learn from a conversation with their CIO that they plan on using Windows NT Server as their network operating system for file sharing and printer sharing tasks. A consultant from a competing consulting firm has recommended that they make use of Windows NT domains, using Microsoft's master domain model to separate user accounts from resources. The primary domain controllers for both the master and resource domains will be located in the central office, with backup domain controllers for each domain located at both remote offices. Windows NT Workstation and Windows 95 will be deployed on the desktop.

To make matters worse, the CIO has a few close friends that he will be hiring as consultants. They have expressed a lack of confidence in Windows NT's ability to host intranet servers and have recommended the use of UNIX-based servers to host the company's intranet and some Telnet-based client-server applications. The simple task assigned to you is to determine their bandwidth needs on the local area networks and on the wide area network links.

This information alone is not enough to begin estimating bandwidth requirements, but it is a good start. You must define exactly which network services will be used. Further, you must determine where the computers that participate in those services will be located, and what types of communications will cross which links.

Estimating Based on Services

The first step is to define the services in use. The company is going to use the NT Master domain structure, which tells us you will need to take into account domain user authentication, domain controller account synchronizations, and intertrust communications, in the very least. You also know they will be using WINS, the Browser service, and the Messenger service. These services all have a certain amount of network overhead that will exist no matter how the users make use of the services.

Other services are more dependent on the specific usage patterns of the individual users. File and printing services will have more impact than any of the preceding services, and their usage will vary on a user-by-user basis. These factors make it more difficult to estimate accurately, but there are still steps you can take to make an educated recommendation.

WINS

WINS, the Windows Internet Name Service, allows NetBIOS name resolution on TCP/IP-based networks. WINS traffic can be broken into two major categories: predictable overhead (background noise) and less predictable usage-based traffic. In large networks, the usage-based portion of the traffic can have a substantial impact on overall network performance.

The overhead portion of the WINS traffic occurs during the initial startup of the system and on a regular basis from that point forward. For example, WINS overhead occurs when machines register their NetBIOS names upon startup and when workstations perform a WINS request looking for the domain controller. This traffic needs to exist for the WINS service to operate properly, but there are many ways it can be adjusted.

WINS traffic also has a usage-based component. For example, each time a desktop system attempts to establish a new connection to a file or print server, that system must perform a WINS query to resolve the computer's NetBIOS name to an IP address. Therefore, some networks may generate more usage-based traffic than other networks. If the network you are attempting to estimate bandwidth requirements for only has a single server, WINS usage-based traffic will be light. Alternatively, if there are hundreds of servers on the network and users are constantly connecting and disconnecting, it can become a significant portion of the total traffic.

In our sample organization, Widgits, Inc., a WINS server will be located in each of the remote sites. Push-pull replication will be performed between the sites to ensure that all NetBIOS names are propagated throughout the enterprise network. In all cases, clients will be configured to use the local WINS server as their primary WINS server.

WINS OVERHEAD

WINS generates a great deal of background noise. Fortunately, the amount of traffic generated by this background noise is completely predictable, if you understand the traffic patterns adequately. In this section, I have broken down the traffic generated by WINS as overhead into three subcategories: traffic generated by workstations, by servers, and by server relationships.

A summary of the traffic generated by WINS on a network is listed in Table 4-5.

TABLE 4-5 WINS OVERHEAD TRAFFIC OVERVIEW

Service	Bandwidth Used	When
NetBIOS client name registrations	approximately 10Kb per client	At startup, shutdown, and every three days
NetBIOS server name registrations	approximately 20Kb per server	At startup, shutdown, and every three days
WINS push/pull relationships	approximately 1Kb per relationship	At startup and as configured

TRAFFIC GENERATED BY WORKSTATIONS   All computers that use NetBIOS computer names must register those names before the TCP/IP stack may be loaded completely. When those computers are configured to use WINS servers (p-node type, m-node type, or h-node type), the name is registered with a WINS server. Generally, computers register multiple NetBIOS names: one for the computer name, one for the workgroup, and one for each service that may use NetBIOS to communicate on the network. For more information on NetBIOS names, please feel free to jump forward to Chapter 10, "NetBIOS: Friend or Foe."

Name registrations are a two-step process. First, the client directs a name registration request to the WINS server. This frame is 110 bytes long. The second step of the two-step process is the WINS confirmation to the client verifying that the name was registered successfully. The response frame is 104 bytes long. Therefore, a total of 214 bytes (1,712Kb) of network traffic is generated for each and every NetBIOS name that is registered by a Windows client. If an average client must register six NetBIOS names, more than 1,200 bytes of traffic are generated. These same names must be released when clients are shut down normally. This is rarely a problem, since Windows desktop machines tend to crash before they have a chance to shut down. (I'm *joking!*)

Further, Windows clients attempt to renew their NetBIOS names every three days. Three days is half of the default Time to Live (TTL) of a NetBIOS name. This detail is configured at the WINS server.

None of this is going to push even a relatively slow LAN such as a 10-Base-T, shared media network anywhere near full utilization. Even 200 clients starting at the same time of day (which is a very possible scenario in organizations where people shut down their desktop computers in the evenings) will only generate about two megabits of network traffic. These requests may swamp a WINS server, but they will not flood the network. Nonetheless, WINS registrations still use bandwidth, especially when you consider they are most likely to be registering during the mornings, when people will also be checking their e-mail and performing other high-bandwidth activities.

This traffic will impact the network the clients reside on and the network the WINS server resides on (if separated). Further, all routers that carry the traffic and any transitory network links will be burdened. This can become significant if performing WINS name registration across a WAN link, particularly a low-bandwidth link such as an analog modem connection, 56k leased line, or ISDN circuits. It can also become significant in a LAN environment where a single WINS server is being used to service large numbers of clients, or where multiple WINS servers are used but they reside on the same physical subnet. Figure 4-13 illustrates a network architecture where traffic convergence could become a problem.

There are several measures you can take to reduce the number of names that must be registered by clients. Because a name must be registered for each service that uses NetBIOS networking, set all unnecessary services to start up manually rather than automatically. The Messenger and Alerter services, in particular, register more names than any other service. There are other benefits to turning off unneeded services, of course, but for now we're just interested in bandwidth issues.

TRAFFIC GENERATED BY SERVERS WINS name registrations and renewals for servers are identical to those for clients; however, servers generally have many more names to be registered. An average server has a dozen NetBIOS names that must be registered, doubling the amount of network traffic generated per host. However, there are usually many more clients than servers on a network, so WINS name registration traffic generated by servers is generally much smaller than what is generated by the clients.

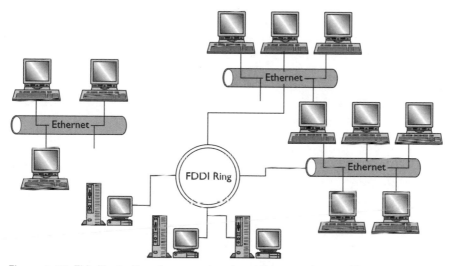

Figure 4-13: This illustration shows a network architecture where traffic convergence could become a problem.

Further, servers are rarely powered down in the evening and started up in the morning, so name renewals once every three days are the only opportunity to generate this type of traffic. Just as with clients, servers will benefit from having as many services set to start up manually as possible.

TRAFFIC GENERATED BY THE PUSH-PULL RELATIONSHIPS There are several scenarios in which it makes sense to have multiple WINS servers within a single organization. Indeed, you may even add WINS servers in an effort to reduce usage-based traffic generated by WINS clients. Though creating multiple WINS servers and moving them logically closer to the clients almost always results in traffic reduction, the communications between WINS servers also generate traffic. This overhead is used to ensure that WINS servers always have a common, accurate copy of the NetBIOS name database.

When you have multiple servers within a single organization, you should consider the following:

Establishing Relationships: When establishing a replication partnership between two WINS servers, you must assure that they greet each other before beginning the regular data exchange. This traffic is generated only at the time of the relationship establishment, so it will not have a significant long-term effect on bandwidth usage. Here is a description of what to expect:

A TCP session and an RPC session are created in turn. This generates seven frames totaling 836 bytes of traffic in a period of less than two seconds. Then the receiving server validates the requesting server, generating 580 bytes of traffic in four frames. At this point, the two servers are ready to begin replicating their databases. In total, eleven frames and 1,416 bytes of traffic are generated during the establishment of a WINS server relationship.

Replicating the Database: Once the servers have established a push or pull relationship, they are ready to begin replicating the database. The amount of traffic generated here is dependent on the size of the database; however, it is predictable.

Anytime a complete WINS database must be transferred, substantial traffic may be generated. This usually happens when the relationship is established, so keep this traffic in mind when setting up WINS servers. The first step in exchanging database information is to establish an RPC session. This requires about nine frames and 600 bytes of traffic. Afterward, the NetBIOS names are transmitted across the network, bundled into as few frames as possible. About fifty names may fit inside a single Ethernet frame.

This information allows us to predict the exact traffic patterns. In the following formulas, the variable Wn represents the number of NetBIOS names in the WINS database. An approximate formula for calculating the bytes of traffic generated by a full database replication is as follows:

```
600 + Wn / 50 * 20
```

An exact formula for calculating the frames generated by full database replication is as follows:

```
9 + Wn / 50 (round down)
```

Verifying the Database: After a full replication of the database occurs, there is no need for the WINS servers participating in a relationship to replicate the entire database. Therefore, WINS includes a feature that allows them to talk to each other and make sure that nothing has happened. This process creates twelve frames and roughly 900 bytes of traffic.

Updating the Database: When updates to the database occur on one WINS server, that update must be propagated to all other WINS servers that have established a relationship with that server. To update a single record, fourteen frames are generated totaling about 1,000 bytes of traffic. The number of bytes is somewhat variable depending on the number of names generated – add twenty bytes per name to the total byte count.

WINS USAGE-BASED TRAFFIC

WINS name resolution converts a computer name to an IP address. This allows a server to be contacted on a TCP/IP-based network when only the server's computer name is known. The amount of traffic generated over a period of time by WINS queries is impossible to estimate, but I will show you how much traffic is generated per query and give you some guidelines for estimating WINS query traffic within an organization.

Each WINS query requires about 200 bytes of traffic, in only two frames. In most cases, this is as simple as it seems: a single frame for the query, a single frame for the response. However, this traffic is compounded if a WINS proxy server is used and does not have the NetBIOS name cached.

The "average" user on a network will generate between 25 and 150 WINS queries in a full day of work, though this number varies greatly. Queries will be generated each time the user accesses a new resource, attempts to access a resource that has not been used recently, accesses an NT domain, or uses pass-through security to protect resources on the local system, as Table 4-6 shows.

TABLE 4-6 WINS USAGE-BASED TRAFFIC OVERVIEW

Service	Traffic Generated	When
Name Query	200 bytes	Each time a NetBIOS name that is not in the cache is needed
WINS Proxy Queries	200 bytes	Each time a WINS proxy attempts to resolve a name it does not have cached

NetBIOS name resolution can happen in one of two ways: NetBIOS broadcasts using the NetBIOS Name service, or WINS queries. In this section, our sample organization is relying on WINS, so I will focus on the impact of name queries on a network.

Similar to the way name registration takes place, name resolution requests are a two-step process initiated by clients. The client sends a single packet to the server, supplying a NetBIOS name to be resolved. Assuming the server receives the packet successfully, it returns a response, which includes the IP address of the server with the requested NetBIOS name. This entire conversation uses 196 bytes of traffic, or 1.5Kb.

To accurately estimate the impact these name requests will have on a network, you must understand how often these requests will be sent and what the traffic patterns look like. Name requests are transmitted from the client to the server every time a server must be contacted and the name does not already exist in the client's NetBIOS name cache. So anytime a user connects to a file server that user did not already have an open connection to, a NetBIOS name query and response are transmitted onto the network, generating 1.5Kb of traffic (before any communications to the file server even begin!). Each time a user prints to a printer that user hasn't used recently, a name query is generated. If a user checks for e-mail on an Exchange server, a name query is generated. This traffic, more than any other WINS-related traffic, uses a significant amount of bandwidth.

To reduce traffic caused by NetBIOS name queries, increase the NetBIOS name cache. The default timeout for the name cache is only ten minutes – this can easily be increased to as much as an hour. Clients will still have to query the WINS server when accessing a server for the first time, but subsequent requests for the same name will be reduced by one-sixth. The NetBIOS name cache can be adjusted by editing the value in the registry key (listed in milliseconds):

```
HKEY_LOCAL_MACHINE\SYSTEM\CurrentControlSet\Services\NetBT\Parameter
s\CacheTimeout.
```

Another method to reduce WINS traffic is to add names to the LMHOSTS file and force them to be preloaded into the name cache. In this way, names will reside permanently in the name cache. This is a real problem if the IP addresses of your servers change often, but it works well in stable environments. The LMHOSTS file, by default, is located in the WINNT\System32\drivers\etc\ directory. To make an entry preload itself into the name cache, add a #PRE to the end of a line.

Clients that have a NetBIOS name in the LMHOSTS file with the #PRE option will *never* perform a WINS query for that server's IP address. Of course, if you implemented LMHOSTS entries for every system on your network, you would not need WINS at all, right? This is really not that bad an idea, but for those who enjoy the benefits of WINS, you should still consider adding the NetBIOS names and IP addresses of your most commonly accessed server to the LMHOSTS files of your clients. Once you start doing this, you need to be sure you will never change an IP address. Of course, you should never change IP addresses around anyway.

DNS

DNS, though much older than WINS, is only beginning to be a common method for name resolution on Microsoft networks. Nonetheless, DNS can be a source of substantial network traffic when Microsoft networks are tightly integrated with the public Internet or when the organization has opted to use DNS for NetBIOS name resolution in lieu of traditional WINS name resolution. DNS, both as a client and as a server, does not generate any overhead. Therefore, all DNS traffic is usage based.

DNS traffic is much simpler than most types of traffic because it relies on UDP as its transport-layer protocol. UDP avoids the handshaking necessary to establish a connection from the client to the server. Because DNS uses UDP, a DNS query requires a minimum of two frames — one for the query and one for the answer.

These frames vary in size depending on the name being queried and the type of result being returned, but a typical query frame is seventy-five bytes long. The response tends to be between 75 and 400 bytes, depending on how many DNS entries have been configured.

At its simplest, a full DNS conversation requires two frames and less than 500 bytes of data. However, it becomes more complicated if the server queried does not have the answer to the query. If the DNS server cannot respond to the query, it performs a recursive lookup — in essence, it becomes a DNS client itself and queries the next DNS server upstream for the answer. These queries are exactly the same as the query that originated from the client, so each recursive query multiplies the total traffic very neatly.

Similar to the recursive query process just described, DNS servers can be configured to query WINS servers if a query from a client fails. In this instance, the total traffic generated is increased by the traffic required for a single WINS lookup — about 200 bytes. The various types of traffic that can be generated as a result of a DNS query are outlined in Table 4-7.

TABLE 4-7 DNS TRAFFIC REQUIREMENTS PER QUERY

Circumstance	Bandwidth Used
The first DNS server that answers the query	150–500 bytes
Each additional DNS server that must be queried	150–500 bytes
Each WINS server that must be queried	196 bytes

BROWSER SERVICE

The Browser service is a method built into Microsoft's Windows-based operating systems to allow them to announce themselves on a network and to enumerate a list of available services. It is a nightmare for anybody who cares about network usage, because it is enabled by default and produces mostly broadcast traffic. So whether or not an organization makes use of the Browser service, it is probably at work, eating your precious bandwidth.

This section describes how much bandwidth the Browser service uses and gives you formulas to be used for capacity planning. If you are reading this section, you should have already decided that the Browser service is a critical part of your network's functionality. If you have not yet made this decision, then skip this section and simply disable the Browser service on all your systems. I have always felt that the Browser service costs more in terms of bandwidth waste than it makes up in convenience. I am of the philosophy that users should only use resources on the network when they are looking for something specific – the Browser service operates on a totally opposite philosophy, encouraging users to poke around and see what others on the network have made available. In this way, the Browser service is not only wasteful but encourages weak security practices.

BROWSER OVERHEAD   Windows NT systems that have the Browser service running generate six frames of traffic upon startup specifically for the Browser service. Thereafter, one 229-byte frame is generated every twelve minutes, as the server reannounces its presence to the network. These frames are broadcast whether or not the system is actually sharing anything to the public.

BROWSER USAGE-BASED TRAFFIC   When a user on a Windows NT system retrieves a browse list (for example, by opening Network Neighborhood), additional traffic is generated. The client computer must locate the local master browser and retrieve a list of backup browsers. Then it must create a connection to a backup browser and retrieve the list of shared resources.

To get a list of backup browsers from the master browser, two frames are transmitted. The first frame is a broadcast frame of roughly 210 bytes. Ideally, the master browser receives this frame and responds with a frame 200 to 300 bytes in length, depending on the number of backup browsers. Once the client has a list of backup browsers, one of these backup browsers will be contacted to retrieve a list of available resources on the network. Retrieving this list requires between fifteen and twenty frames and uses more than 2,000 bytes of traffic.

After the user identifies a specific host he or she wishes to browse, the user will double-click on that computer's name within Network Neighborhood. This initiates a query from the user's system to the server to retrieve a list of available resources. This is part of the network browsing process but is not dependant on the Browser service (that is, you may view a list of available resources on a system regardless of whether or not its Browser service is started). The amount of traffic generated to retrieve this list varies but is roughly eighteen frames totaling more than 4,000 bytes of traffic. The traffic a user generates when using Network Neighborhood is summarized in Table 4-8.

TABLE 4-8 BROWSING A NETWORK

Action	Frames Generated	Bytes Transmitted
Opening Network Neighborhood	~20	~2,500
Viewing available resources on a specific server	~18	~4,000

DOMAIN USER ACCOUNT AUTHENTICATIONS

One of the greatest features of Windows NT is the domain structure, which allows for centralized user authentication. This is very convenient for users and desirable from the perspective of a systems engineer. The network engineer may frown on centralized *anything* on a network, however, because network requests must be made anytime the resource is used.

Authentication requests are made to a domain controller, either the primary domain controller or the backup domain controller. These requests are made under the following circumstances:

◆ A user logs into a Windows system using a domain account.

◆ A user attempts to access a resource on a remote file or printer server using a domain account.

◆ A user attempts to access a resource on a Web server using a domain account.

Windows 95 clients and Windows NT-based clients have similar network authentication mechanisms but produce different amounts of traffic. Table 4-9 provides a summary of the traffic produced on a network when authentication is provided.

TABLE 4-9 TRAFFIC PRODUCED BY AUTHENTICATION

Service	Traffic
Windows 95 domain user authentication	8KB
Windows NT domain user authentication	8KB
Roaming profiles	300KB+
Persistent drives	3KB
Logon scripts	50KB+

WINDOWS 95 NETWORK CLIENTS   The first step in validating a domain user is the same for both Windows 95 and Windows NT. The client computer must establish a session with the computer that will perform the authentication. Windows 95 clients may submit authentication requests to a domain controller or to any Windows NT computer.

Windows 95 clients transmit two frames and receive two frames when a user initially logs on. The first frame requests logon validation from the source specified under the field labeled Obtain List of Users and Groups From in the Network Control Panel applet. The server returns a single frame as a response, carrying either a positive or negative answer. Assuming the authentication request is successful, the Windows 95 machine will query the server to determine the difference in time zones between the two machines, so that file stamps can be dated correctly. This communication requires another packet for the query, and a fourth packet for the response from the server.

These communications alone use approximately 765 bytes (6,120KB) of bandwidth. Above and beyond that, the Windows 95 machine must locate the server that will perform the authentication. If the Windows 95 machine is configured to use WINS, that query will use about 214 bytes (1,712KB) of network traffic.

In total, logging into a Windows 95 machine without downloading a roaming profile or logon script generates about 45 frames of traffic. If the client is configured for b-type or m-type name resolution, seven of these frames are broadcast frames. Five of these broadcast frames are involved in registering the username on the network for the Messenger service, and two are used to locate the domain controller. In total, the Windows 95 client transmits about 3,750 bytes, and the domain controller returns about 3,500 bytes. Table 4-10 summarizes these communications.

TABLE 4-10 WINDOWS 95 CLIENT LOGON

Frame Type	# Frames	# Bytes
Broadcast	7	1,100
Directed, Client to Domain Controller	27	3,750
Directed, Domain Controller to Client	21	3,500

After the authentication has been performed successfully, the Windows 95 machine has other tasks that need to be performed. If the user has a roaming profile, that profile must be downloaded from the server. Though the exact amount of traffic generated varies depending on how much information is stored in the user's roaming profile, a typical profile creates about 850 frames, and 250KB will be used to download the various settings, including the user desktop, start menu, and favorites shortcuts. Naturally, if the user has stored a 10MB file on the desktop, more will need to be transferred. Nonetheless, for estimation purposes, 850 frames/250KB traffic works well.

If the user has been assigned a logon script, it must be downloaded. The client has already created a session to the domain controller's NETLOGON share in order to look for the CONFIG.POL file, so the only traffic involved is the transfer of the logon script itself and the NetBIOS handshaking. Still, this amounts to a total of 12 frames and about 1,600 bytes of traffic, plus the size of the logon script.

If the user has persistent network connections, each of those network connections must be reestablished. In the simplest case scenario, the Windows 95 machine is reestablishing file or printer connections directly to the domain controller to which it is communicating; in this case, only two frames are exchanged: a request from the client and a response from the server, totaling about 230 bytes of traffic per shared directory or printer.

If persistent network connections are not on the domain controller that is validating the user, additional frames are required to create a NetBIOS session and connect to each network directory. This, in turn, can cause the servers to whom the connections are being established to authenticate the user to a domain controller. Nine frames are required for a Windows 95 client to create a NetBIOS session, authenticate itself, and connect to a shared drive on a server. These nine frames account for about 1,100 bytes of traffic. Additionally, the server must pass the authentication request to the domain controller. This dialog involves three frames travelling in each direction, for a total of six frames and almost 1,700 bytes of traffic. This usage is summarized in Table 4-11.

TABLE 4-11 WINDOWS 95 BANDWIDTH USED AFTER AUTHENTICATION

Purpose	# Frames	# Bytes
Transfer logon script	12	1,600+logon script size
Reconnect to share on authenticating domain controller	2	230
Reconnect to share on a domain member computer	15	2,800

In summary, do not forget to count Windows 95 clients in the bandwidth usage analysis. They produce a substantial amount of predictable traffic besides the network applications the users may make use of. This traffic needs to be monitored and optimized just like anything else — it is not significant on networks with only a dozen users. However, enterprise networks with thousands of users can experience heavy bandwidth during periods of exceptionally high authentication frequency — such as early morning, when your users are strolling into the office and logging onto their system. The users on your network and their desktop operating systems cause this "rush hour" network traffic more than anything else.

WINDOWS NT   Validating a user logging onto a Windows NT client is similar to the process used with a Windows 95 client, except a few additional steps are added. The first step is unique to Windows NT, because NT offers a drop-down list of available domains from the Ctrl+Alt+Delete logon prompt, which Windows 95 does not offer. In order to populate this drop-down list, Windows NT clients must perform a query to obtain the list of trusted domains from their domain controller. This query process consists of 15 directed frames, totaling about 2,400 bytes of traffic. This number varies depending on the number of trusts that may exist within your organization.

The next step is to create a NetBIOS communications session between the client and a domain controller capable of validating the logon. The client is forced to validate itself as a member of the proper domain before it may begin to submit logon requests. This conversation creates about 1,400 bytes of traffic.

Finally, the client will submit the logon request itself. This part of the conversation consists of only two frames: one query to the domain controller and one response to the client. These two frames total about 900 bytes. Table 4-12 summarizes Windows NT client logon conversions.

TABLE 4-12 WINDOWS NT CLIENT LOGON SUMMARY

Frame Type	# Frames	# Bytes
Broadcast	7	1,100
Directed, Client to Domain Controller	27	3,750
Directed, Domain Controller to Client	21	3,500

In summary, logging onto a Windows NT workstation or server using a domain account generates a total of about 4,300 bytes of traffic before logon scripts and user profiles are downloaded. After authentication, Windows NT client computers behave much like Windows 95 machines. Traffic generated by NT clients as part of the logon process but after the user has been authenticated are detailed in Table 4-13.

TABLE **4–13** WINDOWS NT BANDWIDTH USED AFTER AUTHENTICATION

Purpose	# Frames	# Bytes
Transfer logon script	12	1,600+logon script size
Reconnect to share on authenticating domain controller	2	230
Reconnect to share on a domain member computer	15	2,800

REDUCING NETWORK TRAFFIC FOR AUTHENTICATIONS   There are several easy steps you can take to reduce the amount of network traffic created during user authentications. First, locate domain controllers as close to the users as possible. Ideally, each network segment would share an interface with a domain controller. An easy way to implement this without having to manage dozens of separate domain controllers is to add additional network interface cards to each domain controller, as shown in Figure 4-14. NICs are inexpensive and simple to implement — if networks are physically close together, take advantage of NT's multihoming ability and add a network card for each of your most busy network segments.

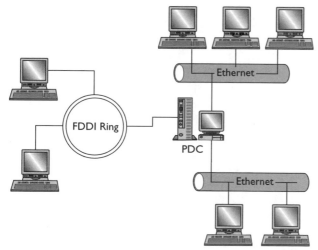

Figure 4–14: This illustration shows the results of adding additional network interface cards to each domain controller.

Besides moving domain controllers closer to the users, you can reduce network traffic during logons by not using services that centralize data. For example, roaming profiles and logon scripts are stored on the domain controllers and downloaded by the clients at the time the user logs onto the system. If you currently have this configuration, do a quick audit of the user profiles. You will find that many users have placed really big files on their desktop — for example, a user may have copied a 6MB QuickTime movie a friend e-mailed. This file must be downloaded each and every time the user logs onto his or her Windows 95 system (which may be quite often, considering how many times a day Windows 95 crashes!).

If you cannot do away with roaming profiles completely, definitely do the audit of the user profiles. Make sure that users are not placing huge files into their user profiles by using the Advanced tab of the Find Files or Folders utility within Windows NT. Try searching for files larger than 200K, and see what you find! Not only is this data transferred to the client when a user logs on, but it is transferred to the server when the user logs off.

Disabling persistent network connections or the Reconnect at Startup option is another way to reduce bandwidth usage during initial logons. NetBIOS connections produce a great deal of network traffic, and many of your users may end up using every drive letter available to mount a remote directory. (*I know I do!!*) If you disable reconnecting these sessions at startup, users may still access every single drive and produce the same amount of traffic, but at least it will be spread out more evenly throughout their sessions, reducing the load on the network during periods of peak usage.

TRUST RELATIONSHIPS

Trust relationships allow domains to exchange user information. They are commonly used in environments that use Microsoft's traditional master domain model, which specifies that user accounts and resource accounts be divided into separate domains. Trusts are also commonly created when two companies merge or when two remote offices begin networking with each other — user accounts in existing domains require access to the other domain's resources, so the administrators configure a trust relationship between the domains. This can become more interesting than it may first appear, however, because these logical trusts often cross physical WAN links — links that have very scarce and possibly very expensive bandwidth. A summary of the bandwidth used is provided in Table 4-14.

TABLE 4-14 SUMMARY OF TRUST-RELATED TRAFFIC

Activity	Frames	Bytes
Establishing the trust	125	17,000
Pass-through authentication	2	850
PDC startup	17	2,300
Assigning access rights	125	22,500

ESTABLISHING THE TRUST   Even organizations that have gone trust-crazy and utilize models such as Microsoft's Complete Trust domain model will not generate so much traffic establishing these trusts that they need to build bandwidth estimates into any kind of network plan. In fact, it only takes a matter of seconds to establish a trust over a 28.8 dial-up link! If you are interested, establishing a trust causes about 125 frames, totaling more than 17,000 bytes of network traffic. Nothing to disregard entirely, but it shouldn't be a daily event, either.

ONGOING BANDWIDTH REQUIREMENTS   Trusts generate very little traffic during their initial creation, but they magnify the bandwidth requirements of many common network activities. Anytime a user logs onto a system using an account that exists in a trusted domain, pass-through authentication must occur. Anytime a user attempts to access a resource in a domain that trusts that user's domain, an intertrust validation takes place. Finally, when administrators assign permissions to resources using user and global group accounts that exist in a trusted domain, the user account list must be transferred.

USER LOGONS   If someone wishes to log onto a machine or access resources on a remote computer using a user account from a domain other than the domain the machine resides in, additional traffic will result as the authentication request is passed from the Windows NT system's domain to the user's domain. The processes used by requests to log onto a computer and requests to access network resources are slightly different, but the bandwidth footprints are very similar. Please keep in mind that the system's domain must trust the user's domain for the option to appear at all.

The bandwidth consumed by logging on using a user account from a trusted domain comes as a result of two distinct processes: establishing a secure communications channel between the primary domain controllers and authenticating each user. The paragraphs that follow describe only the traffic that happens above and beyond the traffic that would occur if the user were logging onto a domain account that was in the same domain as the Windows NT computer.

The first process is fairly costly bandwidth-wise, using about 3,500 bytes of traffic in twenty frames. Fortunately, this does not occur for each authentication attempt: Once a secure channel is established, it will be used for any future authentications.

The second process must be performed each and every time someone from a trusted domain needs to be authenticated. It consists of two frames: a request for an authentication frame and a response from the trusted domain. These two frames require less than 1,000 bytes of data total and are transmitted directly between the primary domain controllers of the trusted/trusting domains.

ASSIGNING PERMISSIONS TO TRUSTED ACCOUNTS   When a user in a trusting domain wants to give a user in a trusted domain access to resources, the user interface provides the trusting user with a list of users and global groups in the trusted domain.

Naturally, this data has to come from somewhere. Specifically, the trusting domain controller requests the list of users and groups from the trusted domain controller. Assuming the trust relationship is still in effect, the list is transferred to the trusting domain controller. The trusting domain controller then returns the list to the user that requested it.

This process generates a substantial amount of traffic between the domain controllers. At a minimum, ninety frames are generated, amounting to about 20,000 bytes of data. Initially, the Windows NT user interface displays only the global groups from the trusted domain; user accounts are not shown. This is done to minimize the amount of data that must be transferred – so, if you need to assign permissions to specific users and press the Show Users button, additional network traffic is generated. If the number of users in the domain is minimal (*really* minimal; small enough for the entire user list to fit inside a packet), only five packets totaling 1,500 bytes are transmitted in the conversation. However, the more users you have, the more packets and data will be transferred.

After you select users and groups to add to the access control list, more data will be exchanged. To add a single user or group, nineteen frames will be exchanged totaling slightly more than 2,300 bytes.

This isn't the end of the bandwidth costs a trust generates. Each and every time someone views or edits the access list of a resource that includes a user or group account from a trusted domain, data transfers must take place. For example, merely viewing the ACL of a protected resource that includes user and group accounts from a trusted domain generates 200 frames of traffic between the domain controllers! If you ever wondered why it takes *soooo* long to view the ACL on a computer, this is why.

SUMMARY: THE REAL COSTS OF A TRUST   The amount of traffic a trust adds to the network depends on the network architecture, how much trusted accounts are used, and the manner in which those accounts are used. There are many factors, making an accurate estimate next to impossible. However, you can create a reasonable estimate if you can anticipate exactly how many of the user accounts in use will be accessing resources through a domain trust.

Now that you have an understanding of the network traffic generated by the various trust-related activities, does it change your perspective on domain design? It should. Microsoft's recommended master domain model is extremely wasteful of network resources. In this model, all "resources" (file, print, and application servers) exist in a resource domain. All user accounts exist in the master domain. Consider the amount of traffic that will be generated when a systems administrator assigns permissions to a resource file server *above and beyond* what would be necessary if the users and resources existed in the same domain. This traffic is summarized in Table 4-15.

TABLE 4-15 EXTRA TRAFFIC GENERATED WHEN ASSIGNING PERMISSIONS USING THE MASTER DOMAIN MODEL

Step	Action	Frames	Bytes
1	Connect to the resource server's shared drive	2	850
2	View the user list from the master domain	200	30,000
3	Assign permissions	25	1,500
Total		257	32,350

Now, consider how many times a day an administrator performs this action!

FILE AND PRINTER SHARING

When Windows NT was first becoming popular as a network operating system, its most common uses were as a file and printer server. The trend towards internetworking and Internet applications instead of traditional Microsoft network applications has changed this somewhat, but many organizations still make use of Windows NT to share files and printers among workgroups and even enterprise networks.

This traffic can consume a significant portion of the total network bandwidth, depending on how it is used. Organizations that make use of centralized file storage may find the performance of their workstations bottlenecked by the performance of the network: If every file request must be sent to a central file server, the network will quickly become saturated. Strong network design can help a great deal. This section will give you the information you need to estimate the total bandwidth used by the different file sharing applications, and it will give you an important understanding of how SMB traffic flows.

NAME RESOLUTION   Anytime a user connects to a new server, name resolution must be performed to translate the friendly name the user knows the server by into the IP address that will be used to identify the server on a network. Exactly how this is done varies depending on the type of request the user makes and the network's configuration. This may consist of a WINS query, a DNS query, or nothing at all, if the host already knows the IP address of the destination server. This traffic is summarized in Table 4-16.

TABLE 4-16 NAME RESOLUTION BANDWIDTH REQUIREMENTS

Service	Frames	Bytes Transmitted
Precached in LMHOSTS	0	0
WINS	2	200
NetBIOS using IP address	25	2,000
DNS	27	2,400

ESTABLISHING A SESSION   Once the client knows the IP address of the server, it is ready to send directed messages and establish a session. Establishing a NetBIOS session requires about 11 frames, totaling 1,300 bytes of network traffic between the client and the server. If the user is accessing the server with a domain user account and the server is not a domain controller, the server will have to authenticate the user to a domain controller at an additional cost of six frames and 1,700 bytes of traffic.

Establishing a session is different from establishing a connection. A client need only establish a single session to a server, regardless of how many connections the user may create. For example, if a user wishes to connect to three shared directories on a single server, the session is established once and three connections are created. Remember, NetBIOS connections are one-way only. More information on NetBIOS sessions and connections can be found in Chapter 10.

ESTABLISHING A CONNECTION   Once a client has established a NetBIOS session to a server, it may begin to create connections. A connection is created every time the client attempts to use a unique share on a particular server. For example, accessing the shares \\server\c$, \\server\d$, and \\server\netlogon requires three individual connections.

To create a connection, two frames are transmitted. The first is a request from the client to the server; the second is the server's response. Together, these frames are about 250 bytes long. Above and beyond the SMB frames the servers exchange, ARP and TCP packets may be transferred. For the purpose of estimating traffic usage, assume that six frames total must be exchanged (two ARP, two TCP, two SMB) for a total of 450 bytes of network traffic.

TRANSFERRING FILES   Ever wonder how much network traffic is generated when a file is transferred using a NetBIOS connection? This section will answer that question, show you how much bandwidth is actually wasted, and describe ways of making the process more efficient.

Have you ever gone to one of those big discount stores? Whenever I go I get excited and end up buying everything in bulk, like 20 boxes of plastic forks. This usually ends up saving me a few dollars compared to what I would pay if I bought all those plastic forks individually. The point I'm getting to here is that waste decreases with size – usually, doing things in a big way is more efficient than doing them on a small scale.

This rule holds true for NetBIOS file transfers. Transfers of files less than 1K use a minimum of 27 frames and about 4,000 bytes of network data. Those extra 3,000 bytes are the overhead that NetBIOS and TCP/IP provide – establishing communications and wrapping the data in data-link, network, transport, and session layer overhead. As the file being transferred gets larger, the protocol overhead takes proportionately less of the total data being transferred. While protocol overhead makes up about 95 percent of the total data transferred when sending a 250-byte file, files more than 100K waste less than 10 percent. Table 4-17 summarizes the data transmitted during various NetBIOS file transfers.

TABLE 4-17 BANDWIDTH USED BY FILE TRANSFER SIZE

File Size	Frames	Bytes from Server	Bytes from Client	Total Bytes	Overhead (%)
250	27	2,162	1,889	4,051	94%
1,000	27	2,898	1,847	4,745	79%
5K	30	6.3K	1.9K	8.2K	39%
10K	36	12.5K	2K	14.5K	31%

Continued

TABLE 4–17 BANDWIDTH USED BY FILE TRANSFER SIZE *(Continued)*

File Size	Frames	Bytes from Server	Bytes from Client	Total Bytes	Overhead (%)
15K	40	17.2K	2.2K	19.4K	23%
25K	51	28K	2K	30K	17%
49K	76	54K	3K	57K	14%
131K	166	137K	5K	143K	9.2%
444K	498	473K	11K	484K	8.3%
10,220K	11,211	11,008K	243K	11,251K	9.1%

DOMAIN SYNCHRONIZATION

Domain synchronization is the process of exchanging security information between the primary domain controller and the backup domain controllers within a single domain. These communications occur when initiated by a systems engineer and on a regular, reoccurring basis. These synchronizations are very configurable, so if you determine that the bandwidth requirements are inappropriate, please keep in mind that they may be adjusted. Further, the domain database is transferred when a new backup domain controller is added to the domain.

Which Protocol Is More Efficient?

There are three popular protocols for transferring files on Windows NT networks—NetBIOS, FTP, and HTTP. Which of these is the most efficient?

For most files, anonymous HTTP is the most efficient protocol. There is very little handshaking that needs to be done—the client simply makes a request and the server returns the file. For a 250-byte file, HTTP has an overhead of 78 percent. This doesn't sound too good, but it's pretty efficient compared to FTP and NetBIOS over TCP/IP. For that same small file, FTP wastes 85 percent of the bytes transmitted on overhead. NetBIOS over TCP/IP is the biggest hog of all—wasting more than 94 percent of the total bandwidth used on overhead. To make matters worse, that 94 percent waste is achieved after a NetBIOS session and connection have already been established—the figures for FTP and HTTP both include establishing a session! Including the overhead of establishing a NetBIOS connection, 5,360 bytes were transferred to copy a 250-byte file! This means that 95.3 percent waste was achieved in the file transfer!

Larger files, of course, are more efficient. All three protocols achieve between 9 and 10 percent wasted bandwidth on files more than 250K in size.

BACKUP DOMAIN CONTROLLER STARTUP TRAFFIC   Several steps are involved in transferring a database between a PDC and a BDC. Several of these steps will seem obvious, because they must occur anytime data is transferring using a NetBIOS connection. These steps are:

1. Locate the PDC. This step is only performed when a backup domain controller is started; once the BDC locates the PDC, it caches the address for later use. This entire conversation creates about 741 bytes of traffic between the PDC and the BDC.

2. Establish a NetBIOS session. The BDC initiates a standard NetBIOS connection to the PDC's IPC$ share. Refer to the section "File and Printer Sharing" later in this chapter for the details of establishing a NetBIOS session, but estimate that 1,200 bytes of traffic and nine frames will be transmitted.

3. Establish a secure channel. The secure channel is established using the NetBIOS session created in step 2. Oddly, this channel will outlive the NetBIOS session — only a single secure channel is created each time a BDC boots. If the NetBIOS session is dropped, the secure channel within it needs to be verified again only when the session is reestablished. In all, the initial connection requires eight frames be exchanged, for a total of 1,550 bytes of information transfer.

4. Verify the database. The user accounts database must be verified each time a BDC starts up, just to make sure nothing has changed since the BDC was last online. This is a complicated process, and the bandwidth used will vary depending on the number of changes that have occurred in the user database since the BDC last synchronized its database. The best-case scenario is that no changes have been made. Even in this case, about 1,500 bytes are transferred between the BDC and the PDC.

BACKUP DOMAIN CONTROLLER ONGOING TRAFFIC   After startup, BDCs verify their user database on a regular basis. The frequency of this verification is configurable through a series of registry parameters, but I will outline the bandwidth requirements for the default configurations. Your results may vary!

A PDC with the default configuration checks its user database every five minutes, and if it finds an update, it sends a message to all BDCs that have a database version older than the PDC's. It is then a BDC's responsibility to retrieve the update from the PDC.

Assuming the BDC has maintained its connection to the PDC, the first step the BDC takes is to establish a NetBIOS connection to the NetLogon share of the PDC and check to see if the account database really does require updating. This exchange uses four frames and about 700 bytes of network traffic. After the connection has been established, the updates must be transferred. The amount of traffic required for updates depends on the amount of updates that have taken place, but a single user account update combined with the protocol overhead amounts to a minimum of ten frames. You can count on this traffic to total more than 2,500 bytes.

TWEAKING DOMAIN SYNCHRONIZATION   Several registry parameters may be adjusted on a domain controller to alter the way network communications take place. These registry parameters can only do so much — when a change is made to the account database, those changes simply have to be replicated outward. You can adjust how much is transferred at a single time, how often the domain controllers check for updates, and how many updates may be transmitted concurrently, but you cannot reduce the amount of data that needs to be transferred — that is entirely dependent on the number of changes and additions made to the PDC's account database.

All the registry values discussed here should be added to the `HKEY_LOCAL_MACHINE\SYSTEM\CurrentControlSet\Services\Netlogon\Parameters` registry key. None of these registry keys exist by default.

Pulse: When the Pulse value is added to the registry of the primary domain controller, the administrator has the ability to control how often the PDC searches its account database for changes that need to be replicated to the backup domain controllers. If this registry value does not exist, this process occurs every five minutes. This value is an excellent place to start when you are attempting to reduce the total bandwidth consumed by directory synchronizations. By reducing the number of times updates are replicated between domain controllers, you arrange that more updates will be sent in each batch of changes. Because protocol overhead makes up the majority of the total traffic in these types of transfers, transmitting more changes at once substantially increases the efficiency of the communications protocol. The fact is, most administrators force a domain synchronization from the Server Manager utility after making a change that needs to take effect right away — in this case, the bandwidth is going to be used anyway. When a change is not forced, the updates may take longer to become available throughout an enterprise network — but apparently there wasn't a hurry anyway.

ReplicationGovernor: The number contained in the ReplicationGovernor registry value is expressed as a percentage — the percentage of the total bandwidth available on a link that will be used by domain synchronization traffic. If this registry value does not exist in the registry, 100 percent of the bandwidth may be used. This value also controls the frequency of synchronization messages. For example, if a value of 75 is entered for the RegistrationGovernor registry value, 75 percent of the available bandwidth may be consumed and synchronization requests from the PDC will occur every three minutes and forty-five seconds (75 percent of five minutes).

ChangeLogSize: Understanding the effects of modifying this registry entry requires understanding how updates are propagated to backup domain controllers. If you are familiar with transaction-oriented databases, then you are already familiar with the concept of a database log, which is nothing more than a file that records recent transactions to a database. The account database on a primary domain controller keeps such a log, using it to remember when certain changes were made to the account database so that it can update backup domain controllers as needed. Because the primary domain controller can examine the log and determine exactly what has changed since it last talked to a particular BDC, the PDC only needs to transmit updates.

So what happens if this log file fills up before a backup domain controller receives the updates? The PDC cannot determine the exact differences between its database and the database located on the BDC, so it must retransmit the entire user database! This is quite a large transaction in an enterprise network, which may have tens of thousands of user and group accounts. So to avoid overfilling the change log, its size may be altered by altering this registry entry. If this entry has not been added, the size of the log is 64K. You should feel comfortable doubling this value in environments where the log file may become entirely filled before all updates have been completed – this may happen as a result of having an extremely slow update frequency (through the modification of the Pulse or Replication Governor values) or of having an extreme number of account database changes (such as changing the value in every user's Full Name field all at once).

PulseMaximum: By default, the PDC sends a pulse message to all its BDCs every two hours, whether they need it or not. This number can be increased, but because it is not a significant source of bandwidth consumption, few bother. The maximum value for this registry entry is forty-eight hours.

PulseConcurrency: By default, a primary domain controller will notify ten backup domain controllers of changes to the account database simultaneously. If you feel that network problems are a result of the primary domain controller flooding the network with huge bursts of updates, feel free to decrease this number. You will not decrease the amount of network traffic that must be sent on the network, but you may spread it around a little more evenly.

DHCP

DHCP, the Dynamic Host Configuration Protocol, allows IP-based clients to be dynamically assigned an IP address at startup. While this process is not a significant source of network traffic, it is worth noting here. DHCP generates network traffic when clients are initially starting and on a regular basis thereafter as they renew their DHCP lease.

DHCP AT STARTUP   The process a DHCP client goes through to retrieve an IP address from a DHCP server is, at its simplest, a two-step, two-way conversation. The first step starts with the client transmitting a packet called a DHCP Discover. This query is the only broadcast frame that will be transmitted during this conversation; it is 342 bytes long. If things are working the way they are supposed to, a DHCP server or proxy agent will see the broadcast DHCP Discovery query and will respond with a DHCP Offer frame. This frame, also 342 bytes long, is directed to the DHCP client. If there are multiple DHCP servers or proxies on a single segment, as there may be if redundancy is desired, each of the servers will transmit a DHCP Offer frame.

At this point in the dialog, the client chooses one of the servers it received DHCP Offers from and returns a directed frame called a DHCP Request. The server that receives the request responds with a DHCP ACK frame, which includes additional information the client will need.

From this information, we can build a formula to determine exactly how much bandwidth a single client will consume when starting up. There are a couple of variables: If a DHCP server does not respond to the first request from a DHCP client, the client will create more DHCP Discovery frames. Each frame is 342 bytes, so this becomes a variable in the formula. The second variable is the number of DHCP servers on the network segment. Each server within the same broadcast domain should respond to the DHCP Discovery request, creating 342 bytes of traffic for each server.

```
684 bytes + (# DHCP servers on the segment) * (342 bytes) + (# DHCP
  Discovery packets required) * (342 bytes) = Total Number of Bytes
  Transmitted across a Network
```

   or

```
8,208 bits + (# DHCP servers on the segment) * (2,736 bits) + (#
  DHCP Discovery packets required) * (2,736 bits) = Total Number of
  Bits Transmitted across a Network
```

A common situation and the best-case scenario is a configuration with a single DHCP server on a subnet that always responds to the first request from a DHCP client. In this case, 1,368 bytes, or 10,944 bits, are transmitted, one-fourth of which are broadcast packets.

DHCP RENEWALS   DHCP clients need to let the DHCP server know, on a regular basis, that they are still using a particular IP address. This process is called the DHCP renewal process; by default, it occurs every thirty-six hours. It also may occur in place of the DHCP Startup procedures described in the previous section if a DHCP client was assigned a DHCP IP address previously — the next time the computer starts up, it will simply attempt to renew the last IP address it had, rather than requesting a brand new one.

DHCP renewals use half the traffic of an initial DHCP request because the first step (DHCP Discovery and DHCP Offer) is skipped. Instead, the client transmits a directed packet to the DHCP server, the DHCP Request, and the server returns an answer indicating that the lease was renewed, the DHCP ACK. Obviously, there are other case scenarios, such as a lease that cannot be renewed or an unresponsive DHCP server — these cases are exceptions to the general rule and do not need to be considered when planning for bandwidth requirements.

While very little can be done to reduce the bandwidth used by DHCP clients at startup, DHCP renewals are very adjustable. It is probably not worth the effort to adjust these, because they generate very little traffic and problems can arise if the lease renewal period is set too long. Nonetheless, if you wish to adjust this value, it can be done using the DHCP Manager by adjusting the value in the Lease Duration field in the Scope Properties dialog box.

Estimating Based on User Type

How your users use your network resources is as important as *what* resources they use. You, the network engineer, have a great deal of control over how much bandwidth is used by your users. As you add features that use the network, users will (hopefully!) take advantage of them. Each feature will increase the load on your network, and the more popular it is, the more of a burden it will be. For example, if you implement file storage standards such that all users connect to a network drive located on a central file server and read and write all documents from that server, network bandwidth consumed by file sharing protocols will be very high.

You can also control how much bandwidth users consume by restricting what they can do. If you are concerned about users wasting bandwidth on the corporate Internet connection by listening to radio transmissions from the Internet, take it away from them! If you think all your bandwidth is being used by people who play Solitaire on the network, take it away!

Your bandwidth requirements will vary wildly depending on who your typical user is. For example, if you are administering a LAN that is used by thirty network engineers, your demands will be much higher than if thirty contract workers use the LAN to perform data-entry. After you profile a "typical" user, keep the figures in Table 4-18 in mind to profile the exceptions.

TABLE 4–18 NON–TYPICAL USER BANDWIDTH REQUIREMENTS

User Type	Bandwidth Requirement Compared to Typical User
Systems administrators	350%
Network administrators	450%
Temporary, short-term, nontechnical employees	30%

Reducing Utilization by Lowering Traffic

The best way to improve the performance of your network is to improve the efficiency of it! In most cases, the only cost is the man-hours required to make the change. Granted, those man hours may be costly and numerous, but tweaking the network for performance is preferable to upgrading hardware.

For most people, NT provides an excellent default configuration. There is no change that I can suggest for every single environment that will make it more efficient. However, I would like to mention several common bandwidth-intensive activities that may be improved on.

Name Resolution

As computers reach out to each other on networks, their names are constantly being resolved. With Microsoft-based networks, name resolution happens at several levels using DNS, NetBIOS name query broadcasts, WINS, and ARP. Besides following the advice in the Network Architecture section that follows, keep these things in mind:

1. Cache as much as possible. All of the protocols previously described can use some form of caching. In each case, the length of time the names are cached should be increased.

2. Reduce the number of protocols. Relying on DNS queries for all name resolutions can eliminate WINS and NetBIOS name queries.

3. Allow each host to resolve names locally. Adding names to the LMHOSTS and HOSTS files can do this.

WWW Intranet

As HTTP-based intranets become more and more common, many administrators are discovering that a great deal of their total network traffic is caused by Web browsers and Web servers. The Webmaster actually has a great deal of control over this traffic. Consider the following points to reduce HTTP-based traffic on an intranet:

1. Enable HTTP-KeepAlives. This reduces the TCP session establishment traffic that must be exchanged.

2. Reduce the size and number of images.

3. Compress files whenever possible. This means using compressed image formats and "ZIPping" large files before allowing them to be downloaded.

4. Implement proxy caching. Proxy caches can be used in large organizations to reduce the amount of traffic bound for an intranet server.

5. Increase the caching on the client. By storing intranet files on the end users' computers, the Web browser does not need to transfer the same file over and over again.

Network Architecture

Network architecture has an impact on every single protocol used on a network. A good network architecture provides full connectivity, keeps network utilization at tolerable levels, and minimizes the number of routers between clients and servers.

Please keep in mind that network traffic essentially doubles when crossing a router. Therefore, the best-case scenario is to place a server and a client on the same subnet, so that traffic will never have to exist on multiple subnets simultaneously. This can be done by multihoming the Web server—placing multiple network interface cards into a single server and connecting it to multiple network segments simultaneously.

If the server and client cannot exist on the same network segment, attempt to reduce the number of hops between any two points. This can be done by implementing a hierarchical, rather than flat, network design.

Reducing Utilization by Growing the Pipe

One of the most common solutions to an overutilized network is to upgrade the hardware. This is not always the best solution, but it is often the quickest alternative to deep analysis. It does require some analysis of its own, though. When adding hardware in an attempt to alleviate network utilization problems, you need to keep cost in mind. It can be a very expensive thing to upgrade hardware on the network because:

◆ Network engineers are expensive.

◆ The work must be done during off-hours to reduce downtime.

◆ Support requirements will increase immediately afterward.

◆ Something always breaks.

Several technologies have come to be common in the quest for greater bandwidth, and I will discuss several.

100-Base-T

Probably the most common upgrade to the most common network is upgrading 10Mbps Ethernet to 100Mbps Ethernet. This has been a savior in many environments, but it has its drawbacks as well. The idea of upgrading from 10-Base-T to 100-Base-T is that the bandwidth increases by a factor of 10. Theoretically, if the network were at 50 percent utilization on a 10-Base-T network, that utilization would drop to 5 percent after the upgrade. Realistically, it never works that well.

Upgrading from 10- to 100-Base-T is a very expensive upgrade path because it requires just about every piece of hardware to be upgraded. Notably, cabling may remain in place if Category 5 cable was used in the original cable plant. Everything else must go!

The most tedious, if not the most expensive, component to upgrade is the network interface card in each of the workstation machines. 100-Base-T is completely incompatible with 10-Base-T networks, although it is still plagued with many of the problems of Ethernet.

100-Base-T is still a shared medium, so electrical transmissions on the network are propagated to every host on the segment. Therefore, if large file transfers are flooding your network, you will still see periodically high utilization on a 100-Base-T network. Granted, the transfer will not take as long to complete, but it will still consume the bandwidth for every single port on both the sending and receiving network segments.

Another problem with a 100-Base-T network is that it may simply shift the bottleneck, depending on your network architecture. If your existing network is entirely 10Mbps, and you upgrade everything to 100Mbps, you will realize the throughput increase throughout your internetwork. However, many organizations have a mixed topology. For example, a company may have 10Mbps for each of the desktop workstations while all servers are on a single 100Mbps FDDI ring. Because all the transfers on a network will be destined for or transmitted from the server's FDDI network, upgrading the clients to 100Mbps will have limited benefits. The bottleneck will simply shift to the FDDI ring, possibly reducing the benefit to 20 percent or 30 percent (much less than the 1,000 percent many hope to achieve!)

Switched Ethernet Networks

Switched Ethernet overcomes some of 100-Base-T's problems. The only upgrade that is necessary is in the wiring closet. Switched Ethernet works by replacing hubs with intelligent, layer-2 Ethernet switches. These switches have the capability to examine the layer-2 header in each frame and transmit that frame only to the network parts that need to receive it.

In other words, if Computer A transmits a 1MB file to Computer B in a series of eight frames, Computer A will send those frames through its network interface card to its network cable, when the frame will be received by the switch. The switch will receive that frame and examine the layer-2 header (for Ethernet, this is always the MAC address). The switch is intelligent enough that it will know which port that MAC address is connected to.

This method is in direct contrast to the traditional hub, which receives an electrical signal on one port and retransmits it to every other port. On a repeated network, if Computer A transmits a 1MB file to Computer B, the available bandwidth on every computer attached to that network segment is reduced.

When switching has been implemented, only the two machines actually transmitting and receiving the data will experience reduced available bandwidth. One notable exception to this is the broadcast frame. Broadcast frames carry a special, reserved layer-2 address that the browser interprets as meaning it should be sent to every node on the network. In the case of Ethernet, this layer-2 address is a MAC address with the value FF FF-FF-FF-FF-FF. Switches cannot forward these frames to a limited number of hosts, because the very definition of a broadcast is that every machine on the subnet must intercept it and process it. So the switch must transmit these frames to every port, in the same way a hub would.

Also beware of network architectures in which all network traffic converges around a central point. This is a common scenario in small to medium-sized client/server networks, where all clients may communicate with a single, centralized server. The problem occurs because the port the server is connected through will continue to be saturated, even if a switched network has isolated different clients from the noise. In this case, the switch must attempt to buffer traffic being transmitted to the server, and some frames may be dropped. In highly centralized networks, many of the benefits of switched networks are completely lost.

The moral of this story: At the very worst, switched networks produce the same amount of traffic as conventional Ethernet networks. At the very best, traffic is only ever transmitted between the client and the server.

SWITCHED 10-BASE-T

One switching technology that is becoming very common in network upgrades is switched 10-Base-T. Switched 10-Base-T has an advantage over other network technologies: It can be used with existing Ethernet nodes, no hardware upgrades required. In other words, all of the desktop systems within an organization may have 10-Base-T network cards. To upgrade to 100-Base-T, someone would have to physically go to each desktop, replace the network card, upgrade the driver on the system, and deal with the problems the next day as various incompatibilities show their ugly faces.

SWITCHED 10/100-BASE-T

For the best of both switched Ethernet and 100-Base-T, a compromise can be made between switched 10Mbps Ethernet and 100-Base-T. This allows for higher total throughput as well as the elimination of the shared media properties of traditional Ethernet. Many modern switches have the capability to supported both switched 10 and 100Mbps Ethernet automatically. In this way, if you have existing 10-Base-T clients that are plugged into 10-Base-T hubs, upgrading them is simply a matter of replacing the hub with a 10/100-Base-T switch. As soon as the client is plugged into the new switch, the switch will detect the network speed and adjust to it automatically. If, in the future, that desktop needs additional bandwidth, the network interface card in the desktop will need to be upgraded, but no other hardware replacements will be necessary — the switch will automatically adjust to the higher speed.

FULL DUPLEX

Switching technologies have another advantage when used with Ethernet: They allow full-duplex communications. Full duplex doubles the theoretical bandwidth on a network port by allowing communications to occur in both directions simultaneously. Because of this, a computer attached to a full-duplex, switched Ethernet port may transmit and receive simultaneously. (Normally, communications may only occur in one direction at any given point in time.) Theoretically, this doubles the available bandwidth.

However, this theoretical advantage is rarely realized. In traditional client/server networks such as the Internet, the traffic is highly asymmetric: The data transmitted by the client is much less than the data transmitted by the server. Consider a typical SQL server, attached to a full-duplex Ethernet port. SQL queries are typically much shorter than the result set. If a SQL server is extremely busy, client requests may total as much as three or four megabits per second. In comparison, the responses may consume 30 or 40Mbps. In this example, 95 percent of the theoretical bandwidth available for incoming requests to the server is wasted because the total network throughput is bottlenecked by the outgoing network capacity.

GUARANTEED BANDWIDTH

Now, don't take the section heading literally. No hardware vendor is going to give you your money back if you don't get the bandwidth you were hoping for. However, switched Ethernet networks do offer much more predictable bandwidth per port than shared media are capable of. Because the only traffic on a switched network port is traffic transmitted from or sent to the computer connected to that port, the connected system should always be capable of consuming the entire bandwidth. So that's why I use the phrase "guaranteed bandwidth": Each system receives a full 10 or 100Mbps connection, without having to worry about uninteresting traffic consuming part of that pipe.

Asynchronous Transfer Mode (ATM)

Asynchronous Transfer Mode (ATM) is a new technology promising extremely high, switched bandwidth. Unfortunately, it has many disadvantages arising from the fact that it is such a new technology. The primary disadvantages are:

◆ **Cost:** Because ATM is such a new technology, companies are attempting to recover their own costs expended during the research and development stages of ATM. Thus, ATM switches and network interface cards are painfully expensive. Further, finding qualified and/or experienced network engineers capable of dealing with ATM is a long shot. For those who find the personnel, their salaries tend to be prohibitively high. (Of course, since I am writing this for network engineers, this may seem like more of an advantage!)

◆ **Compatibility:** As with any new technology, ATM may not be compatible with existing hardware and software platforms. Windows NT does support ATM, but the support is still very limited.

◆ **Reliability:** This is another common problem of new technologies.

Several organizations have actually implemented ATM using Windows NT, but these implementations are primarily within organizations that also invested in the research and development of the technology. For them, the benefits are obvious:

◆ Switching, with 155Mbps to every desktop

◆ Guaranteed quality of service (QOS)

◆ Reliable, redundant networking

At this time, ATM is more of a buzzword than a practical network topology. (I may be eating those words in five years!)

Conclusion

In summary, there are many bandwidth considerations when designing or upgrading a network. In either case, you should take into account several factors:

1. The number of users who will make use of the network

2. How the users will use their connectivity

3. The types of traffic on the network

Windows NT provides many resources for collecting information useful for planning bandwidth requirements. These utilities include Performance Monitor and Network Monitor. Microsoft's Systems Management Server also includes an expanded version of Network Monitor with more robust capabilities.

Accurately anticipating bandwidth requirements is critical to determining the topology of a new network. Likewise, networks that are reaching peak utilization have several different alternatives to choose from, each with its own advantages and disadvantages. The keys to choosing wisely from these technologies are knowledge, understanding, and analysis.

Summary

This chapter covered how to estimate bandwidth by collecting actual statistics and by using speculation. Both of these methods are multifaceted, so you must take into account services or usage as well as number and activities of users. The chapter also showed you how to reduce bandwidth utilization by lowering traffic and by growing the pipe.

You have learned the following:

◆ Windows NT provides many resources for collecting information useful for planning bandwidth requirements. These utilities include Performance Monitor and Network Monitor. Microsoft's Systems Management Server also includes an expanded version of Network Monitor with more robust capabilities.

◆ Networking services such as WINS, DNS, Browser Service, Domain user account authentications, trust relationships, file and printer sharing, and domain synchronization also use bandwidth.

◆ A careful analysis can show you how to help your company reduce traffic, both system and user, especially at peak times.

◆ Growing the pipe with 100-Base-T or switched Ethernet networks can also be a good way to increase bandwidth.

In the next chapter, you'll learn about the necessity of designing a network that can grow and expand (that is, scale up) as demands on its capabilities increase. The very usefulness of a network is in its size and scope – the more you can reach with a network, the more it can do for you. However, scaling a network is a challenging, expensive, and sometimes risky task. Decisions you make today while designing a small network can have a huge impact on the organization's ability to scale into the future.

Chapter 5

Designing Scalable Nets

IN THIS CHAPTER

- ◆ Predicting network growth

- ◆ Recognizing and preventing bottlenecks

- ◆ Enhancing scalability through documentation

- ◆ Automating network management tasks to improve performance

- ◆ Optimizing network reliability through redundant systems

THIS CHAPTER EXAMINES the necessity of designing a network that can grow and expand (that is, scale up) as demands on its capabilities increase. In fact, network designers should preface every decision they make with this question: How well will this work when the size of the company quadruples? The very usefulness of a network is in its size and scope — the more you can reach with a network, the more it can do for you. However, scaling a network is a challenging, expensive, and sometimes risky task. Many things will improve your ability to expand your network's capabilities. Even if you are planning only a small network, you should think big. Decisions you make today while designing a small network can have a huge impact on the organization's ability to scale into the future.

This chapter explains the concepts involved in planning for the future and describes how to scale upward by documenting thoroughly, reducing administration, and improving reliability.

Designing for Growth

How long does it take you to get to work in the morning? Why does it take so long? Does traffic slow you down, or are you limited by the posted speed limit on the roads you travel?

I work in the Boston area and have a two-hour commute every day during which I think about what makes a system scalable. If you have ever lived in the area, you know that the highway systems did *not* scale well at all. This is not intended as an insult to our founding fathers who engineered two-lane highways such as Route 20. Route 20 is the oldest highway in the country; it evolved from wagon trails.

Nonetheless, I spend two hours a day wishing my horse-and-buggy-driving fore-fathers had considered, *just once*, what it was going to be like for Tony driving to work every day in traffic.

Many networks have similar problems as companies grow. The original "network engineer" may have been the office manager who purchased an A/B parallel port switch so that two users could share the same printer. While the solution solved the problem at hand and met the immediate needs of two users, it will not scale well when the office grows to 1,000 users. Indeed, it won't scale past two users!

Networks designed to meet short-term needs often become obstacles to growth. The goal of creating scalable networks is to avoid placing these obstacles in the path between the present and the future of your organization. As a rule of thumb, it takes more effort to replace a poorly designed network than it does to implement it in the first place.

Back to my morning commute. Route 20 was designed around 300 years ago, and I'm sure everyone was just thrilled about it at the time. Instead of my fore-fathers having to pull their wagons across plains and forests, they now had a trail to make travel much faster and easier. Soon, convenience stores were built to sell hay and grain (or whatever horses ate) to travelers. What better place to put these stores than *right on the side of the road*? As my forefathers selfishly built their homes
and businesses conveniently near the highway (*without ever giving any thought to Tony's commute*), they forever bottlenecked traffic to the then-current width of the road.

Naturally, there is no way the first settlers could have anticipated the traffic problems Massachusetts would experience in 300 years. If they had, they probably would have built their homes farther away from Route 20, so that the road could one day be widened. Similarly, everything a systems or network engineer does should consider scalability. The sections that follow will give you suggestions for designing truly scalable internetworks.

Anticipating Bottlenecks

Accurately estimating growth and anticipating bottlenecks is as much an art as a science. It is a skill that experience – the slowest teacher of all – teaches best. You really need to go through the process of scaling a network to large proportions before you have a good feel for the types of things that cause problems during growth. Fortunately, there are guidelines to help you if you lack that experience. The next section discusses several types of bottlenecks that can limit the ability of a network to grow.

System Bottlenecks

The goal of the systems engineer is to make the network the bottleneck. Servers and clients on a network should be capable of generating so much traffic that the network operates at 100 percent utilization. A file server must be capable of generating sharing files at 10Mbps if it resides on a 10Mbps network, and more if it resides on a 100Mbps network. While I do not plan to give detailed information about systems engineering here (the whole book is dedicated to that!), I do need to point out the idea of designing systems to maximize network utilization.

Network Bottlenecks

Years ago, when most networks never had to scale outside of the LAN, the computer systems were always the bottleneck. Most network traffic went between the user's desktop system and a server of some kind. Traffic was generated for the transfer of network documents, print jobs, and messaging. Networks were designed to meet the 80:20 rule, which stated that 80 percent of network traffic should remain local to the network segment, and only 20 percent should need to cross a router. Today the WAN and the Internet receive most of the traffic, and the 80:20 rule is rapidly reversing.

In modern networks, users are likely to communicate with many servers instead of just a single server. Web servers on the Internet provide useful tools and information. E-mail servers no longer reside on a LAN but tend to be centralized for an entire enterprise. The sharing of information is becoming more widespread, and users spend more of their time communicating with distant networks than with their own local network. This trend toward distributed systems throughout enterprise networks is relieving systems of some burden but placing a greater weight on the network.

While network companies strive to meet the increased bandwidth needs of organizations, many companies are beginning to experience performance problems because of network bottlenecks.

NETWORK BANDWIDTH UTILIZATION

The most obvious performance bottleneck that occurs with network growth is network traffic utilization. Broadcast networks such as traditional shared Ethernets scale poorly because each host added to a network segment uses a portion of the shared, total bandwidth. As shared Ethernet networks grow, percent utilization increases, along with collisions and broadcasts. The network must be segmented with a router, as illustrated in Figure 5-1, to make a shared Ethernet network scale beyond 30 to 50 users. Scaling a network by segmenting it is a time-consuming process because network addresses must be reorganized and reassigned.

Figure 5-1: Shared Ethernet networks must be segmented to scale upward.

A shared Ethernet does not scale well for many reasons. Several aspects of the shared Ethernet increase for every user that is added to the network. When enough users are added to the network, more of the resources are consumed until one of the following properties of the shared Ethernet begins to bottleneck the bandwidth:

◆ Total network utilization

◆ Broadcast traffic

Segmenting the network solves both problems. However, there is an alternative to a shared Ethernet. This alternative allows the network to scale without total network utilization becoming the bottleneck. This alternative is a switched Ethernet, which replaces traditional hubs with layer-2 switches that have the intelligence to pass frames only to the systems that need to receive these frames. Because of this, total network utilization becomes less of a consideration – only broadcast traffic affects the entire network segment. All other traffic affects only the two network ports that need to see it – the sending and receiving ports. Therefore, as you scale, network-wide utilization increases only because of broadcast traffic, which is traditionally not enough to cause a bottleneck.

PORT BANDWIDTH UTILIZATION

The ability of switched Ethernet to scale is largely dependent on the network architecture. In particular, switched Ethernet networks scale better when used with distributed server architectures. To illustrate this point, consider two companies that each use shared 10Mbps Ethernet networks. Company A, illustrated in Figure 5-2, uses distributed servers – they have five servers, each serving a specific network service. Company B, as shown in Figure 5-3, uses a single, centralized server for all network services.

Company A

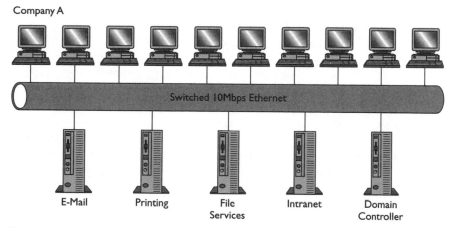

Figure 5-2: Company A has a distributed network service architecture.

Company B

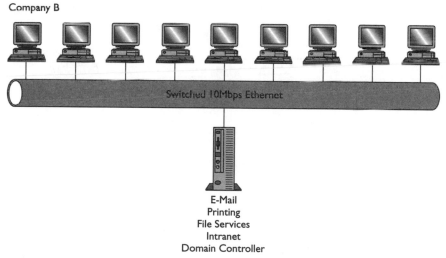

Figure 5-3: Company B has a centralized network service architecture.

The busiest time for most LANs is the early morning — employees show up for work about the same time and all check their e-mail, open documents on the file server, and print a few things. Because the underlying network is switched 10Mbps Ethernet, each host on the network is capable of transmitting and receiving 10Mbps of network traffic at full duplex, for a total of 20Mbps throughput. The system administrator shows up for work and downloads his e-mail, which consists of 500 messages from the fifteen mailing lists he subscribes to. His computer transfers this data from the e-mail server at a full 10Mbps. Simultaneously, an accountant shows up for work and begins printing 200 copies of her résumé. Her computer transfers the print data to the print server at a full 10Mbps. Meanwhile, other users may be taking advantage of the other servers on the network, using the full 10Mbps bandwidth available between their computer and the server.

Network throughput per use will not decrease until multiple users begin to use resources from the same server. For example, consider the vice president of marketing showing up for work and downloading a 50-megabyte movie that was included as an e-mail attachment. He and the system administrator will have to share the 10Mbps bandwidth that the e-mail server has available to it. Because they are both attempting to use the full capacity of a single network port, the bottleneck for their e-mail transfer becomes the switched network port. However, this does not affect the accountant's ability to print. This network traffic is shown in Figure 5-4, with only the servers illustrated.

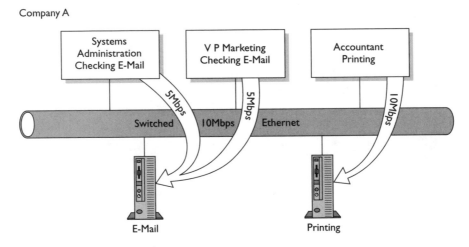

Figure 5-4: Distributed networks make better use of a switched Ethernet.

Now consider the same users, the same situation, and the same underlying switched Ethernet network, but with a single, centralized server. As the system administrator downloads his mail, he receives a full 10Mbps of throughput between his system and the server. As the accountant and the vice-president of marketing begin their work, they must communicate with the same server. Therefore, the single port becomes the bottleneck for *all* network traffic.

As more users begin performing these types of tasks, the 10Mbps of available bandwidth on that port becomes divided further and further. With five users downloading e-mail, printing, and opening files from the file server and from the intranet, each user will receive approximately 2Mbps of total transfer. As a result of having a single switched Ethernet port serving all network services, that port becomes a single bottleneck for throughput on the network, and the advantages of switched Ethernet are hardly realized. This is illustrated in Figure 5-5.

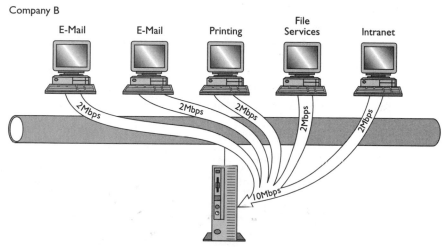

Figure 5-5: Centralized networks bottleneck on a single switched Ethernet port.

NETWORK HARDWARE UTILIZATION

Each full-duplex port on a switched 100Mbps Ethernet network has a 200Mbps potential throughput. This value may very well be realized during large file transfers between fast systems, and most switches would be able to keep up with the switching needs between the two systems. However, consider a switch with 100 individual ports capable of 200Mbps – the total throughput for the Ethernet switch is theoretically 20,000Mbps – or 20 gigabits per second!

Modern Ethernet switches cannot handle that type of load. Consequently, they would be forced to place extra packets in a queue, which would quickly be used up. Once the queue is full, the only option is to drop incoming packets – a worst-case scenario in any network. This will probably never be a problem because 20Gbps network utilization is unlikely in a real network; 100 users will probably not use their network ports at full capacity at the same time.

Network traffic in the real world goes through ups and downs. However, my example illustrates another consideration when planning for the scalability of a network – the switching capability and total throughput of the network hardware.

Ethernet switches typically have limitations on the number of frames they may switch and the total traffic that may traverse the hardware's backbone. Each frame transmitted by any host on a switch must be examined: The destination MAC address must be determined, that MAC address must be correlated to another port on the switch, and the frame must be transmitted on that port. This is a simple process, and the amount of processing overhead is minimal, but it certainly exists. On networks that carry large amounts of traffic, the number of frames an Ethernet switch can process may very well become a bottleneck. Before purchasing a switch, take into account its total switching capacity.

After the switch determines which network port a frame must be transmitted on, the electrical signals that define the bits and bytes of the frame are transmitted onto the physical network port. From the network port, a wire carries the electrical signals to the receiving host. Depending on the size of the switch, it may be carrying these electrical signals between hundreds of individual Ethernet ports. These signals are carried across the backbone (also called the *backplane*) of the switch; this backbone can, in itself, become a bottleneck. Switch vendors usually publish the total throughput of the backbone, and you should consider this figure when purchasing a switch. The total throughput of the network at any given point in time can never exceed the throughput of the backbone.

Documenting for the Future

As networks scale to large proportions, the bottleneck is often much less obvious than bandwidth. Large networks often begin to experience serious problems because of supportability. As the network grows, it becomes impossible for everyone who administers any part of it to understand how all of the pieces work together. Indeed, there may be only one person who understands how it should work and why it was designed that way – the network engineer who originally created the design.

As the network scales, problems with supportability start to crop up. Perhaps the LAN administrator of a remote site decides to replace the network hardware on the LAN with network hardware from a different vendor. While this may not seem like a problem, hardware from a different vendor makes support more complex. Or perhaps an administrator of a particular WAN link upgrades the hardware on a router on a whim – and then questions why the corporate IT group did not warn him of a serious bug in that version of the router's operating system.

The most efficient method for combating these problems is documentation. All aspects of the network must be thoroughly documented to ensure scalability. As engineers and administrators are promoted or leave for other companies, the proprietary information they carry with them *must* be documented so that it can be passed to future generations of engineers and administrators. If the original engineer created a policy of using a particular vendor or a specific version of a router's operating system, these policies must be documented. Further, that documentation must be centralized, available, and well known to others within the organization.

The network itself provides a useful way of storing this documentation. The growing popularity of intranets is largely the result of the need to share information in a structured way. For example, an intranet Web page could be dedicated to the corporate IT group. From this page, a user could reach information regarding network policies. Another link could lead to a page outlining the major concepts used to create the network design. Yet another link could provide detailed information about the network architecture, such as router names and operating system versions.

Often, engineers who are extremely talented at designing scalable networks are resistant to documentation. For many, documentation is a laborious and boring task. It is the manager's responsibility to make sure all staff members document their ideas and creations. This documentation is for the reference of others who will be expected to support the network.

Minimizing Ongoing Management Time

Small organizations use different methods for managing network hardware than large organizations. If a network administrator needs to monitor the use of a single router on a daily basis, a manual process may be acceptable. For example, the administrator may manually connect to the machine, check various performance statistics, and make modifications to the configuration as necessary. However, as the network scales upward, these practices are no longer practical. Imagine an organization with fifteen network administrators manually checking the performance of 500 routers — an easier method must be identified.

There are many tools to aid in management of the systems and network hardware that compose a network. I will not attempt to compare these tools in this book, but I will outline general practices that should be used. For a network to scale upward without the management of that network becoming a serious burden, the following tasks should be automated:

◆ Reactive notification of failed equipment

◆ Reactive logging of management tasks performed on systems

◆ Proactive notification of failing equipment

◆ Proactive monitoring of performance

(*Reactive* means the goal of the task is to help solve a problem after it has occurred. *Proactive* is anticipating problems before they cause downtime.) With these tasks totally automated, a significant portion of the network management burden is relieved. While setting up the systems to automate these tasks will take a significant amount of time, this investment will become worthwhile as the network grows in size.

Increasing Redundancy and Reliability

Failure is more acceptable on small networks. If a router connecting a small remote office to the central office fails in the middle of the day, users will complain to the network administrator, who will promptly walk into the wiring closet and replace the part. The disturbance is still a problem, because twenty or thirty users will lose e-mail connectivity for ten or fifteen minutes while the part is replaced.

However, problems because of failures become much more significant on large networks. When an organization of 10,000 users depends on the network for communications with peers throughout the company, a single point of failure is entirely unacceptable. Further, such problems are typically much more difficult to troubleshoot and resolve in a large network. For these reasons, increasing the reliability and redundancy of the network as a whole is critically important.

It may not be financially justifiable for a small organization to create a redundant network architecture. For scaling purposes, however, the network engineer must keep future redundancy needs in mind when designing a small network. Choose network equipment that has the capability of adding-on redundancy, such as an additional power supply that automatically takes over should the first power supply fail.

Even if the cost of such redundancy is not immediately justifiable, it will be much easier and cheaper to upgrade just the redundant component in the future. If the entire piece of equipment needs replacing because it lacks redundant capabilities, the transition will be more expensive and difficult.

Summary

This chapter examined the benefits of designing networks and systems that can scale upward as your organization grows.

You have learned:

◆ Networks that have been designed to scale up are worth the investment in time and money.

◆ System and hardware bottlenecks can limit a network's ability to grow. Learning to avoid these problems will save a great deal of expense in the future.

◆ Network scalability and reliability are enhanced by thorough documentation and redundant systems.

The next chapter further explores concepts of network design. It focuses on determining needs, choosing business partners, and effectively managing and implementing a network design.

Chapter 6

Network Design

IN THIS CHAPTER

♦ Focusing your network design efforts to create a more effective solution

♦ Choosing vendors with whom you can build strong relationships

♦ Validating and implementing your network design

EVER NOTICE COMPANIES like 3Com, Cisco, and Bay Networks in the headlines of the financial page? Today, organizations spend an incredible amount of money on networking, and as a result, the industry is booming. Ironically, a network administrator's job is to spend *as little* money as possible while still connecting everything to everyone.

Decisions made during the network design phase will have a profound effect on the way all applications that use the network will work in the future. Poor network designs yield extremely high support costs, downtime, and lost business opportunities. On the other hand, a good network design will last a company many years. It will allow a company to upgrade cheaply and easily, and it will provide for backward compatibility, gradual testing of the environment, and modular, gradual transitions.

Most important, a good network design will be easy to support. For many organizations, the greatest costs of a network come from the cost of the support. Good network engineers are difficult to come by, and finding people who can troubleshoot your problems swiftly and efficiently is next to impossible. This is not intended as an insult to the networking community; I just wish there were more of us around.

This chapter will give an overview of network design. More important, it will show you how to take Windows NT and Microsoft networking into account when creating a network design. (No matter what you have heard, the network is never operating system–independent.) Then you will learn the important phases to complete when implementing the design.

Designing the Network

Entire books have been written about network design and network architecture. It's a job that requires many, many weeks of planning, research, testing, and implementation. I will not make an effort to cover all aspects of the technologies and processes necessary to create a good network design, but I do want to provide a general background in network design concepts and cover those aspects specific to the Windows NT Network Operating System.

Network design is an unappreciated art form. Most of the time, a network architecture is chosen arbitrarily (hence, the success of Ethernet!). Unfortunately, these quick decisions can cost organizations hundreds of thousands of dollars in increased maintenance costs and upgrades before they would otherwise be necessary.

Network design includes deciding on a particular network architecture. *Network architecture* refers to the way that routers, switches, and hubs connect clients and servers on a network. All of these aspects together compose the network architecture.

Following are the major phases of a network design and the most important things to consider.

Determining Business Needs

Always start a network design by considering the underlying business needs that are initiating the network implementation or upgrade. These happen at a high level and ultimately serve some purpose for the employees and customers. Understanding the high-level goals ensures that all the low-level decisions will be consistent with the direction of the organization.

Avoid thinking of network design as an opportunity to play with the latest toys; technology for technology's sake may be entertaining, but no company in existence wants to spend that much money to entertain its networking staff. You must have a rational justification for every decision you make relating to the network design. This is especially true when deciding to use new, unproven technologies.

Determining Specific Goals

The job of the network engineer is to grill the management to discover the core requirements of a planned network. Here are two good ways to accomplish this: *core questions* and *needs versus wants*.

CORE QUESTIONS

Before ever considering different technologies, the network engineer must find the answers to some basic, core questions:

- ◆ How many people will use the network?
- ◆ What are the future plans of the company?
- ◆ What are the growth expectations for the company?
- ◆ Who are the users?

The first stages of network design have very little to do with the technical aspects of the network. Indeed, it may be particularly difficult for someone with a technical background to perform the high-level network specification analysis because we tend to get bogged down in the technical details of things, considering the advantages and disadvantages of various network hardware before determining the core business needs.

NEEDS VERSUS WANTS

To help narrow down the specific needs of the business, create a needs versus wants list. Take all the suggestions gathered from management and organize and prioritize them into two categories: needs and wants. "Needs" are the driving forces behind the network initiative. "Wants" are those goals that will benefit the company but are not critical to the functioning of the organization.

The items you add to the "Needs" column will be detailed, specific requirements. A common need might be to have all computers connected to all other computers within the organization. This is a key feature of networking and belongs under the "Needs" column because there would be little purpose in creating the network without this core piece of functionality.

An example of an item that would belong under the "Wants" column would be integrated network faxing. While this may be convenient, the organization probably has an existing method to send faxes. The network would still be useful without this functionality and the organization would not lose its ability to serve customers, so it cannot be considered a "Need."

When Wants Become Needs

"Wants" become "Needs" when they are critical to the business. For example, integrated network faxing is a useful function to any organization. For most, however, it is clearly a "Want." On the other hand, if the company sells faxing capabilities to its customers, then it is a core business requirement and should be considered a "Need."

The needs versus wants list will be a critical reference during the later network design phases. Each aspect of the network must support every item listed under the "Needs" column. Additionally, effort should be extended to ensure that the "Wants" may also be supported. For example, if the organization has placed a high-bandwidth application such as video conferencing under the "Needs" list, major accommodations must be made. The bandwidth will need to be available between any two points in the network, and an application will have to be identified that is compatible with both the network protocol and network architecture.

In that way, the network engineer is taking into account the needs of the organization when creating a network design.

Items under the "Wants" column should receive a "best effort." If they add a great deal of cost to the network design or if they are difficult, are impractical, or add complexity to the design, wants may be discarded. The network engineer will probably discover that the business people "need" just about everything. It is the job of the network engineer to convince the decision makers that not everything is an absolute necessity. Table 6-1 shows a sample of needs versus wants.

TABLE 6-1 EXAMPLES OF NEEDS VERSUS WANTS

Needs	Wants
Complete intranet connectivity	Complete Internet connectivity
E-mail for all users	Network faxing for all users
Emergency, remote dial-in access	Remote access from the Internet
Reliability	Complete redundancy

Choosing a Solution

This section will detail the various aspects of choosing vendors, hardware platforms, and software platforms for network hardware and network operating systems. I will not attempt to recommend specific products; I'll leave that up to you. However, I will spell out what you should look for.

VENDORS

The most important consideration when choosing a hardware or software platform is not the features or functionality of the product – it is the vendor. The vendor is a critical component to any major network implementation, and vendors vary dramatically in several different ways.

RELATIONSHIPS   Most organizations spend very little time building relationships with their vendors. Often, the relationship does not go past the sales meeting. Depending on the product, this may be enough. In many cases, however, it benefits both the customer and the vendor to get to know each other better.

Vendors benefit from strong customer relations because they will have a better understanding of the customers they support. This understanding helps them to steer their products and services in a direction that the customer will find more useful. As a result, the vendor is more likely to keep the customer over a longer period of time, increasing long-term sales.

Customers also benefit from building a relationship with the vendor. Often, a relationship may be leveraged when a problem has been found in the product and vendor cooperation is required. The customer will also be more likely to receive demonstration products and product updates as they become available. In this way, a strong vendor relationship allows the customer to stay ahead of the game.

SUPPORT   Some vendors will have extremely good support policies, while others will have almost no policies in that department. Of those that have good policies in place, some will implement them well and do a good job of keeping their support promises. Others will have a problem providing support people, fixing bugs in their hardware and software, or responding to issues in a timely manner.

To illustrate how different vendors can affect a problem, consider this example: You work for a company that provides Web hosting on the public Internet. A security flaw is found and made public that has the potential to compromise the Web sites you host. You are faced with an immediate problem, and the software vendor is your only source for resolution to that problem. This will require the vendor to dedicate development time and to work with you to ensure that the patch is applied in an efficient, reliable manner.

Different vendors will respond to this problem in different ways. Chances are good that a small vendor may not have the manpower or knowledge to dedicate to solving your problem immediately. They may also not be customer-centric, causing them to put a lower importance on the problem than you associate with it. Larger vendors more often have an understanding that their customers choose their software specifically for their ability to respond to situations such as this. Vendors such as Microsoft and Netscape tend to have the manpower to dedicate to solving high-publicity problems such as the problem described here. On the other hand, large vendors rarely spend a great deal of time with individual customers. Smaller vendors get to know each customer better and may be more capable of fine-tuning their software package to your specific needs.

This is not to say that the only difference in vendors is size. If you are reselling a service to a customer, whether internal or external, you probably have some sort of service guarantee in place. This may state that you will resolve a problem in a certain amount of time, or that you will limit downtime within certain bounds. Your vendor needs to be sensitive to your commitments and willing to work with you to meet them. Good vendors will treat your deadlines as their own.

NETWORK OPERATING SYSTEMS

Servers and clients may be only end nodes on a network, but they still play an important role in the network design. Print servers and clients can have tremendously varied impacts on a network. Depending on the operating systems, they can behave in several different ways. Operating systems such as Windows 95 and Windows NT tend to produce a great deal of broadcast traffic. This is in contrast to the Novell network operating system, which is not well known for producing broadcast traffic, and the traffic it does produce tends to rely on protocols such as IPX rather than TCP/IP.

Another way that operating systems tend to vary is in the amount of traffic they are capable of producing. An example of how this can vary from network operating system to network operating system occurred with NT 3.51. 10-Base-T networking was first becoming popular when NT 3.51 was Microsoft's primary operating system. Vendors began producing 100-Base-T network interface cards for Windows NT 3.51, and they provided drivers as well.

Unfortunately, the architecture of the TCP/IP stack on Windows NT server 3.51 was such that it was incapable of saturating a 100-Base-T network. In fact, it produced only about 20 percent of the capacity of the network interface. Most would agree that this isn't a good thing but does reduce the chances for a network to become entirely saturated. Particularly, it eliminates the possibility of storms. On the other hand, operating systems such as Sun Solaris are capable of taking a 100-Base-T network to near saturation under the same conditions.

This example illustrates the point that different network operating systems are capable of producing different traffic patterns on the network. Such differences can have a profound effect on the way the overall network operates. When designing a network, you will make decisions about two major classes of network operating systems: clients and servers. You may choose multiple operating systems for both clients and servers depending on the specific needs of the system. Obviously, it would be nice if all modern network designs could incorporate only a single network operating system creating entirely homogenous software environments. This is rarely the case, however, as different operating systems seem to excel at different things. Indeed, many personnel may have a particular preference. The following two sections cover the criteria you should consider when choosing both server and client operating systems.

SERVERS   Care should be taken when choosing a server operating system for your network. The server network operating system tends to be far more expensive than the client network operating systems and tends to require the most support time. In planning, a good rule of thumb is to plan to have thirty users for each server on the network.

Servers by their very nature are extremely specialized. Networks are composed of servers that perform various tasks such as print serving, mail services, file services, and application services. Ideally, the same network operating system would be chosen for each of these tasks. Indeed, most operating systems lend some support for each of these tasks, and Windows NT is no exception. Though Windows NT has excelled in each of these areas, it is not necessarily the best for each purpose. The Novell network operating system tends to outperform Windows NT in file services by a large margin. UNIX operating systems such as Sun Solaris tend to serve many more pages from HTTP Web servers than NT is capable of. It can be argued that Windows NT is not the best at any of the typical server roles. If you are reading this book, however, you obviously have a profound interest in the Windows NT network operating system.

I do want to raise the point that Windows NT may not always be the right operating system, particularly for some services that have traditionally been handled by UNIX. While Microsoft has been producing Internet-based server software for 2 or 3 years, UNIX has been doing it for 20 or 30 years. Microsoft has not caught up instantly, either. UNIX systems tend to perform better as e-mail servers, and as Web servers tend to require less maintenance and offer greater reliability. While UNIX systems administrators tend to be scarce, they are much easier to find than Windows NT systems administrators.

Currently, the bulk of networks in the world are made up of heterogeneous operating systems, with Windows NT serving some roles, Novell serving some roles, and UNIX serving other roles, depending on the organization. Ideally, this wouldn't be the case – the entire network would be composed of operating systems from only one vendor.

Having a homogeneous network has many advantages, including allowing the administrators and engineers to learn only the software from a single vendor. It also means that managers need to develop fewer relationships with their software vendors, since all their software could come from a single source. Having a homogenous network is Microsoft's dream as well. Microsoft produces software for many parts of the network in an effort to expand to every point of the network, including clients, servers, and gateways. Five years ago, it was very common to have networks composed entirely of Windows- or MS-DOS-based clients. It was very rare to see any Microsoft product playing a server role in the network. Now, networking often incorporates Windows NT.

When using a server operating system, consider the following criteria:

◆ **Support:** Can you find someone to support the software? When ordering software, carefully consider if anyone in your organization has experience with the software. When planning a new network, consider whether people to support the network are going to be available. The simple fact of the matter is that Windows NT engineers and administrators are in great demand and are very scarce. It may warrant thinking twice before deciding on Windows NT as your server operating system.

◆ **Cost:** As we have discussed before, cost is a multifaceted issue composed of three components: initial cost, cost of maintenance, and upgrade cost. Consider each of these carefully, and keep in mind that the cost of maintenance is going to be the outstanding factor. Many organizations provide studies that detail the cost of maintenance of the various operating systems and provide recommendations on this basis. Just don't trust the sites that are produced by the operating systems vendor!

◆ **Compatibility:** This may seem like an obvious thing to consider, but it is often overlooked. When deciding on a network operating system, be sure that the network operating system is compatible with the hardware platform that you have chosen, or if you plan to choose different platforms depending on the operating system, make sure your clients have the capability to talk to the server. For example, if you plan to use a UNIX-based file server, Windows-based clients will need some sort of additional software, such as Hummingbird, to connect to the NFS shares.

◆ **Performance:** Different network operating systems handle different tasks at widely varying performance levels. If your environment is large enough to have specialized servers, make sure that the network operating system you choose for each of the servers performs adequately. Performance is not a major enough consideration that it should outweigh the desire to have a homogeneous network. In other words, if you find that Novell and UNIX are faster at print services than Windows NT is, this fact alone is not justification to choose another system over Windows NT. Run Windows NT on as many servers as possible simply for the sake of supportability.

CLIENTS   The operating system chosen for the client is also an important consideration, though it has less of an impact on the design. The most important factors for choosing a client do not include its impact on the network; instead, typical criteria are:

◆ **Cost:** Once again, cost is composed of three factors: initial cost, cost of maintenance, and upgrade cost. Support of clients tends to become the most costly component on the network, greatly depending on the operating base.

◆ **Usability:** Choose an operating system your users can use. This will make your users more effective in the work they do, helping to accomplish the overall goals of the organization. It will also work to reduce the cost by reducing the amount of support time needed. The more problems that users are able to avoid or resolve themselves, the less support time will be required.

◆ **Performance:** Always consider the performance of the operating system both on the network and on the desktop system. Operating systems such as Windows 95 and Windows NT, although outwardly very similar, tend to perform very differently.

◆ **Compatibility:** Make sure the client operating system that you choose is capable of communicating with the server operating systems and capable of speaking the proper network protocols. Today, most operating systems are capable of speaking to other operating systems, so this is less of a consideration than it has been in the past.

There are really very few choices for client-side network operating systems today. The vast majority of networks will choose a Microsoft-based client operating system such as Windows 95 or Windows NT. The few sites that choose software other than those two products invariable choose some flavor of Microsoft operating system, be it an older or newer version. Another popular client operating system is UNIX. UNIX-based operating systems tend to be used only in specialized areas. Those already familiar with UNIX may prefer to have UNIX as their main desktop operating system. UNIX is also commonly used in financial organizations because of the wealth of financial software for the platform.

CHOOSING A TELCO: YOU'RE LUCKY IF YOU EVEN HAVE A CHOICE

The majority of modern designs include some kind of wide-area network connectivity. The connection may go to a local Internet service provider, or it may link remote offices together. Nonetheless, the majority of modern networks require some kind of connectivity outside the local office.

Such connectivity requires some form of wide-area network link. In the simplest case, this may be an analog telephone connection using standard modems. As demands increase, these circuits may be upgraded to 56K, T1, or T3 leased lines.

In a few places, you may have a choice between leased line vendors. Unfortunately, most locations in the United States do not offer a choice between telco vendors — you are forced to choose the vendor that services your area. To make matters more complex, you may have to rely on multiple vendors interconnecting to carry a leased line across service areas. Nonetheless, the same concepts apply to circuit vendors as to any other vendors: You need service guarantees, support policies, and a history of reliability. Nonetheless, this will probably not be the basis for your decision. More than likely, you will be limited to choosing the vendor who provides service for your area and the availability of its circuits. As federal regulations change and the communications industry evolves, your options are likely to increase.

SERVER HARDWARE

The focus of this book is networking Windows NT, but I would like to take a few pages to discuss choosing a hardware platform, because the hardware platform you choose to host Windows NT has a significant impact on how it performs on the network. Additionally, I will discuss factors systems engineers tend to overlook when choosing a hardware platform, such as short- and long-term costs and value-added services.

The choice of a server hardware platform deserves even more attention than network hardware and architecture choices. It is not uncommon for organizations to make hardware choices based on a limited set of factors, such as how fast the CPU is or how much memory the computer can hold. Beware taking the simple approach; hardware platform decisions are complex and should be based on many factors. These factors include:

- Initial costs
- Support costs
- Hardware reliability and redundancy
- Software support
- Performance
- Scalability

CHOOSING HARDWARE ON THE BASIS OF COST If there is one concept I want everyone reading this book to take with them, it is that cost goes well beyond the initial purchase price of the system. The price you pay up front for the hardware is almost insignificant compared to the costs for ongoing support, upgrades, and downtime. Different hardware platforms vary tremendously in all four categories, and it is worth the investment in time to choose a platform carefully.

To evaluate these costs, consider the ease with which administrators may maintain the hardware. Simple things, such as memory chips that are difficult to reach, can make maintenance time consuming and therefore costly. Likewise, if the entire server must be disassembled to replace an internal hard drive, the costs associated with both upgrades and downtime will increase.

CHOOSING HARDWARE ON THE BASIS OF PERFORMANCE REQUIREMENT

Choosing a hardware platform on the basis of performance is just like choosing a car on the basis of horsepower: Horsepower is cool, but how much you do really need? Be careful not to over-purchase. Take into consideration the amount of processing power specific applications you intend to deploy will require. Then double those requirements to allow for growth.

In many cases, accurately evaluating your applications will allow you to reduce costs in very specific areas. For example, you may determine that a fast drive subsystem is not necessary if you purchase enough memory for a particular SQL server database to be stored entirely in RAM.

WORKSTATION HARDWARE

The desktop hardware market has become one of the world's largest industries. Companies such as Dell, Compaq, and Gateway go to great lengths to provide reliable, compatible, high-performing desktop hardware platforms. These computers must support popular client-side operating systems such as Windows 95 and Windows NT Workstation. As many factors apply when you are choosing a hardware workstation vendor as do for any other purchase decision. This decision is more important than any other, however, because you will have far more workstations on your network than network hardware components. The factors for choosing a workstation hardware platform are:

- ◆ **Cost:** The cost of the workstation hardware platform is one of the most important decisions you will make in network design. A platform that is not extremely reliable can cause outrageous support costs. Even a single failed hard drive can cause a user days of downtime and can create many hours of work for support personnel while they replace the hard drive and restore the user's data from backup tapes.

- ◆ **Compatibility:** While compatibility will hardly be an issue when choosing from vendors, it does often become an issue with Windows NT Workstation. Microsoft publishes a hardware compatibility list that specifies exactly what hardware Windows NT Workstation is certified to operate on. This does not include all vendors' hardware. There have even been certain platforms from the major vendors that were not compatible. The first versions of Dell Optiplex did not work properly with Windows NT Workstation and could be extremely unreliable. Another example is the Cyrix CPU, which, while it works well under Windows 95, underperforms with Windows NT.

- ◆ **Performance:** How the workstation performs can profoundly affect both the efficiency with which the user can work and the user's satisfaction with the system. A slow CPU, slow hard drive access, lack of memory, or many other factors may be a source of frustration.

> ## HCL on the Web
>
> Microsoft offers an online, up-to-date database containing its latest hardware compatibility list at
> `http://www.microsoft.com/ntworkstation/info/hcl.htm`.

With workstation hardware, it is often a good idea to "jump on the bandwagon" and choose a popular vendor. While popularity should certainly not be the only consideration, a vendor with many customers is likely to find and eliminate bugs and solve reliability problems before you encounter them.

USING YOUR SKILL SET (OR, DO WHAT YOU KNOW)

When making network design decisions, be sure to consider your organization's existing skill set. Since long-term supportability is such an important consideration, you should use network hardware, software, and vendors that you are already familiar with. Avoid entirely new products as often as possible. If an existing product has the functionality you need, stick with it, regardless of whether or not a new product has been released to the marketplace.

I would also not recommend changing products and vendors merely because a price point changes. For example, consider an organization that has been purchasing switches from Cisco Systems and decides to purchase Cabletron switches because Cabletron is charging a lower price. They may save money initially, but almost certainly not enough to make up for the learning curve associated with the different configurations and vendor-specific implementation details of the switch. Additionally, compatibility problems may increase support costs.

It is dangerous to change products simply because you have had noncritical problems with a product. Every piece of hardware or software that you purchase and use will have some kind of problem. No software is perfect. Switching to a product from another vendor will only introduce new problems that you have not yet become familiar with. The time your staff will spend learning new systems and finding workarounds for new problems may be large.

Testing and Implementing the Design

Once you have decided on vendors, products, and policies, it is time to put that work to use. Until the implementation phase is complete, you have nothing tangible to show for your work. There are three stages to implementation: alpha testing, beta testing, and rollout.

The Testing Process: Test, Revise, Repeat

Once you have completed the first stages of the design process and have decided on a set of standards for your network hardware and software, it is time to test the details of your implementation. In this stage, you will test your solution and verify that it works as expected. The testing process should be considered critical and key to any successful implementation. Unfortunately, because it takes a great deal of time, it is often bypassed, overlooked, or given less time than it deserves.

The testing phase has several stages within itself. The first testing phase is to evaluate each individual component of the network in an isolated environment. You should not attempt to introduce products from other vendors to test intercompatibility, and you should not attempt to test backward compatibility with older versions of hardware or software. In the first stage of testing, you are only attempting to determine that the core components specified will work. This is the equivalent of the "Hello World" program a programmer writes to test a new compiler. You wouldn't expect it to use every feature; you just want to make sure the most basic elements are up and running. If you introduce too much complexity right away, it will be difficult to troubleshoot the individual problems.

In the second stage, you will begin introducing products to each other. For example, in the first stage you may have tested out a new switch by connecting it to other switches and "PINGing" across the network interfaces. In stage 2, you would expand on this. If you had chosen to implement Windows NT Server with Windows 95 clients on a switched network based on Cisco Systems layer-2 switches, stage 2 of the testing would involve connecting both a server and a client to the switch and verifying that they can connect to and use the various network applications that are part of your requirements.

Keep in mind that it is best to start small, even in this phase. Plug in components one at a time, and make sure that each component works before you go on. It would be unwise to put all of the network applications on the server and the client, plug them in, and expect everything to work instantly. Verify it one step at a time. Start with a PING across the network interfaces and build to the more complex applications that you plan to use.

Stage 3 of the testing phase involves a simulated rollout. Create an environment that is a near-exact duplicate of your working environment. It should involve putting both hardware and software through the standard provisioning phases, including the mechanism your organization plans to use to configure network hardware, server hardware, desktop hardware, operating systems, and any software packages that may be in use. Have the exact people who will be doing the work in the production environment create your lab environment. This will give you the opportunity to test the processes involved and give the personnel the chance to get their feet wet with the new hardware and software.

It is important to simulate the production environment as closely as possible. Be sure to test each component individually. For example, if you have created a switched Microsoft network, boot up one of the Windows 95 clients and walk though each of the applications you intend to provide to the users. Have someone make sure that every single feature you intend to offer works properly and makes use of the network as you expect it to. If the applications you are offering are client/server by nature, then you will need to test every single feature.

Applications such as Word do not need to be tested as thoroughly, because the network is not integral to them. You may be surprised to find huge problems in this late stage of testing – don't be. You have not tested all of the applications in the exact environment before, and no doubt there will be incompatibilities. All but the simplest network designs will have problems through each of the stages of testing.

This stage of testing should also include some of the users who will be part of the production environment. In this case, users may be the end users or the support people who will be supporting the network hardware and software. Make sure that they do not have any objections to the new environment and that they "buy off" on it. Involving the users will accomplish three things:

◆ It will provide yet another test of the strength of your design.

◆ It will give you a good opportunity to get some feedback from the people who will be working with the various products and may be very knowledgeable with them.

◆ It will cause the end users to "buy off" on your design and help to reduce any resistance that they may have.

Each of these substages should include a cycle of discovering changes, fixing changes, and retesting changes. It is a common mistake to skip the retesting part of the process. Often, people who are testing something will find a problem and think that they have fixed it. Until you have retested it, you will not discover:

◆ First, whether or not you have fixed the problem as you hoped you had

◆ Second, whether your change has created any new problems

Before moving on to any other phase, you should have an entirely successful test. Otherwise, you will only run into the problem at a later stage in testing.

Preproduction Beta Testing

The final phase of testing really overlaps with the first stage of the implementation. It is called a controlled, limited rollout. Controlled, limited rollouts involve isolating a specific section of the company to be "beta" customers. Windows NT systems engineers are familiar with this practice because Microsoft has been doing it for years, issuing copies of their beta products to a select group of their customers for testing and evaluation.

This really accomplishes several things. First, it allows the customers the opportunity to get some exposure to the new product and to verify that it will work in the environment as they hope. It helps Microsoft because they essentially get a great deal of free beta testing that they would otherwise have to pay people to do. In addition, it helps both the users and the engineers because it allows them to work out any problems that they may have before the production release is distributed.

These methods will work in your organization as well. Choose a small, isolated, forward-thinking department and discuss the project with the managers. The department needs to be willing to experience some problems! Despite the fact that you have already gone through four stages of testing, each ending with a perfect score, you will find new problems as you are implementing the design in a production environment.

You must communicate constantly with the people who will be working in the semiproduction beta environment. Direct feedback is essential to a successful full-scale implementation of your design. Finding problems now will allow you to fix them before they grow to be hundreds of times larger. A few users may experience a handful of problems with the beta implementation of your design, but if thousands of users were to experience the problem on an enterprise scale, your problems would be greatly compounded. After this stage of testing is done and you have been able to create an isolated working subsection of the environment, it is time to begin the gradual, full-scale rollout.

Full-Scale Rollout

The final stage is the real implementation of your design. Just as you built from small to large in the testing phases, you will build slowly during the rollout. As you recall, the final stage of the testing was a limited, small-scale rollout. The difference now is that you are no longer in "beta" – it's showtime! Honestly, you shouldn't expect everything to work perfectly, regardless of how much you have tested the design in the previous steps. You are bound to have problems with any large-scale implementation.

Most things will work, but you will have a few isolated problems. These problems may vary in size from very small to very large, and they should be expected and anticipated. You should build extra time into the schedule to resolve problems that will arise during implementation.

Communication is extremely important. Human beings, by nature, are afraid of change. This isn't a bad thing; change, for the most part, causes a lot of trouble. During implementation, your users will be afraid, and their fear will come across as resistance or even anger. Communicating changes to the end users and anyone who will be working with your new network design is critical. They also need to understand not only the types of changes you will be making, but the underlying reasons and how they are going to benefit from the changes.

If there is an existing production environment, you are probably going to have to schedule a long weekend to do the work. Systems administrators and network engineers have come to know the long weekend as basically an extended workday. Long weekends are good because the users tend to go home and not care if the network goes down. Indeed, you will be bringing the network down, probably for a long time, as you make your changes and verify that everything still works.

Determining Success

Once you have completed the implementation phase, it is time to measure the success of the overall project. This is more complicated than merely measuring the success of the individual phases; the "big picture" must be taken into account. For example, if the project consists in upgrading the network hardware, accomplishing that much does not mean that you have been successful in the overall project. However, it does mean that you have successfully completed the implementation stage.

The only real measure of success in a project of this sort is the satisfaction of the people who initiated it. These people should be interviewed carefully after the implementation phase has been completed and again after several months to determine whether the goals they had in mind have been accomplished. If they are happy with it and they feel that it benefits their work on a day-to-day basis, congratulations! You have been successful.

Other factors in success are based on meeting specific criteria that may have been set forth ahead of time. If you accomplish the desired goals but do so late or over budget, the project may be considered only marginally successful. Depending on how much you missed the goals by, the managers of the project may not consider it a success at all.

Planning a network is a daunting task, but great things can be accomplished with a little planning, patience, and experience. Because developing a network is such an incredible investment for any organization, it is worth the time to do it right.

Summary

This chapter covered the phases of designing, testing, and implementing a network. You have learned the following:

◆ A good design starts with determining the business needs and specific goals of the company. Armed with this information, you can then tackle the job of choosing solutions.

◆ Choosing between vendors that offer similar products involves evaluating them on the basis of several different criteria. The vendor you select will have a tremendous impact on the success of the network implementation as a whole.

◆ Network design is like any other engineering process – it requires a methodical engineering and testing process, followed by a gradual implementation.

In the next chapter, you'll learn how Windows NT can help you reduce WAN costs by leveraging the Internet as a corporate backbone. This information will be particularly useful for organizations that currently have long-distance leased lines, have remote users dial into RAS servers long-distance, or need a network connection between remote offices. Several methods will be discussed, including solutions provided by Microsoft and third-party vendors.

Chapter 7

Using the Internet As a Backbone

IN THIS CHAPTER

♦ Using the Internet as a backbone

♦ Reasons for not using the Internet as a backbone

♦ Understanding VPN protocols

TRADITIONALLY, WIDE AREA network links are made from leased lines or packet-switched networks such as frame relay or ATM. Either way, an organization essentially leases part of a larger network from a telco or a network provider. The provider configures a connection between the endpoints of the WAN link and ensures that the connection stays available and consistent.

These days, many companies are considering using the Internet to carry traffic that would traditionally be carried by a dedicated network provider. This is convenient, since most companies maintain Internet connections anyway. Additionally, it is generally much cheaper to lease a connection to the Internet than to lease a connection across the country.

This chapter shows you why so many companies are considering relying on the Internet as their backbone provider, reasons you should *not* do this, and how to get it done once you decide to do it.

Reasons for Using the Internet As a Backbone

Traditionally, companies leased lines between remote offices for interoffice communications. If the company was connected to the Internet, one or more of the remote offices would maintain a leased line to a local Internet service provider. (A simple network of this type is illustrated in Figure 7-1.) As the Internet becomes an essential business tool, more and more companies are considering consolidating their WAN links and their Internet links. Since each of an organization's offices is already connected to the Internet, it sometimes makes sense to use the same links to carry interoffice traffic and Internet traffic.

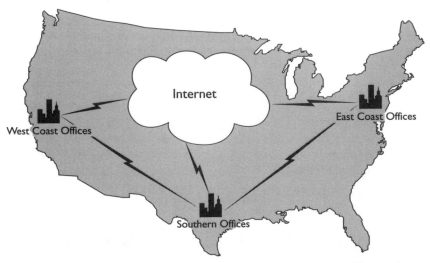

Figure 7-1: The traditional WAN is made up of leased lines between offices and may include Internet connections.

The most common way to use the Internet as a backbone is by using a virtual private network (VPN). VPN is a term used to describe the idea of transmitting private data over a public network. VPNs are not a new concept – they have been used with packet-switched networks for many years under the names "permanent virtual circuit" and "switched virtual circuit." However, sending any private data across the public Internet is definitely a new and experimental concept. Figure 7-2 shows the same organization illustrated earlier, but now relying on the Internet for backbone connectivity.

Lowering wide area networking costs is the primary reason an organization would want to use the Internet as its backbone. Costs are reduced in several ways:

◆ The number of leased lines is lowered, reducing telco charges.

◆ The amount of network hardware required to provide connectivity is reduced, reducing hardware costs.

◆ The overall network complexity is reduced, decreasing maintenance requirements.

◆ Remote users may access the intranet via any ISP, reducing long-distance expenses.

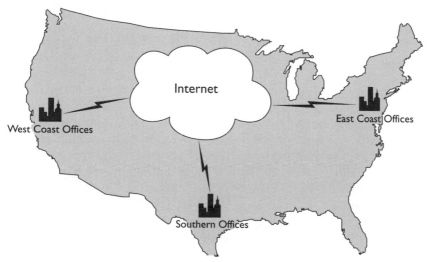

Figure 7-2: Traditional WAN links are being replaced by virtual private network links.

Naturally, the extent to which costs are lowered varies from organization to organization, depending on their current network architecture and the method that organization uses to implement the VPN.

Reasons for Not Using the Internet As a Backbone

It's really not that hard to use the Internet as a corporate backbone. After all, it is just a really big IP network. If two remote offices are both connected to the Internet, all they have to do is exchange traffic and the Internet will carry it back and forth. Users in either remote office can remotely connect to network drives, submit print jobs, browse the remote intranet, or do any other network activity they like. All this can be done across the Internet simply by connecting to an ISP and using valid public IP addresses.

So why dedicate a whole chapter to using the Internet as a backbone? If it is so easy, why bother with such complicated concepts as "virtual private networks"?

Security

Security is the most publicized problem with using the Internet as a backbone. To allow users from other remote offices into your network, you must have very loose security restrictions. Traffic from protocols such as Telnet, HTTP, and FTP would be transmitted across the Internet in clear text, where any ISP that carries traffic between the two offices could (theoretically) eavesdrop and/or alter the data being transmitted.

Reliability

Virtual private networks address the problem of security, but there are other problems inherent in the public Internet that are not so easy to address. First, the Internet is an extremely unreliable network, at least in comparison to leased lines and more traditional packet-switched networks such as frame relay. This is an annoyance when you are surfing the Web to get the latest movie reviews, but it becomes business-critical downtime when an organization is relying on the Internet to carry its backbone traffic. Remember the cliché, "A chain is only as strong as its weakest link"? This statement is very true of the Internet. Traffic that is carried across the Internet may traverse the networks of several different ISPs. Even if the ISPs that provide the organization's Internet connections are 100 percent reliable, the ISP that actually carries the data between the offices may not be so perfect.

For organizations that currently connect offices with leased lines and/or packet-switched networks, the reliability of that connection is limited by several factors. The link is never more reliable than the telco/network provider is, because if a T1 fails (and they do fail), the WAN link is unavailable. Similarly, the routers that connect the organization to the WAN link must be operating properly or the link is lost.

Speed

Sending traffic across a virtual private network involves a lot of processing and overhead. In most cases, the data being transferred is encapsulated within IP datagrams. This adds additional overhead to each packet transmitted. Besides, the data must be encrypted to ensure privacy. Encryption is a very processor-intensive action and can severely bottleneck overall throughput. Even the fastest VPNs currently on the market are not capable of saturating a T1 link (though they come very close). So if your organization requires more bandwidth than about 1Mbps, a VPN will not meet your needs. This is not a major obstacle now because very few (non-ISP) organizations have more bandwidth to the Internet than a T1 provides, and VPN speed will increase as bandwidth does.

For some of the same reasons the Internet is unreliable, its performance also varies. At any given point in time, traffic between two points on the Internet may travel entirely different paths. As network links fail, redundant (and often slower) links take over. As a result, the Internet has a high level of *jitter*. Companies that wish to rely on the Internet to carry their backbone traffic can forget about multimedia applications such as voice and video – the Internet lacks the consistent bandwidth and speed of leased lines. Bandwidth is a concern as always, but it is generally limited by the speed of the organization's ISP connection. This is true of any backbone connection, and as such is not a concern specific to using the Internet.

Understanding VPN Protocols

This section provides a brief overview of some of the virtual private networking protocols and products available for use with Windows NT networks. I have organized it by protocol to avoid showing favoritism to a particular product or vendor. In the end, each of the vendors mentioned will probably support whichever of these protocols survive. Nonetheless, as often happens, each vendor is backing a different protocol while they are in the development stages.

IPSEC

The Internal Protocol Security (IPSEC) working group is a working group within the IETF dedicated to allowing private, secure communications across the public Internet. It is also a general term for a suite of protocols designed to provide privacy, integrity, and authentication to Internet communications. IPSEC is still under development, though it is expected to be standardized some time during 1998. It is an important technology because it is receiving wide support from the networking community. Other organizations offering software- or hardware-based VPN services will adopt the IPSEC standards instead of or in additional to the proprietary protocols currently used.

IPSEC is going to be retrofitted over IPv4, the standard IP protocol in use today. IPSEC is an integral component of IPv6, the future standard for IP. This section covers only the portions of the IPSEC working group that relate to VPNs. For more information on IPSEC, please visit:

```
http://www.ietf.org/html.charters/ipsec-charter.html
```

Encapsulating Security Payload (ESP) is an emerging standard for IP and transport-layer encapsulation, encryption, and validation. It has significant implications for the future of virtual private networks because it is being designed as an open Internet standard. That standard is still under development, however, so I will not cover it in detail here.

IP Authentication Header, or simply AH, is another emerging standard designed to work with ESP. AH complements ESP by validating the sending and receiving hosts. In this way, the possibility of a malicious third party spoofing either end of a virtual private network is practically eliminated.

The primary function of ESP is to encapsulate and tunnel data transferred between two hosts or two networks across another public network, such as the Internet. In addition to tunneling, ESP encrypts and validates data. It also combats replay attacks by sequencing packets and validating that sequence number at the receiving side of the connection.

ESP has the capability to encapsulate data at the transport level or at the network level, as illustrated in Figure 7-3. Because the source and destination IP addresses can be encrypted at the network level, ESP limits the amount of information that can be gathered about an organization's VPN communications.

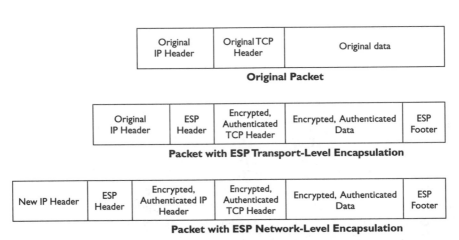

Figure 7-3: ESP is capable of transport- and network-layer encapsulation.

To clarify this point, consider the network in Figure 7-4. Two remote offices have a VPN configured across the public Internet. Host A is communicating with Host C, and Host D is communicating with Host B. Somebody with access to the network equipment carrying the traffic between the two sights could monitor the traffic flow and determine which hosts were talking to which systems and how much data was being transferred. While this may not seem like a serious problem if the data itself is encrypted, it can give away a substantial amount of information about the private networks and the hosts within.

A more secure alternative is to encapsulate the data at the network level. While ESP has the capability, is it certainly not the only option. Notably, the VPN capabilities of Microsoft's Routing and Remote Access Service perform network-level encapsulation without using the ESP standard. Nonetheless, standardized methods are always an improvement over proprietary methods, and I suspect Microsoft will move to adopt ESP once it becomes standardized. ESP is, however, still an IETF draft.

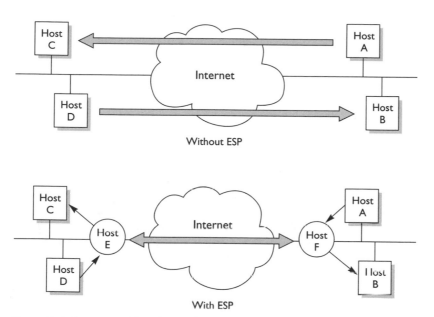

Figure 7-4: Someone with malicious intent could learn a lot about your networks just from the IP headers.

For more information on ESP, visit:

```
http://ds.internic.net/internet-drafts/draft-ietf-ipsec-esp-v2-
  04.txt
```

For more information on AH, visit:

```
http://ds.internic.net/internet-drafts/draft-ietf-ipsec-auth-header-
  05.txt
```

PPTP: Microsoft, 3Com, and Ascend

The Point-to-Point Tunneling Protocol is Microsoft's VPN solution. In a nutshell, PPTP allows PPP traffic to be tunneled within IP. This is useful for many reasons. PPP provides a good foundation to build on top of because it allows any network protocol to be carried between two systems. When the second system receives PPP-encapsulated traffic, it removes the link-layer (HDLC) information and is able to forward the traffic that was contained within: network-layer traffic. The traditional use for PPP is with dial-up networks, as shown in Figure 7-5.

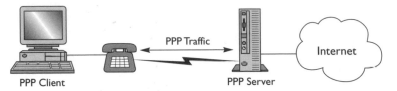

Figure 7-5: PPP is traditionally used to carry traffic across analog phone lines.

The makers of PPTP imagine PPP being extended so that it can carry traffic not only across dial-up links but also across networks as well. Instead of merely being transferred across phone lines, PPP traffic could be transferred from a client to a server on the same network, even a public network such as the Internet. When the server receives the traffic, it could remove the PPP information and transmit the network-layer traffic onto another private network, which would otherwise be unavailable. PPTP in use is shown in Figure 7-6.

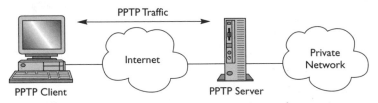

Figure 7-6: Similar to PPP, PPTP carries traffic across public networks.

PPTP works like PPP, but traffic may cross public networks. PPTP is not currently an Internet standard, but an RFC is under development. This lack of standardization is seen as PPTP's biggest drawback — it is uncertain whether it will ever be supported by platforms other than Microsoft's. Companies that are seen more favorably than Microsoft are developing other VPN solutions for multiple platforms. UNIX administrators and engineers often frown on Microsoft-developed Internet solutions, and the Internet is still ruled by UNIX. Whether or not PPTP will succeed as an Internet VPN solution is still undetermined.

PPTP is more flexible than most tunneling protocols because it allows any network-layer protocol to be tunneled. Microsoft has always made an effort to support IPX and AppleTalk, and the multiprotocol capabilities of PPTP are merely an extension of that effort. However, very few of us will need to tunnel the AppleTalk protocol. Even if you did, you could only do so from a Windows 95 or Windows NT system, because only Microsoft platforms support PPTP currently.

Owing to its lack of standardization, PPTP is still a Microsoft-only solution. PPTP clients exist for Windows 95 and Windows NT, and only Windows NT systems may currently act as PPTP servers. 3Com and Ascend network hardware will soon support PPTP, but making the new features functional is still a long way away. Even after 3Com and Ascend release products with PPTP support, ISPs will need to upgrade their equipment before anybody can actually make use of this protocol. Even as PPTP nears standardization, it is being merged with Cisco's L2F protocol to create the L2PT protocol described later in this chapter.

PPTP is and will be an important part of the Windows operating systems. For more information, please review Chapter 13, "Routing and Remote Access Service." RRAS is a freely available upgrade to the PPTP support included in Windows NT 4.0. More features will be added to Windows NT 5.0 when the release product becomes available.

If you would like to review the current draft standard for PPTP, please visit:

```
http://ds.internic.net/internet-drafts/draft-ietf-pppext-pptp-02.txt
```

Cisco's Layer-2 Tunneling: L2F

L2F, Layer Two Forwarding, is Cisco's alternative to PPTP. The functionality provided by the two products is very similar. It was so similar, in fact, that Cisco and Microsoft joined teams. PPTP and L2F are currently being merged into L2TP, the Layer Two Tunneling Protocol. I do not make an effort to cover L2F in detail here because Microsoft does not support it in any way. It is only interesting in the context of this book because it provides part of the foundation of L2TP, the protocol that will replace PPTP when Windows NT 5.0 is released.

L2F is a router-based tunneling protocol. Essentially, a router notices that certain packets are bound for a remote, private network. The traffic bound for that network (which may contain illegal IP addresses) is encapsulated within another IP packet and forwarded to a preconfigured server. L2F is a straightforward tunneling protocol supported by Cisco routing hardware. While Windows NT does not have any explicit support for L2F, it does not need any because the protocol is entirely operating system–independent.

L2TP (Microsoft, Cisco, Ascend, IBM, and 3Com)

The Layer Two Tunneling Protocol is the evolution of PPTP and L2F. A wide range of product vendors, including Microsoft, Cisco, Ascend, IBM, and 3Com, are sponsoring development. Those of you already familiar with PPTP and L2F will find L2TP a natural extension; many of the same goals are being met. I do not cover L2TP in detail here because it is still remote from actual implementation. Cisco plans to include L2TP support in version 11.3 of the Cisco IOS, and Microsoft will include native L2TP support in Windows NT 5.0.

One of the most interesting features new to L2TP is the support of Multilink Point-to-Point Protocol (MPPP). MPPP is an extension of PPP that allows a PPP client to connect to a PPP server over multiple connections and transfer data using all connections. For example, a Windows NT workstation can be configured with two modems, each connected to a separate dial-up link. Both modems could be used to dial into an ISP, and the bandwidth would be effectively doubled. MPPP was built into Windows NT 4.0, and we all need more bandwidth, so why are we not all using it? It is an extremely difficult thing to implement because of a problem called "multilink hunt-group splitting." The PPP servers that accept the calls must be capable of rejoining the data that the client has split between the multiple connections. This is a simple task when the PPP server is a single Windows NT server with multiple modems, but most ISPs use huge banks of hundreds of analog modems to accept dial-up connections. These modems and dial-in servers are generally not connected to each other and so have no way of reuniting the data that was separated by the client.

However, L2TP enables the weakness to be overcome. Because the data must cross a network and arrive at a single point of entry (the L2TP server), all the packets will be combined again before they must be deencapsulated and retransmitted on the private network! Therefore, the packets may enter the network at different analog dial-up connections and do not need to meet together again until they reach the PPTP server that guards the entrance to the private destination network.

For more information on L2TP, visit:

`http://www.masinter.net/~12tp/`

The current draft of the PPTP standard is located at:

`http://ds.internic.net/internet-drafts/draft-ietf-pppext-12tp-09.txt`

Conclusion

Virtual private networks are changing the way companies do wide area networking. As the Internet improves in speed, reliability, and security, it becomes more practical for carrying private data. It will never completely replace current methods of wide area networking such as leased lines and privately owned packet switched networks such as frame relay and ATM, but it will definitely take a large part of the market share.

Many companies currently offer products for creating virtual private networks. Most, though not all, of these support Windows NT. Microsoft itself is building substantial VPN capabilities into the Routing and Remote Access Service. Working as a team, Cisco and Microsoft will change the way companies exchange data over the Internet.

Summary

This chapter discussed why so many companies are considering relying on the Internet as their backbone provider, reasons you should *not* do this, and how to get it done once you decide to do it. Today many companies are considering using the Internet to carry traffic that would traditionally be carried by a dedicated network provider. This is convenient, since most companies maintain Internet connections anyway. Additionally, it is generally much cheaper to lease a connection to the Internet than to lease a connection across the country.

You have learned about:

♦ Using the Internet as a backbone

♦ Reasons for not using the Internet as a backbone

♦ VPN protocols

In the next chapter, you'll learn about the importance of troubleshooting your network when things go wrong. But merely having a deep knowledge of the way a network works is not nearly enough to troubleshoot it successfully; one must also have a skill and a talent for troubleshooting. Troubleshooting is a methodical process of elimination. It must be taken step by step to be effective.

Part III

Implementation

Chapter 8

Troubleshooting and Analysis

IN THIS CHAPTER

- ◆ Using troubleshooting skills to minimize downtime
- ◆ Solving problems methodically by relying on the layered approach to troubleshooting networks
- ◆ Understanding the tools available to assist you in solving problems

TROUBLESHOOTING IS A methodical process of elimination. It must be taken step by step to be effective. This chapter details these steps for you and provides a framework for troubleshooting any network-related problem you run across. It also introduces you to tools of the trade to use when troubleshooting the physical layer, the data-link to presentation layers, and the application layer. At the end of the chapter is an example of how to put these tools to good use.

Throughout the book, I provide information that will help you troubleshoot your network when things go wrong. But merely having a deep knowledge of the way a network works is not nearly enough to successfully troubleshoot it; you must also have a skill and a talent for troubleshooting.

Understanding the Importance of Troubleshooting

We've all been paged at 3 A.M. because someone just determined that something is broken and someone needs to fix it right away. Troubleshooting is the process of taking a general problem, such as a service, system, or network failure, and narrowing it down to one specific component. Once you've isolated the component, you must fix it.

Troubleshooting is especially important because it is rarely done at your leisure. Generally, if something is broken, it needs to be fixed right away. In many cases, outages can cost companies an incredible amount of money. Indeed, they may even cost an administrator his or her job. Because troubleshooting is the best solution for many critical problems, the people responsible must be extremely skilled and efficient at the troubleshooting process.

Troubleshooting is strictly reactive. It only comes into play when proactive measures have failed and something needs to be fixed immediately. It would be nice if all engineers were so perfect that planning and reliable hardware would eliminate the need for troubleshooting. In the meantime, the best to hope for is quick and efficient troubleshooting.

Overall Network Cost Factors

As discussed in Chapter 6, the cost of any network component is made up of many different factors. The simplest to compute is the initial hardware cost and any charges associated with software licenses. While these are the easiest to calculate, however, they usually make up only a small part of the overall cost of a network. Another factor is the ongoing cost, which takes into account the amount of time spent maintaining the equipment and costs incurred when that equipment fails. This is the type of cost we are interested in now, because effective troubleshooting is one way to reduce downtime.

The Cost of Downtime

The cost of downtime can be broken into several subcategories. Downtime costs companies in the following ways:

◆ Repair expenses

◆ Business lost

◆ Reduced productivity

The simplest factor of the cost of downtime is the expense of repairing the problem. This is made up of several components, including hardware replacement costs (which may be covered under warranty) and the salaries of those performing the troubleshooting. While this is the most tangible component of downtime cost, it is generally the least of an organization's concerns. Productivity and revenue lost during periods of downtime can be so great that companies will spend almost unlimited funds to repair failed machinery.

Organizations that have spent money to build a network often rely on that network for business-critical functions. This is especially true for companies such as Internet service providers, which rely on networking as their primary source of revenue. For these organizations, downtime may translate directly into lost revenue. If an ISP sells bandwidth by the byte, losing connectivity for two hours not only irritates the customer but reduces the amount of billable time. This amount is fairly simple to calculate, though the costs vary widely depending on the type of product the company sells.

Anytime a component of the network fails, users complain. However annoying these complaints may be to those of us who receive them, they are a reflection of the user's reduced capacity to work effectively. For example, if a POP/SMTP server fails, users will no longer be able to communicate using e-mail. While another method of communication may be used (such as a telephone), the users are not as effective as they are when they have the option of sending e-mail. It may take twice as long to disseminate a message to employees, a fact that may lead to paid overtime, increased employee stress, missed deadlines, and lost revenue.

As shown, network downtime can cost an organization a significant amount. This underscores the importance of troubleshooting and can be used to justify to higher management the cost associated with troubleshooting tools. Indeed, a particular piece of troubleshooting equipment often pays for itself the first or second time it is needed to help solve a problem.

Analyzing Networks Using the OSI Model

The troubleshooting process must be methodical and organized. The network structure laid out by the OSI model provides a convenient and well known organization.

Whether you begin troubleshooting at the top of the OSI model (the application layer) or the bottom of the model (the physical layer) is a matter of personal preference. The advantages and disadvantages of the two paths are discussed in the next section, "Troubleshooting the Optimistic or Pessimistic Way."

To troubleshoot at the physical layer, verify all aspects of physical connectivity. When troubleshooting a client/server connection, verify that both the client system and the server system have physical connectivity between their network interface cards and the network equipment. Then verify that the network equipment is physically connected to the rest of the network, and include any equipment that participates in the connection between the two nodes. Finally, if everything seems to be plugged in correctly, verify that all cabling works properly using cable-testing equipment. If a single wire within a Cat 5 network cable has become loose from its RJ-45 connector, all network connectivity is lost.

Troubleshooting at the data-link layer is more difficult, though problems with this layer are rare. It is a simple thing to look at cables and determine whether they are plugged in, but it is much more difficult to determine whether a layer-2 protocol is functioning correctly — you cannot simply view the electrical signals on the cabling. More sophisticated tools are necessary, such as protocol analyzers and some utilities that are built into NT, such as ARP. For example, if a system successfully responds to an ARP request, then you know that the system has a bare minimum of data-link-layer capabilities. You have also determined that physical connectivity is fine.

The network layer is a common source of network problems. All IP-related problems fall into this category, including routing problems, mismatched IP addresses, and incorrect subnet masks and IP-based filtering. The primary utilities for troubleshooting the network layer are PING and TRACERT, described in more detail later in this chapter. In general, if you can PING a remote host, you have eliminated the network layer as a potential source of problems. When the network layer has been eliminated, you can be assured that all lower layers (both physical and data-link) are working properly.

Another common source of problems is the transport layer. All TCP- and UDP-related problems will be found by troubleshooting the transport layer. The most common problem is routers that filter based on port number. Protocol analyzers are often used to troubleshoot transport-layer problems, and the Telnet utility can be used to verify that a specific TCP port on a specific host is listening for incoming connections.

The application layer is the most common source of problems in many modern environments. The networking industry is such that network hardware tends to be extremely reliable, but the latest-and-greatest software lures many systems administrators into installing less-than-perfect software. Application services, such as Web servers, tend to be highly unreliable and problematic, especially when initially released. Troubleshooting this layer generally includes testing with application-specific client-side utilities such as Web browsers, though it may also involve protocol analyzers and even the Telnet utility for Telnet-based protocols.

The process of troubleshooting networks based on the OSI model is outlined in Figure 8-1.

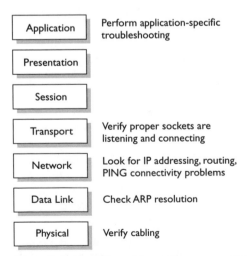

Figure 8-1: The OSI model provides a convenient structure for troubleshooting.

Troubleshooting the Optimistic or Pessimistic Way

Depending on what book you read, different sources recommend troubleshooting starting with the top layer of the OSI model or the bottom layer. If a Web server stops responding, it may seem silly to check the physical layer first by walking behind your computer and checking to make sure the cable is still plugged in. I call this *pessimistic troubleshooting*, because it assumes that absolutely anything may break at any given point, and that everything under the sun should be verified before even checking for the most likely problems.

A method that generally works better in modern internetworks is *optimistic troubleshooting*. With optimistic testing, the troubleshooting starts at the highest layer of the OSI model and works its way down. Given the example of a failed Web server, the troubleshooting would begin at the application layer. Perhaps the first step would be to attempt to connect to another Web server with the same client to ensure that the Web browser is configured properly. If this worked (which it probably would), the troubleshooter will have verified that network connectivity (at least on the client side) is fine and saved lots of time.

As a general rule, optimistic troubleshooting works in environments where the network is reasonably stable. Pessimistic troubleshooting may be used in environments where the network is very new, has recently undergone major modifications (such as recabling), or is fraught with reliability problems. Either method will eventually isolate the problem; the only difference is how quickly.

Troubleshooting the Physical Layer

Especially when you are implementing new networks, physical problems are common. Some of the most common problems administrators experience are faulty wiring, unplugged cabling, and interference. Troubleshooting this layer tends to be a simple but time-consuming task, and most network administrators will want to delegate the job to someone else (if possible!). I avoid the physical layer as a rule in this book, because it is straying too far from the focus. However, this section gives a brief overview of physical-layer troubleshooting.

Cable Testers

Cable-checking equipment comes in all shapes and sizes, and it ranges from very cheap to very expensive. A typical piece of equipment will allow two ends of a cable to be plugged into it and will transmit a signal through one end. It verifies the cable's integrity by watching the traffic it receives on the other side of the cable and ensuring that all the data is received just as it was sent. Other equipment is capable of estimating where a cabling flaw occurs by sending electrical signals down the wire.

It is important to have a collection of this type of equipment on hand should the need arise to troubleshoot at the physical layer. In networks where the cable plant was laid down by a professional, reputable company, physical-layer troubleshooting should rarely go beyond verifying that everything is plugged in.

Loopback Interfaces

A loopback interface is simply a wire that curves back upon itself. The transmit wires loop back and connect to the same interface's receive wires. In this way, any signals generated by the interface will also be immediately received by the interface. This wiring allows the system to communicate only with itself, and therefore it is only useful for troubleshooting. A sample loopback interface is illustrated in Figure 8-2. Most network interface cards and network equipment support using loopback interfaces to diagnose problems with the network card and/or the physical interface.

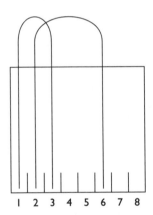

Figure 8-2: Wiring for a 10-Base-T loopback interface

1 2 3 4 5 6 7 8

Using a loopback interface will determine whether or not a particular network interface card is physically okay. Sometimes, one or more pins will become damaged in the transceiver. Without using a loopback interface, this type of problem can be very difficult to uncover.

Troubleshooting Data-Link to Presentation Layer

Network problems often occur between layers 2 and 6. These may be caused by a variety of things, from misconfigured routers to mistyped subnet masks. The following tools are the most important to know for troubleshooting problems of this type.

PING

PING is a simple yet fantastically useful utility that uses the ICMP protocol to verify connectivity on an IP network. To review, ICMP resides at the Internet layer of the model and operates exactly like IP except it is used to carry error messages across TCP/IP-based networks. The PING utility uses this communication channel to verify that the client, the server, and everything in between are connected to the network properly and operating as they should. PING is often the first step in troubleshooting because successfully PINGing a host eliminates the possibility that there has been a failure at the network layer and below. It also tells you that the remote system is online and operating properly.

PING can be used for both optimistic and pessimistic troubleshooting. If you are optimistic, start by PINGing the remote host. A successful PING tells you the system is up and running and the network is okay. A failed PING tells you that either the host is offline or there is a network problem, so you should work your way back through the network. After a failed PING, try PINGing another host residing on the same subnet. If this PING also fails, PING the gateway that connects to that subnet. Eventually, work your way through the network toward the client. If every PING fails, have the client PING itself to verify that the network software has been configured correctly.

If you are pessimistic about the state of the network and the client system, start by PINGing the software loopback interface, 127.0.0.1 (this is a reserved IP address used only for loopback). If this PING fails, you know definitively that there is a problem with the software driver. Try uninstalling TCP/IP and reinstalling it, or reapplying the latest service pack. If that PING succeeds, it indicates that the software has been loaded correctly. Next, try to PING the default gateway of the system. If that PING works, it tells you that the client is connected to the network and the first router is operating properly. Work your way through the network path, PINGing each gateway as you go. The first gateway that fails to respond to PING packets is probably the point of failure. If all PINGs succeed, your problem probably resides at a higher layer.

For more information on Windows NT's implementation of PING and the underlying protocols ICMP and ECHO, please refer to Chapter 9.

TraceRT

The TraceRT utility is closely related to PING because it also relies on the ICMP protocol within the TCP/IP protocol suite. Essentially, TraceRT automates the task described in the previous section; instead of PINGing each gateway on the network, TraceRT sends a series of PINGs with varying TTLs.

If you TraceRT to an IP address and do not use the -d option, the first few packets that TraceRT generates are reverse DNS queries to look up the hostname of the final destination. After the reverse DNS has completed, TraceRT sends three ICMP packets to the destination with the TTL in the IP header set to 1. The first router should receive the ICMP packets and decrement the TTL to zero. Because the packet now has a TTL of zero, the router should return an ICMP error message to the TraceRT utility. This complicated process is illustrated in Figure 8-3.

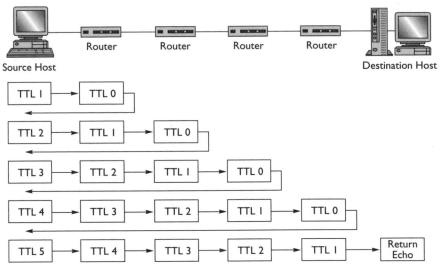

Figure 8-3: TraceRT examined

TraceRT then examines the IP header in each packet and concludes that the source address of the return message is the first hop between itself and the final destination. To make the display friendlier, it performs a reverse DNS lookup on the IP address and displays the DNS name of the gateway. It will then display the total time it took to return each of the three packets. If any of the packets are not returned correctly, TraceRT displays an asterisk instead of the round-trip time.

After the first three packets have either returned to TraceRT or timed out, another three packets are generated. This time, the packets will have a TTL of 2. Therefore, the first gateway will decrement the TTL to 1 and pass it on. However, the second gateway will decrement the TTL to zero and return an error message to TraceRT. Once again, TraceRT will examine the packet and use the source IP address to determine the second hop between itself and the final destination. This process continues until the ICMP packet reaches the IP address of the final destination.

Here is a sample TraceRT execution:

```
C:\ >tracert 10.3.17.74

Tracing route to test.i-made-this-up.com [10.3.17.74]
over a maximum of 30 hops:

  1    *     *      *     Request timed out.
  2   150 ms   140 ms   130 ms router1.level-2-isp.net [10.115.101.254]
```

```
3  130 ms   140 ms   130 ms  router2.level-2-isp.net [10.232.56.65]
4  130 ms   140 ms   131 ms  router3.level-1-isp.NET [10.39.135.213]

5  130 ms   131 ms   140 ms  router4.level-1-isp.Net [10.39.35.6]
6  141 ms   130 ms   140 ms  router5.another-level-1-isp.net
[10.0.2.73]
7  131 ms   150 ms   130 ms  router6.another-level-1-isp.net
[10.0.2.249]
8  140 ms   140 ms   130 ms  router7.another-level-1-isp.net
[10.0.3.54]
9  130 ms   140 ms   140 ms  router8.another-level-1-isp.net
[10.34.78.47]
10  220 ms   140 ms   141 ms  router9.another-level-1-isp.com
[10.3.17.74]
```

```
Trace complete.
```

There are several things you can do to alter the normal behavior of TraceRT. Probably the most useful is the d option, which disables the reverse DNS lookups. This particular option makes TraceRT much faster, and since I never know what the DNS entries mean anyway, it has no drawbacks for me. It also serves to reduce the amount of traffic generated on the network, since several DNS queries are generated for each hop.

TraceRT is a great utility. However, it is often overestimated. Many people use it as a way to diagnose a particular router or network segment as being faulty. Time and time again I have seen a user who performs a TraceRT use a time difference between two hops as proof that a particular gateway is slow. While this would seem like a logical conclusion, it is not necessarily valid, because TraceRT does not follow a single packet through its path; it sends multiple packets, which may even travel completely different paths. For example, consider the following three lines from the TraceRT just described:

```
6   141 ms   130 ms   140 ms router5.another-level-1-isp.net
[10.0.2.73]
7   131 ms   150 ms   130 ms router6.another-level-1-isp.net
[10.0.2.249]
8   140 ms   140 ms   130 ms router7.another-level-1-isp.net
[10.0.3.54]
```

As you can see, the second column of PINGs shows a return time of 130 ms, then 150 ms, and then 140 ms. Obviously, these are not the time it took for a single packet to travel this route — it is the product of three individual packets. Delays that appear to be at a single router may even be the result of latency on the network local to the client — if it happens to be busy while the three ICMP messages are transmitted for that particular hop, the round-trip time shown will be deceiving.

NetStat

Netstat is a useful tool for troubleshooting because it gives you a quick list of all incoming and outgoing connections and a summary of protocol statistics. For example, to determine who is currently connected to a Web server, use the following command:

```
netstat -a -n
```

The -a parameter instructs NetSstat to display all connections both incoming and outgoing and lists all open ports. The -n parameter bypasses the reverse DNS lookups on all IP addresses, greatly speeding the display.

NBTStat

NBTStat provides information about NetBIOS communications on the computer on which it is executed. This has several implications for troubleshooting. First, the commands nbtstat -r and nbtstat -c are useful for determining which NetBIOS names have been resolved. This is a tremendous help if you are attempting to diagnose a NetBIOS connection, because it indicates whether or not the computer was able to resolve the name of a server to an IP address. If the server you are attempting to reach is listed, then the name was resolved successfully and your problem lies elsewhere.

NBTStat is also useful when used in conjunction with the -s parameter. This parameter lists all active NetBIOS sessions and can indicate who is connected to a server or what sessions a client has successfully established.

NBTStat, when used with the -a or -A option, can be used to diagnose remote machines. The lowercase version of the option is used when you wish to name another system using its NetBIOS name. The uppercase version allows you to specify an IP address instead. The following shows a sample run with NBTStat and a remote system named "TERI."

```
D:\WINNT>nbtstat -a TERI

    NetBIOS Remote Machine Name Table

    Name            Type        Status
    ------------------------------------
    TERI        <20> UNIQUE     Registered
    TERI        <00> UNIQUE     Registered
    TONY        <00> GROUP      Registered
    TERI        <1F> UNIQUE     Registered
    TERI        <01> UNIQUE     Registered

    MAC Address = 00-21-78-12-A8-CA
```

IPConfig

The IPCconfig utility is a great way to get a snapshot of the IP configuration on a particular system. To get a full listing of everything you've ever wanted to know about an IP stack, use the -all option. A sample of the IPConfig utility follows:

```
C:\>ipconfig -all

Windows NT IP Configuration

        Host Name . . . . . . . . . : tony.domain-made-up.com
        DNS Servers . . . . . . . . : 10.115.8.20
                        10.115.8.19
        Node Type . . . . . . . . . : Hybrid
        NetBIOS Scope ID. . . . . . :
        IP Routing Enabled. . . . . : Yes
        WINS Proxy Enabled. . . . . : No
        NetBIOS Resolution Uses DNS : No

Ethernet adapter LNEPCI26:

        Description . . . . . . . . : Novell 2000 Adapter.
        Physical Address. . . . . . : 00-21-78-12 7L 3A
        DHCP Enabled. . . . . . . . : No
        IP Address. . . . . . . . . : 10.69.69.1
        Subnet Mask . . . . . . . . : 255.0.0.0
        Default Gateway . . . . . . :
        Primary WINS Server . . . . : 10.111.59.69

PPP adapter NdisWan4:

        Description . . . . . . . . : NDISWAN Miniport
        Physical Address. . . . . . : 00-00-10-b0-05-fC
        DHCP Enabled. . . . . . . . : No
        IP Address. . . . . . . . . : 10.115.33.235
        Subnet Mask . . . . . . . . : 255.255.0.0
        Default Gateway . . . . . . : 10.115.33.235
        Primary WINS Server . . . . : 10.78.64.6
        Secondary WINS Server . . . : 10.78.64.7
```

ARP

Data-link-layer problems are rare, but they do occur. ARP is a useful utility for troubleshooting resolution problems between MAC addresses and IP addresses. If you are unsure whether or not a system is able to find another system on the same subnet, use the arp -a command to retrieve a list of all MAC addresses currently stored in the ARP cache. If a MAC and IP address shows up, it means they were successfully resolved. You should also verify that the IP address and MAC address are correct for the destination.

ARP problems are common when network interface cards change. This is particularly true if the ARP cache timeout has been set to a long period of time. For example, if a client communicates with a server on the same subnet and it has an IP address of 10.10.10.10 and a MAC address of 11-11-11-11-11-11, this IP/MAC address pair will be stored in the client's ARP cache. If the server is then shut down and the network card is replaced, it will have a new MAC address. The next time the client attempts to communicate with the server, it will direct the frames to the *old* MAC address. Therefore, even if the IP address is correct, the client may not be able to communicate with the server. Aside from manually clearing the ARP cache, your only option for solving the problem is to wait until the cache times out.

The next example shows an ARP cache from a system that is not very busy:

```
C:\>arp -a

Interface: 149.111.59.69 on Interface 3
 Internet Address    Physical Address    Type
 10.3.17.74     02-22-72-12-a8-ce   dynamic
```

Route

Problems at the internetwork layer are often caused by misconfigurations in the local routing table of a system. This is very common on systems that are multi-homed because there may be multiple routes to a single destination. I will not go into great detail about routing problems here; they are covered in Chapter 13, "Routing and Remote Access Service." The following example shows output from the route print command, when executed on a system with three network interface cards:

```
C:\> route print

Active Routes:

   Network Address       Netmask Gateway Address     Interface Metric
       0.0.0.0       0.0.0.0  10.115.33.235   10.115.33.235     1
      10.0.0.0      255.0.0.0    10.69.69.1      10.69.69.1     1
     10.69.69.1 255.255.255.255    127.0.0.1      127.0.0.1     1
  10.255.255.255 255.255.255.255    10.69.69.1      10.69.69.1     1
    127.0.0.0     255.0.0.0    127.0.0.1      127.0.0.1     1
   10.115.0.0    255.255.0.0 10.115.33.235   10.115.33.235     1
 10.115.33.235 255.255.255.255    127.0.0.1      127.0.0.1     1
10.115.255.255 255.255.255.255 10.115.33.235   10.115.33.235     1
   10.111.59.0   255.255.255.0 10.111.59.69   10.111.59.69     1
 10.111.59.69 255.255.255.255    127.0.0.1      127.0.0.1     1
10.111.255.255 255.255.255.255  10.111.59.69   10.111.59.69     1
     224.0.0.0    224.0.0.0    10.69.69.1      10.69.69.1     1
255.255.255.255 255.255.255.255    10.69.69.1      10.69.69.1     1
```

Telnet

The Telnet utility is vastly underestimated as a troubleshooting tool. Not only can it be used to make sure that a Telnet server is operating properly at the application level, but it can also be used to ensure that remote systems are listening on specific TCP ports and that they are accessible across the network. For example, if a remote system is configured as a Web server but does not seem to be responding properly, Telnet to the Web server on port 80. To do this, enter the following command (where 10.10.10.10 is the IP address or FQDN of the Web server):

```
telnet 10.10.10.10 80
```

Easy! If Telnet is successful in forming a connection, you know the remote system is listening on port 80 and there is no firewall between the two systems that is filtering that specific port. Once the TCP connection is established properly, you may begin to troubleshoot at the application layer (discussed more later).

Another useful example of using the Telnet application to troubleshoot transport-layer connections involves the NetBIOS Session service. To determine whether a remote machine is listening with the Server service and there is not a filtering router blocking traffic, Telnet to the remote system using TCP port 139. If the remote system is listening for NetBIOS Session service traffic, you will be greeted with a cursor in the upper left corner of the screen. If the remote system has the Server service disabled or has a filtering router blocking NetBIOS traffic, the Telnet application will show an hourglass for the cursor and wait about a minute to time-out before returning an error message.

As a quick exercise, test whether or not Microsoft's Web servers listen for NetBIOS Session service traffic by running the following command:

```
telnet www.microsoft.com 139
```

Isolating Firewall Problems

In modern corporate networks, network administrators typically perform extensive filtering based on TCP port number. This can be frustrating for users who wish to connect to systems, because a remote host may be PINGable but will not respond to HTTP requests. To make matters worse, users on other subnets may be able to reach the server without any problem! Telnet is an excellent utility for determining if a TCP connection can be established between two systems using a specific TCP port; once this is known, you can eliminate packet filtering from the possible causes of the problem you are troubleshooting.

You will notice that Telnet waits for the timeout and then returns an error message. Therefore, Microsoft has done the right thing and blocked NetBIOS traffic.

Performance Monitor

Performance Monitor is not the best tool for nailing down specific problems, but it can be a useful tool for determining the overall state of a system or network. Therefore, if you are concerned that a particular problem may be caused by a network that is experiencing extremely high levels of traffic, use the techniques described in Chapter 4 to determine whether or not this is the case.

Similarly, Performance Monitor can be used if a system doesn't seem to be responding to network requests and you fear it may be an application or service on the system that is consuming all the processor's time. The Performance Monitor utility will provide you with a quick snapshot of the state of the system and verify or invalidate your concerns.

Protocol Analyzers/Network Monitor

Protocol analyzers are the ultimate network troubleshooting tool. They give you a view into the electrical and optical signals as they fly through the wire, allowing you to see exactly what is happening. Of course, this is only really useful to you if you can interpret the data as well. One of the primary goals of this text is to provide you with the knowledge needed to use Network Monitor to troubleshoot networks.

Network Monitor and any protocol analyzer can be used to troubleshoot problems at layer 2 and above. Throughout this text, I have provided examples on how to use this utility to analyze and troubleshoot network problems. If you would like to use the utility to troubleshoot something, please refer to the chapter of this text that refers to that protocol specifically.

Troubleshooting the Application Layer

The application layer is a common source of problems because of the short lifetime application-layer services tend to have. IIS, for example, undergoes a complete revision approximately annually. Each revision is bound to introduce features and/or bugs that did not exist in the previous release. For this reason, troubleshooting application-layer protocols is a common yet difficult task.

Telnet

Telnet is useful for troubleshooting many, but not all, application-layer protocols. Telnet may only be used to troubleshoot application protocols that rely on the Telnet communication mechanism. Fortunately, the most popular application protocols do use Telnet: HTTP, FTP, and (of course) Telnet.

To troubleshoot an application-layer protocol, simply Telnet to the server and specify the port number used by the service. For example, if you wish to troubleshoot an FTP server that is using the default port, enter the command:

```
telnet 10.10.10.10 21
```

where 10.10.10.10 is the IP address of the FTP server. If everything is okay below the application layer, Telnet will connect successfully and greet you with a cursor. At this point, you must pretend to be a normal FTP client and issue regular FTP-like commands. For example, the following conversation logs a user into an FTP server using Telnet rather than an FTP client:

```
( Start | Run ) telnet ftp.microsoft.com 21
user anonymous
pass iloveidg@idgbooks.com
```

Of course, you can't start transferring files this way because the FTP protocol uses a separate connection. However, you have verified that the FTP service is running and allowing a user to connect. The advantage of using Telnet over a standard FTP client is that you eliminate the possibility that the client is introducing a problem. Also, many clients attempt to be "friendly" by hiding messages that are returned from the server. If the server were showing some indication of a problem, a typical FTP client may not give you that information.

Naturally, this approach works well with HTTP, too. Please refer to the chapters on FTP and WWW services for more information on troubleshooting using the Telnet utility.

NSLookup

Use the NSLookup utility any time you need to troubleshoot DNS entries. If you are concerned that a given DNS entry has not been entered correctly, use this utility. If you need to verify that a specific DNS server is returning the right information for a specific DNS record, use this utility. If you want to check and see how round-robin is configured for a particular Web site, use this utility. Chapter 12 provides a great deal of information on the NSLookup utility.

Web Browsers

Not the greatest utilities for detailed troubleshooting of the HTTP protocol, Web browsers are nonetheless useful for determining whether clients on an Internet may connect to a specific Web server. Even if you can get a Web server to respond correctly to HTTP commands using the Telnet utility, this fact does not guarantee that it will accomplish its goal of serving Web pages to the Internet public. For this, your only choice is to connect to the Web server just like anyone else – by using a popular Web browser.

If you manage Web servers, it is a good idea to keep a variety of different Web browsers handy. You should test all Web servers and Web pages with both of the popular Web browsers – Netscape Navigator and Microsoft Internet Explorer. I also recommend keeping older versions of these utilities around, as not everyone has upgraded to the latest and greatest.

FTP Clients

Just as Web servers should be tested with Web browsers, FTP servers should be tested with a variety of popular FTP clients. This will ensure that nothing you have configured on the server will stop a client from connecting to it. For example, some graphical FTP clients have problems with welcome messages that are more than a certain number of characters in length. You would not discover this problem if you used Telnet to diagnose the FTP server.

The most popular anonymous FTP clients are Netscape Navigator and Microsoft Internet Explorer. The most popular graphical FTP clients are Cute FTP, WSFTP, and the command-line FTP utility included with Windows NT and Windows 95.

Troubleshooting in Real-Life Situations

This section provides several examples of troubleshooting at work. My goal is not to give solutions to specific problems, but rather to illustrate the troubleshooting process in real-life situations.

Users call you to complain that they cannot connect to their favorite share, \\SERVER\SHARE. Naturally, this concerns you because it could indicate several very serious things:

♦ The network has failed.

♦ A router has failed.

♦ The file server is unplugged from the network.

♦ The file server has crashed.

◆ The share has been removed from the server.

◆ The client computer has had a network failure.

◆ The client computer could not resolve the computer name.

◆ The user's account has been removed from the domain.

Other possibilities come to mind as well, but these are the most likely possibilities. Because your network tends to be reliable and the majority of problems tend to happen on the client side, you decide to pursue an optimistic method of troubleshooting. Because you are optimistic, you start by attempting to connect to the share from another workstation on the same subnet with your user account. The connection succeeds. This eliminates the possibility that the server and share have been damaged in any way.

To ensure that the client system is connecting to the network properly, you ask the user to PING the server using the IP address. The PING succeeds, eliminating the possibility that the network has failed or that the client computer's TCP/IP stack is not working properly. Next, you want to determine if the user was able to locate the file server, so you have the user issue the command `nbtstat -r` at the command prompt. The server's name does not appear in the list of successfully resolved names, so you determine that there may have been a problem resolving the NetBIOS name.

You know that clients on your network should resolve NetBIOS names using a WINS server, so you want to verify that the client is configured correctly. You ask the user to enter the command `ipconfig /all` and read you the output. With this information, you realize that the user does not have a WINS server configured. After some questioning, the user admits to having removed the IP address on a whim.

To resolve the problem, you ask the user does not have a the WINS server IP address from the Network Control Panel applet and reboot the system. After the reboot completes, the user is once again able to connect to the destination server.

This troubleshooting process was optimistic because it began with an attempt to connect to the destination server. Because this first attempt was successful, the administrator was able to avoid a lot of time-consuming troubleshooting of network connectivity. If a pessimistic path had been chosen, it could have taken hours to verify that the cabling was in place and functioned correctly before you were ready to troubleshoot a high-enough layer to determine the problem.

Summary

This chapter described the importance of troubleshooting and went into some detail about the real cost of downtime. It discussed two different troubleshooting processes: optimistic and pessimistic. It examined the most helpful troubleshooting tools, followed by sample scenarios to illustrate the troubleshooting process at work.

In this chapter you learned:

◆ How to reduce the impact of downtime by using effective troubleshooting

◆ Why the OSI model should be leveraged to make the problem-solving process more methodical

◆ What tools are at your disposal for solving different types of problems

The next chapter examines the inner workings of the Windows NT TCP/IP stack and supported protocols. It builds on and expands your understanding of Windows NT and TCP/IP. It even provides information about the Microsoft implementation of TCP/IP, which has never before been available to the public.

Chapter 9

The Things NT Provides

IN THIS CHAPTER

◆ Defining the full TCP/IP stack

◆ Tuning Windows NT networking

◆ Understanding common TCP/IP protocols and simple TCP/IP services

WINDOWS NT SHIPS with a complete, standards-based TCP/IP stack. This seems like a fairly obvious thing to point out in this book, but it is important to state because not all TCP/IP stacks are created equal. Indeed, network drivers from different operating system vendors often support very different aspects of the TCP/IP protocol. These standards are above and beyond the core protocols – improving performance and efficiency rather than providing core functionality.

The performance and efficiency protocols are the interesting aspects of the Windows NT TCP/IP stack. By learning the details, you will come to better understand why your systems perform the way they do. You will also learn when it will benefit you to modify the configuration of your system's TCP/IP stack, and how it may affect your overall network. To assist in this study, I will provide specific configuration examples and guidelines.

Defining the Full TCP/IP Stack

If you have gotten this far into the book, you already know how to configure your system's TCP/IP configuration from the Network Control Panel applet. You can set the IP address, subnet mask, DNS servers, and more – all the basics. Then when you click OK or Apply, the information you entered into the applet is written to its permanent storage place – the registry.

The registry stores this basic information and a whole lot more. The TCP/IP stack built into Windows NT is extremely configurable, well beyond what is presented to you by the graphical user interface. Adding and modifying these registry entries can often improve the networking speed of systems – it can also hurt it. As always, take care when editing the registry and be sure you have a complete understanding of the effects before making any changes.

Logical Multihoming

Windows NT supports multiple IP addresses assigned to a single network interface card, also called logical multihoming. This is useful because it allows an NT system to assume multiple identities on a single network. Prior to the popularity of Web servers, multiple IP addresses had few purposes. Indeed, in NT 3.51, you could only add a maximum of six IP addresses from the Network Control Panel applet. NT 4.0 expands on that ability, supporting almost unlimited IP addresses on any single network interface card.

One of the most common uses of logical multihoming is to use a single system to support multiple Web sites on the Internet or on an intranet. Multiple IP addresses are required because the destination IP address is the only way an HTTP 1.0 server can distinguish which Web site is being requested. For example, consider two separate intranet sites being hosted on the same IIS server. One of these responds with a corporate accounting database, and the other responds with a human resources database. Human resources people want to use the URL http://hr.company.com, while accounting wants to use the URL http://acct. company.com.

One option for hosting these two sites on the same Web server is to assign both DNS hostnames to the same IP address. To clarify, both hr.company.com and acct.company.com would resolve to 192.168.10.10. Unfortunately, servers using IIS versions 3.0 and earlier cannot distinguish between requests for hr.company.com and acct.company.com because they are both destined for the same IP address. Therefore, the Web server would respond with the default page for only one of the Web sites, regardless of which DNS entry was used. By associating different DNS entries with different IP addresses, IIS can differentiate between requests for hr.company.com and acct.compnay.com. In modern Web hosting environments, it is not uncommon for a single server to assume several hundred such identities. Windows NT and IIS are capable of supporting up to 1,500 IP addresses and virtual servers. This is the upper limit of NT's logical multihoming capabilities.

Another common use for logical multihoming is to allow Windows NT systems to talk to multiple IP subnets that exist on the same physical segment. Indeed, it may even act as a router between logical subnets on the same physical subnet. Figure 9-1 illustrates this concept.

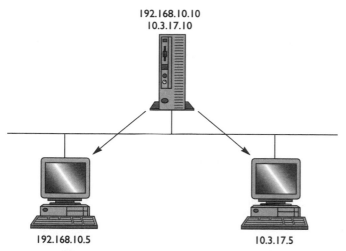

192.168.10.10
10.3.17.10

192.168.10.5   10.3.17.5

Figure 9-1: Windows NT can communicate with two logical subnets on the same wire.

To clarify this point, consider a network with ten hosts on it. Five of these hosts have addresses in the 192.168.10.0 range; the other five hosts have addresses in the network 192.168.20.0. If the subnet mask for these systems is 255.255.255.0, a system without logical multihoming capabilities could not communicate with hosts in different logical subnets without sending the packets through a router. Windows NT does support logical multihoming, and one IP address from each of the logical subnets may be added to the same physical network interface card. For example, if an NT server is assigned the IP addresses 192.168.10.10 and 192.168.20.10, machines on either subnet could address it with the IP address local to their own subnet.

Logical multihoming is a standard part of the TCP/IP stacks implemented in all modern network operating systems.

Physical Multihoming

Logical multihoming allows multiple IP addresses to be assigned to the same physical network interface card. *Physical multihoming* allows multiple physical network cards to be placed inside of the same NT system, each to receive its own unique IP address. This is useful for configuring an NT system to talk to multiple segments simultaneously.

Physical multihoming is a basic concept of the TCP/IP stack in all modern network operating systems, including Windows NT. Network Driver Interface Specification (NDIS) provides the layer of abstraction that allows the TCP/IP software to communicate over multiple interface cards simultaneously.

Implementing physical multihoming requires the network operating system to have a local routing table. This table is used to determine which interface card a packet should be transmitted from based on the destination IP address. Indeed, when configured in a multihomed fashion, the NT system becomes able to route between the network segments. This is an aspect of the operating system that Microsoft is currently expanding with the Routing and Remote Access Service add-on, also known as Steelhead. More information on this product and routing in general may be found in Chapter 13.

IGMP (IP Multicasting) Support

As Internet standards groups continue to make internetworking more bandwidth-efficient, the Internet Group Membership Protocol (IGMP), known more generally as IP multicasting, is becoming more widely used. IP multicasting alters one of the most basic concepts of networking – that packets are sent from a server to a client. Now, datagrams may be sent from a server to *many* clients simultaneously. If traditional unicast networking is similar to a telephone call, multicast networking is similar to radio broadcasts. A single source transmits information, and clients choose whether or not to listen.

This is easier said than done. Just about every component residing at the OSI network layer and above must be designed specifically to support IP multicasting. Applications on the server must be written to transmit to specially reserved IP addresses. Network hardware must be compliant with IGMP standards. Client applications must have the capability of joining a group and listening to the multicasts. These capabilities must be integrated into every component before multicasting will work end to end. The magnitude of upgrading all network hardware on an intranet (and especially the Internet) is the primary reason multicasting has not gone into wider use.

Class D IP Addresses?

Everyone's favorite question in a technical interview is to describe class A, B, and C IP addresses. However, there are a total of five classes – the last two just aren't that popular. Class D addresses fall in the range 224.0.0.0 – 239.255.255.255 and are reserved for IP multicasting. Few people are aware of them, however, because multicasting is rarely used outside of laboratory environments. The range of IP addresses from 240.0.0.0 – 255.255.255.254 are class E addresses, which are reserved for future use (and therefore are even less popular than multicast addresses!)

Today, very few popular protocols make use of IGMP. Of particular interest are WINS and OSPF, which use IGMP to communicate between hosts on the same network segment. Therefore, they do not require multicast support by the network hardware to function. OSPF uses multicasting to exchange routing information between gateways on a network; it provides a convenient way to communicate with multiple hosts on the same network segment without having to transmit broadcasts or individual packets to each host.

Notice that both WINS and OSPF use multicasting to communicate with hosts on the same network only. This greatly simplifies multicasting because network hardware does not have to support IGMP – only the hosts do. The need to address multicast hosts on the same segment is addressed directly in the RFC itself, and an IP address is reserved for the purpose: 224.0.0.1. By definition, all hosts capable of level-2 multicast support must listen for IP address 224.0.0.1 at all times because it corresponds to the IGMP "all-hosts" group. IGMP is defined in detail in RFC 1112 (yes, *another* RFC).

In Windows NT version 3.5 and later, IGMP level 2 support is provided. If you just aren't ready for the fast lane, you can alter the IGMP support provided by your system. Because almost no applications use IGMP, this probably will not affect anyone. However, here is the registry key to modify if you are so inclined:

```
HKEY_LOCAL_MACHINE\System\CurrentControlSet\Services\Tcpip\
    Parameters\IGMPLevel
```

This key contains the value 0, 1, or 2. By default, it is set to 2 – the highest level support defined by the RFC. Level 0, as the name implies, disables IGMP support completely. Level 1 allows the Windows NT system to send IGMP packets but not to listen for them. There is no realistic purpose for ever choosing level-1 support, so I will not cover its features here. Level 2, as described earlier, allows both transmitting and receiving. This is the highest level of support provided for by RFC 1112, and it means the system has full multicasting capabilities. In fact, given the rate at which network weaknesses are discovered in Windows NT, I recommend downgrading systems to level-0 support to limit the security risk. As I mentioned earlier, all level-2 hosts must listen for the IP address 224.0.0.1, and it is always better for security to reduce the traffic a host listens to on the network.

Please keep in mind that while NT supports IP multicasting host capabilities, it is not a multicast router, regardless of how it is configured! Multicast routers must be capable of querying networks to determine which IGMP groups to listen for and forwarding all multicast packets for which one or more connected hosts is listening. These features will no doubt become available as Microsoft continues to position itself as a network software vendor, but you cannot do it yet!

Multicasting and the OSI Model

Multicasting addresses its listeners by defining an IP address in the range 224.0.0.0 – 239.0.0.0. Listening hosts just look for packets with an IP address that corresponds to a multicast they are interested in receiving. But before they can process the OSI network layer address, they must have already recognized the layer-2 address (such as the MAC address on Ethernet networks). So how do you make many hosts on a network segment listen for the same MAC address?

The answer is more complex than you may think. In most current implementations, the layer-2 address for multicast packets is always the broadcast address for the network. Therefore, multicast *packets* are broadcast *frames.* Make sense? What you should know is that every multicast packet on a network results in a CPU interrupt for every host on that network segment – however, hosts that do not support multicasting or are not interested in the specific data stream process the packet only to the network layer. At that point, they process the IP address, realize it is not one of their own, and discard it.

However, RFC 1112 provides for a more elegant approach. It provides a range of MAC addresses that are reserved for multicast frames. Part of the IP address that defines the multicast group is placed into a special Ethernet address. Therefore, hosts that do not support multicasting will not process the frame because the MAC address is neither theirs nor the broadcast MAC address. Hosts that do support level-2 multicasting will only process the frame if they belong to that particular group. While the method described is sound, most modern Ethernet cards do not listen to an indefinite number of MAC addresses. Until this becomes commonplace, the layer-2 address will continue to be the broadcast address.

The lesson to be learned is that multicast packets *do* affect every host on a network, but not enough to cause any noticeable effect on modern computers.

Duplicate IP Address Detection

One feature of Windows NT is its ability to detect other systems on the same network with a duplicate IP address. As you probably already know, two systems on the same network will not behave reliably if they have the same IP address. Some packets will be received by each of the two systems, depending on several circumstances (namely, how the ARP request is resolved).

Duplicate IP addresses are common problems on a network, because IP address management is so difficult. It is very possible for two people to choose the same IP address, and it happens quite often, even in environments that are closely managed. For example, a user who has administrative access to his own Windows NT workstation may decide that he or she needs an additional IP address for some reason. Users often try to PING various IP addresses on the network until they find an IP address that does not respond. Based on this nonresponse, they may assume that the IP address is unused and assign it to their own computer. At a later date, a system that legitimately has that IP address will attempt to use it and both hosts will experience network problems that can be very difficult to track down.

Because of the likelihood of duplicate IP addresses being assigned and the difficulty it can cause, NT provides a feature called duplicate IP address detection, intended to avoid these problems. The way this works is that, when the NT system first begins to load its TCP/IP stack, it performs an ARP request for the IP addresses it has been assigned. If any other system responds to that ARP request, then NT knows that somebody else is attempting to use that IP address. The system that performed the ARP request will be able to load the TCP/IP stack. Upon loading, the graphical user interface will display an error dialog box informing the user at the console that a duplicate IP address was detected. To avoid conflicts, TCP/IP will fail to load. Figure 9-2 shows this dialog box.

Figure 9-2: The duplicate IP address detection warning (we've all seen it!)

Duplicate IP address detection is an extremely useful feature, but it far from eliminates the possibility of two systems booting with the same address. There are many circumstances when two systems can claim the same IP address. First, ARP requests are merely frame-level broadcasts; thus, they are received by every system on the same network, on the same subnet as the system that is attempting to boot. Therefore, if the IP address is claimed by a system on another subnet, an error will be detected. This is not an extremely likely problem, because traffic for that IP address is only going to be routed to a single subnet anyway. Nonetheless, keep it in mind.

Another possibility is that a second system may join the network after its TCP/IP stack has already loaded. For example, if a second system is configured with an already-used IP address and is booted up without being connected to the network, it will boot successfully. The ARP request it transmits upon startup would not have been detected by any other host on the network because it's not connected! Therefore, the TCP/IP stack would continue to load and would create problems once that system is plugged into the network again.

Dead Gateway Detection

Windows NT has the ability to be configured with multiple default routers. Configuring Windows NT this way is simple because the graphical user interface of the Network Control Panel applet supports it, as shown in Figure 9-3.

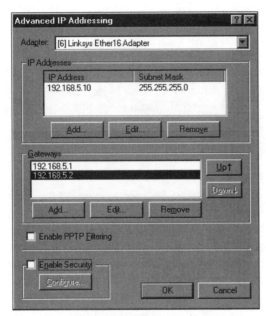

Figure 9-3: Windows NT can be configured to fail-over to a redundant router.

Configuring Windows NT hosts with multiple default gateways is an excellent (and cheap!) way to provide for redundancy on a network. By simply configuring two routers on the same subnet that each have routes to other parts of the network, you assure that any Windows NT host will be able to continue communicating outside of its network segment in the event that one of the two routers fails. Windows NT will detect the failed router and begin forwarding packets destined for external networks to the next router in the list. A sample network with this type of configuration is shown in Figure 9-4. In this network, each of the hosts has two gateways available on the local area network, and any single router may fail without any long-term loss of connectivity.

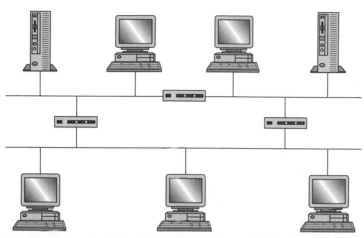

Figure 9-4: A network like this one allows for no single point of failure.

Implementing redundant routers is an extremely expensive and difficult undertaking. By implementing the redundancy logic in the client software, network administrators avoid the cost of redundant routers. Beyond simple monetary expenses, redundant routers are typically difficult to configure and more expensive to manage. Similar features are available in other operating systems, so make sure all systems on your network can support dead gateway detection before relying on it to provide network redundancy.

Dead gateway detection, as implemented in the Microsoft Windows NT TCP/IP stack, is based on *triggered reselection*, a redundancy strategy described in RFC 816 (but *not* an Internet standard). Windows NT will attempt to forward packets through the next gateway in the list only when data transfers begin to fail, specifically when half the value of the registry entry TcpMaxDataRetransmissions has been attempted. Because this value is five by default, Windows NT will send three failed messages to the default gateway and then send the fourth and fifth messages to the second gateway on the list. The time it takes to switch to the second gateway will vary because of Windows NT's ability to dynamically adjust TCP timeouts depending on the connection characteristics, a concept called *smoothed round trip time*. However, if the default TcpMaxDataRetransmissions value is not changed and the three-second default timeout is not affected by SRTT, the second gateway will be contacted after nine seconds.

Tuning Windows NT Networking

The Windows NT TCP/IP stack is largely self-tuning. The defaults it comes configured with work well for most networks, and very few administrators will ever find themselves compelled to modify the out-of-the-box configuration. Microsoft has taken great care to configure the standard TCP/IP stack so that it works efficiently in normal conditions and continues to work even under extremely poor conditions. However, as Windows NT moves out of the local area network and into enterprise networks and the Internet, it is being used for more specialized, performance-critical tasks than before. Under many different situations, tuning the Windows NT TCP/IP stack properly for your environment can realize noticeable effects on both servers and workstations.

This section will cover the most useful ways of fine-tuning the Winsock capabilities built into Windows NT. While the defaults work well, *everyone* will benefit by implementing some or all of the suggestions I outline in this section.

TCP Sliding Windows

The term "windows" is really overused, isn't it? Long before Microsoft began using the term, sliding was an integral feature of the TCP protocol. Sliding windows allow TCP to verify that data was transmitted and received correctly before moving on to the next portion of a transmission. Tuning sliding windows properly allows faster communications on a network by reducing the time dedicated to the handshaking process. I touched on sliding windows in Chapter 2; now I will go into more detail.

TCP is a reliable transport-layer protocol. *Reliable* does not mean that the protocol guarantees that all data will arrive successfully — that is impossible to guarantee on a network. Instead, it means that the protocol itself must always verify that data is received successfully or else notify the higher-layer protocol of the failure. So TCP transmissions may succeed or fail, but you will always know what happened to them.

The mechanism that TCP uses to guarantee delivery is similar to the U.S. Postal Service. When you mail something to somebody using guaranteed delivery, they mail back a little slip that confirms that your package was received successfully. If you *don't* get that little slip back, you know something went wrong. Similarly, stations that receive TCP packets are responsible for returning acknowledgment (ACK) packets after a transmission. When the sending host receives an ACK, it knows that the transmission went okay.

After a transmitting host sends a chunk of data to the receiving host, it must wait for the data to be confirmed with an ACK before sending any more. If it does not receive an ACK after a specific amount of time, it must retransmit all data that has not yet been confirmed. This capability to retransmit data is key to TCP's reliability, and it requires that TCP remember data that it has already transmitted; it must be buffered until receipt has been ACKed by the receiving host. As the transmitting host receives each ACK, it removes that data from its buffer, moves the next block of data from the data stream into the TCP buffer, and begins transmitting again.

From the description, you can see that the buffer "slides" along the data stream, kind of like a "window." Hence the name "sliding windows." Actually, the term is not all that descriptive, but it is an interesting concept and a key part of how TCP works. The TCP sliding windows buffer is illustrated in Figure 9-5.

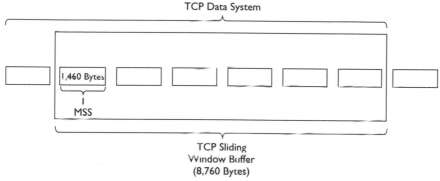

Figure 9-5: The TCP buffer "slides" over the data stream.

Some limited tuning can be done with the sliding windows functionality. As described earlier, the transmitting host must wait for the receiving host to acknowledge packets before removing them from the buffer and transmitting more data. This period of waiting can slow down network transmissions considerably, especially on networks with high latency.

To clarify this point, consider a network that is perfect in every way except for an extremely high latency of one second between the transmitting and receiving hosts. The transmitting host has to send 1MB of data to the receiving host across a standard Ethernet network with an MTU of 1,500. In total, this will require about 700 packets.

If the transmitting host has been configured with an extremely small TCP window size of about 1,500 bytes, it will wait for an ACK after each packet that it transmits. Therefore, each packet will take two seconds to transmit and be ACKed: one-second latency for the transmission, one-second latency for the ACK. The entire transmission will take a little more than 23 minutes (wow, worse than my ISP account).

Calculating Round-Trip Latency

Properly tuning TCP sliding windows on a network has a lot to do with the total latency on a network. Increasing the window size helps the most on networks with high latency and high bandwidth. A quick way to determine the latency between any two points on a network is to do a PING from the command-line. For example:

```
C:\>ping www.idgbooks.com
Pinging leland.idgbooks.com [206.80.51.140] with 32 bytes of
data:

Reply from 206.80.51.140: bytes=32 time=300ms TTL=236
Reply from 206.80.51.140: bytes=32 time=290ms TTL=236
Reply from 206.80.51.140: bytes=32 time=291ms TTL=236
Reply from 206.80.51.140: bytes=32 time=290ms TTL=236
```

This shows that the round-trip latency between the PINGing host and www.idgbooks.com is about 300 milliseconds.

Now consider the same file transfer between hosts that have been configured with a TCP window size large enough to fit eight packets. The transmitting host will send eight packets and wait for an ACK from the sending host. Remembering that this is a perfect network with no constraint besides the latency, let's recalculate the transmission time. Seven hundred packets must still be transmitted, but they will require only about 88 ACKs. Therefore, the calculation becomes 88 times the total round-trip latency of two seconds, yielding a total transmission time of about three minutes — more than seven times faster than was possible with the smaller window size.

The preceding example was exaggerated to prove the point — making the transmitting host wait for acknowledgments from the receiving host slows data transfers. This is especially apparent in networks that have a high latency because latency has the greatest effect on round-trip time. Bandwidth is less of a factor because the ACK packets are typically the minimum size allowed. TCP windows further affect bandwidth because having a larger window size actually *increases* utilization on the network by making better use of it. Now that my point is illustrated, let's move away from sheer theory and consider real-world communications.

By default, Windows NT uses a window size large enough to transfer about six Ethernet packets before requiring an ACK from the receiving host. Please don't let my previous examples confuse you – this does not mean that a Windows NT host will wait to receive a full six packets before transmitting an ACK. Sliding windows allow hosts to avoid "taking turns" communicating on the network. On the contrary, Windows NT normally transmits an ACK for every packet or two it receives, regardless of the window size. If two hosts are on different subnets, the receiving host may be acknowledging a packet it just received at exactly the same time the sending host is transmitting the next packet in sequence. In this way, the sending host is optimistic – it continues to send data on the assumption that an ACK is on the way. The idea that the sending host is transmitting data without waiting for an ACK from the receiving host is the key to understanding sliding windows. This concept is illustrated in Figure 9-6.

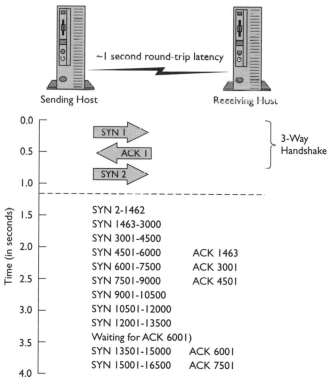

Figure 9-6: Sliding windows allow multiple packets to be transmitted without acknowledgment.

Default Window Size

Most of the networking world connects their Windows NT systems to Ethernet. If you fall in this category, your default TCP window size is 8,760 bytes. However, some of you use other types of networks. If you fall in this category and need to determine your default TCP window size, here is how to do it:

First, find your MSS (maximum segment size). To calculate your MSS, subtract 40 bytes from your MTU (maximum transmission unit). If your MSS is less than 2,228, then round 8,192 up to an even multiple of your MSS — this is your default TCP window size. If your MSS is equal to or greater than 2,228 but less than or equal to 16,383, multiply that number by four to find your default TCP window size. Finally, for extremely large MSSs, greater than 16,383, the maximum value of 65,535 is used.

Figure 9-6 shows two hosts communicating with a TCP window size of 8,760. The size 8,760 means that the TCP transmit buffer may contain six packets total. Therefore, the sending host can transmit six packets of data without receiving an ACK from the receiving host. If it transmits six packets and still has not received an ACK, only then will the transmitting host need to wait for a response. This waiting is what you want to avoid. The goal of sliding windows is to make communications as fast as possible by using as much bandwidth as possible by never forcing the transmitting host to wait idle for an ACK.

Again referencing Figure 9-6, notice that after about 2.5 seconds the transmitting host is forced to wait for an ACK for the fifth packet it transmitted. The transmitting host was forced to wait because its TCP buffer was full of six unacknowledged packets (the fifth, sixth, seventh, eighth, ninth, and tenth packets). Eventually, it does receive an ACK for the fifth packet (labeled ACK 6001). At this point, the sliding window is able to remove the fifth packet from memory and use that space to buffer the next packet (labeled "SYN 13501-15000"), which it transmits. The process of removing the packet from the buffer, reading more data, and transmitting another packet is actually the "sliding window" sliding forward in the data stream.

The network illustrated in Figure 9-6 is a prime candidate for an increased TCP window size. This can be concluded because the transmitting host was forced to wait because it ran out of room in the buffer, not because of bandwidth restrictions or the need to retransmit defective packets. The example is extreme because of the high latency — a full second of latency is unusual even across the Internet.

CALCULATING THE IDEAL SLIDING WINDOW SIZE

As you can see, many factors go into calculating the best window size for a given network. These factors are given in Table 9-1.

TABLE 9-1 FACTORS FOR CALCULATING TCP WINDOW SIZE

Factor	Effect
Latency	Increase latency, increase window size
Jitter	Increase jitter, increase window size
Bandwidth	Increase bandwidth, increase window size
Error rate	Increase error rate, decrease window size

To configure the perfect TCP window size, you must determine how much data the sending host may transmit before it will begin receiving ACKs from the receiving host. If the network has high bandwidth but a great deal of latency, the transmitting host may be able to safely send substantially more than the six packets Windows NT provides by default. If the latency is very low (as it would be on a LAN), then there is never a situation in which the transmitting host would be able to send a full six packets without receiving an ACK. In this circumstance, the default TCP window size is fine and would not need to be adjusted. A simple formula for calculating this "perfect" size is as follows:

```
Bandwidth * Latency
```

Bandwidth is the realized throughput between any two systems on a network. Naturally, this varies depending on how much other traffic there is; when in doubt, choose the highest realistic bandwidth. Similarly, latency is specific to a client/server connection and will vary depending on the current state of the network and the level of jitter present. Choose a value in seconds for latency by finding the average latency over a five-minute period during peak utilization. Once you have found these values, plug them into this formula:

```
(B bits/seconds) * (L seconds) / (8 bits/byte) = Ws bytes
```

For example, consider an analog dial-up link (28,800 bits/second) with a latency of 300 milliseconds (0.3 seconds). Plugging these numbers into the formula yields an "ideal" window size of 1,080 bytes — much lower than the default window size. In this particular case, increasing the window size would not benefit performance because performance will be constrained by the bandwidth. Decreasing the window size will also *not* benefit, unless the network has a high error rate.

However, consider a network connection that is bottlenecked by a T1 link (1,450,000 bits/second) with the same latency (0.3 seconds). These numbers yield a "ideal" window size of 54,375 bytes. This number is significantly higher than the default of 8,760 for Ethernet networks. In this situation, increasing the TCP window size *could* benefit performance significantly. Notice that I used the word "could."

Also notice that I use the term "ideal" to describe the window size calculated by the formula. To find the "perfect" window size, you must round this number up so that a packet will never be sent with less than a full load. For example, the MTU on an Ethernet network is 1,500 bytes. 40 bytes of each packet are used for header information, so a maximum of 1,460 bytes of a TCP segment may be transmitted inside of a single packet (the MSS, or maximum segment size). Therefore, the "perfect" window size will always be an even multiple of 1,460, ensuring that your host will never transmit "five and a half" packets worth of data (wasting half a packet). Therefore, if a system has an MTU of 1,500 and the "ideal" window size is 54,375 bytes, the "perfect" window size is 55,480. I calculated this number by dividing the "ideal" window size (54,375) by the TCP data carried in each packet (1,460). The result was 37.24 – meaning a full window would consist of 37 full packets and one mostly empty packet. So I rounded this up to 38 packets and multiplied by the TCP data carried in each packet (1,460), yielding a "perfect" window size of 55,480.

The MSS (Maximum Segment Size) for PPP is the same as it is for Ethernet — 1,460 bytes.

Another factor in the formula that is not as easy to compute is the error rate. In modern networks errors are uncommon. However, the idea of sliding windows only works because networks are more reliable than unreliable, and data errors occur only rarely. The larger the window size, the more data may need to be retransmitted. Retransmitting the extra data will *not* hurt the performance of that particular session; however, it will waste bandwidth. As a rule of thumb, do not decrease window size out of concern for packets that must be retransmitted. If you have that many errors on your network, you have other, more serious, problems to worry about!

Please keep in mind that the TCP window size can never exceed 65,535. This is a limitation of the 16-bit field size in the TCP header but should rarely be a problem.

To adjust the TCP window size on an NT system, add the following registry key:

```
HKEY_LOCAL_MACHINE\System\CurrentControlSet\Services\Tcpip\
Parameters\TcpWindowSize (REG_DWORD)
```

The value should be set to the number of bytes in the TCP receive window that the system will advertise to clients that connect to it. The server in a client/server TCP connection determines this value. The client's setting has no effect on what will actually be negotiated during the connection setup process, so this value is particularly interesting for network servers. Additionally, it only affects data transfers larger than a single packet. Therefore, systems that perform large file transfers, such as FTP servers and some HTTP servers, will benefit the most.

DELAYED ACKNOWLEDGMENTS

Working in conjunction with TCP sliding windows, delayed acknowledgments help to reduce the number of packets transferred during large data transfers. They even benefit applications that transfer small pieces of information one byte at a time, such as Telnet.

Delayed acknowledgments are a standard part of the TCP/IP stack implemented in Windows NT systems. Instead of sending an ACK packet in response to each and every packet in a data transfer, a Windows NT system will respond to *every other* packet, as illustrated in Figure 9-7.

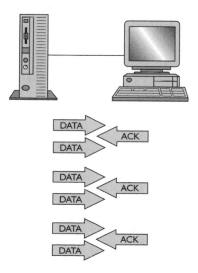

Figure 9-7: Delayed acknowledgments reduce the total number of packets on a fast network.

This approach effectively reduces the number of ACK packets sent during a large data transfer by one-half. It reduces the total number of packets exchanged by one-quarter. However, there is a timer involved in the formula as well. If the receiving host receives a packet and does not need to send an ACK because of the delayed acknowledgment algorithm, it will wait 0.2 seconds. If it has not received another packet in that time, it will transmit an ACK for the first packet.

On network connections with high latency or low bandwidth, such as analog dial-up links, the time between packets during large data transfers may always be greater than 0.2 seconds. In this case, the receiving host will send an ACK after every packet because the timer will expire after each.

Unfortunately, this timer is not configurable. Delayed acknowledgments are defined in RFC 1122, though only general guidelines are specified. The exact implementation used in Windows NT is Microsoft's invention.

Tuning the TCP Connection Process

Microsoft has been kind enough to provide network and systems engineers with settings for just about every timer used in network communications. These are shipped preconfigured with settings that are suitable to the vast majority of networks but not all networks. As networks increase in speed and reliability, many of these settings may be considered too pessimistic for optimal performance. On the other hand, if your network is particularly slow or unreliable, you may benefit by increasing timeouts for the different subsystems of Windows NT.

One registry entry is particularly useful because it controls how long an application waits for a TCP connection to be established. The default configuration results in a time-out period of 45 seconds – way too long for a user to wait after mistyping an IP address. By default, a Windows NT system retransmits a TCP SYN packet a total of three times during an unresponsive TCP connection process. The timeout after each SYN packet retransmission begins at three seconds and doubles after each successive failure. It's important to note that these are retransmissions – the initial request is not counted as one of the retransmissions. Therefore, if your Windows NT system is configured to time-out after three retries (as is the default), it will send a total of *four* SYN connection requests (one initial request followed by three retries).

To clarify, after the first SYN packet, the system waits three seconds for a response. Then the host transmits the second SYN packet (the first *retransmission*) and waits six seconds. Next, the third SYN packet (the second *retransmission*) is sent and the host waits twelve seconds for a response before returning an error. Finally, a fourth SYN packet (the third *retransmission*) is sent followed by a waiting period of 24 seconds. In total, Windows NT systems wait 45 seconds for a TCP connection to be established before returning a time-out error.

This value is somewhat excessive on most modern, reliable networks. Even on the Internet, chances are pretty good that if a system doesn't respond after the first five seconds it's not going to respond at all. Further, 45 seconds is pretty long for a user to wait, and people tend to get annoyed when staring at the hourglass for that amount of time. Therefore, it is advisable that this value be decreased on client systems on which networking is both speedy and reliable. My recommendation is to reduce the number of retries to *one*. In this scenario, the client attempting to connect to the server will send a total of two SYN packets and wait only nine seconds before returning an error message, reducing wait time by 80 percent.

I suggest changing this value on all systems in an enterprise, just to be consistent. However, this value only affects *client outbound* connections. Therefore, you will see the most benefit on desktop workstations (such as those running Windows NT) and very little benefit on servers. To change this value, add the following registry key (of type REG_DWORD) and set the value to the total number of retries desired:

```
HKEY_LOCAL_MACHINE\System\CurrentControlSet\Tcpip\Parameters\
TcpMaxConnectRetransmissions
```

Tuning the ARP Resolution Process

If your goal is to reduce the amount of time an application takes to time-out when attempting to initiate a connection, reducing the number of TCP connection retransmissions is a good way to do it. However, the TCP connection attempt cannot begin until an ARP resolution has taken place. If an ARP request is failing, Windows NT by default will transmit four requests. It waits three seconds between the first and second requests, six seconds between the second and third requests, twelve seconds between the third and fourth requests, and then another twenty-four seconds for the fourth request to time-out completely.

In total, it takes four ARP broadcasts and 45 seconds for an ARP request to time-out and return an error message to the application. If these numbers sound familiar, they should – this is the exact timeout process used for TCP connections. So how do you tune the amount of time a Windows NT system will wait before it gives up broadcasting ARP requests?

Hey, It's Better than Nothing...?

The ability to adjust the number of times a TCP client application attempts to connect to the server is great; thanks, Microsoft! But you didn't give me a way to change the time-out between retries! A better way to reduce the time-out period described in this section would be to reduce the wait between retries. For example, two retries with an initial delay of one second would allow three SYN packets to be transmitted with a total time-out period of only seven seconds.

Perhaps in NT 5.0?

Oddly, the answer is exactly the same as it was for tuning TCP connections (detailed in the previous section): Modify the TcpMaxConnectRetransmissions registry entry. This is odd because it is not documented anywhere (until now). Also, the name implies that it affects TCP protocol timeouts, but ARP is not part of the TCP protocol. In fact, ARP is not even at the same layer as TCP! Now that we have established the illogical behavior of this registry entry, perhaps we can have it fixed in NT 5.0 or the next service pack.

In summary, the ARP time-out process is changed as a side effect of the TCP connection time-out process. I suppose I should view this as a convenience because I don't have to go through the pains of adding a separate registry entry, but I prefer control to convenience when I'm fine-tuning a TCP/IP configuration. I still recommend changing the TcpMaxConnectRetransmissions value to 2.

Maximum Transfer Units

Different types of network media support varying MTUs, or maximum transfer units. The MTU is the highest number of bytes a packet may contain. If more data needs to be transmitted than can fit in a single packet, it must be fragmented between multiple packets. This is a common occurrence because IP datagrams may be as large as 64K but Ethernet can only carry 1,500 bytes in a frame. The data will need to be broken apart, or fragmented, before transmission onto the physical media. Table 9-2 shows common media types and their respective MTUs.

TABLE 9-2 COMMON MTUs

Network Type	MTU
Ethernet	1,500
FDDI	4,352
Token Ring (4Mbps)	4,464
Token Ring (16Mbps)	17,914
X.25	576

It is important to note the use of the term *packet*: the MTU describes the maximum size of the payload of the IP layer—it does not count the IP headers, but it does include the transport-layer headers (such as TCP or UDP information). The MTU is defined at the network layer of the OSI model because fragmentation is the responsibility of the network layer (in this case, IP).

When packets are fragmented, the receiving computer must be able to reassemble them into a single data stream. In order to accomplish this, IP carries four fields in its header. The first is the Identification field, which is 16 bits long and is used to provide a unique identifier for the packet. Two of the three "flag" bits are used during fragmentation: the DF (don't fragment) bit and the MF (more fragments) bit. When the DF bit is set, network equipment must return an error message to the sending host in the event the packet is too large to forward onto the next network segment. When the MF bit is set, it indicates that the IP datagram had to be broken into several pieces. All IP packets that are part of a single, fragmented datagram have the MF bit set to 1 *except* for the last packet. When a receiving host receives a packet with the MF bit set to 0, it knows the data stream is complete. The fourth field is the Fragment Offset field, which tells the computer where in the IP datagram the current packet belongs.

MTU can be important for tuning purposes on a network because the amount of overhead in a packet is fairly high. A higher MTU decreases the number of bytes wasted on header information for large packets. This is particularly important for large file transfers and has absolutely no effect on transfers that would be less than the MTU anyway. Therefore, pay careful attention to configuring the MTU on servers that transmit large data streams, such as file servers and FTP servers.

Further, it is CPU-consuming for network hardware to fragment frames as they pass from a medium that has a high MTU onto a medium that has a low MTU. For example, consider a network composed of both FDDI and Ethernet network segments. Standard Ethernet has an MTU of 1,500 bytes, while FDDI has an MTU of 4,096 bytes. Therefore, packets that must be forwarded from the FDDI network onto the Ethernet network must be fragmented beforehand. This fragmentation can seriously slow down a router and have a severe negative impact on overall network performance.

To alleviate this, it is best to set the MTU of all systems on an enterprise network to the least common denominator. If your enterprise network consists of Ethernet LANs and a server farm based on FDDI, all systems should have the MTU set to 1,500 (the MTU for Ethernet, the lowest common MTU). With this configuration, packets transmitted by servers on the FDDI ring can travel anywhere in the network without requiring fragmentation.

To set the MTU on a Windows NT system, add the following registry entry:

```
HKEY_LOCAL_MACHINE\System\CurrentControlSet\Services\<Adapter>\
  Tcpip\Parameters\MTU
```

The value contained in this registry entry may vary from 68 (the minimum allowable frame size) to the MTU of the underlying network. To comply with standards, NT ignores settings that are smaller than 68 or larger than the MTU reported by the network interface card. Therefore, you cannot increase the MTU on an Ethernet network to 2,000, even though you may be able to improve performance in some cases.

How Are Minimum Transmission Units Determined?

Why is there a minimum frame size at all? Why not allow 20-byte frames?

There really is a logical answer for all of these questions, and it has to do with the speed of light, the bandwidth of the network, and the maximum length of the cable. Ethernet uses Carrier Sense Multiple Access with Collision Detection (CSMA/CD) to determine whether it can transmit on the network without causing a collision and to know when a collision has occurred. Basically, if a system starts to transmit onto the wire and reads the electrical signals from another host, it knows a collision has occurred.

Now consider an Ethernet LAN with a host on either end of a really long Ethernet wire. If you are specifying the Ethernet standards, you need to make sure that these two hosts can transmit at the same time (causing a collision) and know *for sure* that the collision happened. Now, Ethernet information travels as electricity across a copper cable, and as such travels at the speed of light. The speed of light is really fast, but it is not instantaneous. Therefore, it is theoretically possible that two hosts on opposite sides of the wire could each transmit a very short frame and not see the other's frame until after they were completely finished transmitting. In this case, no collision could be detected because the other's frame didn't seem to be transmitted at the same time. However, neither frame would be readable on the network.

What I'm getting at here is why there is a minimum frame size — the frame must be long enough so that the hosts on either end of an Ethernet network can transmit the shortest possible frame (64 bytes) and be *guaranteed* that the other will see the first bytes of the packet before the transmission is complete. Whew!

When choosing an MTU, the rule is to choose the largest possible MTU that will not need to be fragmented during its travels. If your entire network uses a single media type, you will probably never need to adjust it because the default will already be correct. There is no advantage to choosing a smaller MTU than the medium's maximum because the entire IP datagram will need to be retransmitted in the event of an error in any single packet. In other words, it is impossible to retransmit a single fragment.

Automatic Path Maximum Transmission Unit (PMTU) Discovery

Windows NT has the capability to automatically decrease the maximum transmission unit in any IP conversation. While it is still more efficient to manually configure the MTU on all hosts on a network (as described in the previous section), the ability to automatically determine the ideal MTU between two points greatly increases the network performance when the MTU has not been manually optimized.

Windows NT determines this by setting the DF (don't fragment) bit in the IP header to 1 for all Winsock communications. Therefore, it is impossible for packets transmitted from an NT workstation or an NT server to be fragmented before reaching the host – if a router needed to fragment the data, it would have to return an ICMP destination unreachable error to the Windows NT host and drop the packet.

When a Windows NT host receives an ICMP destination unreachable error message and determines that it is a "fragmentation required but DF is set" message, it knows the MTU it is currently using is too large for the existing connection. If the router that returned the error is kind enough to indicate the MTU for the next segment, the Windows NT host will reduce the MTU to the value specified by the router.

Until version 4.0, Windows NT did not include a hint about the MTU on the next network segment when returning ICMP error messages because a packet could not be fragmented. Another case of "Do-as-I-say-not-as-I-do"?

It is important to note that automatic path MTU discovery is dependent on the router returning an ICMP error message – if the router does not return such a message, the connection will simply time-out. If this is the case, there is a registry entry you can add to work around the problem:

```
IIKEY_LOCAL_MACHINE\System\CurrentControlSet\Services\Tcpip\
  Parameters\EnablePMTUBHDetect (REG_DWORD)
```

By adding this registry entry and setting the value to 1, you increase the number of steps a Windows NT host will go through when a TCP connection fails. Therefore, it is not advisable to set this value unless you have determined that you really do have a problem with black hole routers. Even then, it may be better to replace or troubleshoot the black hole routers. When this value is set, Windows NT will turn off the DF bit and retransmit packets that are not acknowledged. If the packet is then acknowledged, Windows NT assumes that the cause of the problem was a black hole router. It will then reduce the MTU for the current session, re-enable the DF bit, and transmit the next packet. This process is repeated until an MTU is found that allows communications with the DF bit set.

If you simply do not want your system to automatically enable the DF bit in outgoing TCP/IP packets, this feature can be entirely disabled through the registry. Changing this value will adversely affect WAN communications from the Windows NT host, however, because the MTU for all communications that must be forwarded through a router is automatically set to 576 – about one-third of the most common network MTU. Disabling this feature does not affect LAN communications – the default is always used. The registry value to add is:

```
HKEY_LOCAL_MACHINE\System\CurrentControlSet\Services\Tcpip\
  Parameters\EnablePMTUDiscovery (REG_DWORD)
```

Setting the value of this registry entry to 0 disables the automatic path MTU features of Windows NT as described in the preceding paragraph.

Understanding Common TCP/IP Protocols

Having a full TCP/IP stack is useless unless you have the proper applications. Windows NT ships with most common client- and server-side Internet applications, with several notable exceptions. This section details each of these applications and their support for the Internet standards.

Telnet Client

In the UNIX environment, the Telnet application is used as one of the primary methods of system administration. For UNIX, Telnet essentially provides a remote console and gives the administrator full control over the system. Telnet is also used as a client-side application window for text-based applications that run on UNIX hosts and may be used by many people simultaneously. Gradually, Telnet-based applications are being converted to HTML, which provides a more flexible user interface.

Telnet is defined in RFC 854, written in 1983. Really, Telnet has been around for much longer than that, but this particular document defines what we know Telnet to be today. When used in the traditional remote command-line fashion, Telnet makes use of TCP port 23. However, Telnet is really much more than a method of remote command line control – it is the underlying standard that most of the Internet's protocols are based on. FTP, HTTP, SMTP, and POP are all based on the Telnet protocol. Each of these protocols use the same ASCII codes and special characters as are defined by the Telnet standards. Because of this, you can use any standard Telnet client to connect directly to one of these servers and send commands by typing them directly into your Telnet client.

Windows NT supports only the client side of Telnet. Therefore, you can use the Telnet application to connect to and control a UNIX host on your network, but you cannot control a remote Windows NT system using Telnet. The lack of a Telnet service for Windows NT is extremely aggravating for UNIX administrators moving into the Windows NT world, because they are accustomed to using the application for remote control of hosts.

Though Windows NT does not include a Telnet service, several third-party Telnet services are available. My favorite is Seattle Lab's Telnet service, available from `http://www.seattlelabs.com`. Please keep in mind that you are still limited to command-line programs, so your ability to administer the systems will be severely limited. However, many administrative tasks can be taken care of from the command line, such as executing batch files, restarting the system, and file management. Seattle Labs also offers an improved Telnet client-side application, which offers several advantages over the extremely limited Telnet client application included with Windows NT.

A Telnet service was included in the Windows NT Resource Kit at one point, but it was too unreliable to be implemented in production networks.

FTP Client and Server

Both client- and server-side FTP applications have been provided with Windows NT since the first release of version 3.1. Initially, it was provided to allow Windows NT systems to exchange files with UNIX hosts. Indeed, it was seen only for UNIX connectivity and only because many hosts did not support SMB-based file sharing. Now, with the rapid growth of the Internet, FTP services are a key part of Microsoft's Windows NT strategy going forward. The FTP services included with IIS 4.0 are much more robust and scalable then the initial implementation in Windows NT 3.1.

Microsoft includes an FTP service with Windows NT 4.0 as part of IIS 2.0. Two Telnet clients are provided: the command-line utility FTP and the graphical utility Internet Explorer 2.0. The command-line utility is essentially the same as it has always been, providing a very thin interface over the FTP protocol itself. This is also its greatest strength — because the user interface is so minimal, the user is afforded a great deal of flexibility and can take advantage of any standard FTP feature. Indeed, the user even has the capability to send FTP protocol commands that the command-line application is not capable of sending.

Internet Explorer 2.0 provides only FTP downloads. While it is capable of authenticating users, it is almost always used as an anonymous FTP client. Internet Explorer 2.0 provides a very thick layer over the FTP protocol and severely limits the features of FTP that may be used. However, it is useful because it allows URLs anchored in HTML Web pages to initiate FTP transfers.

FTP is defined by RFC 959 and is based on the Telnet protocol. Chapter 17 includes a great deal of information on the FTP protocol itself and the services included with Windows NT.

WWW Client and Server

No modern operating system is complete without server-side support for the HTTP protocol. HTTP has become the most popular application-layer communications protocol because of its wide acceptance on the Internet. Indeed, very few large organizations today do not provide HTTP servers for the general public.

Windows NT first supported HTTP services out of the box with the release of Windows NT 4.0, which included IIS 2.0. These services have been greatly expanded with the release of IIS 4.0 and will continue to develop with the release of NT 5.0.

Windows NT provides client-side HTTP services with the Internet Explorer 2.0 application that was included with Windows NT 4.0. Including a Web browser with the operating system is currently the subject of an investigation with the Department of Justice, so the future of this out-of-the-box support is questionable. Regardless, Web browsers will remain available free from the Internet in the foreseeable future. The most popular Web browser is currently published by Netscape Communications and is known as Netscape Navigator.

HTTP/1.0 is defined by RFC 1945. HTTP/1.1 is defined by RFC 2068. For more information of HTTP client and server applications provided with Windows NT, please jump forward to Chapter 16.

DNS Client and Server

Both client- and server-side communications are provided for by Windows NT out of the box. These communications are crucial to internetworking. Surprisingly, DNS services were not provided out of the box until Windows NT version 4.0. For more information on DNS, including RFCs, please skip to Chapter 12.

ICMP and PING Client and Server

Any host that supports TCP/IP must also support ICMP, as defined by RFC 792. ICMP provides many services to IP, such as relaying messages and testing connectivity. Most of these happen behind the scenes. However, users may initiate one particular type of ICMP request at will using the PING (Packet Internet Groper) utility. PING initiates an "echo request" using ICMP type 8. When a remote system receives this request, it should respond with an "echo reply" using ICMP type 0.

The PING client is a pretty basic component of any operating system. The version included with Windows NT includes many useful features, such as the ability to PING a host indefinitely and change the packet size.

The PING server is similarly a required part of the TCP/IP stack. Windows NT places ICMP between IP and TCP/UDP. Per the Department of Defense standards, ICMP is a network-layer protocol that does not need to interact with IP (though it uses the same addressing scheme). For efficiency, however, the Windows NT implementation of ICMP makes calls through IP.

TFTP (Trivial File Transfer Protocol) Client

TFTP, the Trivial File Transfer Protocol, is a UDP-based method of file transfers defined by RFC 783. Windows NT supports only the client-side portion of a TFTP relationship, allowing Windows NT users to upload and download files from TFTP servers. TFTP is not commonly used in the Windows NT world; however, it is commonly used in networking environments. Cisco routers, in particular, have the capability of loading a configuration file across the network from a TFTP server. It would be convenient if Windows NT could act as a TFTP server for this type of network hardware, but it is not currently possible without using a third-party application.

The TFTP client provided by Windows NT is a command-line utility cleverly named "TFTP."

Simple Network Management Protocol (SNMP) Agent

Windows NT comes with the capability of being managed and monitored remotely in several different ways. One of these ways is by use of the Simple Network Management Protocol (SNMP) as defined in RFC 1157. SNMP has long been the standard for management on TCP/IP networks, and the support provided out of the box by Windows NT allows administrators to manage Windows NT systems using the same management utilities they use for UNIX systems.

There are many different aspects of any network host that an administrator will want to monitor and manage. SNMP provides for flexibility and scalability by offering structures called MIBs, or Management Information Bases. A MIB defines what aspects of a host are manageable, similar to the way Performance Monitor counters define what can be monitored. Windows NT supports many standard MIBs, including those defined in RFC 1213. Additionally, any information that can be retrieved using Performance Monitor may be retrieved using SNMP.

A MIB defines the following pieces of information:

◆ An object name and identifier

◆ A specific data type

◆ A description of the object

◆ Whether the object is read- or write-capable

For more information on SNMP, please refer to the NT Server 4.0 Resource Kit *Networking Guide.*

Understanding Simple TCP/IP Services

Windows NT provides an optional set of services called "Simple TCP/IP Services." These services allow Windows NT to serve critical network services normally dominated by the UNIX market, such as the Discard service (which listens for packets and ignores them). Now, thanks to Microsoft, system administrators around the world can throw away those Sun Solaris servers that they were keeping around just to serve up "Quote of the Day" messages. Finally, we can all make the transition to a homogenous Microsoft environment.

I'm actually being a bit sarcastic. The truth is, some environments use these services to test the functionality of their network systems. Of course, it seems odd that Microsoft would provide these services but *not* provide a Telnet service, but enough of my complaining. If you're not sure whether or not you require these services, you don't need them and are better off not installing them at all.

CHARGEN (Character Generator) Server

Defined by RFC 864, the Character Generator service merely listens on TCP port 19, waits for a connection request, and dumps a whole lot of characters across the connection. After it has transmitted a bunch of characters, it sends a bunch more. Then, it sends some more. In fact, it keeps transmitting until the connection is broken. This makes it a useful service in case you ever need to flood your network with ASCII characters, or if you just want to slow a Windows NT system down without having to worry about authentication.

The standard does not specify what characters should be transmitted, but the creative developers at Microsoft decided to display all the ASCII characters in sequence. That way, if you are ever bored, you can Telnet to a Windows NT system and review your alphabet.

The Character Generator service also listens on UDP port 19. When it receives a message on this port, it sends a UDP message back to the sender that has a random number of characters between zero and 512.

If you must install the Simple TCP/IP Services, be sure you disable the Character Generator service. Nobody ever uses it, and it can be considered a security risk. To do this, set the value in either or both of these registry entries to zero:

```
HKEY_LOCAL_MACHINE\System\CurrentControlSet\SimpTcp\Parameters\
  EnableTcpChargen
HKEY_LOCAL_MACHINE\System\CurrentControlSet\SimpTcp\Parameters\
  EnableUdpChargen
```

Daytime Server

This service, defined by RFC 867, might actually appear to be useful because it provides the date and time to anyone who connects. However, it is useful only for testing purposes because the format of the date is not specified in the standard and is therefore not machine-readable. Similar to the other simple TCP/IP services, it listens on both TCP and UDP (port 13).

To disable the Daytime service, set the values of the following registry entries to zero:

```
HKEY_LOCAL_MACHINE\System\CurrentControlSet\SimpTcp\Parameters\
  EnableTcpDaytime
HKEY_LOCAL_MACHINE\System\CurrentControlSet\SimpTcp\Parameters\
  EnableUdpDaytime
```

Discard Server

The Discard service, defined by RFC 863, is, without a doubt, the most useless service of all. It listens on TCP and UDP port 9 and throws away all data it receives. In fairness, it does allow a remote user to initiate a TCP connection and thereby verify that the transport layer is working correctly. Of course, you could only test the data transfer one way, since the server simply discards the service. In its defense, this is probably the easiest RFC ever to read; it's four paragraphs and only half a page. (That's the only nice thing I could think of to say.)

Should you decide you can live without this critical service, set the values of these registry entries to zero:

```
HKEY_LOCAL_MACHINE\System\CurrentControlSet\SimpTcp\Parameters\
  EnableTcpDiscard
HKEY_LOCAL_MACHINE\System\CurrentControlSet\SimpTcp\Parameters\
  EnableUdpDiscard
```

Echo Server

RFC 862 is another good read if you want to make yourself comfortable with reading RFCs. The Echo service accepts both TCP and UDP connections on port 7 and sends back whatever it receives. So you can Telnet to an Echo server and see what you are typing.

Let Me Just Say, "I Told You So!"

To illustrate how important it is to disable this type of service, somebody recently came up with the idea of writing a program that spoofs a system on a network that is running the Echo service and transmits a UDP packet to another system running the Echo server. This packet has both the source and destination port numbers set to 7. As the second system receives the echo packet, it transmits a packet back to the source IP address and port number of the packet — in this case, another system running the Echo service. Now the fun begins, because both systems echo a message back and forth to each other until one of them is interrupted.

If you ever get tired of seeing yourself type and want to remove the Echo service, set these registry values to zero:

```
HKEY_LOCAL_MACHINE\System\CurrentControlSet\SimpTcp\Parameters\
   EnableTcpEcho
HKEY_LOCAL_MACHINE\System\CurrentControlSet\SimpTcp\Parameters\
   EnableUdpEcho
```

QUOTE (Quote of the Day) Server

RFC 865 defines a protocol that accepts a TCP connection or UDP packets and responds to the requester with an unspecified text message. Quote of the day is the most interesting of the Simple TCP/IP protocols because it actually rotates through a list of messages. By default, these messages are stored in the `<winnt_root>\system32\drivers\etc\quotes` text file. The sample file provided gives you an idea of the general format; feel free to replace the default messages with something more clever.

As with the other simple TCP/IP protocols, the quote of the day protocol is most useful for testing purposes. If you want to disable this protocol without removing the service entirely, change the value of these registry entries to zero:

```
HKEY_LOCAL_MACHINE\System\CurrentControlSet\SimpTcp\Parameters\
   EnableTcpEcho
HKEY_LOCAL_MACHINE\System\CurrentControlSet\SimpTcp\Parameters\
   EnableUdpEcho
```

Say What?

Just in case you're looking for some casual reading, here's a listing of all the standard quotes included with Windows NT 4.0. By default, these are contained in the `<winnt_root>\system32\drivers\etc\quotes` file.

"My spelling is Wobbly. It's good spelling but it Wobbles, and the letters get in the wrong places." A.A. Milne (1882–1958)

"Man can climb to the highest summits, but he cannot dwell there long." George Bernard Shaw (1856–1950)

"In Heaven an angel is nobody in particular." George Bernard Shaw (1856–1950)

"Assassination is the extreme form of censorship." George Bernard Shaw (1856–1950)

"When a stupid man is doing something he is ashamed of, he always declares that it is his duty." George Bernard Shaw (1856–1950)

"We have no more right to consume happiness without producing it than to consume wealth without producing it." George Bernard Shaw (1856–1950)

"We want a few mad people now. See where the sane ones have landed us!" George Bernard Shaw (1856–1950)

"The secret of being miserable is to have leisure to bother about whether you are happy or not. The cure for it is occupation." George Bernard Shaw (1856–1950)

"Here's the rule for bargains: 'Do other men, for they would do you.' That's the true business precept." Charles Dickens (1812–1870)

"Oh the nerves, the nerves; the mysteries of this machine called man! Oh the little that unhinges it, poor creatures that we are!" Charles Dickens (1812–1870)

"A wonderful fact to reflect upon, that every human creature is constituted to be that profound secret and mystery to every other." Charles Dickens (1812–1870)

"It was as true as taxes is. And nothing's truer than them." Charles Dickens (1812–1870)

Noting Things That Are Lacking

As I mention throughout this book, Windows NT has evolved from a desktop operating system to a workgroup server and finally to an Internet operating system. While Microsoft has done a commendable job keeping up with this growth, the operating system still lacks severely in several areas.

First, Windows NT lacks native support for several common Internet protocols. Telnet, the most common method for administering UNIX systems on internetworks, is missing. SSH, a more secure form of command-line remote control similar to Telnet, is also missing. Also notable but less critical is the lack of a TFTP server.

Those of us who engineer and administer systems that must be highly tuned for specific network tasks are constantly frustrated with the lack of configurability provided for within the TCP/IP stack. While Windows NT allows for some tuning through the registry, many settings are hard-coded into the operating system. For example, the initial time-out setting for ARP resolution and TCP connections is three seconds, no matter how much you would like to change it. DNS time-outs cannot be adjusted on a system-wide basis, and this fact causes many applications to seem slow to respond when the user mistypes a hostname.

Windows NT was designed to be simple to get up and running, and so the TCP/IP stack was designed to be self-tuning. However, this self-tuning is configured to work well even in unreliable networks, and so many of the settings are too pessimistic for most users. Typically, Microsoft waits for users to complain about missing flexibility before allowing a particular setting to be configurable through the registry — I hope they consider this an open complaint. Any settings for time-outs, retries, and other parameters should be made optional registry entries.

Noting What's New in Windows NT 5.0

A few minor changes have been added to the TCP/IP stack in Windows NT 5.0. All the changes Microsoft has documented to this point help only when TCP sliding windows are being used. Nonetheless, they will improve performance over high latency and unreliable links.

Windows NT 5.0 supports TCP windows larger than 65,535 bytes, as documented in RFC 1323. For most networks, this will not provide a performance increase — only those networks with high bandwidth and extremely high latency, such as satellite links, are likely to benefit.

Another added feature is support for Selective Acknowledgments (SACK). Windows NT 5.0 is now capable of resending a single lost packet. This is not possible in Windows NT 4.0 — if a single packet is lost, that packet and all packets after in the same TCP window must be retransmitted. Windows NT is also capable of inferring the loss of a single packet if it receives multiple ACKs for a single packet — this behavior generally indicates that the next packet in the sequence was expected. By retransmitting only the missing packet, Windows NT avoids retransmitting packets that followed the lost packet but were still part of the TCP window.

Conclusion

Microsoft builds a full-featured TCP/IP stack into Windows NT. It is flexible, configurable, and efficient. Still, it lacks in certain areas. While many parameters may be configured through the Network Control Panel and the registry, many other important aspects of the Microsoft implementation are completely out of the control of the systems engineer. Most of the tools needed to act as either a client or a server on the Internet are part of the standard product, but some of the most important are missing completely: Telnet services, NFS connectivity, X-Window services, and more.

Understanding which internetworking features are and are not supported by Windows NT is critical to the network systems engineer. A strong understanding of the Microsoft implementation will allow us to better tune both clients and servers, making both the systems and the networks more useful and efficient. Knowing its flaws as well as its features, both of which this chapter describes, will allow us to better guide Microsoft in future versions of Windows NT.

Summary

This chapter covered Windows NT, which ships with a complete, standards-based TCP/IP stack. This seems like a fairly obvious thing to point out, but it is important to state because not all TCP/IP stacks are created equal. Indeed, network drivers from different operating system vendors often support very different aspects of the TCP/IP protocol. These standards are above and beyond the core protocols — improving performance and efficiency rather than providing core functionality.

The performance and efficiency protocols are the interesting aspects of the Windows NT TCP/IP stack. By learning the details, you will come to better understand why your systems perform the way they do. You will also learn when it will benefit you to modify the configuration of your system's TCP/IP stack, and how it may affect your overall network.

You have learned about:

♦ Defining the full TCP/IP stack

♦ Tuning Windows NT networking

♦ Common TCP/IP protocols

♦ Simple TCP/IP Services

In the next chapter, you'll learn about Microsoft's implementation of the protocol known as NetBIOS over TCP/IP. Most Windows- and Windows NT–based networks have or will have problems with NetBIOS naming and user authentication. These problems rank among the most troublesome and persistent that networks experience, largely because of lack of knowledge of the inner workings of the protocol.

Chapter 10

NetBIOS: Friend or Foe?

IN THIS CHAPTER

- ◆ Discovering where NetBIOS came from and why we still use it today

- ◆ Breaking NetBIOS down into its different components: the NetBIOS Name service, Datagram service, and Session service

- ◆ Understanding how Windows NT systems use NetBIOS during the startup, logon, logoff, and shutdown processes

- ◆ Examining the different methods of NetBIOS name resolution and how to troubleshoot name resolution problems

THIS CHAPTER EXPLORES in depth Microsoft's implementation of the protocol known as NetBIOS over TCP/IP.

Most Windows- and Windows NT–based networks have or will have problems with NetBIOS naming and user authentication. These problems rank among the most troublesome and persistent that networks experience, largely because of administrators' lack of knowledge of the inner workings of the protocol. This is not the fault of the network managers and systems administrators – documentation from Microsoft on NetBIOS has always been superficial and optimistic. I've geared this chapter specifically to contain information that is difficult or otherwise impossible to obtain, and I've included opinions and impressions gathered from painful experience. My advice to the reader is to avoid learning NetBIOS, as I have, by experience: Those experiences will be painful and costly.

This chapter is intended to provide far more than simply a working knowledge of NetBIOS. It goes beyond spelling out the protocol and examines Microsoft's implementation of NetBIOS and the applications that make use of it. This chapter contains everything a systems engineer or network engineer needs to know about the protocol.

Examining the Origins of NetBIOS

Network Basic Input/Output System was designed for IBM by an organization named Sytek, Inc. It was created to provide an easy-to-use programming interface for connections between computers over a network. Microsoft began developing products for the MS-Net and LAN Manager (the predecessor to Windows NT) using the NetBIOS interface, anticipating the popularity of the standard. Ironically, the standard is only popular today because of Microsoft's implementation of it.

NetBIOS is an application programming interface, providing a set of functions that applications use to communicate across networks. It is similar in function to named pipes and sockets; it allows application programmers to add network capabilities to applications while minimizing the amount of code that must be dedicated to actually transporting the data.

NetBEUI, the NetBIOS Enhanced User Interface, was created as a data-link-layer frame structure for NetBIOS. A simple mechanism to carry NetBIOS traffic, NetBEUI has been the protocol of choice for small MS-DOS- and Windows-based workgroups. NetBIOS no longer lives strictly inside of the NetBEUI protocol, however. Microsoft worked to create the international standards described in RFC 1001 and RFC 1002, NetBIOS over TCP/IP (NBT).

Understanding the Advantages of NBT

One of the greatest advantages of Microsoft's implementation of NetBIOS is that it provides a consistent programming interface regardless of the network protocol used. For those familiar with the OSI model, NetBIOS exists at the Session level, as illustrated in Table 10-1. Because it is completely independent of the protocol, applications such as Server Manager and User Manager work on systems that are running IPX/SPX, TCP/IP, or NetBEUI. This is in contrast to most network applications that are developed specifically for use with a single network protocol, such as the entire Internet suite of applications (Telnet, FTP, and so on). Sound amazing? The drawbacks are equally astounding.

TABLE 10-1 THE OSI MODEL AND NT NETWORKING

Description	Protocol	Layer
Allow management of machines over the network in the same way they manage local machines by relying on the NetBIOS application programming interface.	Server Manager, Event Viewer, Performance Monitor, Registry Editor	Application
Make network directories behave similar to local hard drives.	File Redirection (the Workstation service)	Presentation

Continued

Description	Protocol	Layer
Provide a standardized interface to network applications. Name registration and resolution.	NetBIOS over TCP/IP	Session
Assign NetBIOS TCP port 139 for connection-oriented traffic. UDP ports 137 and 138 are connectionless.	TCP or UDP	Transport
Provide hierarchical, 32-bit IP addresses and DNS hostnames.	IP and ICMP	Network
Provide flat, 48-bit MAC addresses, one per network card. Ethernet, Token Ring, or FDDI.	Data Link	Data Link
Specify how signals are carried between stations on the network.	Cat 5 Copper or Fiber Optics	Physical

Internetworking with TCP/IP is the fastest growing area of modern computing. This is a good thing; soon, we will be able to forget about other network protocols. NetBIOS's advantages no longer outweigh its disadvantages, but we are still required to use it or find other ways to administer our Windows NT machines. Microsoft has promised to phase it out of their operating systems, but only time will tell. In this chapter, I hope to build your understanding of the protocol so that you may better work with it or work around it, whichever you decide.

Now that you have an understanding of what NetBIOS is, where it came from, and why we are still burdened with it, we will begin to explore its most visible aspect. NetBIOS naming causes the majority of problems on networks for a variety of reasons. The next section provides a high level of detail about the naming standards and provides you with the information you need to troubleshoot naming problems. Even better, it will allow you to avoid future naming problems in networks and systems that you engineer.

Exploring NetBIOS Naming Conventions

NetBIOS was designed to be used on the LAN, and the naming architecture reflects that philosophy. The NetBIOS name is often based on the computer name within NT, and it is used to identify servers for most types of communication, including file sharing and domain authentications. It is important to understand how these names work to effectively plan a network using NT servers; name resolution is one of the most common sources of problems on NT-based networks.

NetBIOS names, as specified by the standard, are 16 characters in length. Computer names, as specified by Microsoft, are only 15. The sixteenth character is reserved and is used to identify the type of name during network communications, distinguishing between domain names, computer names, workgroup names, and others. This length is entirely inflexible — if the computer name is "TERI," the remaining 11 characters are padded with 0's. The entire NetBIOS name becomes "TERI [00] [00] [00] [00] [00] [00] [00] [00] [00] [00] [00] [20]."

All NetBIOS names fall into one of two categories: unique names and group names. *Unique names* are just that: they identify a specific entity and cannot be claimed by anyone else on a given network. The most common unique name is the computer name. *Group names* are used to identify workstations as having a membership in a logical organization such as a domain or workgroup.

All NetBIOS communications occur using these names; remember that NetBIOS operates above the network-layer protocol and therefore has no knowledge of such things as IP addresses. However, once the connection is established, the additional overhead of the name no longer needs to be carried: MAC addresses and IP addresses are used instead. Later in this chapter I'll cover, in excruciating detail, how exactly NetBIOS over TCP/IP finds IP addresses given NetBIOS names. Table 10-2 lists the most common NetBIOS name entries and a description of each.

TABLE 10-2 COMMON NETBIOS NAME ENTRIES

Type	Value	Sixteenth Character	Name Type
Unique	Computer name	00h	Workstation service
Unique	"IS" Computer name	00h	IIS server/Internet Service Manager
Unique	Computer name	01h	Messenger service
Unique	Computer name	03h	Messenger service
Unique	User name	03h	Messenger service
Unique	Computer name	06h	RAS Server service
Unique	Domain	1Bh	Domain master browser
Unique	Computer name	1Dh	Master browser
Unique	Computer name	1Fh	NetDDE service

Continued

Type	Value	Sixteenth Character	Name Type
Unique	Computer name	20h	Server service
Unique	Computer name	21h	RAS Client service
Unique	Computer name	BEh	Network Monitor agent
Unique	Computer name	BFh	Network Monitor application
Group	Domain name	00h	Domain name
Group	"\\—__MSBROWSE__"	01h	Master browser
Group	Domain	1Ch	Domain controller
Group	"Inet-Services"	1Ch	IIS server/Internet Service Manager
Group	Domain	1Eh	Browser service elections

NetBIOS Computer Names Versus DNS Hostnames

Perhaps the greatest of the many frustrations of using NBT is that each machine must have *two* names: a NetBIOS computer name and a DNS hostname. The two have several similarities: they both resolve IP addresses to server names, and they are both unique on a network. DNS has several distinct advantages over NetBIOS names, however. DNS hostnames are hierarchical, allowing a fully qualified domain name in the format of "www.idgbooks.com." This also makes DNS more scalable; certainly there is more than one NT server on the Internet with the NetBIOS name of "WWW." True hostnames are used and supported across many platforms besides NT, making DNS more compatible.

So why use NetBIOS names at all? For those of us using homogenous TCP/IP networks, there is no good reason. Microsoft has recognized this and is making efforts to phase out their use in NT 5.0 (no promises!). For the time being, the necessity of using these names can cause several potential problems to arise.

To make your life less complicated, make an effort to synchronize DNS and NetBIOS names on all servers. This only works up to a point, however. Only a single NetBIOS name may be bound to a server at any time; in contrast, a server may have any number of DNS entries. Try to reduce your dependency on NetBIOS names as much as possible; Microsoft was kind enough to include the ability to refer to DNS hostnames within URLs. For example, instead of connecting to a share using the URL \\ELVIS\SHARE, use \\elvis.idgbooks.com\share or \\192.168.10.5\share.

Breaking Down NBT by Service

The services that NetBIOS over TCP/IP provide fall into three categories: the NetBIOS Name service, the NetBIOS Datagram service, and the NetBIOS Session service. Each service provides a distinct set of functions to applications and has a unique impact on a network.

Most applications that use TCP/IP make use of a Well-Known Port, a port that is registered internationally for use with a specific application. For example, Web requests use port 80 and FTP requests use ports 20 and 21. NetBIOS over TCP/IP (NBT) uses a separate port number for each of the three services: two UDP ports (137 and 138) and TCP port 139. Table 10-3 gives a summary of the individual services, the TCP and UDP ports they use by default, and their typical usage.

TABLE 10-3 NETBIOS SERVICES OVER TCP/IP

NetBIOS Service Name	TCP, UDP Port Number	Description
NetBIOS Name service	UDP 137	Used to resolve NetBIOS on a local network segment using broadcasts
NetBIOS Datagram service	UDP 138	Used to transfer data between applications when a broadcast must be used or when speed is more important than data integrity
NetBIOS Session service	TCP 139	Used to transfer data between applications when broadcasts are not required and when data integrity is more important than speed

To better troubleshoot problems with browsing, domain authentication, trusts, and file sharing, it is important to understand, in detail, how and why these three services are used. If you work in a routed environment, pay particular attention to the port numbers to understand what routers should and should not filter to support different functionality. Once you understand the intricacies of each service, you can make use of a protocol analyzer such as Microsoft's Network Monitor to narrow down problems. Network Monitor is an excellent tool for examining frames sent using these services because it automatically decodes many of the cryptic fields within the frames.

NetBIOS Name Service

The NetBIOS Name service provides for name resolution within a single network segment. It is also called upon by services that must listen for a specific NetBIOS name to be used on the network, both to register the name and to release the name. It is used by computers that are part of a domain to locate a domain controller on the local network segment for domain authentication.

NetBIOS connections involve several different steps. When a connection is requested, the first is to resolve the name of the server to something more useful, like an IP address. This step, which sounds simple, causes more NetBIOS problems than anything else! Microsoft recognizes this problem and has provided several different methods of name resolution, outlined in greater detail in the sections to follow. For now, understand that only name resolution through broadcasts uses the NetBIOS Name server. WINS queries and responses use the NetBIOS Datagram service. If the name is currently cached, no request is made.

The NetBIOS Name service always uses the UDP protocol, which exists at the transport layer of the OSI model. The advantages and disadvantages of UDP carry over to the NetBIOS Name service. To its advantage, it carries little overhead by avoiding the three-way handshake of TCP and using fewer header fields. Its connectionless property is also a disadvantage because it provides no method of notifying the sender if a packet is not carried across the network properly.

The specific transport-layer port number that NetBIOS Name service packets use is UDP port 137. Recognizing this port number is important when troubleshooting using tools such as protocol analyzers.

The Messenger service is an excellent example because it uses all three NetBIOS services, depending on the situation. The NET SEND command can be used to direct messages to a specific computer, a specific user, or an entire domain.

If a message is sent to a computer, the NetBIOS Name service is used to find that computer by sending a broadcast on the local network. If a message is sent to a user, a broadcast is sent to the network and is processed by all machines for which the Messenger service has registered a NetBIOS name (consisting of the username and a sixteenth character of <03>). Each machine that has registered that name responds to the query. At this point, the NetBIOS Session service is called upon to actually deliver the message. The three services, their transport layer port numbers, and typical usage of each service are detailed in Table 10-4.

TABLE 10-4 THE THREE NETBIOS SERVICES OVER TCP/IP, THEIR UDP/TCP PORT
NUMBERS, AND TASKS EACH SERVICE PERFORMS ON A NETWORK

NetBIOS Service Name	TCP, UDP Port Number	Description
NetBIOS Name service	UDP 137	Used to resolve NetBIOS names segment using broadcast on a local network
NetBIOS Datagram service	UDP 138	Used to transfer data between applications when a broadcast must be used or when speed is more important than data integrity
NetBIOS Session service	TCP 139	Used to transfer data between applications when broadcasts are not required and when data integrity is more important than speed

The NetBIOS Name service is not extremely well-adapted to typical, routed TCP/IP networks; it was designed to be used on LANs. However, there are several workarounds to smooth out problems. Routers, by default, simply ignore UDP broadcasts. This makes a lot of sense; the whole purpose of a router is to block that type of traffic. Unfortunately, this means that name resolution using the NetBIOS Name service only works on a single network segment, and adding a single router requires the use of an LMHOSTS file at each host or the WINS service.

To avoid this problem, most router manufacturers provide a way to forward these broadcasts between subnets, making the router act more like a bridge. Enabling this feature is a quick way to ensure that name resolution continues to work properly when segmenting a TCP/IP network; without it, users would be able to connect only to servers within their broadcast domain.

NetBIOS Datagram Service

The NetBIOS Datagram service is one of two ways applications may communicate with each other, the alternative being the NetBIOS Session service. The NetBIOS Datagram service provides connectionless and broadcast-oriented communications, making use of the UDP transport-layer protocol, port number 138.

The most common uses for UDP port 138 are for Browser service notifications. These messages are used to build the Network Neighborhood on your users' desktops, and if enabled, they can be mildly useful or extremely frustrating, depending on whether or not the Browser service is working properly on your network. There are many resources on the details of the Browser service, and I will not cover it in detail here. Though the Browser service is the most frequent user of the NetBIOS Datagram service, it is merely an optional application, not a required component of the operating system.

Another common use for the NetBIOS Datagram service is the Messenger service. The Messenger service is an interesting example because it uses either the NetBIOS Datagram service or the NetBIOS Session service, depending on the type of communications required. Messages sent to groups of computers, for example, using the NET SEND * command, make use of UDP's ability to broadcast packets to the local network, as shown in Figure 10-1.

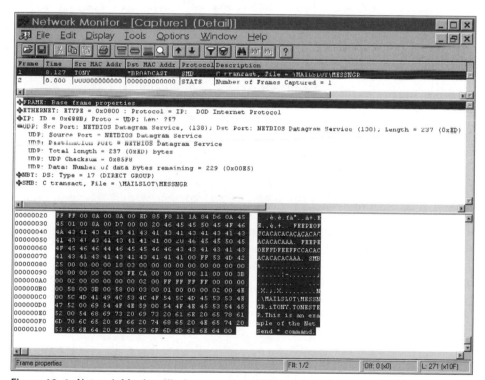

Figure 10-1: Network Monitor displays a captured UDP packet, the result of a Messenger service broadcast.

The NetBIOS Datagram service uses the UDP transport protocol and so suffers from the same problems as the NetBIOS Name service when a routed network is used. To make the Browser service, the Messenger service, and any other applications that use the NetBIOS Datagram service work in a routed network, you must forward broadcasts across routers as described in the previous section.

NetBIOS Session Service

The bulk of all NetBIOS traffic generated on a network occurs using the NetBIOS Session service, which utilizes TCP port 139. The Datagram service, using the connectionless UDP protocol, and the Session service, using the connection-oriented TCP protocol, provide two methods for applications to communicate. The Datagram service, because it uses UDP, is faster and more efficient but does not provide guaranteed delivery of packets. The phrase *guaranteed delivery* does not imply that every packet makes it through every time; it simply means that the computer sending the packets is always notified whether or not they were received.

In modern networks, UDP is an extremely reliable protocol, but it still lacks the capability of notifying the sending application that a packet was not received properly. By utilizing TCP, the NetBIOS Session service allows for small and large transfers where authentication is required, a session must be maintained over a period of time, or delivery of packets must be guaranteed.

File and printer services make up the bulk of traffic generated by the NetBIOS Session service. Another common use is the networked application: Server Manager, User Manager, Event Viewer, Registry Editor, and Performance Monitor all make use of the NetBIOS Session service to interact with remote machines. Therefore, if a router or firewall connecting two machines is blocking TCP port 139, all of these applications fail when used remotely.

The Messenger service makes use of the NetBIOS Session service and Server Message Blocks (SMB) for messages which are directed to a specific computer name. In this way, the Messenger service uses the connectionless NetBIOS Datagram service for broadcasts to groups of computers and the connection-oriented NetBIOS Session service for directed messages to a specific computer. If you are not yet familiar with SMB, it is covered in more detail later in this chapter.

The NetBIOS Session service is far more complex than its UDP counterpart, the NetBIOS Datagram service. Because it is connection-oriented, the NetBIOS Session service includes functions to establish connections, authenticate computers and users, and break connections. The NetBIOS Session service must perform NetBIOS name resolution to locate the IP address of a computer when given the NetBIOS name, and problems while connecting applications may be caused by a problem with either service.

Once the name resolution has been accomplished, a one-way NetBIOS connection is created by the client and maintained until either party terminates it. If the server needs to open a connection to the client, an entirely separate connection must be created. The name and IP address of the server are stored together in the NetBIOS name cache on the client. If you are curious, the names in the cache can be viewed using the command NBTSTAT -c.

NetBIOS Connections

After a single NetBIOS session is established between two hosts on a network, all data transferred thereafter between NetBIOS network applications on those two machines is channeled through the existing session. Because this same session is reused, the overhead of renegotiating a connection is avoided. This has an interesting side effect. When you need to connect to a remote computer that is not in the same domain as your user account, or if you need to access it with a different user account, tools such as the Event Viewer and Server Manager simply give an error and refuse the connection.

These tools do not provide a method to authenticate your connection with a different user account than the one currently in use. However, the Windows Explorer and NET USE commands do allow you to provide a different username and password. Therefore, if you need to connect to a machine using any of the standard administrative tools with a different account than the one you are currently using, start by establishing a network connection to the remote machine using the command NET USE \\SERVER /USER:USERNAME. The NET command prompts you for a password and creates a NetBIOS session. Until that session is broken, the administrative tools and all other NetBIOS networked applications run in the context of the username and password you specified with the NET USE command.

Similarly, if you have an existing connection (such as a connection to a shared directory) and need to perform a task on a remote machine using a different user account, all existing connections must be broken. To view the current NetBIOS sessions, execute the command NBTSTAT -s.

A Final Word on NetBIOS Services

As you learned in the previous sections, the presence NetBIOS has on a network is divided into three individual services. The NetBIOS Name service allows name resolution without using a WINS server but is a common source of problems and delays. The NetBIOS Datagram service is used by applications such as the Messenger service, the Browser service, and other applications that use the mailslots interface. The NetBIOS Session service is the most significant NetBIOS presence on most networks, allowing file transfers, network printing, and remote applications such as Server Manager and User Manager to function. Table 10-5 details the different applications each service is used for and reviews the port assignments.

TABLE 10-5 NETBIOS APPLICATIONS, PORT ASSIGNMENTS, AND SERVICES

Application	Port	Port Name
NetBIOS Name Queries (both directed and broadcast)	UDP 137	NetBIOS Name service
Browsing	UDP 138	NetBIOS Datagram service
File Sharing, Server Manager, User Manager	TCP 139	NetBIOS Session service

Starting Up, Logging In, Logging Off, and Shutting Down

Key to understanding NetBIOS communications and, ultimately, troubleshooting them is understanding how the operating system registers these names on a network. This section describes the process computers go through when configured for b-node-type resolution. (The node type here is important because much of the functionality is replaced in p-node type and h-node type, which rely instead on a WINS server. Node types are covered later in this chapter.)

Two of the most important functions that NetBIOS over TCP/IP provides are name registration and name resolution. Name registration is the process a computer must go through to verify that it has a unique computer name assigned to it and to make sure that others on the network are aware of its presence. Name registration includes verifying that the computer name is unique on a network. All NetBIOS names, including names that are used by a specific service, must be registered to be eligible to receive data from other nodes on the network. Name resolution, therefore, is entirely dependent on the name registration process.

The following sections describe the typical lifetime of a Windows NT session: the startup process, the logon and logoff processes, and finally the shutdown process.

The Startup Process

Anyone who has administered a TCP/IP network with Windows NT has noticed that NT automatically warns you if someone on the network has already claimed the IP address it has been configured with. The first step in loading the TCP/IP stack within Windows NT is to execute an ARP request for the IP address the computer has been configured to use. It should never get a response; each IP address on a network must be unique. Computers are only as perfect as the humans who configure them, however, and mistakes are made from time to time. If the Windows NT computer receives a response to the ARP request, it notifies the user through a dialog box and ceases loading the network protocol. This is not a function of NetBIOS; it is a function of the TCP/IP stack in Windows NT. I've included it here only to explain the ARP request you will see when performing packet-level analysis on a Windows NT system.

Before a computer allows itself to start the Workstation service, it must verify that no other machine is using that same computer name. It does this by sending a broadcast using the NetBIOS Name service on UDP port 137, and it waits for a response from a machine that has already registered that name. Network Monitor displays these registration requests as:

```
'NS: Registration req. for COMPUTERNAME'
```

If the computer is a member of a domain, three requests are sent to the domain controller, separated by a 1.5 second delay. Regardless of the domain association, four registration requests are broadcast to the local subnet, separated by a .75 second delay.

Each computer on the network should be listening to the NetBIOS Name service port, allowing the TCP/IP stack to pass the registration request to NBT. NBT within each networked computer checks to see if the local system has already registered the NetBIOS name in question, and if so, it notifies the machine that was attempting to register the name. Both the query and the response make use of the NetBIOS Name service. Network monitor provides a description for the query that reads:

```
'NS: Registration req. for COMPUTERNAME  <00>' and for the negative
response reading 'NS: Registration (Node Status) resp. for
COMPUTERNAME  <00>, Name Active error., Owner Addr. 192.168.3.17'
```

Once a system registers its name, that name is added to the local name table. The name table is simply a list of names for which the computer should listen; it includes an entry for each NetBIOS-based service running on the machine. To view a simplified version of the name table on a machine, execute the command NBT-STAT -n. Notice that the computer name is probably listed several times; it is listed once for each listening NetBIOS application. Each name is actually different, distinguished by the sixteenth character. The local name table from the author's system, as shown by the command NBTSTAT -n, is shown here:

```
Node IpAddress: [10.3.17.75] Scope Id: []

        NetBIOS Remote Cache Name Table

    Name        Type      Host Address  Life [sec]
    ───────────────────────────────────────────
    ELVIS      <00> UNIQUE    10.3.17.25       120
    ELVIS      <20> UNIQUE    10.3.17.25       480
```

```
PDC        <03> UNIQUE    10.3.22.16      -1
PDC        <00> UNIQUE    10.3.22.16      -1
PDC        <20> UNIQUE    10.3.22.16      -1
```

If the computer starting up is a member of a domain, it registers the NetBIOS group name in the form "DOMAINNAME <00>." Remember that NetBIOS group names do not need to be unique on a network; each machine that is a member of the domain registers this name through the use of broadcasts.

If the computer starting up is an NT server configured as a domain controller, the computer also registers the domain name with the sixteenth character <1C>. From this point forward, the domain controller listens to all communications directed to a domain controller of this domain. This allows member computers to locate a domain controller using broadcasts. Most often, this is done when a domain user needs authentication. Because the primary domain controller and all backup domain controllers on a LAN register this name, they each must be capable of authenticating users and providing logon scripts, if applicable. When a user logs onto that domain, the user's system performs a NetBIOS name resolution request to the domain name, which will be answered by anyone listening for that name – any domain controller.

The machine listens for its own name within future name registration requests. Anyone who has ever booted up two machines on the same network with the same name knows that the second machine to boot up recognizes the fact that the name is already owned. The mechanisms described here allow this seemingly simple task to be accomplished.

Once a machine registers its computer name on the network, it must register itself with the domain controller (if it has been configured as part of a domain). The first step in this process is to locate a domain controller. The system does not record the location of its domain controller between reboots; this is determined dynamically by sending a NetBIOS Name service query request broadcast to the domain name with <1C> as the sixteenth byte. This request is displayed in Network Monitor as:

```
'NS: Query req. for DOMAINNAME <1C>'
```

If there is a domain controller on the local network, it responds.

The final stage of the startup process is to launch those services configured to start automatically. One of the services that performs a NetBIOS name registration is the Messenger service, which uses the sixteenth byte <03>. If the Browser service is set to start automatically, it will generate a substantial amount of traffic during startup.

Once a computer has completed the startup process, several processes generate ongoing NetBIOS traffic. Every two minutes, the NetDDE service transmits three refresh requests, separated by 1.5 seconds, to the domain controller. Host announcements, using the NetBIOS Datagram service, are transmitted periodically to keep the browse list fresh. By default, these transmissions happen every 12 minutes. Because this ongoing traffic occurs whether or not the machine is actively being used, it is worth the effort to reduce it on large networks.

The major points of this process are summarized into a timeline in Table 10-6.

TABLE 10-6 THE WINDOWS NT STARTUP PROCESS: A VIEW FROM THE NETWORK

Time after Startup	Action
0:00.00	Reverse ARP attempt to verify unique IP address
0:05.00	NetBIOS Name service broadcast to register computer name (try #1)
0:05.75	NetBIOS Name service broadcast to register computer name (try #2)
0:06.50	NetBIOS Name service broadcast to register computer name (try #3)
0:07.25	NetBIOS Name service broadcast to register computer name (try #4)
0:08.00	NetBIOS Name service broadcast to register computer name (try #5)
0:08.75	NetBIOS Name service broadcast to register computer name (try #6)
0:09.50	NetBIOS Name service broadcast to register domain name (try #1)
0:10.25	NetBIOS Name service broadcast to register domain name (try #2)
0:11.00	NetBIOS Name service broadcast to register domain name (try #3)
0:11.75	NetBIOS Name service broadcast to register domain name (try #4)
0:12.75	NetBIOS Name service broadcast query for domain name <1C>
0:12.75	NetBIOS Name service response from domain controller listening on <1C>
0:12.75	NT system attempts to log onto domain using NetBIOS Datagram service.
0:12.75	Domain controller responds using NetBIOS Datagram service.
0:12.75	Services start and may register themselves.

The Logon Process

When a user logs onto the console of a Windows NT workstation or server, NetBIOS performs several tasks. If the user has selected a domain from the "Logon To:" drop-down list, domain authentication must be performed.

Regardless of whether the user is authenticated from the local user database or a domain controller, several services may register NetBIOS names on the network. For example, the Messenger service registers the username and <03> as the sixteenth character, listening for both the computer name and the user name. In this way, the Messenger service receives a message for "ELVIS" if either the computer name or username is "ELVIS," or if both are.

The Logoff Process

Each time a user logs off, several NetBIOS communications occur. First, all file sharing (SMB) connections are destroyed. Requests to drop these connections use the SMB protocol and are displayed in Network Monitor with the descriptions "C close file," "C tree disconnect," and "C logoff & X." Acknowledgments from the server to the client are displayed as "R close file," "R tree disconnect," and "R logoff & X."

After SMB connections have been dropped, a release request for services bound to the username is sent. A common example of a service that binds itself to the username of the user currently logged in is the Messenger service. Network Monitor shows these packets as NBT type "NS: Release request for Administrator <03>" (where "Administrator" is the username). Recall that unique names with the sixteenth character <03> are registered by the Messenger service for both the computer name and the user name, when a user has logged on.

The Shutdown Process

The process of shutting down generates very little network traffic. Names that have been registered by servers are released, but the operating system itself has nothing to broadcast. If the Messenger service is running, it must have registered the computer name with the <03> sixteenth character, and it must relinquish it with a packet that Network Monitor describes as "NS: Release request for ComputerName <03>." Other services make noise by announcing their demise, such as the NetDDE service, which uses the sixteenth byte <1F>. Last, the computer name itself is released and removed from the browse list.

Understanding the Name Table

The previous section described the phases that most often cause problems with NetBIOS communications: the startup, logon, logoff, and shutdown processes. Key to these and any other NetBIOS communications is the NetBIOS name table, which stores a list of names a particular host is known by on the network. The name table is covered in depth in this section.

As individual NetBIOS-based services start up on a computer, each registers one or more NetBIOS names in the local NetBIOS name table. NetBIOS applications listen for specific names in the same way that sockets applications listen for specific TCP or UDP ports. Each time a name query is received by a computer, the name table is parsed to find the name in question. If the name in the packet is not found in the name table, the packet is discarded and no further processing is required. If the name is listed in the name table, NBT passes the data to the application that posted the name for further processing.

For example, the Messenger service uses the NetBIOS service-type identifier <03>. Therefore, because it should listen for messages on the network that are directed to the computer name, it registers the name "COMPUTERNAME <03>." From that point forward the Messenger service is associated with the computer's name and the <03> service type. The client that sends a message to the receiving computer already knows that the Messenger service is using the <03> service type. Therefore, when the command NET SEND COMPUTERNAME test_message is issued, the sending computer knows that it should pad the name supplied to a full 15 characters and append the <03> identifier as the sixteenth character before issuing a request.

To see this process in action, stop the Messenger service on a machine. This step ensures that the service is not currently listening and will remove any entries from the name table. To view the current name table, issue the command NBTSTAT -n.

The following example shows a sample name table:

```
Node IpAddress: [146.115.100.1] Scope Id: []

        NetBIOS Local Name Table

    Name          Type        Status
    ---------------------------------
TONY        <00> UNIQUE    Registered
TONY        <20> UNIQUE    Registered
    TONY        <01> UNIQUE    Registered
```

Now start the Messenger service. As the service starts, it registers two names: the computer name and the username. Recall that the Messenger service is assigned the service identifier <03> and so sets the sixteenth bytes of the NetBIOS names to that value. The following example shows the sample name table with the Messenger service started:

```
Node IpAddress: [146.115.100.1] Scope Id: []

        NetBIOS Local Name Table

    Name          Type        Status
    ---------------------------------
TONY        <00> UNIQUE    Registered
TONY        <20> UNIQUE    Registered
```

```
    TONY      <01> UNIQUE    Registered
TONY      <03> UNIQUE    Registered
```

Notice that an additional NetBIOS name has been added, with the service-type identifier <03>, indicating the Messenger service. An entry was also added to the name table for the username, but it is not displayed by the NBTSTAT program.

The name table provides a list of aliases that various processes on a host are identified by on a network. The name table is a component of the NetBIOS Server services on Windows NT systems, defining which NetBIOS messages are accepted and which are ignored. This allows a Windows NT system to accept inbound NetBIOS connections on a network, but it is not used for outbound connections. Outbound, client-side connections use an entirely separate set of components, as the following section describes.

Examining Name Resolution Components

A constant source of trouble and mystery is the process of resolving Microsoft's 15-character computer names into network-layer IP addresses. NetBIOS name resolution exists because hosts on a TCP/IP network cannot speak directly to each other using the computer name but they must rely on IP and MAC addresses for all communications. Ideally, this step is transparent to the user, who connects to network servers using friendly UNC names rather than cryptic, difficult-to-remember IP addresses. Unfortunately, administrators and engineers are cursed to understand the nitty-gritty details of network communications. It is critical to those who design or troubleshoot Microsoft networks to have a detailed understanding of the different methods and processes involved.

NBT provides three methods to resolve computer names to IP addresses: broadcast, the LMHOSTS file, and WINS. Many networks rely on the default configuration: name resolution by broadcast. For slightly more complex configurations including routers and WAN links, an LMHOSTS file is introduced and used to supplement the broadcast method. Complex enterprise internetworks rely on WINS servers for centralized administration and name resolution.

Through the many generations of NT, NetBIOS name resolution has become increasingly complicated. Many components depend on each other to resolve names efficiently and effectively. The components are the NetBIOS name cache, broadcast queries, the LMHOSTS file, WINS servers, and traditional IP addressing mechanisms such as the HOSTS file and DNS.

Name Cache

The NetBIOS name cache is always checked first when name resolution is required. The name cache is a small section of memory dedicated to remembering mappings between NetBIOS names and IP addresses. The purpose of the name cache, like that of any other cache, is to reduce the number of requests that need to be made for the same information. It is entirely independent of the method used to resolve the names; troubleshooting is no different whether name query broadcasts or a WINS server is used. You will probably never lose any sleep over this, but it is important to understand the intricacies of the name cache and the several ways that you can tune its performance.

To view the name cache, use the command NBTSTAT -c. You'll see feedback similar to this:

```
Node IpAddress: [192.168.1.3] Scope Id: []

     NetBIOS Remote Cache Name Table

  Name        Type     Host Address  Life [sec]
  ----------------------------------------------
  TERI       <00> UNIQUE    192.168.3.17     120
  TERI       <20> UNIQUE    192.168.3.17     480
  FILESERVER <03> UNIQUE    192.168.7.7       -1
  FILESERVER <00> UNIQUE    192.168.7.7       -1
  FILESERVER <20> UNIQUE    192.168.7.7       -1
```

Viewing the contents of your computer's name cache is a critical step in troubleshooting name resolution problems. Consider a scenario: You are the administrator of a medium-sized TCP/IP network with several routers. The morning after you change the IP address of a file server, a user complains that he can no longer access a shared directory. You are able to PING the IP address of the server, but you cannot connect a network drive from Explorer.

Successfully PINGing the server indicates that connectivity is intact; the host is able to create a packet, and the routers on the network know how to take it to its proper destination. The inability to connect to a share may be caused by several things, but because an IP address was recently changed, verifying name resolution is a good starting point. It's likely that the Workstation service is still attempting to connect using the old IP address; for some reason, it has not discovered the change.

The NetBIOS name cache in the preceding example indicates that the server "FILESERVER" has a statically mapped, preloaded IP address mapping to "192.168.7.7." The last column shows the amount of time the mapping remains in the name cache. In this case, "-1" is listed, which indicates that it is never removed. This is normally caused by a static mapping in the \<systemroot>\DRIVERS\ETC\LMHOSTS file on the workstation in the format "192.168.7.7 FILESERVER #PRE." The quickest way to resolve the problem is to update the LMHOSTS file with the new IP address and force the workstation to reprocess the file with the command NBTSTAT -R. Afterward, verify that it worked by reexecuting NBTSTAT -c. The name cache should be missing the preloaded names, as seen here:

```
Node IpAddress: [192.168.1.3] Scope Id: []

      NetBIOS Remote Cache Name Table

  Name        Type     Host Address  Life [sec]

  TERI      <00> UNIQUE   192.168.3.17    120
  TERI      <20> UNIQUE   192.168.3.17    480
```

The amount of time a name is retained in the cache is determined by the registry entry HKEY_LOCAL_MACHINE\System\CurrentControlSet\Services\NetBT\Parameters\CacheTimeout. The value of this entry is given in milliseconds and defaults to 600,000 (10 minutes). This entry can be increased if name resolution queries are causing an impact on the network, which is a very possible scenario in networks with large broadcast domains, such as switched networks. If IP addresses are commonly changed during production hours, the value can be lowered to decrease the average time it takes to find the new IP address. Either way, it is best to keep this value consistent enterprise-wide, as setting it differently for different workstations can lead to intermittent, difficult-to-troubleshoot problems.

Broadcasts

Broadcasts are the default method of name resolution for Windows NT, and they are sufficient for small networks that do not span multiple subnets. When a user makes a NetBIOS request to a server on the network, the workstation attempts to resolve the NetBIOS name to an IP address using a query broadcast to all machines on the subnet. This is done using the NetBIOS Name service. Accordingly, all queries and responses use UDP port 137.

As with any broadcast, all network cards on the subnet must interrupt the CPU and pass the packet to the network protocol. In the case of NetBIOS name queries, every machine that receives the requests checks its NetBIOS name table to determine whether or not it needs to listen to the name in the query. If it does not, it simply ignores the packet; there is no need to reply with a negative response. If the name in the query matches, the machine must process it and may send a response with its IP address. Using broadcasts in this way is similar to walking into a crowded room and calling out the name of a friend — everyone in the room hears you, but only your friend responds.

Name resolution by broadcast is suitable for workgroup environments, especially those that use only a single network segment. Many administrators of small networks invest time in creating WINS servers to avoid all the terrible things that come with increased broadcast traffic: broadcast storms, high network utilization, and PCs that must be interrupted. These are all conditions that can occur, but

NetBIOS name resolution by broadcast is often the right answer. *In fact, managing* *LMHOSTS and especially WINS can become so time consuming that I recommend all* *small networks rely on broadcasts for name resolution.* Often, adding complicated technology simply makes things more complicated.

The bulk of NetBIOS broadcast network traffic comes from name queries that are initiated when a user attempts to access a resource using NetBIOS, when connecting to a network drive, for example. At this point it checks the NetBIOS name cache, an area of memory used to remember recently requested names and names stored in the LMHOSTS file with the #PRE option. The best-case scenario is that it finds the name in the cache. If the name is not found, the computer continues attempting to resolve the name with whatever method has been specified.

Name resolution queries, by default, are transmitted every three seconds until a response is received. Each broadcast times-out after $^3/_4$ second. Once the workstation has issued these three queries, it waits 12.75 seconds and then transmits three more queries. After the last query is sent, it waits another 12.75 seconds for a response to be returned. This means that a user should have to wait about twenty-six seconds to determine that a name cannot be resolved when using name resolution by broadcast. However, these times are entirely configurable through the registry. In fact, it is generally a good idea to optimize these settings.

Twenty-six seconds is a long time to wait, and when combined with other types of name resolution that the computer may use, it can seem like a lifetime. For small networks that are not prone to high network utilization, decrease the broadcast query time-out value to $^1/_4$ second (250 milliseconds) on all computers. This has the effect of decreasing the total amount of time spent waiting for a time-out by $^1/_3$.

If you're concerned about the amount of network traffic that this process generates, the packet size is 78 bytes (add this to the frame size; the total size on Ethernet is 92 bytes). The query is simultaneously generated on all interfaces that are bound to the NetBIOS interface, so it is a good idea to manually disable this binding on any interfaces that do not require it, such as dial-up interfaces. The two registry entries to edit to fine-tune this are:

```
HKEY_LOCAL_MACHINE\System\CurrentControlSet\Services\Netbt\Parameter
  s\ BcastNameQueryCount
```

This value represents the number of times a broadcast name query is sent to the local network segment before NetBIOS gives up and moves onto the next method of resolution; it defaults to three.

```
HKEY_LOCAL_MACHINE\System\CurrentControlSet\Services\Netbt\Parameter
  s\ BcastQueryTimeout
```

This value represents the number of milliseconds NetBIOS waits for a response to a broadcast query. It defaults to 750 milliseconds, or $^3/_4$ second.

LMHOSTS File

The LMHOSTS file evolved from the HOSTS file, an early method of TCP/IP host-name-to-IP address resolution used before DNS became popular. In fact, the format of the file is almost exactly the same. The "LM" part of the name is short for LAN Manager, a predecessor to NT. At its simplest, this file is a direct mapping of IP addresses to computer names. At its most complicated, it allows for failover, centralized administration, and registration of full NetBIOS names (including the NetBIOS service type identifier, the sixteenth character).

The default path for the LMHOSTS file is <systemroot>\drivers\etc\lmhosts, though the file is not created by default. A common point of confusion is the LMHOSTS.SAM file located in the same directory – this is a "readme" file; it should be read carefully but should not be used to contain name-to-IP address mappings. Always create a new, blank file; every line of comment must be processed whenever the file is referred to, and LMHOSTS.SAM contains many comments.

The LMHOSTS file can be used for more than mapping simple computer names by explicitly adding a sixteenth hexadecimal byte. To do this, create an entry in the format:

```
"domainname  \0x1b" #PRE
```

The example creates a NetBIOS name of the type Domain Master Browser. In the vast majority of cases, using #DOM:domainname provides all the functionality anyone needs. However, the fine level of control available through statically mapping NetBIOS names of specific types is available if you ever need it.

For more information on how to create centralized and redundant LMHOSTS files, refer to the LMHOSTS.SAM file. The primary advantage of the LMHOSTS file over WINS is that it is distributed. Because of this, I am going to avoid this topic entirely because I feel centralized LMHOSTS files should never be used; if your network is large and dynamic enough to need these features, use a WINS server.

The LMHOSTS file is only used to resolve names if the check box labeled "Enable LMHOSTS Lookup," located in the Network Control Panel applet, is selected. Selecting this check box is equivalent to the setting registry value

```
HKEY_LOCAL_MACHINE\System\CurrentControlSet\Services\Netbt\Parameter
s\EnableLMHOSTS
```

equal to 1. When set, the LMHOSTS file is referenced any time a NetBIOS name could not be resolved through the standard methods. The entire LMHOSTS file is parsed, starting at the first line and working down. To make name resolution as efficient as possible, place commonly used server names at the top of the file and remove all comments. Place infrequently used server names toward the bottom of the list, and avoid adding unused names.

WINS Server

UNIX TCP/IP networks originally relied on the HOSTS file to resolve hostname-to-IP address mappings, eventually introducing DNS to allow centralized administration. Similarly, Microsoft originally relied on the LMHOSTS file and later introduced WINS servers.

A WINS server is any NT Server computer running the WINS Server service. As computers are started on a network, they register their name with the WINS server, the IP address of which has been predefined in their TCP/IP configuration. The WINS server stores these names and IP addresses in its database to be used later to respond to queries from clients that need to locate a particular server by the NetBIOS name. In this way, there is a single, centralized database of names and IP addresses that may span multiple subnets. This overcomes the limitations of broadcasts, which can normally only reach the local subnet, and of LMHOSTS files, which are stored on the clients themselves and can be difficult to update.

WINS has become a common method of name resolution in enterprise networks, but it is not without its problems. It is complicated, troublesome, and susceptible to network attacks. Further, Microsoft has introduced an interesting alternative to WINS in NT 4.0: the ability to use IP addresses and standard UNIX hostnames as part of UNCs instead of computer names.

One or two WINS servers can be used to resolve NetBIOS names when the IP addresses have been added into the Control Panel's Network applet. Messages sent to a WINS server use the NetBIOS Session service and directly replace name resolution broadcasts normally sent by the NetBIOS Name service. Because the requests are directed to a server, they avoid the overhead associated with sending broadcasts to a network. Directed requests are capable of being forwarded past routers to other network segments, a task broadcasts are normally not capable of.

Administrators may find that configuring a WINS server reduces the administrative headaches associated with NetBIOS name resolution. As a rule of thumb, avoid using WINS servers unless absolutely necessary. They are a common point of failure in Microsoft-based networks, and the effects of a missing WINS server can cripple an entire enterprise. Further, the complexity of WINS servers often outweighs the simplicity of centralized control over NetBIOS names. Nonetheless, creating WINS servers and configuring clients to resolve names using them is the best solution for many networks.

For more information on WINS, please refer to Chapter 11.

Deciding When to Use WINS and LMHOSTS

The LMHOSTS file and WINS servers serve the same function: to resolve NetBIOS names to IP addresses. However, the methods used are very different. LMHOSTS files are appropriate for small networks where name resolution through broadcast can be relied upon and only a handful of machines must communicate outside of the local network segment. An organization with centralized administration of user accounts and distributed resources may only require backup domain controllers at each remote site to ever contact servers outside of the local network. In this circumstance, configuring the LMHOSTS file at each of the backup domain controllers allows them to perform domain communications across the wide area network without requiring a WINS server. If the IP addresses of the domain controllers are stable, these files may never have to be updated.

For most other circumstances, a WINS server is appropriate. Anytime desktop machines in a LAN environment need to use NetBIOS to communicate with corporate servers across a WAN, use WINS. Anytime DHCP is used to dynamically allocate IP addresses to servers, use WINS.

Traditional Hostnames Using HOSTS and DNS

With NT 4.0 and the integration of traditional UNIX hostnames into NetBIOS name resolution, the HOSTS file may now be used to resolve names. The HOSTS file is located in the same directory as the LMHOSTS file, <systemroot>\drivers\ etc\lmhosts. This file is a simple text, whitespace-delimited database. Each row contains two fields: IP address and hostname. For example, adding the line "192.168.3.17 this.host.does.not.exist" allows you to successfully PING using the hostname "this.host.does.not.exist." You can also refer to this hostname anytime you would normally use a computer name, such as part of a UNC path. To clarify things a bit, these three commands can all perform the same function: NET USE \\THISHOST\C$, NET USE \\this.host.does.not.exist\C$, and NET USE \\ 192.168.3.17\C$.

Anyone currently using TCP/IP in medium-sized to large networks should seriously consider adopting the usage of HOSTS and DNS with traditional hostnames in lieu of LMHOSTS and WINS with NetBIOS names. Traditional hostnames offer several advantages over NetBIOS names. First, they are not limited to 15 characters – they can have up to 25 characters. Second, they are hierarchical, meaning you can better organize names by region. Combined, these two advantages allow your users to refer to a share as "\\accounting.ny.company.com\forms" instead of "\\ACCT_NY_COMPANY\FORMS."

Other advantages include being able to build on an existing DNS architecture rather than replacing it. Enterprise networks have typically invested a great deal of time and money into reliable, distributed, redundant DNS servers. It is wasteful to build a parallel architecture for WINS. Further, many of the advanced features of DNS can be applied to NetBIOS applications. For example, round-robin DNS is a method of load-balancing wherein a DNS server responds with one of several different IP addresses when queried for a single hostname.

A good example of round-robin DNS is Microsoft's Web site: try PINGing "www.microsoft.com" several times in a row; each PING request that queries a DNS server resolves the fully qualified domain name to a different IP address. Round-robin can also be used to distribute workload between file servers that have identical content. As DNS servers add more complex features, such as Cisco's Distributed Director, NetBIOS applications are able to take advantage of them.

It also makes life simpler to use different servers within a network; users no longer have to memorize separate computer names for file sharing and fully qualified domain names for FTP, HTTP, and Telnet. Further, while NetBIOS limits servers to a single computer name, DNS commonly assigns multiple hostnames to a single IP address. In this way, a single server can respond to multiple hostnames, allowing the tasks to be separated in the future without requiring clients to be reconfigured.

Consider a small company adding a single server to perform file services, printer services, and mail services. Instead of instructing users to connect their printer to the share "\\SERVER\PRINTER," their network drive to the share "\\SERVER\FILES," and their mail client to download mail from "server.my company.com," create a separate CNAME DNS entry for each of these three tasks. Add records for "printer.mycompany.com," "fileserver.mycompany. com," and "mail.my company.com," each with the same IP address. In the future, when a separate printer server is configured, none of the client configurations need to be updated. Simply create a printer server with a new IP address and associate the DNS record for "printer.mycompany.com" with the new IP address. The next time a client queries the DNS database, that client is referred to the new server.

Within the Network Control Panel applet, the hostname and domain name can be configured. The domain name configured here is automatically appended to any hostname. This functionality can be leveraged to shorten the fully qualified domain names into simple hostnames, allowing users to reference a share with "\\server\share" instead of "\\server.mycompany.com\share."

Now that your network has been configured to completely bypass the use of NetBIOS, what NetBIOS names do you give your machines? It is good practice to make the computer name the same as the hostname, but this does not work in enterprise networks where a machine on the west coast may be named "server.west.mycompany.com" and have a peer on the east coast named "server.east.mycompany.com." Consider setting the NetBIOS name on all machines to equal the MAC address in hexadecimal — it is an ugly format, but it is always unique.

The HOSTS file has several lines of comments in it; it is good practice to rename this file and create a new, blank file to store hostname and IP relationships. It is a mystery why Microsoft would create the LMHOSTS.SAM file with comments, forcing the user to create a new blank file, but not use this same practice with the HOSTS file.

This section described the different components Windows NT uses as part of the name resolution process. Each of the components works together to convert friendly NetBIOS names into IP addresses. The next section will show you the different mechanisms for name resolution, and how each of the components described in this section is used with each different mechanism.

Understanding the Major Name Resolution Methods

NetBIOS names can be resolved to IP addresses using broadcast queries, the LMHOSTS file, a WINS server, the HOSTS file, and DNS queries. NT does not simply attempt all methods at once; instead, it has a specific process it follows that can be configured through a well-hidden registry entry. Microsoft provides four different methods, and each has two significant options: to use DNS and/or LMHOSTS to resolve names. This gives us a total of sixteen different methods to consider, each with different advantages and disadvantages.

The following sections outline each of the four major methods for name resolution: b-node, p-node, m-node, and h-node. Each of these methods has its own set of advantages and disadvantages, and each suits some environments better than others.

B-Node

Networks that rely entirely on broadcasts for NetBIOS name resolution should be configured with the b-node (broadcast node) type. This is appropriate for small offices with all computers residing within a single broadcast domain. If the broadcast fails to return an answer, the workstation may attempt to resolve the name using the LMHOSTS file and/or DNS, depending on the configuration.

B-node will become a more common configuration as more and more small networks migrate from traditional LAN protocols like NetBEUI to TCP/IP. Enterprise networks have relied on TCP/IP for its scalability, and small networks are adopting it to connect to the Internet.

B-node-type resolution is best suited to small networks existing in a single segment and medium or enterprise networks where all resources and administration is distributed. To configure a machine to use b-node-type resolution, add the following registry key and set its value to 1:

```
HKEY_LOCAL_MACHINE\CurrentControlSet\Services\NetBT\Parameters\
  NodeType
```

P-Node

Networks that have been configured to rely on WINS servers for all NetBIOS name resolution should be configured with the p-node (point-to-point node) type. By default, when a Windows NT or Windows 95 system is configured to resolve names using a WINS server, the node type is set to h-node (described later). P-node is a better option because it does not attempt to resolve the name through broadcast queries, which extend the time-out for mistyped URLs significantly. When configured with p-node, the computer returns an error message much sooner when a bogus computer name is requested.

P-node-type resolution is best suited to small, medium, and enterprise networks with centralized management of WINS servers. To configure a machine to use p-node-type resolution, set the registry value to 2:

```
HKEY_LOCAL_MACHINE\CurrentControlSet\Services\NetBT\Parameters\
  NodeType
```

M-Node

M-node (mixed node) type resolution is the most rarely used node type. It is a combination of p-node and b-node resolution, first attempting to resolve NetBIOS names using broadcasts, and querying a WINS server in the event the broadcasts do not return an answer. This only makes sense in remote, single-segment networks in which the bulk of connections are to local machines and there is no local WINS server. In this environment, hosts attempt to resolve a name through a local broadcast query, received by every machine on the local network. When a client attempts to connect across the WAN, the broadcast query fails to resolve correctly and a central WINS server is queried. This avoids the necessity of having every desktop and server on an enterprise network register with a WINS server, and it reduces the load placed on a central WINS server. Further, it gives administrators of remote networks the flexibility to add, remove, and rename servers as they see fit without the need to update the central WINS database. It is important to note that the WINS server is only queried after local broadcast queries have failed – forcing users who wish to connect to remote resources to wait an additional twenty-six seconds for the broadcast queries to time-out.

M-node-type resolution is best suited to enterprise networks with distributed WINS administration and both centralized and distributed resources. To configure a machine to use m-node-type resolution, set the following registry value to 4:

```
HKEY_LOCAL_MACHINE\CurrentControlSet\Services\NetBT\Parameters\
  NodeType
```

H-node (hybrid node) type resolution involves a point-to-point query followed by broadcast queries. In a typical scenario, a Windows 95 or Windows NT computer configured to use H-node-type resolution first queries a WINS server for a NetBIOS name and then falls back to broadcast name resolution queries. If both methods fail, the LMHOSTS and/or HOSTS and DNS may be used if configured.

This method is configured by default on all Windows NT and Windows 95 computers that have been configured to use a WINS server. It works well in environments where the majority of NetBIOS name queries can be resolved by a WINS server but computers may be accessed without being registered at the WINS server. Ideally, an organization that commits to use WINS configures every machine in the network to use WINS. In this scenario, resolution by broadcast would never resolve a query that could not be resolved through a WINS query, and the added overhead is not necessary. By using p-node-type resolution instead and eliminating the broadcast query time-out, you assure that URLs that include invalid NetBIOS names return error messages much faster.

To configure a machine to use h-node-type resolution, set the following registry value to 8:

```
HKEY_LOCAL_MACHINE\CurrentControlSet\Services\NetBT\Parameters\
  NodeType
```

The previous section covered the different methods Windows NT systems use to resolve NetBIOS names on a network. Resolving the name is only the first part of NetBIOS communications, however. Once the name is resolved, useful work may be accomplished. One of the most popular mechanisms for this work is SMB, or Server Message Blocks, described in this section.

Microsoft, Intel, and IBM worked as a team to develop the Server Message Blocks (SMB) protocol as a standardized way of exchanging information using NetBIOS. It has been submitted as an open Internet standard, allowing other organizations to create SMB-compliant applications in the future.

SMB provides much of the workgroup functionality that is available in Microsoft operating systems such as MS-DOS, Windows 3.1, Windows for Workgroups, Windows 95, LAN Manager, and Windows NT. It is well suited to workgroup communications, but it is not the most efficient way of exchanging files on a TCP/IP network. However, it has become widely used because it is included with all of Microsoft's desktop and network operating systems, it is easy to configure, and it is free.

Microsoft is not the only organization using SMB, though they are the driving force behind its use. Products such as SAMBA allow UNIX-based systems to connect to shared drives from Windows- and Windows NT–based systems, enabling heterogeneous networks to use a single method of file exchange. Currently there is no method for Macintosh systems to connect to SMB shares. Though Windows NT has the ability to exchange files with Apple systems through the Apple Filing Protocol (AFP), it requires introducing yet another protocol to a network.

The Server Message Blocks protocol has been written to comply with C2 security specifications. It incorporates user authentication and exchanges passwords only in a hashed format to thwart someone with a protocol analyzer from compromising the passwords. The process of exchanging passwords starts with the client, which attempts to initiate a SMB connection to a server. The server determines that the client must supply a username and password, and it sends an authentication challenge including a randomized token. The client uses this token to encrypt a hashed version of the password and returns the result to the server. The server performs the same steps on the password it has stored for the user and matches the results to the answer the client provided. If the answer matches the result of the hash the server computed, the client has started with the correct password and is authenticated.

This security makes it very difficult for someone to listen to a conversation between two different machines and decrypt the password. The client is still vulnerable to attack from the server, however. One method that has been proven to compromise client passwords involves creating a server that challenges the client with the same token every time. In this scenario, the client encrypts the password using the token and returns it to the server. Because the token is not randomized, the server may have constructed a dictionary of hashed passwords to be used to look up the original password based on the client's hashed password. This is a difficult trap to build, but it has been done before. The moral of the story is twofold: Carefully consider which servers you attempt to authenticate with, and consider the security of the client as carefully as security of the server.

Microsoft's Common Internet File System (CIFS), their solution for file sharing across the Internet, is being based on the SMB protocol. This protocol is covered in Chapter 14.

SMB relies on the NetBIOS Session service for all communications. Commands can be broken into four broad categories, discussed in the next sections.

Session Control

A subset of the entire SMB message suite, the Session Control message group, is composed of messages used to establish and break redirector connections (file sharing). These are called when the Windows NT commands NET USE and NET USE /DELETE are issued, or when the Map Network Drive and Disconnect Network Drive commands are called from Windows Explorer.

File

The File message group is a group of commands used to access shared files and directories once a session between a client and a server has already been established. These messages would be sent when copying files from a network drive.

Printer

Similar in function to the File message group, the Print message group is used to send documents to a network print server and provides printer management functions. These messages are used when printing to a network printer or performing management functions from within Printer Manager.

Message

The Message SMB type is used to exchange messages between systems. A command such as NET SEND COMPUTERNAME test_message uses a Message-type SMB packet to transmit a directed message to a specific computer.

SMB is an important topic to understand because it is the underlying mechanism for much of Windows NT's network functionality. While NetBIOS and SMB have proven themselves over time in production networks, they are not without their flaws. The next section will explore these flaws in more detail, with the goal of making you aware before they cause serious problems.

Uncovering NetBIOS's Weaknesses

NetBIOS is not the ideal way for applications on a TCP/IP internetwork to communicate. The most obvious drawback is the additional overhead. When used with TCP/IP, NetBIOS adds yet more headers after the frame header: the IP header and the TCP/UDP header. Another disadvantage is that different applications using NetBIOS all look the same to a router or firewall, limiting an administrator's ability to filter out specific applications. The result is that most simply block NetBIOS entirely – losing the functionality of applications that may be useful.

When designing these applications, did Microsoft simply not take these factors into account? Certainly they did, but NetBIOS was designed in an era before the dominance of TCP/IP in local area networks. In retrospect, Microsoft made a very wise choice; had they built the applications around a single Net protocol, they no doubt would *not* have chosen TCP/IP. In fact, they were so convinced NetBEUI would be the next major protocol that they began development of a routable version called JetBEUI (no joke!).

Network Level Security

Undoubtedly the most publicized flaws of NetBIOS are its security weaknesses. Being aware of the specifics of these weaknesses will make you more able to combat them, and this section will provide you with the information you need to limit your security risks. Securing any network, especially those attached to the public Internet, needs to include security at both the network level and the systems level. Securing at the network level means using firewalls and filtering routers, and it is important specifically because it is independent of the systems operating on the network. For example, if a router has been configured to block all incoming traffic from the Internet to a specific NT server, that system is safe from direct attacks from the Internet, regardless of how the computer itself has been configured.

To avoid the cost of adding a true firewall, most networks make use of packet filtering on routers. Packet filtering allows traffic to be selectively blocked according to the source IP address and the UDP/TCP port number. Port-level filtering allows a network manager to permit certain types of traffic through a router, depending on the application. Because Telnet uses TCP port 23 and HTTP uses TCP port 80, a network manager has the ability, for example, to allow Web requests from the Internet to be forwarded only to the corporate Web server, and to disallow all Telnet access.

Network-level security blocks dangerous packets from ever reaching the system. This concept is illustrated in Figure 10-2.

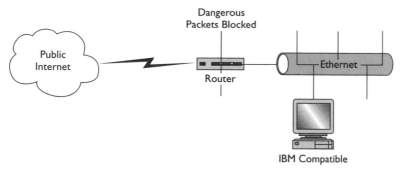

Figure 10-2: Network-level security removes some responsibility from the host.

System-Level Security as Part of Network Security

System-level security is also critical. Every effort must be made to secure individual hosts on a network through methods such as strict share permissions, limiting the services offered to the network, and requiring long, complex passwords for all users. Figure 10-3 shows where in the network system-level security takes place. While system-level security is an important component of overall network security, it cannot be relied upon. Flaws in operating systems are common, and many such flaws allow malicious users to bypass system security. Additionally, all users with legitimate accounts on the server must be entrusted to protect their passwords. To compensate for these weaknesses, system-level security should be used in concert with network-level security.

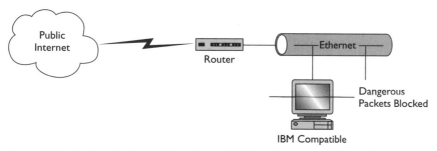

Figure 10-3: System-level security acts as a final barrier to network attacks.

A substantial disadvantage is that all NetBIOS traffic, regardless of the application, relies on the same three TCP ports: UDP 137, UDP 138, and TCP 139. This completely invalidates traditional port-level filtering, a common method of security in TCP/IP networks. This level of granularity is not available with NetBIOS applications. In many cases, an organization with an Internet connection may wish to publish files on the Internet and allow people to connect to that drive as a NetBIOS share. This is very possible, but the organization is forced to allow all NetBIOS traffic through and thereby invite attacks.

To further clarify, for an organization to allow file sharing on the Internet, all public routers must be configured to forward traffic for TCP port 139. Print sharing also uses TCP port 139 and so is automatically accessible. Therefore, if the file server also acts as a printer server, anyone on the Internet may attempt to print to that server. They are forced to authenticate depending on how the share permissions on the printer are configured, but the responsibility for the security of the network has been shifted from the network administrator to the systems administrator. Ideally, security would be provided at both levels.

Security at the network level for NetBIOS is all or nothing. The network manager must decide which computers will and will not act as servers for NetBIOS applications, but he or she has no control over which of the many NetBIOS applications will be available. This weakness makes a strong argument for using Windows sockets for network application programming. Because Windows sockets applications may be filtered out at the network level by specifying a TCP port filter, specific Windows sockets applications may be allowed or disallowed.

Despite these weaknesses, Microsoft continues to leverage NetBIOS for the majority of its administrative utilities. Unfortunately, this trend will continue in Windows NT 5.0. For this reason, understanding the weaknesses and potential problems with NetBIOS is important; until Microsoft changes major parts of the Windows NT operating system, we must continue to accommodate the protocol. However, very few third-party applications make use of NetBIOS. Perhaps third-party developers realize these weaknesses, or perhaps the application programming interface that NetBIOS provides is simply too complicated.

Summary

NetBIOS over TCP/IP (NBT) is a critical, yet problematic component of Windows NT. It is complicated and often misunderstood, lending itself to intermittent problems and difficult troubleshooting sessions. It provides for data transfer and name registration between Windows-based systems and UNIX-based systems when third-party software such as SAMBA is installed.

NBT uses three mechanisms to communicate: the NetBIOS Name service, the NetBIOS Session service, and the NetBIOS Datagram service. Each of these subprotocols uses a different UDP/TCP port number, a feature that is useful for configuring routers to filter traffic.

As Microsoft adapts its operating system software for the Internet, NetBIOS will evolve into CIFS, described in Chapter 14. Support for NetBIOS will continue to be available for backward compatibility, but it will no longer be required. This is good news for network and systems engineers working within homogenous TCP/IP-based networks. In the meantime, you can take several different steps to reduce your dependency on this unreliable, nonsecure protocol.

In this chapter you learned:

♦ NetBIOS was created many years ago for a very different network environment than most of us are using today. Though it is outdated, NetBIOS is a critical part of how Windows NT operates on a network.

♦ The NetBIOS naming scheme includes 16-character names that uniquely identify a host and a process on a network.

♦ Resolving NetBIOS names can be done in several different ways, but the primary methods are name query broadcasts and WINS server queries.

♦ SMB is an important subcomponent of NetBIOS that many network services use. Most important, file and print services are entirely dependent on the SMB protocol.

♦ NetBIOS has many weaknesses, many of which are not present in applications that use the Windows sockets protocols. Understanding the weaknesses of NetBIOS is important for avoiding problems that would otherwise arise.

In the next chapter we continue the discussion of NetBIOS, exploring WINS in more depth. WINS is the most popular form of NetBIOS name resolution on enterprise networks. How WINS is configured has a serious impact on the underlying network; the following chapter will describe the WINS network protocol in detail and show you how to ensure that your WINS configuration operates optimally.

Chapter 11

Windows Internet Naming Service

AS YOU ALREADY KNOW, computers have many different ways to identify each other. At the data-link layer, they refer to each other using the MAC address. At the network layer, they use IP addresses. The transport layer uses TCP and UDP port numbers.

Above that, computers use NetBIOS names to identify each other. Chapter 10 described NetBIOS naming in great detail, and I will not repeat that information in this chapter. However, it is important that you understand the NetBIOS name scheme before reading this chapter because it is an integral part of the WINS protocol; in fact, it is the purpose for WINS's existence.

This chapter will cover WINS from a network viewpoint. I will not show you how to use the WINS Manager, though I may give specific examples. For information on using WINS Manager, please refer to the online help files. I will not tell you every aspect of how to use WINS, unless it relates to networking. Because WINS is a networking protocol and serves no higher purpose than connectivity, this means that I will be covering most of what makes WINS tick.

NetBIOS Networking

As discussed in the previous chapter, NetBIOS is the basis for Microsoft networking. It has been this way for many years, and it has played such an important role that the layer-3 network protocols seemed to have no use besides carrying NetBIOS traffic. This has changed drastically in recent years as TCP/IP has come to dominate the networking industry. Protocols such as Winsock and HTTP now dominate corporate networks, but NetBIOS networking continues to be an important factor.

You are already familiar with NetBIOS names. In fact, if you have gotten through this much of this book, you probably are very familiar with WINS. I hope this is true, because I do not plan to spend any time on WINS basics. Instead, refer to Chapter 10, which covers the NetBIOS protocol in great detail.

Several key concepts in NetBIOS are unique to this set of protocols. One of these is WINS, which will receive the focus for this chapter. The previous chapter gives a broad overview of NetBIOS; this chapter zooms in on WINS clients, servers, and their communications.

NetBIOS Names

NetBIOS naming is the whole purpose for the existence of WINS. To review, NetBIOS naming allows computers on a network to be referred to by a 15-character computer name. This 15-character computer name is really a 16-character NetBIOS name, with an extra character used to identify a specific service. NetBIOS names serve much the same function DNS names do on the Internet: They allow users to identify systems without forcing those users to see the IP address.

I spent a great deal of time in the previous chapter covering the intricacies of NetBIOS naming, so I won't go into a lot of detail here. I do want everyone reading this chapter to keep these items in mind:

◆ NetBIOS names are more than computer names; each service on a system receives a different name.

◆ NetBIOS names may be unique or may identify a group.

◆ NetBIOS names are used to find more than just computers on a network; they are also used to identify services and users.

NetBIOS Name Resolution in a Nutshell

Address resolution happens at many distinct levels. Between layer 2 and layer 3 of the OSI model, ARP is used to translate MAC addresses into IP addresses. Above layer 3, additional address resolution occurs to allow the friendly names that human beings use to identify computers to be translated to the ugly IP addresses that computers use. The process of converting a friendly computer name, such as "ANGIE," into an unfriendly IP address, such as "192.168.10.10," can be a complicated one.

A system can perform this type of name resolution in any of several ways. The node type that has been configured for the system determines which method a system uses. Clients configured as b-nodes rely strictly on broadcasts for name resolution. P-node name resolution relies entirely on querying WINS servers. M- and

H–node: Microsoft Steers Away from the Standards

H-Node is the default node type for all Windows hosts that are configured as WINS clients. However, it is not defined as part of RFC 1001! RFC 1001 defines only b-node, p-node, and m-node. H-Node wasn't seen as necessary because the protocol was intended primarily as a workgroup protocol, and the standards body decided that most network communications would only occur on the local network segment. Who would have imagined that wide area networks like the Internet would become so critical?

h-node types use combinations of WINS and broadcast queries. If the standard method fails to work for a client, the client will query its own LMHOSTS file, or it may attempt to query a DNS server.

The simplest type of name resolution involves sending a broadcast message out to the local network and listening for the computer to respond. This is roughly equivalent to finding someone's phone number by yelling out your window really loud – it works well only if you're right next to each other; otherwise, it's just wasted effort.

Another method of NetBIOS name resolution is accomplished by using the LMHOSTS file. This file keeps a white-space-delimited text database of IP addresses and computer names. Looking up IP addresses in this table is like finding someone's phone number in the phonebook. It's quick and easy, but it doesn't work if that person has moved since you last received a new phonebook. Similarly, LMHOSTS files tend to get outdated quickly in networks where machines may be moved from one subnet to another or IP addresses may be reassigned.

Another method that may be used is name resolution through DNS or the HOSTS file. This adds an extra step, because DNS and the HOSTS file do not store computer names – they store host names and addresses. These are often entirely compatible; however, they may differ as well. This is actually a really good way to do name resolution, because it allows users to identify systems with their host name (such as www.mycompany.com), which they may be more familiar with than the system's computer name.

Finally, WINS is a common method for resolving IP addresses and computer names. WINS is a dynamic, centralized database that stores IP addresses, computer names, and several other pieces of information about the systems on a network. Using WINS for name resolution is similar to finding someone's phone number by calling directory assistance – the operator always knows the latest phone number for an individual because he or she taps directly into the database that stores that information.

Why Use WINS?

WINS was developed to eliminate the requirements to have broadcasts to resolve NetBIOS names on a network. The broadcast method described in detail in Chapter 10 suffers from the same problems broadcast protocols always suffer from:

1. Broadcasts interrupt the processor of every system on the network segments.

2. Routers stop broadcasts, disallowing NetBIOS name resolution on an internetwork.

WINS solves these problems. A WINS server is a centralized database of NetBIOS names on an internetwork. When a client needs to resolve a NetBIOS name, it asks the WINS server directly. The WINS server then responds to the client with another directed packet, indicating the answer to the query or notifying the client of failure. Because directed packets are used for all communications, the weaknesses associated with broadcast-based protocols are eliminated. An example of the differences between broadcast and directed name resolution is shown in Figure 11-1.

The LMHOSTS file is another possible solution, because it stores names and IP addresses in a text file located on each NetBIOS client on the network. This helps by completely eliminating the need for name resolution queries across the network — all questions can be answered by the local system. However, the LMHOSTS file has its own disadvantages as well. It's static, so it gets updated only when someone takes the time to type more information in. To make updating it even more difficult, it's distributed as well. Because each client stores a copy of the LMHOSTS file on its local system, each copy must be updated every time a change is made.

LMHOSTS has the capability to use a centrally located file, but this approach is fraught with problems. Even though the list of computer names and IP addresses may be located centrally, each computer must have a local LMHOSTS file that contains the location of one or more servers from which to retrieve the file. This means that you may still be forced to update that file on all workstations from time to time.

So far, all my justifications for using WINS have been negative. This is like telling you to vote for a specific candidate by telling you about flaws the other candidates have; I have yet to list anything positive about WINS except that it is not as bad as its competitors.

WINS adds a few things, too. By configuring all clients on your network to use WINS, you automatically receive as an added benefit a centralized list of every machine on your network, complete with IP address and computer name. WINS also helps to ensure that no two computers within your organization will ever have the same computer name — it is capable of detecting duplicate computer names by virtue of its definitive database. Your users will like the capability to browse resources on remote domains, a function that would not otherwise be available.

Figure 11-1: Broadcast and directed name resolution queries communicate differently.

Why Not Use WINS?

I am not going to try to sell you on a WINS networking solution. Instead, I will provide you the information you need to decide whether or not the protocol suits your needs. For many people, other solutions will work better.

Many administrators regret implementing WINS in their network because of the high cost of maintenance. In many cases, the time required to maintain WINS servers is greater than the time that would be required to distribute LMHOSTS files. If your network already has a DNS infrastructure, you will almost certainly discover that it is easier to force the network to rely on DNS naming than it is to maintain a separate WINS architecture.

Additionally, WINS can generate a significant amount of traffic on a network. This traffic can cause an already busy network to slow down. Implementing replication relationships (detailed later in this chapter) is another way to generate tons of traffic that you may not otherwise require.

Finally, WINS is a poorly understood protocol. Frankly, if you do not already know how to use WINS, you are probably better off using another method and waiting until Microsoft introduces Enhanced Directory Services with NT 5.0.

You have exactly three alternatives to WINS:

1. NetBIOS name resolutions using broadcasts

2. Relying on the LMHOSTS file

3. Relying solely on a combination of IP addresses, DNS addresses, and the HOSTS file

If this chapter convinces you that WINS is not the right solution, read Chapter 10 for more information about these alternatives.

Understanding How WINS Really Works

Have you ever had a problem with a WINS server? How quickly were you able to solve the problem? Did you really resolve it, or did you have to use a workaround?

WINS is famous for being plagued by mysterious problems. This section will attempt to uncover the mystery. I will provide you with the technical information you need to understand how the WINS protocol works.

For example, this section will tell you exactly what happens when a user connects to a network drive of the server. I will also describe how computers register names to their WINS server upon startup. Further, I will tell you what names they register, what type of traffic that will produce, and how you can optimize it.

WINS servers are Microsoft's implementation of the NetBIOS Name Server (NBNS), as defined in RFC 1001. The standard really specifies very little about a WINS server, leaving most details up to the implementer. While it specifies what the server must accomplish, it does not specify many details, such as interserver communications. If you learned about NBNS strictly from the RFC, you would think of it simply as a network database, allowing the addition and deletion of records that associate NetBIOS names with IP addresses.

I've tried to give you everything you need in this chapter, but you can find the definitive protocol standards at the InterNIC. WINS is defined in RFCs 1001 and 1002.

Client-to-Server Name Registrations

Let's start from the beginning. When a WINS client initializes itself, it must notify the configured primary WINS server of its NetBIOS names and IP address. This action accomplishes several things:

1. It allows the WINS server to reserve that NetBIOS name. The WINS server will not allow other computers on the network to register that same name again.

2. It allows the WINS server to stop the system from starting up its network services if the requested name is already in use.

3. It gives the WINS server the information it needs to resolve future requests for that NetBIOS name. Therefore, when a file server starts up, it must register itself with a WINS server to access the shared resources.

AN OVERVIEW OF THE PROCESS

Requests for new names always go to the primary WINS server, as it has been configured on the client. The WINS server then checks its database to verify that the request is allowed and responds with a confirmation or rejection. If the WINS server accepts the request, it will add the computer name and IP address to its database. This database is available to other WINS servers through the replication process.

If the client requesting a name is using either h-node or m-node, the request must be transmitted to *both* the WINS server and the local subnet via a broadcast datagram. Only if both registration requests succeed will the system register the name.

REFRESHING A NAME

Just because a WINS server confirms with a client that it has successfully registered a particular NetBIOS name does not mean that the client may have that name forever. At regular intervals, the client is required to re-request its own name just to keep its identity. This is done to allow names to be recycled, in case a machine registers a name but then disappears from the network. The process for refreshing a name is very similar to the process for requesting the name originally.

Names within the WINS database are assigned a Time to Live (TTL) when they are registered. The WINS server watches this TTL decrease, and when it reaches zero, begins the process of removing it from the database. In order to avoid losing a registered name, clients re-request the name by sending a Name Refresh Request packet to the WINS server. The WINS server does not send reminders to the clients; the client must be responsible for keeping track of the TTL of a registered name and making sure the WINS server knows that the client is still using it. By default, clients refresh a name after half the total TTL of a name has expired, giving them plenty of time to try again a few times if the WINS server cannot be contacted for the initial refresh request.

The default TTL of a WINS assigned name is four days.

RELEASING A NAME

It's only good manners to clean up after yourself when you are using something, and Windows systems have always been known for their good manners. When a NetBIOS client is shutting down, it sends a message to the WINS server that it is going offline and will no longer need the name. This is called a NetBIOS name release, which frees up the name for someone else on the network to claim. If the client is h-node or m-node, it will send a packet to the WINS server *and* transmit a broadcast packet to the local subnet before considering the name released.

One of the goals of RFC 1001 was to define a protocol that would work correctly in an "uncontrolled environment." Essentially, its drafters wanted NetBIOS over TCP/IP to work correctly even if crazy, ignorant users turned off their machines randomly. Because of this requirement, WINS includes a mechanism to automatically release NetBIOS names if it does not hear from a client system.

For example, if the system crashes (as has been known to happen!), it will simply disappear from the network, without having the opportunity to notify the WINS server that it will be shutting down. This is called a *silent release* and is not detected at the WINS server until the TTL on the name has expired and been removed from the database.

BANDWIDTH IMPACT

The bandwidth impact of registering names with a WINS server varies depending on how many names must be registered. A separate name exists for each NetBIOS service: one for the Messenger service, one for the Alerter service, one for the Server service, and so on. Each registration requires approximately 214 bytes. A typical workstation will have about six NetBIOS names that it must register and will therefore generate about 1,200 bytes of traffic during the NetBIOS name registration process.

ADJUSTING THE BEHAVIOR

While WINS name registration is not a major factor in the bandwidth of most networks, every little bit counts. To reduce the amount of traffic generated while machines register a name initially, reduce the number of names they have to register. Make a point of disabling services such as the Messenger service, and you will save bandwidth during startup of the network systems.

Name renewal is affected by the total number of names as well and can also be adjusted by changing a setting in the WINS server configuration. This can be done by selecting a server in the WINS manager and choosing Configuration from the Server menu. You will be greeted by the dialog box shown in Figure 11-2. Push the spin box up arrow beside the Renewal Interval label to increase the amount of time between renewals. Remember that clients renew names at twice the rate of the number shown here.

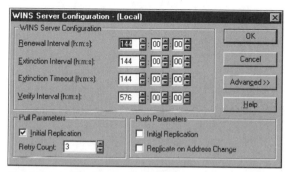

Figure 11-2: The Server Configuration dialog box within the WINS manager

Client-to-Server Name Queries

This section goes into detail on WINS queries. These queries are produced each time a WINS client attempts to find the server on the network using its NetBIOS name. If you already understand how NetBIOS name query broadcasts operate as described in Chapter 10, then you have most of the knowledge required to understand WINS queries. Basically, anytime a client produces a NetBIOS name query, that client instead sends a directed query to the WINS server. In the vast majority of cases, the two services query at the same time.

To review, users of Windows-based systems are able to reference resources on the network using a friendly computer name. So if Rick wants to connect to his share on a network server, he might reference \\SERVER\RICK. In this example, SERVER is the name of the server. Computers cannot simply communicate with each other using these friendly names, though, so it must first be translated to an IP address.

When clients are configured to use a WINS server, they will send that server a name query. This name query will contain the name of the server for which they are looking up the IP address. The WINS server will receive the query, look it up in its database, and respond with the IP address of the destination system. The client server that originally made the query will receive this response and use the specified IP address for all communications with the destination server.

HOW A QUERY WORKS

Name queries made to WINS servers make use of the NetBIOS Datagram service, which uses the underlying UDP protocol and port number 137. The UDP protocol is well suited to name queries because it avoids the overhead of the three-way handshake, characteristic of TCP. By avoiding the overhead associated with setting up a TCP session, UDP queries (which are typically two-packet conversations) can be very efficient.

As described earlier, the process starts when a user attempts to access a network resource using the computer name or NetBIOS name of the system. The client sends a single packet to the primary WINS server, which contains the NetBIOS name being queried. If it does not hear a response within 1.5 seconds, the client will repeat the process up to three times. If it still has not received a response, it will query the secondary WINS server instead. The client will also query the secondary WINS server if the primary WINS server responds with a "name not found" message.

Both the number of queries and the time between the queries is configurable via the registry. To change the retry attempts, modify the value in the following registry key:

```
HKEY_LOCAL_MACHINE\System\CurrentControlSet\Services\NetBT\Parameter
s\NameSrvQueryCount
```

By default, this value is set to 3. It would only be useful to increase the value if your network were extremely unreliable or very slow, in which case you probably have better things to worry about. However, consider changing the value on all clients to 2 to decrease the amount of time it takes for a time-out to be reached.

To configure the amount of time to wait between retries, change the following registry value from its default of 1,500 milliseconds:

```
HKEY_LOCAL_MACHINE\\System\CurrentControlSet\Services\NetBT\Paramete
rs\NameSrvQueryTimeout
```

Queries, because they merely need to carry the NetBIOS name being queried, never require fragmentation at the packet level. Responses are also always one packet in length, and they may contain up to twenty-five IP addresses.

QUERYING THROUGH A PROXY

One option for aiding the migration from NetBIOS name queries using broadcasts to WINS queries is the use of a WINS proxy. A WINS proxy listens for name query broadcasts and forwards the request on to a WINS server. When the response is returned from the server, the proxy forwards it to the client that initiated the query. WINS proxies are discussed in greater detail later in this chapter.

BANDWIDTH IMPACT

WINS queries can have a significant impact on the bandwidth usage of a network. A single WINS query consumes about 200 bytes of traffic if the client and server are on the same network. Remember, each network that the packet must cross to reach the destination adds another 200 bytes of traffic to the total bandwidth impact!

ADJUSTING THE BEHAVIOR

Besides not using WINS, there is really only one thing you can do to reduce the amount of WINS name query traffic generated on your network: You can increase the chance that a name will be found in the NetBIOS name cache. To do this, increase the time-out on all workstations from the default of ten minutes. For most networks, as much as an hour is acceptable. Modifying the following registry value (given in milliseconds) can change the setting:

```
HKEY_LOCAL_MACHINE\SYSTEM\CurrentControlSet\Services\NetBT\Parameter
s\CacheTimeout
```

Server-to-Server Synchronizations

One of the primary goals of WINS is to allow the NetBIOS naming scheme to extend to enterprise networks. In order to scale anything to enterprise scale, this scheme must be able to operate on multiple servers in multiple locations. One of the methods WINS uses to allow this to happen is replication, a process in which servers exchange database information. In this way, servers at remote sites may allow users on the remote network access to the enterprise's NetBIOS name database.

REPLICATION: PUSHES VERSUS PULLS

There are two methods for replication of data between servers: pushing and pulling. These terms are standard networking terms. A *push* refers to the process of sending data to a client without a prior request; in other words, the server that is sending the data initiates the connection. A *pull* works just the opposite: One WINS server requests data from another server and then downloads it.

In most circumstances, WINS servers replicate data between each other by both pushing and pulling.

PULLING DATA   WINS servers keep track of how updated their database is using the version number, similar to the way secondary DNS servers operate. However, DNS stores a single version number for the entire database, while WINS stores the version number with each individual record. When the WINS server starts up, it determines the version number of its database by finding the highest version number from any of the records.

Once a WINS server has determined the highest version number of any record, it queries its partners to determine their highest version number. If one of the partners has a higher version, the querying WINS server will request an update. The responding server will transfer only those records that are newer than the version number provided in the request.

PUSHING DATA   A push replication works exactly like a pull replication, except that the transfer is initiated by the WINS server that will be supplying the changed data. The administrator can use the WINS Manager utility to configure a push partner to initiate a replication after a certain number of WINS records have changed. Alternatively, a push replication may be initiated manually by an administrator in order to immediately propagate changes. Whichever method is used, the push partner sends a message to its pull partner, which receives the message and initiates a pull replication with the push partner.

BANDWIDTH IMPACT

Server-to-server relationships can generate a significant amount of traffic, especially considering they are commonly performed across slow, wide area network links. The formula for this is pretty detailed, so please refer to Chapter 4, "Bandwidth," for more details.

WINS Proxies

To make the entire name resolution process more complicated, Microsoft has provided a way to allow broadcast name queries to be passed to a WINS server. This method is known as a WINS proxy, and it allows broadcast queries to be passed across subnets on a routed network. In this way, it allows for easier migration between broadcast name resolution and WINS name resolution. WINS proxies are one of the services detailed in RFC 1001.

A WINS proxy works by listening on the network for NetBIOS name query broadcasts. This means *all* name broadcasts, not just queries (though queries make up the bulk of the traffic). When it hears a broadcast, it forwards it to its primary WINS server. When the primary WINS server responds (directly to the WINS proxy), the proxy forwards the response on to the server that initially performed the NetBIOS name query broadcast. This process is illustrated in Figure 11-3.

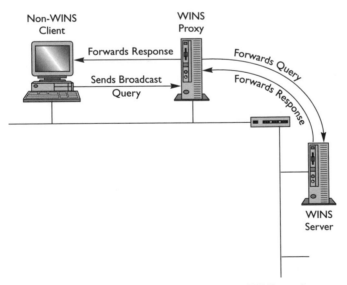

Figure 11-3: Sample network diagram including WINS proxies

Proxy servers will forward NetBIOS name registrations and may even reject a name if it has already been registered on the network. However, the WINS server does not register broadcast name requests in its database. By default, forwarding a name rejection by the proxy server is disabled. To enable it, change the following value in the registry to 1:

```
HKEY_LOCAL_MACHINE\System\CurrentControlSet\Services\Netbt\Parameter
  s\EnableProxyRegCheck
```

Configuring a WINS proxy is really, really easy. Simply set a certain registry value to 1, restart the system, and you've got a WINS proxy! The registry value that you need to change is:

```
HKEY_LOCAL_MACHINE\System\CurrentControlSet\Services\Netbt\Parameter
  s\EnableProxy
```

However, this is one case where planning is much more difficult than implementing. To ensure name resolution works properly and efficiently on your network, take time to plan out a strategy and choose locations on the network for WINS proxy servers to reside. Here are a few general guidelines for placing WINS proxies on your network:

- WINS proxies are never a permanent solution! Plan to use them only during migrations from broadcast to WINS name resolutions.

- Place a WINS proxy on each subnet containing clients that still perform NetBIOS name queries using broadcasts.

- Configure the fewest number of systems possible as WINS proxies. If there is a single system connected to multiple subnets, use it as a WINS proxy for all of the subnets rather than distributing the task between multiple systems.

- Give WINS proxies a fast network connection to the WINS server. This may mean adding an additional network card to the WINS proxy and attaching it to the same network the WINS server is on, but the effort will be worthwhile in terms of bandwidth saved.

- Never connect multiple WINS proxies to the same subnet. Each proxy will forward queries, creating unnecessary traffic.

Planning WINS in Your Network

As with everything related to a network, planning is critical. Effectively planning your WINS architecture will make it easier to support, quicker to implement, and cheaper to upgrade. This section will cover what you need to know to plan a WINS network and provide you with critical planning concepts.

How Many Do You Need?

Unfortunately, there is no simple formula that I can provide you to determine the absolute number of WINS servers in your network. Even the number of users and systems is not enough information, because different hardware platforms can support varying loads of traffic. Many factors go into determining the total number of WINS servers that you need, but here are a few guidelines:

♦ WINS servers should always be implemented in pairs for redundancy and load balancing.

♦ WINS queries should *never* cross a WAN link. Replication traffic should.

♦ If you have less than 100 systems configured to use a specific server as their primary WINS server, you may use the server for other tasks such as performing domain authentications and file and printer sharing.

♦ When calculating WINS server requirements, consider the worst-case scenario. For example, if you have a WINS server pair and half the clients are configured to use each as the primary WINS server, ensure that each server can support the load if one of the servers fails and all clients fail-over to the second server.

Considering Fault Tolerance

WINS servers are *very* critical to a network. WINS clients are configured, by default, to perform NetBIOS name queries using broadcast if a WINS server fails to respond. However, this fail-over capability will only work well if all your clients are on the same subnet, and if that's the case, why are you using WINS at all?

For this reason, I recommend always, *always* implementing WINS servers in pairs. This may seem like a hefty requirement if you merely want to provide a WINS server to a remote office, but you may share WINS server tasks with other tasks on the same server to reduce hardware costs. These servers should have a direct, out-of-band network connection between them to allow almost continuous replication without consuming bandwidth on a subnet.

This systems architecture is rarely used, though it adds a great deal to the reliability of WINS services. Best yet, it is fairly cheap to implement. Assuming you already have two redundant WINS servers and they are both located in the same data center, simply add a network interface card to each system and run a crossover cable between them. Next, assign private, reserved IP addresses to these interface cards. You will need to show the systems that the shortest path between them is through the crossover connection, and this will require modifying the internal routing table in both systems and, additionally, may require you to assign NetBIOS names in the LMHOSTS file to the internal address.

Consider the following example: An organization wants to provide reliable WINS services with no downtime. Rather than choose a clustering solution with an extremely high cost, they have decided to build dual WINS servers. To provide for redundancy in the event of a network failure, each system resides on a different subnet. Through the built-in replication capabilities of WINS, these two servers have been configured to exchange database information with each other. However, because they reside on different subnets, all replication traffic must cross a router and affects two different subnets. This network configuration is illustrated in Figure 11-4.

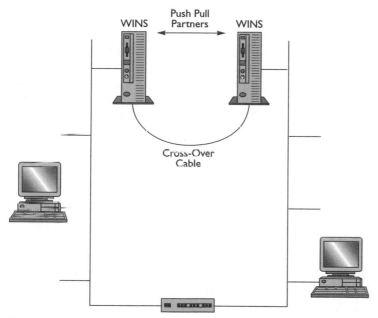

Figure 11-4: Sample network architecture including fault-tolerant WINS servers

The organization does not want to lose any registered NetBIOS names in the event of a server failure, so they set the replication frequency to be very high. Both systems are configured to perform a push replication on *each* change to the database, and pull replication has been configured every two minutes. These settings are shown in Figures 11-5 and 11-6.

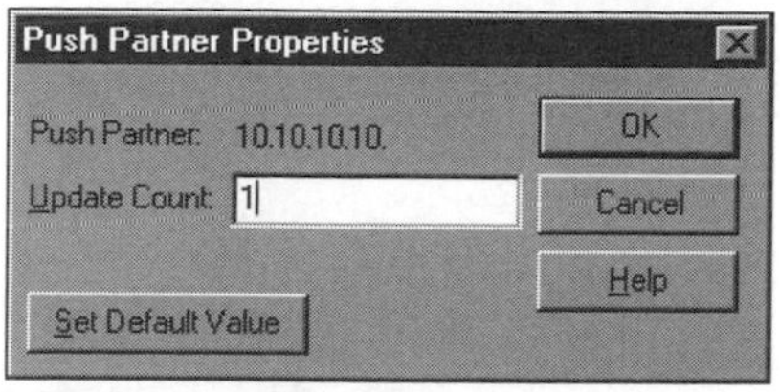

Figure 11-5: The push replication dialog box from the WINS manager

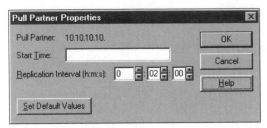

Figure 11-6: The pull replication dialog box from
the WINS manager

Unfortunately, this out-of-control replication scheme will impact the network performance of the networks to which they are directly attached. As just described, the best way to allow for huge amounts of traffic to travel between two physically adjacent servers is through the use of additional network interface cards and a crossover cable.

Considering Time to Convergence

The term "time to convergence" is used throughout this book. To review, time to convergence refers to the time it takes a group of network devices to exchange information and come to total agreement on a particular database. This is an important consideration for DNS, routers, and WINS servers. Time to convergence is always based on the *worst case scenario*. It's pessimistic, but that's the idea. Actually, it's not that pessimistic, because you have to assume all the components are working properly. Time to convergence is the longest time it could possibly take for the information to spread through a working network.

If WINS servers are not converged, clients in different parts of the network may not be able to reach the same set of network resources. For example, consider an enterprise network with five sites around the country. If an administrator changes the IP address of a file server in Atlanta, it will notify its primary WINS server of the updated IP. Therefore, clients that use the same primary WINS server will know about the change the next time they query the WINS server.

However, the name change will take several minutes to propagate to other WINS servers within the organization. Even within the Atlanta office, it will take several minutes for the updated information to be distributed to other WINS servers. By default, WINS servers replicate information every fifteen minutes. Therefore, if there is only one other WINS server in Atlanta, the time to convergence for that office is fifteen minutes.

That is just for a single office, however. If users in the Dallas office attempt to access that file server, they will not be able to, because their local WINS server has a record of an outdated IP address. Remember, WINS is not hierarchical and does not have the concept of iterative queries as DNS does – if a WINS server doesn't know an answer to a question, it simply returns a failure to the client.

So how long does it take for the WINS server in Dallas to be notified of the update to the server in Atlanta? That depends entirely on the replication configuration of the various WINS servers. Let's assume the simplest case scenario, that the primary WINS server in Atlanta is configured to replicate directly to the Dallas WINS server. The administrator has changed the replication period from the default of fifteen minutes to two hours, in order to reduce the traffic traveling over the WAN link. Therefore, the time to convergence is exactly two hours. Easy!

It gets much more complicated as more WINS servers are added. Particularly when WINS servers are configured to replicate in a partial mesh configuration, time to convergence can be difficult to compute. In order to guarantee consistent time to convergence for any point in your network, rely on a star replication configuration.

What Changes Should You Plan to the Clients?

Adding new WINS servers to your network is only the beginning of a WINS rollout. After you complete this phase, your WINS servers will simply sit idle, with nothing but their own computer names registered. To state the obvious, you must reconfigure each of the clients in your network to make use of the WINS servers.

Anytime you have to change the configuration of every client on a network, it will be a time-consuming task. This is true of any change; configuring a WINS server is no more difficult than anything else is. However, there are a few things to know ahead of time that may make the changes easier for you to implement.

First, if you are using DHCP on your network already, converting your entire client base may be as simple as listing the WINS server in the DHCP manager and waiting for the clients to update themselves. Even if you would like different clients to use different WINS servers, DHCP is the easiest method to use. This is one of the nice things about DHCP; it makes simple network configuration changes painless.

Second, depending on the infrastructure you already have in place, it may simplify the process to know the underlying mechanism for storing the address of the WINS server. Like most things in Windows NT and Windows 95, the address of the WINS server is stored in a registry key. Therefore, if you have a software distribution mechanism like SMS or WinInstall already in place, changing a registry value on all the clients within your network should be a simple task.

However, the registry value is buried underneath a key named for the particular model of network interface card on the system. If all the systems on your network are identical, then this will not be a problem because the path to the value in the registry will always be the same. Very few networks have homogenous hardware, so this simple method is hardly realistic. However, the important registry values are:

```
HKEY_LOCAL_MACHINE\System\CurrentControlSet\Services\NetBT\@@@nic
  driver name>\NameServer
```

and

```
HKEY_LOCAL_MACHINE\System\CurrentControlSet\Services\NetBT\@@@nic
  driver name>\NameServerBackup
```

These correspond to the primary and secondary WINS server fields within the TCP/IP Protocol Properties dialog box.

If you are interested in writing a script to edit these values in a network that does not have a homogenous hardware platform, you may parse the registry value:

```
HKEY_LOCAL_MACHINE\System\CurrentControlSet\Services\NetBT\Linkage\B
 ind
```

For a system with two network interface cards, this value will look something like this:

```
\Device\LNEPCI26
\Device\NdisWan4
\Device\ETHER1
```

Remember, `NdisWan#` indicates a dial-up interface. If you write a Perl script to parse this value, finding the correct registry keys is as simple as parsing each row, splitting the row by backslashes, and taking the second value! Well, that only sounds easy if you're a Perl programmer.

Summary

This chapter provided the detail of how the WINS protocol operates, and the impact it has on your network. The goal has been to give you the understanding required to include WINS servers and clients in network designs.

You have learned the following:

♦ WINS can be used to complement or replace broadcast queries and `LMHOSTS` files for NetBIOS name resolution.

♦ WINS fits into many networks, but not all.

♦ Client systems register their own names to WINS servers and query WINS servers to find the IP address of other hosts on the network.

♦ There are two methods for copying name information between WINS servers: push replication and pull replication.

In the next chapter, you'll learn how DNS is used to resolve names on internetworks. You will learn the standards DNS is based on, and the specifics of both the client and server implementations of DNS in Windows NT. Further, I will show you how to best design your network and systems with DNS in mind.

Chapter 12

Domain Name Services

IN THIS CHAPTER

♦ What Domain Name Services are useful for

♦ How DNS came into being

♦ The basics of Windows NT's support for DNS

♦ Planning your Windows NT network to use name services

♦ How to find and resolve problems with DNS

♦ How DNS will change in the future

MOST PEOPLE WHO USE the Internet prefer to refer to systems by their friendly names. This isn't always true for those hard-core engineers among us, who memorize long lists of IP addresses and have no need for "friendly names." Nonetheless, not everyone in the world is as much of a masochist. DNS evolved from HOSTS files. HOSTS files, still used today, relate IP addresses to fully qualified domain names (FQDN) and allow the end user to refer to a system on the Internet as www.idg-books.com instead of 206.80.51.140.

DNS, the Domain Name System, allows users to make use of friendly names instead of IP addresses. Further, it provides for redundancy, scalability, and hierarchy.

DNS is now a big business. Many organizations spend literally tens of thousands of dollars attempting to purchase the best domain names for themselves. This is because DNS is now how everybody in the world recognizes servers on the Internet. Even people who don't know what the Internet is have heard of something with www.something.com. It's everywhere. This is DNS and why DNS is so important.

This chapter provides some history on DNS, describes the underlying protocol, and explains how Windows NT Server implements it. I will also cover how DNS fits into the grand naming convention scheme that includes NetBIOS naming. Then I will tell you what the network considerations are for building DNS clients and servers into your network, and I will provide some tips on testing and troubleshooting DNS. You will end with a look at the future of DNS.

Why Use DNS?

DNS has lots and lots of problems. So why bother using it on your own network? Because that's what all the *cool* kids are doing, and you don't want to be the last one on the block without it. And because DNS is a key part of the Internet, and the Internet is a key part of the future of most businesses. You could probably get by without using DNS, but instead of saying, "Visit our Web site at `www.idgbooks.com`, you would wind up saying, "Visit our Web site at `206.80.51.140`." Not nearly as cool, is it?

Or maybe you don't care about the Internet at all. Even for organizations with an entirely self-contained network (there are a *few* left out there), DNS may play an important part. DNS allows your users to address servers with friendly names rather than IP addresses, and it is much more flexible than using NetBIOS names, a long-standing standard for Windows-based networking. If nothing else, by using DNS now you will be ready for the inevitable day that your network connects into the public Internet.

Finally, DNS works well for NetBIOS name authentication. By configuring DNS within your organization, you can avoid using the 15-character computer names to identify machines, instead relying on fully qualified domain names. For example, using `\\printer.east.mycompany.com` to identify a printer is much more logical than identifying it as `\\east-mycom-pr`. For more information on NetBIOS naming alternatives, please refer to Chapters 10 and 11.

Reviewing the History of DNS

When I was in college, professors told me that learning history was important so that we would not make the same mistakes our forefathers did. I suppose that's a good way to look at it, though it didn't make the classes much more interesting.

The history of DNS is important to understand, though, because many aspects of the protocol will not seem logical unless you understand its roots. I think it's important to understand how a protocol came to be in order to understand how and why it does what it does. DNS is one of the oldest protocols commonly used today, and for that reason I am going to teach you a little history. If you have been through this course already, feel free to skip ahead . . . .

In the beginning of the Internet, everyone identified each other's servers using the IP addresses. This worked out pretty well since there were not many nodes and the people who did the work on it were basically scientists, the first of the network engineers. And you know how network engineers are – they can remember thousands of IP addresses off the top of their heads. Eventually even they became weary of trying to remember all of those 32-bit numbers and came up with the idea to identify systems using host names, such as "ftp." In doing this, they created a name resolution problem. When they referred to a computer using the host name, the computer had to know what that system's IP address was. There was no way it could communicate directly with the other system using just the host name, so the translation had to happen somewhere. Initially these engineers implemented a HOSTS file, which is still carried in most computers today. The HOSTS file was a flat-text database consisting of the IP address of the system and the HOSTS name of the system. This worked really well, and so the HOSTS file was placed on every system on the Internet, and the administrators of each system maintained it independently.

Eventually a few problems appeared in this system that in retrospect seem pretty obvious. First, if the text database changed, there was no way to update it automatically on every system. Essentially, the response was to create a centralized HOSTS file, which would be the definitive HOSTS file on the Internet; on a regular basis, everyone checked this file for any changes. If it were changed, they would update the HOSTS files on their local systems. This worked well, but it was an inconvenience and was still plagued with several problems. For example, with only one HOSTS file on the whole Internet, if that site went down, nobody else knew what any of the DNS names were. Second, that HOSTS file started to get really, really big as more and more systems were added, each becoming a new line in the HOSTS file. So the plan did not scale very well. Third, HOSTS names didn't provide for any kind of hierarchy, so if somebody in one site wanted to have a computer named Tony, nobody else in the whole world could have a computer named Tony. That was it. One host name, one machine.

Even today, a HOSTS file is placed on just about every system connected to an Intranet or the Internet. Windows NT, by default, places an empty HOSTS file in the directory:

```
<winnt_root>\system32\drivers\etc\
```

Now, if you examine that file on a brand-new system, you'll notice that it only contains a single entry for "localhost" that is mapped to the loopback address. This is not all that useful by itself, but it shows that the HOSTS file is ready to go. The HOSTS file in Windows NT is enabled by default.

Most people who use their systems for networking will add entries to this HOSTS file. It's a very convenient way to allow a handful of friendly names to resolve to IP addresses, but life could get pretty difficult if you had to add every host on the Internet to this one file. Further, you would probably want someone else to take care of that work. If you were clever, you might find a way to centralize the HOSTS file so that you and your neighbors could share the same entries.

This is exactly why DNS was created and what it accomplishes. It allows everyone on the Internet or within an organization's intranet to resolve the same friendly names to the same IP addresses, without having to place any burden on the users of the system. I feel that I should mention the name of Dr. Paul Mockapetris, the principal designer of the DNS protocol, and extend a "Thanks!" for being one of the first people to get so annoyed with HOSTS files to actually do something about it.

Those of us who work with Microsoft products are already familiar with how a specific vendor or product can influence a protocol. DNS was influenced in this way by the Berkeley Internet Name Domain (BIND), a version of DNS developed by Berkeley Systems to run on their implementation of the UNIX operating system (BSD UNIX 4.3). BIND had such an incredible influence on the DNS protocol that aspects of the product such as the format of the data files are almost considered part of the protocol itself. Indeed, Microsoft's implementation of the protocol uses the exact same format for its data files, despite the fact that Microsoft is normally inclined to break with tradition, relying on Jet database files instead of a more common text file standard. If Microsoft had not followed the BIND standard, they would have been chastised for being incompatible.

In the years 1986 and 1987, RFCs 974, 1034, and 1035 were written. These RFCs did not define the DNS protocol; they merely reflected its implementation in the real world. The RFCs did help ensure that different vendors' products would interoperate. Today, modifications and improvements to the protocol must be reflected in an updated RFC to receive any industry support. For example, RFC 2181 solved many problems in RFCs 1034 and 1035.

As the Internet grows, so does the DNS protocol. DNS names have become such an important part of day-to-day life in the United States that congressional committees are currently investigating their assignment. Soon, several top-level domain names will be added to allow for the continued expansion of the name space.

Overviewing DNS

This section will provide some background in the workings of DNS. I am not going to attempt to spell out every single aspect of the DNS standards; however, I do want to ensure that all readers have a baseline of certain knowledge. If you already have a good grasp of DNS, feel free to simply skim through this section and ensure there is nothing you may be weak on.

My Favorite Comparison: DNS and the OSI Model

DNS is an OSI application-layer protocol. It is flexible enough to rely on either the connection-oriented TCP or the connectionless UDP transport-layer protocols for name queries and resolutions. Table 12-1 shows DNS, its underlying protocols, and how they fit into the OSI model. Keep in mind that DNS fits better into the DOD model than the OSI model, and so there is no protocol relating to the presentation or session layers.

TABLE 12-1 DNS AND THE OSI MODEL

OSI Layer	Protocol
Application	DNS
Presentation	n/a
Session	n/a
Transport	TCP or UDP
Network	IP
Data Link	Varies
Physical	Varies

DNS on the Internet

DNS is easy to configure, if you don't bother connecting to the Internet. You can make up your own domain names, assign your hosts whatever names you want, and not worry at all about security.

It gets much more complicated once you want to work and play with others on the public Internet. You will have to register your name with the InterNIC, find an ISP to host your primary and/or backup name servers, and make sure it is all safe and reliable enough not to ever fail.

Your DNS Is No More Reliable Than Your ISP

Ultimately, when someone attempts to contact a server using a fully qualified domain name, the name is resolved to an IP address by the primary or backup name server specified for that domain. If these servers should ever disappear from the Internet, as has been known to happen, people attempting to contact your network will lose touch. Even if your sites are hosted on an entirely independent connection, a failed DNS server or network can make an entire domain unusable.

Therefore, choose the ISP you will use to host your DNS carefully. You are at their mercy, and your network cannot be more reliable than their own.

Even merely finding an available domain name from the InterNIC is difficult. Many companies (often small ISPs) have bought huge numbers of domain names that they think will be wanted by somebody at some date in the future – not because they ever plan to use them, but because they hope to make a profit by selling the domain name to the highest bidder. This practice is commonly called "cyber-piracy." This illustrates the importance of domain names to an organization's Internet presence and shows how potentially difficult it can be. Many large companies have engaged companies who buy domain names in legal battles, with varying results. Nonetheless, it is more expensive than it is worth for most small organizations to put up a legal fight for a domain name. Recently, the Ninth U.S. Circuit Court of Appeals ruled that cyber-piracy is a form of extortion and a violation of trademark laws. This ruling may drastically change the way domain names are registered.

For more information on registering a domain name on the Internet, read the section titled "Integrating your DNS into the Internet" later in this chapter.

Domain Hierarchy

One of the keys to understanding how DNS works is understanding that it is intended to be highly distributed. In this way, DNS servers throughout the Internet store only a portion of the entire Internet namespace. Because they store only a small part but are required to resolve names for any host on the Internet, there must be a way for DNS servers to find their neighbors and ask each other for information about a specific host.

This distribution is given order through the DNS hierarchy. Domains, starting with the top-level domains and branching out below, divide the total DNS name space. In this way, the DNS hierarchy looks more like the roots of a tree than the branches of a tree, as illustrated in Figure 12-1.

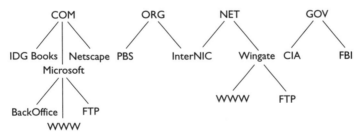

Figure 12-1: An example of the DNS hierarchy

The top-level domain names are closely controlled by the InterNIC, a division of the Internet Assigned Numbers Authority (IANA) responsible for assigning these names. For more information on the IANA, please refer to Chapter 2. In the United States, most people will recognize top-level names because they are part of most URLs: ".com," ".edu," ".net," ".gov," and ".org" to name a few. These top-level domains contain the basis for the rest of the domain naming structure. Individual organizations are granted second-level domain names within one or more of these top-level domains.

When an organization wishes to acquire a second-level domain name, it must submit a request to the Internet Network Information Center (InterNIC). If the domain name is available and the InterNIC doesn't have a problem with the name, it is assigned to the organization in exchange for a biannual fee of $100. The organization itself is responsible for assigning third-level and lower domains.

For example, an organization may register the second-level domain name company under the first-level domain .com. This would allow the organization to call itself company.com on the public Internet. Further, it would be able to create third-level domain names below company.com, such as accounting.company.com or marketing.company.com. Besides creating subdomains, most organizations will add hosts to various domains. For example, when a Web server with the hostname www is added to the accounting subdomain, its fully qualified domain name becomes www.accounting.company.com.

Zone Hierarchy

The DNS name space is also divided into zones, subdivisions of a domain. A zone actually refers to a zone file, which contains the DNS information for that portion of the domain. While a domain is a logical grouping within the DNS name space, the zone is an actual file on DNS server's hard disk, which stores the DNS records themselves. For any given domain, there are one or more zones. Each zone may encompass a domain and/or subdomains, and different zones may manage various subdomains. Make sense? Hopefully the next example will help.

Imagine that you are an administrator for the cleverly named company "MyCompany." Fortunately for you, nobody has registered that name with the InterNIC, so you register and receive the domain name. You are responsible for configuring the organization's internal DNS servers and designing a DNS architecture. In order to divide your portion of the name space, you create four subdomains within mycompany.com, one for each division of the company: pilfering, looting, plundering, and accounting.

You will personally manage the pilfering and looting subdomains, but you know the IT manager for the accounting group will want to manage both the accounting name space and the plundering subdomain's name space. In order to allow that manager to have free reign over his subdomains without bothering you, you create a different zone for them. The zone and domain architectures are illustrated in Figure 12-2.

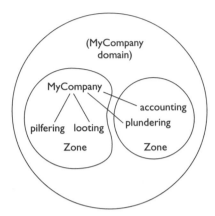

Figure 12-2: The relationship between domains and zones

The Server Hierarchy

As the number and importance of DNS servers increases, it becomes more and more important to ensure that they are both scalable and reliable. The DNS protocol itself has the capability to allow DNS servers to fail-over for each other and to share a load between multiple systems.

There are two levels of name servers: primary and secondary. The primary name server is the definitive source of DNS information for the domain. All other DNS servers for a domain ultimately pull their information from the primary name server, which stores the master copy of the zone file locally.

Secondary name servers exist to provide redundancy, load balancing, and distributed access. Secondary name servers gather all their information from the primary name server. In other words, secondary name servers are not responsible for any unique information; everything they know is handed from the primary name server. Secondary name servers serve a similar role to backup domain controllers in a Windows NT domain.

Secondary name servers transfer the zone file from the primary name server using a process called a zone transfer (cleverly enough!). A zone transfer is little more than a file copy between the two systems, but it gets the job done. Once the secondary name server has a copy of the primary name server's zone file, it is able to answer DNS queries in the same way the primary name server would.

The roles name servers play is both flexible and complicated. Unlike primary and backup domain controllers in a Windows NT domain, name servers can play multiple roles in different domains. For example, the primary name server for the domain `accounting.mycompany.com` can be the secondary name server for the domain `looting.mycompany.com`. This is done merely by specifying the correct properties in the DNS Manager.

Specifically, secondary name servers must be configured with the IP address of the upstream DNS server — either the primary name server or another secondary name server.

PLANNING FOR REDUNDANCY

So as you can see, configuring secondary domain servers can provide a level of redundancy by making an extra copy of the zone file available to network clients. Having an extra copy of the database is only one part of an effective DNS fail-over solution, however. DNS does not take into account how clients that have been configured to query a particular DNS server will contact a different DNS server in the event the first fails. This fail-over is implemented on the client-side operating system. In Windows NT, an unlimited number of DNS servers should be configured on all clients, as illustrated in Figure 12-3.

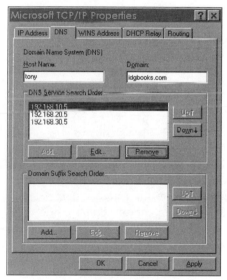

Figure 12-3: The Network Control Panel applet allows a DNS client to be configured to use multiple DNS servers.

The client always begins queries by checking with the first listed server. If that server fails to respond, it will work its way down the list until it finds an active server. By listing multiple DNS servers in the TCP/IP property sheet for each client on your network, you may provide for fail-over of DNS without making any changes to the server configuration. Therefore, if your NT clients were configured as shown in Figure 12-3, they would query 192.168.10.5 until it failed to respond. At that point, queries would instead go to 192.168.20.5.

The two servers should operate as independently as possible. This is not only a good rule of thumb for DNS servers but works well anywhere redundancy is desired. Place your DNS servers on separate networks, on different electrical circuits, and even in separate buildings if at all possible. By separating redundant servers as much as possible, you greatly increase your chance that a secondary name server will still be available in the event of a failure of the primary name server.

PLANNING FOR LOAD BALANCING

Redundancy and load balancing are often thought of together. Redundancy is generally the priority; after all, you should make sure critical systems will be online at all times before you start to worry about their performance. However, once an administrator configures multiple servers to do essentially the same jobs, such as primary and secondary name servers, it becomes tempting to put both machines to work at the same time.

Redundancy is easily configured with name servers because the fail-over responsibilities are placed on the client. As described earlier, DNS clients are generally configured with a list of DNS servers to check, and they will work their way down the list until they find a DNS server that responds appropriately. Creating load balancing between these servers is as simple as configuring different clients with the same list of servers, but in a different order.

For example, consider an organization with three DNS servers. These DNS servers have the IP addresses 192.168.10.5, 192.168.20.5, and 192.168.30.5. The first of these servers is the primary name server; the other two act as secondary name servers. The third server, located at 192.168.30.5, is really just an administrator's desktop system and shouldn't be relied upon, but it could be used in a pinch. The administrator wants to put less of a load on the primary name server, and no load on his desktop machine unless it's an emergency. Therefore, one-third of the clients on the network should be configured with DNS servers as listed in Table 12-2. The other two-thirds should be configured as shown in Table 12-3.

TABLE **12-2 EXAMPLE: ONE-THIRD OF THE DNS CLIENTS
ARE CONFIGURED WITH THIS LIST**

List Sequence	IP Address
1	192.168.10.5
2	192.168.20.5
3	192.168.30.5

**TABLE 12-3 EXAMPLE: TWO-THIRDS OF THE DNS CLIENTS
             ARE CONFIGURED WITH THIS LIST**

List Sequence	IP Address
4	192.168.20.5
5	192.168.10.5
6	192.168.30.5

Of course, this is a simple example. Your networks may be much more complicated and may have a different DNS server configuration for each subnet. As a general rule, configure at least three DNS servers, and place them in the following order:

First DNS Server: The server closest logically to the client. This is often a DNS server with a network interface card on the same subnet.

Second DNS Server: The server second-closest logically to the client. It is preferable that it not be on the same subnet as the first listed DNS server; however, this is not essential. Your primary goal here is to provide for system-level redundancy because the likelihood of the network failing is far lower than that of the system failing.

Third DNS Server: A last-resort. This system should be an authoritative name server and should act as the third name server for all systems within an organization. In this way, if a large section of your network has some kind of failure, clients may still be able to access a DNS server that can respond to their queries. If a nonauthoritative system were listed here, it is possible that the clients would be able to query the DNS server but that the name server would not be able to respond to the queries because it could not reach an authoritative server. The third name server should never be queried unless things are going really, really bad anyway.

PLANNING FOR DISTRIBUTED ACCESS

Another excellent reason to use secondary name servers as part of your DNS architecture is to allow for distributed access in a wide area network environment. An excellent way to reduce the amount of traffic generated by DNS queries across a WAN link is to place a secondary name server at the remote site and configure all clients at the remote site to query their local name server first, as illustrated in Figure 12-4. Naturally, the secondary name server will generate some traffic of its own in the form of zone transfers, but in most cases this will be substantially less than the traffic generated by DNS queries from the clients.

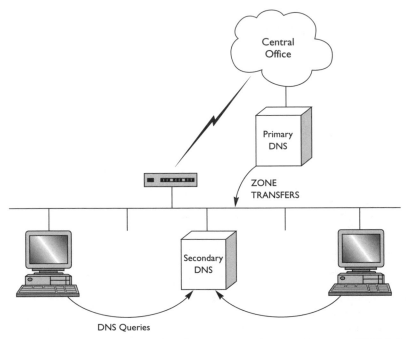

Figure 12-4: Using secondary domain servers to reduce queries across WAN links

Distributing network services is a common method for reducing WAN traffic and is mentioned in several places throughout this book. Earlier in this chapter, I compared secondary name servers to backup domain controllers. To extend this analogy, placing a secondary name server at a remote site is done for the same reasons that most organizations place a backup domain controller at a remote site: to provide services to clients without forcing them to generate traffic across the WAN link, to provide some redundancy, and to reduce the load on the primary system.

Forwarders

In a DNS architecture, a DNS forwarder is similar to a proxy server. Forwarders are used to allow internal name servers the ability to resolve queries for external names, without giving the internal name servers access to the external network (whew!). Forwarders are specified at each name server and are used to help resolve all queries that the queried name server cannot answer directly, as shown in Figure 12-5.

An example is definitely in order....

You are in charge of the internal DNS infrastructure of your organization. You are in the process of connecting the domain to the public Internet and have decided to have only a single entry point, through which all traffic must pass. This server acts as an HTTP and SOCKS4 proxy to the rest of the domain, allowing access for many different types of traffic. Because SOCKS proxy clients require the ability to resolve IP addresses for the external network, your internal DNS servers must be able to resolve names on the public Internet.

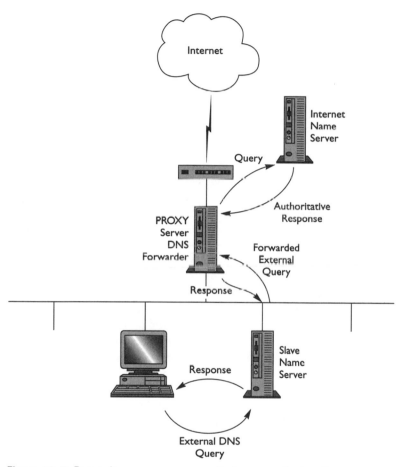

Figure 12-5: Forwarders are name servers that pass queries to other servers.

Because you cannot put them all on the external network, the best method to provide this functionality is to configure the existing proxy server as a *forwarder*. You configure all other DNS servers as slaves to these forwarders. When a client attempts to resolve an external DNS name, such as www.idgbooks.com, it will pass it to the nearest DNS server. That DNS server will check its own zone file for the entry but will not find it. Because it has been configured as a slave, it will forward the request to the name server forwarder, which can resolve the name because it has access to the public DNS servers at your ISP's premises.

Masters and Slaves

I hope you didn't jump to this section after glancing at the table of contents, thinking you finally found an interesting topic in this book (unless, of course, you consider DNS architecture interesting, in which case you're in the right place).

As described earlier, secondary name servers perform zone transfers to retrieve the zone file. The secondary name server may be configured to retrieve this information from either the primary name server or another secondary name server. In either configuration, the systems participating in the relationship receive special titles: *master* and *slave*.

The master name server is the system from which the slave draws its information. You may also think of these systems as being *upstream* and *downstream*.

Caching-Only Servers

There is a simple way to configure a server for a remote site without forcing it to participate in a zone or perform zone transfers. Configuring a name server as a caching-only server, and configuring it with the IP addresses of upstream DNS servers, does this. When configured this way, the name server will accept DNS queries from clients, check its own cache, and return an answer if it was able to resolve the name from the cache. If the name being resolved was not located in the cache, the DNS server will forward the query on to the upstream DNS server, store the result in its cache, and return the answer to the client.

Caching-only DNS servers are really easy to configure in Windows NT. In fact, any default installation of the DNS Server service is automatically configured as a caching-only server. All you need to do to configure a server in this manner is *not* configure it as part of a zone.

There are many ways in which you may use a caching-only DNS server:

◆ They may be used at remote sites to reduce the amount of DNS query traffic that must pass across the WAN link. This is similar to the method I described for configuring a secondary name server at a remote site; however, it eliminates the overhead involved in zone transfers.

◆ Caching-only DNS servers are commonly used on the local side of an Internet connection to reduce the amount of queries that must be sent to the ISP's DNS servers.

◆ Servers that perform a great deal of reverse-DNS lookups, such as Web servers, are often configured as caching-only DNS servers.

How DNS Servers Talk to Each Other

As you already know, primary and secondary servers have methods to exchange data so that they may each have a reasonably accurate copy of the DNS database, known as a zone file. The file transfer between these systems always moves downstream, from the primary name server to the secondary name server(s) within a particular zone.

 ⁻ It is tempting to think of this transfer as taking place in the same way that data is transferred between a primary domain controller and a backup domain controller, but they work in very different ways. While PDC-to-BDC transfers perform a similar function, they are capable of transferring incremental changes. DNS is not this elegant; each time a modification is made, the entire zone file must be transferred. As you can imagine, this can be a bandwidth-consuming transfer in large zones.

ZONE MODIFICATION NOTIFICATION

Zone transfers are inefficient beasts, but they do not happen without some level of intelligence. It would be *really* wasteful if secondary servers simply downloaded the zone file on a prescheduled basis, so DNS has implemented a method of checking for changes. By default, secondary name servers check for a modification to the zone file when the DNS service starts and every three hours thereafter. The administrator can change this default.

This zone modification check is done by comparing a value in the SOA record of the primary name server with the corresponding value stored by the secondary name server. In this way, the SOA record is used to store information about the status of the zone file. Within that SOA record is a field called Serial Number (also referred to as Version Number), which increments each time a change is made to the database.

Using the serial number, the secondary name server is able to determine whether changes have occurred since it last requested a zone transfer. If the secondary name server finds that the serial number of the primary name server is greater than its own, it will request the newer copy of the database.

The impact on the network of merely checking the version of the zone file is minimal. A single packet is transmitted from the secondary name server to the primary name server, and a single packet is returned in response. The first packet is nothing more than a request for the SOA record, and the response is (logically enough) the current SOA record. Because of this clever design, the version of the DNS database may be checked without adding any complexity to the DNS protocol – the standard method of querying DNS records works well.

ZONE TRANSFERS

As described in the previous section, a zone transfer occurs each time the primary name server notifies a secondary name server that an update has occurred. If the database version reported by the primary name server is indeed greater than the version currently stored on the secondary name server, the secondary will send a request for zone transfer packet to the primary. This is a special type of packet, which shows up in Network Monitor with a description of "Std Qry for *domain name* of type Req. for zn Xfer on class INET addr." The response will be the sum total of the zone file, which varies widely in length depending on the size of the database.

The fact that there is no incremental zone file transfer is a great reason to keep your zones small, and primary and secondary name servers close together. If you frequently update the DNS database, zone transfers will happen, at most, every three hours. Keeping the zone file small helps to keep the impact on the network low. This is an especially important consideration for zone transfers that occur across low-bandwidth links.

Name Resolution

So far in this chapter, I've spent a lot of time talking about clients and servers querying each other, but I haven't gone into any detail regarding *how* these queries are performed. There are several different ways, and a lot of complexity, to determine exactly how these queries behave. Essentially, all queries can be divided into one of three families: recursive, iterative, and reverse (or inverse) queries.

Beyond these three types of queries, other functionality can be provided. For example, DNS servers can be configured to return several different IP addresses in response to the same name. Further, Windows NT, since version 4.0, has the ability to resolve NetBIOS name resolution requests using DNS.

RECURSIVE QUERIES

The most common type of query on most networks is the recursive query. This type of query is common because all queries between end-user systems and name servers are recursive. Issuing a recursive query is the client's way of saying to the name server, "Please resolve this name, and don't even *think* about passing the buck!"

When a name server receives a recursive query, it must make a best effort to resolve the name and return an answer to the client. It is not allowed to refer the client to another DNS server: if it can't return an answer, for whatever reason, it must simply return a "not found" type error message.

Slaves also use recursive queries when querying a forwarding server. Because the forwarding server is the slave name server's only chance for resolving a given name, the query must be recursive.

ITERATIVE QUERIES

An iterative query is typically passed from one DNS name server to another in an effort to resolve a hostname. A name server that receives an iterative query is allowed to return a result that merely refers the client to another name server with more authority over the domain given in the request.

A typical scenario in which iterative queries will be used is one in which a name server must resolve a name within an unfamiliar domain. For example, if an ISP's name server is queried for the IP address of the Web server www.idgbooks.com, it will query the root server. The root server will not return the IP address of the site requested but will instead refer the name server to the authoritative name server over the .com top-level domain. The ISP's name server will, in turn, query the .com name server, which may refer it to the `idgbooks.com` authoritative name server. In all likelihood, the authoritative name server for `idgbooks.com` will be able to resolve the name WWW.IDGBOOKS.COM without referring to another name server.

REVERSE LOOKUPS

Commonly used by servers for logging and authentication purposes, reverse lookups resolve an IP address to a DNS name. Ironically enough, they operate exactly the "reverse" of a standard DNS query.

If you don't have any experience with DNS, it may seem that the name servers would simply look through the list of IP addresses in a zone file and return the name associated with that address. Unfortunately, it is not nearly that simple. There is no direct correlation between IP addresses and DNS names, so a special domain was created in order to facilitate reverse lookups. This domain is called `in-addr.arpa`, which may seem somewhat cryptic.

Before I describe exactly how reverse name lookups are performed, let's review a couple of basics of DNS naming. First, a domain name consists of several names separated by dots. These names get less specific as you read them from left to right. Therefore, subdomains within a domain are *prepended* to the domain name. Confusingly enough, IP addresses are organized entirely the opposite way. An IP address also separates octets with dots, but they get *more* specific as you read from left to right. With that in mind, read on....

In order to make the IP and DNS naming schemes more compatible, the order of the octets within an IP address is reversed and added to the `in-addr.arpa` reverse-lookup domain. For example, to allow the IP address `10.3.17.77` to be correctly resolved to the name `www.mycompany.com`, you would add the entry `77.17.3.10.in-addr.arpa` to your DNS servers.

This method works out conveniently for management as well, since administration of the `in-addr` subdomains may be given to each organization as it is assigned a range of IP addresses. Therefore, each company can administer and manage reverse-lookup DNS records individually.

Once subdomains have been built under the `in-addr.arpa` domain, records must be added to the zone files to allow for reverse lookup of individual hosts. A special type of record, called a PTR (pointer) record, is reserved for this type of lookup.

IN-ADDR.ARPA: What?

For the curious, the subdomain used for reverse lookups is named as a shortened form of "inverse address." The "arpa" portion of it refers to the Advanced Research Projects Agency, a division of the government that participated heavily in the development of DNS and the Internet.

ROUND-ROBIN

For many, "round-robin DNS" is the answer to the question, "How do I balance a load between multiple servers?" Others feel it better answers the question, "What is an efficient method of load balancing that can cause numerous, unpredictable, and difficult-to-troubleshoot problems with my end users?" No matter what your opinion, round-robin DNS is a common method of distributing traffic between an array of servers.

Round-robin works by answering DNS queries with an entire list of IP addresses, rather than a single IP address. The application that performed the query generally chooses the first IP address and references that server for all future communications with that server. To ensure that client-side applications do not choose the same IP address, the list is rotated so that a different IP address appears at the top of the list each time. This is considered "round-robin" fashion.

This method of load balancing is extremely common on Internet Web sites. Microsoft is a big fan of round-robin DNS. To get an idea of what these DNS responses look like, perform an NSLOOKUP for www.microsoft.com (a *very* busy site on the Internet).

```
C:\>nslookup www.microsoft.com
Server: dns.this-is-just-an-example.net
Address: 192.168.8.20

Non-authoritative answer:
Name:  www.microsoft.com
Addresses: 207.68.137.56, 207.68.156.51, 207.68.156.52, 207.68.137.62
    207.68.156.53, 207.68.137.65, 207.68.156.73, 207.68.156.61,
  207.68.156.16
    207.68.156.58, 207.68.137.53, 207.68.137.59, 207.68.143.192,
  207.68.143.193
    207.68.156.49
```

As you can see, Microsoft (at the time of this writing) makes use of 15 different IP addresses for the Web server known as www.microsoft.com. To get an idea of how round-robin works, press the Up Arrow key and run the same command again. You will get a very similar response, as shown here:

```
C:\>nslookup www.microsoft.com
Server: dns.this-is-just-an-example.net
Address: 192.168.8.20

Non-authoritative answer:
Name:  www.microsoft.com
Addresses: 207.68.156.51, 207.68.156.52, 207.68.137.62, 207.68.156.53
    207.68.137.65, 207.68.156.73, 207.68.156.61, 207.68.156.16,
  207.68.156.58
    207.68.137.53, 207.68.137.59, 207.68.143.192, 207.68.143.193,
  207.68.156.49
    207.68.137.56
```

Notice the difference between the first and second examples? The second example has the same set of IP addresses, but they have all been shifted up one. I think of it as like geese, flying in a V formation. Each goose takes a turn at the head position, and after that goose gets tired, it moves to the back of the V and the next goose in line takes the first position.

If you get bored, do NSLOOKUPs on a few other sites that use round-robin. You will notice that sometimes these systems are not even on the same subnets! It is even possible to perform round-robin load balancing on systems that are in completely different parts of the country, though it is a really bad idea. Here are a few examples:

♦   www.cnn.com

♦   www.abcnews.com

♦   www.internic.net

♦   www.novell.com

To get an idea of how an application uses round-robin, try PINGing the same hostname over and over again. You will be shown the IP address used each time, and it should rotate through the list shown by NSLOOKUP.

To configure a hostname to map to multiple IP addresses, simply add that hostname in over and over again, once for each IP address. Easy!

DNS Record Properties (Caching and TTL)

As responses are returned from the servers to the clients, they contain more information than the basic IP address. This additional information helps to direct the behavior of the client or secondary name server and can control aspects such as how long they will retain that IP address in their cache, if they may retain it at all. For the person managing the servers, these are simply properties in the Microsoft DNS Manager dialog box. For someone analyzing DNS traffic with a protocol analyzer, these properties are evident within the data portion of the packet.

By default, when a name server is queried using a recursive query, that name server will pass the query on to a more authoritative name server. When the result is finally returned to the original name server, it will store that name and IP address in a cache so that it will not have to query other servers if it is asked for the same information. For those already familiar with proxy servers, this is very similar to the behavior exhibited by an HTTP server: Store all returned data in a cache for later use.

DNS servers communicate how long a given record should be cached using the Time to Live (TTL) property. The TTL of a record is the amount of time that an intermediary name server may retain the record in its cache before purging it. When an intermediary name server or a DNS client caches a record, it must begin to count down the TTL. When the number reaches zero, the record must be purged from cache.

However, there are many circumstances in which DNS addresses should be cached differently or not at all. For example, consider a network that is using DHCP to dynamically assign IP addresses to clients. A properly configured DNS server will return the correct IP address for a dynamically assigned client, but that IP address may not be valid the next time the client starts up. Therefore, it is a good idea to reduce the amount of time that the IP address is stored in the caches of other name servers. This can be done by changing the TTL of a given DNS result using the DNS Manager.

Modifying the TTL of a DNS record can have many side effects. If an administrator wanted to ensure that a DNS server was queried every single time a name from the domain was requested, he or she could configure the DNS records with a TTL of zero. By eliminating caching on intermediate DNS servers, however, the administrator would increase the load on his or her own server—every single request, regardless of where it came from, would have to query the authoritative server. The advantage to this is an increase in the accuracy and freshness of data as it is returned to clients, despite an increase on the load of a server.

To restate that, as you decrease a TTL, you increase the load on a server *and* improve the consistency of the data being returned.

The DNS Database

The data your clients will be querying from your DNS server has to be physically stored *somewhere*, and that place is the DNS database. This database stores all the records within your domain. While the structure of the database itself has very little impact on the network, I feel it is important to provide a general reference to the different types of records and databases you will encounter.

TYPES OF RECORDS

This section gives a brief overview of the most common types of DNS records you will encounter and what they each mean. Again, I do not intend this chapter as a definitive source of information for every aspect of the DNS protocol suite. I am only providing a brief overview of the various record types that you may come across when working with DNS servers.

SOA (START OF AUTHORITY)   The SOA record is always the first record in any zone. It indicates that the server holding the SOA record is the best source of domain information; the "horse's mouth," if you will.

The NS (name server) records exist to provide a list of name servers within a domain. One NS record should exist for each DNS server.

MX (mail exchange) records allow mail destined for a domain to be directed to a mail server, which may not be in the same domain. This is useful in many circumstances, but particularly in cases where a domain is managed by an ISP but mail should be directed to the organization's mail server.

The A record, otherwise known as an address record, maps hosts to IP addresses. This is the most common type of DNS record.

CNAME (canonical name) records are used to provide an alias for a host within a domain's name space. For example, it is common practice for Internet service providers to create CNAME records for "POP" and "SMTP" within their domain. Because both POP and SMTP are often served by the same system, they may both be CNAME records directing traffic to the same IP address.

PTR (pointer) records are used within the in-addr.arpa domain to allow reverse lookups. They map an IP address to a hostname, just opposite what the A record does.

WINS records are not part of the standard DNS configuration but may exist in Windows NT–based DNS servers to allow for integration with a WINS database. These records store NetBIOS names and resolve them to IP addresses.

WINS-R (WINS Reverse Lookup) records are not part of the standard DNS configuration, but may exist in Windows NT–based DNS servers to allow for integration with a WINS database. They store IP addresses and allow them to be resolved to NetBIOS names.

CACHE DATABASE   The cache database is a mechanism built into DNS to allow a name server to store name and IP address relationships that are not part of a zone that the name server is participating in. In other words, the name server may keep IP addresses and names without being authoritative to them. Don't confuse the cache database with similar mechanisms already built into Windows NT, such as the ARP cache. While they are similar in some of their functions, the DNS cache database operates in ways distinct from other caches.

First, the cache database will almost always contain a list of servers that have been statically entered. This static list allows the DNS server to locate other servers that must be queried — for example, for a DNS server to resolve names on the Internet, it must know where the authoritative servers are located. The DNS service built into Windows NT 4.0 includes the following entries by default:

```
.                     2163095040      IN      NS      A.ROOT-SERVERS.NET.
A.ROOT-SERVERS.NET.   2163095040      IN      A       198.41.0.4
.                     2163095040      IN      NS      B.ROOT-SERVERS.NET.
B.ROOT-SERVERS.NET.   2163095040      IN      A       128.9.0.107
.                     2163095040      IN      NS      C.ROOT-SERVERS.NET.
C.ROOT-SERVERS.NET.   2163095040      IN      A       192.33.4.12
.                     2163095040      IN      NS      D.ROOT-SERVERS.NET.
D.ROOT-SERVERS.NET.   2163095040      IN      A       128.8.10.90
.                     2163095040      IN      NS      E.ROOT-SERVERS.NET.
E.ROOT-SERVERS.NET.   2163095040      IN      A       192.203.230.10
.                     2163095040      IN      NS      F.ROOT-SERVERS.NET.
F.ROOT-SERVERS.NET.   2163095040      IN      A       39.13.229.241
.                     2163095040      IN      NS      G.ROOT-SERVERS.NET.
G.ROOT-SERVERS.NET.   2163095040      IN      A       192.112.36.4
.                     2163095040      IN      NS      H.ROOT-SERVERS.NET.
H.ROOT-SERVERS.NET.   2163095040      IN      A       128.63.2.53
.                     2163095040      IN      NS      I.ROOT-SERVERS.NET.
I.ROOT-SERVERS.NET.   2163095040      IN      A       192.36.148.17
```

It's important to understand this database file because it contains entries for the primary servers on the Internet, and if they are wrong or missing, your DNS server will have no idea where to point to resolve names. The latest file can be downloaded from `ftp://rs.internic.net/domain/named.cache`. As you can imagine, it is fairly important that these servers not change their IP addresses very often. Nonetheless, the default cache file provided by Microsoft is already out of date, so I advise you to download the newest from the InterNIC and keep it updated on your DNS servers.

REVERSE LOOKUP DATABASE   The reverse lookup database is very similar to the standard lookup database, except IP addresses are mapped to hostnames, instead of the other way around.

Planning for DNS in Your Network

Designing an effective DNS architecture that can last many years is a very difficult process! It is definitely worth the effort required, and this section will attempt to give you some hints, offer detailed advice, and point you in the right direction.

Integrating Your DNS into the Internet

DNS is useful whether or not you are planning to connect your organization to the Internet. However, the majority of companies require some form of Internet connectivity, and the majority of *those* companies will need to integrate their DNS structures into their ISP and the rest of the Internet.

REGISTERING A DOMAIN NAME
Nowadays, everyone has a domain name on the public Internet. You certainly don't want to be left out of this great big party on the Net, so here's an outline of the steps to take to get yourself registered. These steps are summarized in Table 12-4.

TABLE 12-4 REGISTERING A DOMAIN ON THE INTERNET:
             THREE REALLY DIFFICULT STEPS

Step	Action
Step 1:	Find someone to provide primary and/or secondary DNS services.
Step 2:	Find and register a domain name with the InterNIC.
Step 3:	Configure your domain as desired.

The first step in the process of participating in the public Internet DNS architecture is to find a couple of DNS servers to use. In most cases, organizations that are connecting to the Internet allow their ISP to provide a Primary DNS server. Usually, the company will configure a secondary DNS server on their side of the Internet link to provide local name resolution.

This works out well, unless you *are* the ISP. In this case, you will probably take responsibility for the primary DNS services. It is not as difficult as it may sound, but it requires a solid name server foundation and plenty of redundancy. A single failed DNS server can cause an entire organization to disappear from the Internet – it is very important the your name services be reliable!

The next step, which may already be done for you, is to register a domain name with InterNIC. A good starting place for registration information can be found at `http://rs.internic.net/help/domain/new-domain-reg.html`. This page will allow you to determine whether or not the desired domain name is available, and it contains links to help you register the name.

Registering a name is the second step because you must provide the IP address of an ISP's DNS server that will take primary DNS server responsibilities. The InterNIC will place the IP address of this system in the name space under the top-level domain in which your domain belongs. For example, if you purchased the domain name "`mycompany.com`," the InterNIC would associate the domain entry "`mycompany`" within the "`com`" top-level domain with the IP address of your (or your ISP's) DNS server. The process of registering a domain name is outlined in Figure 12-6.

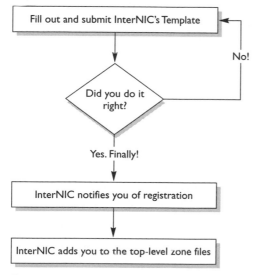

Figure 12-6: Registering domains with the InterNIC is a painful process!

Once you have your domain registered on the Internet, you may begin to add hostnames and subdomains. It is common to add host records for www and ftp that will point to public servers people can use to get information about your organization. You will also want to add several standard records, such as an MX record. The MX record will allow you to receive mail that is destined for that domain at a specific SMTP server. Assuming everything has been configured correctly, your domain information will be available from the public Internet.

NETWORK ARCHITECTURE

Any time an organization connects to the Internet, great care has to be taken. For each service that you provide either *to* or *from* the Internet, consider the risks carefully.

There are several questions you need to answer before you can decide on a network architecture:

◆ Do I want to maintain a separate, internal DNS?

◆ How much information should I reveal about my internal network?

◆ Must I maintain the primary DNS server, or should I let the ISP do it?

◆ How critical is uptime?

◆ How much traffic will I be generating?

Answering these questions before implementing a DNS design will ensure that your design meets your needs and lasts you several years to come. A common configuration, as illustrated in Figure 12-7, places an external DNS server in the non-secure demilitarized zone (DMZ) and a separate, internal DNS server behind the corporate firewall.

SECURITY CONSIDERATIONS   Anything that is connected to the Internet is a security risk. This includes DNS servers. Several bad things can happen when a DNS server is on the public Internet:

◆ It could be the victim of a denial of service attack, which could render your network unreachable via domain names.

◆ It could be modified so that your domain names resolve to IP addresses outside of the realm of control of your administrators.

◆ If the DNS server is connected to both the public Internet and your private network, it could be used as a launching point for attacks against your internal network if compromised.

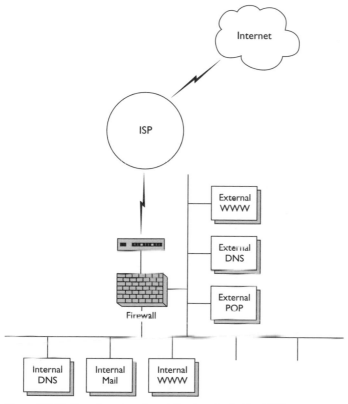

Figure 12-7: Sample network architecture including DNS servers

With these points in mind, read through the rest of the network architecture section. Security is a critical consideration when designing a network.

DESIGN SUGGESTIONS   Most corporate networks that connect to the Internet have both internal and external portions. The external portion may be used by people on the public Internet *and* by users within your corporate network. This area of the network is also called the DMZ (demilitarized zone).

There are several different ways in which DNS may be implemented in your network. One method is to place the DNS server outside of your corporate network, so that people on the Internet and in your intranet may reach it. Another possibility is locating the server strictly within your network where it may serve only internal customers.

CONFIGURING AN EXTERNAL DNS SERVER   To allow users on the public Internet to reach your DNS server, place it on your external network. There are a couple of reasons you may want to do this:

♦ If you wish to provide primary or secondary DNS services for your own organization

♦ If users are supposed to have access to your internal network from the Internet (for example, telecommuters)

This is not a simple configuration to implement! Great care should be taken with public DNS servers because they are a common point of attack. For example, it is possible for a malicious hacker to attack your public DNS server and replace the IP addresses given for specific hosts with IP addresses on other networks! This would allow them to direct users connecting to your Web site to an entirely different server.

A typical network with an external DNS server looks like the diagram shown in Figure 12-8.

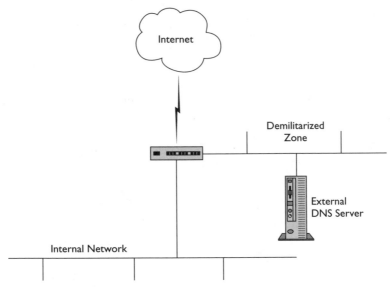

Figure 12-8: An external DNS server

CONFIGURING AN INTERNAL DNS SERVER   There are several reasons to configure a separate DNS server for the inside of a corporate network. First, you may not want the entire Internet to know the names and IP addresses of all the systems within your organization. However, you almost certainly want internal users to be able to gain access to them. Creating a separate internal DNS server allows you to have this compromise between security and accessibility.

Typically, organizations that host separate internal and external DNS servers allow their ISPs to perform name services for their domains. This type of configuration is shown in Figure 12-9.

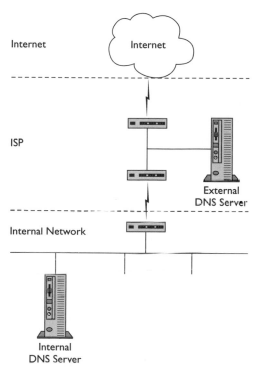

Figure 12-9: An internal DNS server

Capacity Planning and Performance

In smaller companies, DNS servers may never become overloaded. However, in larger organizations or companies that host busy DNS servers (such as Internet service providers), planning the capacity needs of DNS servers is an important consideration. Fortunately, as with all things Microsoft, there are several ways to monitor and anticipate performance requirements.

USING DNS MANAGER

The simplest way is to use the Microsoft DNS Manager that is added to the Administrative Tools folder when DNS services are installed on an NT Server. The information provided by this dialog box is minimal but sufficient for getting a mile-high view of the overall usage of a particular system. Figure 12-10 shows the Server Statistics page of the DNS Manager of a very quiet DNS server.

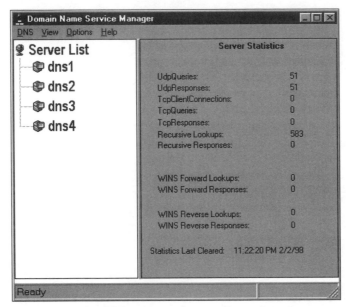

Figure 12-10: The DNS manager gives you a snapshot of
DNS performance.

The DNS Manager is a simple and limited performance analysis tool, providing only a raw listing of the number of queries and responses provided. However, it is useful for determining whether the majority of the queries and responses are happening through UDP or TCP or are being forwarded to a WINS server. The limited amount of information is somewhat frustrating, because there are no Performance Monitor counters specifically for DNS.

Because TCP is used only when UDP queries fail, high numbers of TCP queries in relation to UDP queries can indicate to you that DNS queries are operating inefficiently. If a large number of the total queries are being forwarded to a WINS server, consider a more efficient method. Forwarding queries to a WINS server more than doubles the amount of traffic normally incurred by a DNS query and roughly triples the total latency.

USING PERFORMANCE MONITOR

A more powerful alternative to the DNS Manager is the Performance Monitor, which I refer to throughout this book. Unfortunately, Microsoft has not provided Performance Monitor objects specifically for the DNS service. However, the standard suite of objects are there and, in conjunction with the DNS Manager, sufficient for capacity planning.

Start performance analysis and capacity planning in the same way you would for any system, by monitoring counters for processor, memory, and network utilization. If the system is not a dedicated DNS server, add the following counters to help you separate utilization caused by DNS:

◆ **Process object, % Processor Time counter, DNS instance:** This counter reveals how much of the total CPU time is being consumed by the DNS service. If your DNS server is performing other tasks as well, this will allow you to determine if the DNS process or something else causes high processor utilization. If you see that your server is busy overall but the DNS process shows very low utilization, monitor the performance of other processes to find the culprit.

◆ **Process object, Page Faults/sec counter, DNS instance:** This counter tells you how bad the DNS process is hammering your system's memory. If the number of page faults caused by DNS increases, it is a good indicator that you should add more memory or transfer DNS responsibilities to a different, dedicated server.

LOAD BALANCING

Large networks or those with heavy DNS usage may need to split the responsibilities between multiple servers. If configured correctly, such a system has the advantage of providing fail-over capabilities as well. For this reason, DNS services should always be split between two servers, no matter how small the network. Take this minimal requirement into consideration when planning a DNS structure. As the size of a network increases, you can split the load between an increasing number of servers.

For more information on load balancing, read the section under Planning for Load Balancing earlier in this chapter.

Integrating into Your NT Infrastructure

As if it wasn't confusing enough that Microsoft refers to their administrative model as a domain, now you have to worry about integrating NT domains into the Internet domains, and vice-versa. This is a difficult concept to *read* about, much less write about. Nonetheless, how your Internet domains fit into your NT domains is an important consideration.

In versions of Windows NT 3.51 and earlier, native DNS support was limited to the client-side protocol only. Starting with Windows NT 4.0, a DNS server is provided as part of the operating system. As I have stated earlier in the book, NT 4.0 provides greater support for using DNS names instead of WINS names, an indication of the future direction of the operating system.

Up to this point, however, DNS has not been a critical part of a Microsoft network. If you wanted to use it for compatibility with UNIX hosts or the Internet, you had that option. Nonetheless, Internet domain design did not relate to the way NT domains were designed; the two operated completely independent of each other. All of this is changing, and quickly.

MODELING DNS ARCHITECTURE AFTER DOMAIN ARCHITECTURE

NT 5.0 will incorporate the Enhanced Directory Services, which will integrate tightly with DNS. Exactly how this will work is still somewhat uncertain, but there are guidelines to follow, if you are creating a new NT domain, that will make the migration simpler.

First, make a strong effort to use a single model for both your NT domains and your Internet domains. For example, consider how you would structure your DNS in an NT domain based on the NT master domain model. If you had created a separate resource domain for each remote office and a single user domain, an excellent way to design your Internet domains would be to acquire a second-level domain, such as mycompany.com. Then, you would create a subdomain that corresponded to each NT domain.

It will make your life easier both in the present and in the future with NT 5.0 if the name of the NT domain corresponds to the name of the Internet domain (or subdomain, for multiple-domain designs). For example, if your organization is called MyCompany and has the domain name mycompany.com, the PHOENIX NT domain should correspond to the phoenix.mycompany.com Internet domain. In this way, both NT and Internet domains share the same hierarchy.

In the future, when NT systems are organized by Internet domain names, minimal reorganization will be necessary. Furthermore, systems will be named logically, allowing people in an Internet domain to abbreviate the names of the systems nearest to them. To clarify with an example, if a user on a system named northrup.west.mycompany.com wanted to Telnet to the local mail server called pop.west.mycompany.com, the user would merely have to issue the command telnet pop. Grouping systems logically within Internet domains simplifies the lives of all your users because Windows NT allows FQDNs to be abbreviated with hostnames when accessing systems in the same domain.

INTEGRATING DHCP, WINS, AND DNS

If you are already using WINS (Windows Internet Naming Service) and DHCP (Dynamic Host Configuration Protocol) together and wish to add DNS, make a point of integrating the three together. Really, you only need to integrate WINS and DNS together, since DHCP and WINS are probably already configured on your network. By integrating these services, clients that are assigned an IP address during startup may also be referenced on the network using a domain hostname.

This may seem simple enough; after all, DNS and WINS are just alike, right? If you've read this far, you already know better than that. Nonetheless, it is a common misconception. They perform similar functions but operate entirely differently.

HOW IT WORKS   To explain how DNS can look up WINS records, and how the WINS service adds dynamic IP addresses, I will first provide some background into dynamic WINS records. When a client system starts up using TCP/IP, it either has a statically assigned IP address or is configured to use DHCP. The statically assigned model is more familiar on the Internet, where machines may keep the same IP addresses for decades.

In local area network environments, however, it is common for administrators to make use of DHCP to assign IP addresses. In a DHCP network, systems do not know what their IP address may be until they boot and connect to the network. This makes name resolution difficult, since even the host itself does not know what its IP will be until it is already on the network. Because Microsoft networks typically make use of the WINS service for resolution of NetBIOS names to IP addresses, WINS has the capability to add system names and IP addresses to its database as they boot. In a nutshell, machines contact their configured WINS server and let it know what their IP addresses are after startup.

Nothing in any Windows operating system allows it to contact a DNS server and notify it of an IP address after startup, however. DNS is typically administered differently, by manually adding records one at a time. In order to keep a DNS database up to date when a system booted with a dynamic IP address, an administrator would need to modify the DNS database constantly!

So Microsoft has built a feature into the DNS service in Windows NT to allow it to escalate queries for names to a WINS server. Essentially, if a DNS server is asked for a name to be resolved to an IP address and it does *not* find that name in its zone file, it will forward the query on to a WINS server. If the WINS server recognizes the name, it will return the IP address to the DNS server. The DNS server, in turn, will return the IP address to the client that requested it originally.

This complex process allows the traditionally static DNS database to take on a dynamic characteristic, care of WINS. It only works with Microsoft-based DNS servers, so forget about it if you have an existing UNIX-based DNS infrastructure. Further, it only works with the DNS server built into Windows NT; other Windows NT DNS services will not know how to query WINS servers. All of these problems combined make this a cumbersome and rarely used protocol.

MORE DETAILS, PLEASE   It took some work to allow DNS servers to query WINS servers. First, Microsoft had to add two entirely new record types to DNS, WINS and WINS-R. If this is already sounding a bit hacked together, keep reading . . . .

You already know that DNS is a hierarchical naming standard and WINS is a flat naming standard. For example, two systems may have a hostname `tony` but have different DNS names (such as `tony.west.mycompany.com` and `tony.east.mycompany.com`). However, there can only be a single system named `TONY` in an NT domain. So imagine a scenario where a client queries a DNS server for the hostname `tony`. It just so happens that Tony's system boots using a DHCP-assigned address and so does not have a record in the DNS database.

To which WINS server will the DNS server look to find it? If there are different NT domains for the `east` and `west` subdomains, how does the DNS server know which WINS servers it should ask?

These questions are answered by the first of two types of DNS records that Microsoft retrofitted the DNS "standard" with. This record is called a WINS record, cleverly enough. The mere presence of this record in the root of a DNS zone instructs the DNS server to forward requests for names that cannot be resolved to the WINS server listed.

The format of this record is as follows:

```
<domain> IN WINS <WINS Server IP Address>
```

You may add the record manually as described, or you can use the GUI. To configure a WINS record using the graphical user interface of the DNS Manager:

1. Open the properties sheet for a specific zone by right-clicking on a zone name and picking Properties.

2. The Zone Properties dialog box will appear, as illustrated in Figure 12-11. Select the WINS Lookup tab.

3. Select the Use WINS Resolution check box.

4. Add one or more IP addresses to the list below the check box, clicking the Add button between each.

5. Click OK when done.

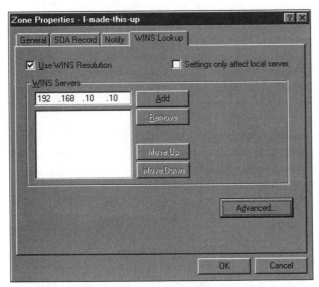

Figure 12-11: WINS records allow DNS servers to forward queries.

Because the WINS record is defined on a per-zone basis, it helps if your zone structure coordinates with the structure of your Windows NT domains.

One more note: If you are using dynamically assigned IP addresses, set the cache time low so that the IP addresses provided by the WINS servers are not retained by the DNS server after they are no longer valid. To do this:

1. Open the properties sheet for a specific zone by right-clicking on a zone name and picking Properties.

2. The Zone Properties dialog box will appear. Select the WINS Lookup tab.

3. Click the Advanced button. You will be greeted with the Advanced Zone Properties dialog box, as illustrated in Figure 12-12.

4. Click the little up and down arrows to change the cache value to something lower, like two minutes.

5. Click OK twice to close the dialog boxes.

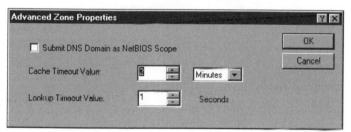

Figure 12-12: Change the cache timeout from the Advanced Zone Properties dialog box.

The second DNS record type that Microsoft added is the WINS-R record, which is used to look up WINS records given the IP address of a system. The format of this type of record is as follows:

```
<domain> IN WINS-R <name of Internet domain>
```

WINS-R records can be added manually to the database or can be configured to work automatically via the GUI. These instructions are similar to adding the records for the standard WINS servers, except that they involve using the in-addr.arpa zone. To configure a WINS-R record using the graphical user interface of the DNS Manager:

1. Open the properties sheet for a specific zone by right-clicking on the in-addr.arpa zone name and picking Properties.

2. The Zone Properties dialog box will appear, as illustrated in Figure 12-13. Select the WINS Reverse Lookup tab.

3. Select the Use WINS Reverse Lookup check box.

4. Add a domain name to append to the hostnames returned from WINS, and click OK.

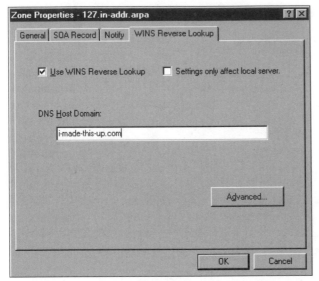

Figure 12-13: The property sheet for a WINS reverse lookup record

WHEN TO AND WHEN NOT TO INTEGRATE THESE SERVICES   For example, integrating these services will be necessary if Elvis's desktop machine (elvis.mycompany.com) is assigned an IP address via DHCP. It would be possible to create a static DNS entry with Elvis's IP address, but it may become invalid the next time the system is rebooted. In this situation, it is very important to integrate WINS and DNS by allowing DNS to look up records in the WINS database.

This is less important if DHCP is used to assign static IP addresses to systems. If all systems are DHCP clients but every system has a static mapping within the DHCP database, you may add static DNS entries for each and every system without too much concern. If these systems are tied to a particular IP address, however, reconsider using DHCP at all.

Testing and Troubleshooting DNS

DNS is a complex and *very* large-scale protocol. Hence, it will break from time to time. This is an inconvenience for the average person, but if you are the administrator, it quickly becomes an emergency. This section is not intended as a complete and thorough how-to guide to troubleshooting DNS, but I do want to introduce you to the primary tools.

PING

I had to mention PING here, though it seems obvious. PING is a great way to determine if a particular host is up and running and whether or not the network is operating properly. The first item to check when you experience DNS problems is the status of the systems and network. I suggest first checking to see if the problematic DNS servers respond at all.

If the DNS server responds to PING, then you have assured yourself that the system is up and running and that the network is operational. Several network-related things can still go wrong – for example, packet filtering may be occurring at some router between the system you use for testing and the DNS server. It is not uncommon for filtering routers or firewalls to allow ICMP traffic (such as PING) through but to filter traffic such as DNS.

If the DNS server does not respond to PING, then the odds are good that the system is down. To verify that it is the system and not a network problem, perform a TRACERT and determine whether the router to which the DNS server is connected is operating properly.

This suggestion will seem obvious to many, but I wanted to point it out anyway. When troubleshooting DNS, make an effort to use the IP addresses instead of the DNS names to eliminate the possibility that the problem is being caused by the DNS server rather than the host.

NSLOOKUP

The definitive utility for testing DNS and diagnosing DNS problems is NSLOOKUP. This has been a part of the UNIX operating environment for years, but it is fairly new to Windows NT. For this reason, many NT administrators may not be familiar with its use – I will take a few pages to describe the command.

First, NSLOOKUP is a command-line utility, so start a command prompt. NSLOOKUP has two execution modes: interactive and noninteractive. Noninteractive is best for looking up information about a single record and for scripting. Interactive mode is less commonly used but is convenient if you are looking up multiple records at a single time or need to make use of the extended command set.

NONINTERACTIVE MODE

To use this mode, provide the NSLOOKUP utility with all the information it needs at the command prompt. These are provided in the standard way, as command-line parameters. For all parameters, preface the option with a hyphen. If the parameters require a string argument, follow it with an equal sign and a value. Table 12-5 shows all the possible parameters for the NSLOOKUP utility.

Table 12-5 NS LOOKUP COMMAND LINE PARAMETERS

Command	Purpose
-all	Shows the default DNS server and any options you have enabled during this session.
-class	Changes the class of the query you wish to submit. This is normally set to Internet, the default.
-d2 or -nod2	Enables or disables exhaustive debugging. This will show you all of the information that is retrieved about the sites you query during your session.
-debug or -nodebug	Enables or disables debugging mode. When enabled, information from some of the packets will be displayed. This option is more commonly used than set d2, which shows more information than most people are interested in.
-defname or -nodefname	Enables or disables automatically appending a dot and the domain name (specified with the set domain option) after each hostname entered into NSLOOKUP that does not already include a domain name.
-domain	Modifies the domain NSLOOKUP appends to the end of hostnames.
-ignore or -noignore	Enables or disables acceptance of packets with truncation errors.
-port	Sets the default TCP/UDP port. This is only used in the very uncommon circumstance of a DNS server that is operating at a port other than the default (53).
-querytype	Sets the type of information query that will be submitted to the DNS servers. This command is the same as set type.
-recurse or -norecurse	Enables or disables asking the DNS name server to query other servers if it does not have the information in its cache or zone files.
-retry	Sets the number of times NSLOOKUP will try the same DNS server before giving up. When NSLOOKUP queries a DNS server, it will try this many times. The timeout value between each query doubles until the retry value is reached.
-root	Sets the name of the root server.
-search or -nosearch	Enables or disables the parsing of the srchlist parameter.
-srchlist	Allows you to configure a list of domain names that NSLOOKUP will automatically append to each hostname you query. It parses the search list.

Continued

Command	Purpose
-timeout	Controls how many seconds NSLOOKUP waits to hear a response from a DNS server. By default, this value is set to 2.
-type	Sets the type of information query that will be submitted to the DNS servers. This command is a synonym for set querytype.
-vc or -novc	Enables or disables forcing NSLOOKUP to use a virtual circuit when submitting queries to the DNS server.

INTERACTIVE MODE

The interactive mode for NSLOOKUP allows you to perform queries for several servers in sequence. It also allows for more flexibility with the command-line arguments. To enter interactive mode, simply execute the NSLOOKUP command without any parameters. Your command prompt will change to a > sign, indicating that NSLOOKUP will be interpreting everything you type. The options are similar to those for the noninteractive mode, and there are many additional commands, as shown in Table 12-6.

TABLE 12-6 NS LOOKUP COMMAND LINE PARAMETERS

Command	Purpose
exit	Quits NSLOOKUP.
finger	Connects with the Finger server on the *current* host. The *current* host is defined when a previous lookup for a host was successful and returned the address information.
help or ?	Shows you a list of the available options with a short description for each.
ls	Retrieves a list of all DNS entries for a domain. The fields returned by default contain host names and IP addresses. Many domains have *hundreds* or *thousands* of hosts, so this could be a pretty big list. To make the output a little more manageable, redirect it to a file just as you would in DOS. NSLOOKUP will echo # signs marking every fifty records.

Continued

TABLE 12-6 NS LOOKUP COMMAND LINE PARAMETERS *(Continued)*

Command	Purpose
lserver	Changes the default server to the specified DNS domain. Lserver uses the initial server to look up the information about the specified DNS domain. (This is in contrast to the server command, which uses the current default server.)
root	Changes the default server to the server for the root of the DNS domain name space. Currently, the host G.ROOT-SERVERS.NET. is used. (This command is a synonym for lserver g.root-server.net.) The name of the root server can be changed with the set root command.
server	Changes the default server to the specified DNS domain. Server uses the current default server to look up the information about the specified DNS domain. (This is in contrast to the lserver command, which uses the initial server.)
set all	Shows the default DNS server and any options you have enabled during this session.
set class	Changes the query class. This is normally set to Internet, the default.
set d2 or set nod2	Enables or disables exhaustive debugging. This will show you all of the information that is retrieved about the sites you query during your session.
set debug or nodebug	Turns debugging mode on or off. When enabled, information from some of the packets will be displayed. This option is more commonly used than set d2, which shows more information than most people are interested in.
set defname or set nodefname	Enables or disables automatically appending a dot and the domain name (specified with the set domain option) after each hostname entered into NSLOOKUP that does not already include a domain name.
set domain	Changes the default DNS domain to the name specified. The default DNS domain name is appended to a lookup request depending on the state of the defname and search options. The DNS domain search list contains the parents of the default DNS domain if it has at least two components in its name. For example, if the default DNS domain is mydomain.mycompany.com, the search list is mydomain.mycompany.com and mycompany.com. Use the set srchlist command to specify a different list. Use the set all command to display the list.

Continued

Command	Purpose
`set ignore` or `no ignore`	Enables or disables acceptance of packets with truncation errors.
`set port`	Sets the default TCP/UDP port. This is only used in the very uncommon circumstance of a DNS server that is operating at a port other than the default (53).
`set querytype`	Changes the type of information query.
`set recurse` or `set norecurse`	Enables or disables asking the DNS name server to query other servers if it does not have the information in its cache or zone files.
`set retry`	Sets the number of times NSLOOKUP will try the same DNS server before giving up. When NSLOOKUP queries a DNS server, it will try this many times. The timeout value between each query doubles until the retry value is reached.
`set root`	Sets the name of the root server.
`set search` or `set nosearch`	If set and the lookup request contains at least one period but does not end with a trailing period, appends the DNS domain names in the DNS domain search list to the request until an answer is received.
`set srchlist`	Changes the default DNS domain name and search list. A maximum of six names separated by slashes (/) can be specified. This command overrides the default DNS domain name and search list of the set domain command. Use the set all command to display the list.
`set timeout`	Changes the initial number of seconds to wait for a reply to a request. When a reply to a request is not received within this time period, the timeout is doubled and the request is re-sent. (The number of retries is controlled with the set retry option.)
`set type`	Changes the type of information query. More information about types can be found in RFC 1035. (The set type command is a synonym for set querytype.)
`set vc` or `set no vc`	If set, forces NSLOOKUP to use a virtual circuit when sending requests to the server.
`view`	Sorts and lists the output of previous ls command(s).

To enter NSLOOKUP interactive mode, simply enter NSLOOKUP at the command prompt. If you want to query a different server (or if you do not have a default DNS server specified), use the format NSLOOKUP - 192.168.8.20, where 192.168.8.20 is the IP address of the DNS server to query. You will be greeted with:

```
Default Server: dns.myisp.net
Address: 192.168.8.20
```

Naturally, the preceding example will vary: The IP address and DNS name of the default DNS server will be your own. The > symbol is your command prompt; you are free to enter in any of the parameters listed for noninteractive mode. However, you do not have to preface the parameters with the '-'; instead, many of the parameters should be prefaced with set. For example, to turn on the debug option and perform a lookup for www.microsoft.com and www.netscape.com, use the following commands:

```
NSLOOKUP
set debug
www.microsoft.com
www.netscape.com
```

EXAMPLE: FUN WITH NSLOOKUP

Have some extra disk space? Try retrieving a list of hostnames within a specific domain with the ls command. To do this, type these commands, where "ispname.net" is a domain name:

```
NSLOOKUP
ls ispname.net
```

Chances are good you will get an error message returned, indicating that the name servers have restricted that type of query. However, if you are successful in retrieving a list (hint: try dialing into your ISP and using its domain name), you will get some insight into the mind of a systems administrator.

Looking at the Future of DNS

DNS, unlike WINS, is here to stay. Long after we have all forgotten what a "NetBIOS name" is, we will still be working with domains and DNS records. In fact, chances are good that it will not change much over the next ten years, though it will be improved.

Microsoft has resisted DNS as long as it can. "If you can't beat 'em, join 'em," though, and Microsoft is doing just that. With the release of Windows NT 5.0, you will have the ability to rely entirely on DNS for all directory services and name resolutions, removing the burden NetBIOS names placed on administrators. If you are designing the DNS architecture for your domain now, you will save yourself headaches in the future if you design it specifically for the Enhanced Directory Services. For those of you simply administering an existing domain structure, it is a good idea to look ahead and find out what Microsoft has in mind, so you can assure you won't be left behind.

Dynamic DNS

I am not a fan of Dynamic Host Configuration Protocol (DHCP), but many in the industry are. In fact, a good number of the Microsoft networks in existence are based on a DHCP infrastructure. I really blame Microsoft for this odd phenomenon – much of their documentation touts DHCP as being the "be-all and end-all" of IP address assignment. In the future, I feel (hope?) that DHCP will go the way of NetBEUI and WINS; dropped from common use in favor of something that makes sense.

Now, DNS and DHCP do not traditionally mix well, because DNS is a static, manually updated method of name resolution. DHCP dynamically assigns IP addresses to systems, so without some sort of communication between the two protocols, it would be impossible for DNS servers to resolve IP addresses to DHCP clients.

To resolve this problem, Microsoft stepped in and integrated WINS and DNS together. Because the WINS database is built dynamically as computers start up and claim their DHCP-assigned IP address, it has no problem with name resolution of dynamic hosts. Microsoft's modifications simply allow the DNS server to query the WINS server if it cannot resolve a particular name.

There are a few problems with their implementation. First, they just thought up the whole idea and stuck it into the software, without bothering to wait for any kind of official standards to be put into place. In Microsoft's defense, they did write a proposal for a standard, but the IETF is still working on finalizing a method for allowing DNS servers to resolve names and IP addresses using a WINS server.

Second, it allows only Windows-based systems to register with the WINS server (and in turn, to be resolved by the DNS server). UNIX boxes that may use DHCP do not speak NetBIOS and so will not bother to register themselves with a WINS server.

Third, it works only with Windows NT-based DNS servers. Naturally, one or two organizations out there have to rebel against Microsoft's homogenous Windows model and throw a UNIX box in as a DNS server. Those wild enough to try this will find that the dynamic DNS updates provided for by Windows NT 4.0 just won't work.

Now that I've told you some great reasons not to use WINS and DNS together, what can we do about it? Microsoft has submitted some suggestions to the IETF, but for now we will just have to wait. The fact of the matter is that organizations will never have to worry about it, because the NT domain model will disappear before any viable method of dynamic DNS updates happens.

IPng/IPv6

Everyone is talking about version 6 of the Internet Protocol, otherwise known as IP: The Next Generation. I've mentioned it here and there throughout this book; it's a new version of the network-layer protocol used on the Internet that has been designed to reduce many of the problems users currently experience.

Because the IP address format changes for IPng, DNS is going to have to adjust as well. Already, an RFC has been written on the topic. This RFC can be found at http://ds2.internic.net/rfc/rfc1886.txt. It defines several changes to the existing DNS structure.

First, a new record type is added to accommodate the 128-bit addresses in IPng. This record type is AAAA, which, by definition, stores a single IPng address encoded from most-significant bit to least-significant bit.

To allow clients to look up this new record type, a AAAA query is defined as well. It works in the same way a normal lookup does, returning all records associated with a particular name.

Finally, a domain is added to facilitate reverse-DNS lookups of IPng addresses. While the reverse-lookup domain for version 4 of IP was called .IN-ADDR.ARPA, the newer version is referred to as .IP6.INT, which makes only slightly more sense. The new version gives the following reverse-lookup records as an example:

b.a.9.8.7.6.5.0.4.0.0.0.3.0.0.0.2.0.0.0.1.0.0.0.0.0.0.1.2.3.4.IP6.INT.

Wow! Now that's a name!

Not to be too pessimistic, we are still several years away from implementing version 6 of the IP network protocol. Fortunately, it will not be too difficult to migrate DNS when the time comes.

Security

DNS servers have always been a popular point for malicious attackers to begin an assault on an organization. The fact is, DNS has very little security built into the protocol itself. As we look to the increased usage of DNS on the public Internet, one of the items on our wish list has to be security.

A couple of standards have been proposed with the intent of providing an increased level of security for DNS. The most popular area of focus seems to be name server–to–name server communications, providing functionality such as authentication of zone transfers. Until these standards are given the stamp of approval by the IETF, refrain from implementing a vendor-specific solution unless absolutely necessary. Otherwise, it is likely that you will end up redoing all of your work in a year to conform to more widely accepted standards of DNS security.

Migration

It is hard to predict the future, but this one is for sure: It will involve a lot of migrating. As new standards develop, administrators and engineers will spend many hours playing catch-up. However, there are some things you can do that will save you time and headaches in the future.

The first DNS-related migration we are all looking forward to is to adopt Microsoft's Enhanced Directory Services. This will be a blessing in the long run, but the initial migration will be painful for most. The first guideline to ease future migrations is to latch onto Internet standards, not vendor standards. If you are still using IPX and/or NetBEUI somewhere on your network, immediately get rid of it! This is so important that I have to recommend putting a sniffer such as Network Monitor on each subnet and monitoring the traffic for any occurrence of these protocols. Any reliance on these archaic standards will cause you tons of problems in the future!

Another rule of thumb that Microsoft recommends is to place a secondary DNS server at each remote site. If you do not make heavy use of DNS servers now, you sure will when they replace all of your WINS servers! Enhanced DS will use DNS servers to locate domain controllers, whereas for most tasks NetBIOS name resolution has traditionally handled that by broadcast or by WINS.

Summary

This chapter has given you the framework to implement, expand, and fix DNS services within your internetwork. It has provided a detailed description of the current implementation of DNS, as well as its history and future.

You have learned the following:

♦ DNS services are used to provide resolution of IP addresses to hostnames from a central server. DNS will continue to evolve as the Internet grows, and it is already being adapted for IPv6.

♦ Windows NT natively supports both client- and server-side DNS functions. Though Windows NT is not yet commonly used for name services, it provides advantages that are not available from more traditional UNIX-based DNS servers, such as WINS integration.

♦ DNS is managed by the InterNIC. Domain names that are used on the public Internet must be registered for a fee, which ensures that no two organizations can claim the same name.

◆ DNS is very hierarchical. Primary servers hold the definitive zone files, listings of DNS records with names and IP addresses. Secondary servers maintain copies of this zone file and can be queried by clients for redundancy and load balancing.

◆ The most useful tool for troubleshooting DNS problems is NSLOOKUP. NSLOOKUP allows you to query a DNS server in many different ways, allowing you to quickly pinpoint errors.

In the next chapter, you'll learn about Routing and Remote Access Service, Microsoft's add-on for Windows NT that replaces RAS and supplements routing capabilities.

Part IV

Noteworthy Products

Chapter 13

Routing and Remote Access Service

IN THIS CHAPTER

- ◆ Understanding how routing works on a TCP/IP internetwork

- ◆ Understanding what a routing protocol does

- ◆ Implementing Microsoft's Routing and Remote Access Service with both the RIP and OSPF routing protocols

- ◆ Using Routing and Remote Access Service and Dial-on-Demand Routing

- ◆ Creating a lab environment to test the features of RRAS

- ◆ Designing a network to include all features of RRAS

THIS CHAPTER COVERS the Routing and Remote Access Service (RRAS) optional component of Windows NT Server. It is different from the other chapters of this book because it includes many step-by-step examples and even covers using the graphical user interface. My philosophy for this chapter remains the same as the rest of the book: to supplement existing documentation rather than duplicate it. Existing documentation for RRAS is incomplete and superficial, and I have made an effort to provide you with the information you need to successfully implement NT servers that use the features provided by RRAS. This includes coverage of the inner workings of the supported routing protocols as well as my personal opinions on situations in which RRAS is not appropriate.

An Introduction to the Routing and Remote Access Service

Microsoft has always been an ambitious company, striving to expand its products into broader and broader marketplaces. The most recent, and one of the most widely questioned, is the company's move into the network hardware market. Microsoft wants Windows NT Server to fill the role Cisco, 3Com, and Bay Networks typically play in a network: the router. Already, a vendor has produced a dedicated piece of hardware based on Windows NT and the Routing and Remote Access Service (RRAS).

Originally called Steelhead, NT 5.0 will use RRAS to replace the Multi-Protocol Router (MPR) version 1.0 included in NT 3.51 and 4.0. MPR v1 provided very limited routing functionality: RIP v1, RIP v2, and static routing were the only options. Nonetheless, many organizations made use of the limited routing functionality to segment small networks and avoid the cost of deploying dedicated routing hardware, which generally costs above $2,000. Using this functionality, it was possible to connect a single Windows NT server to two separate subnets and let machines on both networks fully communicate. Any network card that worked with NT could be used for routing, making expansion very inexpensive. Both TCP/IP and IPX/SPX were fully supported.

The built-in routing in NT 3.51 and 4.0 suffered from many problems, though, including poor performance, incompatibilities with standard RIP routers, and a very limited feature set. These weaknesses were major enough that NT servers were rarely used as routers. The most common complaints about the service were the lack of source-IP filtering and the lack of more robust routing protocols such as Open Shortest Path First (OSPF). Further, since little control was available from the graphical user interface of NT, most work had to be done using the ROUTE ADD commands. This command-line interface was even less robust and more difficult to use than most hardware-based routers.

In order to address these weaknesses and begin its expansion into the router market, Microsoft introduced the Routing and Remote Access Service as a free add-on to Windows NT 4.0. This new service continued to support static routing, RIP v1 and v2 with TCP/IP, and RIP and SAP for IPX/SPX. However, it added one of the most popular and standardized interdomain routing protocols available, OSPF.

In the hope that other vendors would pick up where they left off, Microsoft created a routing application programming interface. This API would enable vendors such as Cisco and 3Com to create drivers for their proprietary routing protocols, making Windows NT servers compatible with their existing hardware-based routers. They also created a management and user interface API to make configuration simpler and provide backward compatibility with SNMP managed routers.

Other new features include support for expanded RAS, virtual private networking using Point-to-Point Transfer Protocol (PPTP), and Dial-on-Demand Routing (DDR). Best of all, it is still completely free.

If you are a systems engineer, Routing and Remote Access Service is also an excellent way for you to raise your knowledge level toward that of a network engineer. For many who have had a difficult time finding routing hardware to play with and learn on, RRAS provides an inexpensive yet robust routing architecture that can be implemented on existing Windows NT Server architecture. If you have already dedicated the time to create a lab environment with NT servers, it is a comparatively simple task to configure these servers and routers. In half a day's work, you can install the RRAS service on four servers, add network cards if they are not already in place, and wire them together. Compared to the cost of purchasing and configuring four new Cisco routers, the cost is insignificant. For more information on setting up an RRAS lab environment, jump to that section within this chapter.

 There is some confusion regarding the official name of the services I discuss in this chapter. As I mentioned earlier in the chapter, the project, while in the beta and development stages, was called Steelhead. The product, as released for public download as an add-on to Windows NT Server 4.0, is called the Routing and Remote Access Service. As integrated into NT 5.0, the features of this service will be called Multi-Protocol Router version 2.0, or MPR v2. In this book I have called the product Routing and Remote Access Service, or RRAS.

Understanding How Routing Works

When two hosts are on physically separated networks, they have no way to communicate. A *router* is the device that connects these two networks and intelligently forwards data between the two segments. The intelligence is a key component: Repeaters, by comparison, also forward data between network segments, but a repeater is only aware of electrical signals and cannot provide filtering or take any action that requires information from the data-link layer or network layer. This is because repeaters operate at the physical layer. Bridges are more intelligent – they are able to read in the frame header, which means they can forward traffic based on the MAC address in the frame. Bridges do not have the intelligence to selectively forward traffic based on network-level information; IPX/SPX, NetBEUI, and TCP/IP packets all look the same at the frame level.

Routers are intelligent enough to analyze the electrical signals on a wire and translate them into meaningful data: a series of bits and bytes. They can then analyze the beginning of the data and determine the MAC address in the data-link-layer header. Just like any network interface card, a router's NIC is able to quickly determine whether the frame is destined for the host. If it is, the router can determine what network-layer protocol is being used and decide what to do with it. Depending on the rules that have been defined for the router, the router will forward the packet out another interface, drop the packet from memory, or process it and respond to it.

You probably already understand how MAC addresses and IP addresses work together, but here is a quick review. Network interface cards on a network segment normally only listen to frames that have one of two MAC addresses: the MAC address of that network card and the broadcast MAC address (FF-FF-FF-FF-FF-FF). So if a host is forwarding a packet through a router, how does that router know that it should take the packet and forward it?

When the source host is preparing to send the packet to the destination, it compares its subnet mask (for example, `255.255.255.0`) to its IP address (for example, `192.168.10.20`) to determine its network number (in this case, `192.168.10.0`). It then compares its subnet mask to the destination IP address (for example, `192.168.30.35`) to determine the destination network number (`192.168.30.0`). If the network numbers differ, then the source host is on a different network than the destination host and a router must be used to forward the packet.

In this example, the transmitting host only has a default router defined (the most common real-world configuration) with an IP address of `192.168.10.1`. It must address the frame to be received by the router, so it performs an ARP request listing the IP address of the default router. The router responds, providing its MAC address. The transmitting host now has enough information to formulate the packet and send it on its way.

In the data-link-layer header, the transmitting host lists the router's MAC address (which it derived via the ARP request) as the destination MAC address and its own MAC address as the source. In the IP network-layer header, the transmitting host provides its own IP address as the source. The packet's destination IP address is given as the IP address of the final destination, not the router's IP address. Despite the fact that the packet must first be processed by the router, the IP address listed is that of the final destination! Here's why.

For the router to be able to perform any action on the frame, the destination MAC address in the frame must be that of the router. When the router receives a frame with its MAC address and a different IP address, it knows that it is not the final destination and that it should forward the frame through another network interface. If both the destination MAC address and the destination IP address are valid for the router, the router is the final destination of the packet and it must process the packet further. This happens when you PING a router or attempt to Telnet directly into it. In almost every case, the IP address will be for a remote host and the router will need to forward it. Figure 13-1 shows the process of sending a packet through a router.

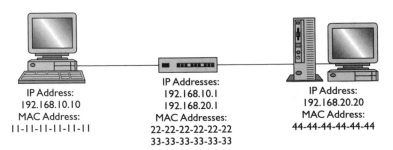

Figure 13-1: Routers change the source and destination MAC addresses when forwarding a packet.

Once the router determines that it is not the final destination for the packet, it must determine what action to perform. In most cases, the router will forward the packet out another network interface to another router or to the final destination, if directly connected. To determine exactly where the packet is to be sent next, the router uses a *routing table*. A routing table is a list of network numbers and next-destination addresses. For example, Figure 13-2 illustrates a router on an IP network and its routing table. As you can see, the routing table (Table 13-1) contains network addresses for networks directly connected and for networks that can only be reached through one or more routers: In this way, packets can "hop" from one router to another to reach their final destination. ("Hop" is a common term to describe each step a packet makes via a router.)

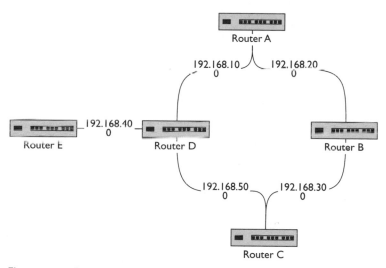

Figure 13-2: Router A maintains a list of its neighboring routers and their distances.

TABLE 13-1 ROUTER A'S ROUTING TABLE

Network	Distance	Next Hop
192.168.10.0	1	Local
192.168.20.0	1	Local
192.168.30.0	2	Router B
192.168.40.0	2	Router D
192.168.50.0	2	Router D

To view a real-life example of a routing table, enter the command ROUTE PRINT at a Windows NT command prompt. This command displays the internal routing table of the local system. If you have more than one network interface card, you can tell which interface will be used to reach which networks. The default gateway is listed with a network of 0.0.0.0.

The router populates the routing table by first adding directly connected networks: Because it can send traffic to those networks without going through another router, it always knows exactly where they are. To add routes to distant networks, the router must have some way of learning about those networks. Routers can be programmed manually, using static routes. With static routes, an administrator programs a router with information like "all packets bound for network 192.168.50.0 should go through the router at 192.168.4.1."

A more elegant approach is to encourage the routers to share information with each other, using their own special language. This language is called a *routing protocol*. Windows NT Server provides support for a variety of such routing protocols using the Routing and Remote Access Service add-on. The next section lists the steps necessary to download and install the free product.

Installing the Routing and Remote Access Service

I've always thought it was important to understand the fundamentals before getting your hands dirty. Certainly, you can dive right in and get RRAS up and running in a few minutes, but you will find yourself spending a great deal of time doing troubleshooting and making configuration changes if you start here. Hopefully, you've read this chapter up to this point and already have a good understanding of how routing works, how the different routing protocols work, and where Windows NT Server fits into all of this.

Now that you know why I've been torturing you, let's dig in.

Downloading RRAS

Routing and Remote Access Service (RRAS) is a free add-on to Windows NT Server and is available from Microsoft's World Wide Web site. To download the software, visit http://backoffice.Microsoft.com/downtrial/moreinfo/rasup.asp.

Starting the Installation Program

Microsoft's setup procedure is simple the first time you install. Start by making sure service pack 3 is installed on the computer. Then simply execute the file you've downloaded from Microsoft (`mpri386.exe` for Intel-based servers). It will decompress the setup files and prompt you to run setup. The RRAS installation program shows a dialog box with three check boxes labeled Remote Access Service, LAN Routing, and Demand Dial Routing. Instinct may tell you to select all three and fire up the setup procedure, but fight this urge. Select them one at a time – this warning comes from experience, not from the setup manuals. I've had problems time and time again when installing multiple components simultaneously.

If you need to run the setup procedure again (for example, to install another component), you must find the `MRPSETUP.EXE` program. It's more complicated than that though, because you must include the full pathname to the setup files as the first argument. For example, if you have extracted the setup files to `C:\Program Files\ Routing\`, pick Run from the Start menu and type `C:\Program Files\Routing\ MPRSETUP` and `C:\Program Files\Routing`.

Installing the Remote Access Service

RAS (Remote Access Service) is one of three components that make up the Routing and Remote Access Service add-on. LAN Routing and Dial-on-Demand Routing are the other two. The RAS component is an upgrade to the RAS already built into Windows NT Server. Like the base Windows NT Server software, it allows both outgoing and incoming connections and may use several modems simultaneously.

The installation procedure is the same as it always has been after this point. You will be prompted to choose which modems to use, and you can configure each modem to allow incoming, outgoing, or Dial-on-Demand connections. One new option is to use Remote Authentication Dial-In User Service (RADIUS) authentication in place of the standard Windows NT authentication. More information on RADIUS can be found in this chapter within the section "Security Considerations."

Installing LAN Routing

After running `MPRSETUP`, select the second check box to install LAN Routing. The LAN Routing option includes packet forwarding, packet filtering, and the RIP and OSPF routing protocols. It also is used for WAN connections when the WAN card includes LAN card emulation.

Installing Demand Dial Routing

Demand Dial Routing allows two RRAS routers to connect to each other over a dialup connection such as an analog phone line or an ISDN circuit. It can also be used to create virtual private networks by using PPTP to connect two remote routers.

When you are using PPTP as a WAN connection, data can be carried privately and transparently over a public network such as the Internet. However, it is only useful if the remote network to which you are connecting also uses RRAS with PPTP.

If you wish to install Demand Dial Routing, run MPRSETUP. You will be prompted to choose which components you wish to install — select only the third check box, Demand Dial Routing, and click OK. The setup routine is straightforward and the user documentation is clear, so I will not cover the process step by step in this text.

Administering the Routing and Remote Access Service

Like most administrative utilities provided by Microsoft, RRAS may be administered from a remote machine running Windows NT. This machine may be a Windows NT workstation in a network operations center, or it may simply be the network manager's desktop system.

To administer a remote router using the graphical utilities, you must install them on the management workstation. To do this, use the copyadmn.cmd utility. This utility is located in the directory to which the RRAS files were extracted on any of your Windows NT Server–based routers. The format for the command is:

```
COPYADMN <source directory> <destination directory>
```

For example:

```
COPYADMN %SYSTEMROOT%\System32\ \\server\c$\winnt\system32\
```

There is no magic to this command; it simply copies over several files. Nonetheless, once these files are copied, they are all you need to run the administrative utilities. Once they are copied, the command MPRADMIN can be executed on the remote machine. Because the utility is copied into the System32 directory, it is automatically in the PATH. Before you can connect to the remote router from the admin utility, establish a NetBIOS connection. A quick way to do this is with the NET USE command, as in the following example:

```
NET USE \\router /user:DOMAIN\USERNAME
```

No icon for the MPRADMIN utility is created in the Start menu when the program is copied to the remote machine.

Like most administrative utilities provided by Microsoft, RRAS uses the NetBIOS over TCP/IP protocol for network communications. In order for the NT-based router to receive the NetBIOS communications from the remote machine running the admin utility, the NetBIOS Session service must be enabled. If any port-based filtering is being used on the NT-based router, be sure TCP port 139 is enabled.

Routing Protocols

Chapter 1 gave an introduction to the concepts of routing and the importance of routing protocols. This section describes the details of specific routing protocols within the TCP/IP protocol suite that Windows NT Server supports.

An autonomous system (AS) is a group of routers that are administered by a single organization. Generally, all the routers within an AS speak the same routing protocols and route traffic for each other. Understanding what an AS is used for is key to understanding the difference between exterior gateway protocols (EGPs) and interior gateway protocols (IGPs).

EGPs are used between ASs, to allow different networks to communicate with each other. EGPs are also commonly used to allow large organizations to share their routes with an ISP. Currently, Windows NT includes no support for any EGP. This is not a major drawback; generally, ISPs add static routes to their routing tables to allow traffic to reach an organization that connects to them, rather than agreeing to use an EGP.

IGPs are used within an AS. Generally, an organization decides on a single routing protocol and uses that same protocol on all internal routers in their network. That organization may also use an EGP to publish selected routes from inside the network to the outside world. For example, BigCo uses OSPF to communicate routes between subnets within its internal network. Several of these networks must have Internet access, because they host a mail server, a DNS server, and several Web servers. BigCo connects to an Internet service provider and uses the BGP protocol to communicate just the routes it wants to allow the rest of the Internet to access. In this way, BigCo allows for complete connectivity within the organization and selected connectivity outside of the company.

Interior gateway protocols allow routers to communicate with each other within a single organization's network. IGPs are characterized by several properties: They are efficient enough to be used on inexpensive routers that may be weak on processing power, they expect their neighbors to be connected via fast LAN links, and they often rely on broadcasts to communicate.

The most common routing protocols used with TCP/IP are RIP, OSPF, and IGRP/Enhanced IGRP. Currently, Windows NT Server's Routing and Remote Access module supports only static routing, RIP, and OSPF. Is this enough? It is certainly not a full suite of protocols, and this deficiency will present problems if you are trying to integrate Windows NT–based routers into an existing routed network. On the other hand, if you are designing a new network that will use Windows NT systems as routers, you have the choice of a distance-vector routing protocol, RIP, or a link-state protocol, OSPF.

Static Routing

Static routing is the simplest and least scalable routing method available. Each path through the network is hard-coded and, with Windows NT, inflexible. For example, consider an NT server with two network interface cards, each connected to different IP networks. With the base install of NT 3.51 or NT 4.0 and IP forwarding enabled, the NT server will automatically route packets that it receives from one network onto the other network, if the packet is destined for the directly attached network. This is simple to configure by following these steps:

1. Bring up the Network Control Panel applet.

2. Click on the Protocols tab, select TCP/IP, and click the Properties button.

3. Click on the Routing tab, and select Enable IP forwarding.

Figure 13-3 shows an example of the Routing tab.

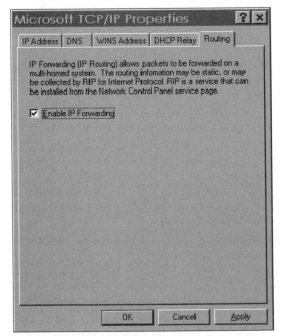

Figure 13-3: Windows NT natively supports static routing; you need only mark this check box.

With this configuration, hosts that are configured to use the NT server's IP address as the default gateway will forward packets to that server. If the NT server receives a packet with its MAC address and an IP address on another subnet, it will replace the MAC address with that of the destination host and forward the packet out the proper network interface. Figure 13-1 illustrates this point.

This is the most simple case scenario and will work for the smallest networks. It is actually more scalable that many people realize because the NT server is not limited to two network cards but can contain quite a few. Consider the following example: You are assigned a single class C address for your internal network. You have 120 hosts that need IP addresses, a single NT server, and no hardware routers.

This problem can be solved with a single NT server. Simply place four network cards into the NT server, assigning each one a valid IP address in each of the four networks and a subnet mask of 255.255.255.192. This 26-bit subnet mask allows for four networks with a maximum of 64 hosts in each network. When you select Enable IP forwarding, the server's configuration is complete. (Note: This is the easy part. The hard part will be going to each of the other hosts and changing the default gateway to be the NT server!) This has the added advantage of making the services provided by the NT server local to each subnet: Any host on any network can communicate with that NT server without having to forward traffic through a router. Therefore, logon validation, file sharing, print sharing, WINS resolution, and DHCP requests can all happen without any traffic being forwarded. Figure 13-4 shows a single NT server routing for four networks.

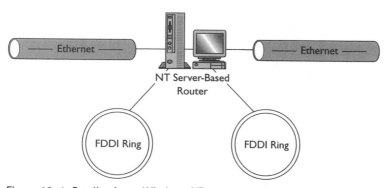

Figure 13-4: By allowing a Windows NT server to act as a router, you assure that traffic to and from the server never has to cross multiple networks.

Much more complex configurations are also possible when using static routes. If there is more than one router on the network, each router will have to know about networks that are *not* directly connected. For traffic to be forwarded to these networks, the packets must be forwarded to another router, rather than directly to the destination host as described in the previous scenario. This object can be accomplished with static routing by using the ROUTE -p ADD command from the Windows NT command line.

For example, consider a network with two NT servers and four networks. The two servers have three network interface cards each and share a connection on a single network, as Figure 13-5 shows. For this example, please suspend your judgment of reality and consider the class A private network 10.0.0.0 to contain addresses actually assigned to the organization and the class C private network (192.168.5.0) to really be a private network. The connection between the two servers is only used for passing traffic between these servers, and so only a private network address is used. Assume that hosts have already been configured to use the nearest NT server as the default gateway.

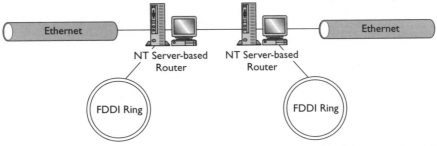

Figure 13-5: Windows NT can participate in a multiple router network by manually adding routing information.

In this scenario, we have a very simple backbone network, 192.168.5.0, and four leaf networks, 10.1.1.0 through 10.1.4.0. Once IP forwarding has been enabled on the servers, only two commands need to be executed on each server to enable full connectivity. Tell Server A to forward traffic bound for networks 10.1.3.0 and 10.1.4.0 through Server B's private network address, 192.168.5.2. To do this, execute the commands:

```
ROUTE -p ADD 10.1.3.0 MASK 255.255.255.0 192.168.5.2
ROUTE -p ADD 10.1.4.0 MASK 255.255.255.0 192.168.5.2
```

To verify that they have been added successfully, use the ROUTE PRINT -p command. This will show the following new lines:

```
Network Address         Netmask  Gateway Address         Interface
  Metric
      10.1.3.0    255.255.255.0  192.168.5.2    192.168.5.100 1
10.1.4.0    255.255.255.0  192.168.5.2    192.168.5.100      1
```

Similar commands must be executed on Server B. After these steps are completed, any servers on any network will be able to communicate with each other. Best of all, no routing protocol need be used.

Persistent Routes

Using the -p option with the ROUTE command causes the route to be added permanently. Persistent routes are stored in the registry, under the key HKEY_LOCAL_MACHINE\System\CurrentControlSet\Services\Tcpip\Parameters\PersistentRoutes.

If the routes in a network are simple (as in the preceding example) and stable, it is better to avoid using a routing protocol entirely. Adding any new feature to a network adds complexity and increases the chances of failure, and routing protocols are a particularly complex and failure-prone feature. There are several reasons you should abandon static routes and use a routing protocol, however:

◆ If you have three or more routers, manually updating routes will become time-consuming. For every network you add or remove, an update must be made on every single router. This means that the work required for each update increases directly proportionally to the total number of routers on a network. For this reason, static routing does not scale above three or four routers.

◆ If you often add or remove subnets from your networks, you will benefit from using a routing protocol. When using a routing protocol, simply add or remove the route from the routers directly attached to the network. These routers will automatically communicate the change to the other routers in the network, substantially reducing the amount of time the administrator must spend.

◆ If redundant paths exist in your network, static routes lack the intelligence to reroute traffic. Redundant paths are a very good thing, allowing interconnectivity to continue in the event a single router dies. Because static routes are hard-coded and inflexible, NT servers will not attempt to forward traffic to another gateway if a network fails. Additionally, there is no mechanism for communicating failures of network links to routers that are not directly connected.

RIP v1

Originally designed for Xerox under the name of GWINFO, the first variation of Routing Information Protocol (RIP) began to be used with TCP/IP in 1982 when it was included with BSD UNIX under the name "routed" (route-dee). As RIP evolved, it became popular because of its compatibility and accessibility, and it is still being used in many networks today. The RIP protocol in use today is defined in RFC 1058, though it was in wide use prior to the writing of the RFC in June 1988. The RFC was written to standardize a protocol that had developed many incompatible variations. A Web link is http://ds1.internic.net/rfc/rfc1058.txt.

RIP, compared to other routing protocols, is very easy to configure and maintain. This has caused it to become a very popular routing protocol on PC-based networks, many of which are primarily Microsoft Windows–based. This makes it a logical choice of routing protocols for Windows NT Server to support, which it has done since version 3.51.

Versions of RIP have been ported to work with AppleTalk and Novell IPX/SPX networks as well. Novell's version of RIP is very similar to the original Xerox standards. The AppleTalk port of RIP is called Routing Table Maintenance Protocol (RTMP), which requires many modifications to work properly with the AppleTalk protocol. Only the TCP/IP variation of RIP will be covered in this book.

RIP belongs to a family of routing protocols most commonly referred to as distance-vector algorithms, though this family is also called Bellman-Ford, named after two of its inventors.

RIP V1 ROUTING TABLES

Different routing protocols exchange different types of information. The type of information a routing protocol exchanges determines what will be stored in that router's routing table. RIP exchanges a very limited amount of information compared to more robust routing protocols, exchanging only destination network, next hop, and distance (in number of hops).

As you learned earlier, a router's routing table is first populated with the routes of directly connected networks. Therefore, when you power on a RIP router, it determines which of its network interface cards are active and adds the network to its routing table with itself listed as the next hop and a distance of one. Figure 13-6 shows a RIP router network. Tables 13-2 through 13-6 show their individual routing tables at the time they start up.

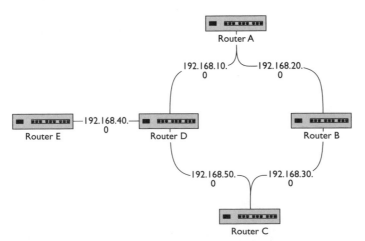

Figure 13-6: An RIP router network, with the routing tables of each router shown in Tables 13-2 through 13-6

TABLE 13-2 ROUTER A'S ROUTING TABLE AT STARTUP

Network	Distance	Next Hop
192.168.10.0	1	Local
192.168.20.0	1	Local

TABLE 13-3 ROUTER B'S ROUTING TABLE AT STARTUP

Network	Distance	Next Hop
192.168.20.0	1	Local
192.168.30.0	1	Local

TABLE 13-4 ROUTER C'S ROUTING TABLE AT STARTUP

Network	Distance	Next Hop
192.168.30.0	1	Local
192.168.50.0	1	Local

TABLE 13-5 ROUTER D'S ROUTING TABLE AT STARTUP

Network	Distance	Next Hop
192.168.10.0	1	Local
192.168.40.0	1	Local
192.168.50.0	1	Local

> ## Convergence
>
> Remember, *convergence* means all the routers on a network agree with each other about the state of the network.

TABLE 13-6 ROUTER E'S ROUTING TABLE AT STARTUP

Network	Distance	Next Hop
192.168.40.0	1	Local

At this point, the router is ready to forward traffic between any directly attached networks, but it will not be able to forward to networks that are not directly attached because it has no knowledge of them. The router will begin to gather this knowledge within the first thirty seconds of its life, however, as it begins to receive routing updates from neighboring routers. Tables 13-7 through 13-11 show the routing tables of the routers illustrated in Figure 13-6 once they have converged.

TABLE 13-7 ROUTER A'S ROUTING TABLE AFTER CONVERGENCE

Network	Distance	Next Hop
192.168.10.0	1	Local
192.168.20.0	1	Local
192.168.30.0	2	Router B
192.168.40.0	2	Router D
192.168.50.0	2	Router D

TABLE 13-8 ROUTER B'S ROUTING TABLE AFTER CONVERGENCE

Network	Distance	Next Hop
192.168.10.0	2	Local
192.168.20.0	1	Router A
192.168.30.0	1	Local
192.168.40.0	3	Router C
192.168.50.0	2	Router C

TABLE 13-9 ROUTER C'S ROUTING TABLE AFTER CONVERGENCE

Network	Distance	Next Hop
192.168.10.0	?	Router B
192.168.20.0	2	Router D
192.168.30.0	1	Local
192.168.40.0	2	Router D
192.168.50.0	1	Local

TABLE 13-10 ROUTER D'S ROUTING TABLE AFTER CONVERGENCE

Network	Distance	Next Hop
192.168.10.0	1	Router A
192.168.20.0	2	Local
192.168.30.0	2	Router C
192.168.40.0	1	Local
192.168.50.0	1	Local

Table 13-11 ROUTER E'S ROUTING TABLE AFTER CONVERGENCE

Network	Distance	Next Hop
192.168.10.0	2	Router D
192.168.20.0	3	Router D
192.168.30.0	3	Router D
192.168.40.0	1	Local
192.168.50.0	2	Router D

In Tables 13-7 through 13-11, the routers have converged. Please note that even though each of the routers has multiple routes to the other networks, the routing table stores only a single entry for each destination. This means that if one of the routers fails, the routing protocol must reconverge before communications can continue through the alternate path.

RIP V1 DATAGRAMS

Routing updates contain every network and the number of hops to that network in the sending router's routing table. Using this information, a router just starting up will know every route that its neighbor router can get to. The RIP process will add these routes, one by one, to its own routing table. Recall that RIP routers keep the number of hops to the destination network within their internal routing tables. In order to calculate the true distance to a network when receiving a routing update, the receiving router must add 1 to the value of every distance given, to take into account that it is one hop farther away than the transmitting router.

These routing updates occur, by default, every thirty seconds. They are broadcast messages and so must rely on the UDP transport-layer protocol. RIP datagrams use the well-known port number 520. In Figure 13-7, two RIP routers and their routing tables are sending out a regular update.

RIP stores any network in its routing table only once. If it finds that two routers have a route to the same network, it will remember only the path with the lowest distance.

These updates are sent within a UDP broadcast packet out every active interface in a router. This transmission is repeated every thirty seconds, whether or not a change has taken place. The data part of this packet contains the information RIP is really interested in: networks and distances.

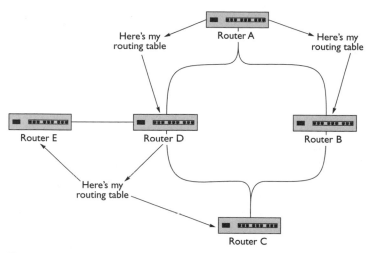

Figure 13-7: The RIP routing protocol uses UDP broadcasts to communicate network topology between routers.

The exact format of this datagram is specified in Section 3.1 of RFC 1058 and summarized in Figure 13-8

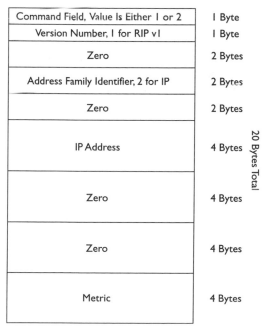

Command Field, Value Is Either 1 or 2	1 Byte
Version Number, 1 for RIP v1	1 Byte
Zero	2 Bytes
Address Family Identifier, 2 for IP	2 Bytes
Zero	2 Bytes
IP Address	4 Bytes
Zero	4 Bytes
Zero	4 Bytes
Metric	4 Bytes

20 Bytes Total

Figure 13-8: The RIP routing protocol specifies a simple packet structure with plenty of room to carry more information.

The first byte contains a RIP command. This byte is set to a value of 1 if it is a request to have the receiving router send all or part of its routing table. A value of 2 in this field indicates a response datagram, either in response to a query or as part of a regular update. Command values greater than 2 are ignored.

The second byte indicates the RIP version number, which ensures that routers of different versions do not confuse each other.

After the version number, the specification pads the datagram with 16 bits (two bytes) of 0s. The two bytes following those zeros, bytes 5 and 6, contain the address type identifier, which allows the RIP routing protocol to exchange information for networks besides simply TCP/IP. However, TCP/IP is the focus of the book and the most common implementation of RIP. The address identifier for TCP/IP is 2.

Two more bytes of all zeros are given. Following this padding, the actual network number is given in the form of an IP address. Conveniently, the address field is four bytes long – the exact length of an IP address.

After the IP address, yet more padding is given. This time, eight bytes are filled with zeros. The last four bytes in the datagram form the metric field. It is interesting that the designers dedicated 32 bits to a metric field yet made the maximum value 15. This means that only the last 4 bits of the 32-bit metric field will ever be used. A metric value of 16 indicates that the distance is infinity – the network is unreachable.

Perhaps more interesting than what the packet contains are the items it *lacks*. Most notably, it lacks a subnet field. In RIP networks, routers must calculate the subnet mask based on the class of the network address – for instance, class A IP addresses receive a 255.0.0.0 subnet mask. This is a serious weakness in any modern network and one of the most significant factors in the demise of RIP v1. By using RIP v1, an organization limits itself to using classful networks – networks that can never be subnetted.

Another notable omission is a more flexible metric field. In RIP, the only metric used is a simple hop count. Hop counts work well in networks on which each link has the same cost and speed, as many LANs do. However, they are insufficient for calculating the most efficient route when multiple links of different speeds or different maximum transfer units exist. Figure 13-9 shows two ways to the same destination, but at different speeds.

The network shown in Figure 13-9 has two paths between router A and the destination network: one path that traverses two 100Mbps links and another that crosses two 10Mbps links. Either route has the same hop count, so RIP will be unable to distinguish the faster route.

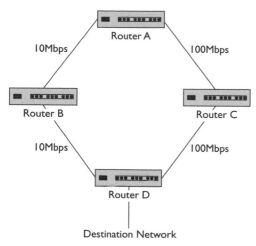

Figure 13-9: There's more than one way to get from here to there; RIP can only determine the shorter path, not the faster path.

RIP v2

The original RIP has not kept up with the times well. In large networks, its broadcast packets generate substantial overhead. Even in small and medium-sized networks, it suffers from problems such as routing loops and slow convergence. Indeed, RFC 1723, which defines RIP v2, begins with a disclaimer stating, "...newer IGP routing protocols are far superior to RIP...." Nonetheless, RIP has the advantage of being widely used and simple to configure. In an effort to keep the benefits of RIP while reducing the problems, RIP v2 was developed. Table 13-12 summarizes the differences between the two versions of the RIP protocol.

TABLE 13-12 DIFFERENCES BETWEEN RIP V1 AND RIP V2

RIP v1	RIP v2
Uses broadcast packets for all communications between routers.	Has the option of using multicast packets (224.0.0.9) for inter-router communications.
Forces classful network allocation.	Allows classless networks to be used by storing the subnet mask in the routing protocol.

Continued

TABLE 13-12 DIFFERENCES BETWEEN RIP V1 AND RIP V2 *(Continued)*

RIP v1	RIP v2
Allows timed updates only.	Timed updates and triggered updates work to decrease convergence delay.
Includes no method for authentication.	Includes simple clear-text password authentication.
All RIP routers automatically communicate with each other.	RIP routers can be placed within different routing domains, creating logically separate routing networks.

RIP V2 DATAGRAMS

The most substantial changes in version 2 of the RIP routing protocol involve making use of all the wasted space in the inter-router datagrams. Most notably, the subnet mask of the networks in the routing table is now communicated, allowing for more efficient use of IP address allocation. Using this feature, CIDR and VLSM can be used with RIP v2 routers.

Remember all of those fields labeled "zero" in the RIP version 1 packet? This feature amounted to a lot of wasted bandwidth in the routing protocol but was created by the designers of the original RIP protocol to make upgrades easier. In the next few paragraphs, I will describe how the designers of RIP v2 used these empty fields to expand the functionality of the protocol while retaining backward compatibility with RIP v1. Figure 13-10 shows the RIP v2 Datagram format.

The first byte of the RIP datagram, the command field, is identical in function and format to the command field in RIP v1.

The second byte of the RIP datagram, the version field, performs the same function but now holds a value of 2. This is a clever way of distinguishing RIP datagrams with the new RIP v2 fields from version 1 datagrams. On a network with a mix of both RIP v1 and RIP v2 routers, RIP v1 routers that comply with the standard will receive datagrams from RIP v2 routers that have been configured to use broadcast messages instead of multicast messages. Believe it or not, RIP v1 routers will correctly process the RIP v2 broadcast packets, ignoring the fields that are new in version 2 of the standard.

The third and fourth bytes of the RIP v2 datagram are described as the *routing domain*. This is a new field introduced in this version of RIP. It allows multiple, logical RIP routing clouds to coexist on the same physical network. This field is normally set to the default value of zero, and when it is not modified, all routers will talk with all other routers. However, if a group of routers should ignore routing updates from another group of routers, distinguish these groups by changing the routing domain number to something other than zero. Unfortunately, there is no way to configure this value from the RRAS Admin utility, and so the field will always contain zero for routes originating from a Windows NT server.

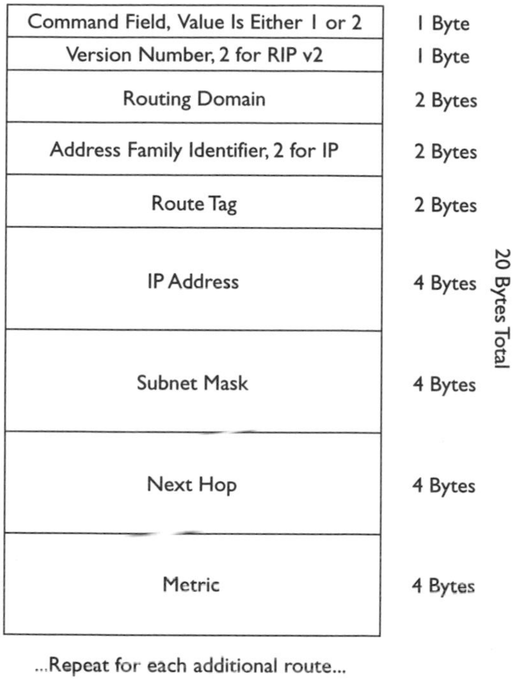

Command Field, Value Is Either 1 or 2	1 Byte
Version Number, 2 for RIP v2	1 Byte
Routing Domain	2 Bytes
Address Family Identifier, 2 for IP	2 Bytes
Route Tag	2 Bytes
IP Address	4 Bytes
Subnet Mask	4 Bytes
Next Hop	4 Bytes
Metric	4 Bytes

20 Bytes Total

...Repeat for each additional route...

Figure 13-10: RIP v2 packets use a similar structure to that in RIP v1, but they make use of the previously unused fields.

The fifth and sixth bytes of the RIP datagram are still the *address family identifier*. A new feature utilizes this field, however. When the value of this field is set to 0xFFFF, it signifies that the next sixteen bytes of the datagram contain authentication information. More information on the authentication field can be found in the "RIP v2 Authentication" section that follows.

The seventh and eighth bytes now contain the route tag field. In most cases, this field will contain zero; however, the intention is to allow RIP to carry information inherited from exterior gateway protocols. For example, if a route is inherited from BGP with an autonomous system number, the AS number will be placed into the route tag field and readvertised with that value. Each RIP v2 router that receives a datagram with a value in the route tag field is required to store that value and retransmit it but will probably never perform any processing on it. The Routing and Remote Access Service in Windows NT does not currently support any exterior gateway protocols, and so RRAS should never insert a value into this field automatically. However, it can be configured on a per-interface basis from the RIP Configuration dialog box. Simply select the General tab and enter a value for the field labeled Tag for Routes Advertised on This Interface. The maximum value for this field is 32,767 – the RRAS interface enforces this. However, there is no reference in the RFC to the first bit being set to zero or the field having a maximum value, so I can only assume that this value restriction is a bug in Microsoft's implementation of the graphical user interface.

Bytes 9 through 12 still carry a 32-bit IP address, as they did in the first version of RIP. However, the following field adds more usefulness to this field.

Perhaps the most significant new feature of RIP v2 is the addition of the subnet Mask field in bytes 13 through 16. These carry a standard 32-bit subnet mask, used to designate the network address portion of the IP address given in the previous field. Instead of forcing routers to make assumptions about the subnet mask when receiving routes via RIP v1, the subnet mask field in RIP v2 allows routers to route to subnetted and supernetted IP networks.

Bytes 17 through 20 hold the value for yet another new field. This field, the next hop field, contains the IP address of the gateway to use to reach the destination network listed in the IP address field. It may seem counterintuitive for a router to advertise a route to a network but not claim itself as the next hop – and in most cases, this field will not be used. However, it is useful when a network contains routers relying on multiple routing protocols. For example, if the best next hop for a network is through a router than speaks only OSPF, a RIP router will never discover that route. This field allows a single router on a network segment to advertise that OSPF router as the next hop and avoids the need to run multiple protocols on a single router.

Bytes 21 through 24 perform the same function they did in RIP v1, storing the distance to the network described in the IP address field.

RIP V2 AUTHENTICATION

When the address family identifier field in the RIP v2 datagram is set to a value of 0xFFF, the following sixteen bytes contain authentication information that can be used to reduce the chance of a malicious person spoofing RIP packets and disturbing the router's routing table. It is very similar to the community name in the SNMP protocol standard – it requires the password be transmitted in clear text but reduces the chances of a successful attack from someone on a different network segment. This is particularly valuable for Internet service providers that are prone to attacks from the public Internet.

To enable this authentication, open the Routing and RAS Admin utility and select RIP for Internet Protocol under the IP Routing folder. Right-click on the interface card you wish to use authentication with, and select Configure Interface.

To enable authentication on this interface, select the check box labeled Enable Authentication and fill in a password in the text box. This password is going to be transmitted in clear text across the network in a broadcast or multicast packet, so do not use a password that is used elsewhere in your organization.

Once you fill in a password and click OK, the RIP routing process on the server will begin to include authentication information on every packet that is sent from that interface. This creates additional overhead – each packet transmitted with authentication enabled will be twenty bytes longer than normal. It is an excellent idea to use authentication, but you must implement it consistently across the entire network — routers with different passwords cannot communicate with each other.

Keep in mind that the password fits into the same data structure as RIP routes do in the RIP datagrams. Because 16 bytes are set aside to carry the information for each route in RIP, the maximum length of this password is 16 characters.

One caveat: If you select the option RIP Version 1 Broadcast as the protocol for outgoing packets, the security information will not be included in the outgoing packets. This is due to the limitation of the RIP v1 protocol itself — including authentication information not complying with the standard. RIP will continue to listen for the password for all incoming updates, however.

RIP V2 ROUTING TABLES

RIP v2 routing tables carry the same information as RIP v1 routing tables but include the additional information that is carried within the datagrams. RIP v1 routing tables already included the subnet mask, but the subnet mask is now based on information carried within the datagram. RIP v2 must propagate the route tag information for each route that it stores, and for most router implementations this is the only new field in the routing table.

RIP V2 MULTICASTING

At some point, everyone learned the difference between class A, B, and C networks in the IP addressing scheme. Many people have not had the opportunity to work with class D networks, though, which start at 224.0.0.0 and end at 239.255.255.255. These networks are used to communicate with several different computers at the same time, similar to the way broadcasts work. In fact, the layer-2 address (the MAC address) used with multicasts is the layer-2 broadcast address (FF-FF-FF-FF-FF-FF). Multicast datagrams offer an advantage over broadcast datagrams: They require less processing by uninterested hosts within the same broadcast domain. In other words, Windows NT systems on a network with a RIP v2 router will receive the multicast datagrams because their network cards are listening for frames with the broadcast MAC address. However, they will spend less time processing the packets, because the IP address will not match a used IP address on that host. In Network Monitor, these IGMP packets will appear with a destination IP address of 224.0.0.9.

The end result is that multicast packets cause less disturbance on a network segment than broadcast packets do. They will *not* reduce the bandwidth utilization on a network segment, however. Even switched networks will transmit the packets to each host — the layer-2 address is still the broadcast address. The broadcast messages that RIP v1 uses to exchange routing tables with neighbors is one of the primary disadvantages of that version of RIP. RIP v2 overcomes this weakness, to some extent, by offering the option of using multicast packets instead.

To maintain compliance with the RFC standard, the Routing and Remote Access Service in Windows NT Server gives the network administrator the option of transmitting multicast RIP v2 packets, broadcast RIP v2 packets, or broadcast RIP v1 packets for backward compatibility. Additionally, each NT Server–based router can listen to any of these packets from its neighbors. Determining which are transmitted and which are listened for is easily configured through the graphical user interface. Figure 13-11 shows the dialog box for RIP configuration.

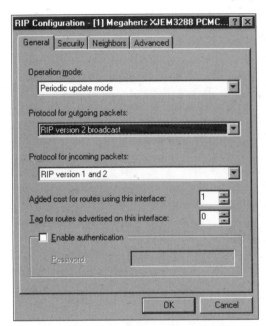

Figure 13-11: This dialog box allows the RIP v2
communication mechanism to be specified.

RIP OPTIONS

The RRAS implementation of RIP includes many optional configurations that alter the behavior of RIP. Each of these options are enabled on an interface-by-interface basis by right-clicking on an interface and selecting Configure Interface when the RIP for Internet Protocol item is selected in the left pane of the RRAS Admin utility. This section describes each of these options and the effects of enabling or disabling each.

ENABLE SPLIT-HORIZON PROCESSING   Just in case the name "split-horizon processing" does not instantly describe to you the meaning of this configuration parameter, I will now describe it. The RIP routing protocol is so prone to routing loops, it can develop a loop when only two routers are involved! Consider a simple network with two routers and three networks. Router A is connected to Networks 1 and 2, and Router B is connected to Networks 2 and 3. A network is shown in Figure 13-12. The routing tables are shown in Tables 13-13 and 13-14.

Figure 13-12: This network illustrates how split-horizon processing can avoid routing loops.

TABLE 13-13 ROUTER A'S ROUTING TABLES

Network	Metric
1	1
2	1
3	2

TABLE 13-14 ROUTER B'S ROUTING TABLES

Network	Metric
1	2
2	1
3	1

As you can see from the routing tables, the routing protocol is in a converged state. An unexpected event causes Network 1 to fail, and Router A removes it from the routing table. The next time Router B transmits a routing update, it will notify Router A that it has a path to Network 1 with a metric of 2. Router A will add this route to its routing table, assuming the path is going through another router. As you can see, a simple routing loop has occurred between Router A and Router B, and any packets destined for Network 1 will bounce between the two routers until the TTL on the packet expires.

Split horizon is a mechanism created to reduce or eliminate the possibility of two-node routing loops. Split horizon forbids a router from advertising a route to a network through the same interface that it learned it. To clarify this, consider the preceding scenario with split horizon enabled on both routers. When Router A removes Network 1 from its routing table, Router B will send an advertisement that includes routes to Network 2 and Network 3 – but it will not advertise the route to Network 1 because of the split-horizon rule: A route cannot be advertised on the same connection from which it was learned.

RRAS enables this option by default, and that is the best configuration for the vast majority of circumstances.

ENABLE POISON-REVERSE PROCESSING   This option forces routers to include failed networks in routing updates with a distance of 16. Without poison-reverse processing enabled, the failed network simply disappears from future updates. Enabling this option reduces the chances of routing loops.

RRAS enables this option by default, and that is the best configuration for most networks. The option is available only when split horizon is also enabled.

ENABLE TRIGGERED UPDATES   One of the greatest disadvantages of the RIP routing protocol is the slow time to convergence. The convergence time is slow because, in most RIP implementations, updates are sent only every thirty seconds. Therefore, if a change is made to the state of a network (such as taking a network interface on the router offline), it may be as long as thirty seconds before the neighboring routers will hear about the change. Then, the neighboring routers will wait as long as thirty seconds before readvertising their routing table with the updated information. In a large network, the delay between broadcasts adds up to a significant amount of time, especially considering the fact that packets may not reach their intended destination until the network converges.

To overcome this delay, RRAS allows for triggered updates. With this option enabled, an update is broadcast to neighboring routers as soon as a network is added or dropped or a metric value is changed. This update is smaller than the normal RIP packets because it includes only the routes that have changed. In a network of routers with triggered updates enabled, changes can propagate much quicker than is otherwise possible and time to convergence is reduced substantially.

The default configuration of RRAS sets the value Minimum Seconds between Triggered Updates to five. This stops a router from consuming a great deal of bandwidth transmitting changes, and it works to limit the number of packets required if several changes are made at one time. This value can be modified from the RIP for Internet Protocol Configuration dialog box.

By default, RRAS enables this option. This setting is suitable to most networks. You may wish to disable this option if your NT-based router will be interoperating with routers that do not support triggered updates – the benefits are reduced when all routers do not propagate the information immediately.

SEND CLEAN-UP UPDATES WHEN STOPPING   This option causes the RIP process within RRAS to transmit a routing update when the routing process is stopped on an interface. All routes are listed in the update with a distance of 16, the equivalent of infinity in the RIP routing protocol. Ideally, another router would be connected to the same networks and would become the most preferable route the next time it transmitted its routing updates.

The on-line help provided with RRAS says this metric is set to 15, which is incorrect. Check it with Network Monitor if you don't believe me!

It is interesting to note that this option does not work as expected when using RIP v2 broadcast or multicast announcements. It does work when using RIP v1 broadcasts, but not all routes are announced with a distance of 16 – some routes are announced with the normal distance. Overall, this option seems to behave unpredictably and I recommend turning it off.

All routing protocols will transmit updates to neighboring routers specifying their routes as being unavailable. This speeds the rerouting of traffic in networks that have some level of redundancy built in. You will not find any value in this option if your network is not redundant, but it does not create a significant amount of network traffic, so it is best to simply leave it enabled.

By default, RRAS enables this option. I recommend disabling this option because of the unpredictable results I have experienced. There is no advantage to enabling it if there is not redundancy in your network. If there is redundancy, it may take a little longer for the network to reconverge after stopping an NT-based router, but it will be more reliable.

OVERRIDE NON-RIP ROUTES WITH RIP-LEARNT ROUTES   This option defines the priority of routes learned through the RIP routing protocol. Consider the situation where multiple routing protocols are running on a network and the NT Server–based router has both OSPF and RIP running. If a route to the network 192.168.20.0/24 is learned through OSPF, that route will, by default, be used. If a route to the same network is learned through the RIP routing protocol, that route will be retained but the next hop listed will not be used to forward traffic – the route learned by OSPF will take precedence. With this option enabled, RIP routes always override OSPF-learned routes.

By default, this option is not enabled in RRAS. Enable it if RIP is more prevalent on your network than OSPF.

PROCESS HOST ROUTES IN PACKETS RECEIVED   *Host routes* are routes to a specific IP address rather than more conventional routes to a network. The difference is that host routes have a 32-bit subnet mask – every bit in their IP address is significant to routing. A few (very few) organizations use host routes to allow employees with laptops to plug into any network within the organization and receive traffic destined for their specific IP address.

Enable this option if you are one of the very few organizations that allow an employee to use the same IP address regardless of the network that employee is currently plugged into. You may also enable this option if you wish to significantly increase a malicious hacker's opportunities to spoof traffic on your network.

Processing host routes increases the opportunity to spoof traffic because traffic destined for the IP address 192.168.20.20 is not necessarily forwarded to the network 192.168.20.0/24. Because of this, spoofing can be accomplished on a different physical network than the host being spoofed – a task normally very difficult to accomplish.

By default, this option is not enabled in RRAS. You will want to leave it that way.

INCLUDE HOST ROUTES IN PACKETS SENT   Enabling this option is just as dangerous as enabling the option directly above it – it facilitates spoofing but allows traffic to be routed to an individual IP address regardless of the physical network it is plugged into.

By default, this option is not enabled in RRAS. In almost every circumstance, you should leave it disabled.

PROCESS DEFAULT ROUTES IN PACKETS RECEIVED   To review, a default route is a route used when no other route is given to a network. Default routes have a zero-bit subnet mask. Default routes are normally not propagated with RIP and can cause undesired results if they are transmitted.

By default, this option is not enabled in RRAS. This setting is suitable for most networks.

INCLUDE DEFAULT ROUTES IN PACKETS SENT   If you have a default route that you need RIP to propagate through your network, enable this option. Chances are extremely good that you will never need to use it, however, so it is best to leave it disabled.

By default, this option is not enabled in RRAS.

OSPF

OSPF (Open Shortest Path First) is a different type of routing protocol from RIP (see Table 13-15). OSPF is a member of a family of routing protocols called *link-state routing protocols*. Link-state routing protocols differ from distance-vector routing protocols like RIP in that link-state routers communicate with each other using directed (TCP) packets to each router with a single area. This is more efficient than broadcast and multicast packets because it does not cause any interruption on other listening hosts within the same broadcast domain. Additionally, when used with switched networks, directed packets between routers avoid congesting the network at all for uninterested hosts because the switch is intelligent enough not to forward these frames to uninterested hosts.

Because link-state routing protocols such as OSPF communicate with every router within their area, they are able to create a map of the entire network. Using this map, they can make intelligent decisions about routes and avoid many of the problems typical of distance-vector protocols, including routing loops and count to infinity. With intelligence comes processor overhead, which leads to one of the primary disadvantages of OSPF: The shortest routes to each network must be recomputed each and every time there is a change in the network topology. The larger an area gets, the greater the processing overhead. This processing overhead can be significant in hardware-based routers, which tend to have minimal processing power. Windows NT servers using Routing and Remote Access Service will generally have more processing power than they can use, and so the overhead created by recomputing the Open Shortest Path First algorithm may never have a significant effect, even in a large network.

I am going to avoid going into a deep description of the details of the way the shortest path first algorithm computes the most efficient path on a network, but those more interested should read Radia Perlman's book *Interconnections: Bridges and Routers* (New York: Addison-Wesley, 1992).

HISTORY

OSPF is a member of a family of routing protocols called link-state routing protocols. These date back to the ARPANET, the precursor to the modern Internet. Since then, link-state routing protocols have gone through many, many iterations. While a great deal can be learned by studying the evolution of technical standards, I will spare you the rest of the history and jump into the good stuff. For those of you interested in a detailed history of link-state routing protocols, seek out section 1.3 of RFC 2178.

The current implementation of the OSPF routing protocol is defined by RFC 1583.

TABLE 13-15 SUMMARY OF DIFFERENCES BETWEEN RIP AND OSPF

RIP	OSPF
Communicates via broadcast or multicast	Communicates via multicast
Flat structure	Hierarchical structure
Communicates with neighboring routers	Communicates with all routers within the same area
Simple to configure	Complex to configure
High network overhead, low processor overhead	High processor overhead, low network overhead
High time to convergence	Low time to convergence

OSPF BACKGROUND

Let's start by discussing a few new vocabulary terms. The OSPF routing protocol introduces several new terms because it has a hierarchical architecture. This is in stark contrast to RIP's flat structure. To illustrate the difference, consider RIP's routing tables. If a network contains 1,000 networks and all routers use the RIP routing protocol, each router on the network must contain 1,000 rows in its routing table. RIP has no ability to define a backbone network or to divide networks into different areas. To make matters worse, it cannot summarize routes, so there is no way to reduce the size of the routing table.

THE FIRST LAYER OF HIERARCHY: AREAS   OSPF has a better way: Each router belongs to a specific *area*. An area is a logical grouping of routers that exchange routing information and are managed by the same group of people. By dividing an enterprise network into areas, you reduce the size of the routing table in each router. For example, consider an enterprise network with 200 networks divided between four different remote sites. With RIP, each router would need to store information in its routing table about all 200 networks. With OSPF, each remote site can be placed within its own area. Additionally, a special area called the *backbone* will be defined.

The area number is a 32-bit number that must be unique within an autonomous system. Because the area number is 32 bits, it is common to write the area number in IP format. For example, the backbone area is always area 0. When using the IP format convention, this is written as 0.0.0.0. Understanding this convention is important because Microsoft insists on using it in all of its documentation for RRAS. Figure 13-13 shows areas in an OSPF-based network.

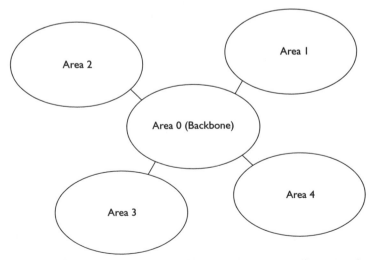

Figure 13-13: Areas are an OSPF concept used to create a hierarchy of groups of routers.

At each point where an area connects to the backbone area, one or more routers perform the routing. These routers are called ABRs (area border routers). An ABR contains the routing information for the area of which it is a member — referring to the preceding figure, note that Router B contains all the routing information for area 2. However, it is also a member of area 0, the backbone area. Because of its membership in both areas, it is able to provide routing between the two areas. Further, because area 0 is connected to all other areas, Router B has the capability to route to each and every area within the enterprise network.

At first glance, this would seem only to add complexity. In theory, each router must still know the path to every other network in the enterprise network. However, the ABRs have the capability of *route summarization*. With route summarization, Router B injects a single route into area 0 — 10.2.0.0. This is pretty good compression, allowing one route to be exchanged instead of the 50 contained in area 2. And because each ABR performs route summarization for its respective area, area 0 contains only five routes — one route for each of the areas.

The ABRs can summarize these five routes even further when communicating with the routers within their own networks. Because the ABR is the only connection to the rest of the enterprise network, each ABR can inject a default route and list itself as the default router. The default route contains a zero-bit subnet mask and can be notated as 0.0.0.0/0.

Route summarization has another advantage — it reduces the number of recomputations that are required. To review, each router must recalculate its link-state database every time a network is added or removed within its area. If the ABRs did not summarize the routes they inject into the backbone, each backbone router would have to recalculate its link-state database if a network were added to any of the areas. However, if a route is added that is included in the summarization, no recalculation must be done. For example, if the network 10.2.100.0/24 is added to area 2, the summarized route 10.2.0.0/16 is still valid. The link-state database must be recomputed if a new network is added to an area that does not fit within the existing summarization. For example, if the network 10.10.0.0/16 were added to area 2, that additional route would need to be injected into area 0 and each ABR would need to recalculate its link-state database.

THE SECOND LAYER OF HIERARCHY: AUTONOMOUS SYSTEMS   Areas are used within enterprise networks to reduce the size of each router's link-state database. However, OSPF can be used on global networks as well. Another layer of hierarchy is needed, and this layer is provided by the AS (autonomous system) number. The AS is shared by an entire enterprise and is globally unique. AS numbers are divvied out by the Internet Assigned Numbers Authority (IANA).

OSPF DATAGRAMS

In this section, you will learn to appreciate RIP's simplicity. OSPF is a very flexible protocol, but complexity and flexibility go hand in hand. I will describe the different methods OSPF uses to communicate between routers and the different options available within the Routing and Remote Access Service Admin utility.

BROADCAST NETWORKS   A broadcast network is the type of network most are familiar with: When a packet is transmitted, that same physical packet has the ability to be received by every host on the same subnet. This is determined by layer 2 of the OSI model – it is entirely independent of network-layer protocols such as IP. If you are using Ethernet, Token-Ring, or FDDI topologies, you are using a broadcast network.

OSPF has separate protocols for broadcast and nonbroadcast networks. On broadcast networks, broadcast messages are used to allow routers to locate each other. This protocol is appropriately named the Hello protocol.

NONBROADCAST NETWORKS   The Hello protocol cannot discover neighboring routers using broadcasts on many popular networks, such as X.25 and many implementations of frame relay and ATM. Therefore, on these nonbroadcast networks, OSPF must be manually configured with the address of each neighboring router. Once it is configured, all packets that are normally broadcast or multicast are sent to neighboring routers individually.

DETERMINING ROUTES THROUGH A NETWORK

As discussed earlier, OSPF uses a different algorithm than RIP for computing the most efficient path through a network. Further, OSPF bases these route computations on its *link-state database*. This link-state database contains a list of every router and each router's directly connected networks. Using this information, OSPF is able to avoid a pitfall of RIP: If a router fails in a RIP network, an incorrect path may be calculated that may result in a routing loop. With OSPF, a router knows exactly what connections are dropped when any given router fails and can immediately calculate the most efficient working path.

Because OSPF keeps track of routers as well as networks, it must have a way to identify each router uniquely. IP addresses are not suitable because each router will have at least two IP addresses, perhaps more. The unique identifier a router uses to identify itself within an autonomous system is a 32-bit number called the router ID. The fact that the number is 32-bits, the same length as an IP address, allows the convenient convention of using the lowest IP address assigned to a router as its router ID. However, this is not required – any 32-bit number can be assigned.

A bug in the current implementation of RRAS does not allow the router ID 0.0.0.0 to be used.

In order to calculate the shortest path to each network within the area, each router running the OSPF routing protocol builds a map of the network. This map takes the form of a tree, with the router itself as the root. Using this tree, the shortest path first algorithm computes the shortest path possible through the routers.

NT's Role As a Router

NT Server 4.0 with the Routing and Remote Access Service add-on is not right for the majority of routing environments. Nonetheless, it does fit in several specific circumstances.

Small, Remote Offices with an Existing Windows NT Network

The Routing and Remote Access Service includes a Dial-On-Demand Routing (DDR) feature. Combined with the Point-to-Point Tunneling Protocol (PPTP), this means that Windows NT can allow remote offices with an existing Windows NT infrastructure full routed connectivity to a central office for nothing more than the cost of a modem, an analog phone line, and an ISP account.

In the simplest variation of this configuration, one Windows NT DDR server dials directly to another Windows NT server running RAS. Do not be misled into thinking that Windows NT is the only way to do this: Hardware-based routers such as the Cisco 2524 have provided this functionality for quite some time. Indeed, networks that require highly available remote connections are probably *not* well suited to Windows NT because the software is still very young — when reliability is a requirement, go with the option that has proven the test of time (*hint: This is not Windows NT DDR*). Also, do not be lured into using Windows NT in this configuration as a cost-saving method; even a small amount of downtime can more than make up for the saved costs. Indeed, losing a remote dial-in server can be a painful experience, especially if the administrators of the server are at the remote site.

Now that we are past the disclaimers, I will describe exactly how to do this and have it work as reliably as possible. The equipment you will need:

♦ **Two modems:** One at either end of the desired remote connection. For best results, purchase two of the exact same modem.

♦ **Two analog phone lines:** To be used by the two modems just described

♦ **Two Windows NT servers, version 4.0:** Presumably, these are part of an existing infrastructure at both sites. This configuration only makes sense costwise if both servers are used for other tasks as well.

♦ **The Routing and Remote Access Service add-on for Windows NT Server:** A free download from Microsoft

Connect each modem to a Windows NT server at either site, and plug them into the phone lines. Install RRAS on both servers, and configure them appropriately. Easy, eh? The difficult part is the "configure them appropriately."

Windows NT Dial-on-Demand Routing As a Backup Circuit

You'll find no check box in the graphical user interface of Windows NT that says "Use DDR as a Backup." Because of the flexibility built into routing protocols and the transparent way Windows NT deals with Demand Dial Routing, however, it is very possible. Consider the following scenario:

A remote office connects to the central office via a dedicated T1 circuit. This T1 circuit is used for all data transfers between the remote office and the central office. Both the central office and the remote office use OSPF as their routing protocol and Windows NT as their network operating system.

A family near the remote office decides to put a swimming pool into their back-yard. In the process, they break through a few wires that were running beneath their yard. One of the many circuits aggregated onto these wires is the T1 line connecting our sample remote office with the central office.

Without a backup circuit, all data communications between the two sites are lost until the telephone company can repair the circuit. It would be nice if we could make use of Windows NT Demand Dial Routing to automatically connect to the central office via an ISDN circuit and begin exchanging data. This network configuration is illustrated in Figure 13-14. The best scenario would have this replacement happen completely transparently to the end users. Well, transparent except for the fact that 1.54Mbps of data throughput will be replaced with 128Kbps of bandwidth. Still, 128Kbps is better than nothing.

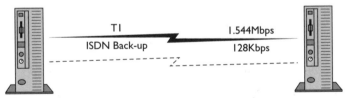

Figure 13-14: Demand Dial Routing allows an ISDN circuit to act as a backup to a leased line.

The whole idea of routing protocols is to allow the routers to redirect traffic should a network connection or a router fail. DDR acts as a network link between two routers, transparently dialing the remote side of the connection and forwarding traffic as needed. This transparency allows us to use a dial-up link as a backup WAN circuit.

We have already covered configuring a Demand Dial Routing circuit, but how do you configure a circuit without forcing traffic across the link when there is a better path? The answer lies in routing protocols and the metrics they use to pick the shortest, fastest path between two points. In RIP, this metric is normally a very simple hop count. It is considered a hop count because normally each link has a distance of 1. In order to make a link extremely unfavorable except when the primary link has failed, increase the distance associated with the link to a number greater than 1. Increasing the distance to 2 is probably not enough: The backup ISDN link would still be chosen over the primary T1 link by routers that were one hop closer to the NT server controlling the ISDN link than to the router connecting the T1 circuit. The exact distance chosen for a backup circuit needs to be chosen on a network-by-network basis; it must be high enough that no router in the network will choose the backup circuit over the T1 circuit, yet low enough to ensure that the total distance between any two points in the remote and central office will never be greater than 15.

Windows NT As a Router Between Two Network Segments

A classic scenario for a Windows NT router has been to segment a single network into two separate networks. There is no reason that this needs to be limited to two segments: Depending on the hardware architecture, a Windows NT server can support as many as half a dozen interface cards and route between all of them. This can improve a network environment in a couple of ways:

◆ **Reduce the broadcast domain:** Windows-based networks typically have a great deal of broadcast traffic, and a router stops this traffic from crossing one segment onto the other. This benefit is often outweighed by the inconvenience of having to use a WINS server and/or a DHCP relay agent to overcome the limitation.

◆ **Improve security:** Sniffers that place the hosts network card into promiscuous mode are common. Microsoft's SMS (Systems Management Server) comes with a version of Network Monitor that allows the host it is installed in to view all traffic on that network segment. When a network is divided into two network segments with a router, traffic can only be sniffed if it is transmitted on the same segment.

This architecture has been supported in Windows NT since version 3.5; one need only check the Enable IP Forwarding check box in the TCP/IP Properties dialog box. This option is still available in Windows NT Server 4.0. To configure an NT server as a router between segments, follow these steps:

1. Configure the NT server with two or more network cards, one connecting to each network you wish to route between.

2. Verify connectivity and assigned IP addresses by PINGing hosts on each of the networks.

3. From the TCP/IP Properties dialog box, select Enable IP Forwarding. Reboot the server.

4. Set the default gateway on all hosts to the IP address of the NT server's local network interface card. Reboot each of the clients.

As you can see, it has always been simple to configure an NT Server as a router, directly out of the box. With the Routing and Remote Access Service add-on to NT Server 4.0, more functionality is available even for this simple scenario.

The most notable new feature is the addition of robust IP filtering capabilities. Using IP filtering, the NT server can be configured to allow only certain types of traffic to cross between network segments. Situations where this may come in handy are described in the sections that follow.

CONFIGURING A WEB SERVER ON A SEPARATE SEGMENT, WITH ONLY TRAFFIC DESTINED FOR THE HTTP AND FTP SERVICES ALLOWED THROUGH

This is a simple exercise in configuring TCP port filters combined with destination IP filtering. In this example, the IP network address of the client network is `192.168.20.0/24`. The IP network address of the Web server is `192.168.10.0/24`. To filter traffic for specific applications, you must know the TCP or UDP port number that the application uses. For HTTP traffic, TCP port 80 is used. For FTP traffic, TCP ports 20 and 21 are used.

CONFIGURING AN E-MAIL SERVER ON A SEPARATE SEGMENT, WITH ONLY TRAFFIC DESTINED FOR THE POP AND SMTP SERVICES ALLOWED THROUGH

This scenario is very similar to the previous scenario, except that a different application's traffic will be allowed through. POP uses TCP port 110; SMTP uses TCP port 25.

Windows NT As a Router in a Large, Existing Network

Large organizations typically find something that works well for them and stick with it. Indeed, this is one of the greatest advantages of a large company: They already have tried-and-true solutions to problems such as routing. NT's RRAS has not been around long enough to be widely implemented in any large organization, and so it seems a bit odd that any company of appreciable size would dedicate the time and effort required to implement routing based on RRAS. Nonetheless, I have talked to people who are implementing NT-based routers alongside hardware-based routers from Bay Networks and Cisco.

Those implementing NT-based routers into existing networks need to be aware of a couple of potential problem areas:

◆ You are going to have to use a routing protocol. If you want people on the enterprise network to be able to find your new subnet, you are going to have to configure RIP or OSPF to communicate with the existing router infrastructure. The very fact that routing protocols implemented by different vendors will have to interoperate should make you nervous. The good news is that Bay Networks had a significant hand in Microsoft's implementation of OSPF, so communication with routers manufactured by Bay Networks should work fairly well. However, different generations of Cisco's implementation of OSPF have always had problems talking to routers from other manufacturers, so whether these routers will work with the NT router is something only time can tell.

◆ Reliability will be substantially lower than for the hardware-based routers on the same networks. NT has always been a reliable operating system, but many hardware routers run for years at a time without missing a packet. NT simply cannot match that level of reliability. Further, many hardware-based routers have hot-swappable network interface cards, a feature very few NT-based servers have implemented. Even if you are using servers like the Compaq 6500 that have hot-swappable PCI cards, the RRAS software component will not handle the change correctly. Figure 13-15 shows hardware-based routers and Windows NT servers configured as routers.

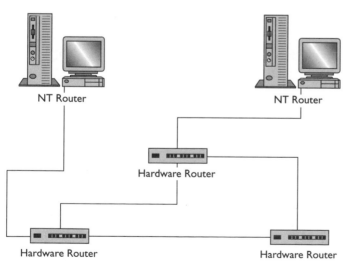

Figure 13-15: Windows NT servers can work side by side with hardware routers.

Protocols Supported

Out of the box, Windows NT Server supports static routing, RIP v1, RIP v2, and the DHCP relay service. The RRAS package supplements this by adding the popular OSPF routing protocol.

Virtual Private Networking

VPN, or virtual private networking, allows two networks to connect securely across another network. Figure 13-16 shows a VPN connection over the Internet. Microsoft also refers to this service as Server-to-Server Point-to-Point Tunneling Protocol. A common scenario is to connect two remote offices of an organization across the Internet. In this way, both networks could connect as if they had a dedicated WAN circuit but with substantially reduced cost.

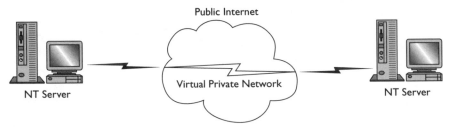

Figure 13-16: A virtual private network allows the exchange of private data across a public network.

This is an exciting prospect to many small companies: full WAN network connectivity, for only the price of an analog phone line and an ISP dial-up account! The cost is just right, being free. (Free is substantially less than other VPN alternatives, such as the Cisco Private Internet Exchange, which costs well into five figures). Indeed, this is the market Microsoft was hoping to capture: small businesses with complicated network demands. For these customers, the ability to use existing NT servers for WAN connectivity adds a great deal of value to the cost of Windows NT.

The primary market for this is limited to small networks because the maximum bandwidth is still very low: VPN relies on RAS and as such must use analog lines or ISDN. Even with support for MPPP (Multilink Point-to-Point Protocol), bandwidth is limited to less than half a megabit per second. A more typical scenario is a single dial-up link, with throughput varying depending on the type of traffic, but generally less than 30Kbps.

To expand this bandwidth, Microsoft offers compression of data over the link with a service called Microsoft Point-to-Point Compression (MPPC). They advertise compression ratios up to 4.1, but take this with a grain of salt when computing expected bandwidth. Keep in mind that the PPTP protocol adds a significant amount of overhead to all traffic transferred: It actually adds an entire layer of headers to each packet. Also, modern analog modems make thorough use of compression already and are less able to support traffic that has been previously compressed. Therefore, MPPC can be used to decrease the amount of data that must be sent, but this advantage is limited because it must be sent at a slower rate. Further, the host server must dedicate CPU cycles to compressing and decompressing the data before transmitting it.

This limited bandwidth still allows a great deal of traffic to operate successfully: e-mail, shared intranet servers, remote network management, and Telnet traffic all require very little bandwidth to function properly. Video conferencing is a definite *no*, however.

Performance Considerations

Performance has greatly increased with the newest generation of routing software from Microsoft. NT Server should never be considered as a high-end backbone router, but it may be appropriate for some small workgroups, and Microsoft claims to switch as many as 30,000 packets per second.

Nobody will choose to use an NT server over a dedicated router based on switching speed, however. Dedicated, hardware-based routers have the edge on efficiency because their architecture is designed specifically for that type of processing.

Security Considerations

Anytime you send something over a public network, you take a measured security risk. The Internet is particularly interesting from a security perspective, because the route your traffic takes between any two hosts may vary from time to time. When choosing a provider to carry virtual private network traffic, consider several factors:

1. Will all traffic stay on a single provider's network?

   Keeping traffic within a single provider's network helps to reduce the chance of someone sniffing the traffic. This is independent of how the traffic is encrypted; much can be learned from traffic patterns without decrypting anything.

2. Where does traffic travel before it is encrypted?

3. How strong is my encryption?

No matter how strong your encryption is, several things cannot be encrypted due to the nature of IP traffic. Traffic must still have the IP header information to traverse the Internet, so encryption normally takes place starting at the transport level: namely, all information carried within the IP header. By examining the headers of packets that are transmitted between two ends of a virtual private network, one can learn the flow characteristics of the traffic. From this, one can learn when the organizations are most active, when people in the organization are working late, and what time of the day backups take place. Someone sniffing the traffic can even tell something about the traffic from the lengths of the packets sent: Even encrypted Web requests will be given away by the asymmetric nature of the traffic — short requests, long responses. These types of analysis are so simple to do that they may very well show up in a billing statement from your ISP! Figure 13-17 shows encryption at the transport level and everything above, but not the IP layer.

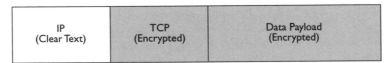

Figure 13-17: Even encrypted IP traffic must leave the IP header unencrypted so that the routers know where to forward the packet.

4. How much am I willing to spend to secure my data?

The bottom line: The greater the security, the greater the cost. How much money are you willing to spend to secure your data? If you work for a financial or government organization, this amount is probably very high. However, if you work for a small company with several remote offices connected by virtual private networks, you may only be exchanging e-mail. The fact is, most traffic on the Internet is simply not interesting to anyone but the person sending or receiving it. As important and interesting as the data may seem to you, consider carefully whether it is worth the additional expense securing it.

SECURING ROUTING PROTOCOLS

Routing protocols are inherently nonsecure. To make matters worse, a failed router generally causes an entire network to fail. With that warning, I will give you guidelines to improve that level of security and reduce your risk of malicious attack against your routers.

When using the RIP protocol, you will find that it is a good idea to explicitly list the neighboring routers' IP addresses. This almost defeats the purpose of RIP, because its biggest advantage is simplicity. However, routers running the RIP routing protocol are extremely susceptible to malicious attacks that may cause entire networks to fail.

To restrict the hosts that RRAS will accept RIP routes from, open the RIP Configuration dialog box. Select the Security tab, and add in each neighboring router's IP address. This is a cumbersome task; it has to be done at each RRAS router individually. Additionally, it will need to be updated each time an IP address changes or additional routers are added. Nonetheless, it eliminates many of the most common attacks against RIP routers and can be worthwhile to organizations that are particularly susceptible to malicious network attacks. Figure 13-18 shows the dialog box for the RIP configuration network.

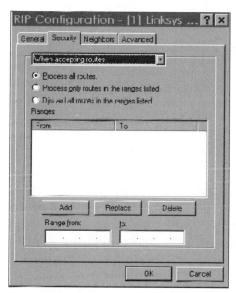

Figure 13–18: RIP may be configured with different levels of security.

RADIUS

RADIUS (Remote Authentication Dial-In User Service) is a protocol designed to allow clients to authenticate to a central server. This section will include the essentials of the protocol but not in a great deal of detail; Microsoft's support of the protocol is still very limited, and deeper coverage would be outside the scope of this book.

RADIUS is supported by the Routing and Remote Access Service RAS component as a method for authenticating users who dial into a RAS server. Traditionally, this task has been performed by a primary domain controller in an NT domain environment or the local RAS server's user database in a workgroup environment. So why would Microsoft offer an alternative to their much-hyped domain environment? Microsoft is competing for money from Internet service providers, and many of the most popular dial-in servers allow use of RADIUS for authentication. RAS has always been useful to small Windows NT–based organizations to provide dial-in capability to their users, but the largest part of the dial-in market today is for Internet access.

Now that we have established *why* Microsoft allows RAS to be a RADIUS client, we will briefly discuss *how* it works. RADIUS is defined in RFC 2138; it provides for a centralized database of users, passwords, and account information. When a dial-in server is configured to use RAS, it follows these steps:

1. Answer an incoming call, and greet the user.

2. Prompt for a username and accept a response.

3. Prompt for a password and accept a response.

4. Forward this information to the central RADIUS server, and wait for a response.

   The response will contain a confirmation or denial of access and may contain account information such as what services the user should have access to.

5. Depending on the response from the RADIUS server and connection type, give the user an IP address and begin a PPP session.

RADIUS uses UDP port 1812 for all communications between the client and the server. All communications are authenticated through the use of a shared secret, and passwords are always encrypted using the RSA's MD5 algorithm before being transmitted on a network. RADIUS also supports load balancing and fail-over capabilities, even more robust than that provided for by NT Server's primary domain controllers and backup domain controllers.

Several third-party vendors already sell software allowing an NT server to be a RADIUS server. Further, as Microsoft continues its "if you can't beat 'em, join 'em" philosophy, NT 5.0 will probably include the server-side RADIUS software out of the box.

Using Microsoft Proxy Server

Microsoft intends RRAS to work side by side with another NT Server–based networking product, Proxy Server. Chapter 18 goes into a great deal of detail about this product, but in this chapter I will cover how it complements and interacts with RRAS.

Consider the organization I described in a previous example that used Demand Dial Routing and the Point-to-Point Tunneling Protocol to create a virtual private network across the Internet simply by dialing into a local Internet service provider.

With that configuration, the remote office has full access to the central office's network. However, it does not have any access to the Internet, despite the fact that its traffic is traversing the Internet. The reason for this is the fact that the ISP assigns only a single IP address to the demand dial router; the other IP addresses on the network are private, reserved addresses such as those described in RFC 1918. If a host on the remote network were to send traffic to a host on the Internet, there would be neither a route to the Internet from the private addresses nor a route to the private network from the Internet.

Microsoft Proxy Server solves this problem. Proxy Server accepts requests from the clients on the private network and uses its public IP address that the ISP assigned to transmit the request onto the Internet. Then it waits for the response back from the Internet host and forwards it on to the host within the reserved network. In this way, an entire network can gain public Internet access with only a single public IP address.

By combining these two products, the remote office can use the same connection for both Internet connectivity and virtual private networking with the central office. This introduces greater complexity, however. Each packet that a client transmits will travel one of three paths: the local network, the virtual private network, or the Internet. If it is destined for a host on the local network, it will be transmitted directly onto the network segment without passing through the NT server.

If it is destined for the central office, it must travel through the virtual private network. This is entirely transparent to the client transmitting the packet: To it, the virtual private network looks like any other router. The NT Server–based router recognizes the destination IP address as belonging to the central office and routes it through the virtual private network.

To distinguish networks that can be routed from those on the Internet that must be handled by Proxy Server, the administrator must define the networks within the MSPCLNT.INI file on the Proxy Server. This is a normal part of Proxy Server setup, but note that both the local network and all networks at the central office that will be handled by the NT Server–based router must be defined as "private." All networks not defined as private – in this case, everything on the Internet – will be recognized as such by the proxy client. The proxy client will forward a request to the proxy server, which will in turn transmit the request onto the public Internet. Figure 13-19 shows DDR combined with MPS.

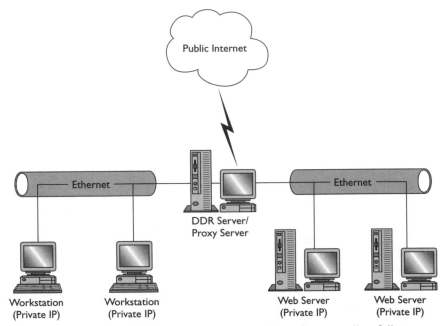

Figure 13-19: DDR may be used in conjunction with Proxy Server to allow fully transparent public Internet connections when both private and public IP addresses have been used.

This is a complicated and confusing concept, but it makes a lot of sense financially. Proxy Server allows an organization to have full Internet connectivity while avoiding the cost of acquiring public IP addresses for its network. Demand Dial Routing allows the organization to have full connectivity with the central office with only the cost of a local call to an ISP. These two functions could be implemented separately by purchasing separate modems, telephone lines, and ISP accounts for each purpose. Combining these two tasks onto the same server and dial-up account allows the same bandwidth to be used for multiple purposes, allowing more efficient use than if separate links were maintained for each purpose. The money saved can be put toward increasing the shared bandwidth.

Even if public Internet access is not desired, Proxy Server can reduce the amount of traffic that needs to cross the virtual private network. The Winsock proxy services do not add any value in this particular scenario, since each IP address on both sides of the network can send and receive routed traffic. However, the Web proxy service can significantly reduce the amount of traffic that must be sent back and forth across the line and improve response time by caching Web requests. This is particularly helpful if the organization relies heavily on intranets, a method that is becoming increasingly popular. Configuring a network to use Microsoft Proxy Server for Web requests instead of making them directly to the Web servers is a simple task: Install Proxy Server on the DDR server and configure the Web browsers on each client machine to use a proxy server.

Using Routing and Remote Access Service for Packet Filtering

The RRAS service includes a great deal of functionality, but one of the most useful features is merely a side effect. Windows NT provides very limited packet filtering capabilities within the Network Control Panel applet. These capabilities are limited to TCP and UDP port numbers and IP protocols. With the filtering capabilities built into Windows NT, for example, an administrator can configure the server to allow in only HTTP traffic by selecting Permit Only within the TCP/IP Security dialog box and adding TCP port 80. Figure 13-20 shows this dialog box configured to allow only Web traffic in or out.

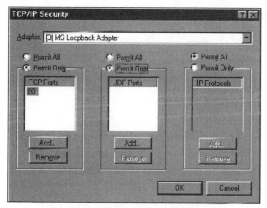

Figure 13-20: Windows NT provides very limited packet filtering capabilities out of the box.

The ability to filter out packets based on port number is a critical part of system-level security. The term *system-level security* means that the hosts themselves, rather than the routers on the network, provide for security. System-level security often means that requests for specific services are only accepted from certain hosts. For example, port filtering may be implemented on a UNIX host so that only hosts originating from a network within the organization may use the Telnet application to access the console of the host. This type of security is commonly relied on within the Internet, where malicious attacks from outside networks are common.

UNIX operating systems have relied on *TCP wrappers* to create system-level security by blocking out packets based on TCP or UDP port number, source IP address, and other factors. Unfortunately, NT's packet filtering capabilities have never been as flexible: It is all or nothing when filtering is based on port number. In the example at the beginning of the section, only TCP port 80 was enabled. This effectively filters out all other types of traffic, including NetBIOS and DNS.

Unfortunately, it filters those types of packets for *all* incoming traffic; not even an administrator on the same network can access the server through NetBIOS. To make matters worse, these filters automatically apply to both incoming and outgoing traffic, so the server in the preceding example will not even be able to FTP to an outside server unless incoming FTP traffic will also be allowed. Finally, port numbers must be added manually, one by one. This means that protocols that rely on ranges of ports, such as DNS, which must be able to receive responses on UDP ports 1024–5000, are almost impossible to implement alongside port filtering. To implement UDP port filtering and allow DNS queries, an administrator would have to add the almost 4,000 required UDP ports.

Fortunately, Microsoft has expanded these capabilities with the release of the Routing and Remote Access Service. Though the packet-filtering capabilities are intended to protect NT servers acting as routers, they can be used in any situation where an NT server requires system-level security. To make use of these features, install the LAN Routing option in RRAS on the server that will implement the filtering. Then follow these steps:

1. Launch the RRAS Admin utility.

2. Open the IP Routing folder.

3. Select Summary Item.

4. Select a network interface and choose Configure Interface. Near the bottom of the dialog box are buttons labeled Input Filters and Output Filters.

Input filters are used to filter packets transmitted to your server. Output filters control packets your server transmits to other hosts on the network. Generally, input filters are more commonly used for host-level security because they stop connections from being established by users on the network.

Consider the common scenario of an NT-based Web server on the public Internet. Certainly, many types of packets should not be allowed to reach the server from just anyone on the Internet. I will start this example by saying I am pessimistic about security: I would rather filter everything except for a few specific services rather than allowing everything through by default. Because the server we are creating filtering on is a Web server, we will start by filtering everything except packets destined for the Web service.

Packets initiated from a Web browser on the Internet to our Web server will have our Web server's IP address as the destination IP, the client's IP address as the source IP, port 80 (the HTTP service) as the destination port number, and an unknown port number (generally 1024–5000) as the source port number.

This is a packet that our Web server should be able to receive, so we are going to create a filter specifically to allow it through. Click the Input Filters button on the Interface Configuration dialog box to view the IP Packet Filters Configuration list. To add a filter, click the Add button at the bottom to add our filter for incoming Web traffic. You will see the Add-Edit IP Filter dialog box, as shown in Figure 13-21.

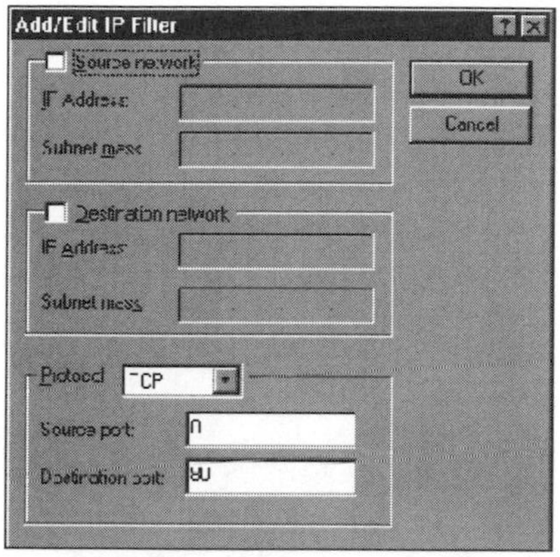

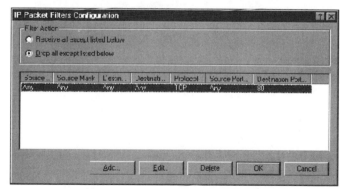

Figure 13-21: Packet filtering with RRAS
may be based on port or IP address.

You are greeted with a simple dialog box prompting you for source and destination network information and protocol information. Because we want to allow incoming traffic from anywhere on the Internet, we can leave the source and destination network information empty. To specify Web traffic on port 80, select TCP from the Protocol drop-down list and fill in 80 as the destination port number. The source port number will be determined by the client, so we cannot perform any filtering on that number. Click OK to accept the settings you have entered. The IP Packet Filters Configuration dialog box now includes a line for the filter we added, as shown in Figure 13-22.

Figure 13-22: This illustration shows a Windows NT server
configured to allow only HTTP traffic.

It will also be helpful if administrators can use utilities such as Server Manager and Internet Services Manager to administer the machine. These utilities rely on NetBIOS over TCP/IP for all communications, so we will need to allow NetBIOS packets through our filter from the internal network only. In this example, the 10.10.0.0/16 network will represent all internal networks.

Add a filter for incoming packets using the NetBIOS Name service by clicking Add... from the IP Packet Filters Configuration dialog box. For Source Network, fill in 10.10.0.0 with a subnet mask of 255.255.0.0. Select the UDP protocol with a destination port of 137. Add a similar filter for the NetBIOS Session service with identical network information but filtering TCP port 139. If we wanted to allow all NetBIOS traffic to and from this machine, we would also add the NetBIOS Datagram service that uses UDP port 138, but that service is not necessary for the administrative utilities.

More filters can be added to allow FTP traffic, RealAudio, and whatever other services are desired, to suite your needs.

The packet filtering included with RRAS is a significant improvement over the out-of-the-box Windows NT Server packet filtering, but it leaves much to be desired. For example, you have no ability to filter packets with the acknowledgment bit set in the TCP header. It may seem odd, but the Windows NT TCP/IP stack will accept all TCP packets with the ACK bit set, regardless of how filtering is configured. More robust routing environments such as the hardware-based Cisco routers force the administrator to explicitly permit established connections.

Another weakness of the existing filtering is the inability to define a filter for a range of port numbers. As I mentioned earlier, DNS queries are returned to the client via a UDP datagram sent to a port number between 1024 and 5000. Given the current filtering capabilities, a Windows NT–based router would have to allow all UDP packets through (very bad) or explicitly allow UDP 1024, UDP 1025, UDP 1026, all the way through UDP 5000. In contrast, Cisco routers can be configured to allow this traffic through with a command as simple as IP ACCESS-LIST ALLOW UDP ANY PORT GT 1023.

In summary, packet filtering is a feature that should be implemented on any NT server that is connected to the public Internet and any other server that requires a high level of security. This can be implemented on a hardware-based router that forwards traffic to the server using network-level security, or it can be implemented on the NT server itself using system-level security. The Routing and Remote Access Service greatly expands the system-level security capabilities of Windows NT Server by allowing packet filtering based on source and destination IP address and port numbers. While this is an improvement over existing features, it still falls short of the feature set provided with a typical hardware-based router.

Configuring an RRAS Lab Environment

It is common practice in the world of systems engineering to piece together a server and place it into a production network with very little testing. This is an acceptable practice, because a server such as a Windows NT server will very rarely damage an entire network. Certainly, if putting an NT server onto a network without testing it first caused every user on the network to lose their Internet connection, we systems engineers would be more inclined to spend time testing the product in a true lab environment. While test servers often have problems, sometimes very serious ones, the scope of the damage is generally limited to that single host.

The same is not true of networking hardware! A misconfigured router, placed innocently onto a production network, has the potential to stop all network traffic. Consider plugging a router into a network that uses the RIP routing protocol: If the new router is advertising the shortest route to a network, it will become a "black hole," accepting packets bound for a network that it cannot route to. Further, routing protocols allow these mistakes to propagate themselves throughout an organization's network like a virus, causing problems that can take several hours to fix. Consider this scenario, and then consider what your boss would say when he found out it was your fault.

The moral of this story is that it is critical to create a lab environment for all sys tems that will participate in routing, and to test them thoroughly in that lab environment before moving them into a production network.

Most organizations that use Windows NT as their network operating system already have some sort of lab environment created. This section will discuss the details of expanding an existing systems engineering lab to accommodate testing routing protocols.

Network Infrastructure

As discussed in the introduction to this section, it is critical to have a separate network for your lab.

If machines are to be located in a geographically distant location (even if it is just across the hallway), products such as Avalan's Remotely Possible and PCAnywhere allow full access to the graphical user interface of Windows NT. This allows an engineer to use the lab environment conveniently and easily, without having to get up from his desk.

PHYSICALLY SEPARATE NETWORKS

The most effective way to set up such an environment is to create an entirely disconnected network; the most effective firewall is air. Unfortunately, this makes it a more difficult environment to work in because the person doing the work must be physically located near the machines. In many cases, servers dedicated to the lab environment may be located in a data center that is geographically distant from the engineer's normal work environment. At the very least, moving a physically separate environment forces the person doing the work to leave the comfort of his or her own desk.

Additionally, because the lab network does not interoperate with the production network, RFC 1918 private addresses can be used. By not consuming additional addresses from the company address space, total cost is reduced. Figure 13-23 shows a production network and a lab network physically separated.

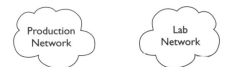

Figure 13-23: The production network and
the lab network should be entirely separate.

PARALLEL NETWORKS

The next safest network architecture implements a parallel network architecture, with each machine that requires network access to the lab adding a network card specifically for that network. Additionally, a static routing table entry may need to be added to these multihomed machines. The advantages to this architecture lie in the fact that it effectively separates the lab environment from the production environment. The disadvantages arise from the fact that it requires every machine that may be used to access the lab network be multihomed, creating additional administrative overhead and adding the cost of network cards. It is not scalable to large lab environments for this reason; it would not be cost effective to add network cards to more than a few desktop machines.

USING PPTP TO ALLOW CONNECTIVITY TO AN ISOLATED NETWORK

One possibility for creating a safe network for testing without requiring modifications to the existing network architecture is to use the Point-to-Point Tunneling Protocol, a feature already built into Windows NT. An engineer needing to access a machine in the lab environment creates a virtual private network between his desktop workstation and the lab environment. A PPTP server acts as a firewall to this environment, allowing users to have access to the lab network it protects without letting traffic through to the production network.

This architecture is advantageous because it provides for security as well as isolation. It still shares a connection to the production network, so the PPTP server that adjoins them needs to be treated as a production machine and should not be used for testing, because it has the potential to damage the rest of the network. Finally, it relies solely on Windows NT servers, reducing the hardware-based routing and firewalling. This design is illustrated in Figure 13-24.

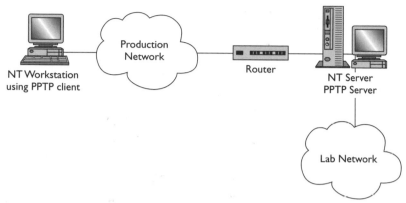

Figure 13-24: You may allow access to a lab environment without risking the production environment by filtering everything but PPTP traffic.

FIREWALLING OFF A NETWORK SEGMENT

Another alternative allows for the most connectivity to the production network at the greatest risk: configuring the lab network as a separate network segment. The router or routers connecting the lab network to the production network should be specially configured to ignore all routing protocols on the interface connecting the lab and to forward only specific types of traffic. In this way, the router behaves like a very simple firewall, stopping routing protocols like RIP and OSPF, which communicate using broadcast messages. Figure 13-25 shows a router that connects a leaf network. The router has routing protocols disabled on the interface connecting to the lab network.

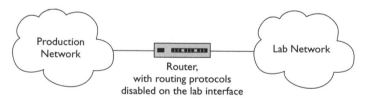

Figure 13-25: Simply disabling routing protocols on the network interface connecting a lab environment reduces the risk that a problem will spread outside the lab.

Modifications to the Systems

NT servers that will be used in a testing environment should be configured as closely to the standard production machines as possible, including both hardware and software configurations. However, several changes need to be made to make it easier to work with the machines in their nonproduction environment.

Lab machines will eventually become difficult to work with because changes are constantly being made, and several people may be working on them simultaneously. After several weeks of these changes, it is impossible to tell whether something breaks because of the changes you were testing or as a result of something that may have been done days before! Additionally, if you finally do get the routing protocols working as you want them to, you may not be able to recreate the environment for production use because you don't know what may have changed! To avoid spending hours reinstalling Windows NT Server and RRAS each time you need to wipe the slate clean, create an extra partition and install Windows NT Server on it. Boot into this partition, create a directory in the root of that partition, and copy over all the files from the primary partition. This backup will be used to recreate your original setup at a later date.

When you want to start testing on your standard install of Windows NT Server again, follow these steps:

1. Boot to the alternate installation of Windows NT.

2. Delete the files on the primary partition.

3. Copy the files you backed up onto the primary partition.

4. Boot to the primary partition again. You will have an installation that is identical to your original!

The Future of RRAS

Microsoft has certainly had products that have failed before, but RRAS is not likely to be one of them. To be successful, it must gain support from the networking industry. To accomplish this elusive goal, it must grow to include a wider variety of routing protocols and greater functionality.

One notable no-show in the current implementation of RRAS is Proxy ARP. Proxy ARP is not a routing protocol but a method a router can use to forward traffic to a subnet without having to be addressed directly. For example, consider a small organization with the single, private class C network `192.168.10.0/24`. The administrator of this network decides to implement packet filtering for four servers on the network that require a high level of security. Proxy ARP is an excellent choice for this particular filtering router because it can be implemented transparently to both the servers behind the router and the clients in front of the router, while filtering packets with its built-in access list capabilities.

Proxy ARP works by listening for ARP requests on each interface. To review, when a client connects to a server, it must perform an ARP request to find the MAC address of the server when it already knows the IP address. For each ARP request a router running Proxy ARP receives, it checks the destination IP address. If the requested IP address is available through another interface than the one the request was received on, the router responds to the ARP request with its own MAC address. In this way, the router impersonates all hosts on the networks it routes for. Clients addressing servers through the router simply perform an ARP request as they always would, and the router responds and automatically forwards packets that it later receives.

Proxy ARP is perfect for small networks and for networks that must be subnetted and secured. If it were implemented, it would allow robust filtering and greater security for small networks that have network servers on the same subnet as the clients. Further, it allows networks to be expanded or divided without reconfiguring the network clients, making a network manager's job simpler. This seems to be the niche that Microsoft is seeking to fill, yet they still do not offer it as a service.

Summary

This chapter has covered routing and routing protocols. While routing may be implemented in many different ways, the focus of this chapter was on one specific method – Microsoft's Routing and Remote Access Service.

You have learned the following:

- ◆ Routers forward packets between physically separate network segments. Routers have a need to communicate in order to know the changing topology of the network around them – routing protocols fulfill this need.

- ◆ Microsoft's free add-on for Windows NT 4.0, the Routing and Remote Access Service (RRAS), is an excellent routing solution for many small environments. It may be downloaded from Microsoft's Web site and installed on almost any Windows NT server.

- ◆ RRAS is much simpler to administer than traditional, hardware-based routers because RRAS offers a graphical user interface. This GUI can be used to control every aspect of the routing software.

- ◆ RRAS supports RIP v1 and v2 as well as OSPF. Each routing protocol has its own set of advantages and disadvantages.

- ◆ Windows NT natively supports only very limited filtering capabilities. RRAS can be used to provide much more flexible filtering and can drop packets based on source or destination IP address and source or destination port number.

- ◆ Routing protocols, if implemented carelessly, can cause serious network-wide problems. Therefore, always test RRAS in a safe, isolated network environment.

- ◆ As Microsoft continues to move into the network hardware market, RRAS capabilities will be expanded to include additional routing protocols.

In the next chapter, you'll learn the inner workings of the Common Internet File System, CIFS. CIFS is being adopted piece by piece in each generation of Windows NT, and much of its functionality is already present in Windows NT 4.0.

Chapter 14

Common Internet
File System

IN THIS CHAPTER

- ◆ Getting acquainted with CIFS
- ◆ Understanding how CIFS will affect your network
- ◆ Exploring the future of CIFS

THE COMMON INTERNET File System, or more simply CIFS, is the next step in the evolution of Microsoft's file and print sharing protocol, Server Message Blocks (SMB). Microsoft is one of the driving forces behind CIFS efforts and bills it as a method of exchanging files on the Internet. It is intended to complement, not replace, HTTP.

Whether you know it or not, you are probably already using CIFS! Portions of the CIFS standards have been added to the Windows operating systems throughout the years. In particular, Microsoft included many CIFS features with service pack 3 for Windows NT. This overlap with the SMB protocol is convenient, because we NT administrators do not have to relearn much. Instead, we merely need to supplement our existing knowledge of Windows file sharing.

This chapter is intended to do just that. It will introduce you to CIFS concepts and take you step by step through what is new. You will learn exactly what features affect you most, and how your network will be improved when you can put these features to use. Security is paramount on any Internet-connected network, and CIFS greatly improves NetBIOS's security. Finally, I will touch on a major competitor to CIFS, Sun's WebNFS. For a thorough background on SMB and NetBIOS, please refer to Chapter 10.

Reviewing the CIFS Background

CIFS, the Common Internet File System, is essentially SMB adapted to the Internet. This may seem odd to some, because SMB works just fine over the Internet. Indeed, many people use it every day. So if it ain't broke, why fix it?

Many problems are associated with using SMB across the Internet, and CIFS is designed to resolve them. In fact, most of the SMB traffic that crosses the Internet today has already integrated some of the feature set of CIFS into it. The fact is, SMB was designed for use in local area network environments. Because of this, security was very weak. CIFS addresses the security weaknesses of SMB by adding encryption and more secure authentication capabilities.

CIFS also adds a more flexible naming schema, allowing the user to name a CIFS file server using the computer name, a DNS entry, or an IP address. These features are already built into Windows NT and Windows 98. As you can imagine, it would be very difficult to connect to systems across the Internet using standard NetBIOS names – either an entry would have to be added to the LMHOSTS file every time a system was accessed or someone would have to manage a global WINS system.

SMB, as a LAN protocol, was not designed to work over slow dial-up links. It has some bad habits that do not work well over dial-up links, such as minimal support for client-side caching, a tendency to open and close a file for multiple writes, and no ability to connect to a different server according to the geographical location.

Together, SMB and these additional features make up the standard called CIFS. It is one of many standards currently being proposed for Internet file sharing, the most notable competitor being Sun's WebNFS (covered briefly later in this chapter). Those who use SMB file sharing currently will find themselves migrating to CIFS whether they like it or not – NT 5.0 will support it exclusively. Fortunately, CIFS is backward compatible with the aging SMB protocols.

The previous paragraphs gave you an overview of CIFS, but the value of this book is in the details. The next section contains all these juicy details, describing the intricacies of CIFS and how it will affect your environment. This information is what you need to effectively design networks that will use the Common Internet File System, both the current version and future releases.

Defining the CIFS Feature Set

I have already hinted at the features that make up the CIFS standards. This section will cover these features in greater detail. I will give you an understanding of the CIFS features you are already using, as well as the features you may look forward to in future releases of Windows operating systems.

Flexible File Locking

A powerful feature of CIFS is the ability for multiple users to access the same file simultaneously. Depending on the implementation of the protocol, several users may even *update* different parts of a single file at the same time.

Key to the concept of CIFS file locking is the idea of *opportunistic locks*. These locks ensure that no client reading a file caches information about the file that is out of date and that no two clients update the same portion of a file at the same time. As you can see, file locking works closely with the CIFS caching mechanisms described in the next section. The client's role in opportunistic locking is to request the conservative opportunistic lock required and to follow the directives provided by the server (for example, to break an existing opportunistic lock). The server's role is to monitor the opportunistic locks on all files within the file system, track who has locked what, and notify clients when an opportunistic lock must be broken for whatever reason.

Opportunistic locks are commonly referred to as *oplocks*. (Well, perhaps they're not "commonly" referred to anywhere in the world besides my office. Nonetheless, that's what I'm going to call them.) There are three different flavors of oplocks: exclusive, batch, and level II.

EXCLUSIVE OPLOCKS

Exclusive oplocks are quite simple. A single client opens a file and nobody else can touch it. This allows the client to update and cache however it sees fit, but it restricts anyone else from using that same file. Exclusive oplocks are the most efficient locking method when a client is performing extensive updates to a file. The server has the right to refuse a request from a client for an exclusive oplock, and it will do so if anyone else is accessing the file.

If another client attempts to access a file that has an exclusive oplock, the server may choose to break the exclusive oplock and allow the sharing of the file. To do this, the server notifies the client that has locked the file that it should send any updates that it has cached to the file. Further, because someone else may update the file, the client must empty any read cache. Once the updates are performed and the file is completely synchronized, the exclusive oplock is broken and the server may grant the request to the second client.

BATCH OPLOCKS

Traditionally, SMB file sharing has been inefficient when only small portions of a file are read at a time. Batch oplocks help to relieve this problem. Instead of opening a connection, reading data, closing the connection, reopening the connection, reading data, closing the connection, reopening the connection, and so on, the client may keep the same connection open and perform several reads at once.

The client may also choose to use read-ahead caching by anticipating the need for the next several lines of a file and reading them before they are actually required. These lines are likely to be transmitted in the same packet, reducing the total load on the network and increasing the perceived response time.

The disadvantage to batch oplocks appears when several clients wish to access the same file simultaneously. They may have to contend with locking conflicts, which are much less likely when a file is opened and closed for each access. To limit the effect of this problem, the server has the capability to notify a client with a batch oplock on a file that it must break the oplock. Thus, it will revert to the more pessimistic form of accessing the file – opening and closing the connection each time the file must be accessed.

LEVEL II OPLOCKS

On the public Internet, it is customary for many users to view the same file simultaneously. HTTP is well suited to this type of access because, traditionally, it is a read-only protocol and files are not kept open for an extended amount of time. Therefore, clients will never run into the problem of contention.

However, one of the problems encountered as file sharing moves onto the public Internet is the frequency of file updates. Additionally, users may keep files open for an extended amount of time. For example, if a user opens a file in Word, it may be kept open for the entire period that the user is working on the file. However, that same file may be opened in Netscape Navigator and only need to remain open long enough to transmit it across the internetwork.

Level II oplocks help to relieve these problems. Level II oplocks allow multiple clients to gain read access to the same file simultaneously. Theoretically, there can be no contention because no client may attempt to update the file. Therefore, all clients may read the identical file without concern for its becoming outdated.

This works well in theory, but the majority of clients (such as Microsoft Word) open a file by requesting read/write access to it, even if the file is opened strictly for read access. This heralds back to the day of standalone PCs, when applications never needed to be concerned about sharing their files with others. However, in the modern world, a single file on a network share may be accessed by dozens of people within a corporate network simultaneously. So how can CIFS help to ensure that applications do not request more privileges to a file than they actually require?

The level II oplocks built into CIFS enable the server to limit the client applications to read-only access when that is all they really need (regardless of what they request). Essentially, the client will still request read/write access when opening a file, but the server will respond with a message saying, "You don't really need write access, do you? Others may want to share that file too, you know." Assuming the client supports level II oplocks, it may choose to settle for read access, allowing other clients to read the file simultaneously.

Suppose a client actually *does* intend to write to a file, but several others already have level II oplocks to read the file. CIFS takes this into account. As part of the level II oplock functionality, CIFS can notify the read-only clients that their oplock has been broken. This allows the end user to modify a file that others are currently viewing and to rest assured that they will be notified of the changes and will not attempt to simultaneously update the file.

Robust Caching

To reduce the amount of traffic generated on the Internet and wide area networks, CIFS supports more robust caching than SMB ever did. This caching ensures that files remain synchronized while generating the least amount of network traffic possible. Several different forms of caching may be used, depending on how a file is being accessed.

Read-ahead caching allows a CIFS client to read a file across a network only once, though it may be accessed many times. The first time the file is read, the client will store the information in memory in case it needs to be used later. Read-ahead caching works well but can cause problems if the file on the server is updated – the client that caches the file will no longer have an accurate copy. CIFS takes this into account; read-ahead caching is considered a form of "safe caching" as long as all clients are accessing the file for reads only.

Write-behind caching speeds updates to a file by not transmitting them from the server to the client immediately – these updates are stored on the client and transmitted at a later time. This type of caching is considered "safe caching" as long as only a single client has requested write access to the file. Indeed, no clients may even request read access to a given file (or portion of the file) and still allow write-behind caching to be safe.

These caching mechanisms are implemented in the client portion of the conversation. It is strictly up to the client to determine when to cache and when to query the server for a portion of the file. However, the CIFS protocol builds in a communications mechanism that allows the server to notify the clients how many users are accessing a file and what type of accesses are being made. Using this information, the CIFS client is capable of making an informed decision about what caching mechanism should be used. Per the protocol, the client should only make use of caching that is considered "safe" at any given point in time.

To clarify this point, consider an organization with a CIFS file server located on the Internet. Bob, a user in the Atlanta office, wishes to view an accounting form located on the file server. Because he is the only user accessing the file at that time, the CIFS client on his computer uses safe read-ahead caching. However, one of the accountants in the New York office needs to update this file. The server knows that Bob's computer may need to be informed that someone is trying to update the file so that it can use a less optimistic form of caching – so it notifies Bob's CIFS client that writes may be occurring to the file. The accountant is able to update the file but cannot use write-behind caching because a user is currently reading the file; all updates must be sent immediately to the server.

Besides being cached on a per-access basis, files accessed using CIFS may be cached much as HTTP proxies cache information from other Web servers. To aid in this, CIFS enables servers to notify clients when a file is changed. This allows the client either to requery the file or to mark it as bad, so as not to inadvertently use an outdated version of a file.

Fault Tolerance

Fault tolerance is key to any scalable protocol, and CIFS has a robust set of fault-tolerant features implemented at both the client and server sides. Because the Internet is an unreliable network, file connections may come and go depending on the state of dial-up connections and leased lines. CIFS clients are capable of losing a connection to a file that is being read or modified and then automatically reopening the same file once the connection is reestablished.

The DFS protocols also provide for fault tolerance within CIFS. Because multiple servers may be listed as sources for a given network share, the client is capable of choosing a server that is still functioning if one or more of the alternates have failed. This feature will become easier to maintain when Windows NT 5.0 is released because it includes the ability to replicate files between servers, ensuring that duplicate copies of files remain duplicated.

Distributed File Services: DFS

When information on a network is tied to a specific server, this fact seriously limits the scalability of that network. Indeed, it may become necessary to move the files, rename the server, or replace the server. This has always been a problem with traditional SMB file sharing; normally, a client establishes a connection to a network share that resides on a specific server. If the file moves to a different server, the user must manually establish another network connection. If the user wishes to access files on a different server, another connection must be established.

To work around these problems, CIFS includes a feature called the distributed file system. DFS is not a new concept, but it is new to Microsoft networking. DFS allows for a single network share to act as the root of a network file system that may span many servers in many different locations. The client is allowed to access files on any of these servers, but the user never has to know that they are located in different places.

More information on DFS and Microsoft's implementation of DFS is provided in the next chapter.

Flexible Naming

SMB is bound to the NetBIOS naming scheme. NetBIOS names do not work well on the Internet for many reasons, as described in Chapter 10, "NetBIOS: Friend or Foe," Chapter 11, "WINS," and Chapter 12, "DNS." CIFS is more flexible than traditional SMB traffic because it allows for open addressing of servers. Therefore, the DNS namespace, which is typically much better suited for use on the Internet, may be used.

Several different naming methods are supported. Most of these are already supported within Windows NT 4.0: traditional NetBIOS naming, DNS hostnames, and IP addresses. When a client references a server using the DNS name, the hostname is separated, padded to 16 characters, and submitted to the server as a NetBIOS name. Clients that attempt to access a CIFS server using the IP address create a session using the generic name "*SMBSERVER." Standard NetBIOS names merely need to be converted to uppercase before being submitted.

You'll notice that NetBIOS names are still relied upon within the CIFS protocol itself. While this may prove to be a limitation in the future, the ability for the clients to initiate sessions without explicit knowledge of the CIFS server's NetBIOS name greatly increases the flexibility of the protocol. This functionality is already present in Windows NT 4.0, Windows NT 5.0, and Windows 98. However, flexible name resolution is not available in MS-DOS or earlier versions of the Windows operating systems.

Understanding CIFS Security

Like most of the CIFS standard, security is a mixture of the old and the new, the "old" being traditional, Windows-based SMB file and printer sharing, and the "new" being the Internet. Windows 95 and Windows for Workgroups are still very popular operating systems, and both provide support primarily for share-level security. Therefore, the functionality has been built into CIFS for backward-compatibility.

The CIFS authentication mechanisms will seem very familiar to anyone already familiar with the way authentication works within Windows NT. Four different methods are available: share level protection, plain text password authentication, LanMan 1.2 challenge/response, and NT LM 0.12 challenge/response. Each of these methods has advantages and disadvantages, as detailed in the next sections.

Share-Level Protection

Share-level security defines a security model based on network share points and passwords. An administrator makes a resource, usually a directory or printer, available to the network. To protect it, a password may be assigned. Any user on the network or any connected network may use the shared resources, provided they have access to the proper password. This security model does not work well for several reasons:

Mostly an Open Standard

It's important to note that the CIFS standards provide a detailed description for creating client applications that will authenticate with servers. Additionally, they document pass-through authentication similar to that provided by Windows 95. However, the server side of the conversation is *not* documented. The server-side portion of the authentication is generally provided by the NetLogon service, and apparently Microsoft wants to keep it this way. This is a real gripe of mine, because it goes against their philosophy of making CIFS an open standard on the Internet. Currently, this information is available to third-party organizations only through the NT code licensing agreement. AT&T has such an agreement with Microsoft, but it will probably never become an "open" standard.

- There is no way to tell which users have accessed a particular share because the username is not required to connect.

- Passwords that protect shared resources have a tendency to be shared between people. However, people are less likely to give out their own personal password.

- Passwords stay with employees after they leave an organization. It is much easier to remove a user.

- The model gives users yet another password to memorize.

- Passwords are transmitted in clear text across the network.

The other, preferred, method of security is user-level security. This is the model used with Windows NT and most enterprise network operating systems. This allows access to be restricted to users and groups that have been defined within an organization. User-level security overcomes the weaknesses of share-level security and provides faster access because users do not have to provide a separate password each time they connect to a share point on the network – they need only be authenticated once.

In order to allow for backward-compatibility with clients that do not support user-level security, CIFS is capable of authenticating operating systems that have only share-level functionality. Because they are not capable of submitting a username to authenticate for access to a share, the computer name is used instead. Therefore, if the user "elvis" is using Windows for Workgroups, his computer should also be given the name "elvis." When Elvis attempts to access a share, he will be prompted for the password. The Windows NT server will then attempt to authenticate the user with the name "elvis" (taken from the computer name) and the password provided.

Plain Text Password Authentication

CIFS, always burdened with backward-compatibility requirements, supports authentication of users using clear-text passwords. If the client shows that it is incapable of performing the requested hash on the password, it may submit it in clear text. The server should be capable of authenticating the password as well. In this scenario, it would be simple to sniff the password from the network. Additionally, the server is capable of recording the password in clear text (which may not be a possibility when encrypted authentication is performed).

These weaknesses are actually not all that bad for many situations. For example, internal, secure networks may use clear-text passwords without worry. Networks that use Ethernet switching greatly reduce the opportunities users have to sniff each other's passwords and as such greatly improve the feasibility of clear-text passwords. Additionally, clear-text passwords require less overhead from the client and the server because CPU-intensive hashing and encrypting are not necessary.

SP3 Kills the Clear-Text Password

Windows operating systems do not make use of clear-text passwords, so most of us never noticed when Microsoft changed the default and disabled the clear-text password capabilities of Windows NT. This was done for security reasons — obviously, sending passwords in clear text is a really bad idea. However, there are a few times when clear-text passwords are required. Most notably, Network Appliance provides excellent support for CIFS file sharing but does not natively support NTLM authentication.

For those who do need to enable clear-text passwords while using SP3, all you have to do is set the value of the following registry key to 1:

```
HKEY_LOCAL_MACHINE\System\CurrentControlSet\Services\Rdr\Parame
ters\EnablePlaintextPassword
```

LanMan 1.2 Challenge/Response

The CIFS specification officially recommends *not* using this form of authentication but supports it for backward compatibility. This method is rarely used in the modern world, so I will not spend a great deal of time discussing it. In fact, a hotfix for service pack 3 for Windows NT — the lm-fix hotfix (see Knowledge Base article Q147706) — provides a way to disable this backward compatibility. Service pack 4 and later will have this built in.

NT LM 0.12 Challenge/Response

With the NT LM 0.12, a challenge/response mechanism, passwords are encrypted using DES encryption in block mode. In a nutshell, when a client attempts to access a resource that requires authentication, the following steps occur:

1. The server responds to the client's request with a unique key.

2. The client uses the key to perform a one-way hash on the user's password.

3. The client transmits this password, which cannot (in theory) be intercepted and decoded, across the network. The fact that it was hashed according to a unique key provided by the server reduces the likelihood that the authentication response can be captured from the network and used again at a later date.

4. The server performs a one-way hash on what it has the user's password listed as. This hash is done using the same key that was initially provided to the client; therefore, the result should be identical to the result the client produced and submitted to the server. If the two hashes match, the password was submitted correctly and the user may be authenticated.

SMB Signing

One of the features of CIFS that is already implemented in Windows NT 4.0 (provided you have installed service pack 3) is SMB signing. This feature reduces the likelihood of an SMB session being hijacked by adding a signature to each segment of the conversation. In a nutshell, the server verifies that each message comes from the client that initially established the connection.

SMB signing helps security but adds computational overhead to the file sharing because the file server and client must constantly compute complicated algorithms to create signatures. Microsoft estimates a reduction in file sharing performance by as much as 10 to 15 percent.

To enable SMB signing, you must edit the registry. The following values must be added to servers:

```
HKEY_LOCAL_MACHINE\System\CurrentControlSet\Services\LanManserv
er\Parameters\EnableSecuritySignature (value of 1)
HKEY_LOCAL_MACHINE\System\CurrentControlSet\Services\LanManserv
er\Parameters\RequireSecuritySignature (value of 1)
```

Once the servers have been configured to require SMB signing, the clients must be modified as well. Add the following values to your workstations:

```
HKEY_LOCAL_MACHINE\System\CurrentControlSet\Services\Rdr\Parame
ters\EnableSecuritySignature (value of 1)
HKEY_LOCAL_MACHINE\System\CurrentControlSet\Services\Rdr\Parame
ters\RequireSecuritySignature (value of 1)
```

Please remember that this feature is only available on Windows NT! Windows 95 clients will not be able to access your server if you add the "RequireSecuritySignature" value with a value of 1. If you want Windows NT systems to use SMB signing when available, set "EnableSecuritySignature" to 1 and "RequireSecuritySignature" to 0 on your file servers.

Understanding CIFS
As It Exists Today

Unfortunately, CIFS is still in development. The most up-to-date version of the standard is defined in an informational RFC that does not currently have a number but is named "Common Internet File System Protocol (CIFS/1.0)." However, several features of CIFS have already worked themselves into the Windows NT operating system. For example, the SMB signing capabilities that were included in service pack 3 are an early release of the CIFS feature set. Even the entire DFS add-on, as described in Chapter 15, is part of the future of CIFS.

Many organizations are developing CIFS implementations. Because the CIFS standards are still evolving, the functionality implemented in each may vary. However, backward-compatibility is a strong point of the CIFS standards, so these varying levels of support should still be provided for transparent functionality.

CIFS implementations currently exist for the following operating systems:

- 3Com® 3+Share®

- AT&T® Advanced Server for UNIX

- DEC Pathworks

- HP® Advanced Server 9000

- IBM LAN Server

- IBM Warp Connect

- LAN Manager for OS/2

- LAN Manager for MS-DOS

- LAN Manager for UNIX

- Macintosh

- Novell® Enterprise Toolkit

- SAMBA (supporting LINUX and other flavors of UNIX)

- SCO UNIX

- Unisys Advanced Server for UNIX

- VMS

- Windows 95

- Windows for Workgroups

- Windows NT Server

- Windows NT Workstation

Outlining Practical Uses for CIFS

Okay, all theory aside – what is CIFS actually good for? First, CIFS will replace any current file sharing occurring in organizations that choose to migrate to the newest version of Windows and Windows NT. So any situation you use file sharing in today will be supported by CIFS.

CIFS's advantage really lies in its ability to internetwork. In this way, organizations may move their existing file sharing structure onto the Internet, forming a true extranet. The security provided for within CIFS will allow users within an organization to access files from anywhere – assuming they can get a connection to the Internet. It is less likely that companies will offer files to the public through CIFS shares. HTTP is better suited to this type of file-sharing because users who are not internal to an organization will require some guidance regarding which files are interesting and which are not – merely connecting to a shared folder and looking at filenames will not suffice.

Theoretically, CIFS could replace anonymous FTP. However, there is no reason *not* to continue to use FTP for anonymous file sharing – at least no reason so compelling that all the Web sites and Web clients on the Internet will stop using the popular and well-standardized FTP protocol. FTP will probably fade as the years go on; however, it is more likely to be replaced by HTTP than CIFS.

CIFS provides speed advantages over SMB. Therefore, it is an excellent candidate anywhere files need to be served rapidly. One vendor, Network Appliance, creates a simple file-sharing system that serves files onto a network faster and with a greater capacity than any other file server is capable of. Network Appliance supports CIFS – thereby allowing any Windows and Windows NT clients to connect and share its resources. One potential use would be a shared file system for multiple front-end Web servers, perhaps based on Windows NT and IIS. In this way, many Web servers could serve the same files to users on the Internet without burdening the administrator with the task of replicating files between each Web server.

Introducing Sun's WebNFS

Who says there is no competition for Microsoft? At the very least, Sun is giving it a real effort. A new product named WebNFS is an Internet extension to the existing NFS file sharing protocols, currently in widespread use by UNIX clients. In this way, it is coevolving with CIFS. While WebNFS and CIFS each have their advantages and disadvantages, neither is likely to be a clear winner. Those who currently rely on Windows-based file sharing are likely to migrate to CIFS. Those who use NFS will choose the path of least resistance, WebNFS.

Understanding the Future of CIFS: NT5

I hope you are ready for CIFS, because Windows NT 5.0 supports it exclusively. The good news is, as I've already discussed, it is really not that big of a change from the traditional NetBIOS file sharing we all know and love (?). NT 5.0 adds true support for DFS, as discussed extensively in the next chapter. NT 5.0 also integrates CIFS into the active directory structure and more flexible forms of authentication.

From now on, I hope you will always call "Windows file sharing" CIFS instead. CIFS is the evolution of Microsoft's flavor of network file and print services and has been adapted to work better over the Internet. CIFS is not going to change anyone's life, as HTTP did. Instead, it will allow organizations to gracefully expand their intranetwork and cautiously extend it to the public Internet.

Summary

This chapter covered the essentials of the Common Internet File System protocol, an evolution of traditional NetBIOS file sharing. A detailed description of all major, new features has been provided. An overview of the security aspects of the protocol has been given so that you may evaluate integrating the protocol into your own network.

In this chapter you learned:

- ◆ CIFS is simply NetBIOS adapted for the Internet.

- ◆ CIFS adds many new features to NetBIOS that will improve the reliability, speed, and security of file sharing. This is of particular interest to those who will be using CIFS to transfer files across the public Internet.

- ◆ CIFS implementations are available for most of the major operating systems.

In the next chapter, we'll explore DFS in more detail. DFS is only one component of CIFS, but Microsoft has released an add-on to Windows NT 4.0 that supports much of the planned CIFS functionality in Windows NT 5.0. Chapter 15 describes the use of this add-on component and reviews third-party DFS offerings.

Chapter 15

Distributed File System

IN THIS CHAPTER

♦ Learning what DFS is, and how it will affect your network

♦ Learning how to implement DFS

♦ Understanding the details of the protocol itself and how to troubleshoot it

♦ Comparing Microsoft's DFS to Transarc/IBM's DFS

♦ Exploring Microsoft's plans for DFS with Windows NT 5.0

MICROSOFT'S DISTRIBUTED FILE system, more commonly known as DFS, brings several welcome new features to Microsoft's age-old file sharing mechanism. DFS hides the boundaries between servers, making the files on a network appear to the user as a single, seamless directory structure. In some cases, DFS can even help organizations provide redundancy and load balancing for network file servers.

DFS is freely available from Microsoft's Web site. It appears to be more of a sneak preview of Windows NT 5.0 than anything mature enough to be deployed in an enterprise network. However, it is an important technology that many organizations are already using. And for those organizations that do choose to deploy DFS with Windows NT 4.0, having a deep understanding of this protocol will assist in the implementation and administration of a sometimes troublesome file sharing mechanism.

The goal of this chapter is to provide you with a detailed understanding of how DFS works, how it should be used, and how to fix it when it breaks. I provide more basic information here than in many of the other chapters in this book because DFS is very new software and I suspect most engineers could use the background.

Defining DFS: Microsoft's Distributed File System

One of the many complaints UNIX administrators have lodged against Microsoft networking is the lack of a unified directory structure for file sharing. Microsoft's answer to this is Windows NT 5.0, which supports a scalable, reliable, and intelligent method of network file services that combines CIFS and Active Directory Services. In the meantime, they offer the DFS add-on for Windows NT 4.0.

Why It's Great

Have you ever run out of drive letters because you have connected to more network shares than there are letters in the alphabet? You know you have too many network connections when you are forced to use the drive letter "B" because that is all that is left. For those of us who like to connect to absolutely everything, DFS is a dream come true. DFS allows a single network connection to branch off into any number of other shares on the network, which may even be on a different file server.

In its simplest form, DFS allows an administrator to hide the structure of the network from the users. For example, consider a network that has file servers for the accounting department, the human resources department, and the legal department. Each organization has several shares configured, and users connect to and disconnect from these shares as they please. This network configuration is shown in Figure 15-1.

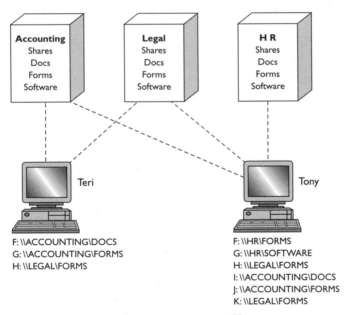

Figure 15-1: Network file services without DFS

As you can see, Teri's computer has a total of three network drives connected to two separate servers. Tony's a little out of control, with a total of six network connections to three different servers. He even has two network drives connected to exactly the same network share. This seems a little wasteful and obviously a bit confusing because Tony has connected to the same share twice.

DFS provides a better way to do this. Using the DFS Administrator utility, you as administrator may create a single tree structure that includes shares from each of the individual departments. If you desire, you can even create individual DFS trees for each NT-based file server. DFS would allow the previously described network diagram to be simplified, as illustrated in Figure 15-2.

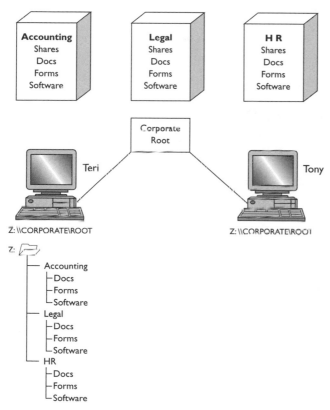

Figure 15-2: Network file services with DFS

As you can see, the network file services are much simpler with DFS enabled. This has widespread effects that go beyond the obvious technical benefits. For example, Teri can now describe a file to anyone on the network by saying, "It's on the Z drive under the Accounting, Docs directory." This is much easier than the alternative, which would include describing a share (which many users would not understand).

DFS has many other "benefits," according to Microsoft. Unfortunately, the rest of the features are poorly implemented; they are discussed in the next section.

What DFS Lacks

Microsoft's DFS add-on has many features but is lacking in several key areas. You will notice these as you begin to implement DFS into your network, each time you say to yourself, "Man, I really wish I could do *that*...."

First, the DFS Administrator is a clumsy utility. It is better in many respects than the command-line interface, but it should really be an integrated part of the Windows Explorer and Server Manager utilities, rather than a standalone executable. When adding a share as shown in Figure 15-3, you will find that the browse buttons are practically useless, and you will probably have to type long pathnames in by hand. I try not to get too bogged down in the graphical user interface provided by Microsoft in this book, but this utility is so difficult to use that it warrants mentioning.

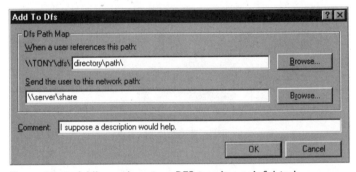

Figure 15-3: Adding a share to a DFS tree is a painful task.

As you may have already gathered, I am not a fan of WINS. Unfortunately, DFS does not allow the use of DNS entries or IP addresses to resolve server names and as such requires WINS or LMHOSTS files. Because LMHOSTS is rarely used on enterprise LANs, DFS is only useful for those also using WINS.

One of the most touted features of DFS is its support for transparent fail-over between two file servers. There is one major problem, however: The individual shares participating in the fail-over DFS branch must be read-only! Currently, Microsoft provides nothing to replicate updated files accurately between two systems. Additionally, while branches of a DFS tree may be configured as redundant, the root of the DFS tree itself is not redundant because each client system must map to it with a single computer name! I cover the details of DFS's fail-over capabilities later in this chapter.

Along with the fail-over capabilities, DFS provides some very limited load-balancing capabilities. These work in exactly the same way as the fail-over capabilities and have the same disadvantage: There is no way to replicate files as they are updated, so load-balanced DFS branches may allow just read-only access by users.

Further, they lack a feature that could be very advantageous: intelligently connecting users based on their geographic or network location. With this feature, which is included with NT 5.0, a user in Los Angeles would be directed to files on a local file server while a user in Tampa Bay would use files located on a server on the same network.

Implementing the Software

The DFS software has really light requirements. Add-on client software must be installed on Windows 95 systems before they may participate as clients. Server software may be installed on Windows NT Workstation and Windows NT Server systems, but it is only required if the system will be hosting a DFS tree, because Windows NT includes the client software out of the box. Sixteen-bit Windows operating systems and non-Microsoft OSs are not supported by DFS. However, 16-bit applications that are running on a 32-bit operating system may make use of DFS shares on the network.

Requirements

The requirements for the DFS server are fairly simple because DFS itself is simple. Hardware requirements are identical to those of the operating system. It does consume a few more megs of disk space, but the software is small enough to fit on a floppy disk. Server software requirements are minimal:

 ◆ Windows NT Workstation or Server v4.0

 ◆ Service pack 3

 ◆ About two megs of hard drive space

Windows NT has the client built into the operating system, so it has no special requirements. Windows 95 requires an add-on component to act as a DFS client, with these requirements:

 ◆ Windows 95

 ◆ About a meg of hard drive space

Installing with Windows NT

First, you should know that you only need to install DFS software on NT systems that will be DFS *servers*. That's because Microsoft had the foresight to build the DFS client software into Windows NT 4.0. Pretty clever, eh? If you are creating a DFS server and you do not already have the DFS software, you may download it from Microsoft. DFS is available at the following URL:

`http://backoffice.microsoft.com/downtrial/moreinfo/dfs.asp`

To install it, follow these steps:

1. Download the software from Microsoft.

2. Execute the file, currently named `dfs_v41_i386.exe`. Executing it extracts the contents into a subdirectory of your system directory, `<winnt_root>\system32\DFS`.

3. Open the Network Control Panel. Select the Services tab and click the Add button. Choose Have Disk and select the directory the files were extracted to. This directory, by default, is `<winnt_root>\system32\DFS`.

4. During the installation, you will be prompted to choose a DFS root. You may do so now (I suggest creating a new directory), or you may do so at a later time by using the DFS Administrator.

5. DFS will be part of the operating system the next time the computer restarts.

Installing with Windows 95

In order for Windows 95 clients to connect to a DFS share from a Windows NT system, a special client must be installed on the Windows 95 computer. This is a simple process because all the software you need is included with the Windows NT client.

To install the Windows 95 agent for DFS:

1. Share the DFS client software from an NT server that has DFS installed. The DFS client software is located in the `<winnt_root>\system32\DFS\win95` directory.

2. Connect a drive on the Windows 95 machine to the Windows 95 DFS share.

3. Open the Network Control Panel applet. Click the Add button, double-click Service, and then press the Have Disk button.

4. Select the drive letter and path for the Windows 95 DFS client, as shared in step 1. Click OK when you have specified the path correctly.

5. Select DFS Services for Microsoft Network Client and click OK.

6. You will be returned to the Network Control Panel applet. Choose OK and restart your computer to make the changes take effect.

Once the system starts up again, you will be able to connect to DFS shares.

Installing with Windows 98

Good news — Windows 98 supports DFS out of the box. Nothing needs to be done! Furthermore, it supports all DFS functionality, just like Windows NT.

Configuring

Most of the configuration for DFS is done from the DFS Administrator, a tool that was added to the Administrative Tools (Common) group within the start menu. The root of the DFS tree is set from the Network Control Panel applet. This section gives a brief overview of how these three tools can be used to configure DFS on an NT server. No configuration is necessary on the client side, so the topic is only touched on.

Once the DFS software has been installed on a server, a DFS root should be created. I recommend following these steps:

1. In Windows Explorer, create a new directory on the server. This directory will act as a DFS root. It requires very little disk space because files do not actually need to be stored here — the DFS root acts more as a table of contents, providing references to other shares on the network.

2. Share that directory with a suitable name, such as "root." Be sure to grant access to everyone who will use any part of the DFS tree. If subdirectories within the DFS tree need stricter permissions, you have the option of applying them only to that particular branch.

3. Specify the share you just created as the root of the DFS tree. This can be done during installation, or by pressing the Properties button with Distributed File System highlighted from within the Services tab of the Network Control Panel. The dialog box used to create the DFS root is shown in Figure 15-4.

4. Restart the computer.

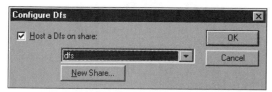

Figure 15-4: The root of a DFS tree is configured from the Network Control Panel.

DFS Gripes 1, 2, and 3

First, why does Microsoft require you to administer DFS from both the Network Control Panel applet *and* the DFS Administrator? They don't do this for WINS or DNS administration. Second, why does the entire server need to be rebooted if the DFS tree changes? In most environments, the server that contains the root of the DFS tree will be extremely critical. In zero-downtime environments, a simple server reboot is a very difficult task. Third, why can there be only one DFS root on an individual server? It would be a lot easier to make servers redundant for each other if you could create multiple DFS trees.

Remember that the computer must be restarted after changing the DFS root. This is a major limitation in the DFS software, as anyone who manages a no-downtime server will appreciate.

Once the server has rebooted, you may begin to build your DFS tree. The tool you will use for this is the DFS Administrator, which allows you to add "volumes" to the tree. The term "volumes" is not very descriptive; the term "virtual directory" describes the concept better, but I will continue to use "volume" to remain consistent with Microsoft. A volume is a subdirectory within a DFS tree that redirects DFS clients to a different network share, which may reside on a different server.

Now that a share has been designated the DFS root for a server, it is time to create a directory structure and link to shared directories and external DFS trees. These tasks are done using Windows Explorer and the DFS Administrator.

It is best that you take some time and plan your DFS tree — it is painful to reconfigure it later. If all subdirectories of the DFS root branch directly to other shares or external DFS trees, then you have no need to create physical directories. However, you will probably want to organize the shares on your network more than they already are. To do this, you should create physical directories within the folder that is shared as the DFS root. For example, if you want to organize all the shares in your network according to the region of the country, you may envision having folders within the DFS root for the east coast, the west coast, and Canada. Therefore, you would create three folders within the DFS root, as shown in Figure 15-5.

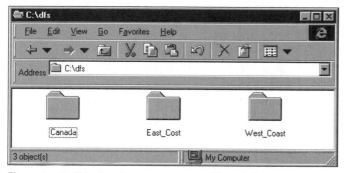

Figure 15-5: This directory structure would work for an organization divided into three regions.

Once you have organized your DFS tree using physical directories, you may begin to add mapped volumes to it. These are added using the DFS Administrator. Continuing our example, consider an enterprise network with separate divisions for the east coast, the west coast, and Canada. In each division are one or more file servers with shares for accounting, human resources, and information systems. You would like these shares to be within the regional subdirectories of the DFS tree. A diagram of the desired tree structure is shown in Figure 15-6.

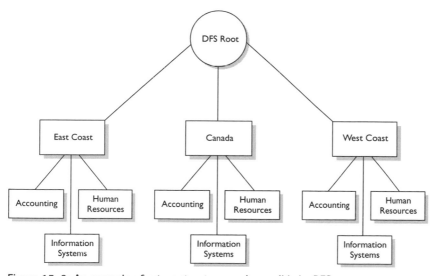

Figure 15-6: An example of a tree structure made possible by DFS

Each level below the second-level directories maps to a share on some server, so they must be added as a mapped volume. To do this, launch the DFS Administrator and follow these instructions:

1. From the DFS menu, select Add to DFS. Alternatively, you may click the first toolbar button.

2. You will be greeted by the Add to DFS dialog box, as shown in Figure 15-3. This dialog box prompts you to enter the desired path within the DFS tree and the network destination it maps to. Both values are entered as UNCs and may contain subdirectories below the root share.

3. Fill in a comment in the Comment field to remind yourself or other administrators why a particular branch exists. Once you have filled in all the fields, click OK.

4. Assuming you completed all required fields correctly, the mapped volume will be added to the DFS tree and become immediately available to all clients. You should save a backup of the DFS tree after all changes by choosing Save As from the DFS menu.

When adding branches to a DFS tree, remember these guidelines:

◆ You may create mapped volumes to shares *and* to subdirectories of shares. For example, `\\server\DFS\documents` could map to `\\server2\documents` or to `\\server2\d$\files\documents`.

◆ If you created mapped volumes to subdirectories of shares, Windows 95 machines cannot connect to them.

◆ You may create mapped volumes to non-Microsoft shares. For example, a subdirectory of a DFS tree could map a directory to a shared volume on a NetWare server.

◆ If you create a mapped volume to a non-Microsoft share, all Windows NT clients that connect to that subdirectory must have the appropriate network client loaded. Windows 95 clients are completely incapable of branching to other types of network file systems.

Understanding the Protocol

DFS is just an evolution of the NetBIOS file transfer mechanism, SMB. Therefore, the only aspects of the protocol that I will cover in detail here are those unique to DFS; otherwise I will assume you have read Chapter 10, which covers NetBIOS in detail.

DFS accomplishes some pretty amazing things, but the underlying mechanism is surprisingly simple. The client and server each have special agents installed on them that allow the server to signal, and the client to understand, instructions to redirect a network connection to a different server or share point.

How It Works

Remember that a DFS share is essentially a standard SMB share with additional functionality. This functionality does not come into play until the client accesses a subdirectory that is actually a mapped volume; until then, it looks and acts just like any other share. However, specifics of the DFS protocol begin to appear the moment a client requests a directory that is actually a mapped volume.

When a client retrieves a directory listing from a DFS share, it is not aware which subdirectories are physical subdirectories and which are mapped volumes. However, as soon as the client attempts to access a mapped volume within a DFS tree, the DFS server returns an SMB error message indicating that the directory does not exist. This is indicated by DFS error number 3, which Network Monitor displays as "DFS PATH_NOT_FOUND." Now it may seem rude that the server would tell the client it could not find a path even though the server just returned the directory name as part of a directory listing. Fortunately, the client knows that the "DFS PATH_NOT_FOUND" error really means, "That directory may be a mapped volume, please check on it."

So after the client receives the "DFS PATH_NOT_FOUND" error, it establishes another connection to the DFS server and attaches to the IPC$ share. Once this connection is established, the client issues a request to look up a DFS reference. This lookup allows the client to determine whether a specific directory is really a DFS mapped volume. This request shows up in Network Monitor with the description "Get DFS Referral." The data portion of the packet includes the full UNC path to the subdirectory within the DFS root. For example, if the client was attempting to determine the real location on the network of the subdirectory map_volume within the DFS root \\server\DFS\, it would send a "Get DFS Referral" packet to the DFS server and name the UNC path "\\SERVER\DFS\MAP_VOLUME*.*."

Assuming that the directory listed really is a DFS volume, the DFS server returns a "Get DFS Referral" response packet. This packet contains some unnecessary data: the directory requested by the client in both long filename format and DOS-compatible 8.3 format. It also contains the UNC path to which the mapped volume is redirected.

The client pulls out the only useful piece of information within the data portion of this packet: the UNC path to which the DFS directory refers. It then establishes an SMB connection to the server and share referenced and does whatever it needs to do in normal SMB fashion. Once the referred computer is connected to, traffic is no longer DFS specific. Because the client returns to using the most basic SMB command set, shares that exist on servers that do not support DFS may be added as mapped volumes. Figure 15-7 gives an overview of the DFS redirection process.

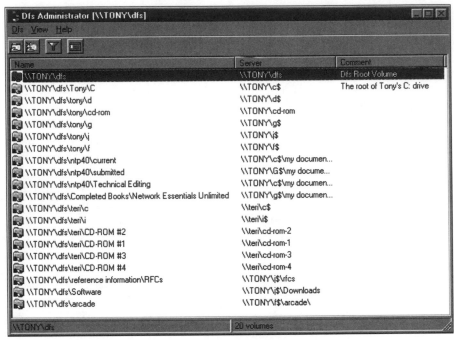

Figure 15-7: The confusing process of a DFS redirection

Things to Know About DFS Referrals

Even if you do not wish to spare the brain cells to memorize the entire DFS referral process, there are several important things to remember about it.

When a server refers a client to another network share, it does so by indicating a generic error. It is then the client's responsibility to requery the server and determine the final network destination. This allows for some level of backward compatibility; if a client that does not support DFS attempts to access a mapped volume, it will receive a valid error message. Theoretically, the server could include the DFS lookup information with the first error message. Including the error message means that two more packets are transmitted than you would expect: the error message and the DFS lookup by the client.

A separate SMB session is created for each and every mapped volume that a client refers to. However, that SMB session is not created until the mapped volume is referenced. Also, if the client already has a connection to a given share, a new connection is not established. Connections are reused whether or not the original connection was established through DFS. The lesson to be learned from this is that you should reference the fewest number of network shares possible. For example, consider a network in which ten directories on a file server need to be mapped to a DFS tree. The less efficient method is to create ten different shares on the file server and map each one to a separate DFS directory. A better method is to create a single share at the root of the file server's drive and reference the single share and each subdirectory within the DFS administrator.

To clarify this point, consider a file server with the shares Accounting, HR, and IS. These shares are physically located on the D:\ drive of the file server, in the physical directories D:\Shares\Accounting, D:\Forms\HR, and D:\Documents\IS. When configuring these as mapped volumes with a DFS tree, reference the UNC path at the lowest possible share point. Instead of creating three mapped volumes as shown in Table 15-1, share the root of the D:\ drive and reference this top-level share instead, as shown in Table 15-2.

TABLE 15-1 DFS MAPPED VOLUMES: THE WRONG WAY

DFS Directory	Referenced Network Path
\\Server\DFS\Accounting	\\Server2\Accounting
\\Server\DFS\IS	\\Server2\IS
\\Server\DFS\HR	\\Server2\HR

TABLE 15-2 DFS MAPPED VOLUMES: THE RIGHT WAY

DFS Directory	Referenced Network Path
\\Server\DFS\Accounting	\\Server2\d$\Shares\Accounting
\\Server\DFS\IS	\\Server2\d$\Documents\IS
\\Server\DFS\HR	\\Server2\d$\Forms\HR

This method increases the speed with which clients may move from one mapped volume to another, because all mapped volumes correspond to the same share on the server. It also reduces the overhead on the client, because it does not need to maintain separate SMB sessions for each share. Remember that Windows 95 clients cannot reference mapped volumes that refer to subdirectories, so this will not work if you still support Windows 95 clients. Also keep in mind that an extra step will be involved if you change the physical path of the shares on the server: You must also change the mapping within the DFS Administrator.

Protocol Analysis

Very little consideration needs to be given to DFS to support it on a network. All DFS traffic is SMB based and relies on the NetBIOS Session service, implemented with TCP port 139. Therefore, if your network supports SMB-based file sharing, you should have no problem supporting DFS.

Bandwidth is hardly a consideration: Each time a client must make a transition between DFS mapped volumes, approximately 1,000 bytes of network traffic are generated. This represents only the traffic that is DFS specific; other traffic will be generated if the client needs to establish a session to the destination server.

REMOTE ADMINISTRATION

Remote administration uses both SMB and the Microsoft Remote Procedure Call protocol. Both of these, as you might expect, utilize the NetBIOS Session service using TCP port 139. Therefore, no special network consideration needs to be given to allow remote administration of a DFS server.

You will probably be surprised at the amount of network traffic that is generated by simply administering the server. The DFS administration tool goes through a particularly inefficient process of enumerating all the shares on the remote system before displaying a listing of DFS mapped volumes that are available.

When you first connect to a remote DFS server using the DFS Administrator, an SMB session is established. Then a request is submitted to the DFS server to enumerate all of the SMB shares that it has available. One of these shares is actually the DFS root, though it is not indicated as anything other than a run-of-the-mill SMB share.

To determine which of the shares listed by the DFS server is the DFS root, the DFS Administrator application requests information about each share that the server has listed as available. It requests this information one share at a time, going in the sequence that was provided by the DFS server. These requests are performed using a "NetrShareGetInfo" via the Microsoft Remote Procedure Call service. The DFS server provides the information about each share and tags the share that is actually the DFS root with something special – a value of 3 in the one hundred twenty-ninth byte after the IP header of the packet. This value is not picked up as anything interesting in Network Monitor, but you can find it if you analyze the data portion of the packet itself. More important, the DFS Administrator recognizes this value and knows it has found the true DFS root. It stops the process of requesting information about every share on the system and begins to request DFS-specific information about the DFS root.

You can recognize that the DFS Administrator has found the DFS root by watching the traffic for a special request to the netdfs object on the DFS server. This shows up in Network Monitor with a packet description similar to "C NT create & X, File = \netdfs." Using the MS-RPC protocol, the DFS Administrator then requests a listing of all DFS mapped volumes within the DFS root. The DFS server responds with all the data that you are accustomed to seeing in the DFS Administrator: DFS path in UNC format, network path in UNC format, and a comment.

When adding or modifying existing mapped volumes within the DFS Administrator, you will observe that all updates take place using the NetBIOS Session service and underlying protocols. This is fairly straightforward, but it is interesting to note that the DFS server itself verifies that each share is accessible before allowing it to be added. Therefore, when you add a mapped volume remotely using the DFS Administrator, your local system establishes an SMB session and provides the information about the new mapped volume. Then the DFS server establishes an SMB session to the server that contains the new mapped volume, just to verify that the shared directory actually exists. This verification is done through a NetrShareGetInfo() MS-RPC call.

ALTERNATE SHARES FOR LOAD BALANCING AND FAIL-OVER

As you may recall from earlier in this chapter, multiple remote shares may correspond to a single mapped volume. The intention is to provide for load balancing and fail-over in enterprise networks. This implementation is similar to round-robin DNS: The client requests information about a mapped volume, and the DFS server provides it with a listing of the servers that it may be connected to. This is shown in the SMB portion of the packet description provided by Network Monitor:

```
SMB: R transact2 NT Get DFS Referral (response to frame 55)
   SMB: Transaction data
      SMB: DFS Path Consumed = 36 (0x24)
      SMB: DFS Number of Referrals = 4 (0x4)
      SMB: DFS Server Function = 2147450878 (0x7FFF7FFE)
 SMB: DFS Version 2 Referral
      SMB: DFS Version Number = 2 (0x2)
      SMB: DFS Server Type = Unknown Server Type
      SMB: DFS Proximity = 0 (0x0)
      SMB: DFS TimeToLive = 604800 (0x93A80)
      SMB: DFS Filename = \TONY\dfs\Test\DFS
      SMB: DFS 8.3 Filename = \TONY\dfs\TEST\DFS
      SMB: DFS Sharename = \TONY\dfs4
    SMB: DFS Version 2 Referral
      SMB: DFS Version Number = 2 (0x2)
      SMB: DFS Server Type = Unknown Server Type
      SMB: DFS Proximity = 0 (0x0)
      SMB: DFS TimeToLive = 604800 (0x93A80)
      SMB: DFS Filename = \TONY\dfs\Test\DFS
      SMB: DFS 8.3 Filename = \TONY\dfs\TEST\DFS
      SMB: DFS Sharename = \TONY\dfs2
    SMB: DFS Version 2 Referral
      SMB: DFS Version Number = 2 (0x2)
      SMB: DFS Server Type = Unknown Server Type
      SMB: DFS Proximity = 0 (0x0)
      SMB: DFS TimeToLive = 604800 (0x93A80)
      SMB: DFS Filename = \TONY\dfs\Test\DFS
      SMB: DFS 8.3 Filename = \TONY\dfs\TEST\DFS
```

```
    SMB: DFS Sharename = \TONY\dfs1
SMB: DFS Version 2 Referral
  SMB: DFS Version Number = 2 (0x2)
  SMB: DFS Server Type = Unknown Server Type
  SMB: DFS Proximity = 0 (0x0)
  SMB: DFS TimeToLive = 604800 (0x93A80)
  SMB: DFS Filename = \TONY\dfs\Test\DFS
  SMB: DFS 8.3 Filename = \TONY\dfs\TEST\DFS
  SMB: DFS Sharename = \TONY\dfs3
```

As you can see, it is left up to the client to determine which network share it will attempt to access. Unlike with round-robin DNS, the client does not necessarily choose the first server listed. Eventually, the client built into Windows NT will be intelligent enough to find the closest network share and connect to it.

A network analysis of a client accessing a DFS branch with multiple mapped volumes showed a serious problem with the way updates take place. The client does not necessarily access the same server/share even during a single session, a fact that can make updates impossible. For example, I connected to a DFS branch that mapped to four shares. I created a new file, which the client created in the \\TONY\DFS2 share. I then immediately attempted to rename that same file; unfortunately, the client issued the rename command through an SMB session connected to a *different* share, which did not have the file. Therefore, the client received an error message. Given this lack of continuity, I cannot imagine how alternate shares could ever work with read/write files, even if they were replicated between different servers, because the updates would have to take place instantaneously to avoid confusing the clients.

The only situation I can imagine in which this would work is that of a mirrored or shared drive. Indeed, there would be little advantage to creating alternate shares that are located on the same system, but two file servers, under certain circumstances, may be able to share the same file system. (Does the name "Wolfpack" mean anything to you?) In this case, alternate DFS shares may be useful. Otherwise, I cannot fathom it working reliably with updatable files.

Noting Transarc/IBM's DFS

Microsoft was not the first company to offer DFS services for Windows-based networks, though it seems likely that they will become the most popular. Other companies have been working on DFS for several years. These third-party products offer a wide variety of features not currently available from the Windows NT 4.0 add-on product offered free from Microsoft. For those organizations that need the power of DFS now, one of these third-party products may be the right solution.

Transarc, a subsidiary of IBM, is the primary competitor in the DFS marketplace. Most compelling among Transarc DFS's features is its ability to connect hosts using different platforms, such as UNIX, VMS, Macintosh, and Windows. In fact, DFS was not even designed for Windows networking; its heritage lies in UNIX and mainframe file sharing. Those organizations that already make use of IBM's DCE software will find DFS a natural extension. Those that do not use DCE will find it cumbersome, difficult, and costly to maintain.

This software really does provide for data replication and redundancy, a feature that Microsoft still just plans to support.

For more information on Transarc's DFS, visit Transarc's Web site at `http://www.transarc.com`.

Outlining the Future of DFS: NT5

The distributed file system as we know it now is still in its infancy. It will only begin to mature with the release of NT 5, which includes most of the features I've been complaining about it lacking. For instance:

- When used in conjunction with NT 5.0's File Replication Service, load balancing between read and write file servers becomes possible.

- Intelligent clients are capable of selecting among a list of alternates and choosing the file server geographically closest.

- Redundancy is provided for the root of the DFS tree.

- The nasty DFS Administrator tool is replaced with the Microsoft Management Console.

- Transitions between junctions in a tree are made faster.

These added features allow DFS to be used in an enterprise environment, adding capabilities that make its implementation worthwhile to end users.

A Final Word

DFS provides a more robust network file system than has been previously available on a Windows network. However, the software currently released by Microsoft is little more than a teaser for what is yet to come. While it is useful for organizations that wish to hide the structure of a network file system, it lacks so much that administrators need – reliability, redundancy, and ease of administration.

For those who like DFS but crave more, alternatives are available from third-party suppliers. The most popular is from Transarc, which currently publishes a robust DFS system that provides the features Microsoft's implementation of DFS lacks most. For those unwilling to pay for third-party software, Microsoft is greatly expanding DFS with the release of Windows NT 5.0.

Summary

You have learned the following:

- ◆ What DFS is, and how it will affect your network
- ◆ How to implement DFS
- ◆ The details of the protocol itself and how to troubleshoot it
- ◆ How Microsoft's DFS compares with Transarc/IBM's DFS
- ◆ Microsoft's plans for DFS with Windows NT 5.0

In the next chapter, you'll learn all about Windows NT's support for Hypertext Transfer Protocol services. This includes an in-depth look at Microsoft Internet Information Server versions 3.0 and 4.0, Netscape Enterprise server, and the various Web browsers. Special attention is given to the underlying standards for HTTP and how they are supported in the real world.

Chapter 16

World Wide Web Services

IN THIS CHAPTER

◆ Reviewing Microsoft's Internet Information Server, versions 3.0 and 4.0

◆ Working with the HTTP/1.0 and /1.1 standards, and both the client and server implementations in Windows NT

◆ Evaluating the impact of Web traffic on the Internet and your intranet

◆ Analyzing and troubleshooting HTTP traffic

THIS CHAPTER IS full of the *good stuff*. The good stuff, of course, is all those nitty-gritty technical details about Microsoft's Internet Information Server the average Joe never discovers. The good stuff is the stuff you learn at 2 A.M. when your Web server has gone on strike and simply refuses to work again, and you start getting e-mail from people who absolutely *must* visit your Web site at 2 A.M. That's the way I learned it; this chapter will make it a little easier for you.

I'm going to assume you have read the documentation for Internet Information Server. If not, you have probably read one of the many books on the market that rehashes the information contained in the documentation. So you probably already know how the user interface works. You probably already know that the only secure way to authenticate yourself to a Web server is by using the Internet Explorer browser. You probably already know when you should enable *Execute* permissions, and when you only need *Read*. So I'm not going to tell you those things.

This chapter covers some details of IIS but spends a lot of time merely discussing the standards IIS is based on. Don't believe everything Microsoft tells you – they did *not* invent the Internet. Protocols like HTTP and FTP have been around for many years, and Microsoft is still just playing catch-up. So it's not going to work right all the time (but you have probably already learned that!).

If you are having a problem with a Web server not serving up a page properly, turn to the section on the HTTP protocol. That section will describe what steps a Web browser goes through when retrieving a page from a Web server, and how the Web server should respond. It will describe how to use Network Monitor to troubleshoot the problem and show you what to look for. And if you understand what is happening, it will help you invent a workaround to appease those night-owl Web surfers.

Much of this information is drawn from the Requests for Comments. The original RFCs can be downloaded from the InterNIC at `ftp://ftp.internic.net/rfc`. Consider this a last resort: I have made a real effort to compile all the useful troubleshooting information from the most important RFCs, specifically so that others don't have to dig through the standards. The chapter ends with some useful troubleshooting information on HTML and URLs.

Introducing Microsoft's Internet Information Server

In 1996, Microsoft realized that the Internet was here to stay. They finally gave up hope that NetBEUI was the protocol of the future, and they released the first version of their Web server — named Internet Information Server. It worked with NT 3.51 and supported WWW (World Wide Web), FTP (File Transfer Protocol), and Gopher. Instantly, they were the laughingstock of the UNIX community, who had been working with Internet services for twenty years. But people used it because it was free and ran on NT. One or two ISPs even began offering hosting services on the platform.

Since then, it has grown up a lot. IIS 4.0 is a robust, high-performance Web hosting platform. For some reason, though, UNIX people still laugh at us . . .

The most used feature of IIS, by far, is the WWW service. "WWW services" is a pretty broad term — encompassing just about everything people use Web servers for. The primary uses for it are the Hypertext Transfer Protocol (HTTP) and Secure Sockets Layer (SSL) services, which are old but constantly evolving standards published by the Internet Engineering Task Force (IETF).

Internet Information Server provides a full suite of standard HTTP features, and several features not available through any other HTTP server. Naturally, it supports HTTP and SSL services. However, it also supports up to 1,500 virtual servers on a single IIS server, filtering based on IP source address, and both basic and NT challenge/response authentication. This chapter covers each of these features in excruciating detail.

Understanding the HTTP Protocol

Hypertext Transfer Protocol, or HTTP, has quickly become one of the most popular protocols in Internetworking. It has been in use on the World Wide Web since 1990. This success is attributable to the success of the Internet's primary method of communication, the World Wide Web. Today, companies deploy HTTP servers for the public to use (Internet Web servers) and for only people internal to the organization to use (intranet Web servers).

The HTTP protocol falls squarely into the application layer of the OSI model, meaning it is available for use by processes running within a computer (for example, Netscape's Navigator Web browser).

Several versions of HTTP are currently in use. RFC 1945 defines HTTP/1.0. RFC 2068 defines HTTP/1.1. These standards are some of the longer ones available — over 150 pages. Fortunately, they are detailed and clearly written. There are many things they do not and cannot tell you, though. RFCs cannot tell you how the real world uses the protocols, and they cannot tell you how different vendor's products support the standards.

HTTP Servers

HTTP is a client-server protocol. The server is a process that runs on a wide variety of hardware platforms and operating systems. For many years, the most common hosts on the Internet were UNIX-based servers, running UNIX operating systems from a variety of vendors such as Sun and Silicon Graphics. Today, Microsoft has a very small piece of the pie: Windows NT servers have become a popular platform for HTTP servers. This success is largely due to Microsoft's willingness to give the Web server away *for free*. Microsoft's Internet Information Server, or IIS, was originally available as a free download from Microsoft's Web site and was considered an add-on to Windows NT Server 3.51. Microsoft included version 2.0 of IIS free with NT Server 4.0, offering organizations an opportunity to launch a Web server without installing any third-party products.

As of the writing of this book, IIS 4.0 is the current production release. IIS 4.0 has added many features and brings the Windows NT platform into competition with the more traditional UNIX-based Web servers. It is more scalable and more robust, particularly in its support for hosting multiple virtual servers. Best of all, it is available for download free on the Internet. Just visit `http://backoffice.microsoft.com/downtrial/optionpack.asp`.

Microsoft does not have the monopoly on Web servers (*yet!*). Netscape, the dominant vendor of professional Web software on the Internet, ports all of their Web server code to the Windows NT platform. It works well, though very few professional hosting services offer it. For more information on Netscape's Web server, including a place to download a copy, visit Netscape's Web site at `http://www.netscape.com/download/`.

When troubleshooting HTTP problems, keep in mind that every HTTP server is different. While all Telnet servers and all FTP servers tend to behave in pretty much the same way, Web server vendors make an effort to differentiate themselves from the market by adding additional features to their Web servers. This factor, combined with the dynamic nature of the HTTP "standards," makes troubleshooting this protocol difficult. These differences make understanding every aspect of the HTTP protocol especially critical for troubleshooting and programming purposes.

HTTP Clients

The IITTP client market has become big business. Legal and marketing battles between Netscape and Microsoft rage on, pushing their respective "Web browsers": Navigator and Internet Explorer. These HTTP clients typically offer the capability to act as clients for other protocols as well, such as FTP, RealAudio, and HTTPS. Nonetheless, HTTP remains the dominant protocol supported by HTTP clients.

The HTTP client often causes problems with the HTTP protocol. Clients from different vendors tend to support different aspects of the HTTP protocol as well as a unique feature set above and beyond the standards specified by RFC 2068. For example, Microsoft's Internet Explorer supports Microsoft's challenge/response authentication over HTTP – Netscape's Navigator client does not.

HTML editors – the modern word processors – are also HTTP clients. They generally allow both reading and writing to a Web site, and they may support additional features. Microsoft's FrontPage allows an administrator to do just about anything to the Web site – create virtual directories, change the default filename, and handle file management, to name a few. Even more interesting is how it accomplishes these tasks – it does not make use of the NetBIOS over TCP/IP like most other Microsoft applications; rather, it relies solely on the HTTP protocol.

Netscape's HTML editor, Composer, supports a smaller set of functions but still allows the user to read and write files to and from a Web server. Like FrontPage, it does all of its magic through the HTTP protocol. Composer and FrontPage have made the job of the Webmaster more complicated by taking advantage of a broader subset of the HTTP protocol. Further, they have eliminated that peace of mind we had knowing that people on the Internet could only read files from our Web server, but never, ever upload anything.

In general, when troubleshooting HTTP and Web server problems, test with multiple Web browsers. Often a problem may be Web browser–specific. Knowing this does not in itself solve the problem, but it does offer a quick workaround – use a different browser. After you determine the problem is browser-specific, you must determine whether it is the browser or the server that is not conforming to the HTTP standards. Knowing who is at fault gives you a starting point at laying blame – situations where products from multiple vendors are not working together are difficult to troubleshoot because vendors tend to blame each other.

Once you lay the blame on one particular vendor, it is much easier to convince that vendor to dedicate development time to solving your problem. Otherwise, it is common to be stuck in the middle of a blame war, where each vendor blames the other vendor's products.

All About Working with HTTP

The knowledge outlined in this section is critical to those of us who work with Web servers and the HTTP protocol on a low level. This includes network administrators, network engineers, systems administrators, systems engineers, and network programmers. For example, to be able to interpret information provided by Performance

Monitor on the number of active connections on a Web server, it is important to understand the nature of HTTP connections, under what circumstances a connection is established, and how long it is retained.

Developers, CGI writers, and anyone doing scripting or development for Web servers or clients must have a low-level knowledge of the HTTP protocol. For example, a system engineer wishing to write a program to performance-test a Web server must understand what command a script should issue to a Web server in order to retrieve a page. He or she must also know how clients determine the end of a file. This information is provided in the sections that follow.

TROUBLESHOOTING HTTP

The text-based nature of the HTTP commands and responses greatly simplifies troubleshooting, but it is far from simple. A great many commands, responses, and header fields are available to the clients and servers. Further, both the commands and the content share the same data stream, which makes using a protocol analyzer more difficult because communication commands cannot be separated from the files being transferred, as can be done with the FTP protocol.

Unfortunately, it is often necessary to troubleshoot the HTTP protocol. Particularly troublesome are the numerous beta software packages released by Microsoft and Netscape. Much of the Internet populace begins to use this software as soon as it is available, and the software is often "not quite ready for prime time."

There are several different ways to troubleshoot the HTTP protocol. The simplest method is to examine the log files on the server. Microsoft's Internet Information Server logs most requests to a text file by default, providing a great way to find malformed client requests. One disadvantage to using this method is that, by default, IIS caches all requests for several minutes before writing them out to the log file – making it more time consuming to track down a problem using these log files.

My favorite method of troubleshooting the HTTP protocol is to use a protocol analyzer such as Network Monitor. Network Monitor allows you to directly examine packets that are transmitted between the client and server, ensuring that no details are missed. You will be able to see every header field in every communication and, using this section of the book, determine the meaning behind it. You will also be able to determine if the client or server is responding appropriately to the messages being exchanged.

Another common method of troubleshooting Web servers is to use a Telnet client to connect to the server and submit queries directly to port 80, the default TCP port for HTTP. Almost any Telnet client can be used to submit queries and retrieve responses from a Web server because the HTTP standards, as defined by the IETF, are based on the Telnet communications protocol. The standard Telnet client built into both Windows 95 and Windows NT has the ability to Telnet to any TCP port number. Viewing the raw response a server provides to a query is useful because Web browsers interpret errors and present the user a more friendly error message than the server provides. This is nice for the average user, but the advanced systems engineer needs to examine the exact response from a server to accurately diagnose a problem.

To aid you in using Network Monitor and Telnet to troubleshoot HTTP, I have included examples and screenshots throughout this section.

WRITING SCRIPTS AND APPLICATIONS THAT USE HTTP

Developers writing applications that communicate with Web servers or act as a Web server must know the HTTP specifications backward and forward. This sounds like a daunting task, but the HTTP protocol is relatively simple to write programs for (in comparison to, say, NetBIOS). HTTP uses clear-text commands that can be issued easily from scripts or even a Telnet window. Because the protocol is so understandable, many systems and network engineers should be taking advantage of the simplicity to create their own HTTP-aware applications.

Potential applications that a systems administrator or engineer may write include client-side scripts that perform load testing on a Web server. A simple form of a load testing application is surprisingly easy to write. Languages such as Perl and C++ have libraries built in for HTTP communications. If you wish to avoid the additional layer of abstraction that these libraries provide, the program can be written to communicate directly at the socket layer. For example, a Perl script to retrieve a Web page from a server is as simple as this:

```
( $them, $port ) = @ARGV;

$port = 80 unless $port;
$AF_INET = 2;
$SOCK_STREAM = 1;

$sockaddr = 'S n a4 x8';

($name,$aliases,$proto) = getprotobyname('tcp');
($name,$aliases,$port) = getservbyname($port,'tcp')
unless $port =~ /^\d+$/;;
($name,$aliases,$type,$len,$thisaddr) =
gethostbyname($hostname);
($name,$aliases,$type,$len,$thataddr) = gethostbyname($them);

$this = pack($sockaddr, $AF_INET, 0, $thisaddr);
$that = pack($sockaddr, $AF_INET, $port, $thataddr);

if (socket(S, $AF_INET, $SOCK_STREAM, $proto)) {
print "socket ok... ";}
else {die "socket failed... \n"; }
```

```
if (bind(S, $this)) {
print "bind ok... ";}
else {die "bind failed... \n";}

if (connect(S,$that)) {
print "connect ok... ";}
else {die "connect failed... \n";}

select(S); $| = 1; select(STDOUT);
print S "GET / HTTP/1.0\n";
while ($a=<S>) {print $a;}
exit 1 ;
```

Besides load testing, many administrators write scripts or programs to monitor a Web server. For example, a script run from a workstation could retrieve a default page from a production Web server every five minutes. If the page was returned successfully, it would indicate that the Web server was up and running. If the page failed to return after several consecutive attempts, the Web server may have crashed. At this point, steps could be taken to alert an administrator or to automatically reboot the server. Such is the magic of coding when the programmer has a little knowledge of how protocols and networks operate.

SNIFFING HTTP

Throughout this book I have given examples from my favorite network sniffer — Microsoft's Network Monitor. Network Monitor is particularly useful for troubleshooting HTTP because of HTTP's simple standards — everything is in readable text. Furthermore, HTTP requests and responses are contained within single packets (unless the data being transferred is too large). Therefore, a single packet generally contains an entire request from a server, making it a simple task to determine exactly what data a Web browser is transmitting.

Perl for Win32

My favorite version of Perl that runs on Windows NT is available from ActiveState — for free! Just visit `http://www.activestate.com`. Additional builds of Perl are available for use with IIS through ISAPI and through ASP. Another implementation has become popular — this core version of Perl can be found at `http://www.perl.com/CPAN-local/ports/win32/Standard/x86/`.

For example, consider the following scenario: Netscape's Navigator browser is attempting to retrieve a Web page from a Web server and you need to determine how it is formatting its request. You'll need to:

1. Make sure the Network Monitor Agent is installed on your Windows NT system. Start Network Monitor, and begin capturing data on the network interface that will be used to make the request.

2. Launch the Web browser, and enter the URL you wish to use to test the browser's requests.

3. After the request has been sent, stop the capture within Network Monitor and examine the traffic.

4. A single packet will contain the entire request from Network Monitor. Figure 16-1 shows a screen from Network Monitor that has such a packet highlighted.

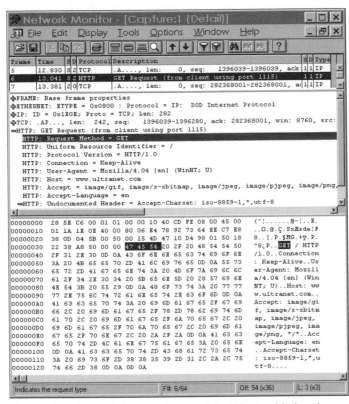

Figure 16–1: Network Monitor is a great tool for troubleshooting HTTP because all requests are in plain text.

As you can see in the figure, the Web browser is retrieving the default page from www.ultranet.com. It is using HTTP version 1.0, requesting HTTP Keep-Alives. The Web browser is Netscape Navigator (a.k.a. Mozilla) version 4.04 running on Windows NT. The following sections will give you the information you need to decode these messages and determine where problems may occur.

HTTP Communication Flow

HTTP has an interesting communications flow, mixing characteristics of both connection-oriented and connectionless traffic. Further, it creates interesting traffic patterns: As a client/server technology, it has traffic flow that is highly asymmetric, with outgoing traffic from the server far outweighing incoming traffic. Because HTTP is capable of both receiving and transmitting files through utilities such as FrontPage, however, traffic patterns vary heavily depending on usage.

Technically, HTTP is a connection-oriented protocol because it makes use of the TCP transport-layer protocol. This ensures that the requests and responses are received exactly as they are sent, and that data arrives intact. HTTP is unlike most connection-oriented protocols, however. Protocols like Telnet and SMTP initiate a TCP connection and then keep that connection open to carry on a dialog between the client and the server. Once the entire dialog has completed, the TCP connection is closed. Typically, HTTP works differently — the client establishes a TCP connection to the server and issues a single request. The server responds and then drops the connection. If the client needs to retrieve another file, it has to establish another TCP connection. This process is illustrated in Figure 16-2.

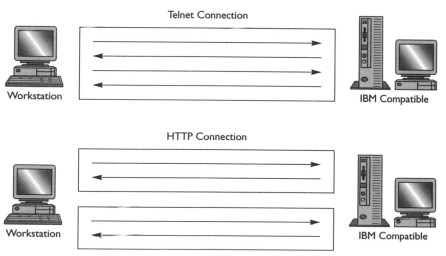

Figure 16-2: Most protocols maintain a connection for several data exchanges. HTTP 1.0 establishes a separate connection for each request.

HTTP and Complex Web Sites

HTTP/1.0's single transaction communication type works particularly poorly with today's typical Web sites: a single page is typically composed of multiple files, including images. For each file, an entirely separate TCP connection must be established. For major Web sites such as www.microsoft.com, as many as 100 separate files must be transferred to complete a single Web page. As you can imagine, this is an inefficient process. Fortunately, HTTP/1.1 provides a solution.

Because of the popularity of the World Wide Web, much has been done to optimize HTTP.

HTTP KEEP-ALIVE OPTIMIZATION

One of these optimizations is the "HTTP Keep-Alive session." When HTTP Keep-Alives are enabled, TCP sessions are not dropped after the Web server returns a file. Instead, the client and server carry on a dialog within a single TCP connection, transferring several files until the entire Web page is done. The connection is dropped when the client disconnects or when the server's preset timeout value expires. The effects of enabling HTTP Keep-Alives are many:

◆ The total number of simultaneous TCP connections on a Web server is significantly reduced.

◆ The ratio of protocol overhead to total bytes transferred between the client and the server is substantially reduced. (The TCP handshaking protocol is used only at the beginning of the TCP connection.)

◆ Complex Web pages are returned to the client faster.

  IIS 4.0 supports HTTP Keep-Alives by default. In IIS 1.0, 2.0, and 3.0, setting the following registry value to 0 will disable this option:

```
HKEY_LOCAL_MACHINE\System\CurrentControlSet\Services\W3SVC\
  Parameters\AllowKeepAlives
```

In IIS 4.0, a check box allows the enabling or disabling of HTTP Keep-Alives. This option is available through the WWW Service property sheet by selecting the Performance tab, as illustrated in Figure 16-3.

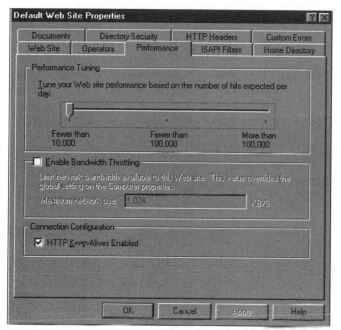

Figure 16-3: The MMC allows HTTP Keep-Alives to be enabled or disabled with IIS 4.0.

CLIENT-SIDE CACHING

Another commonplace optimization is client-side caching. This caching works just like any other cache: When a document is retrieved from the Internet (the slowest possible place to retrieve it from), it is stored in RAM on the client. Should that same file be needed again, it does not have to be retrieved from the Web server. The Web browser that the client is using will recognize the filename of the document being retrieved and display it from memory instead, reducing both latency and the total data that needs to be transferred.

Information from the Web is also stored on the client's hard drive. While it is not as fast to retrieve information from a hard drive as from RAM, it is still much faster than retrieving it from the Internet.

In any read-caching scheme, some mechanism must be in place to ensure that the source data is not updated without the cache being updated. If it were possible to update the source data without updating the cache, the cache would return erroneous information. For example, if you visit your favorite sports site to see the score for the Patriots game, it may report that the Patriots are losing by 14 points. Several minutes later, you return to the site to see that the score has not changed. In reality, your Web browser may have been returning the page from its local cache rather than retrieving it from the Web.

One way to combat this problem is to press the Refresh or Reload button on your Web browser; this forces the Web browser to recheck the information on the Web site for updates and is a useful way of viewing changes. On the other hand, you'll probably just discover the Patriots have fallen farther behind, so don't bother.

To combat this problem, Web pages are tagged with an expiration date. This expiration date allows the server to tell the client how long the page is good before it becomes stale. This is done through two HTTP message headers, Expires and Pragma, described in more detail later in this section.

IIS 4.0 allows you to set the cache expiration parameters that will be transmitted in the HTTP headers to the client. This gives you control over when the client-side application (the Web browser) will re-request pages and when it will simply display the information held in cache. To modify the expiration headers IIS 4.0 sends to the clients, edit the properties for the WWW service and select the HTTP Headers tab, as shown in Figure 16-4.

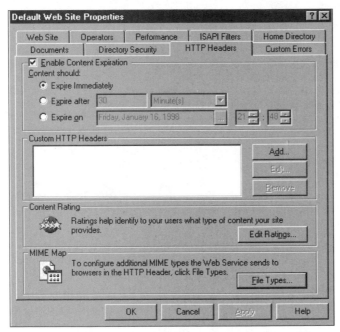

Figure 16-4: How the client is instructed to cache data can be controlled from within the IIS 4.0 MMC interface.

A check box and three option buttons are available, allowing you to enable or disable expiration headers and select the expiration behavior. Pages can be configured to expire immediately, on a certain day, or a number of minutes after being transmitted.

PROXY CACHING

An HTTP proxy acts as an application-layer gateway between the client and server. Proxies are commonly used to allow an entire organization access to the Internet through a single connection, while avoiding the assignment of public Internet addresses to internal clients. I do not intend to provide a full description of HTTP proxying in this section, but I do want to explain how HTTP proxy caching can affect the flow of HTTP information. For a detailed explanation of HTTP proxying, please see Chapter 18.

One of the greatest features of HTTP proxies is the ability to cache information from Web sites for an entire enterprise. As you can imagine, there is a lot of complexity in ensuring that as much caching is done as possible while making sure nobody in the enterprise receives an outdated copy of a Web site. The HTTP protocol has features built into it to allow Webmasters more control over specifying how proxies will cache documents, though most Webmasters do not specify different cache information for proxies than for any other client.

Proxies are important for Webmasters to understand, however, because many of your visitors will be using proxies to access your site and may receive an outdated or altered version as a result. Keep these factors in mind when you receive a complaint from a user who claims to be experiencing a problem you have already resolved: The client's proxy server may be storing data from your Web site that was gathered prior to your changes. Even if the client presses the Reload button on the Web browser, it will only be loading the data from the first proxy server.

Further, LAN administrators who are responsible for client-side HTTP applications, such as Web browsers, must understand the proxy configurations in their own environments. Otherwise, when a proxy breaks, they may be able to work around the problem by rerouting client traffic to another proxy server or directly to the Internet. Further, clients may experience problems as a result of proxy servers: Proxy servers may not be able to support some features of the newest Web browsers, or they may alter data slightly in the handling process.

This chapter does not cover HTTP proxies in great detail because most organizations still do not make use of them. Nonetheless, I've made an effort to provide a foundation of information that will allow you to diagnose and troubleshoot problems with Web servers.

HTTP Protocol Details

The following section describes the nitty-gritty details of the HTTP communications protocol.

I have included a subsection titled "Commands," which describes the different ways a Web browser can ask a server to do something. This section solves the mystery of applications like FrontPage — which do way more than many think is possible with HTTP commands. I will show you which applications use which request methods and tell you what the application is hoping to accomplish. Further, I will give you the information you need to send these requests directly to the Web server to help diagnose HTTP-related problems.

I have included a subsection on HTTP's status messages, which removes the mystery of the numeric codes included with server messages. Further, I'll tell you when they will appear from IIS and what the server is really trying to tell you. I might even tell you how to fix it!

The "MIME Types" subsection describes what a MIME type is and how the HTTP protocol makes use of it. It also tells you what you need to know to configure MIME types in IIS, and in which situations MIME configuration may fix (or cause!) problems.

In the subsection "HTTP Messages," I will cover the various parameters Web browsers may transmit to a Web server and tell you which parameters are used by Microsoft's Internet Explorer and which are used by Netscape's Navigator, the two most common browsers on the Internet today. This section also includes the parameters Web servers return to the browser, and I will describe which of those are used by IIS, which may be configured, and the effects of doing so. Where IIS differs from other Web servers on the Internet, I will contrast the different servers.

A further subsection covers the details of authentication through HTTP. I will show you the differences between what IIS calls "basic authentication" and "challenge/response authentication." I will also give you the information you need to determine which authentication methods a Web server has enabled.

HTTP MESSAGES

HTTP messages are the basis of all communication between clients and servers. Each message is the equivalent of a single statement, and these statements are strung together to form conversations. These conversations convey requests from clients to retrieve specific data from Web servers, what type of data will be returned, how much data to expect, and what software each part of the conversation is using. Messages are broken into several distinct layers. An overview of these layers is provided in Table 16-1.

TABLE 16-1 HTTP MESSAGE LAYERS

Layer	Description
Command or Response	What the server should do, or how the server responds
Message Headers	Information about the server, client, or message body
MIME Type	Describes the format of the message body
Message Body	The useful data — the actual payload

The first of these layers is what I call the "command" or the "response code." If you should ever find it necessary to dig into the actual standards, the RFC refers to these as "request" and "response." Commands are sent from the client to the server. The example I will use most often is a Web browser sending commands to a Web server – in this scenario, the browser sends commands to the server such as "Send me the page" or "Accept this information."

Response codes are the messages servers send back to the clients – they indicate success, failure, or several other alternatives.

The message headers provide specific information in a predefined format. Many, many header fields are defined by the HTTP protocol, and each can be used to communicate information about the state of the client or server, to modify the meaning of the request, or to describe the message body that will follow.

The MIME type is a standard description of the format the message body is being transferred in. Browsers use the MIME type to learn how to display the file they receive on the screen so that the user can understand it. Because MIME types describe message bodies, they are included in an HTTP message only when a message body is also being transmitted.

The message body itself is the data being transferred. In the most common Internet scenario, message bodies are transmitted from the server to the client at the client's request.

COMMANDS

This section describes the commands that a Web browser issues to the Web server. These are the browser's way of saying "Please send me this page" or "Please accept this form data." This section describes the different variations that IIS supports, and the different ways that Navigator, Internet Explorer, and FrontPage make use of them.

GET   The most common of all requests, the GET command retrieves a file from the Web server. In its simplest form it is similar to the TYPE command line utility included with Windows NT, in that it displays the contents of a file. The GET command, when sent from a client to a server, is followed by a Uniform Resource Identifier (URI, discussed near the end of this chapter). As you may recall, the URI is the portion of a URL that describes the directory and filename of a file on a server. For example, the URL http://www.microsoft.com/iis/ default.htm has a URI of /iis/default.htm.

Try a simple request directly to a Web server. First, use a Web browser to find a URL of a Web site and separate the URI from it. Then, Telnet to that server, specifying TCP port 80 instead of Telnet's default TCP port of 23. Next, type a simple GET command. If you have formatted the request properly, the Web server will return the document you requested. This is a simplified version of the command your Web browser would issue to the Web server to retrieve that same page. For example, to retrieve the default page from home.netscape.com, Telnet to home.netscape.com using port 80 and type:

GET / HTTP/1.0

Pretty simple, but you're not ready to give up your Web browser yet, I bet. What you will receive will probably be an HTML file. Nonetheless, you now have a basic understanding of the way browsers and servers communicate.

POST   The `POST` command is another command commonly used in the real-world Internet. The `POST` command may be issued to a server in the following circumstances:

◆ The Web browser is submitting data from an HTML form.

◆ A file is being uploaded to a server, such as with FrontPage.

◆ More data needs to be transmitted to the server than can fit in a single URL.

The `POST` command has one main advantage over the `GET` command: It has the ability to transfer an arbitrary amount of data from the client to the server. The `GET` command can transmit arguments as part of the URL, for example:

```
http://altavista.digital.com/cgi-
  bin/query?pg=q&what=web&kl=XX&q=IDG+books+NT&search.x=40&search.
  y=10
```

The Web server can separate the URI from the arguments by separating everything in the URL after the "?" character.

The `POST` command is much more flexible than the `GET` command. For example, a form may direct a browser to issue a post command when a button is pushed. The `POST` command will include a URI that references a file on the server, often a CGI of some type that will accept and process the data. If the URI is `/scripts/test.cgi`, and the data being submitted is "data=elvislives," the command issued to the server may appear as follows:

```
POST /scripts/test.cgi HTTP/1.1[CR/LF]
Content-Length: 15[CR/LF]
[CR/LF]
data=elvislives
```

Notice that the `POST` command itself is followed immediately by the accepting URI, `/scripts/test.cgi`, then by the HTTP version (similar to the `GET` command). However, more information is supplied, namely the content-length (the length of the data to be accepted by the server) and the actual data itself.

PUT   The `PUT` command is another commonly used HTTP command. It allows a simple file transfer from the client to the server and is commonly used by HTML editors such as Netscape's Composer and the HotDog utility. It may seem unusual that HTTP provides two methods to transfer data from the client to the server: the `POST` and `PUT` commands. The difference lies in the way the commands are used.

The PUT command takes as an argument the destination URI. This is similar to the argument that the POST command takes, except the PUT command is asking the server to place the data at the URI and the POST command is asking the server to send the data to the URI.

The PUT command is used in this manner:

```
PUT /documents/index.html HTTP/1.1[CR/LF]
Content-Length: 150[CR/LF]
Content-Type: text/html[CR/LF]
[...Actual file being transferred...]
```

DELETE   The DELETE command removes a file from a server. It takes a single argument: the URI of the file to be removed. It is used like this:

```
DELETE /documents/index.html HTTP/1.1[CR/LF]
Connection: Keep-Alive
User-Agent: Mozilla/4.04 [en] (WinNT; U)
Host: web13d.bbnplanet.com
Authorization: Basic fdsf32gjw389rugdUhfdsj==
```

The DELETE and PUT commands are most commonly used by Web site management applications, which allow files on a server to be managed. IIS did not natively support this functionality until the release of IIS 4.0, which supports both the PUT and DELETE commands for limited file-management capabilities.

OPTIONS   The OPTIONS command should elicit a response from the server describing all of the features implemented that apply to the resource specified in the Command-URI. The format of the OPTIONS command is similar to that of the other HTTP commands; it is the keyword OPTIONS followed by a URI, a protocol identification string, and a carriage return/linefeed. For example, the following command would retrieve a list of supported features for the default page of a Web site:

PUT and DELETE Using IIS 3.0

Good news! IIS 3.0 can be extended to support the PUT and DELETE HTTP commands using an add-on Microsoft released called Microsoft Posting Acceptor 1.0. This add-on is freely available from their Web site on the Internet, at http://www.microsoft.com/windows/software/webpost/post_accept.htm.

```
OPTIONS / HTTP/1.0[CR/LF]
```

Per the HTTP standards, the URI can be replaced with an asterisk to indicate that the command applies to the Web server as a whole. In this case, the command would look like this:

```
OPTIONS * HTTP/1.0[CR/LF]
```

Unfortunately, the most popular Web servers do not currently implement the OPTIONS functionality and will return a 50x error response-code.

HEAD   First, I've never seen a browser actually issue this command to a server. Further, in my testing, Web servers tend to respond unreliably to the command, as if the developers did not make this their top priority. Nonetheless, it is provided for in the HTTP standards as a way to retrieve the header information for a document without actually retrieving the document – and the format is identical to the GET command. So if a client wanted to retrieve the header information for a file called /documents/sample.htm on the Web server www.example.com, the client would issue the command:

```
HEAD /documents/sample.htm HTTP/1.0[CR/LF]
```

This command would be useful for determining the file sizes of many files on a Web server, and for verifying the existence of a file without actually retrieving it. It is also useful as a method to receive some form of positive response from a server without retrieving an entire page. By definition, output from the HEAD command needs to be identical to the output from the GET command except that the message body itself is excluded. Therefore, if you had a need to check the version of Web server software running on a particular Web server, a quick way to do it would be to issue a HEAD command.

TRACE   TRACE is like a PING command to be used within the HTTP protocol. TRACE is an application-layer loopback interface, allowing an administrator to issue a command such as TRACE ping-a-ding-ding. The receiving server will return the string submitted to it as the message body of a 200 status-code message.

This command would be really great if servers implemented it. Unfortunately, it is not yet available in Microsoft's IIS or Netscape's Enterprise Server.

STATUS MESSAGES

If you have spent any time at all on the Internet, you are familiar with a few of the most basic (and negative) HTTP status codes: 403 (Access Forbidden) and 404 (Not Found). Unfortunately, this is only the beginning. The more you work with the Internet, the more you will find other messages popping up from time to time – these messages are identified with a number and usually some kind of description. The "reason phrases" listed in Table 16-2 are those quoted by the RFC – but the standard allows these to be replaced with something more descriptive, so your results may vary.

HTTP status codes are three numeric digits. The first digit classifies the message into a class of response; the last two digits are used to identify a specific error within a message group.

The format of these messages is simple – first, the version of HTTP is returned, then the error message, a reason phrase, and a carriage return/linefeed. After the actual error message, the server may choose to include more information for the purpose of better explaining the error. For example, many Web servers will show a formatted screen explaining to the end user the reason for the message and directing them to other resources on the Web site.

Consider the following example, returned by a Web server in response to a request for a file that did not exist. The error message returned is 404, which falls into the family of "Client Error" messages. The client is considered in error because it had the gall to ask for a file that the server did not have handy. The 404 message is used for all "Not Found" messages. This example shows the error message that the Web browser interprets (the first line) and then an arbitrary file meant for descriptive purposes, which the Web browser simply displays. As you can see, the Web server has returned a short HTML file:

```
HTTP/1.0 404 Object Not Found
Content-Type: text/html

<body><h1>Sorry, that file isn't available!</h1></body>
```

Status codes with a first digit of 1 indicate an "Informational" error message – not an error at all. They are used to pass a message back to the HTTP client without indicating that the last request is not being completed. It's interesting to note that HTTP/1.0 did not implement *any* 1*xx* status codes – the first was introduced in HTTP/1.1.

Status codes with a first digit of 2 are "Success" messages. These indicate that the last request received was formatted correctly and understood, and it will be processed in some way.

Status codes with a first digit of 3 are "Redirection" messages. Redirection messages indicate that some further action must be taken before the request can be completed.

Status codes with a first digit of 4 are "Client Error" messages. They indicate that the client has formatted something incorrectly or is requesting something the HTTP server cannot – or will not – fulfill.

Status codes with a first digit of 5 are "Server Error" messages. These messages are returned to a client when the server recognizes the request but cannot fulfill it for some reason other than denying the client access. For example, if the server does not support the version of HTTP being requested, it will return a "Server Error" message.

TABLE 16-2 HTTP ERROR MESSAGES

Status Code	Recommended Reason Phrase	Description
100	Continue	*HTTP/1.1 and later.* This message is returned to the client to indicate that it is okay to continue sending the request. After the request is completed, the server is still required to return another status message.
101	Switching Protocols	*HTTP/1.1 and later.* This message is used when the server wishes to use a different protocol than the one currently being used. For example, if the client sent a request in HTTP/1.1, the server may return this message if it is necessary to use HTTP/2.0 to fulfill the request.
200	OK	The request was completed successfully. The meaning of this message is taken in the context of the request — for example, if it is in response to a GET request, it indicates that the file was returned successfully. If it is in response to a POST request, it indicates the information was received correctly.
201	Created	After a client requests that a new file be created on a Web server, the Web server will response with a 201 message after completing the request. If you see the 201 status code, it means resource creation is absolutely complete — the standard dictates that servers return a 202 message if resource creation is still in progress. In addition to the status code, a URI is included to identify the location of the new resource.
202	Accepted	A command was successfully issued to the HTTP server but is still being processed.
203	Non-Authoritative Information	One of the many valid HTTP responses that will probably never be used, 203 is intended to indicate that the server returned a document that was incomplete.

Continued

Status Code	Recommended Reason Phrase	Description
204	No Content	The command was successfully processed, but there is no new information to return. The client should not make any changes to its display or cache based on this type of response.
205	Reset Content	The client should clear the content from whatever form it is currently displaying to the user. The 205 message is rarely, if ever, used.
206	Partial Content	This message indicates a successful response to a partial GET request, a method clients can use to download only part of a file. For example, if a large download is interrupted, the client may request only the portion of the file that was not completed successfully. The server will respond with the 206 message.
300	Multiple Choices	Although it is great in theory, I do not know of any server that uses this feature of the HTTP protocol. If put into use, it would aid end users in choosing between multiple locations that mirror identical content.
301	Moved Permanently	This response indicates that the requested resource is located somewhere else. It is also known as an "HTTP Redirect." The 301 and 302 messages work functionally identically, though their intentions vary. Clients that receive a 301 message should update the links they have stored locally to point to the new location. This response is sent by IIS 4.0 when a particular directory has the A Redirection to a URL option button selected and the A Permanent Redirection for This Resource check box has been checked, as shown in Figure 16-5.

Continued

TABLE 16-2 HTTP ERROR MESSAGES *(Continued)*

Status Code	Recommended Reason Phrase	Description
302	Moved Temporarily	This response indicates that the requested resource is located somewhere else, and the client should redirect its request to the location specified by the server. This response is sent by IIS 4.0 when a particular directory has the A Redirection to a URL option button selected and the A Permanent Redirection for This Resource check box has not been checked.
303	See Other	Similar to 302, 303 is most commonly used to redirect a browser to a Web page after a POST action has been completed. For example, after a user submits a form via a Web browser, the server will return a 303 message, requesting that the browser view a page that displays the results.
304	Not Modified	The command issued by the browser was processed correctly, but a header option such as "if-modified-since" was used and the document request was "not-modified-since." Thus, 304 messages do not need to include a document body, because the browser must have a copy already stored in the cache.
305	Use Proxy	Never used. The intention is that the browser should redirect its request to a particular proxy server.
400	Bad Request	The command sent by the HTTP client was not formatted correctly or was otherwise not understood.

Continued

Status Code	Recommended Reason Phrase	Description
401	Unauthorized	The requested document cannot be returned because the security configuration of the server forbids it. This message is usually associated with a list of potential authentication methods using the WWW-Authenticate header field. For example, if NTFS permissions do not allow the anonymous Web user access to a particular document, IIS will return this error message. Browsers generally prompt the user for a username and password when this message is received, though nothing in the standards require that the client reattempt the request.
402	Payment Required	This isn't actually used. You can guess what the intentions are from the response code description, however.
403	Forbidden	As with the 401 response, access has been denied. However, this differs from the 401 response in that it indicates that the client should not attempt to rerequest the URI, even with some form of authentication.
404	Not Found	The document the browser requested does not exist. Some Web servers may be configured to return this message instead of a 401 message in circumstances where access to certain files is restricted but the server does not want to give away its internal file structure.
405	Method Not Allowed	Theoretically, the browser has attempted to issue an HTTP command and the server doesn't know how to handle it, so it tells the browser a few commands it can accept. Realistically, Web servers respond to unknown methods in unpredictable ways, and browsers don't necessarily know how to handle the response anyway. So it is never used.

Continued

TABLE 16-2 HTTP ERROR MESSAGES *(Continued)*

Status Code	Recommended Reason Phrase	Description
406	Not Acceptable	The browser has included a list of response types that it can accept, and the requested document is not one of those types, so the server does not bother to return it to the client. Instead, the server should return a list of options for the browser — different methods that are available to complete the request.
407	Proxy Authentication Required	This is similar in function to 401 — it indicates that the client needs to prove its identity before the server can return the requested document. The 407 message goes one step further, however, indicating that the client must authenticate itself with a particular authentication server.
408	Request Time-Out	The server did not receive a command from the client before a server-specific timeout period, so the server returns this status code and drops the TCP connection. The reality is that the server (for example, both IIS and Netscape Enterprise Server) normally returns nothing to the client, simply dropping the connection.
409	Conflict	Never used. It would be used in a circumstance where a request, such as a PUT statement, could not be fulfilled because someone else had the file open or had modified the file. The engineers who drafted the HTTP standards intended this to be used as part of a complex HTTP version-control mechanism, though it has not yet been implemented.
410	Gone	Never used. It seems like a far-fetched idea, but this response would be used if the server recognized the requested URI as being a document that it used to have but which is no longer available. Instead of 410, servers will return a 404 status message.

Continued

Status Code	Recommended Reason Phrase	Description
411	Length Required	Never used. This is the server's way of indicating that the last command issued by the client must include the Content-Length header field.
412	Precondition Failed	In general, the client submitted a request that included a conditional header field. The conditional header field conditions evaluated false, so nothing needs to be returned.
413	Request Entity Too Large	Never used. It is intended to be used in conjunction with a max-file-transfer-size parameter on the server, ensuring that files over a certain size cannot be returned to clients.
414	Request-URI Too Large	Never used. The filename and path (the URI) requested is too long to be interpreted properly by the server.
415	Unsupported Media Type	Another response that will never make it into prime time. Supposedly, the format of the file the request specified is not compatible with the document type being requested.
500	Internal Server Error	About as useful for diagnosing problems as "General Protection Fault," "500 Internal Server Error" indicates that something bad just happened at the server, and it is not going to tell you what it was.
501	Not Implemented	The browser made a request of the server that it is unable to support, a possible response if a browser is attempting to use vendor-specific HTTP extensions.
502	Bad Gateway	This message indicates that a proxy server is having a problem responding.

Continued

TABLE 16-2 HTTP ERROR MESSAGES *(Continued)*

Status Code	Recommended Reason Phrase	Description
503	Service Unavailable	This indicates that the server is currently too busy to fulfill your request. I have seen this message many times in the past, particularly from IIS-based Web servers. However, I have never seen it actually meaning that the server was too busy — it often appears as a false indicator, a manifestation of some other problem.
504	Gateway Time-Out	Your proxy server did not receive a response from the destination server before the time-out expired. The server may be offline or may simply not exist.
505	HTTP Version Not Supported	In my testing, I could never induce this response from a Web server, so I suspect it is never implemented. Instead, Web servers process the command as if it were from a version of HTTP they understood. This is really part of the magic of the protocol; both servers and clients do their best to honor a request, regardless of whether it will work or not. If this response code were implemented properly, it would be used when the server could not communicate with the browser's requested version of HTTP.

Redirection As a Hobby

In my research, I stumbled across an odd occurrence of the HTTP redirect header. Anytime you request a URI from a Web server and specify a directory name without specifying a final "/," the Web server redirects the Web browser to the same URI buts completes it properly by adding the ending "/."

That was a mouthful, so let me give an example. Microsoft's download page is located at http://www.microsoft.com/msdownload/. If you type this into your Web browser, Microsoft's Web server knows you are requesting a directory and returns the default Web page for that directory. It knows you are asking for a directory and not a file without a file extension because you ended the URL with a forward slash. It is common practice not to include that final forward-slash, however, instead requesting `http://www.microsoft.com/msdownload`. The Web server cannot handle this, and it will redirect your browser to `http://www.microsoft.com/msdownload/`. It wastes about a quarter of a second while the packets travel back and forth across the Internet, but hardly anyone ever notices it happen.

Unfortunately, I also discovered that it is common practice to create HTML anchors (hyperlinks) to URLs without including the final forward slash. So if I may provide some useful information in this tangent, speed up your Web site by ensuring all hyperlinks that reference directories end in a forward slash.

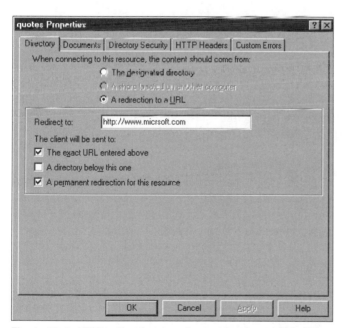

Figure 16-5: HTTP redirections can be enabled from within IIS's MMC interface.

COMMON MESSAGE HEADERS USED IN HTTP/1.0

HTTP message headers are the basis for the text-based command and response exchanges between HTTP clients and servers. The format of these messages is flexible enough that it is used for both client-to-server commands and server-to-client responses. These are defined in RFC 2068, section 14, but I have made an effort to summarize the RFC and provide you all the knowledge you will need about HTTP messages.

The format these messages take is:

```
Message-type: Arguments[CR/LF]
```

For example, the User-Agent message carries as an argument a description of the browser the client is using to access the server. The server receives this message and understands what the client is trying to tell it because the message-type is part of the HTTP standard. For example, the following message sent from a client to a server is equivalent to the sentence, "My browser is Netscape Navigator 4.03, and I am using Windows NT."

```
User-Agent: Mozilla/4.04 [en] (WinNT; U)[CR/LF]
```

Understanding and being able to interpret these messages is a critical part of being able to troubleshoot the HTTP protocol. The sections that follow will describe the common and not-so-common messages that are exchanged in the course of HTTP communications.

Message headers in the HTTP protocol are composed of several fields. The first field is the "field-name;" it tells the receiving process how to interpret the information that follows. For example, a server will often notify the client which HTTP server software it is using. The field-name it will use for this message is "Server."

After the field name, a colon and a space are appended to separate the field name from the data. The data of the message is formally called the "field-value" and is the meat of the message. Finally, a carriage return and linefeed (abbreviated in my examples as "[CR/LF]") indicate the end of a line. To continue the preceding example, if a server was communicating to the client that it is using HTTP server software from Netscape, it would include as part of its reply to the client the line:

```
Server: Netscape Enterprise/2.01[CR/LF]
```

These fields, when combined, create a complete command or response. Furthermore, many message header fields will generally be included within a single request or response. Consider the following dialog between a client and a server:

```
<client request>GET / HTTP/1.0[CR/LF]
Connection: Keep-Alive[CR/LF]
User-Agent: Mozilla/4.04 [en] (WinNT; U)[CR/LF]
Host: www.company.com[CR/LF]
Accept: image/gif, image/x-xbitmap, image/jpeg, image/pjpeg,
  image/png, */*[CR/LF]
Accept-Language: en[CR/LF]
Accept-Characterset: iso-885901,*,utf-8[CR/LF] [CR/LF]
```

```
<server response>HTTP/1.0 200 OK[CR/LF]
Server: Netscape-Enterprise/2.01[CR/LF]
Date: Wed, 10 Dec 1997 06:05:15 GMT[CR/LF]
Content-type: text/html[CR/LF] [CR/LF]
<HTML><HEAD><TITLE>Welcome!</TITLE></HEAD>
<BODY>Welcome to our Web site!</BODY></HTML>
```

Understanding each of these fields is critical in troubleshooting situations and key to anyone writing scripts or programs that act as HTTP servers or clients. The following section describes the meaning and common uses of each of these fields.

AUTHORIZATION   A very popular header field is the Authorization request-header field. The Authorization request-header field is generally used to pass a username and password from an HTTP client to a server. For example, if you restrict NTFS permissions on an NT-based Web server, the Web server will return a 401 message — Unauthorized Request. The Web browser interprets this and prompts the user for a username and password to be submitted to the Web server. After the Web browser collects this information, it resubmits the request to the server, this time including the Authorization request-header field. The format of the field is:

```
Authorization: Type Credentials
```

The most common type of authorization is basic authentication, which transfers the username and password in encoded (*not* encrypted) text. Another method is NTLM authentication, supported only by Microsoft's Internet Explorer. Examples of both types are:

```
Authorization: Basic <base-64 encoded username and password>
Authorization: NTLM <encrypted username and hashed password>
```

For more information on HTTP authentication, see the section titled "Authentication" later in this chapter.

CONTENT-ENCODING   The Content-Encoding header field defines how the original information was modified from its original format. The receiving host uses the Content-Encoding field to determine what method to use to decode the data. It is generally used when transferring data from a server to a client, though it may in theory be used with transfers in either direction.

```
Content-Encoding: x-gzip[CR/LF]
```

CONTENT-LENGTH   Another common header field is the Content-Length field. This field precedes responses from servers and describes the total length of the "payload" of the HTTP response. The payload is the useful data being transferred, aside from any headers and status codes. This is useful to the browser: It knows how much of the remaining response that it receives from the server is part of that particular document. For those writing client-side scripts and applications, this field needs to be processed in order to ensure that your script does not hang waiting for additional information from the server. An example of this header field in use is:

```
Content-Length: 642[CR/LF]
```

Content-Length is not related to the amount of data in any particularly IP packet — it is the entire length of a particular file being transferred. For example, if a GIF file is 1,398 bytes long, the Context-Length header field will contain the value 1398, regardless of how the packet is fragmented.

CONTENT-TYPE   The Content-Type header field is used in almost all HTTP server-to-client transfers. Content-Type defines the document or file type. The most common Content-Types on the Internet are given in the following example:

```
Content-Type: text/html[CR/LF]
Content-Type: image/gif[CR/LF]
```

DATE   The Date header field is passed in the majority of server-to-client transfers. It carries the date and time the document left the server. This may seem pretty useless, at first glance. In cases where there is caching of some sort occurring, however, the Date field is useful because it tells the client when the file was originally sent and can be used to determine whether or not it is "stale."

Believe it or not, there is yet another RFC to tell you exactly how to format the Date field. Dates, as used in HTTP, are defined in RFC 822. I'll leave the reading up to you, but here is an example of the general format:

```
Date: Wed, 10 Dec 1997 02:51:55 GMT[CR/LF]
```

EXPIRES   The Expires header field is useful for determining how long a document should be cached. By definition, the Expires field contains the latest time a client application such as a Web browser or proxy server may cache the file. After that date, the document must be re-requested from the Web server before being displayed again. The Expires field is similar in format to the Date field.

```
Expires: Wed, 11 Dec 1997 02:51:55 GMT[CR/LF]
```

If the date in the Expires header field is equal to or less than the date in the Date header field, the document may not be cached at all. This is useful for Web pages that should not allow any type of client-side caching, such as dynamically produced HTML pages. Please note that the Expires field does not preclude a Web browser from displaying a page from its cache if the user presses the Back button — this is considered part of a history and is excluded from the rule.

IF-MODIFIED-SINCE   The If-Modified-Since request-header field, often used with the `GET` command, is useful and commonly used. It is an easy way for a Web browser to say to the Web server, "Hey, I want to see if this file has been updated since the last time I checked it, five minutes ago. If it has been, send it over!" The Web server reads the If-Modified-Since header field and compares it to the last updated time of the file being requested. If it has not been modified, it returns a status message, "304 Not Updated," declaring that there is nothing new to see and that the browser can use the version it already has in its cache. If it has been modified, the Web server will return the entire file.

Here is an example of the If-Modified-Since header field in use:

```
<client request>
GET /elvis-sightings.html HTTP/1.0[CR/LF]
If-Modified-Since: Tuesday, 09-Dec-97 03:17:50 GMT (...)
<server response>
HTTP/1.1 304 Not Modified (...)
```

LAST-MODIFIED   Servers inform an HTTP client of the time a particular document or file was last updated using the Last-Modified entity-header field. Here is the standard format:

```
Last-Modified: Friday, 03-Jan-97 07:15.20 GMT[CR/LF]
```

LOCATION   Ever wonder what happens when you enter a URL into your Web browser and your Web browser ends up someplace entirely different? This is known as a redirection. Web servers use the Location response-header field to handle redirections. The data carried within this field is the place the Web browser should go. The response may also include a document of some type, such as HTML, for the Web browser to display until the Web browser has loaded the new page. For example, if the client issues a request in the form:

```
GET /berry.html HTTP/1.0[CR/LF]
```

The Web server may prefer the Web browser request a file such as `berry_new.html`. The Web browser might respond:

```
HTTP/1.0 302 Object moved[CR/LF]
Location: http://www.company.com/berry_new.html (...)
Content-Length: 100[CR/LF]
<head><title>You're in the wrong place!</title></head>
<body><h1>That document has moved.</h1></body><0A><0A>
```

PRAGMA   Either the client or the server may use the Pragma header field. It is intended to carry data that is specific to a particular Web server or Web browser. If vendor-specific standards scare you, you will be relieved to know that most arguments are not vendor-specific. An example of Pragma in use is:

```
Pragma: no-cache[CR/LF]
```

REFERER   To allow Web servers to better track the paths people take to get to a Web site and to move around within a Web site, the Referer request-header field is used. Most popular browsers include this field as part of a standard request, unless the user typed the URL into the browser directly. For example, if you clicked on a link from www.company.com to get to another Web site, the request your browser would create would look like this:

```
GET / HTTP/1.0[CR/LF]
(…)
Referer: http://www.company.com/index.html[CR/LF]
```

From the perspective of the Web server, this information is usually captured and placed into log files. It is a commonly used field but is entirely optional and does not generally elicit a different response from a Web browser, so scripts that behave as HTTP clients may simply disregard it.

USER-AGENT   The User-Agent request-header field is used to pass the browser type from the client to the Web server. This information is useful to the Web server in many ways:

◆ It can be logged and the information used by the Webmaster of the site to determine which browsers the majority of the clientele use.

◆ It can be used immediately by the Web server to create different pages for different Web browsers. For example, if you use Microsoft's Internet Explorer to visit Netscape's Web site (www.netscape.com), you will be greeted with an offer to upgrade your browser. Netscape's Web server does this by evaluating the value in the User-Agent request-header field.

◆ It can be used immediately by the Web server to determine what capabilities the client's Web browser has. For example, it may offer a different plug-in for different browsers, or it may suggest that browsers lacking a certain capability (such as frames or cookies) upgrade to something newer with the required features.

The User-Agent request-header field is formatted as:

```
User-Agent: Mozilla/4.04 [en] (WinNT; U)
```

WWW-AUTHENTICATE   The WWW-Authenticate response-header field is used in "access denied" messages the Web server sends to the client's Web browser. It indicates the various methods the Web server supports for authenticating the user.

Almost all Web servers support the "basic" method of authentication. Microsoft's Internet Information Server supports an encrypted method of authentication labeled "NTLM," which is short for NT LAN Manager. Servers that support multiple types of authentication will include multiple occurrences of this header field.

This header field is always included in server responses with the "401 Unauthorized" server message. An IIS server with both types of authentication enabled will return a message such as this:

```
HTTP/1.1 401 Access Denied[CR/LF]
WWW-Authenticate: NTLM[CR/LF]
WWW-Authenticate: Basic realm=""[CR/LF]
```

COMMON MESSAGE HEADERS NEW TO HTTP/1.1

The following message-header fields are new to HTTP/1.1 but commonly used on the Internet. If you are working with browsers and servers that support the new standards, it will pay to be familiar with these. I do not list every message header included in the standards; only the useful and interesting message headers are described in this section. For a complete listing, refer to RFC 2068.

So, Does That Make Internet Explorer "Mothra"?

The way clients identify themselves to servers is through the User-Agent header field. This header field includes an argument that is a unique identifier for that particular browser software. It's kind of funny, though, if you look at what the clients send to the servers: Netscape clients identify themselves as "Mozilla," a play on words formed from "Mosaic," the original Web browser, and "Godzilla," a big lizard that exhales fire. Marc Andreessen, coauthor of Mosaic and author of the original Netscape browser, just thought it was funny. Now his contraction is one of the most commonly-sent-but-rarely-seen words on the Internet.

Even funnier is the fact that Microsoft's Internet Explorer (IE) also identifies itself as Mozilla, impersonating its arch-nemesis. This is done for compatibility purposes: When IE was original written, Web servers would not have recognized other User-Agent parameters and may not have attempted to provide the browser some features of their Web site, such as images! To this day, IE identifies itself using Andreessen's play on words.

CACHE CONTROL   New in HTTP/1.1, the Cache-Control general-header field is commonly included in server-to-client communications. The Cache-Control field is often used when Pragma: no-cache would have been used in HTTP/1.0. It gives the server the ability to direct how and when the client caches data.

The format of the cache-control header field is:

```
Cache-Control: no-store
```

CONNECTION   The Connection header field defines options that are valid only between a single HTTP client and server. In other words, if a proxy server or multiple proxy servers are in use, options defined by the Connection header field are only valid between the HTTP server and the first HTTP proxy.

The most common Connection argument is "Keep-Alive," which indicates the client's preference to use a single TCP session until further notice. An example of this usage is listed here:

```
Connection: Keep-Alive[CR/LF]
```

ACCEPT (AND ACCEPT-*)   The Accept and Accept-Something message headers allow the server and client to notify each other which formats are acceptable for different types of communications. The Accept-Charset header field is used to define the character sets that are acceptable for communications for that particular HTTP session. Accept-Language is used to define languages that may be used; for example, "Accept-Language: En" would be used to notify that server not to transmit messages in any language besides English. Accept-Range and Accept-Encoding are available but are less commonly used and so are not described here.

CONTENT-*   Header fields that have field names beginning with "Content-" are used to notify the receiving agent of properties of the document that is about to be transferred. For example, an HTTP server will always include a Content-Length header field that defines the total length of the file the client is about to receive, allowing the client to know exactly when the file ends. For example, a document that was 1,024 bytes in length would be preceded with the line "Content-Length: 1024."

Another common header field is the Content-Base header field, which is used to notify the client of the absolute URI from which the file is transmitted.

The Content-Language header field carries as an argument the language of the document being transferred. The Internet is a worldwide resource, and, while English is the most common language, many Web pages are in languages other than English. Carrying a Content-Language header field allows the browser to interpret non-English languages correctly, translating codes into characters that may not otherwise be available.

Content-Encoding is included before a file is transferred to indicate that some form of encoding has been performed on it prior to transfer, notifying the client that it must decode the file before interpreting it.

Content-Location is used in responses to tell the browser the complete URL of the file being transferred. The browser should already know, since it must have requested it, but it is included for good measure.

HOST The Host header field is required in all HTTP/1.1 client requests. The value of this field is the hostname of the server from which the data is being requested. It may seem unnecessary – after all, the server should know who it is, right? Realistically, this is not always the case. Many if not most servers on the Internet host multiple virtual servers on the same system. If you are not familiar with virtual servers, they allow two distinct hostnames to return different Web pages but be served by the same system. For example, www.netscape.com and home.netscape.com may be on the same server and yet have distinct IP addresses and return different Web pages.

The problem with this setup is that each virtual server must have a distinct IP address. This is really wasteful – it is not uncommon for a single Web server to host over one hundred different Web sites, each with a unique DNS entry and IP address. HTTP/1.1 added the Host header field to avoid this problem. By requiring the Host header field to be included with all requests, one server can host multiple Web pages with a single IP address. I'll clarify this with an example.

Johnny Proactive is a systems engineer at an Internet, and he has a new customer who wants to host two Web sites on the same Web server: www.company1.com and www.company2.com. The traditional way of hosting multiple sites on a single server is to configure the Web server with two additional IP addresses and associate each DNS entry with a single address. In the traditional method, the IP address 192.168.5.10 would map to www.company1.com and the IP address 192.168.5.11 would map to www.company2.com. However, Johnny wants to take full advantage of the new features in HTTP/1.1. So, Johnny associates both DNS entries with the same IP address. Therefore, 192.168.5.10 would map to both www.company1.com and www.company2.com. When someone surfing the Web enters the URL http://www.company2.com into an HTTP/1.1-compliant browser, the browser will include the header field "Host: www.company2.com." The HTTP/1.1-compliant Web server will interpret this header field and return the default Web page for company 2, not for company 1.

Unfortunately, Johnny lives in a fantasy world, where new technologies work as they're supposed to. As with many things, this is a great concept that is not ready to be relied upon. The fact is, many people on the Internet will still be using older browsers that do not support HTTP/1.1. Further, most Web servers don't support it. IIS 3.0 did not; IIS 4.0 does.

IF-* Several conditional header fields are available to allow the client to request a file to be transferred from the server, but only if certain conditions are met. The most common conditional header field is the If-Modified-Since header field, which browsers use to verify that the cached version of the file stored locally really is the most recent version. If the server determines that the requested file has not been modified since the date supplied in the If-Modified-Since header field, a success response code is returned and the file is not transferred, reducing the delay and total bandwidth required.

Other less common or completely unused conditional header fields include the If-Match, If-None-Match, and If-Range header fields.

The If-Range header field is a combination of the If-Unmodified-Since and Range header fields. They modify a request by asking for only a portion of a particular file, and only if it has not been updated since a given date. Imagine a scenario in which an HTTP transfer was disconnected prematurely. The client would want to continue the transfer where it left off, but only if the file was still the same file – if it had been updated, it would not be able to start in the middle. The If-Range header field was created to address this issue.

Earlier I described the If-Modified-Since header field, which seems useful because it allows a browser to download a file only if a version newer than the one stored in its cache has been posted to the server. If-Unmodified-Since is not as obviously useful as If-Modified-Since, because it is used for less common purposes. Consider a scenario in which a client is uploading content to a server using POST or PUT commands – but they only want to update the content on the server if that version is older than the one stored locally on the client. It would be nice if the client could ask the server, "Please post this document if you haven't modified this file since last week."

This is what the If-Unmodified-Since field allows the client to do. When it is included with an HTTP command, that command will be executed only if a file on the server has not been updated since the date provided with this header field.

VIA   Each proxy server that handles an HTTP request adds one Via header field. For example, if a client makes a request to www.idgbooks.com through an HTTP proxy server, the IDG server will respond to the proxy field with a header field similar to:

```
HTTP/1.0 200 OK[CR/LF]
Content-type: text/html[CR/LF]
Server: Apache/1.1.1[CR/LF]
```

In turn, the proxy server will respond to the client that originated the request with an identical header, with the exception of the Via header field.

```
HTTP/1.0 200 OK[CR/LF]
Via: 1.0 PROXYSERVER[CR/LF]
Content-type: text/html[CR/LF]
Server: Apache/1.1.1[CR/LF]
```

If the architecture includes multiple, nested proxy servers, each will add its own Via header field.

Useless Header Field in Use!

A Web site out there gathers the information from the field and creates statistics on which Web server software is the most popular on the Internet! This Web site is hosted by my friends at Netcraft and can be found at `http://www.netcraft.co.uk/Survey/`.

SERVER   The Server response-header field is used to identify the software and operating system the Web server is using. This field is generally implemented within Web server responses, though Web browsers do not commonly use it. The format of the field is:

```
Server: Microsoft-IIS/4.0 Beta 3
```

LESS COMMON MESSAGE HEADERS

Some message headers are defined by the HTTP standards but are *not* in common use on the Internet. In fact, the majority of these standards are neither supported on the HTTP servers nor implemented on the HTTP clients. Nonetheless, their functionality is interesting and would fulfill some purpose if implemented correctly.

I have left out several header fields entirely. This choice is based on my own opinion of the value of the field; if I thought it was not worth your time to read about, I simply omitted it.

ALLOW   The first of these fields is the Allow entity-header field. This field is used by servers to inform the client of specific methods that may be used during the conversation. For example, an Allow field may be included stating:

```
Allow: GET, POST[CR/LF]
```

This informs the client that the server may accept GET requests and POST messages. It does not necessarily stop the client from attempting other commands. The Allow header field is not commonly used but is included in responses to some commands sent to an IIS server. For example, IIS 4.0 responds to a PUT command and includes the Allow header field, as shown here:

```
HTTP/1.1 201 Created[CR/LF]
Server: Microsoft-IIS/4.0[CR/LF]
Allow: OPTIONS, TRACE, GET, HEAD, PUT, DELETE[CR/LF]
```

FROM   Rarely used on the public Internet, the From request-header field is intended to carry the e-mail address of the user controlling the client-agent. The format of the From request-header field is:

`From:user@organization.com[CR/LF]`

MAX-FORWARDS   The Max-Forwards header field provides an integer that is used to limit the number of times a request may pass through an HTTP proxy. It is very similar in function to the TTL in an IP packet. The Max-Forwards header field is intended to be used with the TRACE HTTP command, similar to the way the TTL is adjusted when using the TRACERT or TRACEROUTE IP diagnostic utility. This header field is currently not commonly implemented.

PROXY-AUTHENTICATE AND PROXY-AUTHORIZATION   These header fields carry values that are used as part of the proxy-authentication scheme. I will only mention it briefly here because proxy authentication has not yet become useful on the public Internet.

PUBLIC   The Public response-header field allows a server to tell a client which subset of the HTTP commands it is capable of understanding. It is not commonly supported.

RETRY-AFTER   The Retry-After header field is used alongside HTTP response error codes such as "503 Service Unavailable." When the Retry-After header field is included, the implication is that the error condition is temporary and may soon be resolved. While it is certainly possible that a Web server would issue this header field as part of a response, no popular Web server makes use of it.

TRANSFER-ENCODING   This header field is included in an HTTP transfer when the file being transferred has been modified in order to be transmitted successfully between the client and the server. Most clients do not support this option, so most servers do not bother with it either.

UPGRADE   The Upgrade header field is used to assist forward compatibility with future versions of the HTTP protocol. It was not introduced until HTTP/1.1, which is still the most recent version, so it is not yet in use. However, the idea is that clients that support future versions of the HTTP protocol may include this header field to let the server know that they are ready to move to a newer version, if the server can support it.

MIME TYPES   After the header fields, the client or server may append a file to be transferred. In order for the agent receiving the file to know what to do with the file, the type of file needs to be communicated. This is communicated through the use of a MIME Type header.

RFC 1521 and RFC 1590 (yes, *more* RFCs) define MIME, or Multipurpose Internet Mail Extensions. MIME is a method of identifying the format of a file before transmitting it. I am not going to cover the details of MIME in this section; I will simply describe the role MIME plays in transmitting documents from IIS and interpreting them within Web browsers.

The first question that pops into the minds of Microsoft followers such as myself is, "Why do we need MIME when we have file extensions? What could be better than a dot and three letters to identify a document?" The answer is simple: We don't need it, but the UNIX guys thought it up and we have to play nicely. The intentions of MIME are so similar to the intentions of the file extension in DOS and Windows that IIS provides a direct mapping between the two. For IIS 3.0, this mapping is located in the registry, in the following key:

```
HKEY_LOCAL_MACHINE\System\CurrentControlSet\SERVICES\InetInfo\
  Parameters\MimeMap
```

In that key, you will find a series of registry values in the following format:

```
MIME type, File Extension, <unused>, <gopher item type, usually
  unused>
```

The strangest thing about this format is that the registry values do not actually contain a value. The useful information is stored in the value name, and the value itself is left empty. Make sense? (Nobody said it would.) Here's an example that may clear things up, a mapping that tells IIS to prepend the text/html mime header to all files with the .htm file extension before they are sent to the client.

```
text/htm,,h
```

Fortunately, IIS 4.0 includes a graphical interface as part of the Microsoft Management Console that allows MIME settings to be changed.

If a file does not have a MIME mapping for its file extension, the Web server will simply transmit it as is, without prepending anything at all. Therefore, it is up to the client to guess what the format of the file is and to decide what to do with it. In most cases, this means the client will attempt to download the file. From a troubleshooting perspective, consider MIME maps as a potential source of trouble anytime files that are supposed to be interpreted by the client's Web browser are downloaded instead.

Here's an example of a Web server returning an HTML file to a Web browser:

```
HTTP/1.1 200 OK[CR/LF]
Server: Stronghold/2.0 Apache/1.2b10[CR/LF]
Content-Length: 93[CR/LF]
Content-Type: text/html[CR/LF] [CR/LF]
<html> <head><title> Welcome! </title></head>
<body>Just a sample HTML file!</body> </html>
```

Notice that the forth line down describes the file to follow as being "text/html." This line is the MIME header. Without it, the browser's response is a bit unpredictable. Netscape's Navigator tends to display files that do not have a MIME Type; IE tends to download them.

MESSAGE BODY   The message body is the meat of an HTTP transaction. It is also the last part of the message, following any commands, response codes, or message headers that may also be part of the message. If the HTTP transaction is a GET request for a Web page from a Web server, the actual HTML will be contained in the message body portion of the message.

The message body, if included in a message at all, is generally the largest portion. It is also the simplest — everything about the message was described in the message headers, so there is nothing left to do but actually transmit the file. The message body can be composed of any type of file: HTML, images, binary files, or whatever your heart desires.

AUTHENTICATION

Authentication is a critical part of most network protocols, and HTTP has better support than most. It has absolutely no standard support for clear-text authentication, as is common with other Internet protocols, including FTP and Telnet. The weakest form of authentication encodes the credentials in a format called Base-64, which, though far from secure, is still a great improvement over clear-text methods. Further, the standard allows room for vendors to create their own authentication methods. The most common of these third-party authentication methods is Microsoft's challenge/response method, which uses encryption and hashing techniques to guarantee that the password is never sent across the network in clear-text form. Finally, add-ons are available for Microsoft IIS to allow one-time passwords (OTP) to be used in lieu of conventional passwords.

Earlier in this chapter I covered the Authentication and WWW-Authenticate header fields. These header fields work together to enable servers to demand a username and password from the client, to enable servers to communicate the different methods that may be used, and to enable the client to actually submit the credentials. I think it is worthwhile to cover in greater detail the way these communications interoperate and how Microsoft's Internet Information Server, Microsoft's Internet Explorer, and Netscape's Navigator applications work together.

Microsoft's Internet Information Server allows both anonymous and nonanonymous access to files on the Web server. During the initial configuration of the Web server software, the administrator configures it with a username and password that will be used by the software to access all files that are requested by users who have not provided another username and password: the anonymous Web user. The vast majority of Internet transactions happen this way — in fact, Web sites on the public Internet that attempt to force the user to submit a username and password have encountered problems because people *like* being anonymous. Allowing these anonymous Web users access to files on your Web server is simple: Assign read permissions to the NT user account configured as the anonymous user.

However, many organizations also have a need to put documents on their Web server but restrict access to people with NT user accounts. IIS makes configuring this as simple as removing NTFS read permissions from the anonymous Web user. I won't bother covering the details of assigning permissions here, but I think it is important to show how different settings in the IIS properties affect what the server actually communicates to Web browsers, and how the different Web browsers respond to different settings.

By default, IIS has both basic authentication and challenge/response authentication enabled.

From this point on, I will refer to challenge/response authentication as NTLM authentication. NTLM stands for NT LAN Manager (okay, I realize there are still acronyms in that definition, but you get the idea) and that is how it is identified in the HTTP communications: with a header field reading "'WWW-Authenticate: NTLM."

So when a client attempts to anonymously access a file that requires a username and password, IIS returns a 401 error message to the client that includes this information:

```
HTTP/1.1 401 Access Denied[CR/LF]
WWW-Authenticate: NTLM[CR/LF]
WWW-Authenticate: Basic realm="www.company.com"[CR/LF]
```

As you can see, the WWW-Authenticate header field is included twice, once for each authentication method available. It is also important to notice that the NTLM method is listed first. Listing this method first causes the browser to submit authentication using the NTLM method, if supported. Currently, the only browser that supports this method is Microsoft's own Internet Explorer.

Unfortunately, some older browsers have problems with this. Instead of reading each of the WWW-Authenticate headers and finding the first supported method, they return an error message to the user after receiving the unrecognized NTLM header field. The only server-side workaround is to disable NTLM authentication on the server.

INTERNET EXPLORER   If Internet Explorer is used, it will automatically submit the current username and password via the Authentication header field. If this authentication is refused, the browser will prompt the user for another username and password and submit them to the server as well. Submitting the credentials is accomplished by adding the Authentication header field to a normal request — an additional packet is not required. For example, the browser's request may look like this:

```
GET / HTTP/1.1[CR/LF]
Authorization = NTLM
 TlRMSVNTUDADAAAAHAAYAGgAAAAZABgAgAAAAKAAEABAAAAAEAATAEAAA[CR/LF]
```

The server recognizes the header field and the four letters "NTLM." IIS will then decode the remainder of the line and compare it against what it knows the user's credentials are. From this point forward, the Authorization header field is *not* included in the requests. If HTTP Keep-Alives are enabled, IIS will only require each TCP session to be authenticated once. If the browser creates a second TCP session and requests a protected file, the server will return a 401 message and require authentication.

The reason you do not have to type your username and password in over and over again is that the Web browser remembers the username and password you entered and will submit them to the server automatically. However, it also means that the browser may send the credentials on pages that do not require them.

There are problems with the way IE handles authentication. First, the fact that it automatically submits the current username and password is a security risk: It is possible for someone to write a mock Web server that would intercept these credentials and learn your password without your knowledge. Second, it means that the server must decline a great many authentication attempts: IIS Webmasters know that IE users, without even knowing it, add errors to the Security Event Log on the Web server if auditing has been enabled for logon failures.

IE also provides support for basic HTTP authentication. IE handles this exactly like Netscape's browser, which is described in the following section.

NETSCAPE COMMUNICATOR Netscape Communicator operates differently, largely because it does not support NTLM authentication. When the first GET request is refused, Netscape prompts the user for a username and password before doing anything else. This is advantageous in some respects, because it reduces the amount of wasted network traffic and eliminates the chance that the browser will disclose your password without your consent. However, it is less convenient if the user account you log onto your system with is identical to the account you use on the Web server.

To submit authentication, Netscape's browser sends a message similar to this:

```
GET / HTTP/1.0[CR/LF]
Authorization = Basic bT3reaQpmhDOX2apI2KbTe==[CR/LF]
```

As you can see, the username and password are not in clear text, as many people think. After the "Authorization =" keyword, the browser sends the word "Basic" to indicate the method of authentication it is attempting to use. Afterward, the base-64 encoded "username:password" is included.

After authentication, Netscape's browser submits the Authorization header automatically for every request that exists within the realm defined in the server's original WWW-Authenticate header. By submitting the username and password automatically, the browser may request files that do not require authentication. However, it reduces network traffic because the server will not have to return another 401 message during that session.

The Impact of HTTP on a Network

HTTP, like most client/server technologies, has highly asymmetric traffic patterns. The term *asymmetric* means that the incoming and outgoing traffic levels are not balanced. In the case of HTTP, this imbalance is severe. How this affects your network depends on whether your network is a LAN or a WAN and, of course, on the network architecture.

On a LAN, HTTP traffic is normally not troublesome. This is due to the typical usage: A user requests a page using a Web browser, resulting in a short (circa 100-byte) request. The server returns a Web page, resulting in a longer transfer (250 bytes–50,000 bytes). Then the user stares at the page for a while before choosing another link and repeating the process. The reason this does not flood the network is that the user stares at the page for a minute or so before issuing another request. The delay between requests ensures that HTTP traffic will not flood the LAN for more than a second.

Naturally, there are exceptions. HTTP is now commonly used to transfer large files. Many corporations are using HTTP for software distribution, allowing users to visit a Web page and click on a link to install an application on their local computer. This process involves transferring the application's setup files across the network encapsulated within the HTTP protocol, and it has the potential to flood the network, as any large file transfer would.

On the global Internet, HTTP traffic becomes a political issue. To understand why this happens, it is important to understand how different Internet backbone providers exchange data. I will avoid going into a great deal of detail in this section, but you should know that tier-1 Internet service providers connect as National Attachment Points (NAPs). At these NAPs, the providers exchange traffic. Because of this arrangement, a user accessing the network through Sprint's connection to the backbone can view a Web site that is connected through MCI.

Now it gets trickier. WAN routing protocols such as BGP define what route traffic will follow on the Internet's backbone, and where that traffic will make the transition between providers. It is costly to carry Internet traffic, so it is each provider's goal to hand packets over to other providers as soon as possible. Internet policy dictates that the provider for which each packet is ultimately destined will carry that packet as far as possible.

Let me clarify. A user on the east coast, connected through Sprint's network, accesses a Web site on the west coast connected through MCI's network. His Web browser sends a request to the distant Web server in the form of packets. Those packets are destined for MCI's network, so MCI has the responsibility to carry them coast-to-coast, a relatively costly journey. At this point, MCI has had to foot the bill for carrying about 100 bytes of traffic, the length of the HTTP command only. This transfer is illustrated in Figure 16-6.

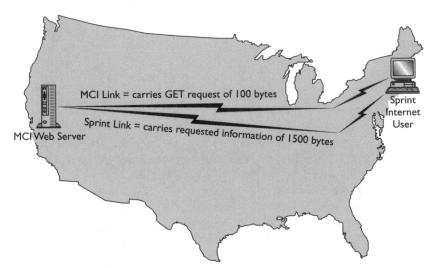

MCI Link = carries GET request of 100 bytes

Sprint Link = carries requested information of 1500 bytes

MCI Web Server

Sprint Internet User

Figure 16-6: Web requests are cheaper to carry than Web responses because requests are so small.

The Web server receives the command and replies with a lengthy HTML document of 1,500 bytes. That Web response is broken into packets and transmitted back to the client. Because the client resides on Sprint's network, the packets are handed off to Sprint to carry coast-to-coast. Therefore, Sprint has to cover the cost of carrying about 1,500 bytes of traffic across the United States.

In summary, the network that supports Web clients must handle the bulk of Web-related traffic. This amounts to about 70 percent of the total Web traffic transmitted on the Internet. Therefore, providers that host many Web servers will have less of a traffic burden than providers that host dial-in services.

Other Protocols of Interest

This section covers each of the major protocols used in NT-based internetworking environments today. The usefulness of this section comes from the high level of detail it contains – this, combined with your own understanding, gives you the tools you need to troubleshoot clients and servers that rely on these protocols.

HTML

It is important to be familiar with HTML standards, because many of the problems that occur with Web servers are actually the result of poor HTML coding. For example, a browser may hang if it attempts to retrieve an HTML file that has a `<html>` tag but lacks a `</html>` tag. Similarly, many symptoms such as those listed here may be caused by either a server misconfiguration or an HTML mistake:

- The Web browser hangs.

- The server seems unresponsive.

- The Web browser attempts to download a file that should be viewed.

- Portions of a single Web page do not appear.

- Frames do not behave properly.

In order to be sure of what causes any of these problems, it is critical to understand how HTML works and feel comfortable enough with it to notice problems when something is wrong. I am going to avoid documenting every aspect of HTML, but I will offer several pointers. For more detailed information on HTML, please refer to RFC 1866.

BEGIN/TERMINATE FORMATTING MARKERS   Formatting commands are contained in "<" and ">" symbols. These formats are started with the command inside those symbols and terminated with the same code except starting with a "</" instead of simply a "<." For example:

```
This text is in <bold>bold</bold>.
```

Only the word "bold" will appear in bold, because the `<bold>` command is terminated afterward with the `</bold>` command. When troubleshooting, look out for starting commands that do not have a matching closing command. For example, if a file begins with `<HEAD>`, make sure there is a `</HEAD>` somewhere later in the file. If it is missing, there could be trouble.

FRAMES ARE BAD   As the title to this section says, frames are bad. They are a real source of problems on Web sites and should generally be avoided. Nonetheless, most Web hosting services have little or no control over their customer's content, so Webmasters will have to learn to deal with them. One method of troubleshooting a Web page that uses frames is to isolate each of the various files that compose the frames page. Then load each page separately by entering the URL of that particular frame into your browser. Your browser will display only one section of the frame, allowing you to narrow down the trouble source.

Once you narrow down the problem to a single file, it is much simpler to troubleshoot. Individual components of a frame are merely HTML files, like any other.

ASPS   ASPs are a common source of problems on Web sites. They grant the creator a significant amount of power to collect, format, and personalize information before presenting it to a Web user. Without your being an ASP programmer, it is very possible to troubleshoot ASP files, if you remember a few pointers.

The server must process ASP files before they are transmitted to the browser. The end result of an ASP file is nothing special – the server translates the code into HTML before sending it anywhere.

`ASP.DLL` is essentially an ISAPI filter, which handles ASP files before they are sent to the client. Versioning problems are extremely common with this particular DLL, and it has been updated frequently. Check Microsoft's FTP site for the latest and greatest version of this file, and update it if your ASP files simply do not seem to be working the way you expect them to.

If a problem happens only with specific browsers, try updating the `browscap.ini` file. The `browscap.ini` file contains a list of browser identification codes (as provided with the User-Agent HTTP header field) and their various capabilities. A really good source for this file can be found at `http://www.browscap.com`. This particular Web site offers a free service that will automatically mail you new versions of this file as they are updated.

If you must isolate a particular portion of an ASP file's HTML results that is causing problems, try saving the results to a separate file. To do this, view the ASP file from a Web browser. You will see the processed results. Now choose Save As from your browser's File menu to save the actual HTML code. I suggest saving it out to a directory on the originating Web server, so that you can eliminate any chance of the problem being server-dependent. Once you have the file in HTML form, it is much simpler to manipulate.

URLS AND URIS

A URL is the primary way resources are identified on the Internet. Just about everyone in the civilized world is familiar with URLs in one form or another; they are all over advertisements. URLs are defined in RFC 1738 and RFC 1808.

URLs are composed of several different components:

♦ **Protocol type:** Generally, HTTP and FTP are the most common protocol types in URLs. However, many other conventions are common, including Gopher, Telnet, and File.

♦ **Server Name:** This is the fully qualified domain name (FQDN), IP address, or NetBIOS name of the server to communicate with, for example, `www.idgbooks.com`.

♦ **Universal Resource Identifier (URI):** The URI is the last portion of the URL and is used to identify a specific file on the destination server. For example, `/documents/index.htm` is a URI.

To put all of these items together, separate the protocol and server name with a colon and two forward slashes. After the server name, list the URI, for example, `http://www.microsoft.com/msdownload/default.htm`. The protocol type is `http`, the FQDN is `www.microsoft.com`, and the URI is `/msdownload/default.htm`.

Summary

This chapter covered how Microsoft Internet Information Server works with the HTTP protocol, including the details of HTTP messages. It also included how Netscape Navigator and Internet Explorer work with HTTP. In addition, the basics of HTML and URLs were covered.

In this chapter you learned:

- ◆ HTTP is the standard upon which most Internet communications are based. The most recent version of HTTP, version 1.1, is defined by RFC 2068.

- ◆ Windows NT supports a wide variety of HTTP clients and servers. The most popular clients are Netscape Navigator and Internet Explorer. The most popular server is Microsoft's own Internet Information Server.

- ◆ A large number of commands, message headers, and status codes are used in HTTP. Fortunately, they all use clear text and are therefore simple to analyze and troubleshoot.

- ◆ The most common type of document that HTTP transfers is the HTML document. HTML is a flexible standard used for transferring formatted text and linking to images and other objects.

In the next chapter, you'll learn all about another important Internet standard, the File Transfer Protocol. Chapter 17 covers the Windows NT implementations of both clients and servers, including Microsoft Internet Information Server. We will go much deeper than simply describing IIS — we will explore the protocol itself, uncovering its weaknesses and building an understanding of its communications.

Chapter 17

File Transfer Protocol Services

IN THIS CHAPTER

- ◆ Learning how FTP works on the Internet and what it is used for

- ◆ Building an understanding of the different FTP products available for Windows NT and the features built into each

- ◆ Developing critical troubleshooting skills to assist in solving complicated FTP problems

- ◆ Understanding FTP well enough to analyze traffic using a protocol analyzer such as Network Monitor

FTP HAS BEEN evolving for decades but has recently become a household name because of its usefulness on the Internet. This chapter will teach you both Microsoft IIS's implementation of FTP services and the FTP standards IIS is based on. It will show you how the protocol *should* work in theory, and how it *does* work in reality.

Information regarding the FTP standards is drawn from the requests for comments. The original RFCs can be downloaded from the InterNIC at `ftp://ftp.internic.net/rfc`. As with previous chapters, I have tried to give you everything you need. Read the RFC only when all else fails!

Overviewing FTP Services

FTP services have been provided with Windows NT since the first version, version 3.1. When IIS 1.0 was released, the FTP service was integrated into IIS, though it continued to run as a separate service.

It remained virtually untouched until IIS 4.0 was released. It can still be considered feature-poor, but it now supports multiple virtual servers, remedying a major drawback of earlier versions.

Microsoft's Internet Information Server 4.0 provides a standard set of FTP server features. It has the capability to have a different FTP server directory structure for each IP address on the machine. It also has the capability to use virtual directories and, for the first time in version 4.0, virtual servers. These features allow the FTP file structure not to be bound by the physical file structure on the machine. The FTP service also supports assigning permissions using Windows NT's built-in NTFS permissions and user accounts.

The FTP Model

The File Transfer Protocol, commonly known as FTP, is another protocol made popular by the public Internet. FTP, as the name implies, allows files of any type to be transferred between a server and a client across a TCP/IP network. If this were the only functionality that FTP provided, it would have been rendered completely obsolete by the HTTP protocol. However, FTP provides for additional functionality that the HTTP protocol does not explicitly accommodate: file and directory management.

FTP, like HTTP and many other Internet protocols, makes use of English text commands between the client and server. This makes it an easy protocol to troubleshoot and to write programs to utilize. Another advantage of FTP is that it acts as a layer of abstraction between the client and the server's operating system. While different vendor's implementations of FTP may vary to some degree, an FTP server looks like any other FTP server, whether it is based on Windows NT or a flavor of UNIX.

FTP has existed in one form or another for more than thirty-five years. The current implementation of FTP is defined by RFC 959, though more than fifty RFCs relate to FTP in one way or another.

FTP Servers

Almost all network operating systems support FTP as a server. Windows NT, the focus of this book, has supported FTP services since version 3.1 – long before an HTTP server was available. When Windows NT 3.1 was created, the FTP server was an attempt at UNIX compatibility and interoperability. Today, the FTP service is integrated into Microsoft's Internet Information Server, which also includes HTTP services. Indeed, Microsoft has slowed development of its FTP service in favor of more modern technologies – the version of FTP included with IIS 2.0 and IIS 3.0 was almost identical to the original FTP released with NT 3.1.

As with most things on the Internet, Windows NT–based systems make up the minority. The majority of FTP sites on the Internet are hosted on UNIX-based systems. Nonetheless, the beauty of FTP is that any client can use any server – making the operating system unimportant.

FTP Clients

Every major desktop operating system includes support for the FTP protocol. Windows NT includes two separate programs for transferring files with FTP:

- ◆ **FTP:** A command-line utility that allows full FTP functionality. It is not as commonly used as other alternatives because it has a clumsy user interface. However, it is flexible and can be used as part of batch files.

- ◆ **Internet Explorer:** A graphical utility that supports only a subset of FTP's functionality. In normal use, it only supports downloading files with the anonymous user account. It allows downloading a single file when provided with a full URL in the form of `ftp://server.net/file.zip`, and it allows navigation of the server's file system when provided with a URL that does not include a filename.

Other common FTP clients include CuteFTP, WSFTP, and Netscape Navigator.

Working with FTP

If your work involves the Internet, you have to work with the FTP protocol. For network administrators, you have to understand the protocol well enough to configure your routers, proxy servers, and/or firewalls to handle it correctly. For ISPs, you have to know the implications of the protocol to troubleshoot problems that your clientele may have. For Webmasters, you have to understand the protocol to troubleshoot problems and to determine when it is appropriate to use FTP, and when it is not.

TROUBLESHOOTING

Troubleshooting FTP is a pleasure, at least compared to troubleshooting some other protocols. FTP is a very understandable protocol because all control communications occur in clear text. Problems you will run into using the FTP protocol usually fall into authentication or permissions categories.

Authentication problems include users who cannot log on, users who *can* log on but shouldn't, and users who are authenticated but not authenticated with the correct permissions. One of the most common authentication problems with any protocol is the mistyped password. These problems carry over into FTP, but fortunately they are easy to troubleshoot. Consider the following scenario: You have just handed off the username and password to a new user, who is having problems FTPing into the server. Using a protocol analyzer, you could watch the commands as they are submitted to the FTP server, and verify that the user is typing the correct username and password. Later in this section I will detail exactly what you need to look for in the packets to distinguish the user's username and password from all the other information being carried on the network.

Along the same lines, malformed usernames are a common source of authentication problems. It may be as simple as the user mistyping his or her name, or it may be more complicated. For example, some proxy servers simply strip out the backslash character from an FTP username, making it impossible for the user to log into FTP using a Windows NT domain user account (which must be submitted in the form *DOMAIN\USERNAME*). No matter what the problem, determining the exact data being submitted to the FTP server can, at the very least, eliminate a few possible sources of problems. This same technique can be used to verify that a user is logging onto FTP with the correct username and password and *not* using an FTP client configured to automatically log on with the anonymous user.

Permission problems are another common complaint of FTP users. These can be difficult to diagnose, because FTP client applications may replace the error message returned by the FTP server with something more user-friendly, such as Error: Command Failed. With the use of a protocol analyzer, you can determine exactly what the client is attempting to do with the server and exactly what error messages the server is returning to the client. By analyzing the protocol communications themselves, you can reduce the amount of time required to decode messages.

WRITING SCRIPTS AND APPLICATIONS THAT USE FTP

Many administrators may wish to automate certain tasks that use the FTP protocol. For example, an administrator may wish to write a script that will download several files from an FTP server on a regular basis. The administrator may even wish to create a script that checks for updated files in a directory and downloads them as needed.

Fortunately, there are many simple ways to script FTP commands. The simplest method is to use the FTP command with the `-s` operator. By executing a command in the form `FTP -s:file.txt`, the administrator can automate simple FTP tasks such as uploading or downloading a previously determined set of files.

If you require greater flexibility, Perl has a full library to simplify FTP communications. Most programming languages that include network support will include libraries for the FTP protocol, largely because of the long history and great stability of the protocol. If you are a truly gung-ho programmer, try writing FTP applications that work at the sockets level. Sure, you will waste a lot of time that could be used productively, but you will develop an extremely deep understanding of the protocols involved!

SNIFFING FTP

FTP is perhaps the easiest protocol to analyze using a sniffer. Commands and arguments are sent all at once in a single packet, so you do not have to piece traffic together from different packets as you may have to with the Telnet protocol, which sends characters as they are entered into the keyboard. All of the commands are in English (albeit many are severely abbreviated). Further, and this points to one of the major weaknesses of FTP, username and password are sent in clear text.

I will cover the way traffic flows in FTP in more detail in the next section, but it is useful to know that FTP exchanges commands with the server using TCP port 21. All data exchanges make use of TCP port 20. Therefore, it is simple to separate the commands, which are human-readable and make up the dialog between the client and the server, and the data transfer, which is probably just a bunch of binary data that nobody but a computer could make sense of. This is in contrast with the HTTP protocol, which uses TCP port 80 for all communications, commands, and data.

As Figure 17-1 shows, FTP is an excellent way to listen to other people's passwords on a network. This is good news for malicious hackers, but bad news for us "good guys." Anybody with a good understanding of the FTP protocol and the ways a network works can write a program that places the network interface card of a system into promiscuous mode and listens to all traffic on port 21. To grab usernames and passwords, it just has to listen to packets with the phrase "USER" (the FTP command that prefaces a valid username) and the phrase "PASS" (which prefaces a valid password). In this way, a host on a network could discretely collect usernames and passwords of any other machine on the same network segment.

This ease with which the service can be monitored is especially bad news for Windows NT, because it allows users to log onto the FTP service using a user account from a domain or from the local user database. Because of this, a stolen password can be used for much more than simply logging onto FTP: If an administrative password is stolen, it could be used on a domain controller to destroy an entire domain.

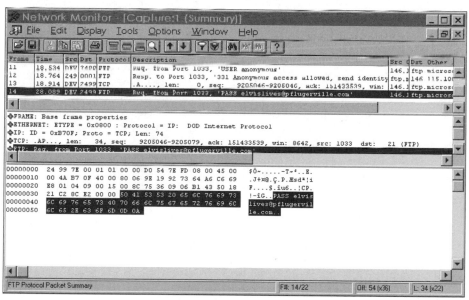

Figure 17-1: Hear any good passwords lately?

FTP Communications Flow

FTP, like most client-server protocols, is characterized by heavily asymmetric traffic patterns. Specifically, traffic generated by the client is typically much, much less than traffic generated by the server. For example, if a client downloads a 500K file from an anonymous FTP server (Internet-style), the client generates less than a dozen packets, each of minimal length. However, the server must transmit the entire file. This relationship is illustrated in Figure 17-2.

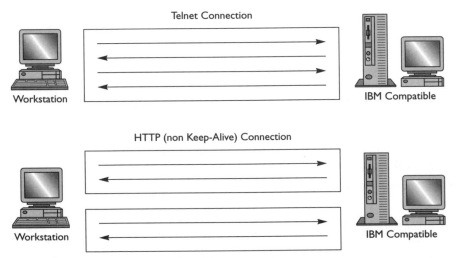

Figure 17-2: How a server transmits a file

The FTP protocol is composed of two distinct communications channels. The first, the FTP Control channel, utilizes TCP port 21. This is a session-oriented dialog, initiated by the client. The second channel, the FTP Data channel, uses TCP port 20.

Once the client establishes a TCP connection to the FTP server, the server typically returns a welcome message (such as "220 ftp Microsoft FTP Service..."), which most FTP clients display on the console to the user. The FTP client must then offer to authenticate itself with the USER command. Unlike in a typical Telnet session, the FTP server does not prompt for a password.

Once the server receives the USER command from the client, it returns a message acknowledging receipt. A positive acknowledgement of 331 is considered a prompt for a password. The client then sends the PASS FTP command across the FTP Control channel, followed by a space and the actual password being submitted. Once again, the server acknowledges receipt with a positive or negative message.

If the client receives a positive message, it may now begin transferring files or issuing other commands that may perform tasks such as file and directory management. If the client requests a file be transferred (either direction), a FTP Data channel is opened from the server's TCP port 20 to a port on the client that was specified at the time the file was requested. This is just opposite of what you would expect to happen – the server actually initiates a connection to the client to transfer data. Once this connection is established, the file is transferred through this communications channel, and the FTP Control channel typically waits until the transfer is completed to begin transferring other data.

TYPICAL DIALOG OF A WEB BROWSER

This section shows a sample dialog between an FTP client and server. Specifically, the client is Netscape Navigator 4.0, the most popular Web browser at the time of this writing. Those running anonymous FTP sites on the public Internet need to understand exactly what will happen in this dialog, as it may happen literally thousands of times in a day, depending on what your business is. A Netscape browser initiated this dialog, but other browsers operate in a very similar fashion.

While reading through this dialog, pay particular attention to the different commands the client passes to the server (always the first word the client transmits, and always in all uppercase) and to the various messages the server returns to the client. The only significant parts of the messages being returned to the client are the numeric codes. Remember, all lines are ended with a carriage return and a line-feed (CR/LF).

```
Client> <Initiates TCP connection to Server's port 21>
Server> 220 ftp Microsoft FTP Service
Client> USER anonymous
Server> 331 Anonymous access allowed, send identity
Client> PASS mozilla@
Server> 230-This is FTP.MICROSOFT.COM
Server> 230-Please see the dirmap.txt file for
Server> 230-more information ( ... )
```

This completes the user logon portion. The 220 server message is simply a greeting to the client that indicates the server is ready for a logon request. The client requests anonymous access by submitting the command USER with the argument anonymous. The server returns a 331 message, indicating that the username was received successfully, and includes a text message that some clients may display to the user (Navigator, however, does not). This prompts the client to return a password — in this case, the generic mozilla@. The 230 messages returned by the server contain a welcome message, which Navigator displays to the user.

```
Client> REST 0
Server> 350 Restarting at 0.
Client> SYST
Server> 215 Windows_NT version 4.0
Client> PWD
Server> 257 "/" is current directory.
```

The REST, SYST, and PWD commands are part of Navigator's normal communication setup. Most FTP clients issue several commands at the beginning of a session to ensure that transfer defaults do not vary from server to server. REST is a command used to pick up a session after an error caused it to end — REST 0 is simply Navigator's way of restarting any session that may have been previously active. The SYST command queries the server to determine what operating system it is running. Presumably, this information is used somewhere inside of Navigator, but I cannot imagine what it could be used for since it does not indicate what type of FTP service the server is running. The PWD (Print Working Directory) command queries the server for the current working directory, and the server returns whatever the default directory is, in this case, "/." Remember that the FTP directory does not necessarily correspond to a directory on the server's file system.

```
Client> PASV
Server> 227 Entering Passive Mode (198,105,232,1,15,47)
```

At this point, the client opens a data connection to the server.

```
Client> TYPE I
Server> 200 Type set to I
Client> SIZE /
Server> 500 'SIZE /': command not understood
Client> MDTM /
Server> 500 'MDTM /': command not understood
Client> CWD /
Server> 250 CWD command successful.
Client> LIST
Server> 125 Data connection already open; Transfer starting
```

Once again, a data connection is opened to allow data to be transferred to the client. Notice that the client has issued the LIST command – this asks the server to transfer a listing of files in the current directory. Once the data has been transferred, the 226 message is returned to the client, and the client will break the TCP connection. This completes the dialog setup between the client and the server.

FTP Services

This section covers the actual commands and responses exchanged between FTP clients and servers. The information contained in this section is very detailed and critical to anyone performing network analysis on the FTP protocol, anyone who writes FTP clients or servers, or anyone who scripts FTP communications.

Terminology

The term *DTP* refers to the data transfer process, the method used to control the data transfer connection.

The term *PI* refers to the protocol interpreter. You will see the terms "server-PI" and "user-PI." The server protocol interpreter is the process listening on TCP port 21 on the FTP server. It must be able to respond to standard FTP commands such as

USER and PASS. The server-PI has control over the server-DTP. The server-PI uses the server-DTP to transfer data to the user. The user-PI is typically a client-side application that knows how to speak the FTP protocol. The user-PI controls the user-DTP.

Common Commands

The commands listed in this section are probably all the FTP commands you need to know. Each one of these commands is commonly used by FTP clients and should be supported in some fashion by all FTP servers.

USER (USER NAME)

All FTP communications begin with the USER command. This command takes a single argument: the username the client wishes to be authenticated with. In a Windows NT environment, this may include both the domain name and the username. For example, when logging onto an NT server that is a member of a domain, the client may transmit the command:

```
USER domain\username
```

The most common argument to the USER command is anonymous. Anonymous logons to FTP are common on the Internet, where a large percentage of FTP servers carry information for the general public.

PASS (PASSWORD)

Generally the second command transmitted by a client to the server, the PASS command carries as an argument the password for the user already specified by the USER command. This command really is as simple as it seems: There is no encoding or encryption of the password, it is simply clear text. An example of transmitting a password from a client to a server:

```
PASS elvislives
```

Analyzing the USER Command for Problems

A common problem with some FTP clients and FTP proxy servers occurs when issuing the USER command. Many do not handle the backslash character correctly; they may translate it into a forward slash or omit it completely. I have even seen a case in which an FTP client translated it into two backslashes, Perl-style.

CWD (CHANGE WORKING DIRECTORY)

The CWD command changes the directory the FTP server is working with. The sole argument for this command is the new directory, in either absolute form or relative form. Examples of both of these forms are given here:

```
CWD /usr/root
CWD /usr/root/
CWD documents
```

The first command changes the current directory to /usr/root, regardless of what the current directory is. The second command illustrates an optional slash at the end of the directory name. The third command moves into a child directory of the current directory named documents; it only works from directories that have a subdirectory named documents.

QUIT (LOG OUT)

The QUIT command is sent to the server to indicate that the FTP session is over. This command takes no arguments.

RETR (DOWNLOAD)

When the RETR command is issued from the client, a data transfer connection is established. The RETR command takes as an argument the path to the file to be transferred. For example, to use the RETR command to transfer the file /documents/file.html, issue the command:

```
RETR /documents/file.html
```

STOR (UPLOAD)

Similar in function and execution to the RETR command, the STOR command sends a file from the client to the server. The only argument for the STOR command is the destination location on the server. If the file already exists in the destination directory, it is automatically overwritten. To upload the file file.html to the /documents directory, issue the command:

```
STOR /documents/file.html
```

REST (RESTART)

The REST command is used to continue a session that has been interrupted. The REST command has an argument, an integer, that represents the position in the file where transfer should begin. For example, to restart a transfer at byte 4096 in a file, the client would issue the following commands to the server:

```
REST 4096
RETR /documents/file.zip
```

It is important to understand that the command that follows the REST command *must* be a transfer of some kind, either a STOR or a RECV.

RNFR, RNTO (RENAME FROM, RENAME TO)

The RNFR and RNTO commands always work together. Rather than issuing two arguments to a single command, as with the MS-DOS command rename file1.txt file2.txt, the rename function is broken into two individual commands. For example:

```
Client> RNFR file1.txt
Server> 350 File exists, ready for destination name
Client> RNTO file2.txt
Server> 250 RNTO command successful.
```

These two commands must always be used together.

ABOR (ABORT)

The ABOR command cancels any command that is currently being executed on the server. If data is currently being transferred in a data session, it is cancelled. This command takes no arguments.

DELE (DELETE)

The DELE command removes a file on the server, assuming the user has the appropriate permissions. It takes a single argument: the relative or absolute path to the file to be removed. For example, the following command will remove the file /documents/file.htm from the server:

```
DELE /documents/file.htm
```

Servers That Support Broken Downloads

Many servers, including the FTP service included with IIS 3.0, do not support restoring broken transfers. To determine whether a server is capable of restoring connections, try issuing a REST command with a nonzero argument. Servers that do not support the REST command will return an error (such as "504 Reply marker must be 0"). Though IIS 3.0 allows the command REST 0 to be issued, it only allows the argument to be zero — which does not really do any good. It is included simply for compatibility.

RMD (REMOVE DIRECTORY)

The RMD command is similar to the DELE command, except that it removes an *empty* directory instead of a file. To remove the directory documents, first make sure that it contains no files whatsoever. Then issue the command:

```
RMD /documents
```

Please note that the RMD command does not let you remove virtual directories created on an IIS server, only physical directories.

MKD (MAKE DIRECTORY)

To create a directory on an FTP server, issue the MKD command with either a relative or absolute path given as the only argument. The path given must include only a single directory that does not yet exist. For example, you cannot issue the MKD command to create two nested directories at once. To create the directory production within the already existing documents directory, you would issue the command:

```
MKD /documents/production
```

PWD (PRINT WORKING DIRECTORY)

The client uses the PWD command to determine the current active directory on the server. The active directory is the default location for all commands that do not include an absolute directory path. In theory, this would only be necessary when a client first establishes a connection to the server; after that, file system navigation is up to the client, so the client should be able to compute its working directory from the commands it issues to the server. This command takes no arguments and forces the server to return a 257 message with the directory path listed as an argument.

LIST (DIRECTORY LISTING)

The LIST command causes a data transfer to occur that will contain the directory listing for the current working directory. An absolute or relative path can be given as an optional argument if a directory listing for another directory is desired.

SYST (EXECUTE SYSTEM COMMAND)

The SYST command is used to determine what operating system the remote FTP server is running. It does *not* tell you what specific FTP service it is running, which is more useful information. The SYST command takes no arguments.

NOOP (NO OPERATION)

This command does nothing except stall the remote server. In many cases, the remote FTP server will close the connection after a certain amount of time has passed with no activity from the client. The NOOP command can be issued to reset this time-out value. Please note that not every Web server will respond the same way: Many will simply ignore the command and will not reset the time-out value.

CDUP

The CDUP command changes the current working directory to its parent directory. It is equivalent to the CD .. command in MS-DOS. Indeed, entering CD .. into the command-line FTP client included with Windows NT will cause it to issue a CDUP command to the server.

This command is considered optional in the FTP standards – any client could perform the equivalent of the CDUP command by issuing a CWD command to the absolute path of the parent directory of the current working directory or by issuing the CWD .. command.

PASV

The PASV command is used when the client wishes to connect to the server to transfer data. This is the method the majority of FTP clients use to transfer data. The server normally returns a 227 message, which includes information about the IP address of the FTP server and the port number to connect to. This command takes no arguments.

PORT

The PORT command is used to set the data communication port and IP address. The argument is somewhat counterintuitive: It is composed of both the IP address and the TCP port number, broken into eight-bit fields and separated by commas. The IP address is obvious when examining this command, but most people will need to pull out a calculator to compute the TCP port number. For example, the command:

```
PORT 10,10,3,17,14,255
```

means that the IP address 10.10.3.17 should be used with the TCP port number 3839. To calculate the TCP port number, use the formula b5 * 256 + b6, where b5 and b6 are the fifth and sixth bytes respectively. In this case, b5 would be 14 and b6 would be 255.

TYPE

Most FTP clients and servers support transferring files either as ASCII text or as binary. To change types, send one of these two commands:

```
TYPE A
TYPE I
```

The argument A means an ASCII file will be transmitted. The argument I means a file image will be transmitted. It is always safe to send a file as an image. Two other types of transfers, E and L, are not commonly used.

Less Common Commands

XCUP, XCWD, XMKD, XPWD, XRMD
These five commands are equivalent in use and function to the commands CDUP, CWD, MKD, PWD, and RMD. They were created in RFC 775, long before the final standards for FTP were written. They are supported by modern FTP servers for backward-compatibility purposes and are rarely used in practice.

ACCT (ACCOUNT INFORMATION)
The ACCT command is used to specify additional information about a user account, above and beyond the USER and PASS commands. If the server responds to the PASS command (or any other command, for that matter) with a 332 message, the user must send the ACCT command with an argument that has some meaning to the server. Nobody ever uses this command.

MODE
FTP can use three transfer modes to transfer data: Stream, Block, and Compressed. Almost all FTP Servers use the Stream method of transferring data. In fact, Microsoft's IIS does not allow any other mode to be selected! Nonetheless, the command is supported. The format for this command is:

MODE S

APPE (APPEND)
The APPE command works almost exactly like the STOR command, except that the destination file is appended to rather than overwritten. If the file does not already exist, a new file is created. FTP is very rarely used for this type of operation, but most FTP clients that support uploading support the append operation.

REIN (REINITIALIZE)
The REIN command is a shortcut, accomplishing the same thing as quitting an FTP session, reestablishing it, and logging on as a different user. The REIN command works similarly to QUIT, except that the TCP connection is not terminated. After issue of the REIN command, the USER and PASS commands must be issued before normal FTP commands can be used.

STOU (STORE UNIQUE)
The STOU command is similar to the STOR command, except that a filename is not provided as an argument. The FTP server is responsible for receiving the file and assigning a name that is not already used by another file in the directory. Nobody ever uses this command, but IIS and all the popular Web servers support it.

ALLO (ALLOCATE)

Another command nobody actually uses, the ALLO command is intended to notify the server to reserve a certain amount of space before a file is uploaded. Most FTP servers, including Microsoft's IIS, simply respond with a positive acknowledgment, regardless of the amount of space they have available.

NLST (NAME LIST)

The NLST command is similar in usage and function to the LIST command, except that it only returns the names of files within a directory. In other words, it filters out subdirectories from the list before returning it to the client.

SITE (EXECUTE SITE COMMAND)

The SITE command executes a server system–dependent command. The arguments available to this command vary from server to server. Issue the SITE HELP command to determine the commands available on a particular FTP server. The server will return a list of arguments that can be issued.

Spying on Microsoft, Spying on You?

An interesting command that is implemented in Microsoft's FTP server is the SITE STATS command. This command returns a list of commands that have been issued to the server and the number of times they have been used. For example, the SITE STATS command, when sent to ftp.microsoft.com, returns:

```
200-ABOR : 955390
    ACCT : 66
    ALLO : 5
    APPE : 37
    CDUP : 1684626
    CWD : 10494165
    DELE : 2188
    HELP : 34908
    LIST : 8853808
    MKD : 2973
    MODE : 257
    NLST : 280820
    NOOP : 3326754
    PASS : 6032361
    PASV : 6282140
    PORT : 8863693
    PWD : 4109938
    QUIT : 1259362
    REIN : 32
    REST : 1045720
```

Continued

Spying on Microsoft, Spying on You? *(Continued)*

```
RETR : 6194984
RMD : 726
RNFR : 488
RNTO : 71
SITE : 18436
STAT : 7989
STOR : 26264
STOU : 2
STRU : 3818
SYST : 1671982
TYPE : 12156200
USER : 6057445
XCUP : 10
XCWD : 458
XMKD : 115
XPWD : 7089
XRMD : 75
```

Interesting, eh? From this information you can see that more than six million FTP connections have been established to ftp.microsoft.com since it was last restarted. I don't know about you, but this makes me nervous — Microsoft might not mind sharing this information with the rest of the Internet, but I don't want everyone knowing what I'm doing on my server! It would be a simple task to write a program that would execute this command against a competitor's FTP site on a regular basis, and chart their FTP traffic. (I do *not* recommend anyone try this!)

To make matters worse, SITE commands are not logged to the FTP log file, so the only way to determine if people are executing the SITE STATS command against your server is to execute SITE STATS against your own server and see!

So how do you disable this "feature" of your FTP server? To my knowledge, you can't! I haven't been able to find any references to it in Microsoft's knowledge base, and there doesn't seem to be any documentation on the command. Nonetheless, it provides a useful insight into how an FTP site is used: The SITE STATS command provides information that cannot be gathered through any other mechanism, even Performance Monitor.

STAT (STATUS)

The STAT command returns information about the current server. This information is returned as part of a 211 status code, and the results are very similar, regardless of the server software. It is an excellent way to find out what version of software an FTP server is using. For example, here is information an FTP server might return:

```
211-server-name Microsoft Windows NT FTP Server status:
   Version 4.0
   Connected to d10.dial-14.idgbooks.com
   Logged in as elvis
   TYPE: ASCII, FORM: Nonprint; STRUcture: File; transfer MODE:
 STREAM
   No data connection
211 End of status.
```

As you can see from this information, the Web server is running Microsoft's FTP Server version 4.0. You can determine what username the connection was authenticated with and whether any data is currently being transferred.

HELP (HELP)

Although useful, the HELP command is rarely used today. It is more useful for people who may Telnet directly into an FTP server and may forget the various commands available—intelligent FTP clients provide help files on the client side and hide the commands available from the user. The HELP command can be used without any arguments, in which case the server generally provides a list of commands available. It can also take any of the commands as an argument, in which case it returns a more detailed description of the specific command. For example, the command:

```
HELP STOR
```

returns information to the user about using the STOR command.

SMNT (STRUCTURE MOUNT)

This command is intended to allow a user to mount a different file system than the current file system at the server. It is not implemented in IIS and is rarely, if ever, used elsewhere.

FTP Server Replies

Similar to HTTP Server replies, FTP replies are three-digit numeric codes categorized by the first digit. Unlike with HTTP, both the first and second digits of an FTP reply code are categorized. Table 17-1 gives a summary of the first-digit codes; Table 17-2 gives a summary of the second-digit codes.

TABLE 17-1 FIRST-DIGIT FTP REPLY CODES

First Digit	Category Description
1xx	"Okay so far, I'll get back to you in a second."
2xx	"All done, everything went well."
3xx	"I got that part, but I still need more information from you."
4xx	"I can't do that now, try again later."
5xx	"Sorry, Dave, I can't do that."

If the first digit is 1, the message is indicating that a command is being processed but the server is not yet ready to process another command. If the first digit is 2, a command has been processed successfully. If the first digit is 3, the command issued by the client was accepted and more information is expected from the client before the server can continue. A first digit of 4 indicates a "transient negative completion" reply, meaning that the error state is only temporary and will soon be resolved. Finally, if the first digit of the response is 5, there was some problem and the requested action could not be completed.

The second digit of the FTP message categorizes the message in greater detail. If the second digit is zero, the information contained in the reply relates to the syntax of the command the server is replying to. For example, the server may respond with a "503 Bad sequence of commands" error message if the RNTO (Rename To) command is issued without a RNFR (Rename From) command first being issued. Similarly, if the server simply wishes to acknowledge that the syntax is okay and the command was understood, the message 200 is used.

A second digit of 1 indicates that the message is informational. For example, replies to the HELP command use the 214 message, and replies to the SYST command (to retrieve system information) use the 215 message.

A second digit of 2 indicates that the message relates to the communication stream in some way. When the FTP Control connection is first established, the user-PI is greeted with a 220 reply from the server. Similarly, when a server acknowledges a successful data transfer, it responds with a 225 message.

When 3 is the second digit of a server reply message, it relates to authentication in some way. For example, 331 confirms a user's username, 230 confirms a user's password and logon, and 530 indicates that the user's username and password are invalid.

You should never see replies with the second digit set to the number 4 — these are reserved for future use.

The second digit of the server reply code is set to 5 to indicate that the reply message relates to the server's file system. For example, if file and/or directory permissions on the FTP server do not allow the user to perform the action requested (such as creating a directory in a read-only virtual directory), the server responds with a "550 Access Denied" message. Responses to the CWD and PWD commands (250 and 257, respectively) also use this format.

These messages are summarized in Table 17-2.

TABLE 17–2 SECOND–DIGIT FTP REPLY CODES

Second Digit	Category Description
x0x	If the first digit indicates an error, this indicates it is a syntax error. If the first digit indicates success, this indicates the command syntax was understood.
x1x	This reply is for informational purposes.
x2x	This reply relates to the control or data connection status.
x3x	Replies with 3 as the second digit refer to authentication messages.
x4x	These replies are currently unused.
x5x	This reply relates to the server's file system in some way.

There are simply too many possible combinations to describe each one in detail in this book. For a complete description of each response, please refer to RFC 959. I have made an effort to give you the information you need to troubleshoot FTP problems with a network analyzer and to code, from scratch, an FTP client.

The following table, Table 17-3, lists some of the most common FTP server replies.

TABLE 17-3 COMMON FTP SERVER REPLIES

Code	Example Usage
150	Starting a data transfer
200	Confirmation of a successful command
214	Replies to the HELP command

Continued

TABLE 17-3 COMMON FTP SERVER REPLIES *(Continued)*

Code	Example Usage
215	Replies to the SYST command
220	The FTP server's greeting to the user
225	A response to a successful ABOR command
226	Note that a data transfer was completed successfully
230	Confirmation of the user's password
250	Successful CWD command
257	A reply to the PWD command
331	Confirmation of the user's username
350	Successful response to a REST command
500	Note that a syntax error has occurred
503	Bad sequence of commands (such as RNTO without RNFR)
504	Unsuccessful response to a REST command
530	Note that the specified username and password are invalid
550	ACCESS denied

Summary

This chapter discussed several FTP servers and how they handle different portions of the FTP standards, particularly Microsoft's Internet Information Server. The other half of the equation, the clients, is covered as well.

You have learned the following:

◆ FTP is and will continue to be commonly used on the Internet to transfer files.

◆ FTP uses two separate TCP sessions during a conversation. One session, called the FTP Control channel, is used for authentication and initiates file transfers. The second session, called the FTP Data channel, is used to actually transfer the files.

◆ The most common type of FTP transfer is an anonymous Web browser request.

◆ The FTP Control channel uses clear-text commands and responses that may be intercepted and easily interpreted with a sniffer. They can also be issued manually to an FTP server using Telnet.

In the next chapter, you'll learn how proxy servers can allow private networks to safely and efficiently access the public Internet. Chapter 18 will provide an overview of the different types of proxy servers, as well as the specific products available for use on Windows NT networks. The two most popular Windows NT–based proxy servers, Microsoft Proxy Server and Netscape Proxy Server, are compared and contrasted.

Chapter 18

HTTP Proxy Services

IN THIS CHAPTER

- ◆ How using proxy servers will benefit your company
- ◆ An overview of the different technologies and methods used to proxy network traffic
- ◆ A comparison of Microsoft Proxy Server, Netscape Proxy Server, and WinGate

PROXY SERVER IS a general term for any node on a network that accepts or intercepts connections from clients and then initializes a new connection to the server. Proxy servers are the middlemen in a client/server relationship. Because proxy servers handle all data that is passed between the client and the server, they are in a position of power. For those of us who need more control over network connections, proxy servers may provide that. An example of a network architecture built around a proxy server is shown in Figure 18-1.

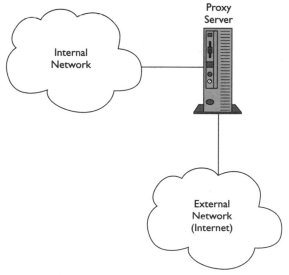

Figure 18-1: Proxies allow safe connections between networks.

We are all familiar with the typical comparison between gateways and the layers of the OSI model. We know that bridges and switches correspond to the data-link layer, and that routers correspond to the network layer. Above layer 3, proxy servers are used as gateways.

Nowadays, proxy servers are most commonly used to connect corporate networks to the Internet. They allow internal clients to securely access the Internet using common applications such as Web browsers and FTP clients. Proxy servers are powerful enough to allow clients to reach the Internet regardless of whether or not they even have legitimate Internet IP addresses, because a proxy server uses only a single IP address for all outbound connections.

This chapter begins with explaining what proxies should be used for and the different methods of proxying. Then the details of Microsoft Proxy Server are explained, followed by Netscape, WinGate, and a few other specific product details.

Reviewing Proxy Background

Proxies connect networks in ways that hubs, bridges, and routers cannot. Proxies connect clients and servers with the intelligence at and above the transport layer of the OSI model. They are capable of looking into the packet at what routers and switches consider merely payload, analyzing it, and taking different actions depending on what is contained in the data.

At the transport layer of the OSI model, circuit-level proxies handle connections based on TCP or UDP port number. Jumping to the highest layer of the OSI model, application-layer proxies transfer data between clients and servers, processing the information with knowledge of application-specific commands. Please keep in mind that the Department of Defense model does not correspond directly to the OSI model; in the former, there are no distinctions between the transport, session, and presentation layers, so the term is the same for all three. The other layers of the OSI model and the term used for gateways at that level are shown in Table 18-1.

TABLE 18-1 GATEWAYS AT VARIOUS LAYERS OF THE OSI MODEL

OSI Layer	Gateway Used
Application	Application-layer proxy
Presentation	Circuit-level proxy
Session	Circuit-level proxy
Transport	Circuit-level proxy

Continued

OSI Layer	Gateway Used
Network	Router
Data-Link	Bridge
Physical	Hub/repeater

Understanding What Proxies Are Good For

Proxies are useful for many purposes. The number-one use of proxy servers is for connectivity. In this respect, proxy servers serve a similar function to routers. However, proxy servers offer many other features, including security, caching, logging, and IP address translation, that are not available to devices that are only capable of analyzing traffic at the OSI network layer.

This section will discuss each of these uses and give you background into why you might need them. Later in this chapter, I will discuss specific products that may be able to fulfill these needs. As you read this section, consider how your organization will make use of each of the different features. Knowing what you want and need will help you choose a proxy server later.

Proxy Servers Instead of Network-Layer Routers

If the primary purpose of a proxy server is connectivity, why not just use a router? The fact is, proxy servers are not nearly as good at connecting networks as routers are. Proxy servers are slower, are more expensive, and require much more administration time. If all you need to do is connect two public or private networks, there's no need for a proxy server.

Proxy servers are only useful because they provide features above and beyond what traditional routers can provide. It is all the other features detailed in this section that give proxy servers their value. Nonetheless, know that proxy servers do provide connectivity and, in most cases, provide all the functionality of the standard router.

Conserving the Public IP Address Space

RFC 1918 (Address Allocation for Private Internet) recommends using private IP addresses for local area networks. This helps to conserve the constantly shrinking pool of public IP addresses. Instead of assigning every node on a network a public IP address, an organization receives only enough public addresses to assign to those systems that will be accessible from the public Internet.

This recommendation has been difficult to implement, because the systems on the local area network will still require access to the Internet. For example, though a user with a desktop machine may receive a private IP address, that user will still want to be able to surf the Net. This is where a proxy comes in handy. The proxy is capable of receiving requests from private IP addresses on a private LAN, retrieving the requested information from the public Internet, and returning it to the original user. An example of a network configured this way is shown in Figure 18-2.

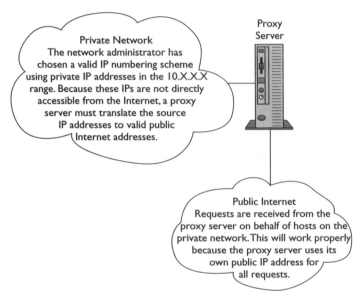

Figure 18-2: Most organizations do not need to assign public IPs to internal networks.

This is also a useful technique for security reasons. Because the IP addresses on the LAN are not publicly accessible, no one on the LAN is capable of bypassing the proxy server. Likewise, it is impossible for a hacker to work around a proxy server that is acting as a firewall and access the systems on your LAN directly. Because the InterNIC has not assigned IP addresses to your network, routes to it do not exist in the Internet's routers.

Hiding Internal Addresses

As discussed earlier, the InterNIC assigns all IP addresses that may be used on the public Internet. If an organization wishes to build an IP-based network, it must use private IP addresses as described in RFC 1918 or be assigned a block of addresses by the InterNIC. The Internet is a chaotic being though, and many organizations have built IP networks without following these rules. In some cases, the administrator has assigned IP addresses to networks based on random information, such as a spouse's birthday.

Everything works just great, until the administrator needs to connect to the public Internet. Then he will discover that someone else has probably already claimed those IP addresses. This is an administrator's nightmare, because there are three possible solutions, and they are all bad:

- ◆ Renumber all nodes on the network with publicly assigned IP addresses.

- ◆ Configure a proxy server to translate the illegal IP addresses to legal IP addresses.

- ◆ Don't connect to the Internet.

The first solution, renumbering each node, is a project that can take months of man-hours. The last solution, not connecting to the Internet, is not much of an answer in today's business world. The only other alternative is to configure a proxy server that will translate traffic coming from the existing, illegal IP addresses into valid Internet requests. In this case, the network configuration will look like that shown in Figure 18-3.

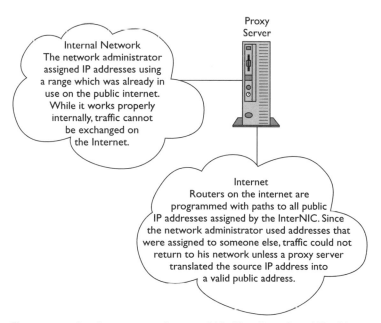

Figure 18-3: Proxies are a good way to hide illegally assigned IP addresses.

For Caching

As traffic on the Internet continues to increase, bandwidth becomes more and more valuable. For organizations that offer an Internet connection to their users, the traffic they create can become very expensive if their ISP bills based on usage. One way to reduce this traffic is to configure a proxy server local to the LAN and enable caching. Caching is a feature available only in application-layer proxy servers.

Businesses with Internet connections are not the only ones trying to reduce the amount of traffic they generate. In fact, ISPs themselves are extremely concerned about the amount of traffic that comes from, and is sent to, their parts of the Internet. It is in the ISP's best interests to reduce this traffic in any way possible, because it will reduce charges from upstream ISPs and reduce the load on the network infrastructure. For these reasons, many ISPs are now offering proxy servers to customers who connect to the Internet through their offices, as illustrated in Figure 18-4.

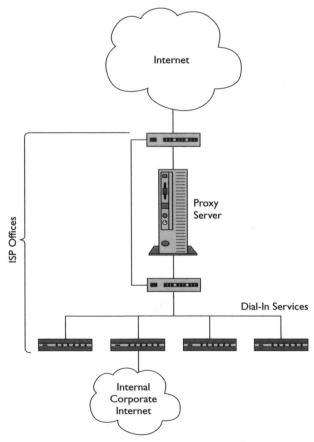

Figure 18–4: Many ISPs take advantage of proxies to reduce the traffic on the Internet.

When considering different proxy servers in terms of their ability to cache data, you should take several different factors into account. Caching is a complex act, and no two proxy servers do it the same way. The sections that follow describe different features that may be available in a particular proxy server.

CACHING DIFFERENT PROTOCOLS

As discussed earlier, the most common type of application-layer proxy is the HTTP proxy. Because of this, most application-layer proxy servers (in fact, all of the products discussed in this chapter) support HTTP caching. However, support for other protocols varies.

FTP is a very cachable protocol, but support is limited. Microsoft Proxy Server only began supporting FTP caching in version 2.0. Netscape Proxy Server now supports it and has supported it since version 2.5. WinGate only began supporting FTP caching in its most recent revision.

When choosing a proxy server, consider which protocols you would like to cache. For most organizations, only HTTP caching is necessary.

PROACTIVE CACHING

Passive or on-demand caching is the mechanism proxy servers use to store remote Web pages so that they may be served directly from the cache, speeding response time. This cache eventually ages and expires. Once Web pages have expired, they must be redownloaded from the Internet before being returned to a client. Waiting for a client to request a Web page before reading it into the cache makes the most efficient use of network bandwidth possible but increases latency by forcing the end user to wait while the page is retrieved.

Proactive caching helps to reduce the time people spend waiting on pages to be refreshed after expiring. The proxy server will watch the files in its cache and, when a file begins to approach its expiration date, will requery the Internet Web server for a newer version of the file. In this way, the cache may receive an updated version of the file without ever making a user wait for the file to be updated. Because the proxy server is capable of timing these proactive updates during nonpeak hours, the total time users spend waiting for a page is reduced. However, the total amount of network traffic generated is actually increased: Because the proxy server is requesting pages without waiting for a user to request them, it may waste time and bandwidth looking for pages that are never again required.

Proactive caching may also be more deliberate. Some proxy servers will allow the administrator to specify Web pages to be updated on a regular basis. They may also support batch updates, wherein specific Web pages are downloaded during off-peak hours and retained in the cache during the normal working day.

Overall, proactive caching is only a useful feature for networks that wish to reduce the amount of time it takes to return Web pages. Organizations that are more concerned about reducing their bandwidth usage will not make use of this feature. However, proactive caching can be used to reduce bandwidth during peak times by moving the task of retrieving Web pages to off-peak hours.

SECURITY

Most application-layer proxy servers will not cache documents that require any form of authentication. For example, if a user must enter a username and password to retrieve a page, the proxy server will notice the header fields in the HTTP communications and make a point of *not* caching those pages. While this will slow future requests for the same page, it increases the level of security for those pages.

The reason the proxy server cannot cache these pages is that it has no way of determining which users may have access to a particular page. This makes a lot of sense, but many proxy servers will cache secure pages anyway. Because of this, subsequent requests for the same page may be served directly from the cache, bypassing the standard authentication mechanisms.

HIERARCHICAL AND DISTRIBUTED CACHING

In enterprise environments where multiple proxy servers are used, it makes sense that the proxy servers cache pages at many different levels. It also makes sense that each proxy server on the network store only a single copy of any particular file on the Internet. This level of intelligence is included in both Microsoft Proxy Server and Netscape Proxy Server, but not WinGate.

Hierarchical and distributed caching features are important for scalability. Conversely, they are not important for small and medium-sized networks that would not have enough traffic to make the features worthwhile. Hierarchical caching divides proxy servers into multiple levels, where "first-level" proxy servers query the Internet directly and "second-level" proxy servers query the first-level proxy servers. Rarely should more than two levels of proxy servers be implemented in a network.

Distributed caching combines multiple proxy servers into one functional array. This is similar in function to a disk array; the servers share a large load and divide it as evenly as possible between them. The concepts of distributed and hierarchical caching are illustrated in Figure 18-5.

ICP (INTERNET CACHE PROTOCOL)   Proxy server caching, in its simplest form, does not scale past a single system. Proxy servers, without additional features, have no way of communicating with other proxy servers to determine whether or not they are storing duplicate information. Indeed, two proxy servers on the same network, which are used by the same groups within an organization, may have as much as 80 percent intersection between their caches. This adds up to a great deal of wasted disk space. Additionally, each proxy server would need to make each original request to the public Internet, not taking advantage of files that may be stored in a neighboring proxy server's cache.

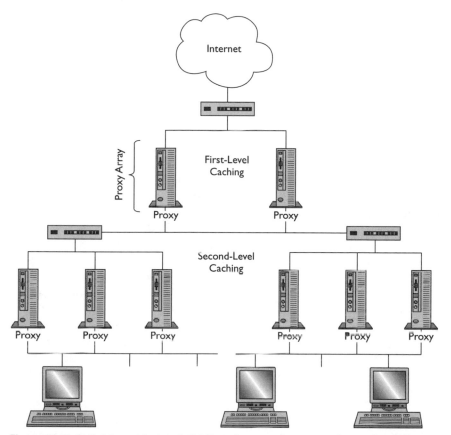

Figure 18-5: Both hierarchical and distributed proxy schemes may be used together.

In order to allow more efficient use of a hierarchy of proxy servers, Internet Cache Protocol (ICP) may be used. This protocol allows a group of proxy servers to share cached documents between each other and specifies a "pecking order" for requested documents that are not within the cache of a set of neighbors. ICP was developed in 1995 to help proxy servers scale beyond a single system.

For example, an organization has implemented a hierarchical caching system. Within each building of the campus networks, three level-two proxy servers act as the first line of defense against Internet requests. Between these proxy servers and the public Internet, an array of five level-one proxy servers receive requests from the level-two proxy servers. This architecture allows for caching for each building (reducing the amount of traffic within the campus network) and caching within the campus (reducing the amount of traffic on WAN links). The Internet Cache Protocol is what makes it all work.

Clients on the internal network are configured to query a proxy server for data existing on an external network such as the Internet. To the client, the ICP proxy array is configured just as if it were speaking to a single proxy, because that single proxy is always used as an interface to the larger ICP cache array. In fact, if a client queries an ICP proxy server for data it already has in its cache, there is absolutely no difference in the way it works. ICP starts to work differently only when a request does not already exist in the cache.

In a nutshell, when the ICP proxy server determines it does not have the requested data, it will ask its neighbors in the ICP array if they have the information cached. If they do have the data on hand, it will be returned to the proxy server that the client originally queried, stored in the cache, and returned to the client. Because the original proxy was able to find the data from a neighboring ICP proxy, a query to the external network was avoided.

If none of the neighboring proxies has the information either, the ICP proxy will send the query "upstream." If hierarchical caching has been configured, the upstream server may be another ICP array that will handle the request. Otherwise, the request will be passed on directly to the external network and handled in the same way any proxy request is handled. As the data is returned to the proxy server, it is added to the cache so that future requests will be fulfilled faster. If an ICP hierarchy exists, the data will be cached at each level as it trickles down through the proxies.

ICP makes proxy servers scale to a much higher level. However, it has its problems as well. First, members of an ICP proxy server array will inevitably cache duplicate information, wasting disk space and memory. In fact, the longer the servers are members of an array, the more information will become duplicated.

Second, queries that are not found in the cache will take longer to return because the ICP proxy server will forward the request to its neighboring proxies, a step that incurs some latency. In this way, ICP arrays have "negative scalability"; the more proxy servers you add to an array, the slower and less efficient it becomes.

Finally, the array allows for scalability but does not provide for redundancy or fail-over in any way: If one of the proxy servers fails, all clients configured to query that server will lose their Internet connections.

CARP (CACHE ARRAY ROUTING PROTOCOL)   CARP is a protocol designed to make large-scale proxy servers' architectures more efficient than is possible with ICP (Internet Cache Protocol). CARP allows content to be cached on an array of proxy servers *without duplication*, and it specifies an algorithm each can use to determine on which server specific content would reside, if indeed it were already cached. An example of a proxy array built around the CARP protocol is shown in Figure 18-6. This hashing algorithm is based on the URL of the cached information.

CARP also allows for some level of fail-over. If a proxy server that is a member of a CARP array stops responding for a specific amount of time, it may be removed from the array automatically. Documents that it had been caching may be distributed to other members of proxy array. Microsoft is currently in the process of making CARP a legitimate IETF-endorsed protocol.

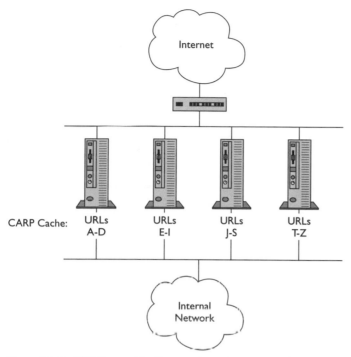

Figure 18-6: CARP is an effective way to scale proxy services.

CARP proxying capabilities are only an important consideration for networks that will be handing large amounts of traffic (greater than 20Mbps) and implementing an array of proxy servers. However, for those who need these features, CARP is a necessity. Microsoft Proxy Server 2.0 and Netscape Proxy Server 3.5 both support CARP functionality, though each has a slightly different implementation. More details on these products and their support for CARP are provided later in this chapter.

Because it avoids the overhead of having to query all of the members' servers in an array, CARP has "positive scalability." The more systems you add to a CARP array, the faster and more efficient it becomes.

CARP does all of this through the HTTP protocol. This is a significant advantage, because each new protocol that is added to a network increases administration overhead. A new protocol may require changes to the firewall and may not work at all through some proxy gateways. Because CARP uses only the widespread HTTP standard to exchange information, most networks will not have to make any adjustments.

The first step in configuring CARP is to create a CARP array. This will add all the CARP proxy servers to an "array membership list." The members of the CARP array are checked on a regular basis to make sure they are still alive, and they are removed from the array if they stop responding.

Hash?

A "hash" is simply a way of converting data into a bunch of numbers. In this way, useful information can be turned into something meaningless to you and me. However, the hashed data is easier for computers to handle, and so it is used as a method of uniquely identifying data without having to work with anything but numbers.

After the servers are added to the array, each CARP proxy server performs a hash on the names of its neighboring proxies. This hash is stored away for later use, when it will be used to determine which server will store a particular URL.

When a client issues a request to a proxy server, that proxy server performs a hash on the URL being requested. A hash of the URL is combined with the hash of each proxy server's name. Using the hash value, the proxy server is able to determine which proxy server in the CARP array would be storing that information. The proxy server then queries *only* that member of the array for the information; it does not even need to check its own cache. If the queried proxy server has that information in its cache, it returns it. If not, the queried proxy server retrieves the information from the public Internet, caches it, and returns it to the first proxy. The first proxy, in turn, returns it to the client.

The preceding example describes the most common task a CARP array will perform. However, CARP does other things as well. If a single server is removed from a CARP array, the servers in the array communicate with each other and redistribute the load the missing server had been carrying. This process is illustrated in Figure 18-7. In this way, CARP arrays include a fail-over capability that allows for the highest reliability possible from a caching system. It also makes administration easy, because no manual changes need to be made when removing a system from the array.

CARP also has the ability to increase cache hits for an enterprise through a *CARP hierarchy*. This can be combined with the distributed method just described, allowing several arrays of CARP systems to query the same upstream servers in the event of a cache failure.

For more information on the CARP protocol, visit Microsoft's Web site at http://www.microsoft.com/proxy/guide/carpspec.asp.

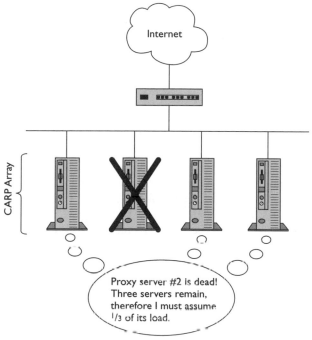

Figure 18-7: CARP arrays automatically adapt when a member server fails.

CARP VERSUS ICP: THE FIGHT NONE WILL NOTICE   Well, I suppose some people will take notice. It is really only of interest to people who are obsessed with making the most of their Internet connections, like myself. CARP is a genuine evolution of ICP, providing much better scalability and performance. Table 18-2 outlines the differences between the two protocols.

TABLE 18-2 CARP AND ICP: A COMPARISON

Task	ICP	CARP
Query neighbors	Must query all neighbors to determine who has a file in cache	Uses an algorithm to determine which neighbor may be caching a file
Fail-over	No fail-over capabilities	Provides for automatic fail-over
Scalability	Negative scalability	Positive scalability

Proxies for Controlling and Filtering

Connecting to the Internet is a scary thing for many organizations because of some rather nasty side effects. Many organizations have noticed that users waste a great deal of time using the Internet for recreation. Others find their way to information that may be illegal or inappropriate in the workplace. The best method of reducing the chances for users to use an Internet connection is to implement filtering at a proxy server.

Most proxy servers have the capability to filter requests from users. Using this feature, an administrator may choose to limit access to Web sites that may not be appropriate for the workplace, such as www.espn.com. All application-layer proxy servers support this feature – it is a key component to ensuring productive use of the Internet connection. Most administrators do not make use of the filtering features, but it's good to know that it is there if you ever need it.

Content filtering is available from proxy servers at any layer. However, application-layer proxy servers will offer the most powerful filtering capabilities, because they can filter based on the actual content being transferred, not just the location being transferred to or from.

Different proxy servers allow different levels of content filtering. Most proxy servers, both circuit-layer and application-layer, allow source-IP filtering. Application-layer proxy servers can provide more intelligent filtering and can disallow content based on the URL, content type, and HTML content. Netscape Proxy Server even includes the ability to scan incoming content for viruses! As you can imagine, this processing increases the amount of overhead involved.

Content filtering is useful if you already know how your users are using your Internet connection, but what do you do if you're not sure what they are up to?

Proxies for Logging

Because Internet traffic passes through a proxy server, the proxy has the ability to log all requests that it processes. This information is useful in many ways. First, it may be logged to track usage information, which may be used for billing, bandwidth analysis, and needs analysis. It can also be used to pinpoint users who are consuming a large portion of the total bandwidth. Finally, administrators may use log file information to isolate Web sites that should be filtered.

Reverse Proxying

So far, I have discussed the reasons people use proxy servers to allow people on a LAN to access larger networks such as the Internet. However, proxy servers are becoming more and more common for inbound connections, as well. When a proxy server handles a connection coming *into* a private network from a public network, the process is called *reverse proxying*. The term "reverse" comes from the fact that the traffic flows in the opposite direction that proxied traffic normally travels. A network that allows reverse proxying is shown in Figure 18-8.

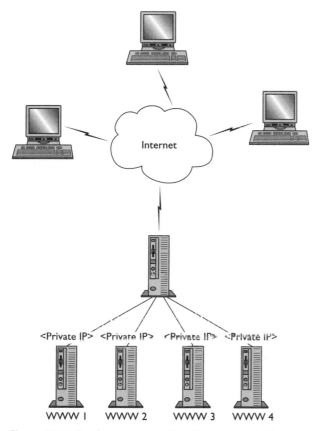

Figure 18-8: Proxies can be used to allow people limited access to internal servers.

LETTING THE PUBLIC INTO A PRIVATE NETWORK

Reverse-proxied traffic is good for many things. First, it can allow an organization to grant some access to its internal resources to users on the Internet. For example, it is common for a company to want to host a Web server on its own premises, through its Internet link. If the company was already using a proxy server, it would be very convenient to place the Web server on the internal network, hidden behind the proxy. Then the proxy could be configured to act as a reverse proxy, accepting connections from the public Internet and forwarding them to the Web server. In this way, the proxy server could provide some filtering and security that might not otherwise be possible if the Web server were placed on the external network.

REVERSE PROXYING FOR LOAD BALANCING

The example in the previous section describes a good way to allow external connectivity to a single internal Web server. However, proxy servers are also used for load balancing between multiple Web servers. In this situation, a company's Web site is so busy that it must spread the load between several Web servers. The proxy server could be configured with a single incoming IP address, and it could distribute incoming queries equally between all servers. Because all requests are funneled through a single proxy server, only a single DNS entry is required on the Internet. Yet, the entire burden is not placed on a single server, allowing increased scalability and performance.

REVERSE PROXYING FOR FAIL-OVER

Another proxy feature commonly used with load balancing is fail-over. In this case, multiple Web servers are configured as described in the previous paragraph. However, the proxy server is intelligent enough to notice if one of the Web servers stops responding. If one does, it no longer submits queries to that Web server. Clients connecting to the Web servers may continue to use the services without noticing any interruption.

PRODUCTS FOR REVERSE PROXYING

The typical use of a reverse-proxy service is for high-end, fast networking for load balancing and fail-over purposes. Because speed is such a high priority for these services, the systems that provide reverse proxying tend to be very specialized. One example of this is the Cisco LocalDirector, which is a hardware-based proxy server capable of both forward and reverse proxying.

Software-based reverse-proxy systems are not as efficient, but they work well for links that are not filled to capacity. Both Netscape's and Microsoft's proxy servers offer reverse-proxy capabilities but operate much slower than more specialized products such as the Cisco LocalDirector.

Understanding Different Methods of Proxying

Proxies come in all shapes and sizes. Application-layer proxies offer the most control over a specific set of Internet protocols, but they are very inflexible and generally do not adapt well as technologies change. Server-dependent transport-layer proxies are less intelligent but more flexible. While they work with most Internet protocols, they do not have any application-specific intelligence. Another type of proxy requires a change to the clients' IP stacks as well as to the servers. This allows for unlimited flexibility but must be implemented separately for each client operating system. This approach is problematic because it may limit future upgrades and offers administrators few choices of desktop operating systems.

To make matters more complicated, many proxy servers will implement a combination of the previously described features. For example, Microsoft Proxy Server implements both application-layer proxies and client/server proxies. The WinGate proxy server implements both application-layer proxies and server-dependent transport-layer proxies. A large part of choosing between proxy applications is choosing the unique feature set that best suits your environment. Understanding each of the different types of proxying available is necessary to the decision process.

I'll start at the top of the OSI model, the application layer, and work my way down to the transport layer.

Application-Layer Proxying

The oldest and most well-known of the proxying methods, application-layer proxying is also known as "classical application proxies." In this scenario, a proxy system is inserted between the traditional client and server. The client must have the intelligence to direct its requests to the proxy and inform the proxy of the final destination. The proxy must be able to act as both the client and a server, though its implementation is typically simpler than either.

Several things are required of the proxy server:

1. It must be able to accept connections from the clients.

2. It must be able to understand the clients' requests and determine the final destination.

3. It must locate and initiate a session to the destination server.

4. Once these connections are established, the proxy server is responsible for relaying information between the clients and the final destination server.

Depending on the application being used, the proxy implementation can be simple or very complex. The simplest proxies simply establish a connection and pass all data directly to the final destination server. More advanced proxies are capable of caching, filtering, logging, and optimizing the data that passes through them.

ACCEPTING CLIENT CONNECTIONS

The process starts with a proxy server's receiving information from a client on the internal network. This request is truly internal; the source IP address is the IP address of the client, and the destination IP address is the internal network interface of the proxy server. This part of the proxy communication mechanism is illustrated in Figure 18-9. Both of these IP addresses may be private or illegal, because the proxy server will change both the source and destination IP addresses before forwarding the request onto the external network.

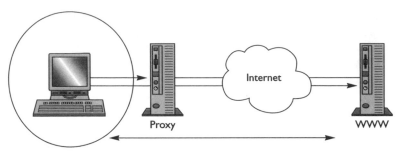

Figure 18-9: Proxy servers act as servers to their internal clients.

For connection-oriented protocols based on the TCP transport-layer protocol, the standard three-way TCP handshake must be negotiated between the client and the proxy server. This step adds some latency, but typically very little since the client and the proxy server are normally connected over the LAN, and network latency is low. Nonetheless, you may reduce the latency involved in this three-way handshake by enabling HTTP Keep-Alives. This will allow clients to maintain a single TCP connection between the client and the proxy server for *all* external Web communications, even if they are for entirely different external servers.

Because the proxy server must act as both the client and a server, it must be capable of accepting incoming client connections. In TCP/IP, this translates to listening to a specific UDP or TCP port. Normally, this does not cause any problems. However, if you like to use the proxy server as both a proxy to a specific application and a server for that application, there may be a conflict.

For example, when configuring a Web proxy that will also behave as a Web server, note that either the proxy or the server, but not both, may claim TCP port 80. To use both a Web server and a Web proxy on the same system, you will have to configure an alternate port for one of the services. The exception to this rule is Microsoft Proxy Server, which has a Web server integrated with a proxy server and is capable of distinguishing between requests destined for the local machine and requests destined for a remote machine.

LOCATING THE SERVER

Often, proxy servers separate the client from the final destination network. This complicates naming and name resolution. For example, if the client is on a private LAN and is requesting a Web page from a Web server on the public Internet, the client probably does not have the capability to resolve the DNS entry for the Web server. The client, in most cases, may have access only to DNS entries that relate directly to the private LAN. Therefore, the proxy server must be capable of receiving requests for servers using the DNS entry for the server and taking responsibility for resolving that DNS entry to an IP address.

This capability allows a Web browser that has been configured to use an HTTP proxy to issue a request such as "GET http://www.cnn.com HTTP/1.0" instead of "GET http://192.168.10.10." While the client does not need to be able to resolve the name of the destination server, it does need to be able to locate the proxy server. For that reason, some method of name resolution is still required on the LAN, unless IP addresses are used.

INITIATING SERVER CONNECTIONS

Once the proxy server has received a request from the client and located the final destination server, it must contact the server to retrieve the requested information. This portion of the proxying mechanism is illustrated in Figure 18-10. The proxy generally requires very little of the client's intelligence because it merely forwards requests. In other words, the proxy does not need to have all of the capabilities of a Web browser in order to proxy for Web browsers.

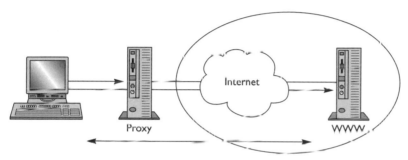

Figure 18-10: Proxy servers act as clients to their external servers.

For connection-oriented protocols such as HTTP, the standard three-way TCP handshake must be negotiated between the proxy server and the Internet server. This adds latency to the transaction, but it may be avoided in certain circumstances. Most HTTP proxy servers have the option to use HTTP Keep-Alives when communicating with a server. This can decrease latency in cases in which the proxy server must retrieve information from the Internet but has retrieved other information recently. This is an advantage of proxy servers because an entirely different user may have initiated the original connection, making the overall transaction faster than it would have been if each user queried the Internet server directly.

All traffic passed between the proxy server and the final destination server on the external network use external IP addresses. If the proxy server is connecting a host on the Internet, outgoing traffic will contain the source IP address of the proxy server's public interface. The destination IP address will be that of the Internet server.

RELAYING INFORMATION

By the time the proxy server reaches this stage, the hard part is over. For most applications, relaying information constitutes simply passing on requests from the client to the server without modification. A proxy server in the process of relaying information between client and server is illustrated in Figure 18-11.

Naturally, certain fields and IP and TCP headers will need to be modified, but normally the application-layer data is not changed.

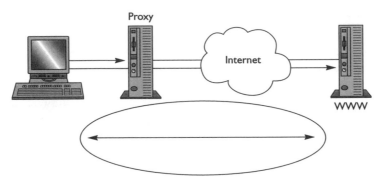

Figure 18-11: After the connection is established, proxy servers must forward data.

One exception to this rule is the HTTP proxy, which adds its own message-header field for each message that it relays. This header field is called Via; it is used to notify both the clients and the servers that the message has passed through a proxy.

SPECIFIC APPLICATIONS

Application-layer proxy servers must be programmed specifically for each different application. For this reason, most proxy servers support only a small set of true application proxies. The most popular of these are HTTP and FTP, with the outdated Gopher protocol occasionally being supported. Configuring and optimizing these proxy servers successfully is very much dependent on having a detailed knowledge of the workings of both the protocols and their proxy methods.

HTTP PROXY CONNECTIONS   HTTP (Hypertext Transfer Protocol) is a brilliantly designed protocol. It has been able to scale larger than any application-layer protocol ever. However, for it to work well in enterprise environments that connect to the Internet, some additions to the protocol have been required. One of these is the HTTP proxy protocol as specified in the RFC standard 1945 and RFC 2068.

Ari Luotonen and Kevin Altis first developed the HTTP proxy while working at the CERN institute. This protocol provides an application-layer gateway between the client and the server, allowing browsers to reach Web servers without speaking directly to each other.

Why are the proxies necessary? They are necessary because when groups of users visit Web pages, they visit many of the same pages. This means that the same data is transmitted from the Web server over and over again. While the HTTP protocol takes into account robust client-side caching and server-side caching controls, this does not help cache data between users that may be closer to each other on the network than they are to the Internet Web server. When an HTTP proxy is placed at the boundary of an organization's connection to the Internet, that proxy is capable of implementing caching for the entire group of users. Therefore, if one user visits CNN's Web page, the next user who visits it may retrieve the information from the proxy server rather than from the Internet CNN Web server.

While the caching features of HTTP proxy servers help to make up for the inefficiency of HTTP transfers, HTTP proxies are also capable of adding a great deal to network security. Unlike network-layer gateways such as routers, application-layer gateways are capable of robust filtering. While they can allow full HTTP access to the Internet, they can also stop all inbound traffic. By putting a proxy server at the boundary of your organization's Internet connection, you can give users full Internet connectivity but eliminate any possibility of someone connecting to their computers from the Internet.

Another advantage of HTTP proxies is that they allow the administrator to implement content filtering. This can stop your users from visiting Web sites that you do not want them visiting, for whatever reason. If you find out that people are wasting a great deal of time at the ESPN Web page, you can eliminate their access to the site. You are also capable of logging each and every request that comes through, so you can see where your users are going the most.

Any HTTP service, including the Web proxy service built into Microsoft Proxy Server, leads a dual life as both a client and a server. To users internal to your organization, HTTP proxies are HTTP servers, accepting inbound connections. However, to the rest of the world, that is, to the Internet, this HTTP proxy appears as any other client, retrieving files and sending data as required from forms.

HTTP proxies work by accepting connections from a client, listening to the command the client issues, and interpreting that command, which initiates an outbound connection to the public Internet. The command from the client is then passed on. For example, if a user attempts to reach the IDG Books Web site, the user would put the URL, `http://www.idgbooks.com`, to a Web browser. Because the Web browser is configured to contact a proxy server, the Web browser sends the following request to the proxy server:

```
GET http://www.idgbooks.com HTTP 1.0
```

As you learned in Chapter 16, this is very similar to a standard `GET` command; however, you'll notice that instead of including simply a URI, it includes a full URL, including the protocol. The proxy server examines the information in the URL, checks the protocol, and notices that the client is requesting a connection to an HTTP server. It then grabs the server name and initiates an HTTP connection on the default port, 80. This connection process is illustrated in Figure 18-12.

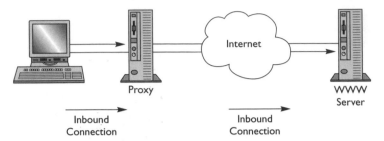

Figure 18-12: A Web browser establishing a connection through a proxy server

Because the client issued a GET command, the server will also issue a GET command. The server initiates a connection on the public Internet to the Web server identified by the DNS entry www.idgbooks.com. Separating the GET command and the URI from the client's request, it issues the following command to the IDG Books Web server:

```
GET / http/1.0
```

The IDG Books Web site interpreting this command returns the default page to the proxy server. The proxy server stores IDG's default Web page in memory and begins to send it back to its internal client. The client displays the file and will begin to request images and referenced objects as necessary.

This was the simplest example of an HTTP proxy connection. Any other command in the HTTP command set is supported as well, including POST, PUT, HEAD.

FTP PROXY CONNECTIONS   FTP proxy connections are not as clear-cut as HTTP proxies. This is because the standards for proxying FTP are not detailed in RFC 959. Instead, several vendor-specific implementations of FTP proxies have been created. These proxies fall into one of two categories: CERN-style proxying and everything else.

CERN-style FTP proxies have an interesting way of avoiding the complexities of proxying the FTP protocol. Essentially, FTP is encapsulated in HTTP. In a manner very similar to the way HTTP proxies work, the FTP client submits an HTTP GET request but includes a URL that begins with ftp://. For example, a client attempting to connect to the Microsoft FTP site through a CERN-style proxy would issue this command to the proxy server:

```
GET ftp://ftp.microsoft.com
```

Both Netscape Navigator and Microsoft Internet Explorer support CERN-style proxying. Because these are the two most popular FTP clients, CERN-style proxying is the method most likely to be useful.

Several vendors have created methods of proxying FTP connections. Some are more elegant than others, but all lack the primary advantage of CERN-style proxying: FTP client support. As an example of this type of proxying, I will describe the method that the WinGate proxy server uses.

The WinGate proxy server supports FTP connections but requires the end user to have knowledge of the proxy server and how to use it. In a nutshell, the user connects his or her FTP client directly to the proxy server. The WinGate proxy server has been configured to listen for FTP connections and return a greeting message as a true FTP server would. Because application-layer proxies require knowledge of the final destination server, the user must somehow supply that FTP server's name to the proxy server. This is where things may get difficult for the end user.

When prompted for a username by the FTP client application, the user must enter the name in the format *username*@ftp.*company*.com. The WinGate proxy server interprets this username, initializes a connection to ftp.*company*.com, and submits the username originally provided by the user. After this, the WinGate proxy server merely relays the information between the clients in the FTP server, watching the FTP commands for data transfers, which will require it to listen on additional ports.

This method is good, in a way, because it works with any standard FTP client. However, it will probably not work with any standard end user. Typically, proxy methods that require special knowledge by the end user do not work out. Imagine an end user surfing the Web with a Netscape browser; instead of clicking on a hyperlink to download a file by FTP, the user is required to launch another FTP client and submit the username in the format just described.

In Wingate's defense, they recommend FTP proxying be done through the SOCKS protocol, described in more detail later in this chapter.

GOPHER PROXY CONNECTIONS   Microsoft Proxy Server supports Gopher proxy connections, but nobody ever actually uses Gopher, so I'm not going to cover it in detail here.

SUMMARY OF APPLICATION-LAYER PROXYING

Application-layer proxies are the best choice when access to the Internet will be limited to a few specific, popular application-layer protocols. You are essentially limited to HTTP, FTP, RealAudio, and Gopher. While this encompasses the majority of Internet traffic, your users will quickly find other applications that are not supported. The majority of these new, leading protocols do not have any application proxy support whatsoever.

Marc Chatel wrote an excellent discussion of application-layer proxying in RFC 1919. In this discussion, application-layer proxies are referred to as "classical proxies" and are contrasted with "transparent proxies."

Circuit-Level Proxies

The concept of application-layer proxying has some serious flaws. First, both the client and the proxy server must have the intelligence built into them to forward and relay traffic through the proxy. This is a serious flaw, because most application-layer protocols do not have this functionality built into them. For example, even the immensely popular Internet e-mail protocols, POP and SMTP, do not support application-layer proxying. Very few new protocols support any kind of application-layer proxy, unless they make use of an existing protocol such as HTTP. For these protocols, the only option is to proxy at a layer below the application layer.

Another problem with application-layer proxying is the demand that it places on the proxy server. The proxy server must do more than simply pass traffic to and from the clients; it must process each command filter and add any proxy directives that exist before sending the information on. When the server retransmits the information on the external network, it must rewrite headers for the first four layers of the OSI model. For these reasons, application-layer proxy servers are able to handle less traffic and fewer connections than other types of proxy servers.

Therefore, some proxy servers support proxying at the transport layer. This means that the proxy server is capable of accepting TCP or UDP packets from clients on the internal network and sending them out another network interface card connected to the external network. When the packets are re-sent, both the source and destination IP addresses are changed. Depending on how the proxy server is configured, the transport-layer headers (TCP or UDP) are also rewritten. The communication process used by circuit-level proxies is illustrated in Figure 18-13. The proxy server keeps track of its connections and can return information to the client when it hears back from the server it is proxying for.

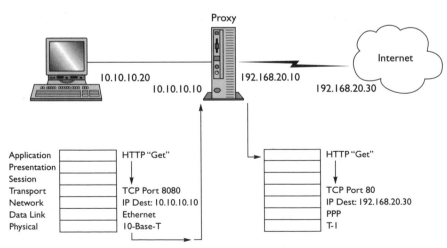

Figure 18-13: Circuit-layer proxies act as gateways at the transport layer.

There are several different methods of circuit-level proxying, and each vendor tends to come up with its own unique solution.

PORT REDIRECTION: MANUALLY CONFIGURED CIRCUIT-LEVEL PROXYING

The simplest method of circuit-level proxying is known as *port redirection* or *port forwarding*. This is very much a brute-force method, but it is simple to understand and requires very little effort on the part of the software developers.

In a nutshell, an administrator configures the proxy server to listen for inbound connections on a specific TCP or UDP port. At the same time, the administrator specifies an outbound IP address and port number. A client who wishes to connect to the external network connects directly to the proxy server using the port number specified for inbound proxy connections. The proxy server opens an outbound connection to the destination IP address and port number that the administrator configured previously. Once the connection is established, all data forwarded to the internal connection is forwarded directly to the external network. This concept is really much more difficult to explain than it is to understand.

Port redirection is reliable and simple to configure but does not scale well. Several separate redirections may need to be configured for each user on the network. Furthermore, every time users want to access a different server, the administrator will be required to change a configuration parameter. For these reasons, port redirection is not even included in the large-scale Microsoft Proxy Server. WinGate, a small-scale shareware product, is the primary example of port redirection on Windows NT and Windows 95 systems. However, most versions of UNIX include port redirection as a component of the operating system.

You cannot configure an application-layer proxy server for the Internet e-mail protocols, POP and SMTP. Instead, you may use a transport-layer proxy. A proxy server will allow you to create a mapping from a particular TCP or UDP port on the internal network interface card of the proxy server to a particular TCP or UDP port of a server on the external network.

So to give an internal user access to an external e-mail server, create a TCP port mapping from the internal interface using TCP ports 25 (for SMTP) and 110 (for POP). On the external interface, map to the same ports on the destination e-mail server.

CLIENT AND SERVER PLATFORM-DEPENDENT CIRCUIT-LEVEL PROXYING

Another proxying scheme allows for complete, transparent connectivity. It allows the end user to use any application his little heart desires, without having to configure it for the proxy in any way. What is this wonderful product? Microsoft Proxy Server.

The Microsoft Proxy Server Winsock service works by implementing both client and server agents. The client operating system must install the client-side program, which completely changes the way the TCP/IP stack works on the system. This is a serious flaw, because it complicates upgrades and increases the chances for problems to occur.

When the user starts a program that communicates with an outside network, the proxy client encapsulates the packets and sends them directly to the proxy server. The proxy server strips off the encapsulation and transmits the packets onto the external network. When it receives a response, it encapsulates the data and forwards it back to the client. This process is illustrated in Figure 18-14.

Figure 18-14: MS Proxy Server allows for dynamic port redirection but requires a special client agent.

This method works well for certain environments but has critical disadvantages. First, Microsoft provides client-side agents for only the following operating systems:

◆ Windows for Workgroups 3.11

◆ Windows 95

◆ Windows NT 4.0 Workstation

◆ Windows NT 4.0 Server

So what do you do if you have a Sun Solaris system on your desktop? You are out of luck! This is the largest problem with any proxying scheme that includes a client-side agent: incompatibilities with alternative operating systems (defined as any operating systems *not* produced by Microsoft).

The SOCKS Proxy: Intelligent Circuit-Level Proxying

SOCKS is the most powerful, flexible proxy standard protocol available. It allows the clients on the internal side of proxy server to have full network connectivity to the server on the external side of proxy server. While SOCKS was originally intended as a firewall technology, it is now also commonly used just for proxying. SOCKS is an important proxy technology simply because it is so powerful and is becoming so popular.

SOCKS: Wannabe Acronym

SOCKS is not actually an acronym, despite the fact that the word has no obvious meaning and is spelled using all capital letters. You will see other terms based on the name SOCKS, such as "SOCKified," which is used to identify an application written to use the SOCKS protocol.

I would let you in on the secret, but I don't know what SOCKS means myself. I suppose it's related to the term "Winsock."

The end user does not have to have any knowledge of the SOCKS proxy server to make use of it. However, client-side applications must be specially written to take advantage of SOCKS. Server-side applications see SOCKS clients just as they do any other clients, because the SOCKS proxy does all the translating.

SOCKS V4 VERSUS SOCKS V5

Currently, the most common version of SOCKS is version 4. However, version 5 is becoming more widely used. SOCKS v5 is defined by RFC 1928 and builds on the foundation of SOCKS v4. It provides the following new features:

- ◆ User authentication
- ◆ UDP proxying

Unfortunately, SOCKS v5 is not backward-compatible with SOCKS v4. Therefore, if you upgrade a proxy server, you will need to simultaneously upgrade all clients. SOCKS v5 has yet to become widely implemented, so this chapter will focus on SOCKS v4.

HOW SOCKS WORKS

SOCKS works by redirecting network connections from an internal network to an external network. SOCKS is an OSI session-layer protocol designed to allow access to an external network using TCP-based client/server applications from the internal network.

Applications use SOCKS in a very similar way to Winsock. Unlike HTTP application-layer proxies, which can connect to a server given only the DNS address, a SOCKS connection requires a legitimate IP address. Therefore, clients on the internal network must have the capability to resolve DNS addresses on the external network. Fortunately, most proxy servers that support SOCKS also provide DNS services.

Once the application knows the IP address of the destination server, it makes a request to SOCKS to communicate with the application server. This request will include the IP address of the server, information about the type of connection, and the user's identity.

This is distinctly different from other application-layer proxy protocols, because it works with any client that has been programmed to use the SOCKS application programming interface. However, it will not work at all if the client has not been specifically programmed to use the SOCKS proxy interface. This fact is illustrated in Figure 18-15.

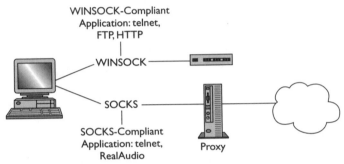

Figure 18-15: SOCKS is a useful method of dynamic port redirection.

At the request of the application, the SOCKS client will initiate a connection to the SOCKS proxy server. By default, this connection makes use of TCP port 1080. Assuming the proxy server is listening on the same port, it initiates a connection to the final destination server.

The final step in the process is relay of the information from the client to the server through the SOCKS proxy. The SOCKS protocol requires no additional bandwidth; the SOCKS proxy server remembers where to forward the traffic from the client.

THE NITTY-GRITTY, ROLL-UP-YOUR-SLEEVES DETAILS

SOCKS is neither the easiest nor the most difficult of protocols to analyze. While it is not clear text as HTTP and FTP are, no data is normally encoded or encrypted. Any standard protocol analyzer is sufficient to analyze the SOCKS protocol, including Network Monitor. However, Network Monitor does not know how to translate the SOCKS data, so keep this book handy!

SOCKS communications, in most cases, begin with a DNS request from the client. Once the client has resolved the desired DNS name to an IP address, it may begin to address the SOCKS proxy server. SOCKS, like most Winsock protocols, can be configured to use a wide range of TCP port numbers, but it resides by default at TCP port 1080.

The SOCKS client initiates a TCP connection to the SOCKS server, just a standard three-way handshake.

After the TCP connection has been established, the SOCKS session-layer connection must be established. To do this, the client transmits a CONNECT request to the SOCKS proxy server. This request includes the version of SOCKS currently in use, the IP address, and the TCP port number of the final destination. The format of the data portion of this request is shown in Table 18-3.

TABLE 18-3 STRUCTURE OF A SOCKS V4 CONNECT REQUEST

Byte	Meaning	Value
1	Version	4
2	Command	1 for connect
3–4	TCP port number	80 for HTTP, 21 for FTP, etc.
5–8	IP address	
9+	Username	
Final	End of data	NULL

In response to this connect packet, the server responds with a confirmation or a denial. The packet structure is very similar to the connect request packet but will be missing the UserID. All fields but the command field will probably be zero. The structure of the connect reply packet is illustrated in Table 18-4.

TABLE 18-4 STRUCTURE OF A SOCKS V4 CONNECT RESPONSE

Byte	Meaning	Value
1	Version	0
2	Command	See Table 18-5
3–4	TCP port number	0
5–8	IP address	0
Final	End of data	NULL

As you can see, the only significant byte in the connect response is the second. The second byte takes on a value from 90 to 93, as illustrated by Table 18-5.

TABLE **18-5 CONNECT REQUEST COMMAND VALUES**

Value	Meaning
90	Request granted
91	Request rejected
92	Request rejected because an identd lookup failed
93	Request rejected because the identd lookup reported a different user id than the SOCKS client

So if everything is going well, the second byte of the command response should be 90 (0x5A). If this is the case, the SOCKS server establishes a connection to the remote server. If the connection was rejected, the TCP connection is also dropped.

BINDs solve a specific problem with several application-layer protocols. Some protocols, such as FTP, require the server to create an inbound connection to the client. Because a proxy that is not aware of the application-layer communication is handling the traffic, the proxy must be explicitly notified that it should begin listening on an external port.

The BIND command in SOCKS v4 allows this to happen. When the client needs to receive an incoming TCP connection, it sends a BIND request to the SOCKS proxy server, which follows the command and listens for incoming TCP traffic on the port indicated.

The structure of the request and response packets is identical to the CONNECT request and response packets. However, different values populate the fields. The SOCKS version stays the same in the request packet. The COMMAND field takes a value of 2, rather than 1, indicating a BIND request. The IP address given is that of the final destination server; the TCP port number describes the port number of the ongoing conversation, not the port number that the proxy server should open. The client doesn't even have the option of requesting a specific port; it must use whatever the SOCKS proxy server gives it.

The reply packet has more interesting information. The first field, as always, carries the value of the SOCKS version. The second field contains a number from 90 to 93, indicating success or failure. The third field is a TCP port number that the server has begun listening on, so that the client may notify the final destination server. The final field, the IP address, is the public IP address that the server listens on.

After a connection is established, the SOCKS server simply redirects the TCP traffic between the client and the server. No filtering, encryption, or caching is performed. So if you are passing FTP traffic through a SOCKS proxy server, all the clear-text FTP traffic will still be available.

There is no RFC for the SOCKS v4 protocol; it did not become an IETF standard until version 5. Instead, I will recommend a document located at NEC's public Web site, typos and all. You can find it at `http://www.socks.nec.com/socks4.protocol`.

SOCKS V5 NITTY-GRITTY

SOCKS v5 is very similar to SOCKS v4 but has a slightly altered packet structure and a couple of new features. Understanding the new fields will give you an incredible understanding of how the functionality has changed between versions.

First, there is an extra step in the Request process. In SOCKS v4, the client's first packet to the server (after the three-way TCP handshake) specified a destination IP address and port number. SOCKS v5 adds a step before that, in which the client communicates to the server a list of acceptable authentication methods. The server then selects one of those methods and returns a packet to the client indicating which method to use. The client's request packet has the fields described in Table 18-6.

TABLE 18-6 STRUCTURE OF A SOCKS REQUEST PACKET

Byte	Meaning	Value
1	Version	4 or 5, depending
2	NMethods	The number of method identifiers in the next field, normally 1
3–257	Methods	See the next table

The NMethods field defines how many bytes will be dedicated to listing various methods. The Methods field actually contains values that describe the different ways the client knows how to speak to the server. Several different methods are described in the standard, as shown in Table 18-7. Other method numbers will be assigned by the IANA on a per-request basis.

TABLE 18-7 VARIOUS METHODS AVAILABLE

Method Value	Meaning
00	No authentication required
01	GSSAPI
02	Username and password required
03–7F	IANA assigned numbers
80–FE	Private, reserved space
FF	No acceptable methods

Because the IANA assigns SOCKS method numbers, various vendors may create their authentication schemes and have them officially recognized. This is the underlying change that allows SOCKS v5 to have a more flexible authentication scheme.

The server receives this request packet from the client and analyzes it to determine which of the listed methods are available to the client. The server then returns a packet that tells the client which method it has chosen to use or rejects its request with the special method number 0xFF. This is a simple packet with only two bytes of data, as described in Table 18-8.

TABLE 18-8 METHOD SELECTION PACKET

Byte	Meaning	Value
1	Version	5
2	Method selected	One of the methods offered by the client, or 0xFF if none are acceptable

After the client receives this message from the server, it may submit a connect request, similar to the first step in the SOCKS v4 protocol. There are a couple of outstanding differences between the SOCKS v5 request packet and the older version. The newer version has an additional command available, which is used for UDP proxying. It also adds a byte to identify a type of address, allowing for network addresses that may be more than four bytes long (like the 128-bit IP addresses in IPng). Network addresses may now even be full DNS names, eliminating the need for clients on an internal network to resolve addresses on the external network. The exact field format is shown in Table 18-9.

TABLE 18-9 STRUCTURE OF A SOCKS V5 CONNECTION REQUEST

Byte	Meaning	Value
1	Version	0
2	Command	See Table 18-11
3	Reserved	0
4	Address Type	1 = IPv4, 3 = DNS name, 4 = IPng
5+	IP address or DNS name	Varies
Last two bytes	TCP/UDP Port number	Varies

To complete the connection request, the SOCKS v5 proxy server returns a reply with a special code indicating the result. This is directly equivalent to the connection reply packet in SOCKS v4, but the format and values have changed. The new format is described in Table 18-10.

TABLE 18-10 STRUCTURE OF A SOCKS V5 CONNECTION RESPONSE

Byte	Meaning	Value
1	Version	5
2	Reply	See Table 18-11
3	Reserved	0
4	Address Type	1 = IPv4, 3 = DNS name, 4 = IPng
5+	IP address or DNS name	Varies
Last two bytes	TCP/UDP Port number	Varies

The most significant byte in the connect response is the second. This byte takes on a value from 00 to 09, as illustrated by Table 18-11. There are more possible values now, allowing a finer grain of error reporting by the SOCKS client.

TABLE 18-11 CONNECT REQUEST COMMAND VALUES

Value	Meaning
00	Succeeded
01	General SOCKS server failure
02	Connection not allowed by rule set
03	Network unreachable
04	Host unreachable
05	Connection refused
06	TTL expired
07	Command not supported
08	Address type not supported

After a 0x00 code is returned, the connection is ready to go and the SOCKS proxy server will relay information between the client and the final destination server. Depending on the method used, this data may be in clear text or may have any kind of encryption, compression, or encoding performed on it.

One additional possibility with SOCKS v5 is that the application will need to create a UDP proxy. UDP proxies allow protocols that depend on UDP to work through a SOCKS proxy. This is more complicated than a TCP proxy, because UDP does not maintain a connection and the proxy server would not otherwise know when to start or stop listeners.

The client requests this from the server by submitting a UDP Associate packet that includes the destination address and UDP port number the client wishes to communicate with on the external network. The UDP request packet, as shown in Table 18-12, is very similar to the TCP request packet.

TABLE 18-12 STRUCTURE OF A SOCKS V5 UDP ASSOCIATE REQUEST

Byte	Meaning	Value
1–2	Reserved	0x0000
3	Fragment number	Varies, 0 if not fragmented

Continued

Byte	Meaning	Value
4	Address type	1 = IPv4, 3 = DNS name, 4 = IPng
5+	IP address or DNS name	Varies
Two bytes after address	TCP/UDP port number	Varies
Remaining data	User data	Determined by the client application

SOCKS v5 supports several new features over SOCKS v4 but is still not widely supported. Clients may now make use of a variety of authentication methods and addressing schemes. The flexibility of the addressing scheme allows a network administrator to limit the exposure internal clients have to the external network — they no longer require access to the external DNS database.

SOCKS v5 also adds support for UDP proxying, through the UDP association mechanism. In this way, SOCKS proxies may forward connectionless UDP data.

SUPPORT FOR SOCKS

SOCKS is almost as widely supported as HTTP proxies. All major Windows NT-based proxy servers, including Microsoft Proxy Server, Netscape Proxy Server, and WinGate, support SOCKS. SOCKS is also supported by proxy servers for alternative operating systems, including all variations of UNIX.

SOCKS clients must be specially coded to work with the proxy protocol. Fortunately, it is common for application developers to allow their application-layer protocols to work with SOCKS. Microsoft Internet Explorer and Netscape Navigator both support SOCKS proxying for HTTP and all other protocols they support. Other applications that may need to pass through a proxy server, such as FTP and RealAudio, support the SOCKS proxy. If you are unsure whether a certain application supports SOCKS, check the documentation for that application.

WHAT SOCKS DOES NOT PROVIDE

SOCKS is a robust protocol, but many users will encounter problems. First, it does not provide any support for network-layer protocols such as ICMP. Because of this, you cannot use utilities like PING or TRACERT through a SOCKS proxy server. Second, SOCKS v4 lacks authentication and UDP support. Both of these features were added to the SOCKS v5 protocol.

SOCKS is definitely designed to help UNIX systems network. The fact is, it does not have any support whatsoever for some critical Microsoft networking protocols, such as NetBIOS and WINS. What this means to those of us who engineer and support NT-based networks is that we can count on SOCKS to give users access to traditional TCP/IP applications, but we cannot use it for the full spectrum of networking needs.

Theoretically, NetBIOS protocols could be written to work with SOCKS v5, because of the robust support for UDP "connections," naming, and authentication. However, don't hold your breath. Microsoft is the only group that has the knowledge and time to "SOCKSify" NetBIOS, and they already have a solution: Microsoft Proxy Server.

For many networks, support for Internet applications is enough. SOCKS will allow an organization to connect itself to the Internet and grant Internet access to users. Users can check e-mail, surf the Web, listen to RealAudio broadcasts, and do just about anything else they want with SOCKS. SOCKS just will not work, however, if you are attempting to use it to connect different organizations and require file sharing or printer sharing access between the two. Figure 18-16 illustrates one possible network architecture.

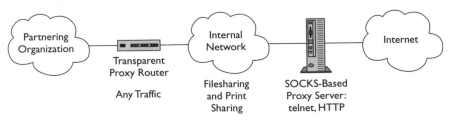

Figure 18-16: An example of a network relying on SOCKS for proxies

THE FUTURE OF SOCKS

SOCKS is destined to continue to be a popular proxy and firewalling protocol. Organizations such as NEC continue constant development and marketing of the protocol as a method for secure access to the Internet. As more and more organizations connect their intranets to the Internet, more and more people will begin to use the SOCKS protocol.

While SOCKS is not the best for NT networking, it is the best option for networks that incorporate both Windows and UNIX systems. Microsoft continues to steer NT away from its NetBIOS dependence, and NetBIOS should be a completely optional protocol by the time NT v5 is released. This will make it more and more feasible to use SOCKS as a method of full connectivity via proxy.

More Info on SOCKS

If you are interested in SOCKS, the best Web site on the Internet for it can be found at `http://www.SOCKS.nec.com`. There you can find downloadable files for alternative operating systems (meaning anything but Windows NT) and several mailing lists you can join. Really brave? Read RFC 1928! (It's actually not that bad.)

Using Application-Layer and Circuit-Level Proxies Together

Wouldn't it be nice to combine the best of application- and transport-layer proxies? Using these two methods in tandem is a very common configuration, because it allows for the robustness of application proxying, while not limiting the users to application protocols that natively support proxy. Some organizations implement this combination in a single software package, such as WinGate. Others choose to use separate products, perhaps on entirely different systems, to provide the different methods of proxy.

For example, an organization may choose to use Microsoft Proxy Server for its robust HTTP proxying features. However, they may rely on hardware-based proxy servers such as Cisco's LocalDirector for transport-layer proxying. If at all possible, find a single method of proxying for the entire enterprise. Proxy servers are a lot of trouble to maintain, so the fewer you have, the better.

Transparent Proxying

Another, more sensible method of proxying provides full network connectivity while not requiring a special client-side agent. This method is known as "transparent proxying," "IP masquerading," or "network address translation (NAT)" and is named such because it is truly transparent to the end users and their system. Many firewalls and several UNIX-based operating systems, notably Linux, support transparent proxying.

HOW DOES TRANSPARENT PROXYING WORK?

To transparently proxy network traffic, the proxy server must pretend to be a router on the network. Routers in the local area network should be configured to route all external traffic to the proxy server, which is treated just like any other router. However, the proxy server behaves very differently once it receives the outbound traffic.

As with any router, the proxy server will receive traffic that must be sent through to another network interface card. This traffic will have a source IP address from the internal network and a destination IP address located within the external network. Most important, neither IP address will directly address the proxy server.

When traditional routers forward traffic, they strip off and replace the data-link-layer header, replacing the MAC address of the proxy server (the last station to receive the frame) with the MAC address of the next router (the next station to receive the frame). While routers are capable of processing data within the network-layer header, they do not attempt to alter the information – the source and destination IP addresses generally stay the same throughout the life cycle of a packet.

When transparent proxy servers forward traffic, they strip off and replace *both* the data-link-layer header and the network-layer header. When the proxy server receives the packet, the source IP address identifies the internal system, which may have a privately assigned address. The destination IP address is already that of the final destination on the external network. Because the proxy server cannot retransmit the packet with the internal IP address, it replaces it with its own external address. It does not need to replace the final destination address; it already contains a valid, public IP address. This arrangement is illustrated in Figure 18-17.

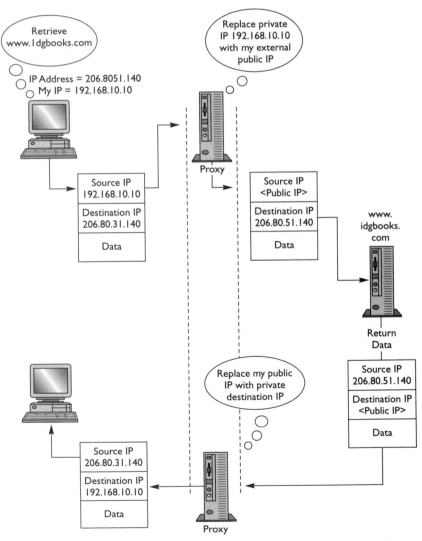

Figure 18-17: Neither the internal clients nor the external servers are aware if a transparent proxy is in use.

The transparent proxy server must remember each connection it proxies to allow the return traffic to be forwarded correctly to the client system. For this reason, processing overhead is significantly more than it would be for a router that handles the same amount of traffic. Because each session is tracked, however, the proxy server may act as a firewall, only allowing incoming traffic that has been requested by a client on the internal network.

WHAT DO I NEED TO BUY?

Systems that support this type of proxying are plentiful but not commonly used on the Windows NT platform. Linux, a free UNIX operating system, includes software to perform IP masquerading. However, it is not a robust or scalable environment. Solaris has an application available called SunScreen, which provides for transparent proxying on busy networks. Cisco offers several specialized hardware systems, including the LocalDirector and Private Internet Exchange (PIX) systems.

TRANSPARENT PROXY DISADVANTAGES

Transparent proxies are very powerful but lack the intelligence of application-layer proxies. For example, most transparent proxies are incapable of filtering Web requests according to the URL. They are also incapable of providing any sort of caching, because that requires knowledge of a specific protocol, and transparent proxies are typically application independent.

Transparent proxies cannot rely on a standard TCP/IP stack. Because the proxy server must masquerade as a server on the external network, the standard TCP/IP stack that does not allow IP spoofing will not work. And replacing key components of an operating system such as the TCP/IP stack can cause real headaches when it comes time to upgrade the system.

Differentiating Proxies and Firewalls

Proxy servers are often confused with firewalls. The two terms are very similar, and many products fit into both categories. What differentiates the two terms is how a product is used: Proxy servers are used primarily for connectivity; firewalls are used primarily for security. So depending on how it is used, Microsoft Proxy Server may be either "a firewall that provides proxy services" or "a proxy server that acts as a firewall."

As I stated in the previous paragraph, proxies and firewalls have a great deal of overlap. Many firewalls include transparent proxying (described previously), which allows clients to access another network through a proxy without requiring knowledge of that proxy. To the client, the firewall merely acts as a router. However, unlike a router, the firewall may translate the IP address in the packet headers as it sends and receives them. Firewalls also include more robust security features. For example, Microsoft Proxy Server allows filtering of outgoing traffic, but firewalls provide for filtering and tracking of sessions that Microsoft Proxy Server cannot handle, such as UDP traffic.

Understanding Automatic Proxy Configuration

It is a difficult and time-consuming project to configure all the browsers in an enterprise to communicate with a particular proxy server. To make this easier, automatic proxy configuration (APC) was created. APC is a method browsers may use to discover the proxy configuration on a network without any form of manual configuration. Netscape Proxy Server supports this functionality, which can greatly reduce the time required to migrate network clients from using a routed Internet connection to using a proxied Internet connection.

APC works via JavaScript. The administrator creates a program with a .PAC file extension and places it at the proxy server. Each time a Web browser is configured, that browser merely needs to be pointed to a proxy server with the .PAC automatic configuration file. The browser has a MIME type listed for the .PAC file extension. The MIME type tells the browser that the file is a special type and that it should be executed in a particular way. Then each and every time the browser is launched, it will requery the proxy server and retrieve a new configuration. This makes the initial configuration of browsers much simpler and minimizes the amount of work that must be done when proxy server configuration changes are made.

APC gives the administrator the ability to create an intelligent script that will direct clients to retrieve requests in different ways depending on their location in the network. For example, clients should generally be configured to query the nearest proxy server for external requests, but they may need to contact a different proxy server for requests within a specific domain. By using the URL and type of request, the PAC script can direct a browser to retrieve a particular URL in a particular way.

PAC scripts contain a function called FindProxyForURL, which receives three arguments: URL, host, and method. In JavaScript, the function definition is:

```
function FindProxyForURL(url, host, method)
```

The meanings of the url and host arguments are obvious; the method argument contains the command within the application-layer protocol that should be executed (such as POST, GET, or PUT). The function returns to the browser a string that contains instructions on how to retrieve the URL. The string is broken into three separate portions and contains the following pieces of information:

- ◆ **Access Method:** This is either PROXY, SOCKS, or DIRECT.

- ◆ **Host:** Used with either the PROXY or SOCKS access method, the host argument tells the browser the name or IP address of the proxy to use.

- ◆ **Port:** The port number indicates where the proxy server is listening for client connections.

For example, if the user enters the URL `http://www.idgbooks.com`, the browser will call the JavaScript query in this way:

```
FindProxyForURL("http://www.idgbooks.com", "www.idgbooks.com",
  "GET");
```

The JavaScript might determine that the request should go through the proxy server named WebProxy at port 8080. The script also wants to indicate to the server that a backup proxy, named WebProxyBackup, is available if the first fails to respond. In case neither proxy is available, the browser should attempt to access the URL directly. In this case, it would return the string:

```
"PROXY WebProxy:8080; PROXY WebProxyBackup:8080; DIRECT";
```

This example illustrates APC's ability to define a fail-over path for browsers by declaring three different methods of accessing the destination Web site, each separated by a semicolon.

Reviewing Specific Proxy Products

Proxy servers come in all shapes and sizes. The product I will focus on this chapter is Microsoft Proxy Server, because I expect it to be the common solution for proxying in enterprise networks that already make use of Windows NT Server. However, it is not the only game in town. Another popular solution is Netscape's proxy server, which is available for both Windows NT and UNIX platforms. For smaller networks and those who just wish to learn about proxying, a shareware product named WinGate is available.

No one product is right for everyone. Each has its own specific set of advantages and disadvantages. An excellent starting point for determining which aspects of a proxy server should be evaluated is the section "Understanding What Proxies Are Good For" earlier in this chapter. I suggest going through this section and deciding which functions you will make the most use of, and picking the product that best supports that feature set.

This section will describe three of the most common Windows NT–based proxy servers and their various features.

Microsoft Proxy Server

Microsoft introduced Microsoft Proxy Server 1.0 in 1996. The company marketed it as both a utility to provide increased connectivity and a method of firewalling.

Now, any time a company tries to sell a new product as a firewall, they are going to receive a great deal of scrutiny from the Internet community. Unfortunately, Microsoft Proxy Server collapsed under scrutiny; people discovered it to be weak in security and found a great deal of flaws. In version 2.0, Microsoft has made an effort to address some of these concerns by providing an increased level of security. They have also supplemented the product with redundancy features, improved caching, and improved clients.

Microsoft Proxy Server is different from other proxy servers because it provides both a standard HTTP proxy, known as the Web proxy service, and a client/server proxy protocol, called the Winsock proxy service. While several products, including Netscape Proxy Server and WinGate, provide different types of proxy services, Microsoft is the only one to develop a client/server type proxy service. The Winsock proxy is important because it allows any Winsock protocol to be used through a proxy server, not limiting the clients to HTTP and other Web-based protocols that the Web proxy does.

CACHING

Who has enough bandwidth? Especially if you are connecting to the Internet, it is never fast enough. You could always download a little quicker. Proxy Server can help you out with this. Proxy Server has the ability to retain information gathered through the Web proxy service and return it to a client at a later date, speeding response time. To make it even better, the larger your organization, the more you benefit from the effects of caching.

Here's an example. Joe's a member of a 500-person organization making use of Proxy Server to cache Web requests for its T1 link to the Internet. Rather than working, Joe is checking out the scores on www.espn.com. When Joe retrieves a Web page, his Web browser makes a request to the proxy server. The proxy server then contacts www.espn.com and retrieves their Web page. Once it is retrieved, the proxy server returns the information from ESPN to Joe. Because the proxy server is in the way, his requests take a little bit longer than they would if he were directly connected to the Internet through the T1 link.

However, the benefits of caching will soon become worthwhile. Many of Joe's coworkers are also wasting time at the sports Web site. As they request the same scores that Joe was looking at, their requests are sent to the proxy server as well. The proxy server then returns those requests from the information it had gathered in the course of processing Joe's request. Because the proxy server was passively caching that information, the request is sped up because it does not have to go onto the public Internet, to be returned by www.espn.com.

It's nice that the other employees' Web requests were returned quicker than they normally would have been thanks to Joe requesting the same pages earlier. However, another benefit is that less traffic has to be transmitted onto the Internet. Depending on the type of link the organization has, this feature can reduce costs. At the very least, this reduces the utilization of the WAN link, speeding up a request that may be business-related.

While Joe is an early riser, many of his coworkers are not. In fact, one of Joe's coworkers does not show up until 1 P.M. Once Sarah arrives, she wants to check out the scores from last week's hockey game. So she goes to visit espn.com. Unfortunately the files that were cached earlier by Joe's request have already expired from the cache. Luckily for Sarah, who has a lot of work to do today and doesn't have time to wait for pages to be received, their administrator has enabled active caching on the proxy server. Active caching monitors the requests that are sent to the public Internet and attempts to reduce future requests by actively gathering information. Between the time that Joe checked out ESPN and the time that Sarah asked to retrieve the pages, the proxy server actively went out onto the Internet and updated the pages. The proxy server was smart enough to retrieve these pages during a time when it was not busy, for example, during a coffee break.

Thanks to the benefits active caching, Sarah did not have to wait as long as she normally would have to retrieve her hockey scores, thus freeing up more of her time to do productive work. Maybe.

PASSIVE CACHING   Passive caching is an important concept because it can have extremely powerful benefits for the overall traffic on an Internet WAN link. This can substantially reduce the costs a company incurs for Internet communications. Further, it has the benefit of improving the response time of Web server requests. In cases where a Web server goes down, the proxy server may even be able to retrieve the pages from its cache, thereby acting on behalf of the dead.

Yet, very few people really understand how proxy server passive caching works. This section will provide you with the technical details of how Proxy Server works, giving you the information you need to optimize the caching strategy on your proxy servers.

Microsoft didn't come up with the idea of HTTP proxy and caching. In fact, RFC 1945 and RFC 2068 spell out every detail on how to implement proxy caching. These gave the Microsoft developers a standard to follow when coding the software to determine whether or not pages are valid or not, that is, what pages can be returned from the cache and what pages must be discarded. While Microsoft has been careful in following these standards, the company has also provided the administrator with the ability to modify the caching behavior for a specific environment.

The Web proxy service does not cache every bit of data that it receives from the external network. Specifically, the following criteria must be met:

◆ The command issued must be the GET command.

◆ The Web page must not require user authentication and must not be encrypted. Storing this type of data would be considered a security risk.

◆ Caching must not be forbidden by an HTTP message-header field.

◆ The HTTP status code must indicate success (200).

ACTIVE CACHING   Passive caching benefits by retaining information that is retrieved from the public Internet and returning it to users who subsequently request it. One of the best benefits of passive caching is that it can reduce the traffic on the Internet link.

Active caching works with passive caching to improve the cache hit ratio. However, active caching actually increases the amount of traffic on a link. It can improve response time on Web pages because it increases the cache hit ratio of the proxy server.

Active caching works by monitoring the files in the Web cache. When a file expires, it will re-request that page from the Web site, caching it again. In this way, the next time the page is requested from the cache, the proxy server does not have to retrieve from the Web page on the user's request. This would slow response time by adding in the latency incurred by contacting the Web site before being able to return the page to the user.

As I mentioned in a previous paragraph, active caching actually increases the traffic on a WAN link, because it is trying to update its cache continually without user requests. Therefore, it is bound to retrieve pages for its cache that are never called for by a user. The traffic generated in requesting these pages is completely wasted. There is no benefit to anyone whatsoever.

So to decide whether or not you want to enable active caching on your server, you have to decide which is the higher priority: reducing network traffic or improving response time.

SMALL-NETWORK INTERNET ACCESS THROUGH PROXY SERVER

The most simple and obvious Proxy Server configuration allows a small to medium-sized network to connect to a larger network, probably the Internet, through a SQL dial-up connection. I expect this to be the most common proxy server configuration because so many small organizations out there would like to have full Internet capabilities but cannot afford to get an entire network of public IP addresses or more bandwidth than a dial-up connection allows. The minimal hardware and network requirements are detailed in Table 18-13.

TABLE 18-13 HARDWARE REQUIREMENTS FOR A SMALL NETWORK PROXY

Pentium 120+

1GB Hard Drive

64MB RAM

An analog modem

Monthly network fee: $50

This configuration will work with networks ranging from 2 nodes to 30 nodes and is the least costly option for allowing full Internet connectivity to a small network. In this configuration, an NT server is configured with a modem, a phonebook entry that points to an ISP where the server has been granted dial-up access, and a local area network where all hosts are running the TCP/IP protocol.

One of the reasons this is such an inexpensive alternative is because the proxy server will be configured to gain Internet access through a common ISP dial-up account. These accounts range in price from $10 to $40 a month. Above and beyond the ISP account fees, a monthly fee must be paid for the analog phone line. Depending on the region, these fees range from $20 to $50. Therefore, an average monthly cost for unlimited Internet access via a standard analog phone line is about $50.

This configuration will work well for many organizations; however, bandwidth will quickly become a problem. Even if a single user begins a file transfer, bandwidth for every other user on the network will be significantly impacted. A typical analog phone line is only capable of carrying about 35Kbps of bandwidth. If one user attempts to transfer a large file, the available bandwidth for the other users will be cut down to between 10 and 15Kbps. As more users begin transferring data simultaneously, the bandwidth per user continues to decrease until it gets so slow that either users begin to lose their patience or connections time out due to its nonresponsiveness. Therefore, when you are dealing with such limited bandwidth, it is important to monitor the usage carefully in anticipation of the time when bandwidth restrictions become overwhelming and a more powerful link must be investigated.

MEDIUM-SIZED NETWORKS WITH INTERNET CONNECTIVITY

Most medium to large organizations that require full Internet connectivity for users provide it by assigning public IP addresses to all users and then connecting to an Internet service provider through a wide area network link such as a T1 leased line. While this is the most common method, it has substantial drawbacks:

1. IP addresses must be used. These can be difficult to manage and difficult to acquire from the InterNIC.

2. Users on the public Internet may be able to attack the internal hosts because their access is not restricted in any way and the internal IP addresses are publicly accessible.

3. Administrators have no way to manage the types of traffic that are carried from the local area network to the Internet.

4. Administrators have no way of logging the types of activities that users are carrying out on the Internet.

For these reasons, many medium-sized organizations have begun to implement proxy servers such as Microsoft Proxy Server to provide Internet connectivity to their users. Proxy servers provide solutions to all of the problems just listed. Furthermore, with the release of Microsoft Proxy Server version 2.0, the product has become more scalable, allowing medium-sized organizations to deploy multiple proxy servers for each section of their network. By deploying multiple proxy servers, an organization can take advantage of both load balancing and fail-over capabilities, improving the performance and reliability of its Internet access.

For many medium-sized organizations, a single system may very well suffice. Table 18-14 outlines suggested hardware and network configuration for a Microsoft Proxy Server to be used by this type of organization.

TABLE 18-14 HARDWARE REQUIREMENTS FOR MEDIUM-SIZED NETWORK PROXY

Pentium 166+

4GB Hard Drive

96MB RAM

A T1 connection or adapter

Monthly network fee: $2,000

Many medium-sized organizations provide for wide area network redundancy by purchasing multiple leased lines. In many cases, the organizations may have multiple leased lines to their ISP. In this way, they will benefit from having twice the regular bandwidth and can configure the routers for some sort of fail-over capabilities.

In the following example, the organization has two T1 links to the local ISP and has been assigned only two public static IP addresses. Because only two public IP addresses have been assigned to the organization, proxy servers must be used to allow access from the internal network to the public Internet. One possible configuration is to place one proxy server on each Internet connection. The proxy server will act as the sole gateway to that connection.

To provide for load balancing and fail-over, half of the clients will have proxy server A listed as their primary proxy server and proxy server B listed as their secondary proxy server. The remaining clients will work just the opposite. Proxy server B will be listed as the primary server, while proxy server A will be listed as the secondary server. In this way, if either of the proxy servers fail, all the clients that have been configured to use that proxy server as the primary proxy will fail-over to the redundant proxy. Assuming that both lines don't fail at the same time, Internet connectivity will only be lost for a matter of minutes while the clients determine that the primary link has failed.

It is important to note that only the Winsock proxy client has this fail-over feature built in. Application-layer proxies and the SOCKS proxy normally do not provide for fail-over, though it is determined entirely by the client application.

ENTERPRISE NETWORKS
Small and medium-sized organizations have many simple options for Internet connectivity through proxy servers. However, as a network scales to enterprise levels, providing proxy services to all users becomes more and more challenging. Specifically, the enterprise will be faced with these unique challenges:

♦ Lack of redundancy in proxy servers means a single point of failure for all Internet traffic.

♦ The more users on a network, the greater the chance for malicious attacks.

♦ Proxy servers may become overloaded with traffic.

♦ WAN connections may not provide the bandwidth or redundancy required.

Microsoft has made an effort to address each of these issues through their Proxy Server product and the Windows NT operating system.

BUILDING IN REDUNDANCY   As your network grows, it is especially important to ensure that your users never lose their Internet connections. Even if the Internet connection is only provided as a convenience to the users, for many people it will quickly become a critical resource for their jobs. Companies in the modern business world can be seriously damaged if they lose their Internet e-mail services for a day or two, for example.

Microsoft Proxy Server provides for redundancy of the Winsock service by allowing both primary and secondary proxy servers to be specified in the client configuration file (MSPCLNT.INI). In the event the client can no longer contact its primary Winsock proxy server, it will redirect communications to the secondary server.

Providing fail-over services for application-layer proxy protocols is more complicated. This is because the application, a Web browser for example, does not incorporate any fail-over capabilities. Because the requests are not intercepted by the operating system in the way Winsock proxy requests are, the application must be intelligent enough to know the location of both primary and secondary servers. Until applications become that smart, redundancy must be entirely transparent to the client application.

This is easier said than done with Microsoft Proxy Server. I will not go into a great deal of detail here, because the problem is not specific to the proxy server application. However, consider providing for redundancy within each system using highly reliable hardware components such as RAID arrays, redundant power supplies, and redundant network cards. Also consider clustering solutions as they become more feasible.

INCREASING SECURITY   Proxy servers are often used as firewalls, providing a layer of protection between the external network and the internal network. As an organization grows, it becomes a more likely target for malicious attacks. There are many things an administrator can do to tighten the security on a Windows NT–based proxy server, but for the best results I suggest including a physically separate, dedicated firewall between the proxy server and the external network. An example of this architecture is shown in Figure 18-18.

REDUCING SERVER LOAD   As your enterprise grows, that 486 system you were using to run the proxy server for the organization is no longer going to be sufficient. Eventually, it will become bogged down with requests, and your bottleneck will no longer be bandwidth — it will be the proxy. For large organizations, no single proxy server will be high-powered enough to support proxy requests from the entire organization.

In these circumstances, the best method for reducing the load on any single proxy server is to distribute the load between multiple proxy servers. CARP is an excellent way to do this and is supported by Microsoft Proxy Server natively. In the future, when the member servers of the CARP array become overloaded, scaling is as simple as adding additional servers to the array.

INCREASING NETWORK BANDWIDTH AND STABILITY   Your proxy servers may not be the first bottleneck you encounter in an enterprise network. Often, network bandwidth becomes saturated before the proxy servers do. There are several ways you can counteract this effect:

◆ Add more bandwidth.

◆ Increase the cache hit ratio of proxy servers.

◆ Decrease network usage.

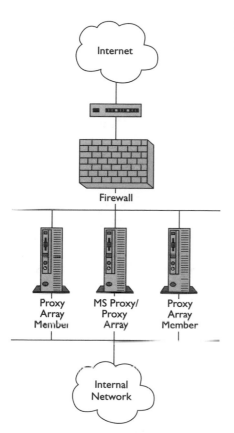

Figure 18-18: Add a firewall in front of your proxy server(s) for the highest level of security.

Only the second option applies to this section; the others are taken into account in Chapters 4 and 5. If you decide to reduce bandwidth utilization by improving the performance of your proxy server(s), start by gathering information on the server. Performance Monitor and the proxy server logs will provide you with information about the total number of hits, the number of hits that must be referred to the external network for resolution, where people tend to be visiting, and how often objects must be refreshed for particular sites.

Given this information, you may begin to tweak some performance settings. For example, if you discover that a popular Web site is being constantly required, it may be that the administrator of that Web site has configured the cache expiration date to be too soon. By changing a setting in Microsoft Proxy Server, you can make the cached files for that site remain in the cache for a longer period before being required.

Active caching is another alternative for reducing utilization during peak times. A proxy server may be configured to query a set of Web sites during nonpeak hours and retain the files it retrieves in a cache. Because the transfers are done during off-hours, the bandwidth usage is less likely to slow down anyone's work.

WEAKNESSES OF MS PROXY SERVER

Microsoft Proxy Server is a great product, but it has its downside as well. First, it does not support SOCKS v5 (though support for SOCKS v4.3a is provided). Therefore, all the great things you've read about SOCKS v5 are unattainable if you use MPS as your network proxy. This isn't all that bad, because very few client applications support the protocol yet.

Second, Microsoft Proxy Server cannot proxy everything. Any traffic that is handled by the Windows redirector, such as file and print sharing and all remote administration tools, bypass the Winsock interface. Therefore, they are not handled by the Winsock proxy and cannot reach the external network. This is a serious disadvantage given NT's reliance on the NetBIOS interface.

WEB PROXY DETAILS

The HTTP, FTP, and Gopher application-layer proxies provided by Microsoft Proxy Server are all CERN-compliant and operate as described earlier in the section "HTTP proxy connections." Microsoft Proxy Server, when used in conjunction with IIS 4.0, is HTTP/1.1 compatible.

One feature of the Web proxy service is particularly noteworthy and is not part of the standard CERN compliance: HTTP Keep-Alives. As you may recall from Chapter 16, HTTP Keep-Alives reduce the latency associated with Internet requests by maintaining a single TCP connection for multiple HTTP requests. This is a great feature when Web browsers are speaking directly to the Web servers, but the advantage is multiplied when proxy servers are used.

When HTTP Keep-Alives are configured on Microsoft Proxy Server, the Web proxy service can maintain a single TCP connection for multiple transfers, even for entirely separate user transactions. For example, if Mary visits www.cnn.com, the Web proxy service will initiate a TCP connection to the Web server and transfer the requested files. Now, if Joe then queries that same server for different data, the Web proxy service will make use of the existing TCP connection. Therefore, Joe does not have to wait while the TCP handshaking occurs before the proxy server begins to return data.

WINSOCK PROXY DETAILS

The Winsock proxy service implemented as part of Microsoft Proxy Server includes both client- and a server-side components. The client-side component is essentially a modified Winsock layer, which has the capability of forwarding Winsock requests to a remote proxy server for handling. The client-side component is available for Windows 3.1, Windows for Workgroups 3.11, Windows 95, Windows NT Workstation, and Windows NT Server. It is compatible with Windows Sockets 1.1, but not Windows Sockets 2.0.

The server-side component, the Microsoft Winsock proxy service, listens on a predetermined port for these Winsock requests. It operates on Windows NT Server only and is independent of the IIS service (unlike its sibling, the Microsoft Web proxy service).

Before we get our hands dirty, here is a little refresher on Windows Sockets. Windows Sockets, abbreviated Winsock, is a method for clients and servers to communicate with each other across a network. In this way, it is similar in function to other network communications mechanisms such as Mail Slots and NetBIOS over TCP/IP. Winsock is a set of application programming interfaces used to initiate outgoing connections, listen for incoming connections, transfer data across open connections, and destroy active connections.

Applications communicate across the network by identifying each other with an IP address and a port number. These two identifications, when combined, are called a *socket*. A socket defines a process on a computer on a network. For example, the socket for one of Microsoft's Web services is `207.68.137.65:80`, where `207.68.137.65` is the IP address and `80` is the TCP port number.

THE WINSOCK PROXY TAKES CONTROL   When the Winsock proxy is installed on a client, it must replace the existing Winsock API. This API is implemented on Windows machines as a DLL, which is named `winsock.dll` on 16-bit operating systems and `wsock32.dll` on 32-bit operating systems. The Winsock proxy client installation program first renames the existing Winsock DLL file and then places a new, proxy-aware DLL file in its place. This proxy DLL will receive all Winsock calls, determine whether or not the call should be sent to a proxy server, and then pass it on. If an application such as a Web browser makes a Winsock proxy call to a system on an external network, the Winsock proxy DLL will forward the API call directly to the proxy server. If the call is to a system on the internal network, the call is forwarded instead to the renamed Winsock DLL file and handled just like any other call.

A word of warning: This intervention incurs additional overhead for all network calls, even those to an internal network. It also adds an additional point of failure. These are things to keep in mind, but for the most part the performance and reliability of the Winsock client is excellent.

WINSOCK PROXY AT STARTUP   The first time an application makes a Winsock call, the Winsock proxy client DLL is loaded into memory. It will stay in memory until the system is shut down, which is not a terrible waste considering the fact that most users make use of network connections continually through a session. During initialization of the DLL, it contacts the Winsock proxy server as configured in the `MSPCLNT.INI` file using the Winsock control channel.

After establishing communications over the Winsock control channel, the client transfers a copy of the local address table (LAT) from the server to the local system. This is not done using the Winsock control channel – instead, standard NetBIOS file sharing mechanisms are used. This is an important consideration, because the process requires a separate port (TCP 139) from the one used for control channel communications. When configuring port-based packet filtering on a network, ensure that both TCP 139 and UDP 1745 (for the Winsock proxy control channel) are enabled.

WINSOCK PROXY COMMUNICATIONS   As soon as a system that has been outfitted with the Winsock proxy client starts up, it loads its Winsock proxy DLL. This DLL establishes a connection with the Microsoft Proxy Server using the Winsock proxy control channel. This control channel is a datagram-based communications mechanism used to establish and break down communications between the client and the server.

The Winsock control channel is primarily used when TCP connections need to be established from the client to the proxy server. The steps in the process are as follows:

1. An application begins the process by making a socket call to establish an outgoing connection to a server on an external network.

2. This socket request is intercepted by the Winsock proxy client DLL, which determines that the destination IP address resides on a distant network.

3. The Winsock proxy client sends a message to the Winsock proxy server, via the Winsock control channel, indicating the destination address and port number of the external server.

4. The Winsock proxy server receives this message and configures a TCP port redirection from the internal network interface card to the destination server on the external network. It chooses a port to accept further data on its internal interface and returns that information to the Winsock proxy client.

5. The Winsock client takes note of what port number the proxy server will use to receive this particular connection's traffic. From this point forward, when the application that initiated the connection attempts to send data to the remote server, the Winsock proxy DLL will receive the traffic and change the destination IP address to be that of the proxy server. It will also modify the TCP port number to match the one that the proxy server is listening on. With these modifications made, it will forward the Winsock request to the standard Winsock DLL. If you recall, the standard Winsock DLL was renamed during installation but is still used for most communications. The important concept to grasp here is that the Winsock proxy client DLL does very little after the initial connection is established, instead passing all data to the standard Winsock DLL.

The Winsock control channel is also used for DNS resolutions. It should not be necessary for internal clients to have access to external DNS databases, so the Winsock clients have the capability to forward DNS requests to the Winsock proxy server. These requests are made using the Winsock proxy control channel.

I mentioned earlier that the client connects to the server and transfers data via TCP. These TCP communications bind to the Winsock proxy server using a port number between 1024 and 5000, the default upper bound of available port numbers. The upper bound of 5000 can be adjusted to a maximum of 65534 by increasing the value in this registry key:

```
HKEY_LOCAL_MACHINE\System\CurrentControlSet\Services\Tcpip\
  Parameters\MaxUserPort
```

WINSOCK INTERNAL COMMUNICATIONS The Winsock proxy client DLL replaces the standard DLL and is used to allow the proxy client to connect to external networks through the proxy server. However, the proxy client still needs to be able to communicate with systems on the internal network and has no reason to go through a proxy server to do this. Understanding how local communications occur after the Winsock proxy has been installed is important for the troubleshooting process, should something ever break. And it's pretty interesting.

As I said earlier, the Winsock proxy client DLL renames the standard Winsock DLL and then takes its place. Thus, the proxy client must handle each and every Winsock call. The application making the call does not even know it is using anything but the standard Winsock DLL, so there is no way the application can determine whether it needs to use the Winsock proxy DLL or the standard Winsock DLL.

Accordingly, for every socket connection request, the Winsock proxy DLL checks its local address table (LAT) and determines whether the IP address listed in the sockets request is internal or external. If the request is internal, the Winsock proxy DLL passes the request on to the standard Winsock DLL. This process is compared to the process of communicating with an external network in Figure 18-19.

INCOMING CONNECTIONS Up to this point, I've covered the mechanics of Winsock proxy connections, but only for outgoing client connections. Winsock proxy would be pretty limited in its usefulness if it did not support inbound server connections as well.

When a system that has the Winsock proxy client installed starts an application (such as a Web server) that must listen for incoming connections, it issues a Winsock "listen" command. If the Winsock proxy client were not installed, the standard Winsock DLL would accept the command and start listening on the specified port. Even with the Winsock proxy client installed, this is what happens in most cases.

Any "listen" request that does not include a specific IP address is passed directly to the standard Winsock DLL and handled that way. Therefore, if a user starts a Web server on a system that has the Winsock proxy client installed, a listener will be started on the local system — not on the proxy server. Because the listener is within the internal network, users on the external network cannot get to the connection. From a security standpoint, this is a really good idea.

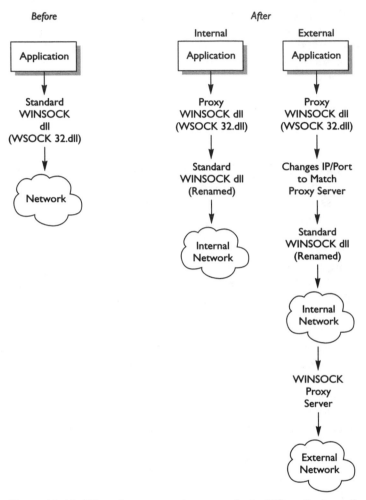

Figure 18-19: Winsock proxy agents communicate differently depending on whether the destination is internal or external.

There are many cases, however, when the proxy client needs to accept inbound connections from systems on the external network. For example, FTP transfers often require the FTP server to establish a data connection with the FTP client. For these circumstances, an IP address is provided with the "listen" Winsock command. The Winsock proxy client notices that the IP address is on the external network and sends a request to the proxy server to open a listener on the external network and pass data received on that port back to the client. This request is issued using the command channel.

In summary, listeners for incoming connections that are not for a specific system on the external network are created on the local system. Inbound connections waiting for data from a client on the external network are passed to the proxy server, which will listen for and forward data as needed.

WINSOCK SUMMARY   The Winsock proxy services provided with Microsoft Proxy Server are incredibly useful but fairly simple. Essentially, they are merely a method of dynamic port redirection. I use the term "dynamic" because the Winsock proxy server does not begin to redirect ports until an application requests to make use of the connection. It is the dynamic nature of the Winsock proxy that makes it superior to static port redirectors such as those provided with the shareware proxy server WinGate.

Netscape Proxy Server

For most Internet-related software, both Microsoft and Netscape have an offering. In the case of proxy servers, Netscape has been offering proxying services for many more years than Microsoft; their first product was released in spring 1995. Netscape Proxy Server supports many of the same functions as Microsoft Proxy Server, with several key differences.

NETSCAPE VERSUS MICROSOFT

Microsoft's Proxy Server is very similar to Netscape's. So how do you choose between the two offerings? My advice is to choose the software that is most consistent with the rest of your network. If your administrators are already familiar with the Netscape Web servers, Netscape Proxy Server will be much easier for them to learn. However, if you use Microsoft Internet Information Server on your network, adding Microsoft Proxy Server will be easier.

It is interesting that both Microsoft's and Netscape's proxy server offerings make use of the same methods of administration as their respective Web servers. Netscape Proxy Server uses a strictly Web-based administrative tool, whereas Microsoft Proxy Server makes use of the Internet Service Manager or the Microsoft Management Console. Which of the two methods you prefer is really a personal decision; either interface gets the job done.

Another notable difference is that Netscape's Proxy Server lacks the Winsock service, Microsoft's circuit-level proxy method that allows any client network application to work through a proxy server. Instead, Netscape offers the SOCKS v5 protocol, which provides much of the same functionality but requires client applications to be specifically written to use the protocol. Microsoft Proxy Server 1.0 did not support any version of SOCKS, but MPS 2.0 now supports SOCKS v4.

Oh, and if you are not using Windows NT on your servers, Microsoft Proxy Server is not even an option.

FEATURES

Netscape Proxy Server has a broad range of features centered around proxying application traffic. These features help to authenticate users, improve network performance, ease implementation, and increase scalability. The most outstanding of these features are:

- Windows NT domain synchronization

- Automatic proxy configuration

- Clustered management

- Reverse proxying

For the same reasons that Microsoft implemented the domain model, Netscape Proxy Server supports LDAP (Lightweight Directory Access Protocol). LDAP provides for centralized authentication of usernames and passwords. LDAP makes use of TCP port 636 for network communications. Netscape Proxy Server does not allow clients to be authenticated directly to the Windows NT domain. It does, however, allow the LDAP database to be synchronized with the Windows NT domain, allowing NT users to use a single username and password for both types of authentication.

In order to ease the configuration and roll-out of proxy services to a network, Netscape Proxy Server supports automatic proxy configuration (APC). This is supported by all major proxy server vendors and greatly simplifies configuring Netscape Navigator or Microsoft Internet Explorer to make use of a proxy server.

The ability to manage a group of servers as a single unit is critical when you are configuring large arrays of proxy servers. Netscape Proxy Server allows this to happen through the use of clustered management, which allows the following features:

- Starting, stopping, and restarting an array of proxy servers

- Transferring configuration files to an entire array of servers at once

- Automatic combining of error and access logs for all servers within an array

Netscape Proxy Server is capable of providing proxy services for inbound connections as well as outbound connections. This configuration is common when an organization wishes to share a Web server with the rest of the Internet but does not want to place the Web server outside of the proxy server. Essentially, the proxy server will be configured to receive requests exactly as if it were the Web server. After the proxy receives the request, it checks its cache for the data and returns it to the client if found. If the data was not found in the cache, the request is forwarded to the Web server. When the Web server returns the data to the proxy, the proxy stores a copy in the cache and forwards the result to the client on the public Internet.

CACHING PERFORMANCE

HTTP caching is all about performance, and Netscape has managed to extend the standard HTTP proxy specifications to allow for a higher cache hit ratio. First, the proxy server is capable of dynamically determining which pages will be cached the longest. For example, it is capable of keeping documents in the cache for longer periods of time if it finds that users request them more often. The administrator may also configure it to cache specific Web pages or Web sites.

CACHING SECURITY

Netscape Proxy Server has an odd policy regarding caching Web pages for which the remote server requires authentication. Netscape's product will cache secured documents and store them on the local proxy server system. However, it requires each user who requests the document to authenticate with the remote server. This is an odd compromise between convenience and security: The system is convenient because it allows secured documents to be returned more quickly, but it is insecure because those documents are stored on the local proxy server in the cache, where they may not be as secure as they are on the remote Web server.

SCALING CACHING

Netscape Proxy Server, like all of Netscape's products, has been designed with scalability in mind. Through the use of hierarchical caching, Netscape Proxy Server can use multiple proxy servers as one collective group. Because of this feature, it is able to make more efficient use of an array of proxy servers, allowing it to scale better.

An interesting feature included with hierarchical caching is the option to forward requests using the client's IP address instead of the server's IP address. Normally, proxy servers replace the client's IP address with their own when they issue requests. In order to allow source-IP filtering and other network functions an administrator may use within a network, Netscape Proxy Server has the unique ability to enable "client IP forwarding." The process of forwarding connections while retaining the client's IP address is shown in Figure 18-20. Essentially, the proxy server acts as a network-layer router rather than an application-layer proxy.

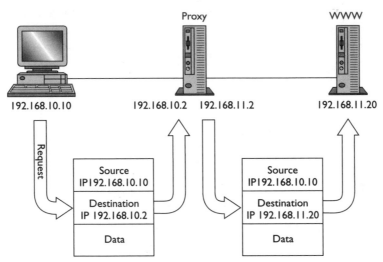

Figure 18-20: Netscape Proxy Server can forward the client IP address to the destination.

Netscape Proxy Server also supports Cache Array Routing Protocol (CARP), which, as described earlier, allows for intelligent distributed caching in an enterprise network.

PLATFORMS

Unfortunately for Microsoft, the entire world is not (yet!) using Windows. Currently, Microsoft Proxy Server is only available for Windows NT on the Intel and Alpha architectures. Netscape, on the other hand, supports Netscape Proxy Server on the following platforms:

- Digital UNIX

- HP-UX

- AIX

- IRIX

- Solaris

- BSDI

- AIX

- Reliant UNIX

- MP-RAS

- SCO OpenServer

- ◆ SCO UnixWare

- ◆ Windows NT (Intel only)

Microsoft has begun to support alternative platforms on much of its client software but currently supports no other server platforms. So if you are using anything but Windows NT or are working in a heterogeneous environment, Netscape may be the way to go.

WinGate

While Microsoft Proxy Server scales well for both small and large environments, it is not right for many small organizations. First, it is a costly alternative: The software alone costs about $900 on top of Windows NT Server. Second, hardware resource demands are high. The proxy server must have a large section of a hard disk assigned to do nothing but store cache files, and it requires a fairly expensive processor and plenty of memory. For organizations and workgroups that do not want to invest in an expensive proxy server solution, a shareware alternative has been popular for many years.

This proxy server is called WinGate. WinGate provides both standards-based HTTP proxy services and TCP proxy services. WinGate may run under Windows 95, Windows NT Workstation, or Windows NT Server. Memory requirements are very minimal, RAM being needed only for a disk cache. While WinGate may act as a member of a caching hierarchy, it does not support distributing caching features such as ICP and CARP.

WinGate's HTTP proxy service is based on the HTTP standards defined in RFC 1945. Because of this, the raw functionality it provides is identical to any standards-based HTTP service. It contains the ability to create a few simple content filters but lacks high-end content control. Again, WinGate is a small-scale solution for open environments.

WinGate also provides a port redirection service. This provides some of the same functionality as the Winsock proxy service built into Microsoft Proxy Server. However, it works in a very different way. First, the Winsock proxy service is automatic and dynamic, whereas WinGate's port redirector is manual and dynamic. The Winsock proxy service that Microsoft Proxy Server provides works as both a server and a client component, whereas there is no client-side component to the WinGate TCP proxy service. Instead, a mapping is created in WinGate associating an incoming port to an outgoing IP address and port. Therefore, when the WinGate service receives an incoming connection from an internal client, it opens an outgoing connection to a client on the external network at a predefined port number. This arrangement allows for support of proxying applications that do not have an application-layer proxy protocol, such as POP and SMTP. To clarify this, consider the following example:

Teri is a member of a small workgroup with five computers and a local area network. One of these machines, a Windows NT server, has a dial-up connection to the

Internet. None of the other systems have a modem or an analog phone line to use to connect to the Internet. Teri would like to check her Internet e-mail on a Web server provided by the ISP. Her workgroup has a very limited budget and would like to spend as little as possible to solve this problem.

Because WinGate does not include a client component, the client has no way of knowing to use the proxy server. Additionally, there is no standard proxy service for the POP mail protocol, so Teri will have to reconfigure her e-mail client. Her e-mail client should be configured to check her mail at the internal IP address of the proxy server. The way it works: When Teri checks her e-mail, her computer will send a packet to the proxy server's internal IP address using the port number 110. The server, because WinGate is listening to that port, will create a TCP connection.

At this point, Teri's computer will begin to issue POP commands to retrieve her e-mail. The proxy server will receive these commands on its own internal interface using TCP port 110. It will then initiate an outgoing connection to the ISP's mail server with the TCP port number of 110. All data transmitted by Teri's mail client will be forwarded directly to the server without being interpreted at all. When the server receives the data, it will return a response to the proxy server's public IP address that was assigned at the time the proxy server dialed the Internet service provider. The proxy server will then transfer all data that is returned to Teri's e-mail client. Therefore, Teri's mail client will be able to retrieve the mail from the ISP even though she has the IP address of the proxy server listed as her mail server.

If you are interested in downloading WinGate, visit Wingate's Web site at `http://www.wingate.net.`

Other Products

Proxies are not simple to create, but they are based on well-defined standards and so can be created with some skill and patience. Consequently, you have many options for using a Windows NT system as a proxy server. None of these are excellent solutions for corporate networks, but they may be a good fit for your network at home. They all work great if you just need to let your kid get to the Internet through your dial-up connection.

NetCache, from Network Appliance, is a simple but scalable option for both forward and reverse proxying. You will not find many advanced proxy features, but you will find a great user interface. Most important, NetCache scales incredibly high and performs extremely well. This makes it well-suited to ISPs that may allow dial-in clients the use of a proxy server. It doesn't do much, but it does it right. For more information on NetCache, visit `http://www.netapp.com/products/level3/netcache/datasheet.html`. There you will find a downloadable evaluation version of the software.

Spaghetti Proxy and Gateway is a server for Windows NT and Windows 95. It has a caching HTTP and HTTPS proxy, and it supports both SOCKS 4 and SOCKS 5, Internet e-mail and news, Telnet, RealAudio/Video, and more. It also provides for TCP port redirection and hierarchical caching. For more information on Spaghetti Proxy and Gateway, visit `http://www.dceng.demon.co.uk/spaghetti/features.htm`.

Viking Proxy and WWW Server provides HTTP and HTTP proxy services, Internet mail services, SSL Tunneling, SOCKS 4 services, DNS services, and port redirection. It offers limited caching capabilities but does not work as a member of a caching hierarchy. It is compatible with both the Windows 95 and Windows NT platforms. For more information and to download an evaluation copy, visit `http://www.robtex.com/viking/`.

Purveyor provides a Web server and HTTP proxy that works under Windows 95, Windows NT, NetWare, and OpenVMS. It allows HTTP, FTP, and Gopher proxying through a single or hierarchical proxies. Unfortunately, their NT software is not available for download at the time of this writing. For more information on Purveyor, visit the company's Web site at `http://www.process.com/prod/purveyor.htp`.

Conclusion

Proxy servers will play an important role in the future of Internetworking. Proxy servers make the Internet more efficient by reducing traffic and increasing response time. Many organizations also use proxy servers to increase the security of their networks, to closely monitor the types of traffic being requested from the Internet, and to carefully filter incoming content.

Proxy servers are not the invention of any particular vendor, and many different vendors have proxy server offerings. Table 18-15 describes the key features to look for in a proxy server and details the support of three major proxy server products: Microsoft Proxy Server, Netscape Proxy Server, and WinGate.

TABLE 18-15 KEY FEATURES OF A PROXY SERVER

Feature	Microsoft	Netscape	WinGate
HTTP proxy	*	*	*
FTP proxy	*	*	*
Gopher proxy	*	*	.
SOCKS 4 proxy	*	*	*
SOCKS 5 proxy	.	*	.
Winsock proxying	*	.	.
HTTP passive caching	*	*	*
HTTP active caching	*	*	.

Continued

TABLE 18-15 KEY FEATURES OF A PROXY SERVER *(Continued)*

Feature	Microsoft	Netscape	WinGate
FTP caching	*	*	*
Logging	*	*	*
Filtering	*	*	*
Security	*	*	*
Reverse proxying	*	*	.
Caching arrays	*	*	.
Hierarchical caching	*	*	*
Client automatic configuration	*	*	.
Supports IPX	*	.	.

Summary

This chapter has covered a wide range of information on network proxying. All types of proxies have been explained, including application-layer proxies, circuit-level proxies, and transparent proxies. Additionally, a summary of the most popular proxy servers was provided with a comparison of the features available in each product.

You have learned the following:

◆ Proxy servers are used to reduce bandwidth utilization, mask internal network architecture, filter traffic, and improve the response time for network requests.

◆ Several technologies are available to allow proxy servers to scale higher. ICP and CARP are the two predominant technologies, and both allow the burden of proxying network traffic to be shared between multiple servers.

◆ Reverse proxying is a technique whereby a proxy server is associated with a Web server, rather than a Web client. Some reverse proxies are capable of balancing the burden of incoming traffic between multiple servers.

◆ Microsoft Proxy Server and Netscape Proxy Server both are capable of providing robust proxying capabilities to medium-sized networks. WinGate provides simple proxying for smaller networks.

Appendix A

TCP/UDP Well-Known Port Numbers

TCP PORT NUMBERS

Port Number	Description
7	Echo (PING)
9	DIscard
13	Daytimer
19	Character generator
20	FTP data
21	FTP control
23	Telnet
25	SMTP (Simple Mail Transfer Protocol)
53	Domain Name Service
70	Gopher
80	WWW (World Wide Web)
110	POP (Post Office Protocol)
119	NNTP (Network New Transfer Protocol)
139	Nbsession (NetBIOS Sessions service)
636	LDAP (Lightweight Directory Access Protocol)
1080	SOCKS

UDP PORT NUMBERS

Port Number	Description
7	Echo (PING)
9	Discard
13	Daytimer
19	Character generator
69	TFTP (Trivial File Transfer Protocol)
137	Nbname (NetBIOS Name service)
138	Nbdatagram (NetBIOS Datagram service)
161	SNMP (Simple Network Management Protocol)

Appendix B

Requests for Comments

RFC Number	Description
775	Directory-oriented FTP commands
783	TFTP Protocol
792	ICMP (Internet Control Message Protocol)
816	Fault isolation and recovery
022	Standard for the format of ARPA Internet text messages
826	ARP (Address Resolution Protocol Ethernet)
854	Telnet
862	Echo
863	Discard
864	Character generator
865	Quote of the Day
867	Daytime
903	RARP (Reverse Address Resolution Protocol)
959	FTP (File Transfer Protocol)
974	Mail Routing and the Domain System
1001	NBT (NetBIOS over TCP/IP)
1002	NBT (NetBIOS over TCP/IP)
1034	Domain Names — concepts and facilities
1035	Domain Names — implementation and specification
1058	RIP (Routing Information Protocol)
1112	Host extensions for IP multicasting
1157	SNMP (Simple Network Management Protocol)

Continued

RFC Number	Description
1160	IAB (Internet Activities Board)
1213	MIB-II (Management Information Base-II)
1323	TCP Extensions for high performance
1521	MIME (Multipurpose Internet Mail Extensions)
1661	PPP (Point-to-Point Protocol)
1700	Assigned numbers
1738	URLs (Uniform Resource Locators)
1808	RURLs (Relative Uniform Resource Locators)
1866	HTML (Hypertext Markup Language)
1886	Text/Enriched MIME
1918	Address allocation for private Internets
1919	Classical versus transparent IP proxies
1928	SOCKS protocol v5
1945	HTTP 1.0 (Hypertext Transfer Protocol)
1990	PPP Multilink Protocol
2068	HTTP 1.1 (Hypertext Transfer Protocol)
2070	Internationalization of HTML (Hypertext Markup Language)
2138	RADIUS (Remote Authentication Dial-In User Service)
2178	OSPF v2 (Open Shortest Path First)

Appendix C

Headers

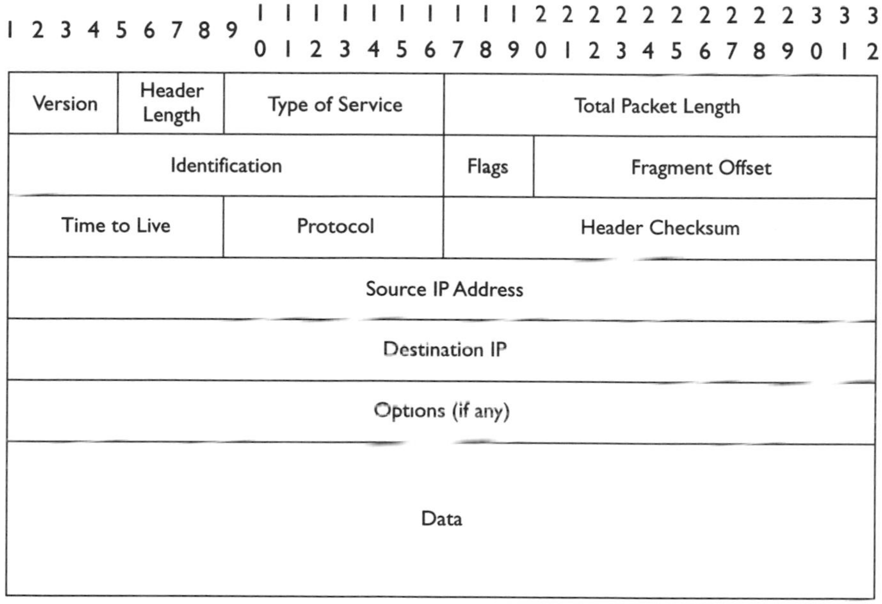

| 1 2 3 4 5 6 7 8 9 | 1 1 1 1 1 1 1 1 1 1 1 2 2 2 2 2 2 2 2 2 2 3 3 3 |
| | 0 1 2 3 4 5 6 7 8 9 0 1 2 3 4 5 6 7 8 9 0 1 2 |

Version	Header Length	Type of Service	Total Packet Length
Identification		Flags	Fragment Offset
Time to Live		Protocol	Header Checksum
Source IP Address
Destination IP
Options (if any)
Data

Figure C-1: IP header

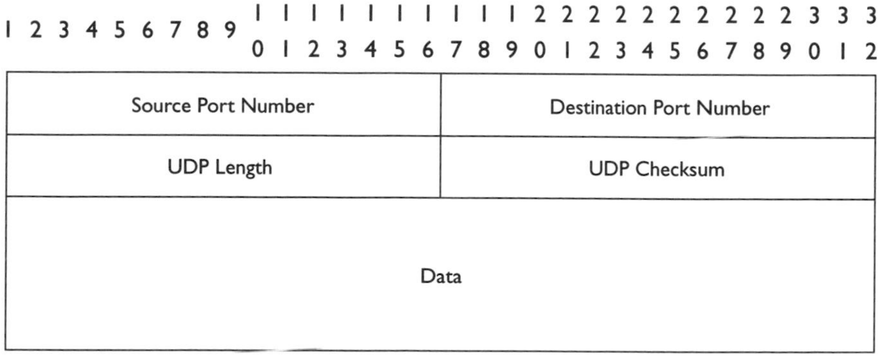

| 1 2 3 4 5 6 7 8 9 | 1 1 1 1 1 1 1 1 1 1 1 2 2 2 2 2 2 2 2 2 2 3 3 3 |
| | 0 1 2 3 4 5 6 7 8 9 0 1 2 3 4 5 6 7 8 9 0 1 2 |

| Source Port Number | Destination Port Number |
| UDP Length | UDP Checksum |
| Data |

Figure C-2: UDP header

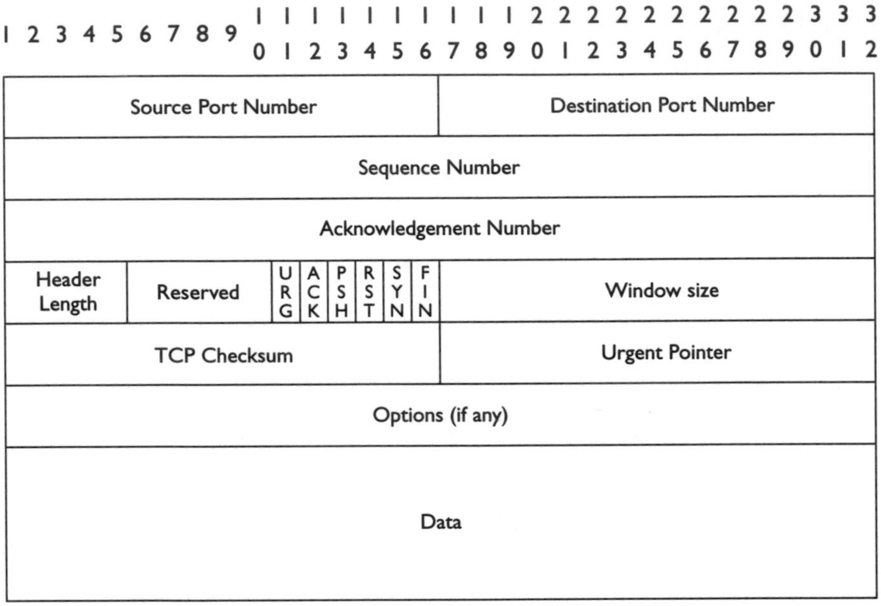

```
                                 1 1 1 1 1 1 1 1 1 1 2 2 2 2 2 2 2 2 2 2 3 3 3
   1 2 3 4 5 6 7 8 9  0 1 2 3 4 5 6 7 8 9 0 1 2 3 4 5 6 7 8 9 0 1 2
```

Source Port Number	Destination Port Number
Sequence Number	
Acknowledgement Number	

Header Length	Reserved	U R G	A C K	P S H	R S T	S Y N	F I N	Window size

TCP Checksum	Urgent Pointer
Options (if any)	
Data	

Figure C–3: TCP header

Appendix D

Common Acronyms and Their Definitions

Acronym	Real Name
ACK	Acknowledge
API	Application Programming Interface
ARP	Address Resolution Protocol
ARPA	Advanced Research Projects Agency
ATM	Asynchronous Transfer Mode
BDC	Backup domain controller
BIND	Berkeley Internet Name Domain
b-node	Broadcast node
BOOTP	Boot Protocol
DHCP	Dynamic Host Configuration Protocol
DLL	Dynamic link library
DNS	Domain Name System
DOD	Department of Defense
ESP	Encapsulating Security Payload
FQDN	Fully qualified domain name
FTP	File Transfer Protocol
h-node	Hybrid node
HTML	Hypertext Markup Language
HTTP	Hypertext Transfer Protocol
IAB	Internet Architecture Board

Continued

Acronym	Real Name
IANA	Internet Assigned Numbers Authority
ICMP	Internet Control Message Protocol
IETF	Internet Engineering Task Force
IGMP	Internet Group Membership Protocol
IIS	Internet Information Server
IP	Internet Protocol
IPng	Internet Protocol: Next Generation
IPSec	IP Security
IRTF	Internet Research Task Force
ISAPI	Internet Server Application Programming Interface
ISDN	Integrated Services Digital Network
ISO	International Standards Organization
ISOC	Internet Society
ISP	Internet service provider
Kbps	Kilobits per second
KBps	Kilobytes per second
L2F	Layer-2 Forwarding
L2TP	Layer-2 Tunneling Protocol
LAN	Local area network
LANA	Local area network adapter
MAC	Media access control
MAN	Metropolitan area network
Mbps	Megabits per second
MBps	Megabytes per second
MIB	Management information base
m-node	Mixed node
MPPP	Multilink PPP

Continued

Acronym	Real Name
MTU	Maximum transfer unit
NBNS	NetBIOS name server
NBT	NetBIOS over TCP/IP
NDIS	Network Device Interface Specification
NetBEUI	NetBIOS Enhanced User Interface
NetBIOS	Network Basic Input/Output System
NIC	Network Interface Card
NS	Name Server
OSI	Open Systems Interconnection
OSPF	Open Shortest Path First
PACKET-SWITCHED NETWORK	Packet-Switched Network
PDC	Primary domain controller
PING	Packet Internet Groper
PNA	Private network address
P-Node	Peer-to-Peer node
PPP	Point-to-Point Protocol
PPTP	Point-to-Point Tunneling Protocol
PTR	Pointer record
RAS	Remote access server, Remote Access Service
RCP	Remote Copy Protocol
RFC	Request for Comments
RIP	Routing Information Protocol
RRAS	Routing and Remote Access Service
RSH	Remote Shell
SLIP	Serial Line Internet Protocol
SMB	Server message block

Continued

Acronym	Real Name
SMS	Systems Management Server
SMTP	Simple Mail Transfer Protocol
SNMP	Simple Network Management Protocol
SOA	Start of Authority
TCP	Transmission Control Protocol
TDI	Transport Driver Interface
TFTP	Trivial File Transfer Protocol
TTL	Time to Live
UDP	User Datagram Protocol
URI	Universal Resource Identifier
URL	Universal Resource Locator
VPN	Virtual private network
WAN	Wide area network
WINS	Windows Internet Name Service
WWW	World Wide Web

Appendix E

CIDR (Classless Interdomain Routing)

Number of Available Networks	Prefix	Dotted Decimal Subnet Mask	Binary Subnet Mask
128 A	/1	128.0.0.0	1000 0000 0000 0000 0000 0000 0000 0000
64 A	/2	192.0.0.0	1100 0000 0000 0000 0000 0000 0000 0000
32 A	/3	224.0.0.0	1110 0000 0000 0000 0000 0000 0000 0000
16 A	/4	240.0.0.0	1111 0000 0000 0000 0000 0000 0000 0000
8 A	/5	248.0.0.0	1111 1000 0000 0000 0000 0000 0000 0000
4 A	/6	252.0.0.0	1111 1100 0000 0000 0000 0000 0000 0000
2 A	/7	254.0.0.0	1111 1110 0000 0000 0000 0000 0000 0000
1 A or 256 Bs	/8	255.0.0.0	1111 1111 0000 0000 0000 0000 0000 0000
128 Bs	/9	255.128.0.0	1111 1111 1000 0000 0000 0000 0000 0000
64 Bs	/10	255.192.0.0	1111 1111 1100 0000 0000 0000 0000 0000
32 Bs	/11	255.244.0.0	1111 1111 1110 0000 0000 0000 0000 0000
16 Bs	/12	255.240.0.0	1111 1111 1111 0000 0000 0000 0000 0000

Continued

Number of Available Networks	Prefix	Dotted Decimal Subnet Mask	Binary Subnet Mask
8 Bs	/13	255.248.0.0	1111 1111 1111 1000 0000 0000 0000 0000
4 Bs	/14	255.252.0.0	1111 1111 1111 1100 0000 0000 0000 0000
2 Bs	/15	255.254.0.0	1111 1111 1111 1110 0000 0000 0000 0000
1 B or 256 Cs	/16	255.255.0.0	1111 1111 1111 1111 0000 0000 0000 0000
128 Cs	/17	255.255.128.0	1111 1111 1111 1111 1000 0000 0000 0000
64 Cs	/18	255.255.192.0	1111 1111 1111 1111 1100 0000 0000 0000
32 Cs	/19	255.255.224.0	1111 1111 1111 1111 1110 0000 0000 0000
16 Cs	/20	255.255.240.0	1111 1111 1111 1111 1111 0000 0000 0000
8 Cs	/21	255.255.248.0	1111 1111 1111 1111 1111 1000 0000 0000
4 Cs	/22	255.255.252.0	1111 1111 1111 1111 1111 1100 0000 0000
2 Cs	/23	255.255.254.0	1111 1111 1111 1111 1111 1110 0000 0000
1 C	/24	255.255.255.0	1111 1111 1111 1111 1111 1111 0000 0000
_ C	/25	255.255.255.128	1111 1111 1111 1111 1111 1111 1000 0000
_ C	/26	255.255.255.192	1111 1111 1111 1111 1111 1111 1100 0000

Continued

Number of Available Networks	Prefix	Dotted Decimal Subnet Mask	Binary Subnet Mask
1/8 C	/27	255.255.255.224	1111 1111 1111 1111 1111 1111 1110 0000
1/16 C	/28	255.255.255.240	1111 1111 1111 1111 1111 1111 1111 0000
1/32 C	/29	255.255.255.248	1111 1111 1111 1111 1111 1111 1111 1000
1/64 C	/30	255.255.255.252	1111 1111 1111 1111 1111 1111 1111 1100
1/128 C	/31	255.255.255.254	1111 1111 1111 1111 1111 1111 1111 1110
1/256 C	/32	255.255.255.255	1111 1111 1111 1111 1111 1111 1111 1111

Index

(continued)

(continued)

my2cents.idgbooks.com

Register This Book — And Win!

Visit **http://my2cents.idgbooks.com** to register this book and we'll automatically enter you in our fantastic monthly prize giveaway. It's also your opportunity to give us feedback: let us know what you thought of this book and how you would like to see other topics covered.

Discover IDG Books Online!

The IDG Books Online Web site is your online resource for tackling technology — at home and at the office. Frequently updated, the IDG Books Online Web site features exclusive software, insider information, online books, and live events!

10 Productive & Career-Enhancing Things You Can Do at www.idgbooks.com

- Nab source code for your own programming projects.

- Download software.

- Read Web exclusives: special articles and book excerpts by IDG Books Worldwide authors.

- Take advantage of resources to help you advance your career as a Novell or Microsoft professional.

- Buy IDG Books Worldwide titles or find a convenient bookstore that carries them.

- Register your book and win a prize.

- Chat live online with authors.

- Sign up for regular e-mail updates about our latest books.

- Suggest a book you'd like to read or write.

- Give us your 2¢ about our books and about our Web site.

You say you're not on the Web yet? It's easy to get started with IDG Books' *Discover the Internet,* available at local retailers everywhere.